REREADING AMERICA

Cultural Contexts for Critical Thinking and Writing

ELEVENTH EDITION

EDITED BY

Gary Colombo
Emeritus—Los Angeles City College

Robert Cullen
Emeritus—San Jose State University

Bonnie Lisle
University of California, Los Angeles

 bedford/st.martin's
Macmillan Learning
Boston | New York

For Bedford/St. Martin's

Vice President, Editorial, Macmillan Learning Humanities: Edwin Hill
Executive Program Director for English: Leasa Burton
Senior Program Manager for Readers and Literature: John E. Sullivan III
Executive Marketing Manager: Joy Fisher Williams
Director of Content Development, Humanities: Jane Knetzger
Developmental Editor: Cara Kaufman
Editorial Assistant: William Hwang
Content Project Manager: Pamela Lawson
Senior Workflow Project Manager: Jennifer Wetzel
Production Supervisor: Brianna Lester
Media Project Manager: Allison Hart
Manager of Publishing Services: Andrea Cava
Project Management: Lumina Datamatics, Inc.
Composition: Lumina Datamatics, Inc.
Text Permissions Manager: Kalina Ingham
Text Permissions Editor: Mark Schaefer, Lumina Datamatics, Inc.
Photo Permissions Editor: Angela Boehler
Photo Researcher: Candice Cheesman/Krystyna Borgen, Lumina Datamatics, Inc.
Director of Design, Content Management: Diana Blume
Text Design: Janis Owens/Lumina Datamatics, Inc.
Cover Design: William Boardman
Cover Image: American Landscape #1, Nabil Mousa
Printing and Binding: LSC Communications

Manufactured in the United States of America.

1   2   3   4   5   6   23   22   21   20   19   18

For information, write: Bedford/St. Martin's, 75 Arlington Street, Boston, MA 02116

ISBN 978-1-319-05636-0

Acknowledgments
Text acknowledgments and copyrights appear at the back of the book on pages 715–716, which constitute an extension of the copyright page. Art acknowledgments and copyrights appear on the same page as the art selections they cover.

At the time of publication all Internet URLs published in this text were found to accurately link to their intended website. If you do find a broken link, please forward the information to cara.kaufman@macmillan.com so that it can be corrected for the next printing.

PREFACE FOR INSTRUCTORS

ABOUT *REREADING AMERICA*

Designed for first-year writing and critical thinking courses, *Rereading America* anthologizes a diverse set of readings focused on the myths that dominate U.S. culture. This central theme brings together thought-provoking selections on a broad range of topics — family, education, technology, success, gender, and race — topics that raise controversial issues meaningful to college students of all backgrounds. We've drawn these readings from many sources, both within the academy and outside of it; the selections are both multicultural and cross-curricular and thus represent an unusual variety of voices, styles, and subjects.

The readings in this book speak directly to students' experiences and concerns. Every college student has had some brush with prejudice, and most have something to say about education, the family, or the gender stereotypes they see in films and on television. The issues raised here help students link their personal experiences with broader cultural perspectives and lead them to analyze, or "read," the cultural forces that have shaped and continue to shape their lives. By linking the personal and the cultural, students begin to recognize that they are not academic outsiders — they too have knowledge, assumptions, and intellectual frameworks that give them authority in academic culture. Connecting personal knowledge and academic discourse helps students see that they are able to think, speak, and write academically and that they don't have to absorb passively what the "experts" say.

FEATURES OF THE ELEVENTH EDITION

A Cultural Approach to Critical Thinking   Like its predecessors, the eleventh edition of *Rereading America* is committed to the premise that learning to think critically means learning to identify and see beyond dominant cultural myths — collective and often unconsciously held beliefs that influence our thinking, reading, and writing. Instead of treating cultural diversity as just another topic to be studied or "appreciated," *Rereading America* encourages students to grapple with the real differences in perspective that arise in a pluralistic society like ours. This method helps students to break through conventional assumptions and patterns of thought that hinder fresh critical responses and inhibit dialogue. It helps them recognize that even the most apparently "natural" fact or obvious idea results from a process of social construction. And it helps them to develop the intellectual independence essential to critical thinking, reading, and writing.

Timely New Readings   To keep *Rereading America* up to date, we've worked hard to bring you the best new voices speaking on issues of race, gender, class, family, education, and technological progress. As in past editions, we've retained old favorites like Gary Soto, Stephanie Coontz, John Taylor Gatto, Mike Rose, Sherry Turkle, Barbara Ehrenreich, Jamaica Kincaid, Jean Kilbourne, Rebecca Solnit, Sherman Alexie, and Ta-Nehisi Coates. But you'll also find a host of new selections by authors such as Amy Ellis Nutt, Nikole Hannah-Jones, Peggy Orenstein, Yuval Noah Harari, Jean M. Twenge, Ellen K. Pao, Carlos Andrés Gómez, Marc Lamont Hill, Amani Al-Khatahtbeh, and José Orduña. And like earlier versions, this edition of *Rereading America* includes a healthy mix of personal and academic writing, representing a wide variety of genres, styles, and rhetorical strategies.

Visual Portfolios   In addition to frontispieces and cartoons, we've included a Visual Portfolio of myth-related images in every chapter of *Rereading America*. These collections of photographs invite students to examine how visual "texts" are constructed and how, like written texts, they are susceptible to multiple readings and rereadings. Each portfolio is accompanied by a series of questions that encourage critical analysis and connect portfolio images to ideas and themes in chapter reading selections. As in earlier editions, the visual frontispieces that open each chapter are integrated into the prereading assignments found in the chapter introductions. The cartoons, offered as a bit of comic relief and as opportunities for visual thinking, are paired with appropriate readings throughout the text.

Focus on Struggle and Resistance   Most multicultural readers approach diversity in one of two ways: either they adopt a pluralist approach and conceive of American society as a kind of salad bowl of cultures or, in response to worries about the lack of "objectivity" in the multicultural curriculum, they take what might be called the "talk show" approach and present American culture as a series of pro-and-con debates on a number of social issues. The eleventh edition of *Rereading America*, like its predecessors, follows neither of these approaches. Pluralist readers, we feel, make a promise that's impossible to keep: no single text, and no single course, can do justice to the many complex cultures that inhabit the United States. Thus the materials selected for *Rereading America* aren't meant to offer a taste of what "family" means for Native Americans or the flavor of gender relations among immigrants. Instead, we've included materials like excerpts from Sheryll Cashin's *Loving: Interracial Intimacy in America and the Threat to White Supremacy* or Ta-Nehisi Coates's "The Case for Reparations" because they offer us fresh critical perspectives on the common myths that shape our ideas, values, and beliefs. Rather than seeing this anthology as a mosaic or kaleidoscope of cultural fragments that combine to form a beautiful picture, it's more accurate to think of *Rereading America* as a handbook that helps students explore the ways that the dominant culture shapes their ideas, values, and beliefs.

This notion of cultural dominance is studiously avoided in most multicultural anthologies. "Salad bowl" readers generally sidestep the issue of cultural dynamics: intent on celebrating America's cultural diversity, they offer a relatively static picture of a nation fragmented into a kind of cultural archipelago. "Talk show" readers admit the idea of conflict, but they distort the reality of cultural dynamics by presenting cultural conflicts as a matter of rational — and equally balanced — debate. All of the materials anthologized in *Rereading America* address the cultural struggles that animate American society — the tensions that result from the expectations established by our dominant cultural myths and the diverse realities that these myths often contradict.

Extensive Apparatus   *Rereading America* offers a wealth of features to help students hone their analytic abilities and to aid instructors as they plan class discussions, critical thinking activities, and writing assignments. These include:

- *A Comprehensive Introductory Essay*   The book begins with a comprehensive essay, "Thinking Critically, Challenging Cultural Myths," that introduces students to the relationships among thinking, cultural diversity, and the notion of dominant cultural myths, and that shows how such myths can influence their academic performance. We've also included a section devoted to active reading, which offers suggestions for prereading, prewriting, note taking, text marking, and keeping a reading journal. Another section helps students work with the many visual images included in the book.

- *"Fast Facts" Begin Each Chapter*   Several provocative statistics before each chapter introduction provide context for students and prompt discussion. For example, "Following the 2016 presidential election, 64% of Americans said that fake news stories online had left the nation confused about basic facts. However, 84% also feel either 'very confident' or 'somewhat confident' that they can recognize fake news when they see it."

- *Detailed Chapter Introductions*   An introductory essay at the beginning of each chapter offers students a thorough overview of each cultural myth, placing it in historical context, raising some of the chapter's central questions, and orienting students to the chapter's internal structure.

- *Prereading Activities*   Following each chapter introduction you'll find prereading activities designed to encourage students to reflect on what they already know about the cultural myth in question. Often connected to the images that open every chapter, these prereading activities help students to engage the topic even before they begin to read.

- *Questions to Stimulate Critical Thinking*   Three groups of questions following each selection encourage students to consider the reading carefully in several contexts: "Engaging the Text" focuses on close reading of the selection itself; "Exploring Connections" puts the selection into dialogue with other selections throughout the book; "Extending the Critical Context" invites students to connect the ideas they read about here with sources of knowledge outside the anthology, including library and Internet research, personal experience, interviews, ethnographic-style observations, and so forth. As in past editions, we've included a number of questions linking readings with contemporary television shows and feature films for instructors who want to address the interplay of cultural myths and the mass media. Also as in past editions, we've included a number of questions focusing on writers' rhetorical and stylistic strategies. Identified as "Thinking Rhetorically" for easy reference, these questions typically appear as the final item under "Engaging the Text."

- *"Further Connections" Close Each Chapter* Located at the end of each chapter, these questions and assignments invite students to undertake more challenging projects related to the chapter's theme. They often provide suggestions for additional in-depth research or activities that require community engagement.

ACKNOWLEDGMENTS

Critical thinking is always a collaborative activity, and the kind of critical thinking involved in the creation of a text like *Rereading America* represents collegial collaboration at its very best. Since publication of the last edition, we've heard from instructors across the country who have generously offered suggestions for new classroom activities and comments for further refinements and improvements. Among the many instructors who shared their insights with us as we reworked this edition, we'd particularly like to thank James Allen, College of DuPage; Deborah Bertsch, Columbus State Community College; Ruth Blandon, East Los Angeles College; Nancy Botkin, Indiana University South Bend; Tony Bowers, College of DuPage; Michael Duncan, University of Houston–Downtown; Irene Faass, Minneapolis Community and Technical College; Rebecca Fleming, Columbus State Community College; Karen Forgette, University of Mississippi; Melanie Gagich, Cleveland State University; Rick Garza, Reedley College; Joshua Giorgio-Rubin, Indiana University South Bend; Sara Heaser, University of Wisconsin–La Crosse; Owen Kaufman, Quinebaug Valley Community College; Julia Klimek, Coker College; David McCracken, Coker College; Alisea McLeod, Rust College; Ilona Missakian, Fullerton College; Stan Porter, Merced College; Pegeen Powell, Columbia College Chicago; Edwin Sams, San Jose State University; Jasna Shannon, Coker College; Abha Sood, Monmouth University; Jeffrey Susla, University of Hartford; Kerry Taylor, Anne Arundel Community College; Bronte Wieland, Iowa State University.

For their help with the tenth edition, we'd like to thank the following: Douglas Armendarez, East Los Angeles College; Tolu Bamishigbin, University of California, Los Angeles; Sheena Boran, University of Mississippi; David Bordelon, Ocean County College; Jane Carey, Quinebaug Valley Community College; Kirsti Cole, Minnesota State University; Rachelle Costello, Indiana University South Bend; Virginia Crisco, California State University, Fresno; Peter DeNegre, Tunxis Community College; Tiffany Denman, Sacramento City College; Peter Dorman, Central Virginia Community College; Chip Dunkin, University of Mississippi; Randa Elbih, Grand Valley State University; Maria Estrada, Mt. San Antonio College; Karen Forgette, University of Mississippi; JoAnn Foriest, Prairie State College; Kimberly Hall, Harrisburg Area Community College; Barbara Heifferon, Louisiana State University; Cristina Herrera, California State University, Fresno; Robert Imbur, University of Toledo; Danielle Lake, Grand Valley State University; Catherine

Lamas, East Los Angeles College; Danielle Muller, Los Angeles City College; Pamela McGlynn, Southwestern College; Charlotte Morgan, Cleveland State University; Eduardo Munoz, East Los Angeles College; Kylie Olean, University of Hartford; Heather Seratt, University of Houston–Downtown; Phil Wagner, University of California, Los Angeles; Jessica Walsh, Harper College; Vallie Watson, University of North Carolina at Wilmington; Judith Wigdortz, Monmouth University; Mary Williams, San Jose State University.

For their help with the ninth edition, we'd like to thank the following: Janice Agee, Sacramento City College; Fredric J. Ball, Southwestern College; Chantell M. Barnhill, Indiana University South Bend; Norka Blackman-Richards, Queens College, City University of New York; Candace Boeck, San Diego State University; Mark Brock-Cancellieri, Stevenson University; Audrey Cameron, North Idaho College; Catheryn Cheal, Oakland University; Kirsti Cole, Minnesota State University, Mankato; Sean P. Connolly, Tulane University; Jackson Connor, Guilford College; Myrto Drizou, State University of New York at Buffalo; David Estrada, Fullerton College; Jacquelyn Lee Gardner, Western Michigan University; Rochelle Gregory, North Central Texas College; Gwyn Fallbrooke, University of Minnesota; Philip Fishman, Barry University; Naomi E. Hahn, Illinois College; Rick Hansen, California State University, Fresno; Nels P. Highberg, University of Hartford; Amy Lynn Ingalls, Three Rivers Community College; Asao B. Inoue, California State University, Fresno; Amanda Katz, Worcester State University; O. Brian Kaufman, Quinebaug Valley Community College; Barbara Kilgust, Carroll University; Carolyn Kremers, University of Alaska Fairbanks; Catherine Lamas, East Los Angeles College; Sharon A. Lefevre, Community College of Philadelphia; Alisea Williams McLeod, Indiana University South Bend; Tanya Millner-Harlee, Manchester Community College; Ilona Missakian, Rio Hondo College; Roxanne Munch, Joliet Junior College; Katrina J. Pelow, Kent State University; M. Karen Powers, Kent State University at Tuscarawas; Kevin Quirk, DePaul University; Alex Reid, State University of New York at Buffalo; Brad C. Southard, Appalachian State University; Terry Spaise, University of California, Riverside; Sarah Stanley, University of Alaska Fairbanks.

We are also grateful to those reviewers who helped shape previous editions.

As always, we'd also like to thank all the kind folks at Bedford/St. Martin's, who do their best to make the effort of producing a book like this a genuine pleasure. We're especially grateful to Edwin Hill, Leasa Burton, and John Sullivan. We thank Cara Kaufman, our editor, whose patience and professionalism have helped us immensely throughout the development of this new edition. We also want to thank Pamela Lawson, who served as content project manager; Lumina Datamatics, Inc., who managed copyediting and composition; William Boardman, who produced our new cover; Mark Schaefer, for clearing text permissions; Candice Cheesman and Krystyna Borgen, for researching and tracking down art; and editorial assistant William Hwang who helped out with many of the hundreds of details that go into a project such as this. Finally, we'd like to acknowledge our spouses, Elena Barcia, Liz Silver, and Roy Weitz, for their love and support.

Gary Colombo
Robert Cullen
Bonnie Lisle

WE'RE ALL IN. AS ALWAYS.

Bedford/St. Martin's is as passionately committed to the discipline of English as ever, working hard to provide support and services that make it easier for you to teach your course your way.

Find **community support** at the Bedford/St. Martin's English Community (community.macmillan.com), where you can follow our *Bits* blog for new teaching ideas, download titles from our professional resource series, and review projects in the pipeline.

Choose **curriculum solutions** that offer flexible custom options, combining our carefully developed print and digital resources, acclaimed works from Macmillan's trade imprints, and your own course or program materials to provide the exact resources your students need. Our approach to customization makes it possible to create a customized project uniquely suited for your students and, based on your enrollment size, return money to your department and raise your institutional profile with a high-impact author visit through the Macmillan Author Program ("MAP").

Rely on **outstanding service** from your Bedford/St. Martin's sales representative and editorial team. Contact us or visit macmillanlearning.com to learn more about any of the options below.

Choose from Alternative Formats of *Rereading America*

Bedford/St. Martin's offers a range of formats. Choose what works best for you and your students:

- *Paperback*   To order the paperback edition, use ISBN 978-1-319-05636-0.

- *Popular e-book formats*   For details of our e-book partners, visit **macmillanlearning.com/ebooks**.

Select Value Packages

Add value to your text by packaging a Bedford/St. Martin's resource, such as Writer's Help 2.0, with *Rereading America* at a significant discount. Contact your sales representative for more information.

Writer's Help 2.0 is a powerful online writing resource that helps students find answers, whether they are searching for writing advice on their own or as part of an assignment.

- **Smart search**
  Built on research with more than 1,600 student writers, the smart search in Writer's Help provides reliable results even when students use novice terms, such as *flow* and *unstuck*.

- **Trusted content from our best-selling handbooks**
  Choose *Writer's Help 2.0, Hacker Version,* or *Writer's Help 2.0, Lunsford Version,* and ensure that students have clear advice and examples for all of their writing questions.

- **Diagnostics that help establish a baseline for instruction**
  Assign diagnostics to identify areas of strength and areas for improvement and to help students plan a course of study. Use visual reports to track performance by topic, class, and student as well as improvement over time.

- **Adaptive exercises that engage students**
  Writer's Help 2.0 includes LearningCurve, game-like online quizzing that adapts to what students already know and helps them focus on what they need to learn.

Student access is packaged with *Rereading America* at a significant discount. Order ISBN 978-1-319-24513-9 for *Writer's Help 2.0, Hacker Version*, or ISBN 978-1-319-24515-3 for *Writer's Help 2.0, Lunsford Version* to ensure your students have easy access to online writing support. Students who rent or buy a used book can purchase access and instructors may request free access at **macmillanlearning.com/writershelp2**.

Instructor Resources

You have a lot to do in your course. We want to make it easy for you to find the support you need — and to get it quickly.

   Resources for Teaching Rereading America: Cultural Contexts for Critical Thinking and Writing, Eleventh Edition, is available as a PDF that can be downloaded from **macmillanlearning.com**. Visit the instructor resources tab for *Rereading America*. In addition to chapter overviews and teaching tips, the instructor's manual includes sample syllabi.

CONTENTS

①

HARMONY AT HOME   15

Myths of Family

② LEARNING POWER 107

The Myth of Education and Empowerment

3

THE WILD WIRED WEST

Myths of Progress on the Tech Frontier

④ MONEY AND SUCCESS   **341**

The Myth of Individual Opportunity

TRUE WOMEN AND REAL MEN   471

Myths of Gender

6

CREATED EQUAL   597

Myths of Race

not just the sins of the past but the sins of the present and the certain sins of the future."

THINKING CRITICALLY, CHALLENGING CULTURAL MYTHS

BECOMING A COLLEGE STUDENT

Beginning college can be a disconcerting experience. It may be the first time you've lived away from home and had to deal with the stresses and pleasures of independence. There's increased academic competition, increased temptation, and a whole new set of peer pressures. In the dorms you may find yourself among people whose backgrounds make them seem foreign and unapproachable. If you commute, you may be struggling against a feeling of isolation that you've never faced before. And then there are increased expectations. For an introductory history class you may read as many books as you covered in a year of high school coursework. In anthropology, you might be asked to conduct ethnographic research — when you've barely heard of an ethnography before, much less written one. In English, you may tackle more formal analytic writing in a single semester than you've ever done in your life.

College typically imposes fewer rules than high school, but also gives you less guidance and makes greater demands — demands that affect the quality as well as the quantity of your work. By your first midterm exam, you may suspect that your previous academic experience is irrelevant, that nothing you've done in school has prepared you to think, read, or write in the ways your professors expect. Your sociology instructor says she doesn't care whether you can remember all the examples in the textbook as long as you can apply the theoretical concepts to real situations. In your composition class, the perfect five-paragraph essay you turn in for your first assignment is dismissed as "superficial, mechanical, and dull." Meanwhile, the lecturer in your political science or psychology course is rejecting ideas about country, religion, family, and self that have always been a part of your deepest beliefs. How can you cope with these new expectations and challenges?

There is no simple solution, no infallible five-step method that works for everyone. As you meet the personal challenges of college, you'll grow as a human being. You'll begin to look critically at your old habits, beliefs, and values, to see them in relation to the new world you're entering. You may have to re-examine your relationships to family, friends, neighborhood, and heritage. You'll have to sort out your strengths from your weaknesses and make tough choices about who you are and who you want to become. Your academic work demands the same process of serious self-examination. To excel in college work you need to grow intellectually — to become a critical thinker.

WHAT IS CRITICAL THINKING?

What do instructors mean when they tell you to think critically? Most would say that it involves asking questions rather than memorizing information. Instead of simply collecting the "facts," a critical thinker probes them, looking for underlying assumptions and ideas. Instead of focusing on dates and events in history or symptoms in psychology, she probes for motives, causes — an explanation of how these things came to be. A critical thinker cultivates the ability to imagine and value points of view different from her own — then strengthens, refines, enlarges, or reshapes her ideas in light of those other perspectives. She is at once open and skeptical: receptive to new ideas yet careful to test them against previous experience and knowledge. In short, a critical thinker is an active learner, someone with the ability to shape, not merely absorb, knowledge.

All this is difficult to put into practice, because it requires getting outside your own skin and seeing the world from multiple perspectives. To see why critical thinking doesn't come naturally, take another look at the cover of this book. Many would scan the title, *Rereading America*, take in the surface meaning — to reconsider America — and go on to page one. There isn't much to question here; it just "makes sense." But what happens with the student who brings a different perspective? For example, a student from El Salvador might justly complain that the title reflects an ethnocentric view of what it means to be an American. After all, since America encompasses all the countries of North, South, and Central America, he lived in "America" long before arriving in the United States. When this student reads the title, then, he actually does *reread* it; he reads it once in the "commonsense" way but also from the perspective of someone who has lived in a country dominated by U.S. intervention and interests. This double vision or double perspective frees him to look beyond the "obvious" meaning of the book and to question its assumptions.

Of course you don't have to be bicultural to become a proficient critical thinker. You can develop a genuine sensitivity to alternative perspectives even if you've never lived outside your hometown. But to do so you need to recognize that there are no "obvious meanings." The automatic equation that the native-born student makes between "America" and the United States seems to make sense only because our culture has traditionally endorsed the idea that the United States *is* America and, by implication, that other countries in this hemisphere are somehow inferior — not the genuine article. We tend to accept this equation and its unfortunate implications because we are products of our culture.

THE POWER OF CULTURAL MYTHS

Culture shapes the way we think; it tells us what "makes sense." It holds people together by providing us with a shared set of customs, values, ideas, and beliefs, as well as a common language. We live enmeshed in this cultural web: it influences the way we relate to others, the way we look, our tastes, our habits; it enters our dreams and desires. But as culture binds us together it also selectively blinds us. As we grow up, we accept ways of looking at the world, ways of thinking and being that might best be characterized as cultural frames of reference or cultural myths. These myths help us understand our place in the world — our place as prescribed by our culture. They define our relationships to friends and lovers, to the past and future, to nature, to power, and to nation. Becoming a critical thinker means learning how to look beyond these cultural myths and the assumptions embedded in them.

You may associate the word "myth" primarily with the myths of the ancient Greeks. The legends of gods and heroes like Athena, Zeus, and Oedipus embodied the central ideals and values of Greek civilization — notions like civic responsibility, the primacy of male authority, and humility before the gods. The stories were "true" not in a literal sense but as reflections of important cultural beliefs. These myths assured the Greeks of the nobility of their origins; they provided models for the roles that Greeks would play in their public and private lives; they justified inequities in Greek society; they helped the Greeks understand human life and destiny in terms that "made sense" within the framework of that culture.

Our cultural myths do much the same. Take, for example, the American dream of success. Since the first European colonists came to the "New World" some four centuries ago, America has been synonymous with the idea of individual opportunity. For generations, immigrants have been lured across the ocean to make their fortunes in a land where the streets were said to be paved with gold. Of course we don't always agree on what success means or how it should be measured. Some calculate the meaning of success in terms of six-figure salaries or the acreage of their country estates. Others discover success in the attainment of a dream — whether it's graduating from college, achieving excellence on the playing field, or winning new rights and opportunities for less fortunate fellow citizens. For some Americans, the dream of success is the very foundation of everything that's right about life in the United States. For others, the American dream is a cultural mirage that keeps workers happy in low-paying jobs while their bosses pocket the profits of an unfair system. But whether you embrace or reject the dream of success, you can't escape its influence. As Americans, we are steeped in a culture that prizes individual achievement; growing up in the United States, we are told again and again by parents, teachers, advertisers, Hollywood writers, politicians, and opinion makers that we, too, can achieve our dream — that we, too, can "Just Do It" if we try. You might aspire to become an Internet tycoon, or you might rebel and opt for a simple life, but you can't ignore the impact of the myth.

Cultural myths gain such enormous power over us by insinuating themselves into our thinking before we're aware of them. Most are learned at a deep, even unconscious level. Gender roles are a good example. As children we get gender role models from our families, our schools, our churches, and other important institutions. We see them acted out in the relationships between family members or portrayed on television, in the movies, or in song lyrics. Before long, the culturally dominant roles we see for women and men appear to us as "self-evident": for many Americans it still seems "natural" for a man to be strong, competitive, and heterosexual, just as it may seem "unnatural" for a man to shun competitive activity or to be romantically attracted to other men. Our most dominant cultural myths shape the way we perceive the world and blind us to alternative ways of seeing and being. When something violates the expectations that such myths create, it may even be called unnatural, immoral, or perverse.

CULTURAL MYTHS AS OBSTACLES TO CRITICAL THINKING

Cultural myths can have more subtle effects as well. In academic work they can reduce the complexity of our reading and thinking. A few years ago, for example, a professor at Los Angeles City College noted that he and his students couldn't agree in their interpretations of the following poem by Theodore Roethke:

> My Papa's Waltz
>
> The whiskey on your breath
> Could make a small boy dizzy;
> But I hung on like death:
> Such waltzing was not easy.
>
> We romped until the pans
> Slid from the kitchen shelf;
> My mother's countenance
> Could not unfrown itself.
>
> The hand that held my wrist
> Was battered on one knuckle;
> At every step you missed
> My right ear scraped a buckle.
>
> You beat time on my head
> With a palm caked hard by dirt,
> Then waltzed me off to bed
> Still clinging to your shirt.

The instructor read this poem as a clear expression of a child's love for his blue-collar father, a rough-and-tumble man who had worked hard all his life ("a palm caked hard by dirt"), who was not above taking a drink of whiskey to ease his mind, but who also found the time to "waltz" his son off to bed. The students didn't see this at all. They saw the poem as a story about an abusive father and heavy drinker. They seemed unwilling to look beyond the father's roughness and the whiskey on his breath, equating these with drunken violence. Although the poem does suggest an element of fear mingled with the boy's excitement ("I hung on like death"), the class ignored its complexity — the mixture of fear, love, and boisterous fun that colors the son's memory of his father. It's possible that some students might overlook the positive traits in the father in this poem because they have suffered child abuse themselves. But this couldn't be true for all the students in the class. The difference between these interpretations lies, instead, in the influence of cultural myths. After all, in a culture now dominated by images of the family that emphasize "positive" parenting, middle-class values, and sensitive fathers, it's no wonder that students refused to see this father sympathetically. Our culture simply doesn't associate good, loving families with drinking or with even the suggestion of physical roughness.

Years of acculturation — the process of internalizing cultural values — leave us with a set of rigid categories for "good" and "bad" parents, narrow conceptions of how parents should look, talk, and behave toward their children. These cultural categories work like mental pigeonholes: they help us sort out and evaluate our experiences rapidly, almost before we're consciously aware of them. They give us a helpful shorthand for interpreting the world; after all, we can't stop to ponder every new situation we meet as if it were a puzzle or a philosophical problem. But while cultural categories help us make practical decisions in everyday life, they also impose their inherent rigidity on our thinking and thus limit our ability to understand the complexity of our experience. They reduce the world to dichotomies — simplified either/or choices: either women or men, either heterosexuals or homosexuals, either nature or culture, either animal or human, either "alien" or American, either them or us.

Rigid cultural beliefs can present serious obstacles to success for first-year college students. In a psychology class, for example, students' cultural myths may so color their thinking that they find it nearly impossible to comprehend Freud's ideas about infant sexuality. Ingrained assumptions about childhood innocence and sexual guilt may make it impossible for them to see children as sexual beings — a concept absolutely basic to an understanding of the history of psychoanalytic theory. Yet college-level critical inquiry thrives on exactly this kind of revision of common sense: academics prize the unusual, the subtle, the ambiguous, the complex — and expect students to appreciate them as well. Good critical thinkers in all academic disciplines welcome the opportunity to challenge conventional ways of seeing the world; they seem to take delight in questioning everything that appears clear and self-evident.

QUESTIONING: THE BASIS OF CRITICAL THINKING

By questioning the myths that dominate our culture, we can begin to resist the limits they impose on our vision. In fact, they invite such questioning. Often our personal experience fails to fit the images the myths project: a young woman's ambition to be a test pilot may clash with the ideal of femininity our culture promotes; a Cambodian immigrant who has suffered from racism in the United States may question our professed commitment to equality; a student in the vocational track may not see education as the road to success that we assume it is; and few of our families these days fit the mythic model of husband, wife, two kids, a dog, and a house in the suburbs.

Moreover, because cultural myths serve such large and varied needs, they're not always coherent or consistent. Powerful contradictory myths coexist in our society and our own minds. For example, while the myth of "the melting pot" celebrates equality, the myth of individual success pushes us to strive for inequality — to "get ahead" of everyone else. Likewise, our attitudes toward education are deeply paradoxical: on one level, Americans tend to see schooling as a valuable experience that unites us in a common culture and helps us bring out the best in ourselves; yet at the same time, we suspect that formal classroom instruction stifles creativity and chokes off natural intelligence and enthusiasm.

These contradictions infuse our history, literature, and popular culture; they're so much a part of our thinking that we tend to take them for granted, unaware of their inconsistencies.

Learning to recognize contradictions lies at the very heart of critical thinking, for intellectual conflict inevitably generates questions. Can both (or all) perspectives be true? What evidence do I have for the validity of each? Is there some way to reconcile them? Are there still other alternatives? Questions like these represent the beginning of serious academic analysis. They stimulate the reflection, discussion, and research that are the essence of good scholarship. Thus whether we find contradictions between myth and lived experience, or between opposing myths, the wealth of powerful, conflicting material generated by our cultural mythology offers a particularly rich context for critical inquiry.

THE STRUCTURE OF *REREADING AMERICA*

We've designed this book to help you develop the habits of mind you'll need to become a critical thinker — someone who recognizes the way that cultural myths shape thinking and can move beyond them to evaluate issues from multiple perspectives. Each of the book's six chapters addresses one of the dominant myths of American culture. We begin with the myth that's literally closest to home — the myth of the model family. In Chapter One, "Harmony at Home," we begin with readings that show what makes the mythical nuclear family so appealing and yet so elusive. Subsequent readings enrich our understanding of family by exploring the intersections of family life with race, class, and gender — key themes that resonate throughout *Rereading America*. These selections ask fascinating questions: How can a family best help a transgender daughter navigate her adolescence? When should child protection agencies or courts intervene in a family's affairs, and are their life-altering decisions swayed by racial bias? Is choosing a partner of a different ethnicity a political as well as a romantic act? And what about setting monogamy aside and choosing two or more partners? Chapter Two, "Learning Power," gives you the chance to reflect on how the "hidden curriculum" of schooling has shaped your own attitudes toward learning. You'll also encounter readings here that address problems currently associated with higher education, including campus sexual assault and student debt. We begin our exploration of American cultural myths by focusing on home and education because most students find it easy to make personal connections with these topics and because they both involve institutions — families and schools — that are surrounded by a rich legacy of cultural stories and myths. These two introductory chapters are followed by consideration of one of the most durable American myths — our national belief in progress. In Chapter Three, "The Wild Wired West: Myths of Progress on the Tech Frontier," you'll have the chance to explore how technologies like the Internet and social media are reshaping American lives. You'll also be invited to consider how technologies like data mining and artificial intelligence may threaten our privacy, our ability to make a living, and even our sense of personal agency.

The second portion of the book focuses on three cultural myths that offer greater intellectual and emotional challenges because they touch on highly charged social issues. Chapter Four introduces what is perhaps the most famous of all American myths, the American Dream. "Money and Success" addresses the idea of unlimited personal opportunity that brought millions of immigrants to our shores and set the story of America in motion. It invites you to weigh some of the human costs of the dream and to reconsider your own definition of a successful life. The next chapter, "True Women and Real Men," considers the socially constructed categories of gender — the traditional roles that enforce differences between women and men. This chapter explores the perspectives of Americans who defy conventional gender boundaries. Chapter Six, "Created Equal," critically examines the meaning of race and the myth of racial and ethnic superiority. It looks at the historical and contemporary consequences of racism, offers personal perspectives on racial and religious discrimination, and explores antiracist activism. Each of these two chapters questions how our culture divides and defines our world, how it artificially channels our experience into oppositions like black and white, male and female, straight and gay.

THE SELECTIONS

Our identities — who we are and how we relate to others — are deeply entangled with the cultural values we have internalized since infancy. Cultural myths become so closely identified with our personal beliefs that rereading them actually means rereading ourselves, rethinking the way we see the world. Questioning long-held assumptions can be an exhilarating experience, but it can be distressing too. Thus you may find certain selections in *Rereading America* difficult, controversial, or even downright offensive. They are meant to challenge you and to provoke classroom debate. But as you discuss the ideas you encounter in this book, remind yourself that your classmates may bring with them very different, and equally profound, beliefs. Keep an open mind, listen carefully, and treat other perspectives with the same respect you'd expect other people to show for your own. It's by encountering new ideas and engaging with others in open dialogue that we learn to grow.

Because *Rereading America* explores cultural myths that shape our thinking, it doesn't focus on the kind of well-defined public issues you might expect to find in a traditional composition anthology. You won't be reading arguments for and against affirmative action, bilingual education, or the death penalty here. We've deliberately avoided the traditional pro-and-con approach because we want you to aim deeper than that; we want you to focus on the subtle cultural beliefs that underlie, and frequently determine, the debates that are waged on public issues. We've also steered clear of the "issues approach" because we feel it reinforces simplistic either/or thinking. Polarizing American culture into a series of debates doesn't encourage you to examine your own beliefs or explore how they've been shaped by the cultures you're part of. To begin to appreciate the influence of your own cultural myths, you need new perspectives: you need to stand outside the ideological machinery that makes American culture run to begin to appreciate its power. That's why we've included many strongly dissenting views: there are works by community activists, gay-rights activists, socialists, libertarians, and more. You may find that their views confirm your own experience of what it means to be an American, or you may find that you bitterly disagree with them.

We only hope that you will use the materials here to gain some insight into the values and beliefs that shape our thinking and our national identity. This book is meant to complicate the mental categories that our cultural myths have established for us. Our intention is not to present a new "truth" to replace the old but to expand the range of ideas you bring to all your reading and writing in college. We believe that learning to see and value other perspectives will enable you to think more critically — to question, for yourself, the truth of any statement.

You may also note that several selections in *Rereading America* challenge the way you think writing is supposed to look or sound. You won't find any "classic" essays in this book, the finely crafted reflective essays on general topics that are often held up as models of "good writing." It's not that we reject this type of essay in principle. It's just that this kind of writing has lost its appeal for many authors who stand outside the dominant culture, and it is being supplanted today by new forms of expression evolving in academia, in the business world, and on the Internet.

Our selections, instead, come from a wide variety of sources: professional books and journals from many disciplines, popular magazines, college textbooks, personal memoirs, literary works, nonfiction best sellers, and online publications. We've included this variety partly for the very practical reason that you're likely to encounter texts like these in your college coursework. But we also see textual diversity, like ethnic and political diversity, as a way to multiply perspectives and stimulate critical analysis. For example, an academic article like Jean Anyon's study of social class and school curriculum might give you a new way of understanding Mike Rose's personal narrative about his classroom experiences. On the other hand, you may find that some of the teachers Rose encounters don't neatly fit Anyon's theoretical model. Do such discrepancies mean that Anyon's argument is invalid? That her analysis needs to be modified to account for these teachers? That the teachers are simply exceptions to the rule? You'll probably want to consider your own classroom experience as you wrestle with such questions. Throughout the book, we've chosen readings that "talk to each other" in this way and that draw on the cultural knowledge you bring with you. These readings invite you to join the conversation; we hope they raise difficult questions, prompt lively discussion, and stimulate critical inquiry.

THE POWER OF DIALOGUE

Good thinking, like good writing and good reading, is an intensely social activity. Thinking, reading, and writing are all forms of relationship — when you read, you enter into dialogue with an author about the subject at hand; when you write, you address an imaginary reader, testing your ideas against probable responses, reservations, and arguments. Thus you can't become an accomplished writer simply by declaring your right to speak or by criticizing as an act of principle: real authority comes when you enter into the discipline of an active exchange of opinions and interpretations. Critical thinking, then, is always a matter of dialogue and debate — discovering relationships between apparently unrelated ideas, finding parallels between your own experiences and the ideas you read about, exploring points of agreement and conflict between yourself and other people.

We've designed the readings and questions in this text to encourage you to make just these kinds of connections. You'll notice, for example, that we often ask you to divide into small groups to discuss readings, and we frequently suggest that you take part in projects that require you to collaborate with your classmates. We're convinced that the only way you can learn critical reading, thinking, and writing is by actively engaging others in an intellectual exchange. So we've built into the text many opportunities for listening, discussion, and debate.

The questions that follow each selection should guide you in critical thinking. Like the readings, they're intended to get you started, not to set limits; we strongly recommend that you also devise your own questions and pursue them either individually or in study groups. We've divided our questions into three categories. Here's what to expect from each:

- Those labeled "Engaging the Text" focus on the individual selection they follow. They're designed to highlight important issues in the reading, to help you begin questioning and evaluating what you've read, and sometimes to remind you to consider the author's choices of language, evidence, structure, and style. Questions in this category are labeled "Thinking Rhetorically," and we've included more of them in this edition.

- The questions labeled "Exploring Connections" will lead you from the selection you've just finished to one or more other readings in this book. When you think critically about these connecting questions, though, you'll see some real collisions of ideas and perspectives, not just polite and predictable "differences of opinion."

- The final questions for each reading, "Extending the Critical Context," invite you to extend your thinking beyond the book — to your family, your community, your college, the media, the Internet, or the more traditional research environment of the library. The emphasis here is on creating new knowledge by applying ideas from this book to the world around you and by testing these ideas in your world.

ACTIVE READING

You've undoubtedly read many textbooks, but it's unlikely that you've had to deal with the kind of analytic, argumentative, and scholarly writing you'll find in college and in *Rereading America*. These different writing styles require a different approach to reading as well. In high school you probably read to "take in" information, often for the sole purpose of reproducing it later on a test. In college you'll also be expected to recognize larger issues, such as the author's theoretical slant, her goals and methods, her assumptions, and her relationship to other writers and researchers. These expectations can be especially difficult in the first two years of college, when you take introductory courses that survey large, complex fields of knowledge. With all these demands on your attention, you'll need to read actively to keep your bearings. Think of active reading as a conversation between you and the text: instead of listening passively as the writer talks, respond to what she says with questions and comments of your own. Here are some specific techniques you can practice to become a more active reader.

Prereading and Prewriting

It's best with most college reading to "preread" the text. In prereading, you briefly look over whatever information you have on the author and the selection itself. Reading chapter introductions and headnotes like those provided in this book can save you time and effort by giving you information about the author's background and concerns, the subject or thesis of the selection, and its place in the chapter as a whole. Also take a look at the title and at any headings or subheadings in the piece. These will give you further clues about an article's general scope and organization. Next, quickly skim the entire selection, paying a bit more attention to the first few paragraphs and the conclusion. Now you should have a pretty good sense of the author's position — what she's trying to say in this piece of writing.

At this point you may do one of several things before you settle down to in-depth reading. You may want to jot down in a few lines what you think the author is doing. Or you may want to make a list of questions you can ask about this topic based on your prereading. Or you may want to freewrite a page or so on the subject. Informally writing out your own ideas will prepare you for more in-depth reading by recalling what you already know about the topic.

We emphasize writing about what you've read because reading and writing are complementary activities: being an avid reader will help you as a writer by familiarizing you with a wide range of ideas and styles to draw on; likewise, writing about what you've read will give you a deeper understanding of your reading. In fact, the more actively you "process" or reshape what you've read, the better you'll comprehend and remember it. So you'll learn more effectively by marking a text as you read than by simply reading; taking notes as you read is even more effective than marking, and writing about the material for your own purposes (putting it in your own words and connecting it with what you already know) is better still.

Marking the Text and Taking Notes

After prereading and prewriting, you're ready to begin critical reading in earnest. As you read, be sure to highlight ideas and phrases that strike you as especially significant — those that seem to capture the gist of a particular paragraph or section, or those that relate directly to the author's purpose or argument. While prereading can help you identify central ideas, you may find that you need to reread difficult sections or flip back and skim an earlier passage if you feel yourself getting lost. Many students think of themselves as poor readers if they can't whip through an article at high speed without pausing. However, the best readers read recursively — that is, they shuttle back and forth, browsing, skimming, and rereading as necessary, depending on their interest, their familiarity with the subject, and the difficulty of the material. This shuttling actually parallels what goes on in your mind when you read actively, as you alternately recall prior knowledge or experience and predict or look for clues about where the writer is going next.

Keep a record of your mental shuttling by writing comments in the margins as you read. It's often useful to gloss the contents of each paragraph or section, to summarize it in a word or two written alongside the text. This note will serve as a reminder or key to the section when you return to it for further thinking, discussion, or writing. You may also want to note passages that puzzled you. Or you may want to write down personal reactions or questions stimulated by the reading. Take time to ponder why you felt confused or annoyed or affirmed by a particular passage. Let yourself wonder "out loud" in the margins as you read.

The following section illustrates one student's notes on a passage from Mike Rose's "I Just Wanna Be Average" (p. 123). In this example, you can see that the reader puts glosses or summary comments to the left of the passage and questions or personal responses to the right. You should experiment and create your own system of note taking, one that works best for the way you read. Just remember that your main goals in taking notes are to help you understand the author's overall position, to deepen and refine your responses to the selection, and to create a permanent record of those responses.

—Who says this?

"I JUST WANNA BE AVERAGE"

MIKE ROSE

A **professor** in the **UCLA Graduate** **School of Education and Information Studies**, Mike Rose (b. 1944) has won awards from the National Academy of Education, the National Council of Teachers of English, and the John Simon Guggenheim Memorial Foundation. Below you'll read the story of how this highly successful teacher and writer **started high school in the vocational education track**, learning dead-end skills from teachers who were often underprepared or incompetent.

Like tech-ed or woodshop?

Not public school

Intro: Trip to school

IT TOOK TWO BUSES TO GET TO Our Lady of Mercy. The first started deep in South Los Angeles and caught me at midpoint. The second drifted through neighborhoods with trees, parks, big lawns, and lots of flowers. The rides were long but were livened up by a group of South L.A. veterans whose parents also thought that Hope had set up shop in the west end of the county. There was Christy Biggars, who, at sixteen, was dealing and was, according to rumor, a pimp as well. There were Bill Cobb and Johnny Gonzales, grease-pencil artists extraordinaire, who left Nembutal-enhanced[1] swirls of "Cobb" and "Johnny" on the corrugated walls of the bus. And then there was Tyrrell Wilson. Tyrrell was the coolest kid I knew. He ran the dozens[2] like a metric halfback, laid down a rap that outrhymed and outpointed Cobb, whose rap was good but not great—the curse of a moderately soulful kid trapped in white skin. But it was Cobb who would sneak a radio onto the bus, and thus underwrote his patter with Little Richard, Fats Domino, Chuck Berry, the

Goes from inner city to suburbs?

Friends = his street cred?

[1]**Nembutal:** Trade name for pentobarbital, a sedative drug. [All notes are the editors'.]
[2]**the dozens:** A verbal game of African origin in which competitors try to top each other's insults.

Coasters, and Ernie K. Doe's[3] mother-in-law, an awful woman who was "sent from down below."....

My homeroom was supervised by <u>Brother Dill</u>, a troubled and unstable man who also taught freshman English. When his class drifted away from him, which was often, his voice would rise in paranoid accusations, and occasionally he would lose control and <u>shake or smack us</u>. I hadn't been there two months when one of his brisk, face-turning slaps had my glasses sliding down the aisle. <u>Physical education</u> was also pretty harsh. Our teacher was a stubby ex-lineman who had played old-time pro ball in the Midwest. He routinely had us grabbing our ankles to <u>receive his stinging paddle across our butts</u>. He did that, he said, to make men of us. "Rose," he bellowed on our first encounter; me standing geeky in line in my baggy shorts. "'Rose'? What the hell kind of name is that?"

"Italian, sir," I squeaked.

"Italian! Ho. Rose, do you know the sound a bag of shit makes when it hits the wall?"

"No, sir."

"Wop!"[4]

Abuse, sexism, prejudice (Not my H.S.!)

Classes + Teachers

Keeping a Reading Journal

You may also want (or be required) to keep a reading journal in response to the selections you cover in *Rereading America*. In such a journal you'd keep all the freewriting that you do either before or after reading. Some students find it helpful to keep a double-entry journal, writing initial responses on the left side of the page and adding later reflections and reconsiderations on the right. You may want to use your journal as a place to explore personal reactions to your reading. For example, you might make notes about ideas or lines in the reading that surprise you. Or you might want to note how the selection connects to your own experiences or why you found it particularly interesting or dull. You can do this by writing out imaginary dialogues — between two writers who address the same subject, between yourself and the writer of the selection, or between two parts of yourself. You can use the journal as a place to rewrite passages from a poem or an essay in your own voice and from your own point of view. You can write letters to an author you particularly like or dislike or to a character in a story or poem. You might even draw a cartoon that comments on one of the reading selections.

Many students don't write as well as they could because they're afraid to take risks. They may have been repeatedly penalized for breaking "rules" of grammar or essay form; their main concern becomes avoiding trouble rather than exploring ideas or experimenting with style. But without risk and experimentation, there's little possibility of growth. One of the benefits of journal writing is that it gives you a place to experiment with ideas, free from worries about "correctness." Here

---

[3]**Little Richard . . . and Ernie K. Doe:** Popular black musicians of the 1950s.
[4]**Wop:** Derogatory term for Italian.

are two examples of student journal entries, in response to Mike Rose's "I Just Wanna Be Average" (we reprint the entries as they were written):

Entry 1: Personal Response to Rose

It's interesting that Rose describes how school can label you and stifle your dreams and also how it can empower you and open doors in your life. When he goes to Our Lady, they put him in a crappy Voc-Ed. track by mistake — incredible because this could mess up his entire life. I knew lots of kids who were forced into ESL back in middle school just because they spoke Spanish. What a waste! Still, when Rose meets Mr. MacFarland, his whole life changes cause the guy makes learning exciting and he knows how to hook the kids on ideas. Mr. Moore was my Mr. Mac. He used to push us to read stuff way beyond grade level, things like Fight Club and Malcolm X. He was also like MacFarland because he made everything personal. We used to spend weeks doing research on big issues like police brutality — and then we'd hold day-long debates that'd get really heated. But then there were a-hole teachers too — the ones who didn't care and would just sit there and read the paper while we did homework drills in our books. We had some nut-jobs like Brother Dill, but nobody'd dare hit us or call us names. All that's changed since Rose was in school — or maybe it's changed at least in public school. Maybe the nuns still can get away with it?

Entry 2: Dialogue Between Rose and Ken Harvey

Rose: I never really understood why you said that you just wanted to be average. It always seemed to me that you were just buying into the bull that the Voc-Ed. teachers were handing out about us. Why would you give up when you were obviously smarter than most of them?

Harvey: You wouldn't understand 'cause you were one of MacFarland's favorites. You were a hipster-nerd and that was the ID that got you through school. Mine was different. I was a jock and a rebel—and both seemed better than being a brain. We thought you guys were just kissing up—and that you read books because you couldn't make it on the field.

Rose: But you just threw your future away. We all knew you were a leader and that you could've done anything if you tried.

Harvey: Yeah, but why try? I wasn't interested in postponing my life the way you were. I had girlfriends and people thought I was cool. My parents didn't expect much out of me except sports. So why not just do the minimum in school and enjoy my life? Reading a lot of weird books on religion and philosophy didn't make me particularly happy. Maybe we just wanted different things. Have you thought about that?

Rose: I just figured you were protecting yourself against being classified as a Voc-Ed. Protecting yourself against being seen as working class.

Harvey: Maybe I wasn't. Maybe I was happy being who I was and I didn't need school to change me the way you did. School just isn't for everybody.

You'll notice that in the first entry the writer uses Rose's memoir as a point of departure for her own reflections on school and education. She also uses the journal as a place to pose questions about Rose's essay and about schooling in general. In the second entry she explores how a shift in perspective might challenge Rose's conclusions about Ken Harvey and his attitude toward education. Rose sees the damage schooling can do, but he ultimately accepts the idea that education can empower us. That's why he assumes that Harvey has given up on himself when he won't try to be more than just average. But what if Harvey's choice isn't just a matter of self-protection? What if it's a rational expression of who he is? Here, the writer uses an imaginary dialogue to explore alternatives to Rose's own thinking about school as a means of self-transformation.

WORKING WITH VISUAL IMAGES

The myths we examine in *Rereading America* make their presence felt not only in the world of print — essays, stories, poems, memoirs — but in every aspect of our culture. Consider, for example, the myth of "the American family." If you want to design a minivan, a restaurant, a cineplex, a park, a synagogue, a personal computer, or a tax code, you had better have some idea of what families are like and how they behave. Most important, you need a good grasp of what Americans *believe* about families, about the mythology of the American family. The Visual Portfolio in each chapter, while maintaining our focus on myths, also carries you beyond the medium of print and thus lets you practice your analytic skills in a different arena.

Although we are all surrounded by visual stimuli, we don't always think critically about what we see. Perhaps we are numbed by constant exposure to a barrage of images on TV, in films, and in social media and other websites. In any case, here are a few tips on how to get the most out of the images we have collected for this book. Take the time to look at the images carefully; first impressions are important, but many of the photographs contain details that might not strike you immediately. Once you have noted the immediate impact of an image, try focusing on separate elements such as background, foreground, facial expressions, and body language. Read any text that appears in the photograph, even if it's on a T-shirt or a belt buckle. Remember that many photographs are carefully *constructed*, no matter how "natural" they may look. In a photo for a magazine advertisement, for example, everything is meticulously chosen and arranged: certain actors or models are cast for their roles; they wear makeup; their clothes are really costumes; the location or setting of the ad is designed to reinforce its message; lighting is artificial; and someone is trying to sell you something.

Also be sure to consider the visual images contextually, not in isolation. How does each resemble or differ from its neighbors in the portfolio? How does it reinforce or challenge cultural beliefs or stereotypes? Put another way, how can it be understood in the context of the myths examined in *Rereading America*? Each portfolio is accompanied by a few questions to help you begin this type of analysis. You can also build a broader context for our visual images by collecting your own, then working in small groups to create a portfolio or collage.

Finally, remember that both readings and visual images are just starting points for discussion. You have access to a wealth of other perspectives and ideas among your family, friends, classmates; in your college library; in your personal experience; and in your imagination. We urge you to consult them all as you grapple with the perspectives you encounter in this text.

HARMONY AT HOME
Myths of Family

Self-portrait with family in SUV, Michigan (2007)

FAST FACTS

1. Among adults younger than 35, roughly 61% live without a spouse or partner. In 2017 the median household income for partnered adults was $86,000, versus $61,000 for unpartnered adults.

2. Nearly 33% of the U.S. adult population share a household with at least one "extra adult" (e.g., an adult child, a sibling, an elderly parent, or an unrelated housemate). This percentage, measured in 2017, is up from 14% in 1995.

3. Since the 2015 U.S. Supreme Court ruling legalizing same-sex marriage nationwide (*Obergefell v. Hodges*), the percentage of same-sex cohabiting couples who are married has risen from 38% to 61%. LGBTQ Americans who marry are twice as likely as the general public to cite legal rights and benefits as a very important reason to marry.

4. Ten percent of Americans today say they would oppose a close relative marrying someone of a different race or ethnicity—down from 32% in 2000. The percentage of nonblack Americans who would oppose a relative marrying a black person has dropped from 63% in 1990 to 14% today.

5. Among 41 countries studied by the Organization for Economic Development and Cooperation, the United States is the only country that does not mandate any paid leave for new parents. Several countries offer a year or more of paid leave.

6. Nearly 450,000 American children live in foster care. Drug abuse by a parent is associated with roughly a third of the cases in which a child is removed from home.

7. Estimates of the number of Americans in polyamorous (multiple-partner) relationships vary widely—from 1.2 to 9.8 million people, according to Internet polyamory sites.

Data from (1), (2), (3), (4) Pew Research Center, http://www.pewresearch.org/fact-tank/2017/10/11/the-share-of-americans-living-without-a-partner-has-increased-especially-among-young-adults/; http://www.pewresearch.org/fact-tank/2018/01/31/more-adults-now-share-their-living-space-driven-in-part-by-parents-living-with-their-adult-children/; http://www.pewresearch.org/fact-tank/2017/06/26/same-sex-marriage/; http://www.pewresearch.org/fact-tank/2017/06/12/key-facts-about-race-and-marriage-50-years-after-loving-v-virginia/; (5) Organization for Economic Cooperation and Development, https://www.oecd.org/els/soc/PF2_1_Parental_leave_systems.pdf; (6) "Number of Children in Foster Care Continues to Increase," US Department of Health and Human Services, Administration for Children & Families, November 30, 2017; (7) Elisabeth Sheff, *The Polyamorists Next Door: Inside Multiple-Partner Relationships and Families* (New York: Rowman & Littlefield, 2014), 3.

THE FAMILY MAY BE THE ORIGINAL CULTURAL INSTITUTION; people lived in families long before they invented the wheel, began farming, or founded cities. You might think that by now we would have clear and stable ideas about what defines a family, how families form and dissolve, what forms they can take, and how they can best raise their children, but such absolutely fundamental elements of family life have shifted dramatically through the centuries and continue to change today — perhaps faster than ever before. The most dramatic recent change in the United States is the groundswell of support for same-sex marriage: marriage equality, a concept almost unheard of thirty years ago, is now being claimed as a fundamental human right. Other changes are garnering fewer headlines but nonetheless are reshaping the values and behaviors we associate with family life. Both divorce and cohabitation have become more common and less stigmatized, and "singlehood" has gained traction as a perfectly normal alternative to marriage. An increasing number of adult Americans are now living in multigenerational families, whose larger households help them economize in tough times as well as provide for elderly members. Meanwhile, birth control, reproductive technologies, surrogacy, and genetic screening for heritable diseases are giving people more choices about whether, when, and how to have children.

Although experts agree that family and marriage are changing, there is little consensus about what these changes mean. Are we witnessing the collapse of family values, or a welcome evolution beyond restrictive and discriminatory models of family life? Central to this cultural debate is the traditional nuclear family — Dad, Mom, a couple of kids, maybe a dog, and a spacious suburban home. Millions of Americans aspire to this middle-class "model family," while others see it as limiting, unattainable, or simply outdated. Whatever value you, your family, or your community may place on the nuclear family, it's important to recognize that it has been around only a short time, especially when compared with the long history of the family itself.

In fact, what we call the "traditional" family, headed by a breadwinner-father and a housewife-mother, has existed for little more than two hundred years, and the suburbs came into being only in the 1950s. But the family as a social institution was legally recognized in Western culture at least as far back as the Code of Hammurabi, created in ancient Mesopotamia some four thousand years ago. To appreciate how profoundly concepts of family life have changed, consider the absolute power of the Mesopotamian father, the patriarch: the law allowed him to use any of his dependents, including his wife, as collateral for loans or even to sell family members outright to pay his debts.

Although patriarchal authority was less absolute in Puritan America, fathers remained the undisputed heads of families. Seventeenth-century Connecticut, Massachusetts, and New Hampshire enacted laws condemning rebellious children to severe punishment and, in extreme cases, to death. In the early years of the American colonies, as in Western culture stretching back to Hammurabi's time, unquestioned authority within the family served as both the model for and the basis of state authority. Just as family members owed complete obedience to the father, so all citizens owed unquestioned loyalty to the king and his legal representatives. In his influential volume *Democracy in America* (1835), French aristocrat Alexis de Tocqueville describes the relationship between the traditional European family and the old political order:

> Among aristocratic nations, social institutions recognize, in truth, no one in the family but the father; children are received by society at his hands; society governs him, he governs them. Thus, the parent not only has a natural right, but acquires a political right to command them; he is the author and the support of his family; but he is also its constituted ruler.

By the mid-eighteenth century, however, new ideas about individual freedom and democracy were stirring the colonies. And by the time Tocqueville visited the United States in 1831, they had evidently worked a revolution in the family as well as in the nation's political structure. He observes: "When the condition of society becomes democratic, and men adopt as their general principle that it is good and lawful to judge of all things for one's self, . . . the power which the opinions of a father exercise over those of his sons diminishes, as well as his legal power." To Tocqueville, this shift away from strict patriarchal rule signaled a change in the emotional climate of families: "as manners and laws become more democratic, the relation of father and son becomes more intimate and more affectionate; rules and authority are less talked of, confidence and tenderness are oftentimes increased, and it would seem that the natural bond is drawn closer." In Tocqueville's view, the American family heralded a new era in human relations. Freed from the rigid hierarchy of the past, parents and children could meet as near equals, joined by "filial love and fraternal affection."

This vision of the democratic family — a harmonious association of parents and children united by love and trust — has mesmerized popular culture in the United States. From the nineteenth century to the present, popular novels, magazines, music, and advertising images have glorified the comforts of loving domesticity. For several decades we have absorbed our strongest impressions of the family from television. In the 1950s we watched the Andersons on *Father Knows Best*, the Stones on *The Donna Reed Show*, and the real-life Nelson family on *The Adventures of Ozzie & Harriet* — shows which portrayed the mythical American family as happy, healthy, and modestly affluent. Over the next three decades the model stretched to include single parents, second marriages, and interracial adoptions on *My Three Sons*, *The Brady Bunch*, and *Diff'rent Strokes*, but the underlying ideal of wise, loving parents and harmonious happy families remained unchanged. More recently, our collective vision of the family has grown more complicated. In shows like *The Sopranos*, *Sister Wives*, *Here and Now*, *Transparent*, *The Fosters*, and *This Is Us*, we encounter not only diverse families (for example, same-sex, multiracial, or polygamous households), but also a wide range of social issues including adoption, foster care, infidelity, substance abuse, domestic abuse, immigration status, and transgenderism. Although media portrayals of family have evolved dramatically since the 1950s, our never-ending fascination with television families underscores the cultural importance of family dynamics and family boundaries.

There are a few reasons why *Rereading America* begins with this chapter on myths of family. First, we all know a lot about families from living in our own families, observing our communities, and consuming various media. We may not be licensed experts, but we are deeply knowledgeable. In addition, the notion of an ideal nuclear family is a perfect example of a cultural myth that held sway for decades despite its dubious relation to real life. As you proceed through the chapter you can judge for yourself how much power that myth retains today. Finally, other key topics in *Rereading America*— notions about gender, race, and success, for example— are powerfully shaped by family life.

The myth of the idealized nuclear family is explored in the chapter's first reading selection, "Looking for Work," in which Gary Soto recalls his boyhood desire to transform his working-class Chicano family into a facsimile of the Cleavers on *Leave It to Beaver*. Stephanie Coontz, in "What We Really Miss About the 1950s," then takes a close analytical look at the 1950s family, explaining its lasting appeal to some Americans but also documenting its dark side. Together these selections describe and then reread a complex set of cultural assumptions.

The next few selections draw on sociology, public policy, law, and the visual arts to provide broader and more recent perspectives on the meanings of family. "The Color of Family Ties: Race, Class, Gender, and Extended Family Involvement," by Naomi Gerstel and Natalia Sarkisian, challenges common misconceptions by carefully examining how ethnicity and social class shape the behaviors of American families. The next reading—"When Should a Child Be Taken from His Parents?"— asks us to consider one of the most difficult and consequential decisions a society can make, the decision to break apart a family to guarantee the safety or even the survival of its children. The need to separate some parents from their children is in itself a troubling reality, but as author Larissa MacFarquhar reveals, such decisions about child welfare may also reflect racial or class bias. Next, midway through the chapter, the Visual Portfolio offers you a chance to practice interpreting images; the photographs in this collection suggest some of the complex ways the contemporary American family intersects with gender, ethnicity, and social class.

The chapter ends with three readings that explore twenty-first century challenges and opportunities for American families. First, Amy Ellis Nutt tells the story of how a family supports the transition of one of their identical twin boys, Wyatt, into a young transgender woman, Nicole. Next, in a selection from *Loving: Interracial Intimacy in America and the Threat to White Supremacy*, Sheryll Cashin explains why the growing number of interracial marriages may foster healthier race relations and serve as a powerful counterforce to white supremacism. The chapter concludes with a short reading by sociologist Mimi Schippers that questions our cultural assumption that a monogamous couple is the best or only foundation of family life.

Sources

Lerner, Gerda. *The Creation of Patriarchy*. New York: Oxford University Press, 1986. Print.
Mintz, Steven, and Susan Kellogg. *Domestic Revolutions: A Social History of American Life*. New York: Free Press, 1988. Print.
Tocqueville, Alexis de. *Democracy in America*. 1835. New York: Vintage Books, 1990. Print.

BEFORE READING

- Spend ten minutes or so jotting down every word, phrase, or image you associate with the idea of "family." Write as freely as possible, without censoring your thoughts or worrying about grammatical correctness. Working in small groups, compare lists and try to categorize your responses. What assumptions about families do they reveal?

- Draw a visual representation of your family. This could take the form of a graph, chart, diagram, map, cartoon, symbolic picture, or literal portrait. Don't worry if you're not a skillful artist: the main point is to convey an idea, and even stick figures can speak eloquently. When you're finished, write a journal entry about your drawing. Was it easier to depict some feelings or ideas visually than it would have been to describe them in words? Did you find some things about your family difficult or impossible to convey visually? Does your drawing "say" anything that surprises you?

- Write a journal entry about how you think attending college has changed, or will change, your relationship to your family.

- Study the frontispiece to this chapter on page 15 and discuss the way photographer Julie Mack has chosen to portray her family. Is this a "typical" family? How do you read the expressions of the people and the emotional tone of the image as a whole? Why is the family posing in their SUV, in their driveway, seemingly at dusk?

LOOKING FOR WORK

GARY SOTO

> **"Looking for Work" is the narrative of a nine-year-old Mexican American boy who wants his family to imitate the "perfect families" he sees on TV. Much of the humor in this essay comes from the author's perspective as an adult looking back at his childhood self, but Soto also respects the child's point of view. In the marvelous details of this midsummer day, Soto captures the interplay of seductive myth and complex reality. Gary Soto (b. 1952) grew up "on the industrial side of Fresno, right smack against a junkyard and the junkyard's cross-eyed German shepherd." Having discovered poetry almost by chance in a city college library, he has now published more than forty books of poetry, fiction, and nonfiction for children, young adults, and adults. He has also received fellowships from the National Endowment for the Arts and the Guggenheim Foundation, in addition to numerous other awards. His recent publications include *Meatballs for the People: Proverbs to Chew On* (2017) and *The Elements of San Joaquin* (2018).**

ONE JULY, WHILE KILLING ANTS ON THE KITCHEN SINK with a rolled newspaper, I had a nine-year-old's vision of wealth that would save us from ourselves. For weeks I had drunk Kool-Aid and watched morning reruns of *Father Knows Best*, whose family was so uncompli-cated in its routine that I very much wanted to imitate it. The first step was to get my brother and sister to wear shoes at dinner.

"Come on, Rick—come on, Deb," I whined. But Rick mimicked me and the same day that I asked him to wear shoes he came to the dinner table in only his swim trunks. My mother didn't notice, nor did my sister, as we sat to eat our beans and tortillas in the stifling heat of our kitchen. We all gleamed like cellophane, wiping the sweat from our brows with the backs of our hands as we talked about the day: Frankie our neighbor was beat up by Faustino; the swimming pool at the play-ground would be closed for a day because the pump was broken.

Such was our life. So that morning, while doing-in the train of ants which arrived each day, I decided to become wealthy, and right away! After downing a bowl of cereal, I took a rake from the garage and started up the block to look for work.

We lived on an ordinary block of mostly working class people: ware-housemen, egg candlers,[1] welders, mechanics, and a union plumber. And there were many retired people who kept their lawns green and the gutters uncluttered of the chewing gum wrappers we dropped as we rode by on our bikes. They bent down to gather our litter, muttering at our evilness.

At the corner house I rapped the screen door and a very large woman in a muu-muu answered. She sized me up and then asked what I could do.

"Rake leaves," I answered smiling.

"It's summer, and there ain't no leaves," she countered. Her face was pinched with lines; fat jiggled under her chin. She pointed to the lawn, then the flower bed, and said: "You see any leaves there—or there?" I followed her pointing arm, stupidly. But she had a job for me and that was to get her a Coke at the liquor store. She gave me twenty cents, and after ditching my rake in a bush, off I ran. I returned with an unbagged Pepsi, for which she thanked me and gave me a nickel from her apron.

I skipped off her porch, fetched my rake, and crossed the street to the next block where Mrs. Moore, mother of Earl the retarded man, let me weed a flower bed. She handed me a trowel and for a good part of the morning my fingers dipped into the moist dirt, ripping up runners of Bermuda grass. Worms surfaced in my search for deep roots, and I cut them in halves, tossing them to Mrs. Moore's cat who pawed them play-fully as they dried in the sun. I made out Earl whose face was pressed to the back window of the house, and although he was calling to me I couldn't understand what he was trying to say. Embarrassed, I worked without looking up, but I imagined his contorted mouth and the ring of keys attached to his belt—keys that jingled with each palsied step. He scared me and I worked quickly to finish the flower bed. When I did

5

---

[1]**egg candler:** One who inspects eggs by holding them up to a light. [All notes are the editors'.]

finish Mrs. Moore gave me a quarter and two peaches from her tree, which I washed there but ate in the alley behind my house.

I was sucking on the second one, a bit of juice staining the front of my T-shirt, when Little John, my best friend, came walking down the alley with a baseball bat over his shoulder, knocking over trash cans as he made his way toward me.

Little John and I went to St. John's Catholic School, where we sat 10 among the "stupids." Miss Marino, our teacher, alternated the rows of good students with the bad, hoping that by sitting side-by-side with the bright students the stupids might become more intelligent, as though intelligence were contagious. But we didn't progress as she had hoped. She grew frustrated when one day, while dismissing class for recess, Little John couldn't get up because his arms were stuck in the slats of the chair's backrest. She scolded us with a shaking finger when we knocked over the globe, denting the already troubled Africa. She muttered curses when Leroy White, a real stupid but a great softball player with the gift to hit to all fields, openly chewed his host[2] when he made his First Communion; his hands swung at his sides as he returned to the pew looking around with a big smile.

Little John asked what I was doing, and I told him that I was taking a break from work, as I sat comfortably among high weeds. He wanted to join me, but I reminded him that the last time he'd gone door-to-door asking for work his mother had whipped him. I was with him when his mother, a New Jersey Italian who could rise up in anger one moment and love the next, told me in a polite but matter-of-fact voice that I had to leave because she was going to beat her son. She gave me a home-made popsicle, ushered me to the door, and said that I could see Little John the next day. But it was sooner than that. I went around to his bedroom window to suck my popsicle and watch Little John dodge his mother's blows, a few hitting their mark but many whirring air.

It was midday when Little John and I converged in the alley, the sun blazing in the high nineties, and he suggested that we go to Roosevelt High School to swim. He needed five cents to make fifteen, the cost of admission, and I lent him a nickel. We ran home for my bike and when my sister found out that we were going swimming, she started to cry because she didn't have the fifteen cents but only an empty Coke bottle. I waved for her to come and three of us mounted the bike—Debra on the cross bar, Little John on the handle bars and holding the Coke bottle which we would cash for a nickel and make up the difference that would allow all of us to get in, and me pumping up the crooked streets, dodging cars and pot holes. We spent the day swimming under the afternoon sun, so that when we got home our mom asked us what was darker, the floor or us? She feigned a stern posture, her hands on her hips and her mouth puckered. We played along. Looking down, Debbie and I said in unison, "Us."

---

[2]**his host:** The wafer that embodies, in the Catholic sacrament of Communion, the bread of the Last Supper and the body of Christ.

That evening at dinner we all sat down in our bathing suits to eat our beans, laughing and chewing loudly. Our mom was in a good mood, so I took a risk and asked her if sometime we could have turtle soup. A few days before I had watched a television program in which a Polynesian tribe killed a large turtle, gutted it, and then stewed it over an open fire. The turtle, basted in a sugary sauce, looked delicious as I ate an afternoon bowl of cereal, but my sister, who was watching the program with a glass of Kool-Aid between her knees, said, "Caca."

My mother looked at me in bewilderment. "Boy, are you a crazy Mexican. Where did you get the idea that people eat turtles?"

"On television," I said, explaining the program. Then I took it a step further. "Mom, do you think we could get dressed up for dinner one of these days? David King does."

"*Ay, Dios,*" my mother laughed. She started collecting the dinner plates, but my brother wouldn't let go of his. He was still drawing a picture in the bean sauce. Giggling, he said it was me, but I didn't want to listen because I wanted an answer from Mom. This was the summer when I spent the mornings in front of the television that showed the comfortable lives of white kids. There were no beatings, no rifts in the family. They wore bright clothes; toys tumbled from their closets. They hopped into bed with kisses and woke to glasses of fresh orange juice, and to a father sitting before his morning coffee while the mother buttered his toast. They hurried through the day making friends and gobs of money, returning home to a warmly lit living room, and then dinner. *Leave It to Beaver* was the program I replayed in my mind:

"May I have the mashed potatoes?" asks Beaver with a smile.

"Sure, Beav," replies Wally as he taps the corners of his mouth with a starched napkin.

The father looks on in his suit. The mother, decked out in earrings and a pearl necklace, cuts into her steak and blushes. Their conversation is politely clipped.

"Swell," says Beaver, his cheeks puffed with food.

Our own talk at dinner was loud with belly laughs and marked by our pointing forks at one another. The subjects were commonplace.

"Gary, let's go to the ditch tomorrow," my brother suggests. He explains that he has made a life preserver out of four empty detergent bottles strung together with twine and that he will make me one if I can find more bottles. "No way are we going to drown."

"Yeah, then we could have a dirt clod fight," I reply, so happy to be alive.

Whereas the Beaver's family enjoyed dessert in dishes at the table, our mom sent us outside, and more often than not I went into the alley to peek over the neighbor's fences and spy out fruit, apricots or peaches.

I had asked my mom and again she laughed that I was a crazy *chavalo*[3] as she stood in front of the sink, her arms rising and falling

[3]**chavalo:** Kid.

with suds, face glistening from the heat. She sent me outside where my brother and sister were sitting in the shade that the fence threw out like a blanket. They were talking about me when I plopped down next to them. They looked at one another and then Debbie, my eight-year-old sister, started in.

"What's this crap about getting dressed up?"

She had entered her *profanity* stage. A year later she would give up such words and slip into her Catholic uniform, and into squealing on my brother and me when we "cussed this" and "cussed that."

I tried to convince them that if we improved the way we looked we might get along better in life. White people would like us more. They might invite us to places, like their homes or front yards. They might not hate us so much.

My sister called me a "craphead," and got up to leave with a stalk of grass dangling from her mouth. "They'll never like us."

My brother's mood lightened as he talked about the ditch — the 30 white water, the broken pieces of glass, and the rusted car fenders that awaited our knees. There would be toads, and rocks to smash them.

David King, the only person we knew who resembled the middle class, called from over the fence. David was Catholic, of Armenian and French descent, and his closet was filled with toys. A bear-shaped cookie jar, like the ones on television, sat on the kitchen counter. His mother was remarkably kind while she put up with the racket we made on the street. Evenings, she often watered the front yard and it must have upset her to see us — my brother and I and others — jump

FUTURE SALMON

from trees laughing, the unkillable kids of the very poor, who got up unshaken, brushed off, and climbed into another one to try again.

David called again. Rick got up and slapped grass from his pants. When I asked if I could come along he said no. David said no. They were two years older so their affairs were different from mine. They greeted one another with foul names and took off down the alley to look for trouble.

I went inside the house, turned on the television, and was about to sit down with a glass of Kool-Aid when Mom shooed me outside.

"It's still light," she said. "Later you'll bug me to let you stay out longer. So go on."

I downed my Kool-Aid and went outside to the front yard. No one was around. The day had cooled and a breeze rustled the trees. Mr. Jackson, the plumber, was watering his lawn and when he saw me he turned away to wash off his front steps. There was more than an hour of light left, so I took advantage of it and decided to look for work. I felt suddenly alive as I skipped down the block in search of an overgrown flower bed and the dime that would end the day right. 35

ENGAGING THE TEXT

1. Why is the narrator attracted to the kind of family life depicted on TV? What, if anything, does he think is wrong with his life? Why do his desires apparently have so little impact on his family?

2. Why does the narrator first go looking for work? How has the meaning of work changed by the end of the story, when he goes out again "in search of an overgrown flower bed and the dime that would end the day right"? Explain.

3. As Soto looks back on his nine-year-old self, he has a different perspective on things than he had as a child. How would you characterize the mature Soto's thoughts about his childhood family life? (Was it "a good family"? What was wrong with Soto's thinking as a nine-year-old?) Back up your remarks with specific references to the narrative.

4. Review the story to find each mention of food or drink. Explain the role these references play.

5. Review the cast of "supporting characters" in this narrative — the mother, sister, brother, friends, and neighbors. What does each contribute to the story and in particular to the meaning of family within the story?

EXPLORING CONNECTIONS

6. Look ahead to the excerpt from *Becoming Nicole: The Transformation of an American Family* (p. 73). Compare Soto's family to the Maines family, being sure to consider ethnicity, gender roles, levels of affluence, and the different

time periods and locations. What would it be like to live in each of these families — particularly as a young boy like Gary or like Nicole's brother Jonas? Can you see any important similarities in addition to the numerous differences?

7. Compare and contrast the relationship of school and family in this narrative to that described by Mike Rose in "I Just Wanna Be Average" (p. 123).

EXTENDING THE CRITICAL CONTEXT

8. Write a journal entry about a time when you wished your family were somehow different. What caused your dissatisfaction? What did you want your family to be like? Was your dissatisfaction ever resolved?

9. "Looking for Work" is essentially the story of a single day. Write a narrative of one day when you were eight or nine or ten; use details as Soto does to give the events of the day broader significance.

WHAT WE REALLY MISS ABOUT THE 1950s

STEPHANIE COONTZ

Popular myth has it that the 1950s were the ideal decade for the American family. In this example of academic writing at its best, Stephanie Coontz (b. 1944) provides a clear, well-documented, and insightful analysis of what was really going on and suggests that our nostalgia for the 1950s could mislead us today. Coontz teaches family studies and history at The Evergreen State College in Olympia, Washington; she also serves as Director of Public Education at the Council on Contemporary Families, a nonprofit association based at the University of Texas, Austin. An award-winning writer and internationally recognized expert on the family, she has testified before a House Select Committee on families, appeared in several television documentaries, and published extensively for both general and scholarly audiences. Her recent books include *Marriage, a History: How Love Conquered Marriage* and *The Way We Never Were: American Families and the Nostalgia Trap* (both 2016); this excerpt is from her earlier study *The Way We Really Are: Coming to Terms with America's Changing Families* (1997).

IN A 1996 POLL BY THE KNIGHT-RIDDER NEWS AGENCY, more Americans chose the 1950s than any other single decade as the best time for children to grow up.[1] And despite the research I've done on the underside of 1950s families, I don't think it's crazy for people to feel nostalgic about the period. For one thing, it's easy to see why people might look back fondly to a decade when real wages grew more in any single year than in the entire ten years of the 1980s combined, a time when the average 30-year-old man could buy a median-priced home on only 15–18 percent of his salary.[2]

But it's more than just a financial issue. When I talk with modern parents, even ones who grew up in unhappy families, they associate the 1950s with a yearning they feel for a time when there were fewer complicated choices for kids or parents to grapple with, when there was more predictability in how people formed and maintained families, and when there was a coherent "moral order" in their community to serve as a reference point for family norms. Even people who found that moral order grossly unfair or repressive often say that its presence provided them with something concrete to push against.

I can sympathize entirely. One of my most empowering moments occurred the summer I turned 12, when my mother marched down to the library with me to confront a librarian who'd curtly refused to let me check out a book that was "not appropriate" for my age. "Don't you *ever* tell my daughter what she can and can't read," fumed my mom. "She's a mature young lady and she can make her own choices." In recent years I've often thought back to the gratitude I felt toward my mother for that act of trust in me. I wish I had some way of earning similar points from my own son. But much as I've always respected his values, I certainly wouldn't have walked into my local video store when he was 12 and demanded that he be allowed to check out absolutely anything he wanted!

Still, I have no illusions that I'd actually like to go back to the 1950s, and neither do most people who express such occasional nostalgia. For example, although the 1950s got more votes than any other decade in the Knight-Ridder poll, it did not win an outright majority: 38 percent of respondents picked the 1950s; 27 percent picked the 1960s or the 1970s. Voters between the ages of 50 and 64 were most likely to choose the 1950s, the decade in which they themselves came of age, as the best time for kids; voters under 30 were more likely to choose the 1970s. African Americans differed over whether the 1960s, 1970s, or 1980s

[1]Steven Thomma, "Nostalgia for '50s Surfaces," *Philadelphia Inquirer*, February 4, 1996. [All notes are Coontz's.]

[2]Frank Levy, *Dollars and Dreams: The Changing American Income Distribution* (New York: Russell Sage, 1987), p. 6; Frank Levy, "Incomes and Income Inequality," in Reynolds Farley, ed., *State of the Union: America in the 1990s*, vol. 1 (New York: Russell Sage, 1995), pp. 1–57; Richard May and Kathryn Porter, "Poverty and Income Trends, 1994," Washington, DC: Center on Budget and Policy Priorities, March 1996; Rob Nelson and Jon Cowan, "Buster Power," *USA Weekend*, October 14–16, 1994, p. 10.

were best, but all age groups of blacks agreed that later decades were definitely preferable to the 1950s.

Nostalgia for the 1950s is real and deserves to be taken seriously, but it usually shouldn't be taken literally. Even people who *do* pick the 1950s as the best decade generally end up saying, once they start discussing their feelings in depth, that it's not the family arrangements in and of themselves that they want to revive. They don't miss the way women used to be treated, they sure wouldn't want to live with most of the fathers they knew in their neighborhoods, and "come to think of it" —I don't know how many times I've recorded these exact words— "I communicate with my kids *much* better than my parents or grandparents did." When Judith Wallerstein recently interviewed 100 spouses in "happy" marriages, she found that only five "wanted a marriage like their parents'." The husbands "consciously rejected the role models provided by their fathers. The women said they could never be happy living as their mothers did."[3]

People today understandably feel that their lives are out of balance, but they yearn for something totally *new*—a more equal distribution of work, family, and community time for both men and women, children and adults. If the 1990s are lopsided in one direction, the 1950s were equally lopsided in the opposite direction.

What most people really feel nostalgic about has little to do with the internal structure of 1950s families. It is the belief that the 1950s provided a more family-friendly economic and social environment, an easier climate in which to keep kids on the straight and narrow, and above all, a greater feeling of hope for a family's long-term future, especially for its young. The contrast between the perceived hopefulness of the fifties and our own misgivings about the future is key to contemporary nostalgia for the period. Greater optimism *did* exist then, even among many individuals and groups who were in terrible circumstances. But if we are to take people's sense of loss seriously, rather than merely to capitalize on it for a hidden political agenda, we need to develop a historical perspective on where that hope came from.

Part of it came from families comparing their prospects in the 1950s to their unstable, often grindingly uncomfortable pasts, especially the two horrible decades just before. In the 1920s, after two centuries of child labor and income insecurity, and for the first time in American history, a bare majority of children had come to live in a family with a male breadwinner, a female homemaker, and a chance at a high school education. Yet no sooner did the ideals associated with such a family begin to blossom than they were buried by the stock market crash of 1929 and the Great Depression of the 1930s. During the 1930s domestic violence soared; divorce rates fell, but informal separations jumped; fertility plummeted. Murder rates were higher in 1933 than they were

[3]Judith Wallerstein and Sandra Blakeslee, *The Good Marriage: How and Why Love Lasts* (Boston: Houghton Mifflin, 1995), p. 15.

in the 1980s. Families were uprooted or torn apart. Thousands of young people left home to seek work, often riding the rails across the country.[4]

World War II brought the beginning of economic recovery, and people's renewed interest in forming families resulted in a marriage and childbearing boom, but stability was still beyond most people's grasp. Postwar communities were rocked by racial tensions, labor strife, and a right-wing backlash against the radical union movement of the 1930s. Many women resented being fired from wartime jobs they had grown to enjoy. Veterans often came home to find that they had to elbow their way back into their families, with wives and children resisting their attempts to reassert domestic authority. In one recent study of fathers who returned from the war, four times as many reported painful, even traumatic, reunions as remembered happy ones.[5]

By 1946 one in every three marriages was ending in divorce. Even 10 couples who stayed together went through rough times, as an acute housing shortage forced families to double up with relatives or friends. Tempers frayed and generational relations grew strained. "No home is big enough to house two families, particularly two of different generations, with opposite theories on child training," warned a 1948 film on the problems of modern marriage.[6]

So after the widespread domestic strife, family disruptions, and violence of the 1930s and the instability of the World War II period, people were ready to try something new. The postwar economic boom gave them the chance. The 1950s was the first time that a majority of Americans could even *dream* of creating a secure oasis in their immediate nuclear families. There they could focus their emotional and financial investments, reduce obligations to others that might keep them from seizing their own chance at a new start, and escape the interference of an older generation of neighbors or relatives who tried to tell them how to run their lives and raise their kids. Oral histories of the postwar period resound with the theme of escaping from in-laws, maiden aunts, older parents, even needy siblings.

The private family also provided a refuge from the anxieties of the new nuclear age and the cold war, as well as a place to get away from the political witch hunts led by Senator Joe McCarthy and his allies. When having the wrong friends at the wrong time or belonging to any "suspicious" organization could ruin your career and reputation, it was safer to pull out of groups you might have joined earlier and to focus on your family. On a more positive note, the nuclear family was where

---

[4]Donald Hernandez, *America's Children: Resources from Family, Government and the Economy* (New York: Russell Sage, 1993), pp. 99, 102; James Morone, "The Corrosive Politics of Virtue," *American Prospect* 26 (May–June 1996), p. 37; "Study Finds U.S. No. 1 in Violence," *Olympian*, November 13, 1992. See also Stephen Mintz and Susan Kellogg, *Domestic Revolutions: A Social History of American Family Life* (New York: The Free Press, 1988).

[5]William Tuttle Jr., *"Daddy's Gone to War": The Second World War in the Lives of America's Children* (New York: Oxford University Press, 1993).

[6]"Marriage and Divorce," *March of Time*, film series 14 (1948).

people could try to satisfy their long-pent-up desires for a more stable marriage, a decent home, and the chance to really enjoy their children.

The 1950s Family Experiment

The key to understanding the successes, failures, and comparatively short life of 1950s family forms and values is to understand the period as one of *experimentation* with the possibilities of a new kind of family, not as the expression of some longstanding tradition. At the end of the 1940s, the divorce rate, which had been rising steadily since the 1890s, dropped sharply; the age of marriage fell to a 100-year low; and the birth rate soared. Women who had worked during the Depression or World War II quit their jobs as soon as they became pregnant, which meant quite a few women were specializing in child raising; fewer women remained childless during the 1950s than in any decade since the late nineteenth century. The timing and spacing of childbearing became far more compressed, so that young mothers were likely to have two or more children in diapers at once, with no older sibling to help in their care. At the same time, again for the first time in 100 years, the educational gap between young middle-class women and men increased, while job segregation for working men and women seems to have peaked. These demographic changes increased the dependence of women on marriage, in contrast to gradual trends in the opposite direction since the early twentieth century.[7]

The result was that family life and gender roles became much more predictable, orderly, and settled in the 1950s than they were either twenty years earlier or would be twenty years later. Only slightly more than one in four marriages ended in divorce during the 1950s. Very few young people spent any extended period of time in a nonfamily setting: They moved from their parents' family into their own family, after just a brief experience with independent living, and they started having children soon after marriage. Whereas two-thirds of women aged 20 to 24 were not yet married in 1990, only 28 percent of women this age were still single in 1960.[8]

Ninety percent of all the households in the country were families 15 in the 1950s, in comparison with only 71 percent by 1990. Eighty-six percent of all children lived in two-parent homes in 1950, as opposed to just 72 percent in 1990. And the percentage living with both biological

---

[7]Arlene Skolnick and Stacey Rosencrantz, "The New Crusade for the Old Family," *American Prospect*, Summer 1994, p. 65; Hernandez, *America's Children*, pp. 128–32; Andrew Cherlin, "Changing Family and Household: Contemporary Lessons from Historical Research," *Annual Review of Sociology* 9 (1983), pp. 54–58; Sam Roberts, *Who We Are: A Portrait of America Based on the Latest Census* (New York: Times Books, 1995), p. 45.

[8]Levy, "Incomes and Income Inequality," p. 20; Arthur Norton and Louisa Miller, *Marriage, Divorce, and Remarriage in the 1990s*, Current Population Reports Series P23-180 (Washington, DC: Bureau of the Census, October 1992); Roberts, *Who We Are* (1995 ed.), pp. 50–53.

parents—rather than, say, a parent and stepparent—was dramatically higher than it had been at the turn of the century or is today: seventy percent in 1950, compared with only 50 percent in 1990. Nearly 60 percent of kids—an all-time high—were born into male breadwinner–female homemaker families; only a minority of the rest had mothers who worked in the paid labor force.[9]

If the organization and uniformity of family life in the 1950s were new, so were the values, especially the emphasis on putting all one's emotional and financial eggs in the small basket of the immediate nuclear family. Right up through the 1940s, ties of work, friendship, neighborhood, ethnicity, extended kin, and voluntary organizations were as important a source of identity for most Americans, and sometimes a *more* important source of obligation, than marriage and the nuclear family. All this changed in the postwar era. The spread of suburbs and automobiles, combined with the destruction of older ethnic neighborhoods in many cities, led to the decline of the neighborhood social club. Young couples moved away from parents and kin, cutting ties with traditional extrafamilial networks that might compete for their attention. A critical factor in this trend was the emergence of a group of family sociologists and marriage counselors who followed Talcott Parsons in claiming that the nuclear family, built on a sharp division of labor between husband and wife, was the cornerstone of modern society.

The new family experts tended to advocate views such as those first raised in a 1946 book, *Their Mothers' Sons*, by psychiatrist Edward Strecker. Strecker and his followers argued that American boys were infantilized and emasculated by women who were old-fashioned "moms" instead of modern "mothers." One sign that you might be that dreaded "mom," Strecker warned women, was if you felt you should take your aging parents into your own home, rather than putting them in "a good institution . . . where they will receive adequate care and comfort." Modern "mothers" placed their parents in nursing homes and poured all their energies into their nuclear family. They were discouraged from diluting their wifely and maternal commitments by maintaining "competing" interests in friends, jobs, or extended family networks, yet they were also supposed to cheerfully grant early independence to their (male) children—an emotional double bind that may explain why so many women who took this advice to heart ended up abusing alcohol or tranquilizers over the course of the decade.[10]

[9]Dennis Hogan and Daniel Lichter, "Children and Youth: Living Arrangements and Welfare," in Farley, ed., *State of the Union*, vol. 2, p. 99; Richard Gelles, *Contemporary Families: A Sociological View* (Thousand Oaks, Calif.: Sage, 1995), p. 115; Hernandez, *America's Children*, p. 102. The fact that only a small percentage of children had mothers in the paid labor force, though a full 40 percent did not live in male breadwinner–female homemaker families, was because some children had mothers who worked, unpaid, in farms or family businesses, or fathers who were unemployed, or the children were not living with both parents.

[10]Edward Strecker, *Their Mothers' Sons: The Psychiatrist Examines an American Problem* (Philadelphia: J. B. Lippincott, 1946), p. 209.

The call for young couples to break from their parents and youthful friends was a consistent theme in 1950s popular culture. In *Marty*, one of the most highly praised TV plays and movies of the 1950s, the hero almost loses his chance at love by listening to the carping of his mother and aunt and letting himself be influenced by old friends who resent the time he spends with his new girlfriend. In the end, he turns his back on mother, aunt, and friends to get his new marriage and a little business of his own off to a good start. Other movies, novels, and popular psychology tracts portrayed the dreadful things that happened when women became more interested in careers than marriage or men resisted domestic conformity.

Yet many people felt guilty about moving away from older parents and relatives; "modern mothers" worried that fostering independence in their kids could lead to defiance or even juvenile delinquency (the recurring nightmare of the age); there was considerable confusion about how men and women could maintain clear breadwinner-homemaker distinctions in a period of expanding education, job openings, and consumer aspirations. People clamored for advice. They got it from the new family education specialists and marriage counselors, from columns in women's magazines, from government pamphlets, and above all from television. While 1950s TV melodramas warned against letting anything dilute the commitment to getting married and having kids, the new family sitcoms gave people nightly lessons on how to make their marriage or rapidly expanding family work — or, in the case of *I Love Lucy*, probably the most popular show of the era, how *not* to make their marriage and family work. Lucy and Ricky gave weekly comic reminders of how much trouble a woman could get into by wanting a career or hatching some hare-brained scheme behind her husband's back.

At the time, everyone knew that shows such as *Donna Reed*, *Ozzie* [20] *and Harriet*, *Leave It to Beaver*, and *Father Knows Best* were not the way families really were. People didn't watch those shows to see their own lives reflected back at them. They watched them to see how families were *supposed* to live — and also to get a little reassurance that they were headed in the right direction. The sitcoms were simultaneously advertisements, etiquette manuals, and how-to lessons for a new way of organizing marriage and child raising. I have studied the scripts of these shows for years, since I often use them in my classes on family history, but it wasn't until I became a parent that I felt their extraordinary pull. The secret of their appeal, I suddenly realized, was that they offered 1950s viewers, wracked with the same feelings of parental inadequacy as was I, the promise that there were easy answers and surefire techniques for raising kids.

Ever since, I have found it useful to think of the sitcoms as the 1950s equivalent of today's beer ads. As most people know, beer ads are consciously aimed at men who *aren't* as strong and sexy as the models in the commercials, guys who are uneasily aware of the gap between the ideal masculine pursuits and their own achievements. The promise is that if the viewers on the couch will just drink brand X, they too will be able to run 10 miles without gasping for breath. Their bodies will firm up, their complexions will clear up, and maybe the Swedish bikini team will come over and hang out at their place.

Similarly, the 1950s sitcoms were aimed at young couples who had married in haste, women who had tasted new freedoms during World War II and given up their jobs with regret, veterans whose children resented their attempts to reassert paternal authority, and individuals disturbed by the changing racial and ethnic mix of postwar America. The message was clear: Buy these ranch houses, Hotpoint appliances, and child-raising ideals; relate to your spouse like this; get a new car to wash with your kids on Sunday afternoons; organize your dinners like that—and you too can escape from the conflicts of race, class, and political witch hunts into harmonious families where father knows best, mothers are never bored or irritated, and teenagers rush to the dinner table each night, eager to get their latest dose of parental wisdom.

Many families found it possible to put together a good imitation of this way of living during the 1950s and 1960s. Couples were often able to construct marriages that were much more harmonious than those in which they had grown up, and to devote far more time to their children. Even when marriages were deeply unhappy, as many were, the new stability, economic security, and educational advantages parents were able to offer their kids counted for a lot in people's assessment of their life satisfaction. And in some matters, ignorance could be bliss: The lack of media coverage of problems such as abuse or incest was terribly hard on the casualties, but it protected more fortunate families from knowledge and fear of many social ills.[11]

There was tremendous hostility to people who could be defined as "others": Jews, African Americans, Puerto Ricans, the poor, gays or lesbians, and "the red menace." Yet on a day-to-day basis, the civility that prevailed in homogeneous neighborhoods allowed people to ignore larger patterns of racial and political repression. Racial clashes were ever-present in the 1950s, sometimes escalating into full-scale antiblack riots, but individual homicide rates fell to almost half the levels of the 1930s. As nuclear families moved into the suburbs, they retreated from social activism but entered voluntary relationships with people who had children the same age; they became involved in PTAs together, joined bridge clubs, went bowling. There does seem to have been a stronger sense of neighborly commonalities than many of us feel today. Even though this local community was often the product of exclusion or

---

[11]For discussion of the discontents, and often searing misery, that were considered normal in a "good-enough" marriage in the 1950s and 1960s, see Lillian Rubin, *Worlds of Pain: Life in the Working-Class Family* (New York: Basic Books, 1976); Mirra Komarovsky, *Blue Collar Marriage* (New Haven, Conn.: Vintage, 1962); Elaine Tyler May, *Homeward Bound: American Families in the Cold War Era* (New York: Basic Books, 1988).

repression, it sometimes looks attractive to modern Americans whose commutes are getting longer and whose family or work patterns give them little in common with their neighbors.[12]

The optimism that allowed many families to rise above their internal difficulties and to put limits on their individualistic values during the 1950s came from the sense that America was on a dramatically different trajectory than it had been in the past, an upward and expansionary path that had already taken people to better places than they had ever seen before and would certainly take their children even further. This confidence that almost everyone could look forward to a better future stands in sharp contrast to how most contemporary Americans feel, and it explains why a period in which many people were much worse off than today sometimes still looks like a better period for families than our own.

Throughout the 1950s, poverty was higher than it is today, but it was less concentrated in pockets of blight existing side-by-side with extremes of wealth, and, unlike today, it was falling rather than rising. At the end of the 1930s, almost two-thirds of the population had incomes below the poverty standards of the day, while only one in eight had a middle-class income (defined as two to five times the poverty line). By 1960, a majority of the population had climbed into the middle-income range.[13]

Unmarried people were hardly sexually abstinent in the 1950s, but the age of first intercourse was somewhat higher than it is now, and despite a tripling of nonmarital birth rates between 1940 and 1958, more than 70 percent of nonmarital pregnancies led to weddings before the child was born. Teenage birth rates were almost twice as high in 1957 as in the 1990s, but most teen births were to married couples, and the effect of teen pregnancy in reducing further schooling for young people did not hurt their life prospects the way it does today. High school graduation rates were lower in the 1950s than they are today, and minority students had far worse test scores, but there were jobs

---

[12]See Robert Putnam, "The Strange Disappearance of Civic America," *American Prospect*, Winter 1996. For a glowing if somewhat lopsided picture of 1950s community solidarities, see Alan Ehrenhalt, *The Lost City: Discovering the Forgotten Virtues of Community in the Chicago of the 1950s* (New York: Basic Books, 1995). For a chilling account of communities uniting against perceived outsiders, in the same city, see Arnold Hirsch, *Making the Second Ghetto: Race and Housing in Chicago, 1940–1960* (Cambridge, Mass.: Harvard University Press, 1983). On homicide rates, see "Study Finds United States No. 1 in Violence," *Olympian*, November 13, 1992; *New York Times*, November 13, 1992, p. A9; and Douglas Lee Eckberg, "Estimates of Early Twentieth-Century U.S. Homicide Rates: An Econometric Forecasting Approach," *Demography* 32 (1995), p. 14. On lengthening commutes, see "It's Taking Longer to Get to Work," *Olympian*, December 6, 1995.

[13]The figures in this and the following paragraph come from Levy, "Incomes and Income Inequality," pp. 1–57; May and Porter, "Poverty and Income Trends, 1994"; Reynolds Farley, *The New American Reality: Who We Are, How We Got Here, Where We Are Going* (New York: Russell Sage, 1996), pp. 83–85; Gelles, *Contemporary Families*, p. 115; David Grissmer, Sheila Nataraj Kirby, Mark Bender, and Stephanie Williamson, *Student Achievement and the Changing American Family*, Rand Institute on Education and Training (Santa Monica, Calif.: Rand, 1994), p. 106.

for people who dropped out of high school or graduated without good reading skills—jobs that actually had a future. People entering the job market in the 1950s had no way of knowing that they would be the last generation to have a good shot at reaching middle-class status without the benefit of postsecondary schooling.

Millions of men from impoverished, rural, unemployed, or poorly educated family backgrounds found steady jobs in the steel, auto, appliance, construction, and shipping industries. Lower-middle-class men went further on in college during the 1950s than they would have been able to expect in earlier decades, enabling them to make the transition to secure white-collar work. The experience of shared sacrifices in the Depression and war, reinforced by a New Deal–inspired belief in the ability of government to make life better, gave people a sense of hope for the future. Confidence in government, business, education, and other institutions was on the rise. This general optimism affected people's experience and assessment of family life. It is no wonder modern Americans yearn for a similar sense of hope.

But before we sign on to any attempts to turn the family clock back to the 1950s we should note that the family successes and community solidarities of the 1950s rested on a totally different set of political and economic conditions than we have today. Contrary to widespread belief, the 1950s was not an age of laissez-faire government and free market competition. A major cause of the social mobility of young families in the 1950s was that federal assistance programs were much more generous and widespread than they are today.

In the most ambitious and successful affirmative action program ever adopted in America, 40 percent of young men were eligible for veterans' benefits, and these benefits were far more extensive than those available to Vietnam-era vets. Financed in part by a federal income tax on the rich that went up to 87 percent and a corporate tax rate of 52 percent, such benefits provided quite a jump start for a generation of young families. The GI Bill paid most tuition costs for vets who attended college, doubling the percentage of college students from prewar levels. At the other end of the life span, Social Security began to build up a significant safety net for the elderly, formerly the poorest segment of the population. Starting in 1950, the federal government regularly mandated raises in the minimum wage to keep pace with inflation. The minimum wage may have been only $1.40 as late as 1968, but a person who worked for that amount full-time, year-round, earned 118 percent of the poverty figure for a family of three. By 1995, a full-time minimum-wage worker could earn only 72 percent of the poverty level.[14]

[14]William Chafe, *The Unfinished Journey: America Since World War II* (New York: Oxford University Press, 1986), pp. 113, 143; Marc Linder, "Eisenhower-Era Marxist-Confiscatory Taxation: Requiem for the Rhetoric of Rate Reduction for the Rich," *Tulane Law Review* 70 (1996), p. 917; Barry Bluestone and Teresa Ghilarducci, "Rewarding Work: Feasible Antipoverty Policy," *American Prospect* 28 (1996), p. 42; Theda Skocpol, "Delivering for Young Families," *American Prospect* 28 (1996), p. 67.

MORE NONTRADITIONAL FAMILY UNITS

Guy, Chair, Three-Way Lamp

A Woman, Her Daughter, Forty-four My Little Ponies

The Troy Triplets and Their Personal Trainer

Two Guys, Two Gals, Two Phones, a Fax, and a Blender

R. Chast

An important source of the economic expansion of the 1950s was that public works spending at all levels of government comprised nearly 20 percent of total expenditures in 1950, as compared to less than 7 percent in 1984. Between 1950 and 1960, nonmilitary, nonresidential public construction rose by 58 percent. Construction expenditures for new schools (in dollar amounts adjusted for inflation) rose by 72 percent; funding on sewers and waterworks rose by 46 percent.

Government paid 90 percent of the costs of building the new Interstate Highway System. These programs opened up suburbia to growing numbers of middle-class Americans and created secure, well-paying jobs for blue-collar workers.[15]

Government also reorganized home financing, underwriting low down payments and long-term mortgages that had been rejected as bad business by private industry. To do this, government put public assets behind housing lending programs, created two new national financial institutions to facilitate home loans, allowed veterans to put down payments as low as a dollar on a house, and offered tax breaks to people who bought homes. The National Education Defense Act funded the socioeconomic mobility of thousands of young men who trained themselves for well-paying jobs in such fields as engineering.[16]

Unlike contemporary welfare programs, government investment in 1950s families was not just for immediate subsistence but encouraged long-term asset development, rewarding people for increasing their investment in homes and education. Thus it was far less likely that such families or individuals would ever fall back to where they started, even after a string of bad luck. Subsidies for higher education were greater the longer people stayed in school and the more expensive the school they selected. Mortgage deductions got bigger as people traded up to better houses.[17]

These social and political support systems magnified the impact of the postwar economic boom. "In the years between 1947 and 1973," reports economist Robert Kuttner, "the median paycheck more than doubled, and the bottom 20 percent enjoyed the greatest gains." High rates of unionization meant that blue-collar workers were making much more financial progress than most of their counterparts today. In 1952, when eager home buyers flocked to the opening of Levittown, Pennsylvania, the largest planned community yet constructed, "it took a factory worker one day to earn enough money to pay the closing costs on a new Levittown house, then selling for $10,000." By 1991, such a home was selling for $100,000 or more, and it took a factory worker *eighteen weeks* to earn enough money for just the closing costs.[18]

The legacy of the union struggle of the 1930s and 1940s, combined with government support for raising people's living standards, set limits

35

---

[15]Joel Tarr, "The Evolution of the Urban Infrastructure in the Nineteenth and Twentieth Centuries," in Royce Hanson, ed., *Perspectives on Urban Infrastructure* (Washington, DC: National Academy Press, 1984); Mark Aldrich, *A History of Public Works Investment in the United States*, report prepared by the CPNSAD Research Corporation for the U.S. Department of Commerce, April 1980.

[16]For more information on this government financing, see Kenneth Jackson, *Crabgrass Frontier: The Suburbanization of the United States* (New York: Oxford University Press, 1985); and *The Way We Never Were*, chapter 4.

[17]John Cook and Laura Sherman, "Economic Security Among America's Poor: The Impact of State Welfare Waivers on Asset Accumulation," Center on Hunger, Poverty, and Nutrition Policy, Tufts University, May 1996.

[18]Robert Kuttner, "The Incredible Shrinking American Paycheck," *Washington Post National Weekly Edition*, November 6–12, 1995, p. 23; Donald Bartlett and James Steele, *America: What Went Wrong?* (Kansas City: Andrews McMeel, 1992), p. 20.

on corporations that have disappeared in recent decades. Corporations paid 23 percent of federal income taxes in the 1950s, as compared to just 9.2 percent in 1991. Big companies earned higher profit margins than smaller firms, partly due to their dominance of the market, partly to America's postwar economic advantage. They chose (or were forced) to share these extra earnings, which economists call "rents," with employees. Economists at the Brookings Institution and Harvard University estimate that 70 percent of such corporate rents were passed on to workers at all levels of the firm, benefiting secretaries and janitors as well as CEOs. Corporations routinely retained workers even in slack periods, as a way of ensuring workplace stability. Although they often received more generous tax breaks from communities than they gave back in investment, at least they kept their plants and employment offices in the same place. AT&T, for example, received much of the technology it used to finance its postwar expansion from publicly funded communications research conducted as part of the war effort, and, as current AT&T Chairman Robert Allen puts it, there "used to be a lifelong commitment on the employee's part and on our part." Today, however, he admits, "the contract doesn't exist anymore."[19]

Television trivia experts still argue over exactly what the fathers in many 1950s sitcoms did for a living. Whatever it was, though, they obviously didn't have to worry about downsizing. If most married people stayed in long-term relationships during the 1950s, so did most corporations, sticking with the communities they grew up in and the employees they originally hired. Corporations were not constantly relocating in search of cheap labor during the 1950s; unlike today, increases in worker productivity usually led to increases in wages. The number of workers covered by corporate pension plans and health benefits increased steadily. So did limits on the work week. There is good reason that people look back to the 1950s as a less hurried age: The average American was working a shorter workday in the 1950s than his or her counterpart today, when a quarter of the workforce puts in 49 or more hours a week.[20]

So politicians are practicing quite a double standard when they tell us to return to the family forms of the 1950s while they do nothing to restore the job programs and family subsidies of that era, the limits on corporate relocation and financial wheeling-dealing, the much higher share of taxes paid by corporations then, the availability of

[19]Richard Barnet, "Lords of the Global Economy," *Nation*, December 19, 1994, p. 756; Clay Chandler, "U.S. Corporations: Good Citizens or Bad?" *Washington Post National Weekly Edition*, May 20–26, 1996, p. 16; Steven Pearlstein, "No More Mr. Nice Guy: Corporate America Has Done an About-Face in How It Pays and Treats Employees," *Washington Post National Weekly Edition*, December 18–24, 1995, p. 10; Robert Kuttner, "Ducking Class Warfare," *Washington Post National Weekly Edition*, March 11–17, 1996, p. 5; Henry Allen, "Ha! So Much for Loyalty," *Washington Post National Weekly Edition*, March 4–10, 1996, p. 11.

[20]Ehrenhalt, *The Lost City*, pp. 11–12; Jeremy Rifken, *The End of Work: The Decline of the Global Labor Force and the Dawn of the Post-Market Era* (New York: G. P. Putnam's Sons, 1995), pp. 169, 170, 231; Juliet Schorr, *The Overworked American: The Unexpected Decline of Leisure* (New York: Basic Books, 1991).

union jobs for noncollege youth, and the subsidies for higher education such as the National Defense Education Act loans. Furthermore, they're not telling the whole story when they claim that the 1950s was the most prosperous time for families and the most secure decade for children. Instead, playing to our understandable nostalgia for a time when things seemed to be getting better, not worse, they engage in a tricky chronological shell game with their figures, diverting our attention from two important points. First, many individuals, families, and groups were excluded from the economic prosperity, family optimism, and social civility of the 1950s. Second, the all-time high point of child well-being and family economic security came not during the 1950s but *at the end of the 1960s.*

We now know that 1950s family culture was not only nontraditional; it was also not idyllic. In important ways, the stability of family and community life during the 1950s rested on pervasive discrimination against women, gays, political dissidents, non-Christians, and racial or ethnic minorities, as well as on a systematic cover-up of the underside of many families. Families that were harmonious and fair of their own free will may have been able to function more easily in the fifties, but few alternatives existed for members of discordant or oppressive families. Victims of child abuse, incest, alcoholism, spousal rape, and wife battering had no recourse, no place to go, until well into the 1960s.[21]

At the end of the 1950s, despite ten years of economic growth, 27.3 percent of the nation's children were poor, including those in white "underclass" communities such as Appalachia. Almost 50 percent of married-couple African American families were impoverished—a figure far higher than today. It's no wonder African Americans are not likely to pick the 1950s as a golden age, even in comparison with the setbacks they experienced in the 1980s. When blacks moved north to find jobs in the postwar urban manufacturing boom they met vicious harassment and violence, first to prevent them from moving out of the central cities, then to exclude them from public space such as parks or beaches.

In Philadelphia, for example, the City of Brotherly Love, there were 40 more than 200 racial incidents over housing in the first six months of 1955 alone. The Federal Housing Authority, such a boon to white working-class families, refused to insure homes in all-black or in racially mixed neighborhoods. Two-thirds of the city dwellers evicted by the urban renewal projects of the decade were African Americans and Latinos; government did almost nothing to help such displaced families find substitute housing.[22]

---

[21]For documentation that these problems existed, see chapter 2 of *The Way We Never Were.*

[22]The poverty figures come from census data collected in *The State of America's Children Yearbook, 1996* (Washington, DC: Children's Defense Fund, 1996), p. 77. See also Hirsch, *Making the Second Ghetto*; Raymond Mohl, "Making the Second Ghetto in Metropolitan Miami, 1940–1960," *Journal of Urban History* 25 (1995), p. 396; Micaela di Leonardo, "Boys on the Hood," *Nation*, August 17–24, 1992, p. 180; Jackson, *Crabgrass Frontier*, pp. 226–27.

Women were unable to take out loans or even credit cards in their own names. They were excluded from juries in many states. A lack of options outside marriage led some women to remain in desperately unhappy unions that were often not in the best interests of their children or themselves. Even women in happy marriages often felt humiliated by the constant messages they received that their whole lives had to revolve around a man. "You are not ready when he calls—miss one turn," was a rule in the Barbie game marketed to 1950s girls; "he criticizes your hairdo—go to the beauty shop." Episodes of *Father Knows Best* advised young women: "The worst thing you can do is to try to beat a man at his own game. You just beat the women at theirs." One character on the show told women to always ask themselves, "Are you after a job or a man? You can't have both."[23]

The Fifties Experiment Comes to an End

The social stability of the 1950s, then, was a response to the stick of racism, sexism, and repression as well as to the carrot of economic opportunity and government aid. Because social protest mounted in the 1960s and unsettling challenges were posed to the gender roles and sexual mores of the previous decade, many people forget that families continued to make gains throughout the 1960s and into the first few years of the 1970s. By 1969, child poverty was down to 14 percent, its lowest level ever; it hovered just above that marker until 1975, when it began its steady climb up to contemporary figures (22 percent in 1993; 21.2 percent in 1994). The high point of health and nutrition for poor children was reached in the early 1970s.[24]

So commentators are being misleading when they claim that the 1950s was the golden age of American families. They are disregarding the number of people who were excluded during that decade and ignoring the socioeconomic gains that continued to be made through the 1960s. But they are quite right to note that the improvements of the 1950s and 1960s came to an end at some point in the 1970s (though not for the elderly, who continued to make progress).

Ironically, it was the children of those stable, enduring, supposedly idyllic 1950s families, the recipients of so much maternal time and attention, that pioneered the sharp break with their parents' family forms and gender roles in the 1970s. This was not because they were led astray by some youthful Murphy Brown in her student rebel days or inadvertently spoiled by parents who read too many of Dr. Spock's child-raising manuals.

[23]Susan Douglas, *Where the Girls Are: Growing Up Female with the Mass Media* (New York: Times Books, 1994), pp. 25, 37.

[24]*The State of America's Children Yearbook, 1966*, p. 77; May and Porter, "Poverty and Income Trends: 1994," p. 23; Sara McLanahan et al., *Losing Ground: A Critique*, University of Wisconsin Institute for Research on Poverty, Special Report No. 38, 1985.

Partly, the departure from 1950s family arrangements was a logical extension of trends and beliefs pioneered in the 1950s, or of inherent contradictions in those patterns. For example, early and close-spaced childbearing freed more wives up to join the labor force, and married women began to flock to work. By 1960, more than 40 percent of women over the age of 16 held a job, and working mothers were the fastest growing component of the labor force. The educational aspirations and opportunities that opened up for kids of the baby boom could not be confined to males, and many tight-knit, male-breadwinner, nuclear families in the 1950s instilled in their daughters the ambition to be something other than a homemaker.[25]

Another part of the transformation was a shift in values. Most people would probably agree that some changes in values were urgently needed: the extension of civil rights to racial minorities and to women; a rejection of property rights in children by parents and in women by husbands; a reaction against the political intolerance and the wasteful materialism of 1950s culture. Other changes in values remain more controversial: opposition to American intervention abroad; repudiation of the traditional sexual double standard; rebellion against what many young people saw as the hypocrisy of parents who preached sexual morality but ignored social immorality such as racism and militarism.

Still other developments, such as the growth of me-first individualism, are widely regarded as problematic by people on all points along the political spectrum. It's worth noting, though, that the origins of antisocial individualism and self-indulgent consumerism lay at least as much in the family values of the 1950s as in the youth rebellion of the 1960s. The marketing experts who never allowed the kids in *Ozzie and Harriet* sitcoms to be shown drinking milk, for fear of offending soft-drink companies that might sponsor the show in syndication, were ultimately the same people who slightly later invested billions of dollars to channel sexual rebelliousness and a depoliticized individualism into mainstream culture.

There were big cultural changes brewing by the beginning of the 1970s, and tremendous upheavals in social, sexual, and family values. And yes, there were sometimes reckless or simply laughable excesses in some of the early experiments with new gender roles, family forms, and personal expression. But the excesses of 1950s gender roles and family forms were every bit as repellent and stupid as the excesses of the sixties: Just watch a dating etiquette film of the time period, or recall that therapists of the day often told victims of incest that they were merely having unconscious oedipal fantasies.

Ultimately, though, changes in values were not what brought the 1950s family experiment to an end. The postwar family compacts

[25]For studies of how both middle-class and working-class women in the 1950s quickly departed from, or never quite accepted, the predominant image of women, see Joanne Meyerowitz, ed., *Not June Cleaver: Women and Gender in Postwar America, 1945–1960* (Philadelphia: Temple University Press, 1994).

between husbands and wives, parents and children, young and old, were based on the postwar social compact between government, corporations, and workers. While there was some discontent with those family bargains among women and youth, the old relations did not really start to unravel until people began to face the erosion of the corporate wage bargain and government broke its tacit societal bargain that it would continue to invest in jobs and education for the younger generation.

In the 1970s, new economic trends began to clash with all the social expectations that 1950s families had instilled in their children. That clash, not the willful abandonment of responsibility and commitment, has been the primary cause of both family rearrangements and the growing social problems that are usually attributed to such family changes, but in fact have *separate* origins.

ENGAGING THE TEXT

1. According to Coontz, what do we really miss about the 1950s, and what don't we miss? Explain how it might be possible for us to miss an era that's now half a century in the past.

2. In Coontz's view, what was the role of the government in making the 1950s in America what they were? What part did broader historical forces or other circumstances play?

3. Although she concentrates on the 1950s, Coontz also describes the other decades from the 1920s to the 1990s, when she wrote this piece. Use her information to create a brief chart naming the key characteristics of each decade. Then consider your own family history and see how well it fits the pattern Coontz outlines. Discuss the results with classmates or write a journal entry reflecting on what you learn.

4. Consider the most recent ten years of American history. What events or trends (e.g., same-sex marriage, immigration policies, and the Black Lives Matter and #MeToo movements) do you think a sociologist or cultural historian might consider important for understanding our current mythologies of family? How do you think our ideas about family have changed in this decade?

EXPLORING CONNECTIONS

5. The mythic nuclear family of the 1950s included kids. Do you think people today place less emphasis on raising children, and if so, why? How might Coontz respond to the "Future Salmon" cartoon on page 24 or to the frontispiece to this chapter (p. 15)?

6. Review "Looking for Work" by Gary Soto (p. 20). How does this narrative evoke nostalgia for a simpler, better era for families? Does it reveal any of the problems with the 1950s that Coontz describes?

7. Look at the image on page 525 and discuss which elements of the photo — and of the 2016 Trump-Pence campaign more generally — could be considered nostalgic. Do you think the title "What We Really Miss about the 1850s" would be an apt one for this image?

EXTENDING THE CRITICAL CONTEXT

8. Watch an episode of a 1950s sitcom such as *Father Knows Best*, *The Donna Reed Show*, *Leave It to Beaver*, or *I Love Lucy*. Analyze the extent to which it reveals both positive and negative aspects of the 1950s that Coontz discusses — for example, an authoritarian father figure, limited roles for wives, economic prosperity, or a sense of a secure community.

9. Coontz suggests that an uninformed nostalgia for the 1950s could promote harmful political agendas. What connections do you see between her analysis and the campaign slogan "Make America Great Again" or other recent political stances or events? Do you agree with Coontz that nostalgia can be dangerous? Why or why not?

THE COLOR OF FAMILY TIES: RACE, CLASS, GENDER, AND EXTENDED FAMILY INVOLVEMENT

NAOMI GERSTEL AND NATALIA SARKISIAN

The myth of the nuclear family is not just a harmless cliché; rather, it can lock us into fundamental misunderstandings of how American families live, misunderstandings that can divide groups and promote simplistic public policy. In this study, sociologists Naomi Gerstel and Natalia Sarkisian examine data on black, white, and Latino/a families to challenge the popular notion that minority families have weaker ties and are more fragmented than white families. They find that social class is more important than ethnicity; moreover, while differences between ethnic groups do exist, each group has developed ways to cope with the practical, emotional, and financial challenges they face and to maintain family solidarity. Gerstel is Distinguished University Professor and professor of sociology at the University of Massachusetts, Amherst; she has published widely on such topics as the changing American family,

elder care, child care, and work schedules. Sarkisian is Associate Profes-
sor of Sociology at Boston College. The two coauthored the 2012 book
*Nuclear Family Values, Extended Family Lives: The Importance of Gender,
Race, and Class.* "The Color of Family Ties" appeared in *American Fami-
lies: A Multicultural Reader,* edited by Stephanie Coontz (see p. 26) with
Maya Parson and Gabrielle Raley (2008).

WHEN TALKING ABOUT FAMILY OBLIGATIONS and solidarities,
politicians and social commentators typically focus on the ties between
married couples and their children. We often hear that Black and Lati-
no/a, especially Puerto Rican, families are more disorganized than
White families, and that their family ties are weaker, because rates of
non-marriage and single parenthood are higher among these minority
groups. But this focus on the nuclear family ignores extended family
solidarities and caregiving activities. Here we examine these often
overlooked extended kinship ties.[1]

Taking this broader perspective on family relations refutes the myth
that Blacks and Latinos/as lack strong families. Minority individuals are
more likely to live in extended family homes than Whites and in many
ways more likely to help out their aging parents, grandparents, adult
children, brothers, sisters, cousins, aunts, uncles, and other kin.

According to our research using the second wave of the National
Survey of Families and Households, as Figures 1 and 2 show, Blacks
and Latinos/as, both women and men, are much more likely than
Whites to share a home with extended kin: 42 percent of Blacks and 37
percent of Latinos/as, but only 20 percent of Whites, live with relatives.
Similar patterns exist for living near relatives: 54 percent of Blacks and
51 percent of Latinos/as, but only 37 percent of Whites, live within two
miles of kin. Blacks and Latinos/as are also more likely than Whites to
frequently visit kin. For example, 76 percent of Blacks, 71 percent of

[1]For the extensive analysis underlying this discussion, see: (1) Natalia Sarkisian, Mar-
iana Gerena, and Naomi Gerstel, "Extended Family Integration Among Mexican and Euro
Americans: Ethnicity, Gender, and Class," *Journal of Marriage and Family,* 69 (2007), 1
(February), 40–54. (2) Natalia Sarkisian, Mariana Gerena, and Naomi Gerstel, "Extended
Family Ties Among Mexicans, Puerto Ricans and Whites: Superintegration or Disinte-
gration?," *Family Relations,* 55 (2006), 3 (July), 331–344. (3) Natalia Sarkisian and Naomi
Gerstel, "Kin Support Among Blacks and Whites: Race and Family Organization," *Amer-
ican Sociological Review,* 69 (2004), 4 (December), 812–837. (4) Amy Armenia and Naomi
Gerstel, "Family Leaves, The FMLA, and Gender Neutrality: The Intersection of Race
and Gender," *Social Science Research,* 35 (2006), 871–891. (5) Naomi Gerstel and Natalia
Sarkisian, "A Sociological Perspective on Families and Work: The Import of Gender, Class,
and Race," in Marcie Pitt Catsouphes, Ellen Kossek, and Steven Sweet (eds.), *The Work
and Family Handbook: Multi-disciplinary Perspectives, Methods, and Approaches* (Mah-
wah, NJ: Lawrence Erlbaum, 2006), pp. 237–266. (6) Naomi Gerstel and Natalia Sarkisian,
"Marriage: The Good, the Bad, and the Greedy," *Contexts,* 5 (2006) 4 (November), 16–21.
(7) Naomi Gerstel and Natalia Sarkisian, "Intergenerational Care and the Greediness of
Adult Children's Marriages," in J. Suitor and T. Owens (eds.), *Interpersonal Relations
Across the Life Course. Advances in the Life Course Research,* Volume 12 (Greenwich, CT:
Elsevier / JAI Press, 2007). [Gerstel and Sarkisian's note.]

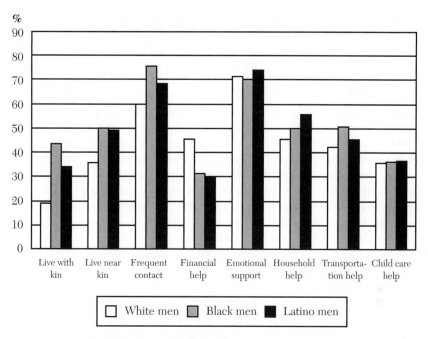

Figure 1.   Ethnicity and extended kin involvement among men.
Data from National Survey of Families and Households, 1992–1994.

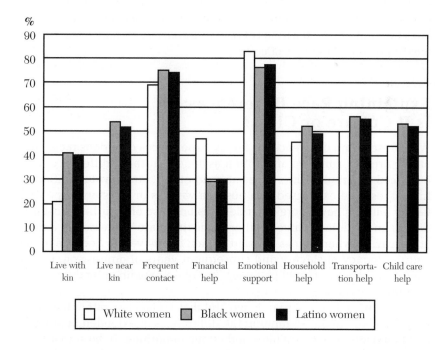

Figure 2.   Ethnicity and extended kin involvement among women.
Data from National Survey of Families and Households, 1992–1994.

Latinos/as, but just 63 percent of Whites see their relatives once a week or more.

Even if they don't live together, Blacks and Latinos/as are as likely as Whites — and in some ways more likely — to be supportive family members. But there are important racial and ethnic differences in the type of support family members give each other. Whites are more likely than ethnic minorities to give and receive large sums of money, and White women are more likely than minority women to give and receive emotional support, such as discussing personal problems and giving each other advice. When it comes to help with practical tasks, however, we find that Black and Latino/a relatives are more likely than Whites to be supportive: they are more likely to give each other help with household work and child care, as well as with providing rides and running errands. These differences are especially pronounced among women.

This is not to say that Black and Latino men are not involved with kin, as is implied in popular images of minority men hanging out on street corners rather than attending to family ties. In fact, Black and Latino men are more likely than White men to live near relatives and to stay in touch with them. White men, however, are more likely to give and receive large-scale financial help. Moreover, the three groups of men are very similar when it comes to giving and getting practical help and emotional support.

These data suggest that if we only consider married couples or parents and their young children, we are missing much of what families in general and families of color in particular do for each other. A focus on nuclear families in discussions of race differences in family life creates a biased portrait of families of color.

Explaining Race Differences: Is It Culture or Class?

When discussing differences in family experiences of various racial and ethnic groups, commentators often assume that these differences can be traced to cultural differences or competing "family values." Sometimes these are expressed in a positive way, as in the stereotype that Latino families have more extended ties because of their historical traditions and religious values. Other times these are expressed in a negative way, as when Blacks are said to lack family values because of the cultural legacy of slavery and subsequent years of oppression. Either way, differences in family behaviors are often explained by differences in cultural heritage.

In contrast, in our research, we find that social class rather than culture is the key to understanding the differences in extended family ties and behaviors between Whites and ethnic minorities. To be sure, differences in cultural values do exist. Blacks and Latinos/as are more likely than Whites to say they believe that extended family is important; both groups are also more likely to attend religious services. Blacks tend to hold more egalitarian beliefs about gender than Whites, while Latinos/as, especially Mexican Americans, tend to hold more "traditional" views. But these differences in values do not explain racial differences in actual involvement with relatives. It is, instead, social class that matters most in explaining these differences.

It is widely known (and confirmed by U.S. Census data presented in Table 1) that Blacks and Latinos/as tend to have far less income and education than Whites. Families of color are also much more likely than White families to be below the official poverty line. In our research, we find that the differences in extended family ties and behaviors between Whites and ethnic minorities are primarily the result of these social class disparities.

Simply put, White, Black, and Latino/a individuals with the same   10
amount of income and education have similar patterns of involvement with their extended families. Just like poor minorities, impoverished Whites are more likely to exchange practical aid and visit with extended kin than are their wealthier counterparts. Just like middle-class Whites, middle-class Blacks and Latinos/as are more likely to talk about their personal concerns or share money with relatives than are their poorer counterparts.

More specifically, it is because Whites tend to have more income than Blacks and Latinos/as that they are more likely to give money to their relatives or get it from them. And the higher levels of emotional support among White women can be at least in part traced to their higher levels of education, perhaps because schooling encourages women to talk out their problems and makes them more likely to give (and get) advice.

Conversely, we find that the relative economic deprivation of racial/ethnic minorities leads in many ways to higher levels of extended family involvement. Individuals' lack of economic resources increases their need for help from kin and boosts their willingness to give help in return. Because Blacks and Latinos/as typically have less income and education than Whites, they come to rely more on their relatives for

TABLE 1 Education, Income, and Poverty Rates by Race			
	WHITES	BLACKS	LATINOS/AS
Median household income	$50,784	$30,858	$35,967
Percentage below poverty line	8.4%	24.7%	22.0%
Education:			
Less than high school	14.5%	27.6%	47.6%
High school graduate	58.5%	58.1%	42.0%
Bachelor's degree or higher	27.0%	14.3%	10.4%

Data from U.S. Census Bureau, 2005.

daily needs such as child care, household tasks, or rides. The tendency of Blacks and Latinos/as to live with or near kin may also reflect their greater need for kin cooperation, as well as their decreased opportunities and pressures to move away, including moving for college.

Social Class and Familial Trade-Offs

How do our findings on race, social class, and familial involvement challenge common understandings of minority families? They show that poor minority families do not necessarily lead lives of social isolation or lack strong family solidarities. The lower rates of marriage among impoverished groups may reflect not a rejection of family values but a realistic assessment of how little a woman (and her children) may be able to depend upon marriage. Sociologists Kathryn Edin and Maria Kefalas (2007) recently found that because disadvantaged men are often unable to offer women the kind of economic security that advantaged men provide, poor women are less likely to marry. Instead, these women create support networks beyond the nuclear family, regularly turning to extended kin for practical support.

Reliance on extended kin and lack of marital ties are linked. In another analysis of the National Survey of Families and Households, we found that, contrary to much rhetoric about marriage as a key source of adult social ties, marriage actually diminishes ties to kin. Married people—women as well as men—are less involved with their parents and siblings than those never married or previously married. These findings indicate a trade-off between commitments to nuclear and extended family ties. Marriage, we have found, is a "greedy" institution: it has a tendency to consume the bulk of people's energies and emotions and to dilute their commitments beyond the nuclear family.

On the one hand, then, support given to spouses and intimate part-   15
ners sometimes comes at the expense of broader kin and community ties. Indeed, married adult children take care of elderly parents less often than their unmarried siblings. Marriage can also cut people off from networks of mutual aid. Married mothers, for example, whether Black, Latina, or White, are often unable to obtain help from kin in the way that their single counterparts can. Although the "greedy" nature of marriage may pose a problem across social class, it is especially problematic for those less well off economically, as these individuals most need to cultivate wider circles of obligation, mutual aid, and reciprocity.

On the other hand, support to relatives sometimes comes at the expense of care for partners, and can interfere with nuclear family formation or stability. Indeed, individuals who are deeply immersed in relationships with extended families may be less likely to get married or, if they marry, may be less likely to put the marital ties first in their loyalties. Several decades ago in her observations of a poor Black community, anthropologist Carol Stack (1974) found that the reciprocal patterns of sharing with kin and "fictive kin" forged in order to survive hardship often made it difficult for poor Blacks either to move up economically or to marry. To prevent the dilution of their social support networks, some extended families may even discourage their members from getting married, or unconsciously sabotage relationships that threaten to pull someone out of the family orbit. As sociologists Domínguez and Watkins (2003) argue, the ties of mutual aid that help impoverished individuals survive on a day-to-day basis may also prevent them from saying "no" to requests that sap their ability to get ahead or pursue individual opportunities.

Overall, we should avoid either denigrating or glorifying the survival strategies of the poor. Although social class disparities are key to understanding racial and ethnic variation in familial involvement, it is too simple to say that class differences create "more" involvement with relatives in one group and "less" in another. In some ways economic deprivation increases ties to kin (e.g., in terms of living nearby or exchanging practical help) and in other ways it reduces them (e.g., in terms of financial help or emotional support). These findings remind us that love and family connections are expressed both through talk and action. Equally important, focusing solely on the positive or on the negative aspects of either minority or White families is problematic. Instead, we need to think in terms of trade-offs—among different kinds of care and between the bonds of kinship and the bonds of marriage. Both trade-offs are linked to social class.

Why Do These Differences in Family Life Matter?

Commentators often emphasize the disorganization and dysfunction of Black and Latino/a family life. They suggest that if we could "fix" family values in minority communities and get them to form married-couple households, all their problems would be solved. This argument misunderstands causal connections by focusing on the family as the source of problems. Specifically, it ignores the link between race and class and attributes racial or ethnic differences to cultural values. Instead, we argue, it is important to understand that family strategies and behaviors often emerge in response to the challenges of living in economic deprivation or constant economic insecurity. Therefore, social policies should not focus on changing family behaviors, but rather aim to support a range of existing family arrangements and improve economic conditions for the poor.

Social policies that overlook extended family obligations may introduce, reproduce, or even increase ethnic inequalities. For example, the relatives of Blacks and Latinos/as are more likely than those of Whites to provide various kinds of support that policymakers tend to assume is only provided by husbands and wives. Such relatives may need the rights and support systems that we usually reserve for spouses. For instance, the Family and Medical Leave Act is an important social policy, but it only guarantees unpaid leave from jobs to provide care to spouses, children, or elderly parents requiring medical attention. Our findings suggest that, if we really want to support families, such policies must be broadened to include adult children, needy grown-up brothers and sisters, cousins, aunts and uncles. Similarly, Medicaid regulations that only pay for non-familial care of ill, injured, or disabled individuals implicitly discriminate against Blacks and Latinos/as who provide significant amounts of care to extended kin. "Pro-marriage" policies that give special incentives to impoverished women for getting married may penalize other women who turn down marriage to a risky mate and rely instead on grandparents or other relatives to help raise their children.

Extended family obligations should be recognized and accommo- 20 dated where possible. But they should not be counted on as a substitute for antipoverty measures, nor should marriage promotion be used in this way. Policymakers must recognize that support from family — whether extended or nuclear — cannot fully compensate for the disadvantages of being poor, or minority, or both. Neither marital ties nor extended family ties can substitute for educational opportunities, jobs with decent wages, health insurance, and affordable child care. Instead of hoping that poor families pull themselves out of poverty by their own bootstraps, social policy should explicitly aim to rectify economic disadvantages. In turn, improvements in economic opportunities and resources will likely shape families.

References

Domínguez, Silvia, and Celeste Watkins. "Creating Networks for Survival and Mobility: Examining Social Capital Amongst Low-Income African-American and Latin-American Mothers." *Social Problems*, 50 (2003), 1 (February), 111–135.

Edin, Kathryn, and Maria Kefalas. *Promises I Can Keep: Why Poor Women Put Motherhood Before Marriage* (Berkeley, CA: University of California Press, 2007).

Stack, Carol B. *All Our Kin: Strategies for Survival in a Black Community* (New York: Harper and Row, 1974).

ENGAGING THE TEXT

1. In paragraph 1, what might politicians and social commentators mean when they describe black and Latino/a families as "more disorganized" than white families? How accurate is this label in Gerstel and Sarkisian's view? Why might a politician find the term "disorganized" useful?

2. What evidence do Gerstel and Sarkisian give that social class is even more important than ethnicity in understanding differences among families? Why is this a critical distinction to the authors?

3. What examples of "extended family solidarities and caregiving activities" (para. 1) do the authors provide? How common or uncommon are these in your own family or community? Do your personal experiences and those of your classmates tend to support, refute, or complicate Gerstel and Sarkisian's analysis?

51

MACFARQUHAR • WHEN SHOULD A CHILD BE TAKEN FROM HIS PARENTS?

4. Explain why you agree or disagree with the claim that "social policy should explicitly aim to rectify economic disadvantages" (para. 20). What would this abstract language mean in practice?

EXPLORING CONNECTIONS

5. Read or review Gary Soto's "Looking for Work" (p. 20), Larissa MacFarquhar's "When Should a Child Be Taken from His Parents?" (below), or the excerpt from *Becoming Nicole* by Amy Ellis Nutt (p. 73). To what extent could each family be described as "disorganized" (para. 1) and to what extent does it exhibit "extended family solidarities and caregiving activities" (para. 1)?

6. Carefully study the frontispiece to Chapter Four on page 341. What symbols of affluence does the photograph contain? How might Gerstel and Sarkisian read the importance of family background in the man's level of economic achievement?

7. How might Gerstel and Sarkisian read the cartoon on page 36?

EXTENDING THE CRITICAL CONTEXT

8. In this article, Gerstel and Sarkisian focus on just three groups — blacks, Latinos/as, and whites. What do you think the data would look like for other groups such as Asian Americans, Pacific Islanders, Native Americans, or recent immigrants? Find data to support or refute your guesses.

9. Study the footnote on page 44, which lists seven articles by Gerstel, Sarkisian, and others. Based on the journal and article titles in the footnote, what can you say about the scope, purpose, and methodologies of Gerstel and Sarkisian's research? To extend the assignment, read one of the articles and report its key findings to the class.

WHEN SHOULD A CHILD BE TAKEN FROM HIS PARENTS?

LARISSA MACFARQUHAR

In the idealized families of television sitcoms, child-protective services never shows up at night to remove kids from their home. Yet this is a common occurrence in America today, as it has been for decades. Through the story of a single mom trying to hold on to her kids, this essay introduces us to the complexities of a system that balances the sanctity of family with the urgent need to protect some children from their own parents. **Larissa MacFarquhar (b. 1968) is a staff writer at the** *New Yorker* **and an Emerson Fellow at New America, a think tank of writers, researchers, activists, and technologists. Before joining the** *New Yorker* **she wrote and edited for numerous publications, including the** *Paris Review, Artforum, Slate,* **the** *New Republic,* **and the** *Nation.* **MacFarquhar is author of the 2015 book** *Strangers Drowning: Grappling with Impossible Ideals, Drastic Choices, and the Overpowering Urge to Help.*

What should you do if child-protective services comes to your house?

You will hear a knock on the door, often late at night. You don't have to open it, but if you don't the caseworker outside may come back with the police. The caseworker will tell you you're being investigated for abusing or neglecting your children. She will tell you to wake them up and tell them to take clothes off so she can check their bodies for bruises and marks. She will interview you and your kids separately, so you can't hear what she's asking them or what they're saying. She opens your fridge and your cabinets, checking to see if you have food, and what kind of food. She looks around for unsafe conditions, for dirt, for mess, for bugs or rats. She takes notes. You must be as calm and deferential as possible. However disrespectful and invasive she is, whatever awful things she accuses you of, you must remember that child protection has the power to remove your kids at any time if it believes them to be in danger. You can tell her the charges are not true, but she's required to investigate them anyway. If you get angry, your anger may be taken as a sign of mental instability, especially if the caseworker herself feels threatened. She has to consider the possibility that you may be hurting your kids, that you may even kill one of them. You may never find out who reported you. If your child has been hurt, his teacher or doctor may have called the state child-abuse hotline, not wanting to assume, as she might in a richer neighborhood, that it was an accident. But it could also have been a neighbor who heard yelling, or an ex-boyfriend who wants to get back at you, or someone who thinks you drink too much or simply doesn't like you. People know that a call to the hotline is an easy way to blow up your life. If the caseworker believes your kids are in imminent danger, she may take them. You may not be allowed to say goodbye. It is terrifying for them to be taken from their home by a stranger, but this experience has repercussions far beyond the terror of that night. Your children may hear accusations against you—you're using drugs, your apartment is filthy, you fail to get them to school, you hit them—and even if they don't believe these things they will remember. And, after your children see that you are powerless to protect them, this will permanently change things between you. Whatever happens later—whether the kids come back the next week, or in six months, or don't come back at all—that moment can never be undone.

The caseworker has sixty days to investigate the charges against you. She will want you to admit to your faults as a parent, and you should, because this tells her you have insight into your problems and that you have a sincere desire to accept her help and change your life. But you should admit only so much, because she is not just there to help you: she is also there to evaluate and report on you, so anything you say may be used against you in court. The Administration for Children's Services—A.C.S., as child-protective services is known in New York City—has to prove its allegations against you only by "preponderance of the evidence." It can bring in virtually anything as evidence—an old drug habit, even if you've been clean for years; a D.U.I.; a diagnosis of depression. While the court case is proceeding, you may be asked to submit to drug testing or a mental-health evaluation, to attend parenting classes or anger-management classes or domestic-violence classes and some kind of therapy. These services are intended to help you, but, if you want to get your kids back, they are not really voluntary, even though they may be so time-consuming and inflexibly scheduled that you lose your job. The more obedient you are, the better things will go for you. Even if you are innocent and can prove it, it could be more than a year before you get a hearing, and during those crucial months your compliance and deference are the currency that buys you visits with your children.

When should you take a child from his parents?

You must start your investigation within twenty-four hours of the hotline call. Go at night—people are more likely to be home. As you look around, you have to be very, very careful, because if you miss something it will be partly your fault if a child ends up hurt, or dead. You may be shocked by the living conditions you encounter, but you're not allowed to remove children solely because of poverty—if, for instance, there's no food in the kitchen because the parent's food stamps have run out—only for "imminent risk" due to abuse or neglect. But it's often difficult to draw a line between poverty and neglect. When a child has been left alone because his mother can't afford childcare and has to go to work, is that poverty or neglect? What if the child has been injured because there wasn't an adult there to prevent it? Unless you've become desensitized through repetition, emergency removals are awful. Parents may scream at you and call you terrible names. Sometimes a parent will get violent. When you suspect in advance that a situation is going to be dicey, you can bring a colleague or a police officer, but sometimes things turn very fast and you're on your own. If you remove the children that night, you will take them to a processing center to be assigned to a temporary foster home. Once you get there, it could take a long time for a home to be found—many hours. The children sit and wait, along with other children in the same situation. They may be crying, but it's unlikely you will be able to comfort them, because you may never have met them before, and you have just separated them from their parents. If the children ask you where they're going next, or when they'll go home, or if they'll stay together with their brothers and sisters, you can't answer them, because you don't know.

After that first visit, you have sixty days to investigate the charges. You should interview the child's teacher, his pediatrician, and anyone else you think relevant. You should seek out neighbors and relatives; they may be too wary to talk to you, or else so eager to talk that you suspect they're trying to get the parent in trouble. You must also draw out the parent herself; this is tricky, because you must play two conflicting roles—helper and investigator. Even if you feel for the parent and believe her kids should not be taken away, that is not the end of the story, because the final decision to ask in court for the removal of children is not yours to make; your supervisor, or your supervisor's manager, will make it. Even though this manager has likely never met the parent or her kids, she may override your recommendation and take what she believes to be the safer course of action. Many at A.C.S. believe that taking kids from their parents is the cautious thing to do. Nobody wants to end up on the front page of the *Daily News.* You are working to protect children, and you will remind yourself of that when your job gets really difficult. Maybe once or twice a parent will thank you, and tell you that the services you provided made a difference in her life, and you will feel that those thanks make up for all the other parents who cursed at you and called you a baby snatcher. But that's unlikely. The turnover among A.C.S. caseworkers is very high.

This is how Mercedes describes what happened. She was running a bath for her children. It was 2009, so Leslie was eleven months old and Camron was two. (To protect her kids' privacy, Mercedes provided pseudonyms.) She plugged in her curling iron, because she was planning to curl and wrap her hair while they were in the tub. The kids were playing with toys in the living room. She left the curling iron on the side of the sink and went to fetch towels. She heard crying and, running back to the bathroom, she saw that Leslie had pulled the hot curling iron off the sink by its dangling cord, and it had fallen on her legs and burned them. She looked at the burns and they weren't blistering, so she figured they were O.K.

The next day, at her cousin's house, she saw that the burns had blistered, and announced that she was going to take Leslie to the E.R., but her aunt told her, Do not go to the E.R. If they see those burns, child services will take your kids. So she didn't. The next day, she went to her mother's house. She and her mother started fighting, as they usually did, and she left the apartment with Leslie and sat with her outside. It was a warm night. She saw two women she didn't know walk past her and into the building. Her mother called her phone and told her to come upstairs. The two women were in her mother's apartment, they told her they were from A.C.S., and had come to see what happened to the baby.

She answered a few questions, growing increasingly outraged, and then, guessing her mother had called A.C.S. to get back at her, began

55

1

MACFARQUHAR · WHEN SHOULD A CHILD BE TAKEN FROM HIS PARENTS?

cursing at her and screaming that she would never see her grandchildren again. She started putting on Leslie's clothes to leave, but the A.C.S. women told her that first they had to take photographs of Leslie's burns. Mercedes said no, she was going, and one of the women said, Miss, you are making me real nervous right now. The women left, but a few minutes later they came back, accompanied by a couple of policemen. Mercedes sat on the floor crying, holding Camron and Leslie and begging the women, Don't take my kids, please don't take my kids. But her mother, believing it was best to comply, picked up Camron and then Leslie and gave them to the women, both kids wailing, and the women took them away.

Mercedes grew up in Brooklyn. Her father was a drunk, who beat her and her mother. One time he nearly killed them, trying to run their car off the road as they fled from him on the Belt Parkway. When Mercedes was old enough to understand what was going on, she started calling the cops on him. When she was older still, she started running away, at which point her mother called the authorities on her. When she was a teenager, her mother sat the kids down and they voted on whether they should kick their father out of the house. Mercedes's younger brother, who was six, voted no, but Mercedes and her older brother and her mother voted yes, so her father left. Mercedes got pregnant when she was fourteen, but her boyfriend beat her up and she lost the baby. When she was eighteen she got pregnant again. Her father turned up and beat her, but she didn't miscarry, and in 2007 she had her first baby, Camron.

Camron's father had told her to get an abortion, and was violent with her, too, so her mother came and brought her home. "She told me, 'I'm going to help you with the baby, I got you,' " Mercedes says. But although Mercedes and her mother were best friends when they weren't living together — they talked every day on the phone, spent every weekend together — when they were in the same house they fought constantly, and when Camron was eight months old Mercedes's mother threw her out, so Mercedes and the baby moved into a shelter. When she got pregnant again, with Leslie, the same thing happened: she moved in with her mother and then ended up in a shelter again six months later. It was in this second shelter that the incident with the curling iron occurred.

At the Bronx Family Court, A.C.S. argued that Mercedes had burned Leslie with the curling iron on purpose, but the judge was not persuaded. Rejecting the charges of abuse, she issued a lesser finding of neglect, because Mercedes had failed to supervise her children properly and had not taken Leslie to the hospital. The children were put into foster care with Mercedes's cousin, and Mercedes set about doing what A.C.S. told her she had to do to get them back—going to parenting class, submitting to inspections by a caseworker. By this time, she was pregnant again. "The first thing that caseworker said to me when she met me was not 'Hello' but 'Oh, you're pregnant again? They ain't going to do nothing but take that baby, too.' That was the first thing that came out of her mouth." But the caseworker was wrong: shortly before Mercedes gave birth to her third child, Tiana, the judge gave Camron and Leslie back to Mercedes, on the condition that she live with her mother.

A.C.S. was still uneasy about Mercedes, however. Right after Tiana was born it requested that the court find "derivative neglect" of Tiana by Mercedes, on the ground that she had been found to neglect Camron and Leslie, and argued that all three children should be taken into foster care. It pointed out that Mercedes's home had been observed to be unsanitary on at least two occasions, that she had refused to participate in drug treatment despite admitting that she smoked marijuana "whenever I get the urge," and had missed two child-safety conferences, and therefore posed an imminent risk to Tiana's life or health. But the children's attorney argued that Mercedes should be allowed to keep the baby, and the judge agreed.

Six months later, A.C.S. filed another petition to remove the children: Leslie had cellulitis and eczema, and Tiana was seriously underweight, and A.C.S. argued that the persistence of these problems suggested that Mercedes was failing to care for them properly. The judge pointed out that since Tiana had not gained weight even during a two-week stay in the hospital, it was not clear that Mercedes had anything to do with it. (Years later, Tiana was given a diagnosis of growth-hormone deficiency.) Moreover, she said, there was a strong bond between mother and infant, the disruption of which would only make things worse. Three months after that, A.C.S. tried to remove Tiana a third time, but again the judge said no.

Mercedes fought with her mother and moved with the kids to a   15 shelter again, but there were bedbugs, so she left. The next day she took Leslie and Tiana to the doctor, and he told her they were so sick he wanted to admit them both to the hospital. For a couple of nights she and Camron slept in the girls' hospital room, but the hospital kicked them out. Then, soon afterward, Mercedes's mother and a woman friend of hers from church turned up at the hospital, along with a caseworker from A.C.S. The caseworker told Mercedes that since she didn't have anywhere for Camron to go she had to give him to either her mother or the friend, or else A.C.S. would take all three kids. As Mercedes understood the arrangement, the caseworker promised her that, if she gave up Camron temporarily, then when the girls were released from the hospital A.C.S. would get the family on a priority list for proper housing and she would get Camron back. Mercedes desperately needed housing, and she didn't have anywhere else for Camron to go, so she said O.K. Because she was still angry with her mother, she told the caseworker that Camron could go with the friend. That turned out to be the wrong decision.

Leslie was released from the hospital a few days later, and she was given to the friend, too. Mercedes kept calling A.C.S., asking when

57

1

MACFARQUHAR · WHEN SHOULD A CHILD BE TAKEN FROM HIS PARENTS?

she was getting her kids back. Tiana was still in the hospital—were they waiting for her to be released? Why did she not have Leslie? When was she going to get her housing? What was going on? But now a caseworker was telling her that she had given up all three children of her own free will.

The judge on Mercedes's case was Carol Sherman, who had worked in family court in various capacities for nearly forty years. As a law student, she had studied reformatories in Massachusetts and was appalled by what she saw—children being held in prisonlike conditions, with only the most rudimentary attempts at education—so when she graduated she looked for an organization that defended children in court. She found only one, the Juvenile Rights Division of the Legal Aid Society in New York, and went to work there in the summer of 1971. The reason she could find only one such organization was that, until a few years before, juvenile defense had not been thought necessary. The Progressive Era[1] creators of family court had imagined its judges as quasi-parents, helping rather than punishing, ruling benevolently in a child's best interest. But, in 1967, the Supreme Court ruled that it was irrelevant whether a judge felt benevolent or not: family court had the power to deprive citizens of their liberty, and that kind of state power had to be restrained by the law, so a juvenile delinquent was entitled to an attorney.

The mission to protect children, combined with the excitement of creating a whole new field of law, made the Juvenile Rights Division in the early seventies a thrilling place to be. Martin Guggenheim, now a professor of law at N.Y.U., arrived at the same time that Sherman did, and together they felt themselves to be part of a righteous crusade on behalf of their underage clients. "We defended murderers and muggers with zeal," he says. "And if our client was found guilty and sent away, we'd say, That fucking judge. We were warriors!"

When Sherman and Guggenheim started out, their caseload was almost all delinquencies. But then growing awareness of "battered-child syndrome"—an awareness that the abuse of children at home was not a rare pathology but a frequent occurrence that demanded attention—led, in 1974, to the Child Abuse Prevention and Treatment Act. The Juvenile Rights Division saw more and more abuse and neglect cases, and as this happened a divide opened among the warriors. To Sherman, it seemed clear that these new cases were very different—that whereas in the delinquency cases children accused of crimes had to be protected from the state, in the neglect and abuse cases the state itself was protecting children, from their parents. But to Guggenheim the child-welfare cases and the delinquency cases looked all too similar: in both, the state

---

[1]**Progressive Era:** The period from 1890 to 1920, which saw numerous reform movements arise in response to the problems of rapid industrialization. Activists pushed ambitious agendas to battle poverty, malnutrition, alcoholism, government corruption, the exploitation of children, and other social ills. [Eds.]

possessed the fearsome power to remove children from their homes, and so in both that power had to be kept in check.

By the time Sherman became a judge, in 2008, a great deal had changed in family court. In the eighties and nineties, putting children in foster care was very common: in 1991, there were nearly fifty thousand children in care in New York City. But study after study had shown how harmful foster care could be, and judges had become leery of it; by 2005, the number had dropped to eighteen thousand. (It is now under nine thousand.) But this didn't mean that all the children who were no longer in foster care had stayed with their parents: many experts in the field had come to believe that the solution to the problem of children spending years in foster care was to speed up adoption. In 1997, Congress passed the Adoption and Safe Families Act, which required states to file for termination of parental rights in most cases when a child had been in foster care for fifteen of the previous twenty-two months. This gave parents far less time to satisfy child-protection agencies that they had adequately reformed, and made it far more likely that they would never get their children back.

Sherman knew that foster care could be harmful, so she felt more comfortable removing children if there was a relative who could pass a background check and take them—she believed that children almost always did better with family. . . . She worked tirelessly, aware that she now had more power than ever to affect children's lives. She read every report in advance, she took detailed notes and reviewed them, she interrogated. . . . When it came to abuse, she tried to parse the different sorts of violence. Was the parent whipping with a belt, which was painful but not usually dangerous, or choking, which was? And why was the parent doing these things in the first place? . . .

Sherman became known in family court for examining the tiniest of details. When inquiring how a child was doing, she wanted to know everything there was to know about him. "I want to see every report card, and if the child isn't doing well in school I order tutoring in the home," she says. "I will order P.S.A.T. and S.A.T. review courses. Information about scholarships. My experience is that unless I give a very detailed order the things that need to be done won't necessarily get done." She was notorious among caseworkers for her obsession with summer camp: if a child was not enrolled by the middle of spring, she would issue an order requiring it. She found out that one boy loved science but had never been to the natural-history museum, so she issued a court order requiring his foster mother to take him there. When he was adopted, she bought him a book about atoms and tickets to the planetarium to celebrate.

Although she issued dozens of orders in every case, she kept track of all of them, and excoriated the caseworkers when they weren't carried out. Some judges seemed to be concerned chiefly that their cases proceeded according to schedule; Sherman was not one of them. "Judge Sherman cares very deeply for children," Mary Anne

1

MACFARQUHAR · WHEN SHOULD A CHILD BE TAKEN FROM HIS PARENTS?

Mendenhall, Mercedes's lawyer, says. "That is something you can never doubt."

Sherman would often say, "All the children before me are entitled to everything that my child's entitled to." To her, this was a matter of social justice: she believed that it was not right for poor children to be deprived of the after-school activities and therapy and evaluations and tutoring and domestic orderliness that middle-class children had, so when a child came into her purview she did her utmost to insure that the child's life and prospects were substantially improved before she was done with him. The trouble was, what to her seemed like helpful services could feel to a parent like intrusion, and the high standards she set could become barriers to reunification. "It moved into social control very quickly, in her courtroom," Emma Ketteringham, the managing director of the Family Defense Practice at the law firm the Bronx Defenders, says. "I will never forget one case where a case planner had put in her report that there was a lot of stuff in the crib. Judge Sherman issued an order that nothing be allowed in the crib except the baby." . . .

"Carol does not see intervention as a terrible cost," Guggenheim says. "She sees it as a price to pay to avoid what is for many in this field the thing to avoid above all else: wrongfully failing to protect a child. She really has a Progressive mind-set, in that she sees herself as the instrument of power to improve children's lives. But, on the privileged side of town in all parts of America, children are raised by drunks, by drug addicts, by violent people. We don't care how privileged children are raised, because we've arranged our world around the fundamental principle that the state doesn't intrude on the family. Equality requires that we give the same freedom to underprivileged children as we give to privileged children—to be raised by crappy parents."

For a long time after she lost her children, Mercedes was homeless. She couldn't sleep at her mother's anymore, and she didn't have close friends, so she floated from place to place, staying in each as long as her host would let her, sometimes staying with someone she had met that day. She refused to go to a shelter for single women—she had heard there were fights in those places, and people stole things. She was used to this. Her life had been this way since she was sixteen—staying with her mother, getting thrown out, staying with a friend, getting in an argument, moving on. Besides, she didn't have her kids, so she barely cared what happened to her. "When they take your kids, it's like everything stops," she says. "Your heart stops. Everything stops. Then you're trying to figure out what the hell to do next. What do I do? Once they take them, you don't have no reason to be here no more. Your kids give you purpose."

She was permitted to see her children each week in a room at the foster-care agency, but she came to dread these visits, because they were so short and saying goodbye was awful for everyone, and because someone from the agency would watch them, taking notes on how she and the kids behaved together. But mostly she dreaded them because the kids had started saying things about her. They said that their foster mother had told them that Mercedes was bad, that she was a drug addict, that she didn't want them back. Mercedes started coming late to visits, and sometimes she wouldn't show up at all, and the kids would get very upset. Sherman ruled that if Mercedes was late for a visit it would be cancelled, and Mercedes was late. She was late for court dates, too. "Mercedes has no sense of time," her mother says. "I tell her, Don't leave when you feel like it, stop getting up when you feel like it, you got to be in court at twelve, how dare you get there when it's over?" The foster agency warned the foster mother not to disparage Mercedes in front of the children, but she continued to do it. (A.C.S., Judge Sherman, and the foster agency all have a policy of not discussing open cases.)

Before she took in Mercedes's kids, the foster mother had been earning a little money cleaning houses and watching people's children, but now she began receiving foster-care benefits. Mercedes's children were medically complicated, so the payments were higher than usual. For "special children" in New York, foster parents are paid up to $1,289 a month; for "exceptional children," the payment is $1,953; so to take care of all three of them the foster mother was likely being paid between forty-six and sixty-two thousand dollars a year, plus up to seventeen hundred dollars a year in clothing allowance. If she ended up adopting the children, she would receive benefits until each child turned twenty-one.

She wanted to adopt them. In the past, foster parents often did not want to adopt, so if a parent's rights were terminated the children were forced to go to yet another home. To overcome this problem, the foster agency that was supervising Mercedes's children had a policy of encouraging foster parents to consider adoption. The trouble with this solution was that foster parents were prompted from the start to form attachments to the children, and their hopes were pitted against those of the biological parents.

While the case dragged on and Mercedes drifted, the agency was helping the foster mother with housing. "They done moved this lady three times, and every time the apartment's getting bigger," Mercedes said bitterly. "But you can't help the biological mother who's showing you that she wants her kids? If they would have done that for me in the first place, I wouldn't be in the situation that I'm in now, and I'd have my kids." Between constantly moving from place to place and feeling that A.C.S. had it in for her, and wasn't going to return her kids no matter how hard she tried or how many parenting classes she enrolled in, Mercedes had started to fray. "By this time, I'm tired. I love my kids, but I'm tired. My mind is tired. My body is tired. I keep getting—excuse my language—dicked around by A.C.S. They're lying to me, they're being disrespectful. So I start to disappear for a while."

Every time she came to court she felt surrounded by people who were convinced that she was a bad mother and a bad person, although

61

MACFARQUHAR · WHEN SHOULD A CHILD BE TAKEN FROM HIS PARENTS?

they barely knew her. "At one point, we had a court date when the lawyer for the foster-care agency first came on," she says. "And when we met outside he kept saying, 'Oh, you're really clean.' What the fuck does that mean? 'I don't see nothing wrong with you, you look clean.' Because I'm black I'm supposed to be dirty?" She would sit in the courtroom resentfully listening to the caseworker note when she'd been late to a visit, or missed a therapy appointment, but not mention when the foster mother was late, or when she missed the kids' doctors' appointments, or that she had been telling the kids terrible and untrue things about their mother. The lawyers only ever brought up the bad stuff about her, she felt; never the good. One time when she was at a conference at the foster-care agency, Leslie burst into the room and said, "I have an announcement to make—I love my mommy"; and then next time they were in court there was Leslie's attorney advocating against reuniting her with her mother, and there was no mention of what Leslie had said until Mary Anne Mendenhall, representing Mercedes, brought it up.

The judge kept saying she understood Mercedes, because they had been encountering each other in court for years, but she knew only a few things about her life. "It always bothered Mercedes when Judge Sherman would look at her and say, 'I know you very well,'" Mendenhall says. "Mercedes would walk out crying and say, 'She doesn't know me! She only knows what they say about me! She's never talked to me, she doesn't know anything about who I am.' Just because of the number of pages she'd read about Mercedes, to feel entitled to look her in the eye and say, 'I know you very well.' I don't think Judge Sherman recognized what that meant to Mercedes. And how wrong it was. And how many times she said it." . . .

Because A.C.S. continued to complain in court about Mercedes's marijuana use, and because she hoped that a dramatic demonstration of compliance and sacrifice might convince them that she was determined to reform, in 2012 she enrolled in a yearlong in-patient drug-treatment program called La Casita. At first, it was hard. "I didn't have no phone," she says. "You got to get rid of everything—no nails, no hair, no makeup, nothing, you're in there Plain Jane. I didn't really understand the logic of why you got to take my weave out, or why I can't wear earrings. I cried about my hair. They said, 'To strip you down to nothing and build you back up.' But you already feel like shit because your kids are in the system. Why would you want me to feel like nothing? I already feel like nothing." She couldn't believe she was there in the first place—she looked around and saw dope fiends and crackheads, and all she'd done was smoke some pot.

But then she grew close to a couple of the counsellors; she felt they understood her and gave her good advice. They believed in her and thought she should get her children back. Little by little, she started to unfurl. "Like most women that enter treatment, she didn't trust, she came from a broken home, she was always fighting," Yolanda

Stevenson, one of the counsellors, says. "She was angry at herself, and at the system. I also think that she suffered from some form of depression, which was taboo for her. For a lot of African-Americans, we feel it's taboo—we're not crazy, why should we have therapy? But when you're fighting with your mother like boxers, that's a little off." Mercedes felt that, after months of shutting down and running away from her life, this was her last chance, and she seized it.

Judge Sherman saw how hard she was trying, and how far she'd   35 come, and said that the kids could visit her on weekends. She said that soon they'd be able to come for overnight visits, so La Casita moved Mercedes to a bigger room, with enough beds for all the kids to sleep there. Tiana was being fed through a tube into her stomach now, and Mercedes studied up on it so she would know how to take care of her. "I knew how to flush it, I knew how to mix it, I knew how to put the milk and cereal together and put the tube in and everything," she says. Mendenhall argued that the only remaining barrier to reuniting the family was housing, and Sherman charged the foster-care agency with arranging it. The agency resisted—it believed that the children should be adopted by their foster mother—but she ordered it to comply. Now it was only a matter of finding an apartment: after three and a half years, it would be just a few more months before the family could be together.

That year—2013—Mercedes brought her kids to Thanksgiving dinner at her aunt's house. "Thanksgiving was beautiful," she says. "My aunt and my grandfather hadn't seen Leslie, Camron, and Tiana since they were babies. We ate, we laughed, we talked. My aunt has one of them big dummies with no arms that they have in defense classes, and Camron was fighting that—they put boxing gloves on him and he went at it and had a ball. He was play-wrestling with my brother. Tiana, she was playing with toys with my cousin. Leslie was eating, talking to my mother, talking to my aunt."

Then, two days later, the agency told Mercedes that Camron had said that during the Thanksgiving dinner she had taken him into the bathroom and punched him in the stomach while her mother held his shirt up. More accusations followed: Leslie said that she had been abused, sexually and otherwise, by Mercedes and other people in her family. Later, Camron admitted to Mercedes and a caseworker at La Casita that the punching at Thanksgiving hadn't happened, that his foster mother had told him to say that, and the caseworker recorded his statement, but the foster-care agency said the statement sounded coerced.

A.C.S. investigated each of these reports but pursued none of them in court. But as soon as one was closed another accusation would be made, and no reunion could take place before the new report was properly looked into. It seemed that nobody really believed that Mercedes had abused her children, because she was never arrested, and during this period she gave birth to a fourth child, Amaya, and Amaya was never taken away. But the reports continued. . . .

63

1

MACFARQUHAR · WHEN SHOULD A CHILD BE TAKEN FROM HIS PARENTS?

By the spring of 2017, Mercedes hadn't seen her children in nearly two years. She was living with Amaya in a shelter in Manhattan, near the F.D.R. Drive. "So much time has gone past, I don't even know what my kids look like right now," she said. "I look at them old pictures, I know Camron looks older. He's taller. I know Leslie looks older and she's taller. I don't know what they look like." The foster-care agency was advocating strenuously for adoption. The point of no return was getting closer. . . .

For Mercedes, spring was the hardest time of year, because of birthdays. Camron's was March 21st, Tiana's March 30th, Leslie's May 5th. Each year, she braced herself for this dark period by going all out for Amaya's birthday, in January. She would spend her food stamps on a birthday cake and they would celebrate together. "Your birthday is special," she would tell her. "That's the day you changed me. That's the day you made me feel like I need to be here. Because I didn't feel like I needed to be here for a long time. They always made me feel like my kids never needed me, they didn't want me, they was better off with this lady. I just lost the will to live. It was like, whatever happened to me happened to me, I'm on the streets until whatever. But, when I saw Amaya, that was my purpose—to make sure she didn't go into care. I made sure that that baby stayed with me, and I'm going to continue to make sure that my baby stay with me. I refuse to lose her. I fucking refuse to. They will have to kill me."

"The reckless destruction of American families in pursuit of the goal of protecting children is as serious a problem as the failure to protect children," Martin Guggenheim, Sherman's former colleague, says. "We need to understand that destroying the parent-child relationship is among the highest forms of state violence. It should be cabined and guarded like a nuclear weapon. You use it when you must." He believes the tide is turning in his direction—nine thousand children in foster care in New York City compared with fifty thousand, changing views on drugs—but each time a child is murdered by a parent some gain is lost. After the death of Zymere Perkins, last year, Mayor de Blasio spoke on the radio about the case. "Our mission is to save every child," he said. "Unlike pretty much any other area in government—we do not set a standard for perfection in policing or so many other areas—in this case we do set a standard of perfection." He said, "Our job is to get there first and intervene and stop it." . . .

Children are killed all the time. But when confronted with one particular dead child and asked if there is no limit to what we should do to prevent another from dying like that—if perfection should be the goal of child-protective services, and if the state should intervene before bad things happen, just in case—it is very difficult to say no, even if the price is other children and parents suffering while alive.

Mercedes knows that, at this point, she has very little chance of getting her kids back. She knows that they will probably grow up without her, and that she may not even be allowed to see them. The foster mother and Mercedes's mother aren't friends anymore. The photographs she has will get more and more out of date, and Camron, Leslie, and Tiana will become people she doesn't know. What she hopes for now is that when they're grown, when they're adults and can do as they like, one day they will come and find her. "I will always be looking for that phone call, for that hit up on Facebook: 'Mommy, what happened?' " she says. It will be years till then, but it's been years already, and she'll survive as long as she has Amaya. "I'm waiting for it," she says. "I got time. Camron, that's eight more years till he's eighteen. Leslie is, what, nine more years. Tiana is six now. So I'm waiting for it. I'm waiting for it."

ENGAGING THE TEXT

1. Who are the key players in Mercedes's story? Where do their interests align, and where do they conflict? With whose views and actions are you most and least sympathetic, and why? To what extent do you think MacFarquhar reveals her own sympathies?

2. Can you imagine a story like this unfolding in the community where you grew up? Why or why not? What elements here seem universal, and which are specific to Mercedes's personal history, family relationships, or social class?

3. Discuss the decisions made by Carol Sherman, the judge assigned to Mercedes's case. What are her guiding principles, and do they strike you as reasonable and laudable? Do you think she is overzealous or guilty of micromanaging people's lives as a kind of "social engineering"?

4. MacFarquhar quotes Martin Guggenheim as arguing that "Equality requires that we give the same freedom to underprivileged children as we give to privileged children — to be raised by crappy parents" (para. 25). Consider the roles A.C.S., the courts, and foster-care agencies play in Mercedes's story. Debate whether they have too much power over her life and whether she seems to be treated unjustly because of her ethnicity or poverty.

5. **Thinking Rhetorically**   Jot down several of the important issues raised in this reading — for example, the difficulty of knowing whose account of an event is more accurate. Then review the opening paragraphs of the article, before MacFarquhar introduces Mercedes (paras. 1–6). Which of the essay's main themes are prefigured in the opening? How effective do you find the strategy of beginning by creating the dual perspectives of parent and caseworker?

EXPLORING CONNECTIONS

6. In "Looking for Work" (p. 20), Gary Soto recollects that Little John's mother "told me in a polite but matter-of-fact voice that I had to leave because she was going to beat her son" (para. 11). Does MacFarquhar's serious and extended discussion of child abuse cause you to reread Soto's brief description of this incident? Why or why not?

65

1

MACFARQUHAR · WHEN SHOULD A CHILD BE TAKEN FROM HIS PARENTS?

7. If you are not already familiar with the idea of a universal basic income, read "Why We Should Give Free Money to Everyone" by Rutger Bregman (p. 456). How and to what extent do you think simply having more money might have helped Mercedes deal with some of the challenges she faced?

8. Using "Looking for Work" by Gary Soto (p. 20) as a rough model, write a fictional account of a single day in Mercedes's life from the perspective of her mother, her son Camron, or Judge Sherman. Compare your narrative with those of classmates to see how you interpret the personalities and motivations of the people around Mercedes.

EXTENDING THE CRITICAL CONTEXT

9. Dividing the work among teams, research child-protective services in your state. How many children are removed from their families each year, either temporarily or permanently, and is the number trending up or down? What demographic information can you find about which families are most commonly affected (e.g., data by region, ethnicity, income, or dual- vs. single-parent household)? What laws govern protective services, and when were they passed? What agencies are involved, and what information do they publish about their missions, guidelines, and procedures? How do foster care and adoption work?

10. What resources are available in your community for women dealing with any of Mercedes's challenges (e.g., free counseling, legal aid, or temporary housing)? How robust and accessible are these resources?

VISUAL PORTFOLIO

READING IMAGES OF AMERICAN FAMILIES

Freedom from What (2014), by Pops Peterson.

Mariette Pathy Allen

Patryce Bak/Getty Images

CSP_desertsolitaire/AGE Fotostock

VISUAL PORTFOLIO:
READING IMAGES OF AMERICAN FAMILIES

1. The illustration on page 66 by artist Pops Peterson closely mirrors *Freedom from Fear*, an iconic painting by Norman Rockwell (1894–1978) that depicts two American children being safely tucked into bed while World War II rages in Europe. Find *Freedom from Fear* online and list all the similarities and differences you can see between the original painting and Peterson's recreation. Then explain how you read the relationship between the two pieces, accounting not only for Peterson's switch to showing an African American family but also for details like the doll, the facial expressions, the body language, and the newspaper headlines (the partially visible headline "Bombings Ki . . . Horror Hit" in *Freedom from Fear* and "I Can't Breathe!" in Peterson's reinterpretation). What is Peterson saying about freedom, fear, and race in America?

2. The young women pictured on page 67 are Lucy and Maria Aylmer; they are sisters—in fact *twin* sisters born to a white father and half-Jamaican mother. Explain how this image of biracial twins may complicate our understanding of racial and family identity. Do you think Maria's and Lucy's divergent appearances are likely to impact their life experiences? Why or why not?

3. The image on page 68 was taken in April 2015 during demonstrations after Freddie Gray Jr., a twenty-five-year-old African American, died while in Baltimore Police custody. What emotions can you read in the faces pictured? How do you read the signs and symbols in the image—the children's hands, the father's Baltimore Orioles T-shirt, and the photograph itself in its racially charged context? Compare this image to the portrait of Lucy and Maria Aylmer, who are also members of a multi-ethnic family (p. 67).

4. In the photo of Rachel watching her dad transforming into Paula (p. 69), how would the meaning and the impact of the image change if Rachel were not included? What claims do Rachel's dad and the photographer, Mariette Pathy Allen, seem to be making about families, parenting, and gender, and to what extent do you accept or challenge their perspectives?

5. What strikes you first in the photo on page 70—perhaps the cat, the cute kids, or all the smiling faces? Or perhaps you notice right away that the family is interracial. In any case, you likely don't see that the father here is transgender. Discuss this photo and others in the Visual Portfolio as images designed to disrupt our notions of family by combining everyday or even clichéd elements with controversial ideas about gender, race, religion, or immigration.

6. What do you imagine the relationships to be among the three people pictured on page 71? Assuming the photograph has been carefully staged, explain details such as the positioning of the three bodies, the camera angle, the furniture, the partially concealed faces, and the man's ring. To extend your analysis, read the excerpt from *Beyond Monogamy* on page 100 and explain any changes in your assessment of the photo.

FROM *BECOMING NICOLE: THE TRANSFORMATION OF AN AMERICAN FAMILY*

AMY ELLIS NUTT

In 1997, Wayne and Kelly Maines adopted identical twin boys, Wyatt and Jonas. From a very young age, Wyatt identified as female, and she is now Nicole Maines, a transgender actress and activist. The excerpt below describes key events in Nicole's adolescence — her move away from a school where she suffered harassment; the family's emerging activism on transgender issues; and the twins' enrollment at a progressive school where Nicole could come out about her gender. Nicole was featured in the 2016 HBO documentary *The Trans List*, and in 2018 was cast as the first transgender superhero in the CW television series *Supergirl*. Journalist Amy Ellis Nutt (b. 1955) is currently a science writer at the *Washington Post*. She won the 2011 Pulitzer Prize in feature writing for her series "The Wreck of the *Lady Mary*." Her 2009 series, "The Accidental Artist," was a Pulitzer Prize finalist and later became the book *Shadows Bright as Glass: The Remarkable Story of One Man's Journey from Brain Trauma to Artistic Triumph* (2014). *Becoming Nicole,* the source of this selection, was a 2016 *New York Times* notable book and was named the Stonewall Honor Book in nonfiction.

Going Stealth

THE MAINESES WERE ABOUT TO ESSENTIALLY shred the world they'd lived in for the past decade and trade it for an unknown one. Time was not on their side. They had to put their house on the market, then find a home for Kelly and the kids in Portland.[1] They had to register Jonas and Nicole at King Middle School, meet with the principal and teachers, pack up everything they owned and put some of it in storage—and they had two months to do it. The easiest part was registering the kids and meeting with more than two dozen of the staff and teachers at King. No one, except this group of adults at King Middle School, could know about Nicole. If anyone found out she was transgender the family would have to come up with a new game plan, perhaps even move again, and that seemed unimaginable. Could Kelly and Wayne trust the school to keep Nicole's secret? Yes, the administrators said. But there was one other worry: Kelly wasn't 100 percent sure Nicole could keep the secret.

---

[1]**Portland:** Portland, Maine. Orono, mentioned below, is also in Maine, roughly 140 miles northeast of Portland. [All notes are the editors'.]

The temperature hovered around ninety degrees the day of the move, and the heat baked the blacktop on the roads out of Orono. Wayne was getting over a bout with pneumonia, and when he finally slid behind the wheel of the rented U-Haul he was already exhausted. There was little joy and a lot of frayed nerves and the whole family couldn't help but feel as if they were somehow sneaking out of town. On the highway, the truck whined louder the faster Wayne drove.

"Dad, it sounds like it's going to blow up," Jonas said.

Wayne tried not to push the truck. It had clearly seen better days, and the last thing he needed was for the engine to break down. Nearly three hours later he finally pulled into the driveway of the Portland duplex they'd rented, and the moment the truck came to a stop, the engine's manifold loudly disconnected from the exhaust system. On top of everything else, Wayne now had a useless U-Haul he had to get back to Orono.

The University of Southern Maine is located in Portland and its law school was just two blocks from the duplex. Generations of students living in off-campus housing gave the neighborhood a worn, dilapidated feel. There was more traffic on the street in front of the house, including police cars and ambulances at all hours, than either Kelly or Wayne had ever experienced, and it took them quite a while to learn how to sleep through the noise, especially with Wayne visiting only on weekends.

The entrance to the house had two doors, separated by a few feet, with the inner door secured by two locks. That was something Wayne had never seen before. Then again, he and Kelly had never felt the need to lock their house in Orono. Immediately inside was the living room, with just enough space for a couch and an armchair, wedged around a large cast-iron radiator. Layers of paint from one tenant after another coated the walls, and cracks in the plaster spidered across the ceiling. Three windows opened up one side of the living room to a bit of light, but the house sat so close to the one next door, occupied by six female college students, that Kelly and the kids could watch them ironing their clothes in the morning. The back door of the house was only thirty feet from the girls' porch, which was the scene of many raucous parties. Once, when Wayne was cooking dinner, a drunken young man stumbled through the back door and began talking to Wayne as if they were both at the party.

"You better turn around and walk away before you get shot," Wayne told him.

The young man quickly sobered up and scampered out.

When they finally finished unloading that first day in Portland, Wayne took a moment to lean against the bumper of the truck. From the other side of the street he watched Jonas and Nicole lug their toys into the tired old apartment. The bright blue wallpaper was peeling, the attic bedroom had no heat, and the only emergency exit was a small window with no outside staircase. After more than a decade of marriage, he and Kelly weren't moving up in the world, they were moving down. They'd bought the house in Orono when real estate prices were sky-high and it was going to take a long time to sell. They were paying a mortgage on a house only Wayne was living in and rent on a new one where Wayne would only ever be a visitor.

Wayne found himself vacillating between panic and depression. 10 They were breaking up the family. How was he going to leave them here and drive home alone to Orono? He didn't want to let the kids see him crying. They really didn't know how serious it all was, and now Kelly was going to have to shoulder everything alone. In truth, she was used to it. She'd pretty much steered the family through one crisis after another on her own. In a way, she thought, living apart might be good for both of them. Now she could focus all her attention on Nicole and Jonas without worrying about her husband's obstinacy.

Wayne shook off the mood. His self-pity wouldn't do anyone any good. Kelly was already trying to make the best of things. While his wife scrubbed the apartment from attic to basement, he went out and bought a small hot-oil heater, a thermometer to keep track of the temperature in Nicole's attic bedroom, and a fire escape ladder for her little window. He also tried to glue the wallpaper back into place—a losing battle.

Closing up the truck that first night in Portland, Wayne could hear the faint sounds of a sports announcer floating over the treetops from the high school football field a few blocks away. Taking the kids to University of Maine games was something he'd enjoyed when they all lived in Orono. So a few weeks after the move, on one of his weekend visits, he suggested to Jonas and Nicole they all walk over to the high school to watch the football game. At halftime Jonas said he was going to the snack bar for a hot dog. Nicole wanted to watch the cheerleaders closer to the field. During a break in the cheerleaders' routine, Nicole hiked back up into the stands and sat down next to her father. Jonas was still nowhere in sight.

Nicole looked up at her dad.

"Sometimes I hate being transgender," she said. "Transgender kids commit suicide or they're killed."

Wayne was caught by surprise. It had been a hard year, with all the 15 harassment in school and the lawsuit, then this move to a new city. But this seemed different.

"Why do you say that?"

"It was in a movie I saw. They said most transgender kids commit suicide or are killed."

Nicole had seen a documentary called *Two Spirits: Sexuality, Gender, and the Murder of Fred Martinez*, about a transgender Native American teenager. It had been shown at a meeting of the Proud Rainbow Youth of Southern Maine, or PRYSM. Kelly had pressed hard to find a place in Portland where Nicole could be herself, and PRYSM was the only group that seemed like it might be a good fit. The PRYSM meetings were held at Portland's Community Counseling Center, in a neighborhood just north of shabby, and were mostly attended by older LGBT individuals.

As PRYSM members filtered into a room at the center to watch the film, the smell of stale cigarettes lingered in the air. When the room darkened and the movie started, interviews with experts on hate crimes were interspersed with pictures and videos of Fred and his mother, scenes from the reservation, including the place where Fred was killed, and a close-up of the bloody twenty-five-pound rock that was used to bash in his skull.

Nicole sunk lower in her chair. On screen an activist described other 20 hate crimes against transgender people: a man who was repeatedly run over by the same car, another person who was set on fire. Nicole felt sick to her stomach. Fred Martinez, the murder victim, hadn't been a troubled teen; he was described by someone who knew him as having "a high degree of self-acceptance about who he was," just like Nicole. Fred's eighteen-year-old killer, who was eventually convicted of the crime, had bragged to his friends before his arrest that he'd "bug-smashed a fag."

Nicole didn't tell her parents or Jonas about the movie when she got home. She didn't want to talk about it, and not too long afterward she stopped going to PRYSM meetings, primarily because she had failed to meet any other transgender teens.

"Many of the trans kids mentioned in that movie didn't have parents who loved and accepted them and were supportive of their children," he told Nicole. "They didn't let them be who they needed to be."

Wayne wasn't sure if this was the right thing to say, because being who you are was, in many ways, more dangerous. It had proved fatal for Fred, and it was that danger that chiefly worried Kelly and Wayne.

"That doesn't mean there aren't mean, dangerous people out there who can hurt you," he said. "You have to be very careful about who you let into your circle of trust. You have to watch where you go and who you are with at all times. Never go anywhere alone." . . .

On the Outside Looking In

On the first day of seventh grade, the twins walked the half mile to 25 King Middle School under a chilly, overcast sky, saying little to each other. The school, a sprawling two-story brick and concrete building, sat at the bottom of a hill in a working-class neighborhood. Two years earlier King had made the news when it became the first middle school in Maine (and one of the first in the nation) to offer birth control to students as young as eleven years old. The decision was made after Portland's three middle schools reported seventeen pregnancies over a four-year span.

When Nicole and Jonas arrived at King that September morning, they were told they had to wait in the parking lot with about five hundred other students before the first bell signaling the start of the school day. This would be a daily ritual. To Jonas, the other students looked much older and, for some reason, unhappy. Many were children of recent immigrants—Africans, East Asians, Muslims, and Sikhs. In fact, there were more minorities in their middle school than Jonas and Nicole had ever seen in Orono. It was hard not to feel both intimidated and terrified, and all the twins wanted to do was blend into the background. The seventh graders were split into two sections and assembled on opposite sides of the parking lot. They also ate lunch and had recess at different times. So from the second day of school, Jonas and Nicole actually saw very little of each other.

Nothing about King Middle School felt right. It was large and unfriendly, especially if you didn't belong to one of the many cliques. Having to hide who they were, and why they were there, only added to the twins' sense of not belonging.

Nicole was always acutely aware of leading a kind of double life, never more so than the time, only two months into the seventh grade, when a boy in one of her classes asked her out on a date as they stood talking in the hallway. The boy was lean and lanky with short hair and braces. And he was the first boy to ever ask her out on a real date, to go to a concert. It took her aback. She knew she couldn't say yes, and yet she also didn't want to hurt the boy.

"I'm sorry, I can't," she said as gently and politely as she could.

No explanations were asked for. "Can't" was better—or at least 30 easier—to say than "won't," and it had the added benefit of being true. There was no way she could go out on any dates for the next two years, a source of both sadness and frustration. But it was more than that. It hurt deeply because it confirmed for Nicole the reason she'd never been asked out on a date in Orono, where all her schoolmates knew who she was: It was because she was transgender. The word, the identity— she had already fought long and hard for them. And yet, it was precisely that identity that seemed to prevent any boy who really knew her from getting too close. It was that distance she dreaded she'd never overcome, and, ironically, this boy had just reminded her of it.

There was an edginess to the school that made it hard for the twins to let their guard down. Several times during the seventh grade, brawls broke out. Neither Jonas nor Nicole had ever seen someone their age in a fistfight, much less partaken in one, but that soon changed. Jonas had developed a crush on a girl and, trying to fit in, had made it known to some of the other boys in his class that he was interested in her. Unfortunately, one of the other boys decided he liked this girl, too, and asked her out. Jonas felt betrayed and quietly seethed. Not long afterward, when his class was playing a vigorous game of floor hockey, Jones singled out the student he was angry at, and was a bit more physical with him than he should have been. Arms and elbows flew, shoulders crunched. Finally Jonas called the other boy a "bitch" and the other boy retaliated. Before he knew what he was doing, Jones turned around and punched the kid in the face. Immediately he realized he'd done something very wrong. Fighting was something he generally didn't do, but his anger had gotten the best of him.

Maybe that's why Jonas withdrew into music and playing the guitar—things he could do on his own. At Asa Adams[2] he'd played the drums in the school band and orchestra. Maybe he'd try that again. He signed up for band class, but on the first day, when he walked into the room, he immediately felt out of place, as if everyone was looking at him. When Jonas began drumming, another student mocked him loudly. Wounded, Jonas simply stood up and walked out.

As attuned as they were to what was happening with Nicole on a day-to-day basis, Kelly and Wayne both knew they needed to be more aware of what was going on with Jonas. He had a tendency to be passive, to step aside and let the world—or Nicole—not only rush by him, but overwhelm him. Their whole lives, Kelly had made sure each child had the same opportunities. What one received the other received, and most of the time the twins were in sync, not only sharing toys and games but most of their friends as well. But where Nicole was impulsive, explosive, and domineering, Jonas was reflective and intellectual. Sometimes indolent, he let others make decisions for him. What worries he had, he usually buried, but every now and then the came surging to the fore, sometimes with disastrous results.

Toward the end of April 2010, almost eight months after Wayne and Kelly and the kids started living apart, Wayne lingered on the phone with his son a bit longer than usual. That's when Jonas admitted to his father that some kids at school had punched him.

"Why didn't you say something earlier to your mother?" Wayne asked. 35

"Because Mom would have gotten upset and she would want to do something."

"Do something" meant calling the school or the parents of the boy who punched Jonas, and that was the last thing he wanted. What he did want, just like Nicole, was to fit in, to be a normal kid, not the brother of a transgender sister, and especially not the identical twin of a transgender sister. Jonas understood that at King Middle School you didn't tell anyone anything or you'd be labeled for life. But Jonas's sense of justice was acute. He told his father that when he heard another student refer to someone as a fag, he couldn't just stand there, even if it wasn't directed at his sister. So he'd confronted the kid and the kid threw a punch.

Wayne told him he understood, but he still needed to deal with things differently.

"I don't want you to fight. You need to look the kid in the eye and tell him not to do it again and if he does, then walk away and tell someone. There are better ways to deal with things."

[2]**Asa Adams:** Asa C. Adams, the school Jonas and Nicole had attended in Orono. The Maineses filed a civil lawsuit against the school in 2009, saying it had "intentionally and negligently inflicted emotional distress on Nicole and the family." Encouraged by his grandfather, a boy had repeatedly followed Nicole into the girls' bathroom, asserting he had as much right to be there as she did; the school's remedy was to direct Nicole to use a single-stall staff bathroom and not the girls' restroom. In 2014 a Superior Court order settled the suit, forbidding discrimination against students like Nicole and awarding $75,000 to the plaintiffs.

Nicole knew this, too. And while she never wanted to respond physically to someone, there were many times she wanted to say exactly how she felt but couldn't for fear that it would inevitably lead to being outed. Being true to her beliefs, and not just about being transgender, had never felt this dangerous. The hardest times were keeping her mouth shut when she'd hear someone say "Oh, that's so gay," which kids often did. She knew if she tried to object, the other person would only say, "Why do you care? Are you gay?" And then she'd be stuck. She had good reason to challenge others' prejudices, but she couldn't because they hit too close to home. So she kept her mouth shut, buttoned down her anger, and sealed off her sense of self-righteousness.

Jonas, like Nicole, walked to school every day, and nearly every day walked home right afterward and watched TV or played video games. He had a couple of friends, who were also Nicole's, but neither twin hung out with them much after the school day was over. No one could get too close for fear they'd find out too much. It was strange and stressful, trying to be "half friends" with certain classmates. As for classwork, Jonas found it hard to motivate himself. He was extraordinarily bright, but being around so many other disinterested kids sapped him of his normal curiosity and love of knowledge. King was an expeditionary learning school, modeled on the reforms of Kurt Hahn, the German educator who also founded Outward Bound.[3] The central idea was project-based learning, which involved multidiscipline group activities. The theme that year was invasive species, but as far as Jonas could tell, neither the students nor the teachers seemed all that excited about the project. There was very little joy in learning, on either side of the desk, Jonas thought. By the end of the year he'd sunk into a deep depression and admitted to his mother he felt like cutting himself. Kelly immediately called Wayne. What could he do two hundred miles away? He would talk to Jonas on the phone, but Kelly would have to handle it with the school. She sat down and sent an email to school officials:

> Yesterday, Jonas came home and said he felt like cutting himself. My husband and I have decided to pursue counseling for him and I will arrange that today. Meanwhile, we would appreciate all of you keeping a close eye on him while he is in school. I will be giving him a ride to school and walking with him after school until we are sure he is not truly going to hurt himself. Thanks for your help, and any insight you may have would be greatly appreciated.

Wayne and Kelly both realized that hormones were likely playing a big part in Jonas's life at that moment. Jonas was also a thinker, and sometimes he was just too far inside his head for his own good.

[3]**expeditionary learning school/Outward Bound:** The expeditionary learning model encourages the development of values such as discovery, collaboration, and empathy through direct exploration of the natural world. Outward Bound is an international non-profit that operates some forty schools which strive to build participants' physical and emotional strength through outdoor expeditions and collaborative problem-solving.

Kelly set him up with a therapist, and he appeared to benefit from having someone to talk to outside the family. But Jonas also liked figuring things out for himself, turning them over in his mind until he'd explored every nook and cranny and felt satisfied he understood the issue. It was a tool he had to use frequently at King Middle School because nearly every day something got under his skin. He couldn't abide meanness in others, or stupidity, but he also knew it was pointless and self-defeating to expend the energy to lash out every time something bothered him.

Jonas knew this acutely because he had that same strange ability his mother had, the capacity to look at himself as if he were floating outside his own body, and when he did, he came to the conclusion that it was unreasonable to respond to every single thing that irritated him. Instead, he needed to keep things at a low simmer, to suppress his frustrations and let them out slowly. It was all about self-control, and Jonas saw himself as immensely self-controlled. So he examined the slights as they came his way, first figuring out why others felt the need to act the way they did. Next he examined how those acts or words made him feel. Then he put them away. Puzzles solved, frustrations defused. It was all very neat and clean—until it wasn't.

Nicole isolated herself in her own thoughts as well. She read, played video games, and talked online with former classmates in Orono. But the house in Portland was almost too quiet when the kids were home.

Jonas stayed in his room, Nicole in hers. Concentrating on home- 45 work was hard for both of them. Jonas, an excellent science and math student, had let his grades slip, and Nicole was flunking Spanish. She brooded about her future, convinced she'd never be loved and never find someone who'd marry her. Nicole was not only afraid of getting close to a person, she was afraid of getting close to the "wrong" person and the secret suddenly becoming very public.

It almost happened twice. The first time it came from outside the school, just after Nicole had joined a club called A Company of Girls, or ACOG, an organization that seeks to empower teenage girls primarily through theater and the arts. Nicole, who already enjoyed drawing, also wanted to explore acting. At one of the meetings, out of the blue, another student asked her if she was transgender.

"What?" Nicole responded.

Her heart was pounding so loud she was certain everyone in the room could hear it, but she tried to remain low-key and reacted as if she didn't understand what the girl was talking about. How had she found out? Nicole tried to be as blasé as possible, and prayed the other girl would drop the subject, which she did, but not before Nicole had spent a few anxious moments worrying her cover had been blown. Another time, in the girls' locker room, a girl asked Nicole why she always dressed and undressed for gym in a stall, not out in the open like the others. Before she could answer, though, another student distracted the girl and she wandered off without waiting for Nicole's reply.

Eighth grade was not much better than seventh. The twins had each other, and that was about it. Jonas watched TV. Nicole played video games. Sometimes she closed the door at the bottom of the staircase to the attic and curled up on one of the lower steps to read a book. Her favorites were *Luna* and *Almost Perfect*, two young adult novels about transgender youth her father had given her.

Nicole had been miserable her final two years at Asa Adams when she was out of the closet, and she was miserable her first two years at King when she was in it. It was all so bewildering and depressing, like never having a sense of balance. How could she, when she and Jonas felt as isolated as they did and were actively hiding a part of their lives from people who might otherwise have become their friends? Friendships, in fact, were more tease than reality. Just when Nicole seemed on the verge of making a good connection with someone, she'd ask her mother, "Can't I tell anyone?" And every time her mother said, "No." When Nicole balked once and asked why she couldn't at least tell just one person, since it was *her* life after all, Kelly answered her in no uncertain terms.

"It's not just about you. It's about the whole family, Nicole. If you tell someone and it all goes downhill, we'll all have to move again."

After the ACOG incident, there was really only one other close call, and it came on one of those rare occasions when Nicole invited someone over to the house after school. On the stairway leading up to her bedroom, Nicole had lined the walls with drawings and photos. One of the photographs was a still from *The Wizard of Oz*, autographed by one of the Munchkins. The twins' uncle Andy had gotten it for Nicole years earlier, and it was inscribed "To Wyatt."[4]

"Who's Wyatt?" the friend from King asked Nicole as she passed the photo on the staircase.

"Oh, that's my uncle Wyatt. He gave me the picture because he didn't want it anymore."

Nicole barely missed a beat, but her heart was pounding. When her classmate left she took the photo down and hid it in a drawer.

The oddest part about being in the closet at King was that anything even remotely related to being transgender felt threatening. One day, Kelly received a call from Nicole's teacher, who wanted her to know that the following week there was going to be a bullying-awareness day and a film shown to all students that included transgender issues. Nicole might feel uncomfortable during the discussion afterward, the teacher said, so she was being given permission to call in sick that day if she wanted. She did.

Even when things were going well, it wasn't about the danger of slipping up so much as the sense of always having to hold back. Eventually Nicole and Jonas developed a small, select group of friends, but they were always held at an emotional distance. For Nicole, it wasn't

[4]**"To Wyatt":** Wyatt was Nicole's original name.

about shutting people out so much as shutting herself down. It felt especially hard one weekend when she and about five others gathered at a friend's house and built a campfire in the backyard, then watched movies. Everyone was so relaxed and the conversations often veered toward the intimate. These were people who knew Nicole, and yet didn't. She knew them well enough to know she could probably trust them, but not saying anything was a promise she'd made to her mother—to her whole family—and she couldn't break that. . . .

We Can't Lose

A middle-aged man wearing reading glasses stood silently at the microphone before the House Judiciary Committee of the 124th Maine legislature. Then he cleared his throat and began:

> My name is Wayne Maines, I live in Old Town. I have a thirteen-year-old transgender daughter. In the beginning, I was not on board with this reality. Like many of you I doubted transgender children could exist, I doubted my wife, and I doubted our counselors and doctors. However, I never doubted my love for my child. It was only through observing her pain and her suffering and examining my lack of knowledge about these issues did I begin to question my behavior and my conservative values. . . .
>
> When my daughter lost her privileges at school and both children and adults targeted her, I knew I had to change and I have never looked back. . . . When she was told she could no longer use the appropriate bathroom her confidence and self-esteem took a major hit. Prior to this my daughter often said, "Dad, being transgender is no big deal, my friends and I have it under control." I was very proud of her. It was only when adults became involved with their unfounded fears that her world would be turned upside down. . . . This bill tells my daughter that she does not have the same rights as her classmates and reinforces her opinion that she has no future. Help me give her the future she deserves. Do not pass this bill.

Trembling, Wayne wiped away the tears streaming down his face. It was Tuesday, April 12, 2011, and he felt like he'd just come out of his own closet. He had spoken openly and honestly about his transgender daughter, about himself and his family, and now there was no turning back.

State representative Ken Fredette was the conservative legislator 60 sponsoring the bill with the support of the Republican governor, Paul LePage. The Maine Civil Liberties Union and several other organizations had gone on record opposing it. The hearing before the Judiciary Committee was a chance for the public to speak, and it was an overflow crowd. Before Wayne addressed the committee, Jennifer Levi, one of the Maineses' lawyers in their suit against the Orono school district, spoke:

The only way a business could enforce LD 1046[5] in a consistent and nondiscriminatory fashion without resorting to gender profiling would be through physical inspections, which raises serious privacy and medical confidentiality concerns and, again, risk of litigation. Not to mention that a person's anatomy is personal, private information that nobody would want to be required to disclose (or worse, viewed) before being given access to a public facility.

Levi set out not only the reasons why transgender people should be allowed to use the bathroom of their gender identity, but logically, pragmatically, and legally why enforcing a biological-sex accommodation rule would not work. Everything Nicole, Kelly, Wayne, and Jonas had fought for, sued for, been harassed for, was suddenly at stake, and not just for Nicole, but for every transgender person in the state of Maine. Before he spoke, Wayne wasn't sure how he was going to do it, or even if he could. Now he knew there had never been any other option. For years Kelly had quietly borne the family burden of protector and provider for Nicole's needs. Now it was Wayne's turn to step up and speak out. He was oddly ebullient, as if he'd finally rid himself of some suffocating weight, and it was all he could do to keep himself tethered to the ground. All those values he'd been taught growing up—defending the defenseless, helping the downtrodden—he'd always thought they meant standing up for a friend or a neighbor or a stranger in need, not his own child.

No one, however, was confident LD 1046 would be defeated. In fact, Wayne was worried enough it might pass that just days after he spoke at the hearing he called Kelly from work and said he'd been thinking about the state legislators and the upcoming vote.

"I think they have to meet Nicole," he told his wife. "We can't lose."

Wayne liked to write things down. Partly it was an organizational habit. He had many thoughts running through his mind. In a way, he talked more to himself than to Kelly, but it was how he worked things out. When he first began to do his own searches on the Internet he was stunned to find so little information for fathers of transgender children. Being the self-starter he was, he realized that maybe he could fill the void. It wasn't that he knew any better than anyone else how to raise a transgender child; he just thought it could help other fathers if he shared his own questions and experiences. Maybe he'd even hear back from someone. Every few months he wrote a piece for the Huffington Post blog called *Gay Voices*. At first he posted anonymously, but, encouraged by responses from other bloggers and readers, he began to write more personally. The responses were often a means for further discussion, such as the column he wrote about allowing Nicole to wear dresses. After reading the post, one person wrote:

---

[5]**LD 1046:** Proposed legislation that said "Unless otherwise indicated, a rest room or shower facility designated for one biological sex is presumed to be restricted to that biological sex." LD 1046 explicitly stated that such restrictions based solely on biological sex were not discriminatory, but it never became law.

You may be correct. However, is it not a parent's job to show a kid some direction in life and not just giving in to what they say?

Sorry, I would never let my son wear a dress at five because I would not have given up on him so early in the process, but that is the manly side of me talking. Whatever he develops into later, I would accept, but it wouldn't be because I decided to throw him over the fence to the other side at an early age.

Wayne and Kelly had heard all this before. It had taken them both 65 time to realize that it didn't matter how much they'd encouraged or discouraged Nicole's feminine behavior. The truth was going to win out no matter what. Wayne was reminded of something Kelly had said when a friend "kindly" suggested that perhaps Nicole was transgender because her parents had given her dolls at such a young age.

"Are you kidding?" Kelly asked. "So what you're saying is, every man is just one doll away from being a woman?"

Nicole never flinched. For two days, along with her father, she walked around the statehouse, a thirteen-year-old kid, knocking on doors and stopping representatives in the hallways.

"Hi, my name is Nicole Maines, and I really want your support to defeat this bill," she'd tell each person she met.

A few walked away when they saw her coming, but most were polite and listened. Of the 151 state representatives, she spoke with 60 or 70. What bothered Nicole wasn't simply the injustice of the bill; it was the stupidity of it. She asked the politicians, "How are you going to know if a person is transgender in order to stop them from using the bathroom of their choice?" For the past two years, she'd been just another teenage girl at Helen King Middle School. No one knew her story, no one knew she was transgender, and so no one thought twice about her using the girls' restroom.

Accompanying Nicole to the statehouse, Wayne made his own 70 personal pleas, distributing leaflets that began with a single, simple declaration:

> Today I am announcing I am the proud father of identical twins.
> One is a boy and one is a girl.

Included in the handouts were photographs of Nicole in her sparkly tutus, with scarves over her head or wearing her princess costume.

Wayne went on to describe how, as a child, when Nicole first began talking she tried to tell her parents she was a girl, not a boy. He asked others to imagine how painfully hard that must have been for a toddler.

> We have tried to live our lives privately, but the stakes are now too high to sit on the sidelines. . . . Nicole is not alone. Children as young as age four will experience severe consequences [if the bill is passed]. . . . These children deserve better. They deserve unconditional love and support. . . . Transgender children deserve the same level of safety and same basic human rights that their friends and their parents often take for granted. If each of us does our part, other children, like Nicole, will not have to say, "Daddy, what did I do wrong?"

Kelly was proud of both her husband and her daughter. Public speaking was not something she was comfortable doing, and she didn't like her family's life suddenly being pried open, but it was all worth it if they could help defeat the proposed restrictions on public accommodation.

There was one positive development for both Jonas and Nicole, and that was the prospect of starting over at a new school in ninth grade. The experience of going stealth at King had drained them both, and Kelly and Wayne knew they couldn't keep it up. They still needed to be protected, but they also needed to be in an environment where they could be themselves, freely and without reservation. Casco Bay, a public high school in Portland, appeared to be a good fit. Kelly met with the principal and found the school was both progressive and welcoming. But because there were never enough slots for the number of kids who wanted to attend, a lottery was held every year. Jonas and Nicole put their names in, but only Jonas was offered a slot. Kelly and Wayne had assumed the twins were entered into the lottery together, as a family unit, but when they contacted the school and asked them how they could accept one and not the other, they were told those were the rules. The options were dwindling. There was another public school in Portland as well as a Catholic school, but the former did not have as good a reputation as Casco Bay, and neither Kelly nor Wayne was particularly religious, so their last best hope was Waynflete, a private school, pre-K through twelfth grade, of fewer than six hundred total students. Nicole and Jonas passed the entrance tests easily and were accepted as ninth graders for the 2010–11 school year.

Waynflete, named by its two female founders after a British educator, opened in 1898 with forty-nine students. The curriculum was based on the progressive educational ideals of American philosopher John Dewey, who emphasized the need for a balance of physical, social, emotional, and intellectual development in young people. Its mission, according to the school's website, is to "engage the imagination and intellect of our students, to guide them toward self-governance and self-knowledge, and to encourage their responsible and caring participation in the world."

Waynflete's mission embodied ideals that had become the family's watchwords. At King, Jonas and Nicole had arrived as strangers and, for the most part, stayed that way for the next two years. But they arrived at Waynflete on the first day of classes having already made friends during Wilderness Week, an outing held every year for incoming students. Chewonki is an environmental education camp on a 400-acre peninsula in Wiscasset, fifty miles north of Portland. The incoming ninth graders canoed, kayaked, played games, and hiked for miles.

"Hi, how are you?" more than one person asked Jonas as he walked down the path to the campsite with a book under his arm. One kid even stopped to ask him what he was reading. It took Jonas a moment to compute what had just happened. At King no one went out of their way to talk to you, unless it was to make fun of you. Jonas had nearly forgotten how

Joe Dator/Conde Nast/The Cartoon Bank

JOEDATOR

"Son, your mother and I, Grandpa Jack, Grandma Kate, Uncle Danny, Aunt Sue, Grandpa Sy, Grandma Jenny, Cousin Rhonda, Tugger, and Sprinkles are gay."

to socialize. There had been the harassment in the fifth and sixth grades, then the depression of the seventh and eighth grades, when he and Nicole couldn't tell their friends why they'd moved to Portland. It was tiring keeping secrets, and it had exhausted everyone in the family. Sometimes it had been so hard Jonas didn't want to get out of bed in the morning. Now, all that seemed to vanish. Life didn't feel like a battle anymore.

Nicole's biggest worry was no longer about keeping a secret, but about how to finally share it, now that she and Jonas were in a small, progressive school. She'd forgotten how to talk about herself, something that had always come naturally to her, growing up as an effusive, self-confident child who thought there was nothing unusual about saying she was a boy-girl. But as a teenager, especially after two years of burying her identity, she didn't know how to resurrect it, to let people back in. Nicole desperately wanted to, but she bottled it in, looking for an opening that didn't come until the class was on its way back to Portland. She'd bonded with another girl on one of the first nights at Chewonki when they both broke out in song, singing Lady Gaga's "Bad Romance." So the two sat next to each other for the hour-long bus ride home. Nicole was feeling comfortable; her worries about being at a new school were slowly melting away. There was just this one last hurdle. That was when her new friend told her she was pansexual. Yes! Nicole thought to herself. She smiled and nodded and told the other girl she was transgender.

"Cool."

And that was it. Relief, joy — every good feeling she'd ever had about herself, poured right back in. When classes began the following

80

week, Nicole came out to someone nearly every day. No one had an issue; no one turned away. One classmate did ask her if that meant she was now going to start dressing like a boy. Nicole laughed so hard she almost cried.

ENGAGING THE TEXT

1. Review the opening few pages of this reading. What dislocations did the family have to cope with when Kelly and the twins moved from Orono to Portland? Discuss the impact of each of these disruptions. Is it an exaggeration to describe them as a "shredding" of the Maineses' prior lives?

2. Why might Nicole herself be the most likely person to reveal her secret after the move to Portland? Why does Kelly forbid her to tell even a single friend (para. 50), and what do you make of Kelly's decision?

3. Paragraphs 14–24 recount Nicole's response to the documentary film *Two Spirits: Sexuality, Gender, and the Murder of Fred Martinez*. When you consider how and what you have learned about gender in your own life, can you think of times when you were surprised, confused, or frightened? Write a journal entry or short essay about such a moment.

4. As the subtitle of Nutt's book emphasizes, Nicole's transgenderism was deeply important to the entire family. How would you assess Kelly and Wayne's parenting? What did they get right, and where may they have made mistakes? Also discuss Jonas's experience of being the identical twin of a transgender girl. How well did he handle the challenges he faced?

5. Compare the middle school you attended to King Middle School, addressing size, ethnic makeup, educational philosophy, social cliques, discriminatory language, bullying/fights, and the degree to which LGBTQ students were welcomed, safe, and supported.

6. Nutt writes that Waynflete's mission statement "embodied ideals that had become the family's watch words" (paras. 75–76). What specific moments in this reading reflect the ideals of the mission statement? To extend the assignment, learn more about the school at waynflete.org and write a few paragraphs comparing it to one of the schools you attended.

EXPLORING CONNECTIONS

7. Look ahead to "How to Do Gender" by Lisa Wade and Myra Marx Ferree (p. 480) and discuss how the concept of "doing gender" sheds light on Nicole's performances of gender as a transgender girl. For example, you might focus on the need to have "more than one pair of gender binary glasses" (para. 11); gender policing and self-policing; or ways of bending and breaking gender rules.

8. Look ahead to Ruth Padawer's "Sisterhood Is Complicated" (p. 505), which describes the experiences of transgender students at women's colleges. Write a dialogue between Nicole and one of the students profiled by Padawer in which they discuss the complexities of being transgender in an educational setting.

EXTENDING THE CRITICAL CONTEXT

9. *Becoming Nicole* is far from the only source of information about Nicole and her family. Learn more about the story from one or more of the media resources below and share what you learn with classmates.

- Nicole's TEDxSMCC talk, "Transgender: You're Part of the Story" — a moving overview of Nicole's story in her own words: https://www.youtube.com/ watch?v=bXnTAnsVfN8&feature=share

- Nicole's interview with Terry Gross on NPR's *Fresh Air:* http://freshairnpr.npr .libsynfusion.com/transgender-activists-nicole-maines-kylar-broadus

- The segment about Nicole included in the HBO documentary *The Trans List* (2016)

- The ABC *Nightline* segment "'Becoming Nicole': Born Identical Twin Boys, Now Brother and Sister": http://abcnews.go.com/Nightline/video /nicole-born-identical-twin-boys-now-brother-sister-34539470

- An ABC *Good Morning America* segment which uses some of the *Nightline* footage but also covers issues of nature/nurture and parenting: http://abcnews .go.com/GMA/video/identical-male-twins-brother-sister-34517564

- A conversation featuring Nicole, Jonas, and Dr. Norman P. Spack, cofounder of the Gender Management Service clinic at Boston Children's Hospital. The symposium was hosted by the Boston Museum of Science: https://www .youtube.com/watch?v=YNvTFH0uHHU

10. The National Conference of State Legislatures tracks legislation on dozens of issues, including the so-called bathroom bills that have been proposed in many states. Check their website (ncsl.org) to see the history of LD 1046 in Maine (para. 60) and similar legislation in other states. Do you think the battle over bathrooms is over, either nationally or in particular states or regions?

FROM *LOVING: INTERRACIAL INTIMACY IN AMERICA AND THE THREAT TO WHITE SUPREMACY*

SHERYLL CASHIN

It's common to think of intimacy as closeness within a family, as romantic attachment, or perhaps as bonding among a circle of friends, teammates, or fellow worshippers. Sheryll Cashin expands the notion of intimacy to consider its role in America's race history. In the example of the interracial couple Richard and Mildred Loving, who were banished

from Virginia in 1958 for the felony of marrying across race lines, Cashin finds not only a particular courageous couple, but also a model of a powerful antiracist practice — the nourishing of what she calls "cultural dexterity." This excerpt from *Loving* recounts some of our history's most shameful moments but also finds hope in the increasing number of Americans ready to abandon hate and embrace diversity. Sheryll Cashin is Professor of Law at Georgetown University. An expert on civil rights and race relations in America, she has published widely in academic journals as well as in the *New York Times, Los Angeles Times,* the *Washington Post,* and other media. Her 2014 book *Place Not Race: A New Vision of Opportunity in America* was nominated for an NAACP Image Award for Outstanding Non-Fiction. *Loving,* the source of this selection, was published in 2017, fifty years after the Supreme Court struck down bans on interracial marriage in *Loving v. Virginia.*

To love beyond boundaries is the most radical of acts. It also requires optimism. Richard Loving must have followed the light of his surname. In news clips he didn't smile much, perhaps because his teeth were irregular. He didn't look the part of an ardent integrator. His buzz cut, rugged face, and tobacco-scarred Southern accent marked him as a white, working rural man of simple means and tastes.

Like many Southerners, Loving knew people of color. But his relations with them were more intimate than most whites were willing to countenance. His father worked on a farm for a prosperous man of color, and his parents' home was "down in the community where all the Indians lived," according to a resident. Loving and friends would gather at a favorite bend in the road or at the back of a general store they had turned into a juke joint.[1] Someone would bring a guitar or a fiddle, and this motley crew would play music and hang out together. They were black, white, racially ambiguous "high yellow", or "Indian," depending on the perspective of who was observing and who was claiming labels. Their crossing of color lines irritated the county sheriff, who literally was the race police and tried to break up their fun. Loving was perhaps the most culturally dexterous among this group. He could blend in with anybody, people said.[2] He was playful and lived the life he wanted, loved the red-brown girl he wanted, drag-raced cars with his high-yellow friends. In the 1950s, in Central Point, Virginia—a hamlet with a penchant for race mixing—he and others willfully defied the old Jim Crow.[3]

---

[1]**juke joint:** An informal establishment featuring entertainments such as music, dancing, drinking, and gambling. [Eds.]

[2]These statements about Richard Loving and his interracial friendships are presented in a documentary film about the couple: Nancy Buirsky, *The Loving Story*, HBO Documentary Films LLC, April 15, 2011.

[3]**Jim Crow:** The system of laws that enforced racial segregation in the South between the end of Reconstruction in 1877 and the civil rights movement of the 1950s and 1960s. [Eds.]

Mildred Jeter Loving accorded with central casting. In a documentary about the couple and the Supreme Court case that she and her husband brought fifty years ago, she played herself better than any actress could.[4] She was dignified, slender, and pretty, with a quiet voice that made people lean in to hear her. Richard called her "Bean," short for "String Bean." She dressed like the housewife that she was; her short, bobbed hair was fuzzy at the roots but ended in shiny curls that betrayed either her complicated lineage or the pressing comb. She appeared to be a Negro or colored, words then used to describe African Americans, although she identified herself as a descendant of an indigenous nation rather than slaves.

In 1958, Mildred and Richard were arrested and jailed for the felony crime of marrying. Virginia was among sixteen states in that era still sufficiently obsessed with the purity of its white citizens' bloodlines to ban whites from marrying nonwhites, with varying definitions for who could claim whiteness. From 1661 until the Supreme Court ruled against such measures in the *Loving* case, forty-one states had enacted statutes that penalized interracial marriages.[5] Every state with such laws discouraged or prohibited whites from marrying blacks, but many statutes also named other groups that could not intermarry with whites: Chinese, Japanese, Filipinos, American Indians, native Hawaiians, and South Asians, among others.[6]

There were legal bans, and there were social ones. Marrying, loving, and having sex across lines of phenotype were not considered normal or acceptable among most people in pre-civil-rights America. In 1958, only 4 percent of Americans approved of marriages between blacks and whites.[7]

On June 12, 1967, the Supreme Court sided with the Lovings. The civil rights revolution had roiled from a Woolworth's lunch counter in Greensboro, North Carolina, to a thousand similar nonviolent protests in over one hundred Southern cities, resulting in over twenty thousand arrests.[8] When Police Commissioner Bull Connor turned water hoses and attack dogs on child protesters in Birmingham, Alabama, people of goodwill supported the protesters, as did moderate Republicans in Congress, who added their votes to overcome the staunch opposition of segregation-forever Southern Democrats. The Civil Rights Act of 1964 barred discrimination in education and employment and allowed

5

---

[4]Ibid.

[5]Laurence C. Nolan, "The Meaning of *Loving*: Marriage, Due Process and Equal Protection (1967–1990) as Equality and Marriage, from *Loving* to *Zablocki*," *Howard Law Journal 41* (1998): 248.

[6]Peggy Pascoe, *What Comes Naturally: Miscegenation Law and the Making of Race in America* (New York: Oxford University Press, 2009), 6, 8, 10–12.

[7]Joseph Carroll, "Most Americans Approve of Interracial Marriages," Gallup News Service, August 16, 2007, http://www.gallup.com/poll/28417/most-americans-approve-interracial-marriages.aspx; Hazel Erskine, "The Polls: Interracial Socializing," *Public Opinion Quarterly* 37 (Summer 1973): 283.

[8]Paul Osterman, *Gathering Power: The Future of Progressive Politics in America* (Boston: Beacon Press, 2002), 18–19.

people of color to dine, shop, and travel where they wanted. The Voting Rights Act of 1965 began to desegregate politics. In *Loving v. Virginia*, the Supreme Court added to the movement's momentum.

Chief Justice Earl Warren, writing for his unanimous brethren, plainly stated that Virginia's ban on interracial marriage was "designed to maintain White Supremacy," an objective no longer permitted by the Constitution. It was the first time the court used those potent words to name what the Civil War and the resulting Fourteenth Amendment should have defeated. Twice Warren mentioned "the doctrine of White Supremacy" animating these laws, implicitly acknowledging that the case was not only about intermarriage but also the ideology itself. This idea, created and propagated by patriarchs, had required separation in all forms of social relations. The ideology told whites in particular that they could not marry, sleep with, live near, play checkers with, much less ally politically with a black person. It built a wall that supremacists believed was necessary to elevate whiteness above all else. A dominant whiteness, constructed by law, was embedded in people's habits. Perhaps Warren thought being transparent about this pervasive racial dogma would help cure the nation of its mental illness.

The onset of the long hot summer of 1967 may also have hastened the court's desire to help dismantle the architecture of division. A race riot had erupted in the Roxbury neighborhood of Boston on June 2 and raged for three days. The day before the court announced its *Loving* opinion, Tampa, Florida, had ignited. By the end of the year, 159 race riots had roiled the United States, most lethally in Detroit, where a police raid on an after-hours bar set off a revolt that ended five days later with forty-three deaths and two thousand injuries.[9]

There was an "impasse in race relations," as Dr. Martin Luther King Jr. delicately phrased it—a wide gap in perception between blacks and most whites about the aims of the civil rights movement and the riots.[10] Black people were outraged by the inequality they suffered. They wanted opportunity and freedom from police harassment, squalor, and isolation. According to Dr. King, whites wanted improvement for the Negro, but not necessarily economic equality. When black folks moved beyond sitting down to order a hamburger to trying to integrate the neighborhoods, workplaces, and schools that whites dominated, a firm, even violent resistance ensued. Black people trapped in high-poverty ghettos expressed rage at their limited possibilities, and white people considered riots evidence that blacks were unconstructive and undeserving. This was the impasse Dr. King described, alas, solely in terms of Negro and white.[11] In 1967, the many-hued people of the United

[9]Jack Tager, *Boston Riots: Three Centuries of Social Violence* (Boston: Northeastern University Press, 2001), 178–84; John S. Dempsey and Linda S. Forst, *An Introduction to Policing*, 8th ed. (Boston: Delmar Cengage Learning, 2015), 24–25.

[10]Martin Luther King Jr., *The Trumpet of Conscience* (Boston: Beacon Press, 2010), 1–18, which includes a transcript of King's Massey lecture, "Impasse in Race Relations."

[11]Ibid.

States were more focused on the Vietnam War and ameliorating or flee-ing the aftermath of the riots than on the Lovings' victory for quiet acts of interracial love.

Mildred Loving was motivated more by her desperation to end her family's years of exile from Virginia than by the civil rights movement. In lieu of prison, a Virginia judge had banished them from the state for twenty-five years. They had settled, unhappily, in Washington, DC, a world away from tight-knit Central Point. For Mildred, the last straw came when one of her children was hit by a car. At her cousin's urging, she wrote a letter to Attorney General Robert Kennedy, asking for help. This infant step toward her personal liberation ultimately led to a trans-formation in national consciousness about the freedom to love.

Loving v. Virginia was one of a series of antiracist decisions by the Warren Court. Neither it, nor its famous predecessor, *Brown v. Board of Education*, would dismantle segregation, the enduring structures of white supremacy. While *Loving* removed legal barriers to interracial intimacy, the true import of the case is only beginning to emerge, as social barriers to interracial love have fallen and will continue to play out in coming decades.

In the long arc of history, the meaning of the case becomes clearer. It is impossible to understand America's persistent race business with-out examining its origins, and antimiscegenation was an enduring pro-tagonist. Enacting laws to ban or penalize interracial sex and marriage and stoking loathing about race mixing were key legal and rhetorical tools for constructing and propagating white supremacy. This ideol-ogy, in turn, was the organizing plank for regimes of oppression that were essential to American capitalism and expansion—from slavery, to indigenous and Mexican conquest, to exclusion of Asian and other immigrants, and, later, to Jim Crow. . . .

Before *Loving*, lawgivers constructed whiteness as the preferred identity for citizen and country and then set about protecting this fic-tional white purity from mixture. Over three centuries, our nation was caught in a seemingly endless cycle of political and economic elites using law to separate light and dark people who might love one another or revolt together against supremacist regimes the economic elites cre-ated. After *Loving*, the game of divide and conquer continues, but ris-ing interracial intimacy could alter tired scripts.

White people who have an intimate relationship with a person of color, particularly a black person, can lose the luxury of racial blindness if they really are in love with their paramour, their adopted child, their "ace" in that nonsexual way that one can adore a friend. They can lose their blindness and gain something tragic, yet real—the ability to see racism clearly and to weep for a loved one and a country that suffers because of it. For the culturally dexterous, race is *more* salient, not less, and difference is a source of wonder, not fear.

This transition from blindness to seeing, from anxiety to familiarity, that comes with intimate cross-racial contact is a process of acquiring *dexterity*. And if one chooses to undertake the effort, the process is never-ending. Some folks are more dexterous than others. Some, like Richard Loving, are more adventurous and get more practice than others at crossing boundaries or immersion in another culture. I do not make the simplistic and silly claim that interracial intimacy in and of itself will destroy white supremacy or eliminate race. Instead, I argue that a growing cohort is acquiring dexterity and race consciousness through intimate interracial contact, especially in dense metropolitan areas. Although I do not claim that every interracial relationship automatically confers such knowledge, many do, leading us on an arc toward less emotional segregation, of many but obviously not all whites choosing to work at adjusting to difference.

With proximity, race mixing has always occurred in America. In every generation, some people defied color lines to love, befriend, or agitate with racial others. From the founding of Jamestown in 1607, throughout much of the seventeenth century in colonial Virginia, indentured and enslaved people were allies and sometimes lovers without much distinction among themselves about color. After 1660, their masters began to introduce a color line to transition to and sustain the American institution of black chattel slavery. Laws prohibiting miscegenation encouraged struggling whites to see black people as inferior and to police black slaves. The investor class, those with the power to own people and write laws, began to assess special penalties for interracial sex and interracial cooperation, such as when servants and slaves ran away together.

Lawgivers enacted Virginia's first comprehensive slave code in 1705, stripping African slaves of rights they had enjoyed along with indentured servants in the previous century and bolstering the white bonded[12] with new privileges. The code also included penalties against interracial marriage and fornication among bonded people. There was no penalty, however, for master-slave sex, which would become the dominant form of interracial sex in the eighteenth and nineteenth centuries. Mixed-race people were common. The one-drop rule that rendered them black or Negro has roots in the Virginia slave code. Under that law, the child of a slave, no matter how fair the baby's skin or elevated the status of the father, was also a slave.

Virginia's slave code became a model for other states. As the state with the most slaves and the most to lose economically from any efforts to undermine slavery, Virginia relentlessly policed interracial intimacy and interracial cooperation among people who were not themselves slaveholders. The miasma of racism that suffused legal code would soon spread to the consciousness of men without political or economic power. The 1705 code helped reconcile rich and working whites, classes that had been economic antagonists. Race pride would emerge as a source of unity for all who could claim whiteness.

---

[12]**the white bonded:** Indentured servants obliged by a contract, or "bond," to a period of servitude. [Eds.]

The color line and a discourse against race mixing had a political function as well. In *Notes on the State of Virginia*, Thomas Jefferson expounded on his belief in supremacy of whites over Africans and offered his fear of amalgamation of whites with blacks as part of his justification for not championing black freedom. Slavery was an evil, Jefferson admitted. Blame it on King George, he wrote in his first draft of the Declaration of Independence, for introducing this stain and thousands of dark bodies into the colonies. Jefferson couldn't imagine a country where whites would accept blacks as citizens, much less intermix with them, his relationship with Sally Hemings[13] notwithstanding.

Jefferson's arguments with himself in *Notes* and with others in correspondence are consistent with nearly two centuries of subsequent discourse about the perceived problem of race mixing and American identity. These questions arose in the debate about whether and how the US should conquer northern Mexico, which was replete with Spanish-speaking, mixed-race people. The ideology of white supremacy that animated slavery and Manifest Destiny placed politicians on the horns of an American dilemma. What to do with adventurous people who defied this ideology and muddied the lines? Hence, dog-whistling[14] in the nineteenth century was often about interracial sex and, in turn, American identity.

In seven debates with Stephen Douglas in their bid for senator from Illinois, Abraham Lincoln was forced to address the issue. He countered Douglas with humor and played to the electorate's racism. "Now I protest against the counterfeit logic which concludes that, because I do not want a black woman for a slave, I must necessarily want her for a wife," he said, to laughter.

The Party of Lincoln prosecuted the Civil War, ended slavery, and extended citizenship to black males. During Reconstruction, the Radical Republicans offered the world its first glimpse of racially integrated democracy, and several Reconstruction governments repealed miscegenation laws. But in an odd twist of logic, white supremacy Democrats equated black voting power with black male sexuality, and the myth of the black man as sexual predator was born. Supremacist-orchestrated hysteria about black bodies would soon ferment the regular if strange public ritual of lynching. And when Southern Democrats retook control, they reinstated miscegenation laws throughout the states of the former Confederacy. Lawgivers in Midwestern and Western states also adopted miscegenation laws in an attempt to insulate whites from myriad groups they might mix or compete with economically. White political power translated into separate social worlds.

For a brief moment in the 1890s, the South saw a resurgence of biracial politics. Economically oppressed whites joined with blacks to create

[13]**Sally Hemings:** The mulatto house servant whose six children were fathered by Jefferson. [Eds.]

[14]**dog-whistling:** In politics, using a form of coded language, sometimes to make prejudices more abstract and thus more palatable. For example, a travel ban on Muslims might be called "enhanced homeland security." [Eds.]

a biracial farmers' alliance that challenged unfair financial policies. Seeing such alliances as a threat, economic elites destroyed them with the offer of supremacy to the white working class. Jim Crow became the only political game to play, and Southern politicians competed with one another by proposing ever-more-ingenious forms of racial apartheid. Voting and full citizenship were reserved for whites who could afford poll taxes. Race mixing was banned in politics and life.

By the early twentieth century, interracial violence seemed much more normal than interracial love. Lynching continued, mainly though not exclusively in the South, and race riots broke out in three dozen cities in the Red Summer of 1919. Violent mobs enforced social codes about the lowly place of the Negro in America's racial pecking order. As Gunnar Myrdal explained two decades later in *An American Dilemma*, his classic treatise on American race relations, the regime of Jim Crow proliferated on the fear of black men having sex with white women.[15] It was easy to use this ruse to garner widespread support for segregation, and false accusations against black men would regularly incite public lynching. Families brought picnic baskets to these ritual atrocities, and people fought over body parts after a body was cut down from the noose. In this context, the Virginia legislature niggardly redrew the color line to narrow the class of people who could claim whiteness.

The state's Racial Integrity Act of 1924, which would cause Mildred and Richard Loving's arrest years later, was enacted at the apex of the American eugenics[16] movement. The ideology of supremacy supported not only Jim Crow but also eugenics laws authorizing state-enforced sterilization of undesired populations and constricted immigration. In 1924, a federal law banned or severely restricted immigration for all nationalities except people from northern Europe. For much of the twentieth century, the nation would continue to limit immigration of colored and olive-skinned people and promote forced sterilization and racial segregation—all of it to the benefit of white upper classes.   25

Much has changed, although segregation, inequality, and race-baiting endure. Today, the *Loving* decision has a fan base, and most people in the United States now approve of interracial marriage.[17] *Loving* has been chronicled in films, and the decision has its own annual worldwide celebration, Loving Day, on June 12. *Loving* was also a progenitor of the Supreme Court's 2015 decision *Obergefell v. Hodges*, which constitutionalized same-sex marriage.

Since *Loving* was decided, race mixing and same-sex marriage have gained acceptance, and social tolerance is rising for people and lifestyles that diverge from white, patriarchal, heterosexual norms. At least that is what removal of legal and social restrictions against

---

[15]Gunnar Myrdal, *An American Dilemma: The Negro Problem and American Democracy* (New York: Harper & Bros. 1944), 589–91.

[16]**eugenics:** The attempt to improve a human population through genetic selection. Eugenics has been used as a rationale for discriminatory immigration policies, forced sterilization, and genocide. [Eds.]

[17]Carroll, "Most Americans Approve of Interracial Marriages."

mixing is beginning to mean. Racist or insensitive people often capture our attention. Millennials make news for hanging a noose on a campus, chanting a frat-boy song about lynching, wearing gangsta'-blackface to a Halloween party, or murdering nine African Americans at a Wednesday night Bible study.[18] The majority of millennials, however, are more open to our majority-minority future than are their parents and grandparents. Much less attention is paid to the 54 percent of millennials who have friends of a different race or the 67 percent who say that they view increasing diversity as a good thing.[19]

In the 2010s, the American people changed their minds about same-sex marriage with seemingly lightning speed, although the patrons at the Stonewall Inn rose up against homophobia in 1969. Acceptance spread as straight people had conversations with gay people or their allies about their hardships and dreams for equality. Attitudes about race will also undergo exponential change in coming decades in part because countless individuals will have acquired the scar tissue of seeing how race affects a loved one or a friend. Many already recognize that we are all trapped in the architecture of division supremacists and cynics created. The rise of the culturally dexterous offers a possibility for breaking free, for creating something that might have been, had the first Reconstruction, or the second,[20] been allowed to stand.

Most who love interracially take the time to understand and value racial and cultural differences. I believe that rising interracial intimacy, combined with immigration and demographic and generational change, will contribute to the rise of what I call the *culturally dexterous class*. From cross-racial marriage, adoption, and romance to the simple act of entering the home of someone of another race or ethnicity to have a meal, the dexterous cross different cultures daily and are forced to practice pluralism. Though relatively few today, ardent integrators will inevitably create a tipping point, as Malcolm Gladwell defines it.[21] In this case, integrators are spreading the social epidemic or virus of

---

[18]See, for example, Susan Svrlunga, "Noose Is Found Hanging from Tree on Duke's Campus," *Washington Post*, April 1, 2015, https://www.washingtonpost.com/news/grade-point/wp/2015/04/01/noose-is-found-hanging-from-tree-on-dukes-campus; Manny Fernandez and Richard Pérez-Peña, "As Two Oklahoma Students Are Expelled for Racist Chant, Sigma Alpha Epsilon Vows Wider Inquiry," *New York Times*, March 10, 2015, http://www.nytimes.com/2015/03/11/us/university-of-oklahoma-sigma-alpha-epsilon-racist-fraternity-video.html; Justin Ellis, "Blackface Halloween: A Toxic Cultural Tradition," *Atlantic*, October 30, 2015, http://www.theatlantic.com/entertainment/archive/2015/10/blackface-halloween-a-toxic-cultural-tradition/413323; Eliza Gray, "What We Know About South Carolina Shooting Suspect Dylann Roof," *Time*, June 18, 2015, http://time.com/3926263/charleston-church-shooting-dylann-roof.

[19]Tom Rosentiel, "Almost All Millennials Accept Interracial Dating and Marriage," Pew Research Center, February 1, 2010, http://www.pewresearch.org/2010/02/01/almost-all-millennials-accept-interracial-dating-and-marriage; "Millennials' Judgments About Recent Trends Not So Different," Pew Research Center, last modified January 7, 2010, http://www.pewresearch.org/2010/01/07/millennials-judgments-about-recent-trends-not-so-different/.

[20]**second Reconstruction:** Although Cashin refers above to the "resurgence of biracial politics" in the 1890s, this more likely points to the civil rights movement of the 1950s and 1960s (paras. 6–10). [Eds.]

[21]Malcolm Gladwell, *The Tipping Point: How Little Things Can Make a Big Difference* (Boston: Little, Brown and Company, 2000).

cultural dexterity—an enhanced capacity for intimate connections with people outside one's own tribe, for seeing and accepting difference rather than demanding assimilation to an unspoken norm of whiteness. For whites in particular, intimate contact reduces prejudice and anxiety about dealing with an out-group.[22]

In a fast future, culturally dexterous people will redefine American culture and, hopefully, politics. The descriptor "American" will no longer imply a dominant norm of English-speaking whiteness. Instead, the majority of "We the People of the United States" will accept that the country is and should be a pluralistic mash-up of myriad human strains, a gorgeous multicolored quilt, not a melting pot of assimilation. It is the difference, say, between those who loved and those who hated a Super Bowl commercial featuring "America the Beautiful" sung in seven languages. The nondexterous recoiled at this montage. No matter. As older generations die, as racial demographics change, and as cultural dexterity proliferates, math will overtake haters. The haters will continue to fight and fear the future, but when a third or more of whites have acquired cultural dexterity, it will be much easier to create a functional, multiracial politics for the common good. . . .

Today the ranks of tolerant, culturally dexterous people are exploding even as non-dexterous reactionaries rage. Activists for #BlackLives, for example, have more allies than they might imagine. About 60 percent of whites under age thirty support this movement and agree with its critique of law enforcement.[23] That the other 40 percent are more circumspect should not diminish the potential power of people not wedded to old ways of thinking. Culturally dexterous whites are quite similar to people of color in their vision for this country. Those who live integrated lives are less racist and more likely to support policies designed to promote diversity and reduce inequality.

Of course, there are potent reasons to be skeptical about the political and cultural influence of racial intimacy. As Brazil and other examples throughout Latin America demonstrate, intense racial mixing does not lead necessarily to racial or economic equality. If America is to be exceptional, a critical mass of whites must act with allies of color to dismantle supremacy. And so I offer suppositions that are both radical and modest.

In his 1967 lecture on race relations, Dr. King spoke of the "millions who have morally risen above prevailing prejudices," people who were "willing to share power and to accept structural alternations of society even at the cost of traditional privilege."[24] Such culturally dexterous,

[22]See, generally, Thomas F. Pettigrew and Linda R. Tropp, "A Meta-Analytic Test of Intergroup Contact Theory," *Journal of Personality and Social Psychology* 90 (2006): 751–83.

[23]Juliana Horowitz and Gretchen Livingston, "How Americans View the Black Lives Matter Movement," Pew Research Center, July 8, 2016, http://www.pewresearch.org/fact-tank/2016/07/08/how-americans-view-the-black-lives-matter-movement/.

[24]Martin Luther King Jr., "A New Sense of Direction," Carnegie Council for Ethics in International Affairs, http://www.carnegiecouncil.org/publications/articles_papers_reports/4960.html, accessed October 18, 2016; King, *Trumpet of Conscience.*

other-regarding souls were not a majority in 1967 and still are not in 2017. I suggest that in the future, there will be a tipping point at which a critical mass, though not a majority, of white people accepts that structural change and sharing power is what rejecting supremacy, with its embedded notions of white cultural and political dominance, actually means and requires. . . .

The ultimate question is whether more loving and more pluralism will lead to the dismantling of stubborn structures born of supremacist thinking. I dare to imagine what the culturally dexterous class could deliberately dismantle and create. Many a cynic will believe that we cannot overcome supremacy constructed and reified for centuries or the plutocracy that results. Some people are too disappointed by the America they live in to hope for or imagine anything different, too grief stricken by too many killings of innocents, too beaten down by racial or economic oppression. Those who still have hope for a beautiful America owe it both to themselves and to those who have lost faith to keep fighting. This is an agitator's burden. You never get to stop fighting for your vision for this country. And when you tire, you pass the baton to the next generation, which is hopefully more creative at agitation and more open-minded than yours.

ENGAGING THE TEXT

1. What does Cashin mean by "cultural dexterity"? How is it gained, and why does she consider it so valuable?

2. Aside from romantic relationships, what kinds of "intimate cross-racial contact" (para. 15) might promote cultural dexterity? What settings do you consider most and least likely to promote dexterity, and why?

3. What is Cashin implying when she describes whiteness as something people "claimed" (paras. 18 and 24)? What does she suggest when she notes that whiteness was "constructed" as the ideal "identity for citizen and country" (para. 13)?

4. In paragraph 7 Cashin stresses that Chief Justice Earl Warren viewed laws banning interracial marriage as motivated by "the doctrine of White

Supremacy." Why was it important for him to frame the Loving case this way instead of interpreting it as a matter of injustice or discrimination? What point was he trying to make?

5. **Thinking Rhetorically**   Cashin writes that "we are all trapped in the architecture of division supremacists and cynics created" (para. 28). What do the metaphors of "trap" and "architecture" suggest about race relations? Similarly, explain why Cashin stresses the importance of Chief Justice Warren using the words "white supremacy."

6. Is Cashin suggesting that only those who have had personal experience with interracial relationships can move beyond the structural racism she sees as defining American culture? Do you think people who haven't had such relationships are perhaps less tolerant and/or more likely to harbor racist attitudes?

EXPLORING CONNECTIONS

7. Look ahead to "From a Tangle of Pathology to a Race-Fair America" (p. 382), which focuses on the African American experience from 1965 to the present — that is, the half century after *Loving v. Virginia*. What elements of Cashin's overview of race history carry over into the more modern era, and what elements were fundamentally changed by the civil rights movement? Overall, do you think Aja and his coauthors see white supremacist ideology in roughly the same way as Cashin does? Is their vision of a "race-fair America" compatible with hers?

8. Although Cashin acknowledges that some young people commit racist acts, she thinks "the majority are more open to our majority-minority future than are their parents and grandparents" (para. 27). With this in mind, how do you think she might react to the photo of Trump/Pence supporters on page 525? Is using a Confederate flag in a twenty-first century campaign clearly racist? Will shifting demographics mean that we won't see something similar in another ten or twenty years?

EXTENDING THE CRITICAL CONTEXT

9. Cashin cites a 1924 law which "banned or severely restricted immigration for all nationalities except people from northern Europe" (para. 25). To what extent have president Trump's attitudes toward people of color and policies on immigration undermined the development of cultural dexterity in America today?

10. Watch the film *Loving* and discuss how well the film conveys Cashin's appreciation of the historical significance of the Lovings' story.

FROM *BEYOND MONOGAMY: POLYAMORY AND THE FUTURE OF POLYQUEER SEXUALITIES*

MIMI SCHIPPERS

The classic American marriage was once assumed to be both heterosexual and monogamous. "Traditional marriage," we've been told, is a union between "one man and one woman." As the title of this selection suggests, however, Americans are beginning to embrace a view of relationships that goes *Beyond Monogamy*. According to Mimi Schippers, some Americans see "polyamory" — the practice of having intimate relationships with more than one other person — as a welcome alternative. Polyamory, in her view, liberates those who practice it and challenges the cultural dominance of white heterosexual men. Schippers (b. 1964) is Associate Professor of Sociology and Gender and Sexuality Studies at Tulane University and author of *Rockin' Out of the Box: Gender Maneuvering in Alternative Hard Rock* (2002). Her new book, *The Poly Gaze* (expected 2018), focuses on how monogamy and polyamory are represented in the media. *Beyond Monogamy*, the source of this reading, appeared in 2016.

A man and woman are in an open relationship.[1] They have agreed that having sexual partners outside of their couple relationship is permissible. One night, when her partner is in another city, the woman has sex with the man's best friend.

A man is in love with two people at the same time. He is under tremendous pressure from his family and community to be a respectable black man by attending church, having a successful career, and marrying a beautiful, talented, and smart black woman. The woman he loves is perfect, and he wants to marry her. However, he is also in love with his best friend, with whom he has a sexual relationship. While he loves this man and has loved other men, he has never felt at home in the "gay community" and does not identify as gay. His best friend is well aware of his relationship with the woman, but the woman has no idea he is in love with his best friend.

A woman has a twelve-year affair with a man other than her husband. Over the twelve years, despite pleas from her lover to leave her husband, she refuses because she loves them both. One evening, her husband — knowing he shouldn't, but unable to resist the temptation — listens to a voicemail message on his wife's cell phone. It is a message

---

[1] **open relationship:** A relationship whose partners agree that sexual intimacy with others is permissible; consensual non-monogamy. [All notes are the editors'.]

from her lover saying that he can't live without her and needs to see her. Enraged, the husband swears to himself that he will find the other man and kill him.

A married man tells a friend that he and his wife had a threesome with another woman. With pride, he tells the friend that it was "every guy's dream" and that he had a great time. When the friend asks him if he'd ever have a threesome with his wife and another man, he balks with repulsion and says, "No way. I'm not gay, and I would never want to see my wife have sex with someone else."

What do these vignettes have in common? With whom do you iden- 5 tify, if anyone? Do you judge some and sympathize with others? While most people might read these vignettes and cringe and shake their heads in disgust at the disruption and possible destruction of the heterosexual couple through sexual infidelity, I see potentialities.

Advocating for queer utopian politics, José Esteban Muñoz (2009) writes, "Unlike a possibility, a thing that simply might happen, a potentiality is a certain mode of nonbeing that is eminent,[2] a thing that is present but not actually existing in the present tense" (9). No doubt, what is present in these scenarios is non-monogamy, and we assume that what is eminent is some kind of violation of the integrity of the couple.

We all know how these stories should unfold. A man is expected to reject the woman who becomes lovers with his best friend; choose one or the other — the perfect woman *or* a gay identity; if not kill his wife's lover, use violence to get him out of the picture; and vociferously decline the invitation for a threesome with another man. The woman, in contrast, should expect to lose her partner and her new lover — his best friend; live a "lie" because her partner is "on the down low";[3] end the love affair or lose her family; enjoy a threesome with another woman but never entertain the possibility of, let alone request, a threesome with another man. The only viable path is one of *either* relationship destruction and emotional trauma *or* restoring the couple through monogamy.

In her book *Queer Phenomenology: Orientations, Objects, Others,* Sara Ahmed (2007) offers a phenomenological[4] approach to thinking about sexual orientation. According to Ahmed, heteronormativity[5] is a "straight" line from one's position as a gendered and sexual subject to objects in the world, not just in terms of objects of desire, but also in choosing a life. She writes, "The lines we follow might . . . function as forms of 'alignment,' or as ways of being in line with others. We might say that we are orientated when we are in line. We are 'in line' when

---

[2]**eminent:** Schippers quotes Muñoz accurately, but the intended word here is presumably "imminent," meaning close at hand, near, impending.

[3]**on the down low:** A man having a secret relationship with another man. The phrase is used primarily in African American communities.

[4]**phenomenological:** Related to consciousness, self-awareness, or states of mind.

[5]**heteronormativity:** The idea that heterosexuality is the normal, natural, or preferred sexual orientation.

we face the direction that is already faced by others" (15). In order to be "in line" with the direction faced by others, the individuals in the vignettes above must choose monogamy. Ahmed goes on to write,

> In the case of sexual orientation, it is not simply that we have it. To become straight means that we not only have to turn toward the objects that are given to us by heterosexual culture, but also that we must "turn away" from objects that take us off this line. . . . The concept of "orientations" allows us to expose how life gets directed in some ways rather than others, through the very requirement that we follow what is already given to us. For a life to count as a good life, then it must return the debt of its life by taking on the direction promised as a social good, which means imagining one's futurity in terms of reaching certain points along a life course. A queer life might be one that fails to make such a gesture of return. (21)

One of the objects given to us by heterosexual culture is the *monogamous couple.* In order to live a "good life" of sexual and emotional intimacy, we must turn away from other lovers. Perhaps, then, a queer life would mean reorienting oneself toward other lovers, and non-monogamy would constitute a queer life.

The people described in the situations above could "fail to make   10 such a gesture of return" to monogamy and choose a different line. A man could accept a love affair between his partner and best friend or enthusiastically say "yes" to a threesome with another man. What if the man who is simultaneously in love with a woman and a man were honest with himself and his lovers, refuses to identify as straight or gay, and insists on being openly polyamorous with both of them, and what if they both agree? Even the man whose wife is having a twelve-year affair could, if he chose, somehow learn to accept the "other" man as part of the family; after all, the wife and "other" man have also been in a long-term relationship and, in that sense, their relationship has been part of the family all along. What if having more than one long-term partner was available to wives as well as husbands, and tolerated or even expected across and within all races and classes? . . .

I approach compulsory monogamy in a similar way to how Adrienne Rich (1983) interrogated compulsory heterosexuality. According to Rich, compulsory heterosexuality is a network or system of social beliefs, customs, and practices that compel women into intimate relationships with men. As an institution, compulsory heterosexuality systematically ensures men's access to and "ownership" of women's bodies, labor, and children. According to Rich, compulsory heterosexuality is characterized by male identification[6], androcentrism,[7] and the erasure of lesbian existence,

---

[6]**male identification:** Acceptance by women of men's dominant cultural position—a kind of false consciousness that sees male privilege as normal or unavoidable. Woman identification, in contrast, involves consciousness-raising and resistance to patriarchal dominance or control.

[7]**androcentrism:** The practice of making male values and perspectives central or primary.

and, as such, prevents women from bonding with each other sexually, emotionally, and politically. In her groundbreaking essay, Rich suggests that woman-identification and lesbian sexuality are important to feminist practice because they refuse and disrupt compulsory heterosexuality as a central mechanism of men's dominance over and access to women.

> But whatever [compulsory heterosexuality's] origins, when we look hard and clearly at the extent and elaboration of measures designed to keep women within a male sexual purlieu, it becomes an inescapable question whether the issue we have to address as feminists is not simply "gender inequality," nor the domination of culture by males, nor mere "taboos against homosexuality," but the enforcement of heterosexuality for women as a means of assuring male right of physical, economical, and emotional access. One of the means of enforcement is, of course, the rendering invisible of the lesbian possibility, an engulfed continent that rises fragmentedly to view from time to time only to become submerged again. (191)

. . . As a sociologist, I follow in Rich's feminist footsteps but reorient my theoretical focus away from radical feminist theory, where men are the oppressors and women are the oppressed, and toward gender sociology and queer theory to theorize the monogamous couple as central to white heteromasculine privilege and superiority and to social and cultural *regimes of normalcy* implicated in power relations and sexual stratification. I argue that consensual non-monogamy, like lesbian sexuality according to Rich, "rises… to view from time to time" in the feminist consciousness and feminist theory "only to become submerged again." Given the emergence in the mainstream media of polyamory as a viable relationship form, it is imperative that feminist, queer, and critical race theorists take this opportunity to unpack mono-normativity, develop an interest in the queer, feminist, and anti-racist potential of polyamory, and advocate and cultivate *polyqueer* sex and relationships.

Bibliography

1. Ahmed, Sara. 2007. *Queer Phenomenology: Orientations, Objects, Others.* Durham, NC: Duke University Press.
2. Muñoz, José Esteban. 2009. *Cruising Utopia: The Then and There of Queer Futurity.* New York: New York University Press.
3. Rich, Adrienne. 1983. "Compulsory Heterosexuality and Lesbian Existence." In Ann Snitow, Christine Stansell, and Sharon Thompson (Eds.), *Powers of Desire: The Politics of Sexuality.* New York: Monthly Review Press.

ENGAGING THE TEXT

1. After presenting four polyamorist vignettes, Schippers herself poses three questions about them in paragraph 5. Write a journal entry in response to one or more of her questions.

2. When you first read the four vignettes, did you "see potentialities" or perhaps "cringe and shake [your] head in disgust" (para. 5)? What do you make

of the alternative outcomes Schippers describes in paragraph 7? How plausible and how desirable do you consider each of these? Having finished the reading and perhaps discussed it with classmates, do you now see opportunities in the vignettes?

3. One simple view of polyamory is that whatever adults do is nobody's business but their own. How strong an argument do you consider this, and what counterarguments can you think of? When, if ever, might the state have a legitimate interest in governing the romantic or sexual behavior of consenting adults? Furthermore, if you accept polyamory as a choice some people make, explain why you would or would not support legal recognition of polyamorous marriages.

4. The passage by José Esteban Muñoz that Schippers quotes is challenging: it describes a paradoxical situation in which something is present, but not quite fully present. Discuss why Schippers uses this slippery idea to explain how nonmonogamy functions in the vignettes she is analyzing.

5. Discuss the metaphor of the "straight line" that appears in the quotations from Sara Ahmed (paras. 8–9). What does it mean for a person to line up — not just in terms of gender and sexual desire, but also life choices? Do you find "the straight line" a useful metaphor for investigating conformity versus nonconformity? What influences in our lives work most powerfully to keep us in line, oriented, conforming? What do we risk when we step out of line?

6. Echoing Adrienne Rich's analysis of lesbianism, Schippers suggests that polyamory is rarely visible (para. 13). Brainstorm with classmates to identify places where polyamory *is* visible in American culture today, even if only temporarily or incompletely.

EXPLORING CONNECTIONS

7. Read or review the excerpts from Sheryll Cashin's *Loving* (p. 88) and Amy Ellis Nutt's *Becoming Nicole* (p. 73). Discuss how each author connects a private, personal, intimate realm to a public, legal, political sphere. Do you find these connections as substantive and important as the authors claim they are? Would you go so far as to say that sex and gender are always political? Why or why not?

8. Look ahead to "How to Do Gender" by Lisa Wade and Myra Marx Ferree (p. 480). How do their descriptions of gender policing help explain mainstream attitudes about polyamory?

9. How do you think Schippers might respond to the cartoon on p. 86?

EXTENDING THE CRITICAL CONTEXT

10. **Thinking Rhetorically** Mimi Schippers is author of the blog marxindrag.com, billed as "Karl Marx's social critique and utopian vision all dolled up in queer drag." Read one of her blog posts and compare it to this excerpt from *Beyond Monogamy* — both in subject matter and in authorial voice or "persona."

11. Look online for a glossary of polyamorous terminology. What picture of poly-amorous relationships does the glossary paint? What words and concepts do you find most surprising, instructive, revealing, or creative?

12. Adultery — sex with someone other than one's spouse — could be consid-ered a form of polyamory. It is also a crime in some states. Research the legal situation in your own state plus two or three others from this list: Arizona, Florida, Idaho, Kansas, Michigan, New York, North Carolina, Oklahoma, South Carolina, Utah, Wisconsin. In which states is adultery legal, a misdemeanor, or a felony, and how often are people prosecuted or convicted? Then dis-cuss whether you think your state's legislation should be kept as is, revised, or repealed.

FURTHER CONNECTIONS

1. Family relationships are a frequent subject for novels and films, perhaps because these extended forms can take the time to explore the complexities of family dynamics. Keeping in mind the issues raised in this chapter, write an essay analyzing the portrayal of family in a single contemporary novel or film.

2. Writers and analysts routinely use data from the U.S. Census Bureau to get a "snapshot" of the American population as a whole or to track national trends over time. However, the bureau also provides a wealth of information at the state and county levels. Choose two counties in your state that you think are substantially differ-ent demographically; explore the Census Bureau website (www.census.gov) and gather statistical data on items like size of house-holds, their median income, the number of households headed by women, and so on. Report your findings to the class, or collaborate with classmates to build an overview of your state.

3. Tolstoy wrote that all happy families are alike, but that each unhappy family is unhappy in its own way. Taking into account your own experience and the readings in this chapter, write a jour-nal entry or an essay articulating your views of what makes families happy or unhappy, and assessing your own experiences of family up to this point in your life.

LEARNING POWER
The Myth of Education
and Empowerment

Richard Stacks/Baltimore Sun/TNS/Getty Images

FAST FACTS

1. In 2017, recent U.S. high school graduates had an unemployment rate of 16.9% and earned, on average, only $10.89 an hour, while recent college graduates had an unemployment rate of 5.6% and earned $19.18 an hour.

2. According to the latest international school assessment results, American students rank 35th out of 72 nations in math — behind students in countries such as Singapore, Japan, China, Canada, Finland, Slovenia, Germany, Russia, Spain, Latvia, and Lithuania.

3. Between 1993 and 2014, college enrollment among 18- to 24-year-olds rose from 22% to 35% for Latinos, from 25% to 33% for African Americans, from 37% to 42% for whites, and from 55% to 64% for Asians.

4. Among undergraduate students, about 23% of females and 5% of males have experienced rape or sexual assault through physical force, violence, or incapacitation. Only 20% of female student victims, age 18–24, report assaults to law enforcement. For every 100 rapes committed, only two rapists will ever serve a day in prison.

5. As of January 2018, U.S. college students shouldered a total debt load of $1.48 trillion. More than 44 million U.S. college students currently have student loans, with the average student borrower owing more than $37,000.

6. Between 1980 and 2011, states cut college budgets, on average, by 40.2%. Colorado reduced funding the most (by 69%), followed by South Carolina (67%), Arizona (62%), and Minnesota (56%). Extrapolating this trend, the national average state investment in higher education will reach zero by 2059.

7. As of 2016, over 4,180 Massive Open Online Courses (MOOCs) offered by private companies and universities such as Harvard, MIT, and Stanford had enrolled millions of students worldwide. The completion rate for MOOCs ranges between 5% and 15% of those enrolling.

Data from (1) Economic Policy Institute, "The Class of 2017," https://www. epi.org/publication/the-class-of-2017/; (2) "PISA Results in Focus," Organization for Economic Cooperation, https://www.oecd.org/pisa/pisa-2015-results-in-focus.pdf; (3) "5 facts about Latinos and education," Pew Research Center, http://www.pewresearch.org/fact-tank/2016/07/28/5-facts-about-latinos-and-education/; (4) *Rape, Abuse & Incest National Network,* https://www.rainn.org/statistics/campus-sexual-violence; *KnowyourtitleIX,* https://www.knowyourix.org/issues/statistics/; (5) Board of Governors of the Federal Reserve System, https://www.federalreserve.gov/releases/g19/current/default.htm; Center for Microeconomic Data Fed Res Bank of NY, https://www.newyorkfed.org/microeconomics/

databank.html; *Wall Street Journal*, "Student Debt Is About to Set Another Record," May 2, 2016; (6) American Council on Education, "State Funding: A Race to the Bottom," http://www.acenet.edu/the-presidency/columns-and-features/Pages/state-funding-a-race-to-the-bottom.aspx; (7) "Who Is Studying Online, and Where?" *Inside Higher Education*, January 5, 2018, https://www.insidehighered.com/digital-learning/article/2018/01/05/new-us-data-show-continued-growth-college-students-studying; "Completion Rates Are the Greatest Challenge for MOOCs," edu4me, May 19, 2016, http://edu4.me/en/completion-rates-are-the-greatest-challenge-for-moocs.

MOST AMERICANS TEND TO SEE EDUCATION as something intrinsically valuable or important. After all, education is the engine that drives the American Dream. The chance to learn, better oneself, and gain the skills that pay off in upward mobility has sustained the hope of millions of Americans. As a nation we look up to figures like Abraham Lincoln and Frederick Douglass, who learned to see beyond poverty and slavery by learning to read. Education tells us that the American Dream can work for everyone. It reassures us that we are, in fact, "created equal" and that the path to achievement lies through individual effort and hard work, not blind luck or birth.

But American attitudes toward teachers and teaching haven't always been overwhelmingly positive. The Puritans who established the Massachusetts Bay Colony viewed education with respectful skepticism. Schooling in Puritan society was a force for spiritual rather than worldly advancement. Lessons were designed to reinforce moral and religious training and to teach children to read the Bible for themselves. Education was important to the Puritan "Divines" because it was a source of order, control, and discipline. But when education aimed at more worldly goals or was undertaken for self-improvement, it was seen as a menacing, sinful luxury. Little wonder, then, that the Puritans often viewed teaching as something less than an ennobling profession. In fact, teachers in the early colonies were commonly treated as menial employees by the families and communities they served, performing duties like serving summonses, ringing bells for church service, and digging graves. Frequently, they came to the New World as indentured servants. Once here, they drilled their masters' children in spiritual exercises until they earned their freedom — or escaped.

The reputation of education in America began to improve with the onset of the Revolutionary War. Following the overthrow of British rule, leaders sought to create a spirit of nationalism that would unify the former colonies. Differences were to be set aside, for, as George Washington pointed out, "the more homogeneous our citizens can be made...the greater will be our prospect of permanent union." The goal of schooling became the creation of uniformly loyal, patriotic Americans. In the words of Benjamin Rush, one of the signers of the Declaration of Independence, "Our schools of learning, by producing one general and uniform system of education, will render the mass of people more homogeneous and thereby fit them more easily for uniform and peaceable government."

Thomas Jefferson saw school as a training ground for citizenship and demo-cratic leadership. Recognizing that an illiterate and ill-informed population would be unable to assume the responsibilities of self-government, Jefferson laid out a comprehensive plan in 1781 for public education in the state of Virginia. Accord-ing to Jefferson's blueprint, all children would be eligible for three years of free public instruction. Of those who could not afford further schooling, one prom-ising "genius" from each school was to be "raked from the rubbish" and given six more years of free education. At the end of that time, ten boys would be selected to attend college at public expense. Jeffersonian Virginia may have been the first place in the United States where education so clearly offered the penniless boy a path to self-improvement. However, this path was open to very few, and Jefferson, like Washington and Rush, was more concerned with benefiting the state than serving the individual student: "We hope to avail the state of those talents which nature has sown as liberally among the poor as the rich, but which perish with-out use, if not sought for and cultivated." For leaders of the American Revolution, education was seen as a tool for nation-building, not personal development.

In the nineteenth century two great historical forces — industrialization and immigration — combined to exert pressure for the "homogenization" of young Americans. Massive immigration from Ireland and Eastern and Central Europe led to fears that "non-native" peoples would undermine the cultural identity of the United States. Many saw school as the first line of defense against this per-ceived threat, a place where the children of "foreigners" could become Amer-icanized. In a meeting of educators in 1836, one college professor stated the problem as bluntly as possible:

> Let us now be reminded, that unless we educate our immigrants, they will be our ruin. It is no longer a mere question of benevolence, of duty, or of enlightened self-interest, but the intellectual and religious training of our foreign population has become essential to our own safety; we are prompted to it by the instinct of self-preservation.

Industrialization gave rise to another kind of uniformity in nineteenth-century public education. Factory work didn't require the kind of educational preparation needed to transform a child into a craftsman or merchant. So, for the first time in American history, school systems began to categorize students into different edu-cational "tracks" that offered qualitatively different kinds of education to different groups. Some — typically students from well-to-do homes — were prepared for professional and managerial positions. But most were consigned to education for life "on the line." Increasing demand for factory workers put a premium on young people who were obedient and able to work in large groups according to fixed schedules. As a result, leading educators in 1874 proposed a system of schooling that would meet the needs of the "modern industrial community" by stressing "punctuality, regularity, attention, and silence, as habits necessary through life." History complicates the myth of education as a source of personal empowerment. School can bind as effectively as it can liberate; it can enforce conformity and limit life chances as well as foster individual talent.

But history also supplies examples of education serving the idealistic goals of democracy, equality, and self-improvement. Nineteenth-century educator and reformer Horace Mann worked to expand educational opportunity for all.

Perhaps more than any other American, Mann helped fashion the myth of personal empowerment through education. Born on a farm in Franklin, Massachusetts, in 1796, Mann raised himself from poverty to a position of national importance through study and hard work. His own early educational experiences left an indelible imprint: the ill-trained and often brutal schoolmasters he encountered in rural Massachusetts made rote memorization and the power of the rod the hallmarks of their classroom practice. After graduating from Brown University and a successful career in politics, Mann became Secretary of the Massachusetts Board of Education in 1837, a role that gave him the opportunity to design what he called the "common school," the model of the first comprehensive public school in the United States.

Mann sketched his vision of democratic public education in the "Report of the Massachusetts Board of Education, 1848." In this famous document, he claimed that if the people were to govern themselves, every citizen had to be sufficiently educated to make independent judgments about the issues of the day. Education, according to Mann, "must prepare our citizens to become municipal officers, intelligent jurors, honest witnesses, legislators, or competent judges of legislation — in fine, to fill all the manifold relations of life." Mann saw the school as "the most effective and benignant of all the forces of civilization." In his view, schooling fulfills an almost sacred social mission:

> In teaching the blind and the deaf and dumb, in kindling the latent spark of intelligence that lurks in an idiot's mind, and in the more holy work of reforming abandoned and outcast children, education has proved what it can do by glorious experiments. These wonders it has done in its infancy, and with the lights of a limited experience; but when its faculties shall be fully developed, when it shall be trained to wield its mighty energies for the protection of society against the giant vices which now invade and torment it, — against intemperance, avarice, war, slavery, bigotry, the woes of want, and the wickedness of waste, — then there will not be a height to which these enemies of the race can escape which it will not scale, nor a Titan among them all whom it will not slay.

The common school, according to Mann, would empower students by providing them with the physical, moral, intellectual, and political tools they would need to lead socially productive lives. Compulsory public education would target every major social ill — including what Mann saw as a dangerous, growing division between the classes:

> Now, surely nothing but universal education can counterwork this tendency to the domination of capital and servility of labor. If one class possesses all the wealth and the education, while the residue of society is ignorant and poor, it matters not by what name the relation between them may be called: the latter, in fact and in truth, will be the servile dependants and subjects of the former. But, if education be equably diffused, it will draw property after it by the strongest of all attractions, for such a thing never did happen, and never can happen, as that an intelligent and practical body of men should be permanently poor... Education, then, beyond all other devices of human origin, is the great equalizer of the conditions of men, — the balance-wheel of the social machinery... I mean that it gives each man the independence and the means by which he can resist the selfishness of other men. It does better than to disarm the poor of their hostility towards the rich: it prevents being poor.

At the turn of the century, philosopher and educational theorist John Dewey made even greater claims for educational empowerment. A fierce opponent of the kind of "tracking" associated with industrial education, Dewey proposed that schools should strive to produce thinking citizens rather than obedient workers. As members of a democracy, all men and women, according to Dewey, are entitled to an education that helps them make the best of their natural talents and enables them to participate as fully as possible in the life of their community: "only by being true to the full growth of the individuals who make it up, can society by any chance be true to itself." Most of our current myths of education echo the optimism of Mann and Dewey. Guided by their ideas, most Americans still believe that education leads to self-improvement and can help us empower ourselves — and perhaps even transform our society.

In recent decades, however, the reputation of schools has also been deeply questioned. In 1983, a special commission appointed by President Ronald Reagan published *A Nation at Risk*, an assessment of public schools that portrayed them as failing students and their families at every level. Since then, the country has experienced more than thirty years of federal and state educational reform efforts aimed at improving the "mediocre" performance of our schools. Interventions like the 2001 No Child Left Behind Act, the 2009 Race to the Top grant program, and the 2010 Common Core Standards Initiative have invested billions of taxpayer dollars to "fix" our educational system. Charter schools have proliferated, and high-stakes testing has become a staple of American education, often taking up time that once was dedicated to art, music, and physical education.

Higher education in the United States has also experienced its share of challenges. Over the past two decades college costs have skyrocketed as states have systematically reduced funding for higher education, and, as a result, students have often been left with crippling levels of debt. Smartphones and laptops have disrupted and transformed the classroom, and innovations like the Massive Open Online Course (MOOC) now offer an alternative to the old-fashioned brick-and-mortar college. Even student social life has become a topic of passionate debate. Once seen as a sanctuary for learning and personal growth, the college campus lost much of its allure in the early 2000s following a series of harshly critical reports on the issue of campus rape. As a result, many students today recognize that college may be a place for reflection and self-improvement, but it's also become a "hunting ground" where students of all orientations are vulnerable to sexual assault.

We find ourselves, then, still asking the central question: Does education empower us, or does it stifle personal growth? This chapter takes a critical look at what American education can do and how it shapes or enhances our identities. The first four readings focus on schooling in elementary and secondary classrooms. In "Against School," award-winning teacher and libertarian John Gatto offers a provocative analysis of how public education "cripples our kids" by training them to be "employees and consumers." The next selection, by renowned educator Mike Rose, offers a counterpoint to Gatto. In "I Just Wanna Be Average," Rose provides a moving personal account of the dream of educational success and pays tribute to a teacher who never loses sight of what can be achieved in the classroom. Next, Jean Anyon's "Social Class and the Hidden Curriculum of Work" explores how schools program students for success or failure according to their socioeconomic status. Nikole Hannah-Jones rounds off the first half of the chapter by discussing the resegregation of America's public schools and her reasons for sending her own daughter to an "intensely segre-gated" elementary school in New York City.

Following these initial readings, the chapter's Visual Portfolio opens with the image of a 1950s classroom that echoes both the idyllic and nightmarish aspects of the school experience. The photographs that follow raise questions about our national and personal educational priorities and about the current state of U.S. college campuses.

The second half of the chapter focuses on some of the recent challenges confronting higher education in America. In "Education: Attentional Disarray," the founder of MIT's Initiative on Technology and the Self, Sherry Turkle, asks us to consider how smartphones and social media are changing the way students focus and relate to each other in the classroom. Next, in "Blurred Lines, Take Two," Peggy Orenstein explores issues surrounding the campus sexual assault crisis, including the role played by binge drinking and the prospects for change offered by the adoption of "affirmative consent" policies. The chapter concludes with "City of Broken Dreams," Sara Goldrick-Rab's account of how students strug-gle with the rising price of college and how the costs of higher education stack the deck against the aspirations of low-income students.

Sources

Best, John Hardin, and Robert T. Sidwell, eds. *The American Legacy of Learning: Readings in the History of Education*. Philadelphia: J. B. Lippincott Co., 1966. Print.

Dewey, John. "The School and Society" (1899) and "My Pedagogic Creed" (1897). *John Dewey on Education*. New York: Modern Library, 1964. Print.

Jefferson, Thomas. *Notes on the State of Virginia*. Chapel Hill: University of North Carolina Press, 1955. Print.

Mann, Horace. "Report of the Massachusetts Board of Education, 1848." *An American Primer*. Ed. Daniel Boorstein. New York: Penguin Books, 1966. Print.

Pangle, Lorraine Smith, and Thomas L. Prangle. *The Learning of Liberty: The Educational Ideas of the American Founders*. Lawrence: University Press of Kansas, 1993. Print.

Stevens, Edward, and George H. Wood. *Justice, Ideology, and Education: An Introduction to the Social Foundations of Education*. New York: Random House, 1987. Print.

Vallance, Elizabeth. "Hiding the Hidden Curriculum: An Interpretation of the Language of Justification in Nineteenth-Century Educational Reform." *Curriculum Theory Network*, Vol. 4, No. 1. Toronto: Ontario Institute for Studies in Education, 1973–1974. 5–21. Print.

Westbrook, Robert B. "Public Schooling and American Democracy." *Democracy, Education, and the Schools*. Ed. Roger Soder. San Francisco: Jossey-Bass Publishers, 1996. Print.

BEFORE READING

• Freewrite for fifteen or twenty minutes about your best and worst educa-tional experiences. Then, working in groups, compare notes to see if you can find recurring themes or ideas in what you've written. What aspects of school seem to stand out most clearly in your memories? Do the best expe-riences have anything in common? How about the worst? What aspects of your school experience didn't show up in the freewriting?

• Work in small groups to draw a collective picture that expresses your experience of high school or college. Don't worry about your drawing skill—just load the page with imagery, feelings, and ideas. Then show your work to other class members and let them try to interpret it.

- Write a journal entry about the first graders reciting the Pledge of Allegiance back in 1955 on the title page of this chapter (p. 107). What does this photo suggest about the role of education in American society? How realistic is this depiction of public schooling?

AGAINST SCHOOL

JOHN TAYLOR GATTO

The official mission statements of most American schools brim with good intentions. On paper, schools exist to help students realize their full potential, to equip them with the skills they'll need to achieve success and contribute to society, or to foster the development of independence, critical thinking, and strong ethical values. But as John Taylor Gatto (b. 1935) sees it, public schools actually exist to fulfill six covert functions meant to "cripple our kids." The frightening thing is that Gatto might know what he's talking about. An award-winning educator and ardent libertarian, Gatto taught in New York public schools for more than two decades. In 1989, 1990, and 1991, he was named New York City Teacher of the Year, and in 1991 he was also honored as New York State Teacher of the Year. His publications include *Dumbing Us Down: The Hidden Curriculum of Compulsory Schooling* (1992), *A Different Kind of Teacher* (2000), *The Underground History of American Education* (2001), and *Weapons of Mass Instruction: A Schoolteacher's Journey through the Dark World of Compulsory Schooling* (2008). This selection originally appeared in *Harper's* magazine in 2003.

I TAUGHT FOR THIRTY YEARS in some of the worst schools in Manhattan, and in some of the best, and during that time I became an expert in boredom. Boredom was everywhere in my world, and if you asked the kids, as I often did, *why* they felt so bored, they always gave the same answers: They said the work was stupid, that it made no sense, that they already knew it. They said they wanted to be doing something real, not just sitting around. They said teachers didn't seem to know much about their subjects and clearly weren't interested in learning more. And the kids were right: their teachers were every bit as bored as they were.

Boredom is the common condition of schoolteachers, and anyone who has spent time in a teachers' lounge can vouch for the low energy, the whining, the dispirited attitudes, to be found there. When asked why *they* feel bored, the teachers tend to blame the kids, as you might expect. Who wouldn't get bored teaching students who are rude and interested only in grades? If even that. Of course, teachers are themselves products of the same twelve-year compulsory school programs that so thoroughly bore their students, and as school personnel they are trapped inside structures even more rigid than those imposed upon the children. Who, then, is to blame?

We all are. My grandfather taught me that. One afternoon when I was seven I complained to him of boredom, and he batted me hard on the head. He told me that I was never to use that term in his presence again, that if I was bored it was my fault and no one else's. The obligation to amuse and instruct myself was entirely my own, and people who didn't know that were childish people, to be avoided if possible. Certainly not to be trusted. That episode cured me of boredom forever, and here and there over the years I was able to pass on the lesson to some remarkable student. For the most part, however, I found it futile to challenge the official notion that boredom and childishness were the natural state of affairs in the classroom. Often I had to defy custom, and even bend the law, to help kids break out of this trap.

The empire struck back, of course; childish adults regularly conflate opposition with disloyalty. I once returned from a medical leave to discover that all evidence of my having been granted the leave had been purposely destroyed, that my job had been terminated, and that I no longer possessed even a teaching license. After nine months of tormented effort I was able to retrieve the license when a school secretary testified to witnessing the plot unfold. In the meantime my family suffered more than I care to remember. By the time I finally retired in 1991, I had more than enough reason to think of our schools—with their long-term, cell-block-style, forced confinement of both students and teachers—as virtual factories of childishness. Yet I honestly could not see *why* they had to be that way. My own experience had revealed to me what many other teachers must learn along the way, too, yet keep to themselves for fear of reprisal: if we wanted to we could easily and inexpensively jettison the old, stupid structures and help kids *take* an education rather than merely *receive* a schooling. We could encourage the best qualities of youthfulness—curiosity, adventure, resilience, the capacity for surprising insight—simply by being more flexible about time, texts, and tests, by introducing kids to truly competent adults, and by giving each student what autonomy he or she needs in order to take a risk every now and then.

But we don't do that. And the more I asked why not, and persisted in 5 thinking about the "problem" of schooling as an engineer might, the more I missed the point: What if there is no "problem" with our schools? What if they are the way they are, so expensively flying in the face of common sense and long experience in how children learn things, not because they are doing something wrong but because they are doing something right?

Is it possible that George W. Bush accidentally spoke the truth when he said we would "leave no child behind"? Could it be that our schools are designed to make sure not one of them ever really grows up?

Do we really need school? I don't mean education, just forced schooling: six classes a day, five days a week, nine months a year, for twelve years. Is this deadly routine really necessary? And if so, for what? Don't hide behind reading, writing, and arithmetic as a rationale, because 2 million happy homeschoolers have surely put that banal justification to rest. Even if they hadn't, a considerable number of well-known Americans never went through the twelve-year wringer our kids currently go through, and they turned out all right. George Washington, Benjamin Franklin, Thomas Jefferson, Abraham Lincoln? Someone taught them, to be sure, but they were not products of a school *system*, and not one of them was ever "graduated" from a secondary school. Throughout most of American history, kids generally didn't go to high school, yet the unschooled rose to be admirals, like Farragut;[1] inventors, like Edison; captains of industry, like Carnegie[2] and Rockefeller;[3] writers, like Melville and Twain and Conrad;[4] and even scholars, like Margaret Mead.[5] In fact, until pretty recently people who reached the age of thirteen weren't looked upon as children at all. Ariel Durant, who cowrote an enormous, and very good, multivolume history of the world with her husband, Will, was happily married at fifteen, and who could reasonably claim that Ariel Durant[6] was an uneducated person? Unschooled, perhaps, but not uneducated.

We have been taught (that is, schooled) in this country to think of "success" as synonymous with, or at least dependent upon, "schooling," but historically that isn't true in either an intellectual or a financial sense. And plenty of people throughout the world today find a way to educate themselves without resorting to a system of compulsory secondary schools that all too often resemble prisons. Why, then, do Americans confuse education with just such a system? What exactly is the purpose of our public schools?

---

[1]**Farragut:** Admiral David Glasgow Farragut (1801–1870), American naval officer who won several important victories for the North in the Civil War, including the capture of the port of New Orleans in 1862. [All notes are the editors'.]

[2]**Carnegie:** Andrew Carnegie (1835–1919), American businessman and philanthropist who made his enormous fortune in the steel industry.

[3]**Rockefeller:** John D. Rockefeller (1839–1937), American industrialist who founded Standard Oil and who was for a time the richest man in the world.

[4]**Melville and Twain and Conrad:** Herman Melville (1819–1891), American novelist best known as the author of *Moby-Dick* (1851); Mark Twain, the pen name of American writer Samuel Langhorne Clemens (1835–1910), author of *Adventures of Huckleberry Finn* (1884); and Polish-born writer Joseph Conrad (1857–1924), best known for the novella "Heart of Darkness" (1899).

[5]**Margaret Mead:** American anthropologist (1901–1978) and author of the groundbreaking book *Coming of Age in Samoa* (1928).

[6]**Ariel Durant:** With husband Will (1885–1981), Ariel (1898–1981) won the Pulitzer Prize for literature for volume ten of their eleven-volume *The Story of Civilization*, published from 1935 to 1975.

Mass schooling of a compulsory nature really got its teeth into the United States between 1905 and 1915, though it was conceived of much earlier and pushed for throughout most of the nineteenth century. The reason given for this enormous upheaval of family life and cultural traditions was, roughly speaking, threefold:

1. To make good people.

2. To make good citizens.

3. To make each person his or her personal best.

These goals are still trotted out today on a regular basis, and most of us accept them in one form or another as a decent definition of public education's mission, however short schools actually fall in achieving them. But we are dead wrong. Compounding our error is the fact that the national literature holds numerous and surprisingly consistent statements of compulsory schooling's true purpose. We have, for example, the great H. L. Mencken,[7] who wrote in *The American Mercury* for April 1924 that the aim of public education is not

> to fill the young of the species with knowledge and awaken their
> intelligence....Nothing could be further from the truth. The aim...
> is simply to reduce as many individuals as possible to the same
> safe level, to breed and train a standardized citizenry, to put down
> dissent and originality. That is its aim in the United States...and
> that is its aim everywhere else.

Because of Mencken's reputation as a satirist, we might be tempted to dismiss this passage as a bit of hyperbolic sarcasm. His article, however, goes on to trace the template for our own educational system back to the now vanished, though never to be forgotten, military state of Prussia. And although he was certainly aware of the irony that we had recently been at war with Germany, the heir to Prussian thought and culture, Mencken was being perfectly serious here. Our educational system really is Prussian in origin, and that really is cause for concern.

The odd fact of a Prussian provenance for our schools pops up 10 again and again once you know to look for it. William James[8] alluded to it many times at the turn of the century. Orestes Brownson,[9] the hero of Christopher Lasch's[10] 1991 book, *The True and Only Heaven*, was publicly denouncing the Prussianization of American schools back in the 1840s. Horace Mann's[11] "Seventh Annual Report" to the

---

[7]**H. L. Mencken:** American social critic and commentator known for his satiric wit (1880–1956).

[8]**William James:** American psychologist and philosopher (1842–1910).

[9]**Orestes Brownson:** American philosopher and essayist (1803–1876).

[10]**Christopher Lasch:** American historian and social critic (1932–1994), probably best known for *The Culture of Narcissism: American Life in an Age of Diminished Expectations* (1979) and *The Revolt of the Elites: And the Betrayal of Democracy* (1994).

[11]**Horace Mann:** U.S. politician and Secretary of the Massachusetts State Board of Education from 1837 to 1847.

Massachusetts State Board of Education in 1843 is essentially a paean to the land of Frederick the Great[12] and a call for its schooling to be brought here. That Prussian culture loomed large in America is hardly surprising given our early association with that utopian state. A Prussian served as Washington's aide during the Revolutionary War, and so many German-speaking people had settled here by 1795 that Congress considered publishing a German-language edition of the federal laws. But what shocks is that we should so eagerly have adopted one of the very worst aspects of Prussian culture: an educational system deliberately designed to produce mediocre intellects, to hamstring the inner life, to deny students appreciable leadership skills, and to ensure docile and incomplete citizens—all in order to render the populace "manageable."

It was from James Bryant Conant—president of Harvard for twenty years, World War I poison-gas specialist, World War II executive on the atomic-bomb project, high commissioner of the American zone in Germany after World War II, and truly one of the most influential figures of the twentieth century—that I first got wind of the real purposes of American schooling. Without Conant, we would probably not have the same style and degree of standardized testing that we enjoy today, nor would we be blessed with gargantuan high schools that warehouse 2,000 to 4,000 students at a time, like the famous Columbine High[13] in Littleton, Colorado. Shortly after I retired from teaching I picked up Conant's 1959 book-length essay, *The Child, the Parent, and the State*, and was more than a little intrigued to see him mention in passing that the modern schools we attend were the result of a "revolution" engineered between 1905 and 1930. A revolution? He declines to elaborate, but he does direct the curious and the uninformed to Alexander Inglis's 1918 book, *Principles of Secondary Education*, in which "one saw this revolution through the eyes of a revolutionary."

Inglis, for whom a lecture in education at Harvard is named, makes it perfectly clear that compulsory schooling on this continent was intended to be just what it had been for Prussia in the 1820s: a fifth column[14] into the burgeoning democratic movement that threatened to give the peasants and the proletarians a voice at the bargaining table. Modern, industrialized, compulsory schooling was to make a sort of surgical incision into the prospective unity of these underclasses. Divide children by subject, by age-grading, by constant rankings on tests, and by many other more subtle means, and it was unlikely that the ignorant

---

[12]**Frederick the Great:** King of Prussia (now part of present-day Germany), who reigned from 1740 to 1786.
[13]**Columbine High:** Site of April 20, 1999, massacre by students Eric Harris and Dylan Klebold, who killed twelve and wounded twenty-four others before killing themselves.
[14]**a fifth column:** Secret group of infiltrators who undermine a nation's defenses.

mass of mankind, separated in childhood, would ever re-integrate into a dangerous whole.

Inglis breaks down the purpose—the *actual* purpose—of modern schooling into six basic functions, any one of which is enough to curl the hair of those innocent enough to believe the three traditional goals listed earlier:

1. The *adjustive* or *adaptive* function. Schools are to establish fixed habits of reaction to authority. This, of course, precludes critical judgment completely. It also pretty much destroys the idea that useful or interesting material should be taught, because you can't test for *reflexive* obedience until you know whether you can make kids learn, and do, foolish and boring things.

2. The *integrating* function. This might well be called "the conformity function," because its intention is to make children as alike as possible. People who conform are predictable, and this is of great use to those who wish to harness and manipulate a large labor force.

3. The *diagnostic and directive* function. School is meant to determine each student's proper social role. This is done by logging evidence mathematically and anecdotally on cumulative records. As in "your permanent record." Yes, you do have one.

4. The *differentiating* function. Once their social role has been "diagnosed," children are to be sorted by role and trained only so far as their destination in the social machine merits—and not one step further. So much for making kids their personal best.

5. The *selective* function. This refers not to human choice at all but to Darwin's theory of natural selection as applied to what he called "the favored races." In short, the idea is to help things along by consciously attempting to improve the breeding stock. Schools are meant to tag the unfit—with poor grades, remedial placement, and other punishments—clearly enough that their peers will accept them as inferior and effectively bar them from the reproductive sweepstakes. That's what all those little humiliations from first grade onward were intended to do: wash the dirt down the drain.

6. The *propaedeutic* function. The societal system implied by these rules will require an elite group of caretakers. To that end, a small fraction of the kids will quietly be taught how to manage this continuing project, how to watch over and control a population deliberately dumbed down and declawed in order that government might proceed unchallenged and corporations might never want for obedient labor.

That, unfortunately, is the purpose of mandatory public education in this country. And lest you take Inglis for an isolated crank with a rather too cynical take on the educational enterprise, you should know that he was hardly alone in championing these ideas. Conant himself, building on the ideas of Horace Mann and others, campaigned tirelessly for an American school system designed along the same lines. Men like George Peabody, who funded the cause of mandatory schooling throughout the South, surely understood that the Prussian system was useful in creating not only a harmless electorate and a servile labor force but also a virtual herd of mindless consumers. In time a great number of industrial titans came to recognize the enormous profits to be had by cultivating and tending just such a herd via public education, among them Andrew Carnegie and John D. Rockefeller.

There you have it. Now you know. We don't need Karl Marx's con- 15 ception of a grand warfare between the classes to see that it is in the interest of complex management, economic or political, to dumb people down, to demoralize them, to divide them from one another, and to discard them if they don't conform. Class may frame the proposition, as when Woodrow Wilson, then president of Princeton University, said the following to the New York City School Teachers Association in 1909: "We want one class of persons to have a liberal education, and we want another class of persons, a very much larger class, of necessity, in every society, to forgo the privileges of a liberal education and fit themselves to perform specific difficult manual tasks." But the motives behind the disgusting decisions that bring about these ends need not be class-based at all. They can stem purely from fear, or from the by now familiar belief that "efficiency" is the paramount virtue, rather than love, liberty, laughter, or hope. Above all, they can stem from simple greed.

There were vast fortunes to be made, after all, in an economy based on mass production and organized to favor the large corporation rather than the small business or the family farm. But mass production required mass consumption, and at the turn of the twentieth century most Americans considered it both unnatural and unwise to buy things they didn't actually need. Mandatory schooling was a godsend on that count. School didn't have to train kids in any direct sense to think they should consume nonstop, because it did something even better: it encouraged them not to think at all. And that left them sitting ducks for another great invention of the modern era—marketing.

Now, you needn't have studied marketing to know that there are two groups of people who can always be convinced to consume more than they need to: addicts and children. School has done a pretty good job of turning our children into addicts, but it has done a spectacular job of turning our children into children. Again, this is no accident. Theorists from Plato to Rousseau[15] to our own Dr. Inglis knew that if children could be cloistered with other children, stripped of responsibility and

---

[15]**Plato to Rousseau:** Plato (c. 427–c. 347 B.C.E.), extraordinarily influential Greek philosopher. Jean-Jacques Rousseau, Swiss philosopher and writer (1712–1778).

independence, encouraged to develop only the trivializing emotions of greed, envy, jealousy, and fear, they would grow older but never truly grow up. In the 1934 edition of his once well-known book *Public Education in the United States*, Ellwood P. Cubberley detailed and praised the way the strategy of successive school enlargements had extended childhood by two to six years, and forced schooling was at that point still quite new. This same Cubberley—who was dean of Stanford's School of Education, a textbook editor at Houghton Mifflin, and Conant's friend and correspondent at Harvard—had written the following in the 1922 edition of his book *Public School Administration*: "Our schools are...factories in which the raw products (children) are to be shaped and fashioned.... And it is the business of the school to build its pupils according to the specifications laid down."

It's perfectly obvious from our society today what those specifications were. Maturity has by now been banished from nearly every aspect of our lives. Easy divorce laws have removed the need to work at relationships; easy credit has removed the need for fiscal self-control; easy entertainment has removed the need to learn to entertain oneself; easy answers have removed the need to ask questions. We have become a nation of children, happy to surrender our judgments and our wills to political exhortations and commercial blandishments that would insult actual adults. We buy televisions, and then we buy the things we see on the television. We buy computers, and then we buy the things we see on the computer. We buy $150 sneakers whether we need them or not, and when they fall apart too soon we buy another pair. We drive SUVs and believe the lie that they constitute a kind of life insurance, even when we're upside-down in them. And, worst of all, we don't bat an eye when Ari Fleischer[16] tells us to "be careful what you say," even if we remember having been told somewhere back in school that America is the land of the free. We simply buy that one too. Our schooling, as intended, has seen to it.

Now for the good news. Once you understand the logic behind modern schooling, its tricks and traps are fairly easy to avoid. School trains children to be employees and consumers; teach your own to be leaders and adventurers. School trains children to obey reflexively; teach your own to think critically and independently. Well-schooled kids have a low threshold for boredom; help your own to develop an inner life so that they'll never be bored. Urge them to take on the serious material, the *grown-up* material, in history, literature, philosophy, music, art, economics, theology—all the stuff schoolteachers know well enough to avoid. Challenge your kids with plenty of solitude so that they can learn to enjoy their own company, to conduct inner dialogues. Well-schooled people are conditioned to dread being alone, and they

---

[16]**Ari Fleischer:** Press secretary for George W. Bush from 2001 to 2003 (b. 1960).

seek constant companionship through the TV, the computer, the cell phone, and through shallow friendships quickly acquired and quickly abandoned. Your children should have a more meaningful life, and they can.

First, though, we must wake up to what our schools really are: laboratories of experimentation on young minds, drill centers for the habits and attitudes that corporate society demands. Mandatory education serves children only incidentally; its real purpose is to turn them into servants. Don't let your own have their childhoods extended, not even for a day. If David Farragut could take command of a captured British warship as a preteen, if Thomas Edison could publish a broadsheet at the age of twelve, if Ben Franklin could apprentice himself to a printer at the same age (then put himself through a course of study that would choke a Yale senior today), there's no telling what your own kids could do. After a long life, and thirty years in the public school trenches, I've concluded that genius is as common as dirt. We suppress our genius only because we haven't yet figured out how to manage a population of educated men and women. The solution, I think, is simple and glorious. Let them manage themselves.

ENGAGING THE TEXT

1. Why does Gatto think that school is boring and childish? How does Gatto's depiction of school compare with your own elementary and secondary school experience?

2. What, according to Gatto, are the six unstated purposes of public schooling? To what extent does your own prior educational experience support this bleak view of American education?

3. To what extent would you agree that we really don't need to go to school? Given the current state of technology and a globalizing economy, do you think most people would gain the abilities they need to survive and thrive through homeschooling?

4. How would you go about teaching your own children to be "leaders and adventurers," to think "critically and independently," and to "develop an inner life so that they'll never be bored" (para. 19)? How many parents, in your estimation, have the time, experience, and resources to make Gatto's ideal education a reality?

5. **Thinking Rhetorically** When does Gatto introduce his thesis in this essay, and why does he postpone it so long? What kinds of evidence does he offer to support his thesis, and how effective is this support? For example, how persuasive are his allusions to the Prussian approach to education or the influence of James Conant and Alexander Inglis? What other types of evidence could he have used to support his critique of American education?

EXPLORING CONNECTIONS

6. Given his belief that public education exists to "ensure docile and incomplete citizens ... in order to render the populace 'manageable'" (para. 10), how might you expect Gatto to view the image of children reciting the Pledge of Allegiance that opens this chapter (p. 107)? What lessons might this daily ritual teach children, and how might it shape their behavior? What else might this image suggest about the functions and purposes of schooling?

7. Look ahead to Jean Anyon's excerpt from *Social Class and the Hidden Curriculum of Work* (p. 136), and compare Anyon's analysis of the real agenda of American public education with that described by Gatto. To what extent does Anyon's class-based analysis of education in America support Gatto's description of the unspoken purposes of public schooling?

EXTENDING THE CRITICAL CONTEXT

8. Working in groups, write a proposal for a school that wouldn't be boring or childish and that would create the kind of independent, critical, active thinkers that Gatto prizes. What would a day in such a school be like? What would the students do? What would they learn? Who would teach them?

9. Research the state of Prussia and Frederick the Great to learn more about Prussian history and culture. How might your findings change your response to Gatto's argument? Would you agree that the Prussian influence on American schooling is really a "cause for concern"? Why? What other nineteenth-century nation might have offered a better model?

"I JUST WANNA BE AVERAGE"

MIKE ROSE

Mike Rose is anything but average: he has published poetry, scholarly research, a textbook, and several widely praised books on education in America. A professor in the UCLA Graduate School of Education and Information Studies, Rose (b. 1944) has won awards from the National Academy of Education, the National Council of Teachers of English, and the John Simon Guggenheim Memorial Foundation. Below you'll read the story of how this highly successful teacher and writer started high school in the vocational education track, learning dead-end skills from teachers who were often underprepared or incompetent. Rose shows that students whom the system has written off can have tremendous

unrealized potential, and his critique of the school system specifies several reasons for the failure of students who go through high school belligerent, fearful, stoned, frustrated, or just plain bored. This selection comes from *Lives on the Boundary* (1989), Rose's exploration of America's educationally underprivileged. His publications also include *Possible Lives* (1996), an examination of nationwide educational innovation; *The Mind at Work* (2006), a study of the complex thinking involved in vocational fields; *Back to School: Why Everyone Deserves a Second Chance at Education* (2012); and, with Michael B. Katz, *Public Education Under Siege* (2013). A member of the National Academy of Education, Rose has been honored with more than a dozen awards for his research on schooling.

IT TOOK TWO BUSES TO GET TO Our Lady of Mercy. The first started deep in South Los Angeles and caught me at midpoint. The second drifted through neighborhoods with trees, parks, big lawns, and lots of flowers. The rides were long but were livened up by a group of South L.A. veterans whose parents also thought that Hope had set up shop in the west end of the county. There was Christy Biggars, who, at sixteen, was dealing and was, according to rumor, a pimp as well. There were Bill Cobb and Johnny Gonzales, grease-pencil artists extraordinaire, who left Nembutal-enhanced[1] swirls of "Cobb" and "Johnny" on the corrugated walls of the bus. And then there was Tyrrell Wilson. Tyrrell was the coolest kid I knew. He ran the dozens[2] like a metric halfback, laid down a rap that outrhymed and outpointed Cobb, whose rap was good but not great—the curse of a moderately soulful kid trapped in white skin. But it was Cobb who would sneak a radio onto the bus, and thus underwrote his patter with Little Richard, Fats Domino, Chuck Berry, the Coasters, and Ernie K. Doe's[3] mother-in-law, an awful woman who was "sent from down below." And so it was that Christy and Cobb and Johnny G. and Tyrrell and I and assorted others picked up along the way passed our days in the back of the bus, a funny mix brought together by geography and parental desire.

Entrance to school brings with it forms and releases and assessments. Mercy relied on a series of tests, mostly the Stanford-Binet,[4] for placement, and somehow the results of my tests got confused with those of another student named Rose. The other Rose apparently didn't do very well, for I was placed in the vocational track, a euphemism for the bottom level. Neither I nor my parents realized what this meant. We

---

[1]**Nembutal:** Trade name for pentobarbital, a sedative drug. [All notes are the editors'.]

[2]**the dozens:** A verbal game of African origin in which competitors try to top each other's insults.

[3]**Little Richard, Fats Domino, Chuck Berry, the Coasters, and Ernie K. Doe:** Popular black musicians of the 1950s.

[4]**Stanford-Binet:** An IQ test.

had no sense that Business Math, Typing, and English-Level D were dead ends. The current spate of reports on the schools criticizes parents for not involving themselves in the education of their children. But how would someone like Tommy Rose, with his two years of Italian schooling, know what to ask? And what sort of pressure could an exhausted waitress apply? The error went undetected, and I remained in the vocational track for two years. What a place.

My homeroom was supervised by Brother Dill, a troubled and unstable man who also taught freshman English. When his class drifted away from him, which was often, his voice would rise in paranoid accusations, and occasionally he would lose control and shake or smack us. I hadn't been there two months when one of his brisk, face-turning slaps had my glasses sliding down the aisle. Physical education was also pretty harsh. Our teacher was a stubby ex-lineman who had played old-time pro ball in the Midwest. He routinely had us grabbing our ankles to receive his stinging paddle across our butts. He did that, he said, to make men of us. "Rose," he bellowed on our first encounter; me standing geeky in line in my baggy shorts. "'Rose'? What the hell kind of name is that?"

"Italian, sir," I squeaked.

"Italian! Ho. Rose, do you know the sound a bag of shit makes   5
when it hits the wall?"

"No, sir."

"Wop!"[5]

Sophomore English was taught by Mr. Mitropetros. He was a large, bejeweled man who managed the parking lot at the Shrine Auditorium. He would crow and preen and list for us the stars he'd brushed against. We'd ask questions and glance knowingly and snicker, and all that fueled the poor guy to brag some more. Parking cars was his night job. He had little training in English, so his lesson plan for his day work had us reading the district's required text, *Julius Caesar*, aloud for the semester. We'd finished the play way before the twenty weeks was up, so he'd have us switch parts again and again and start again: Dave Snyder, the fastest guy at Mercy, muscling through Caesar to the breathless squeals of Calpurnia, as interpreted by Steve Fusco, a surfer who owned the school's most envied paneled wagon. Week ten and Dave and Steve would take on new roles, as would we all, and render a water-logged Cassius and a Brutus that are beyond my powers of description.

Spanish I—taken in the second year—fell into the hands of a new recruit. Mr. Montez was a tiny man, slight, five foot six at the most, soft-spoken and delicate. Spanish was a particularly rowdy class, and Mr. Montez was as prepared for it as a doily maker at a hammer throw. He would tap his pencil to a room in which Steve Fusco was propelling spitballs from his heavy lips, in which Mike Dweetz was taunting Billy Hawk,

[5]**Wop:** Derogatory term for Italian.

a half-Indian, half-Spanish, reed-thin, quietly explosive boy. The vocational track at Our Lady of Mercy mixed kids traveling in from South L.A. with South Bay surfers and a few Slavs and Chicanos from the harbors of San Pedro. This was a dangerous miscellany: surfers and hodads[6] and South-Central blacks all ablaze to the metronomic tapping of Hector Montez's pencil.

One day Billy lost it. Out of the corner of my eye I saw him strike   10 out with his right arm and catch Dweetz across the neck. Quick as a spasm, Dweetz was out of his seat, scattering desks, cracking Billy on the side of the head, right behind the eye. Snyder and Fusco and others broke it up, but the room felt hot and close and naked. Mr. Montez's tenuous authority was finally ripped to shreds, and I think everyone felt a little strange about that. The charade was over, and when it came down to it, I don't think any of the kids really wanted it to end this way. They had pushed and pushed and bullied their way into a freedom that both scared and embarrassed them.

Students will float to the mark you set. I and the others in the vocational classes were bobbing in pretty shallow water. Vocational education has aimed at increasing the economic opportunities of students who do not do well in our schools. Some serious programs succeed in doing that, and through exceptional teachers—like Mr. Gross in *Horace's Compromise*[7]—students learn to develop hypotheses and troubleshoot, reason through a problem, and communicate effectively—the true job skills. The vocational track, however, is most often a place for those who are just not making it, a dumping ground for the disaffected. There were a few teachers who worked hard at education; young Brother Slattery, for example, combined a stern voice with weekly quizzes to try to pass along to us a skeletal outline of world history. But mostly the teachers had no idea of how to engage the imaginations of us kids who were scuttling along at the bottom of the pond.

And the teachers would have needed some inventiveness, for none of us was groomed for the classroom. It wasn't just that I didn't know things—didn't know how to simplify algebraic fractions, couldn't identify different kinds of clauses, bungled Spanish translations—but that I had developed various faulty and inadequate ways of doing algebra and making sense of Spanish. Worse yet, the years of defensive tuning out in elementary school had given me a way to escape quickly while seeming at least half alert. During my time in Voc. Ed., I developed further into a mediocre student and a somnambulant problem solver, and that affected the subjects I did have the wherewithal to handle: I detested Shakespeare; I got bored with history. My attention flitted here and there. I fooled around in class and read my books indifferently—the intellectual equivalent of playing with your food. I did what I had to do to get by, and I did it with half a mind.

---

[6]**hodads:** Nonsurfers.
[7]***Horace's Compromise:*** A 1984 book on American education by Theodore Sizer.

But I did learn things about people and eventually came into my own socially. I liked the guys in Voc. Ed. Growing up where I did, I understood and admired physical prowess, and there was an abundance of muscle here. There was Dave Snyder, a sprinter and halfback of true quality. Dave's ability and his quick wit gave him a natural appeal, and he was welcome in any clique, though he always kept a little independent. He enjoyed acting the fool and could care less about studies, but he possessed a certain maturity and never caused the faculty much trouble. It was a testament to his independence that he included me among his friends—I eventually went out for track, but I was no jock. Owing to the Latin alphabet and a dearth of *R*s and *S*s, Snyder sat behind Rose, and we started exchanging one-liners and became friends.

There was Ted Richard, a much-touted Little League pitcher. He was chunky and had a baby face and came to Our Lady of Mercy as a seasoned street fighter. Ted was quick to laugh and he had a loud, jolly laugh, but when he got angry he'd smile a little smile, the kind that simply raises the corner of the mouth a quarter of an inch. For those who knew, it was an eerie signal. Those who didn't found themselves in big trouble, for Ted was very quick. He loved to carry on what we would come to call philosophical discussions: What is courage? Does God exist? He also loved words, enjoyed picking up big ones like *salubrious* and *equivocal* and using them in our conversations—laughing at himself as the word hit a chuckhole rolling off his tongue. Ted didn't do all that well in school—baseball and parties and testing the courage he'd speculated about took up his time. His textbooks were *Argosy* and *Field and Stream*, whatever newspapers he'd find on the bus stop—from the *Daily Worker* to pornography—conversations with uncles or hobos or businessmen he'd meet in a coffee shop, *The Old Man and the Sea*. With hindsight, I can see that Ted was developing into one of those rough-hewn intellectuals whose sources are a mix of the learned and the apocryphal, whose discussions are both assured and sad.

And then there was Ken Harvey. Ken was good-looking in a puffy way and had a full and oily ducktail and was a car enthusiast...a hodad. One day in religion class, he said the sentence that turned out to be one of the most memorable of the hundreds of thousands I heard in those Voc. Ed. years. We were talking about the parable of the talents, about achievement, working hard, doing the best you can do, blah-blah-blah, when the teacher called on the restive Ken Harvey for an opinion. Ken thought about it, but just for a second, and said (with studied, minimal affect), "I just wanna be average." That woke me up. Average? Who wants to be average? Then the athletes chimed in with the clichés that make you want to laryngectomize them, and the exchange became a platitudinous melee. At the time, I thought Ken's assertion was stupid, and I wrote him off. But his sentence has stayed with me all these years, and I think I am finally coming to understand it.

Ken Harvey was gasping for air. School can be a tremendously disorienting place. No matter how bad the school, you're going to

15

encounter notions that don't fit with the assumptions and beliefs that you grew up with—maybe you'll hear these dissonant notions from teachers, maybe from the other students, and maybe you'll read them. You'll also be thrown in with all kinds of kids from all kinds of backgrounds, and that can be unsettling—this is especially true in places of rich ethnic and linguistic mix, like the L.A. basin. You'll see a handful of students far excel you in courses that sound exotic and that are only in the curriculum of the elite: French, physics, trigonometry. And all this is happening while you're trying to shape an identity, your body is changing, and your emotions are running wild. If you're a working-class kid in the vocational track, the options you'll have to deal with this will be constrained in certain ways: you're defined by your school as "slow"; you're placed in a curriculum that isn't designed to liberate you but to occupy you, or, if you're lucky, train you, though the training is for work the society does not esteem; other students are picking up the cues from your school and your curriculum and interacting with you in particular ways. If you're a kid like Ted Richard, you turn your back on all this and let your mind roam where it may. But youngsters like Ted are rare. What Ken and so many others do is protect themselves from such suffocating madness by taking on with a vengeance the identity implied in the vocational track. Reject the confusion and frustration by openly defining yourself as the Common Joe. Champion the average. Rely on your own good sense. Fuck this bullshit. Bullshit, of course, is everything you—and the others—fear is beyond you: books, essays, tests, academic scrambling, complexity, scientific reasoning, philosophical inquiry.

The tragedy is that you have to twist the knife in your own gray matter to make this defense work. You'll have to shut down, have to reject intellectual stimuli or diffuse them with sarcasm, have to cultivate stupidity, have to convert boredom from a malady into a way of confronting the world. Keep your vocabulary simple, act stoned when you're not or act more stoned than you are, flaunt ignorance, materialize your dreams. It is a powerful and effective defense—it neutralizes the insult and the frustration of being a vocational kid and, when perfected, it drives teachers up the wall, a delightful secondary effect. But like all strong magic, it exacts a price.

My own deliverance from the Voc. Ed. world began with sophomore biology. Every student, college prep to vocational, had to take biology, and unlike the other courses, the same person taught all sections. When teaching the vocational group, Brother Clint probably slowed down a bit or omitted a little of the fundamental biochemistry, but he used the same book and more or less the same syllabus across the board. If one class got tough, he could get tougher. He was young and powerful and very handsome, and looks and physical strength were high currency. No one gave him any trouble.

I was pretty bad at the dissecting table, but the lectures and the textbook were interesting: plastic overlays that, with each turned page, peeled away skin, then veins and muscle, then organs, down to the very bones that Brother Clint, pointer in hand, would tap out on our hanging skeleton. Dave Snyder was in big trouble, for the study of life—versus the living of it—was sticking in his craw. We worked out a code for our multiple-choice exams. He'd poke me in the back: once for the answer under *A*, twice for *B*, and so on; and when he'd hit the right one, I'd look up to the ceiling as though I were lost in thought. Poke: cytoplasm. Poke, poke: methane. Poke, poke, poke: William Harvey. Poke, poke, poke, poke: islets of Langerhans. This didn't work out perfectly, but Dave passed the course, and I mastered the dreamy look of a guy on a record jacket. And something else happened. Brother Clint puzzled over this Voc. Ed. kid who was racking up 98s and 99s on his tests. He checked the school's records and discovered the error. He recommended that I begin my junior year in the College Prep program. According to all I've read since, such a shift, as one report put it, is virtually impossible. Kids at that level rarely cross tracks. The telling thing is how chancy both my placement into and exit from Voc. Ed. was; neither I nor my parents had anything to do with it. I lived in one world during spring semester, and when I came back to school in the fall, I was living in another.

Switching to College Prep was a mixed blessing. I was an erratic 20 student. I was undisciplined. And I hadn't caught onto the rules of the game: why work hard in a class that didn't grab my fancy? I was also hopelessly behind in math. Chemistry was hard; toying with my chemistry set years before hadn't prepared me for the chemist's equations. Fortunately, the priest who taught both chemistry and second-year algebra was also the school's athletic director. Membership on the track team covered me; I knew I wouldn't get lower than a C. U.S. history was taught pretty well, and I did okay. But civics was taken over by a football coach who had trouble reading the textbook aloud—and reading aloud was the centerpiece of his pedagogy. College Prep at Mercy was certainly an improvement over the vocational program—at least it carried some status—but the social science curriculum was weak, and the mathematics and physical sciences were simply beyond me. I had a miserable quantitative background and ended up copying some assignments and finessing the rest as best I could. Let me try to explain how it feels to see again and again material you should once have learned but didn't.

You are given a problem. It requires you to simplify algebraic fractions or to multiply expressions containing square roots. You know this is pretty basic material because you've seen it for years. Once a teacher took some time with you, and you learned how to carry out these operations. Simple versions, anyway. But that was a year or two or more in the past, and these are more complex versions, and now you're not sure. And this, you keep telling yourself, is ninth- or even eighth-grade stuff.

Next it's a word problem. This is also old hat. The basic elements are as familiar as story characters: trains speeding so many miles per hour or shadows of buildings angling so many degrees. Maybe you know enough, have sat through enough explanations, to be able to begin setting up the problem: "If one train is going this fast . . ." or "This shadow is really one line of a triangle . . ." Then: "Let's see . . ." "How did Jones do this?" "Hmmmm." "No." "No, that won't work." Your attention wavers. You wonder about other things: a football game, a dance, that cute new checker at the market. You try to focus on the problem again. You scribble on paper for a while, but the tension wins out and your attention flits elsewhere. You crumple the paper and begin daydreaming to ease the frustration.

The particulars will vary, but in essence this is what a number of students go through, especially those in so-called remedial classes. They open their textbooks and see once again the familiar and impenetrable formulas and diagrams and terms that have stumped them for years. There is no excitement here. *No* excitement. Regardless of what the teacher says, this is not a new challenge. There is, rather, embarrassment and frustration and, not surprisingly, some anger in being reminded once again of long-standing inadequacies. No wonder so many students finally attribute their difficulties to something inborn, organic: "That part of my brain just doesn't work." Given the troubling histories many of these students have, it's miraculous that any of them can lift the shroud of hopelessness sufficiently to make deliverance from these classes possible.

Through this entire period, my father's health was deteriorating with cruel momentum. His arteriosclerosis progressed to the point where a simple nick on his shin wouldn't heal. Eventually it ulcerated and widened. Lou Minton would come by daily to change the dressing. We tried renting an oscillating bed — which we placed in the front room — to force blood through the constricted arteries in my father's legs. The bed hummed through the night, moving in place to ward off the inevitable. The ulcer continued to spread, and the doctors finally had to amputate. My grandfather had lost his leg in a stockyard accident. Now my father too was crippled. His convalescence was slow but steady, and the doctors placed him in the Santa Monica Rehabilitation Center, a sun-bleached building that opened out onto the warm spray of the Pacific. The place gave him some strength and some color and some training in walking with an artificial leg. He did pretty well for a year or so until he slipped and broke his hip. He was confined to a wheelchair after that, and the confinement contributed to the diminishing of his body and spirit.

I am holding a picture of him. He is sitting in his wheelchair and smiling at the camera. The smile appears forced, unsteady, seems to quaver, though it is frozen in silver nitrate. He is in his mid-sixties and looks eighty. Late in my junior year, he had a stroke and never came out of the resulting coma. After that, I would see him only in dreams, and to this day that is how I join him. Sometimes the dreams are sad and grisly and primal: my father lying in a bed soaked with his suppuration,[8]

25

---

[8]**suppuration:** Discharge from wounds.

holding me, rocking me. But sometimes the dreams bring him back to me healthy: him talking to me on an empty street, or buying some pictures to decorate our old house, or transformed somehow into someone strong and adept with tools and the physical.

Jack MacFarland couldn't have come into my life at a better time. My father was dead, and I had logged up too many years of scholastic indifference. Mr. MacFarland had a master's degree from Columbia and decided, at twenty-six, to find a little school and teach his heart out. He never took any credentialing courses, couldn't bear to, he said, so he had to find employment in a private system. He ended up at Our Lady of Mercy teaching five sections of senior English. He was a beatnik who was born too late. His teeth were stained, he tucked his sorry tie in between the third and fourth buttons of his shirt, and his pants were chronically wrinkled. At first, we couldn't believe this guy, thought he slept in his car. But within no time, he had us so startled with work that we didn't much worry about where he slept or if he slept at all. We wrote three or four essays a month. We read a book every two to three weeks, starting with the *Iliad* and ending up with Hemingway. He gave us a quiz on the reading every other day. He brought a prep school curriculum to Mercy High.

MacFarland's lectures were crafted, and as he delivered them he would pace the room jiggling a piece of chalk in his cupped hand, using it to scribble on the board the names of all the writers and philosophers and plays and novels he was weaving into his discussion. He asked questions often, raised everything from Zeno's paradox to the repeated last line of Frost's "Stopping by Woods on a Snowy Evening." He slowly and carefully built up our knowledge of Western intellectual history — with facts, with connections, with speculations. We learned about Greek philosophy, about Dante, the Elizabethan world view, the Age of Reason, existentialism. He analyzed poems with us, had us reading sections from John Ciardi's *How Does a Poem Mean?*, making a potentially difficult book accessible with his own explanations. We gave oral reports on poems Ciardi didn't cover. We imitated the styles of Conrad, Hemingway, and *Time* magazine. We wrote and talked, wrote and talked. The man immersed us in language.

Even MacFarland's barbs were literary. If Jim Fitzsimmons, hung over and irritable, tried to smart-ass him, he'd rejoin with a flourish that would spark the indomitable Skip Madison — who'd lost his front teeth in a hapless tackle — to flick his tongue through the gap and opine, "good chop," drawing out the single "o" in stinging indictment. Jack Mac-Farland, this tobacco-stained intellectual, brandished linguistic weapons of a kind I hadn't encountered before. Here was this *egghead*, for God's sake, keeping some pretty difficult people in line. And from what I heard, Mike Dweetz and Steve Fusco and all the notorious Voc. Ed. crowd settled down as well when MacFarland took the podium. Though a lot of guys groused in the schoolyard, it just seemed that giving trouble to this particular teacher was a silly thing to do. Tomfoolery, not to mention assault, had no place in the world he was trying to create for us, and instinctively everyone knew that. If nothing else, we all recognized MacFarland's considerable intelligence and respected the hours he put into his work. It came to this: the troublemaker would look foolish rather than daring. Even Jim Fitzsimmons was reading *On the Road* and turning his incipient alcoholism to literary ends.

There were some lives that were already beyond Jack Mac-Farland's ministrations, but mine was not. I started reading again as I hadn't since elementary school. I would go into our gloomy little bedroom or sit at the dinner table while, on the television, Danny McShane was paralyzing Mr. Moto with the atomic drop, and work slowly back through *Heart of Darkness*, trying to catch the words in Conrad's sentences. I certainly was not MacFarland's best student; most of the other guys in College Prep, even my fellow slackers, had better backgrounds than I did. But I worked very hard, for MacFarland had hooked me. He tapped my old interest in reading and creating stories. He gave me a way to feel special by using my mind. And he provided a role model that wasn't shaped on physical prowess alone, and something inside me that I wasn't quite aware of responded to that. Jack MacFarland established a literacy club, to borrow a phrase of Frank Smith's, and invited me—invited all of us—to join.

There's been a good deal of research and speculation suggest- 30 ing that the acknowledgment of school performance with extrinsic rewards—smiling faces, stars, numbers, grades—diminishes the intrinsic satisfaction children experience by engaging in reading or writing or problem solving. While it's certainly true that we've created an educational system that encourages our best and brightest to become cynical grade collectors and, in general, have developed an obsession with evaluation and assessment, I must tell you that venal though it may have been, I loved getting good grades from MacFarland. I now know how subjective grades can be, but then they came tucked in the back of essays like bits of scientific data, some sort of spectroscopic readout that said, objectively and publicly, that I had made something of value. I suppose I'd been mediocre for too long and enjoyed a public redefinition. And I suppose the workings of my mind, such as they were, had been private for too long. My linguistic play moved into the world; . . . these papers with their circled, red B-pluses and A-minuses linked my mind to something outside it. I carried them around like a club emblem.

One day in the December of my senior year, Mr. MacFarland asked me where I was going to go to college. I hadn't thought much about it. Many of the students I teach today spent their last year in high school with a physics text in one hand and the Stanford catalog in the other, but I wasn't even aware of what "entrance requirements" were. My folks would say that they wanted me to go to college and be a doctor, but I don't know how seriously I ever took that; it seemed a sweet thing to say, a bit of supportive family chatter, like telling a gangly daughter she's graceful. The reality of higher education wasn't in my scheme of things: no one in the family had gone to college; only two of my uncles had completed high school. I figured I'd get a night job and go to the local junior college because I knew that Snyder and Company were going there to play ball. But I hadn't even prepared for that. When I finally said, "I don't know," MacFarland looked down at me—I was seated in his office—and said, "Listen, you can write."

My grades stank. I had A's in biology and a handful of B's in a few English and social science classes. All the rest were C's—or worse. MacFarland said I would do well in his class and laid down the law about doing well in the others. Still, the record for my first three years wouldn't have been acceptable to any four-year school. To nobody's surprise, I was turned down flat by USC and UCLA. But Jack MacFarland was on the case. He had received his bachelor's degree from Loyola University, so he made calls to old professors and talked to somebody in admissions and wrote me a strong letter. Loyola finally accepted me as a probationary student. I would be on trial for the first year, and if I did okay, I would be granted regular status. MacFarland also intervened to get me a loan, for I could never have afforded a private college without it. Four more years of religion classes and four more years of boys at one school, girls at another. But at least I was going to college. Amazing.

In my last semester of high school, I elected a special English course fashioned by Mr. MacFarland, and it was through this elective that there arose at Mercy a fledgling literati. Art Mitz, the editor of the school newspaper and a very smart guy, was the kingpin. He was joined by me and by Mark Dever, a quiet boy who wrote beautifully and who would die before he was forty. MacFarland occasionally invited us to his apartment, and those visits became the high point of our apprenticeship: we'd clamp on our training wheels and drive to his salon.

He lived in a cramped and cluttered place near the airport, tucked away in the kind of building that architectural critic Reyner Banham calls a *dingbat*. Books were all over: stacked, piled, tossed, and crated, underlined and dog eared, well worn and new. Cigarette ashes crusted with coffee in saucers or spilling over the sides of motel ashtrays. The little bedroom had, along two of its walls, bricks and boards loaded with notes, magazines, and oversized books. The kitchen joined the living room, and there was a stack of German newspapers under the sink. I had never seen anything like it: a great flophouse of language furnished by City Lights and Café le Metro. I read every title. I flipped through paperbacks and scanned jackets and memorized names: Gogol, *Finnegans Wake*, Djuna Barnes, Jackson Pollock, *A Coney Island of the Mind*, F. O. Matthiessen's *American Renaissance*, all sorts of Freud, *Troubled Sleep*, Man Ray, *The Education of Henry Adams*, Richard Wright, *Film as Art*, William Butler Yeats, Marguerite Duras,

Redburn, A Season in Hell, Kapital. On the cover of Alain-Fournier's *The Wanderer* was an Edward Gorey drawing of a young man on a road winding into dark trees. By the hotplate sat a strange Kafka novel called *Amerika,* in which an adolescent hero crosses the Atlantic to find the Nature Theater of Oklahoma. Art and Mark would be talking about a movie or the school newspaper, and I would be consuming my English teacher's library. It was heady stuff. I felt like a Pop Warner[9] athlete on steroids.

Art, Mark, and I would buy stogies and triangulate from   35 MacFarland's apartment to the Cinema, which now shows X-rated films but was then L.A.'s premier art theater, and then to the musty Cherokee Bookstore in Hollywood to hobnob with beatnik homosexuals — smoking, drinking bourbon and coffee, and trying out awkward phrases we'd gleaned from our mentor's bookshelves. I was happy and precocious and a little scared as well, for Hollywood Boulevard was thick with a kind of decadence that was foreign to the South Side. After the Cherokee, we would head back to the security of MacFarland's apartment, slaphappy with hipness.

Let me be the first to admit that there was a good deal of adolescent passion in this embrace of the avant-garde: self-absorption, sexually charged pedantry, an elevation of the odd and abandoned. Still it was a time during which I absorbed an awful lot of information: long lists of titles, images from expressionist paintings, new wave shibboleths,[10] snippets of philosophy, and names that read like Steve Fusco's misspellings — Goethe, Nietzsche, Kierkegaard. Now this is hardly the stuff of deep understanding. But it was an introduction, a phrase book, a Baedeker[11] to a vocabulary of ideas, and it felt good at the time to know all these words. With hindsight I realize how layered and important that knowledge was.

It enabled me to do things in the world. I could browse bohemian bookstores in far-off, mysterious Hollywood; I could go to the Cinema and see events through the lenses of European directors; and, most of all, I could share an evening, talk that talk, with Jack MacFarland, the man I most admired at the time. Knowledge was becoming a bonding agent. Within a year or two, the persona of the disaffected hipster would prove too cynical, too alienated to last. But for a time it was new and exciting: it provided a critical perspective on society, and it allowed me to act as though I were living beyond the limiting boundaries of South Vermont.[12]

---

[9]**Pop Warner:** A nationwide youth athletics organization.
[10]**new wave shibboleths:** Trendy phrases or jargon.
[11]**Baedeker:** Travel guide.
[12]**South Vermont:** A street in an economically depressed area of Los Angeles.

ENGAGING THE TEXT

1. Describe Rose's life in Voc. Ed. What were his teachers like? Have you ever had experience with teachers like these?

2. What did Voc. Ed. do to Rose and his fellow students? How did it affect them intellectually, emotionally, and socially? Why was it subsequently so hard for Rose to catch up in math?

3. Why is high school so disorienting to students like Ken Harvey? How does he cope with it? What other strategies do students use to cope with the pressures and judgments they encounter in school?

4. What does Jack MacFarland offer Rose that finally helps him learn? Do you think it was inevitable that someone with Rose's intelligence would eventually succeed?

EXPLORING CONNECTIONS

5. To what extent do Rose's experiences challenge or confirm John Taylor Gatto's critique of public education in "Against School" (p. 114)? How might Gatto account for the existence of truly remarkable teachers like Rose's Jack MacFarland?

6. Read Gregory Mantsios's "Class in America" (p. 347) and write an imaginary dialogue between Rose and Mantsios about why some students, like Rose, seem to be able to break through social class barriers and others, like Dave Snyder, Ted Richard, and Ken Harvey, do not.

EXTENDING THE CRITICAL CONTEXT

7. Rose explains that high school can be a "tremendously disorienting place" (para. 16). What, if anything, do you find disorienting about college? What steps can students at your school take to lessen feelings of disorientation? What could your college do to help them?

8. Review one or more of Rose's descriptions of his high school classmates; then write a description of one of your own high school classmates, trying to capture in a nutshell how that person coped or failed to cope with the educational system.

9. Watch any one of the many films that have been made about charismatic teachers (for example, *Dangerous Minds, Renaissance Man, Stand and Deliver,* or *Dead Poets Society*) and compare Hollywood's depiction of a dynamic teacher to Rose's portrayal of Jack MacFarland. What do such charismatic teachers offer their students personally and intellectually? Do you see any disadvantages to classes taught by teachers like these?

FROM *SOCIAL CLASS AND THE HIDDEN CURRICULUM OF WORK*
JEAN ANYON

It's no surprise that schools in wealthy communities are better than those in poor communities, or that they better prepare their students for desirable jobs. It may be shocking, however, to learn how vast the differences in schools are — not so much in resources as in teaching methods and philosophies of education. Jean Anyon observed five elementary schools over the course of a full school year and concluded that fifth graders of different economic backgrounds are already being prepared to occupy particular rungs on the social ladder. In a sense, some whole schools are on the vocational education track, while others are geared to produce future doctors, lawyers, and business leaders. Anyon's main audience is professional educators, so you may find her style and vocabulary challenging, but, once you've read her descriptions of specific classroom activities, the more analytic parts of the essay should prove easier to understand. Anyon (1941–2013) was a social activist and professor of educational policy in the Ph.D. Program in Urban Education at The City University of New York. Her publications include *Radical Possibilities: Public Policy, Urban Education and a New Social Movement* (2005) and *Theory and Educational Research: Toward Critical Social Explanation* (2009). This essay first appeared in the *Journal of Education* in 1980.

SCHOLARS IN POLITICAL ECONOMY and the sociology of knowledge have recently argued that public schools in complex industrial societies like our own make available different types of educational experience and curriculum knowledge to students in different social classes. Bowles and Gintis,[1] for example, have argued that students in different social-class backgrounds are rewarded for classroom behaviors that correspond to personality traits allegedly rewarded in the different occupational strata—the working classes for docility and obedience, the managerial classes for initiative and personal assertiveness. Basil Bernstein, Pierre Bourdieu, and Michael W. Apple,[2] focusing on school knowledge, have argued that knowledge and skills leading to social power and regard (medical, legal, managerial) are made available to the advantaged social groups but are withheld from the working classes, to whom a more "practical" curriculum is offered (manual skills, clerical knowledge). While there has been considerable argumentation of these points regarding education in England, France, and North America, there has been little or no attempt to investigate these ideas empirically in elementary or secondary schools and classrooms in this country.[3]

This article offers tentative empirical support (and qualification) of the above arguments by providing illustrative examples of differences in student *work* in classrooms in contrasting social-class communities. The examples were gathered as part of an ethnographical[4] study of curricular, pedagogical, and pupil evaluation practices in five elementary schools. The article attempts a theoretical contribution as well and assesses student work in the light of a theoretical approach to social-class analysis....It will be suggested that there is a "hidden curriculum" in schoolwork that has profound implications for the theory—and consequence—of everyday activity in education. . . .

The Sample of Schools

. . . The social-class designation of each of the five schools will be identified, and the income, occupation, and other relevant available social characteristics of the students and their parents will be described. The first three schools are in a medium-sized city district in northern New Jersey, and the other two are in a nearby New Jersey suburb.

---

[1]S. Bowles and H. Gintis, *Schooling in Capitalist America: Educational Reform and the Contradictions of Economic Life* (New York: Basic Books, 1976). [All notes are Anyon's, except 4 and 11.]

[2]B. Bernstein, *Class, Codes and Control*, Vol. 3. *Towards a Theory of Educational Transmission*, 2d ed. (London: Routledge & Kegan Paul, 1977); P. Bourdieu and J. Passeron, *Reproduction in Education, Society and Culture* (Beverly Hills, Calif.: Sage, 1977); M. W. Apple, *Ideology and Curriculum* (Boston: Routledge & Kegan Paul, 1979).

[3]But see, in a related vein, M. W. Apple and N. King, "What Do Schools Teach?" *Curriculum Inquiry* 6 (1977): 341–58; R. C. Rist, *The Urban School: A Factory for Failure* (Cambridge, MA: MIT Press, 1973).

[4]**ethnographical:** Based on an anthropological study of cultures or subcultures—the "cultures" in this case being the five schools observed. [Eds.]

The first two schools I will call *working-class schools*. Most of the parents have blue-collar jobs. Less than a third of the fathers are skilled, while the majority are in unskilled or semiskilled jobs. During the period of the study (1978–1979), approximately 15 percent of the fathers were unemployed. The large majority (85 percent) of the families are white. The following occupations are typical: platform, storeroom, and stockroom workers; foundrymen, pipe welders, and boilermakers; semi-skilled and unskilled assemblyline operatives; gas station attendants, auto mechanics, maintenance workers, and security guards. Less than 30 percent of the women work, some part-time and some full-time, on assembly lines, in storerooms and stockrooms, as waitresses, barmaids, or sales clerks. Of the fifth-grade parents, none of the wives of the skilled workers had jobs. Approximately 15 percent of the families in each school are at or below the federal "poverty" level;[5] most of the rest of the family incomes are at or below $12,000, except some of the skilled workers whose incomes are higher. The incomes of the majority of the families in these two schools (at or below $12,000) are typical of 38.6 percent of the families in the United States.[6]

The third school is called the *middle-class school*, although because of neighborhood residence patterns, the population is a mixture of several social classes. The parents' occupations can be divided into three groups: a small group of blue-collar "rich," who are skilled, well-paid workers such as printers, carpenters, plumbers, and construction workers. The second group is composed of parents in working-class and middle-class white-collar jobs: women in office jobs, technicians, supervisors in industry, and parents employed by the city (such as firemen, policemen, and several of the school's teachers). The third group is composed of occupations such as personnel directors in local firms, accountants, "middle management," and a few small capitalists (owners of shops in the area). The children of several local doctors attend this school. Most family incomes are between $13,000 and $25,000, with a few higher. This income range is typical of 38.9 percent of the families in the United States.[7]

The fourth school has a parent population that is at the upper income level of the upper middle class and is predominantly professional. This school will be called the *affluent professional school*. Typical jobs are: cardiologist, interior designer, corporate lawyer or engineer, executive in advertising or television. There are some families who are not as affluent as the majority (the family of the superintendent of the district's schools, and the one or two families in which the fathers

---

[5]The U.S. Bureau of the Census defines *poverty* for a nonfarm family of four as a yearly income of $6,191 a year or less. U.S. Bureau of the Census, *Statistical Abstract of the United States: 1978* (Washington, DC: U.S. Government Printing Office, 1978), 465, table 754.

[6]U.S. Bureau of the Census, "Money Income in 1977 of Families and Persons in the United States," *Current Population Reports* Series P-60, no. 118 (Washington, DC: U.S. Government Printing Office, 1979), p. 2, table A.

[7]Ibid.

are skilled workers). In addition, a few of the families are more affluent than the majority and can be classified in the capitalist class (a partner in a prestigious Wall Street stock brokerage firm). Approximately 90 percent of the children in this school are white. Most family incomes are between $40,000 and $80,000. This income span represents approximately 7 percent of the families in the United States.[8]

In the fifth school the majority of the families belong to the capitalist class. This school will be called the *executive elite school* because most of the fathers are top executives (for example, presidents and vice-presidents) in major United States–based multinational corporations—for example, AT&T, RCA, Citibank, American Express, U.S. Steel. A sizable group of fathers are top executives in financial firms on Wall Street. There are also a number of fathers who list their occupations as "general counsel" to a particular corporation, and these corporations are also among the large multinationals. Many of the mothers do volunteer work in the Junior League, Junior Fortnightly, or other service groups; some are intricately involved in town politics; and some are themselves in well-paid occupations. There are no minority children in the school. Almost all the family incomes are over $100,000, with some in the $500,000 range. The incomes in this school represent less than 1 percent of the families in the United States.[9]

Since each of the five schools is only one instance of elementary education in a particular social-class context, I will not generalize beyond the sample. However, the examples of schoolwork which follow will suggest characteristics of education in each social setting that appear to have theoretical and social significance and to be worth investigation in a larger number of schools....

The Working-Class Schools

In the two working-class schools, work is following the steps of a procedure. The procedure is usually mechanical, involving rote behavior and very little decision making or choice. The teachers rarely explain why the work is being assigned, how it might connect to other assignments, or what the idea is that lies behind the procedure or gives it coherence and perhaps meaning or significance. Available textbooks are not always used, and the teachers often prepare their own dittos or put work examples on the board. Most of the rules regarding work are designations of what the children are to do; the rules are steps to follow. These steps are told to the children by the teachers and are often written on the board. The children are usually told to copy the steps

[8]This figure is an estimate. According to the Bureau of the Census, only 2.6 percent of families in the United States have money income of $50,000 or over. U.S. Bureau of the Census, *Current Population Reports* Series P-60. For figures on income at these higher levels, see J. D. Smith and S. Franklin, "The Concentration of Personal Wealth, 1922–1969," *American Economic Review* 64 (1974): 162–67.

[9]Smith and Franklin, "The Concentration of Personal Wealth."

as notes. These notes are to be studied. Work is often evaluated not according to whether it is right or wrong but according to whether the children followed the right steps.

The following examples illustrate these points. In math, when two-digit division was introduced, the teacher in one school gave a four-minute lecture on what the terms are called (which number is the divisor, dividend, quotient, and remainder). The children were told to copy these names in their notebooks. Then the teacher told them the steps to follow to do the problems, saying, "This is how you do them." The teacher listed the steps on the board, and they appeared several days later as a chart hung in the middle of the front wall: "Divide, Multiply, Subtract, Bring Down." The children often did examples of two-digit division. When the teacher went over the examples with them, he told them what the procedure was for each problem, rarely asking them to conceptualize or explain it themselves: "Three into twenty-two is seven; do your subtraction and one is left over." During the week that two-digit division was introduced (or at any other time), the investigator did not observe any discussion of the idea of grouping involved in division, any use of manipulables, or any attempt to relate two-digit division to any other mathematical process. Nor was there any attempt to relate the steps to an actual or possible thought process of the children. The observer did not hear the terms *dividend, quotient,* and so on, used again. The math teacher in the other working-class school followed similar procedures regarding two-digit division and at one point her class seemed confused. She said, "You're confusing yourselves. You're tensing up. Remember, when you do this, it's the same steps over and over again—and that's the way division always is." Several weeks later, after a test, a group of her children "still didn't get it," and she made no attempt to explain the concept of dividing things into groups or to give them manipulables for their own investigation. Rather, she went over the steps with them again and told them that they "needed more practice."

In other areas of math, work is also carrying out often unexplained fragmented procedures. For example, one of the teachers led the children through a series of steps to make a 1-inch grid on their paper *without* telling them that they were making a 1-inch grid or that it would be used to study scale. She said, "Take your ruler. Put it across the top. Make a mark at every number. Then move your ruler down to the bottom. No, put it across the bottom. Now make a mark on top of every number. Now draw a line from . . ." At this point a girl said that she had a faster way to do it and the teacher said, "No, you don't; you don't even know what I'm making yet. Do it this way or it's wrong." After they had made the lines up and down and across, the teacher told them she wanted them to make a figure by connecting some dots and to measure that, using the scale of 1 inch equals 1 mile. Then they were to cut it out. She said, "Don't cut it until I check it."

In both working-class schools, work in language arts is mechanics of punctuation (commas, periods, question marks, exclamation points), capitalization, and the four kinds of sentences. One teacher explained to me, "Simple punctuation is all they'll ever use." Regarding punctuation, either a teacher or a ditto stated the rules for where, for example, to put commas. The investigator heard no classroom discussion of the aural context of punctuation (which, of course, is what gives each mark its meaning). Nor did the investigator hear any statement or inference that placing a punctuation mark could be a decision-making process, depending, for example, on one's intended meaning. Rather, the children were told to follow the rules. Language arts did not involve creative writing. There were several writing assignments throughout the year, but in each instance the children were given a ditto, and they wrote answers to questions on the sheet. For example, they wrote their "autobiography" by answering such questions as "Where were you born?" "What is your favorite animal?" on a sheet entitled "All About Me."

In one of the working-class schools, the class had a science period several times a week. On the three occasions observed, the children were not called upon to set up experiments or to give explanations for facts or concepts. Rather, on each occasion the teacher told them in his own words what the book said. The children copied the teacher's sentences from the board. Each day that preceded the day they were to do a science experiment, the teacher told them to copy the directions from the book for the procedure they would carry out the next day and to study the list at home that night. The day after each experiment, the teacher went over what they had "found" (they did the experiments as a class, and each was actually a class demonstration led by the teacher). Then the teacher wrote what they "found" on the board, and the children copied that in their notebooks. Once or twice a year there are science projects. The project is chosen and assigned by the teacher from a box of 3-by-5-inch cards. On the card the teacher has written the question to be answered, the books to use, and how much to write. Explaining the cards to the observer, the teacher said, "It tells them exactly what to do, or they couldn't do it."

Social studies in the working-class schools is also largely mechanical, rote work that was given little explanation or connection to larger contexts. In one school, for example, although there was a book available, social studies work was to copy the teacher's notes from the board. Several times a week for a period of several months the children copied these notes. The fifth grades in the district were to study United States history. The teacher used a booklet she had purchased called "The Fabulous Fifty States." Each day she put information from the booklet in outline form on the board and the children copied it. The type of information did not vary: the name of the state, its abbreviation, state capital, nickname of the state, its main products, main business, and a "Fabulous Fact" ("Idaho grew twenty-seven billion potatoes in one year. That's enough potatoes for each man, woman, and . . ."). As the children finished copying the sentences, the teacher erased them and wrote more. Children would occasionally go to the front to pull down the wall map in order to locate the states they were copying, and the teacher did not dissuade them. But the observer never saw her refer to the map; nor did the observer ever hear her make other than perfunctory remarks concerning the information the children were copying. Occasionally the children colored in a ditto and cut it out to make a stand-up figure (representing, for example, a man roping a cow in the Southwest). These were referred to by the teacher as their social studies "projects."

Rote behavior was often called for in classroom work. When going over math and language arts skills sheets, for example, as the teacher asked for the answer to each problem, he fired the questions rapidly, staccato, and the scene reminded the observer of a sergeant drilling recruits: above all, the questions demanded that you stay at attention: "The next one? What do I put here? . . . Here? Give us the next." Or "How many commas in this sentence? Where do I put them . . . The next one?" 15

The four fifth-grade teachers observed in the working-class schools attempted to control classroom time and space by making decisions without consulting the children and without explaining the basis for their decisions. The teacher's control thus often seemed capricious. Teachers, for instance, very often ignored the bells to switch classes — deciding among themselves to keep the children after the period was officially over to continue with the work or for disciplinary reasons or so they (the teachers) could stand in the hall and talk. There were no clocks in the rooms in either school, and the children often asked, "What period is this?" "When do we go to gym?" The children had no access to materials. These were handed out by teachers and closely guarded. Things in the room "belonged" to the teacher: "Bob, bring me my garbage can." The teachers continually gave the children orders. Only three times did the investigator hear a teacher in either working-class school preface a directive with an unsarcastic "please," or "let's," or "would you." Instead, the teachers said, "Shut up," "Shut your mouth," "Open your books," "Throw your gum away — if you want to rot your teeth, do it on your own time." Teachers made every effort to control the movement of the children, and often shouted, "Why are you out of your seat??!!" If the children got permission to leave the room, they had to take a written pass with the date and time. . . .

Middle-Class School

In the middle-class school, work is getting the right answer. If one accumulates enough right answers, one gets a good grade. One must follow the directions in order to get the right answers, but the directions often call for some figuring, some choice, some decision making. For example, the children must often figure out by themselves what the directions ask them to do and how to get the answer: what do you do first, second, and perhaps third? Answers are usually found in books or by listening to the teacher. Answers are usually words, sentences, numbers, or facts and dates; one writes them on paper, and one should be neat. Answers must be given in the right order, and one cannot make them up.

The following activities are illustrative. Math involves some choice: one may do two-digit division the long way or the short way, and there are some math problems that can be done "in your head." When the teacher explains how to do two-digit division, there is recognition that a cognitive process is involved; she gives you several ways and says, "I want to make sure you understand what you're doing—so you get it right"; and, when they go over the homework, she asks the *children* to tell how they did the problem and what answer they got.

In social studies the daily work is to read the assigned pages in the textbook and to answer the teacher's questions. The questions are almost always designed to check on whether the students have read the assignment and understood it: who did so-and-so; what happened after that; when did it happen, where, and sometimes, why did it happen? The answers are in the book and in one's understanding of the book; the teacher's hints when one doesn't know the answers are to "read it again" or to look at the picture or at the rest of the paragraph. One is to search for the answer in the "context," in what is given.

Language arts is "simple grammar, what they need for everyday life." The language arts teacher says, "They should learn to speak properly, to write business letters and thank-you letters, and to understand what nouns and verbs and simple subjects are." Here, as well, actual work is to choose the right answers, to understand what is given. The teacher often says, "Please read the next sentence and then I'll question you about it." One teacher said in some exasperation to a boy who was fooling around in class, "If you don't know the answers to the questions I ask, then you can't stay in this *class!* [pause] You *never* know the answers to the questions I ask, and it's not fair to me—and certainly not to you!"

Most lessons are based on the textbook. This does not involve a critical perspective on what is given there. For example, a critical perspective in social studies is perceived as dangerous by these teachers because it may lead to controversial topics; the parents might complain. The children, however, are often curious, especially in social studies. Their questions are tolerated and usually answered perfunctorily. But after a few minutes the teacher will say, "All right, we're not going any farther. Please open your social studies workbook." While the teachers spend a lot of time explaining and expanding on what the textbooks say, there is little attempt to analyze how or why things happen, or to give thought to how pieces of a culture, or, say, a system of numbers or elements of a language fit together or can be analyzed. What has happened in the past and what exists now may not be equitable or fair, but (shrug) that is the way things are and one does not confront such matters in school. For example, in social studies after a child is called on to read a passage about the pilgrims, the teacher summarizes the paragraph and then says, "So you can see how strict they were about everything." A child asks, "Why?" "Well, because they felt that if you weren't busy you'd get into trouble." Another child asks, "Is it true that they burned women at the stake?" The teacher says, "Yes, if a woman did anything strange, they hanged them. [*sic*] What would a woman do, do you think, to make them burn them? [*sic*] See if you can come up with better answers than my other [social studies] class." Several children offer suggestions, to which the teacher nods but does not comment. Then she says, "Okay, good," and calls on the next child to read.

Work tasks do not usually request creativity. Serious attention is rarely given in school work on *how* the children develop or express their own feelings and ideas, either linguistically or in graphic form. On the occasions when creativity or self-expression is requested, it is peripheral to the main activity or it is "enrichment" or "for fun." During a lesson on what similes are, for example, the teacher explains what they are, puts several on the board, gives some other examples herself, and then asks the children if they can "make some up." She calls on three children who give similes, two of which are actually in the book they have open before them. The teacher does not comment on this and then asks several others to choose similes from the list of phrases in the book. Several do so correctly, and she says, "Oh good! You're picking them out! See how good we are?" Their homework is to pick out the rest of the similes from the list.

Creativity is not often requested in social studies and science projects, either. Social studies projects, for example, are given with directions to "find information on your topic" and write it up. The children are not supposed to copy but to "put it in your own words." Although a number of the projects subsequently went beyond the teacher's direction to find information and had quite expressive covers and inside illustrations, the teacher's evaluative comments had to do with the amount of information, whether they had "copied," and if their work was neat.

The style of control of the three fifth-grade teachers observed in this school varied from somewhat easygoing to strict, but in contrast to the working-class schools, the teachers' decisions were usually based on external rules and regulations—for example, on criteria that were known or available to the children. Thus, the teachers always honor the bells for changing classes, and they usually evaluate children's work by what is in the textbooks and answer booklets.

There is little excitement in schoolwork for the children, and the assignments are perceived as having little to do with their interests and feelings. As one child said, what you do is "store facts up in your head

25

like cold storage—until you need it later for a test or your job." Thus, doing well is important because there are thought to be *other*, likely rewards: a good job or college.[10]

Affluent Professional School

In the affluent professional school, work is creative activity carried out independently. The students are continually asked to express and apply ideas and concepts. Work involves individual thought and expressiveness, expansion and illustration of ideas, and choice of appropriate method and material. (The class is not considered an open classroom, and the principal explained that because of the large number of discipline problems in the fifth grade this year they did not departmentalize. The teacher who agreed to take part in the study said she is "more structured" this year than she usually is.) The products of work in this class are often written stories, editorials and essays, or representations of ideas in mural, graph, or craft form. The products of work should not be like everybody else's and should show individuality. They should exhibit good design, and (this is important) they must also fit empirical reality. Moreover, one's work should attempt to interpret or "make sense" of reality. The relatively few rules to be followed regarding work are usually criteria for, or limits on, individual activity. One's product is usually evaluated for the quality of its expression and for the appropriateness of its conception to the task. In many cases, one's own satisfaction with the product is an important criterion for its evaluation. When right answers are called for, as in commercial materials like SRA (Science Research Associates) and math, it is important that the children decide on an answer as a result of thinking about the idea involved in what they're being asked to do. Teacher's hints are to "think about it some more."

The following activities are illustrative. The class takes home a sheet requesting each child's parents to fill in the number of cars they have, the number of television sets, refrigerators, games, or rooms in the house, and so on. Each child is to figure the average number of a type of possession owned by the fifth grade. Each child must compile the "data" from all the sheets. A calculator is available in the classroom to do the mechanics of finding the average. Some children decide to send sheets to the fourth-grade families for comparison. Their work should be "verified" by a classmate before it is handed in.

Each child and his or her family has made a geoboard. The teacher asks the class to get their geoboards from the side cabinet, to take a handful of rubber bands, and then to listen to what she would like them

---

[10]A dominant feeling, expressed directly and indirectly by teachers in this school, was boredom with their work. They did, however, in contrast to the working-class schools, almost always carry out lessons during class times.

to do. She says, "I would like you to design a figure and then find the perimeter and area. When you have it, check with your neighbor. After you've done that, please transfer it to graph paper and tomorrow I'll ask you to make up a question about it for someone. When you hand it in, please let me know whose it is and who verified it. Then I have something else for you to do that's really fun. [pause] Find the average number of chocolate chips in three cookies. I'll give you three cookies, and you'll have to *eat* your way through, I'm afraid!" Then she goes around the room and gives help, suggestions, praise, and admonitions that they are getting noisy. They work sitting, or standing up at their desks, at benches in the back, or on the floor. A child hands the teacher his paper and she comments, "I'm not accepting this paper. Do a better design." To another child she says, "That's fantastic! But you'll never find the area. Why don't you draw a figure inside [the big one] and subtract to get the area?"

The school district requires the fifth grade to study ancient civilization (in particular, Egypt, Athens, and Sumer). In this classroom, the emphasis is on illustrating and re-creating the culture of the people of ancient times. The following are typical activities: the children made an 8mm film on Egypt, which one of the parents edited. A girl in the class wrote the script, and the class acted it out. They put the sound on themselves. They read stories of those days. They wrote essays and stories depicting the lives of the people and the societal and occupational divisions. They chose from a list of projects, all of which involved graphic representations of ideas: for example, "Make a mural depicting the division of labor in Egyptian society."

Each child wrote and exchanged a letter in hieroglyphics with a 30 fifth grader in another class, and they also exchanged stories they wrote in cuneiform. They made a scroll and singed the edges so it looked authentic. They each chose an occupation and made an Egyptian plaque representing that occupation, simulating the appropriate Egyptian design. They carved their design on a cylinder of wax, pressed the wax into clay, and then baked the clay. Although one girl did not choose an occupation but carved instead a series of gods and slaves, the teacher said, "That's all right, Amber, it's beautiful." As they were working the teacher said, "Don't cut into your clay until you're satisfied with your design."

Social studies also involves almost daily presentation by the children of some event from the news. The teacher's questions ask the children to expand what they say, to give more details, and to be more specific. Occasionally she adds some remarks to help them see connections between events.

The emphasis on expressing and illustrating ideas in social studies is accompanied in language arts by an emphasis on creative writing. Each child wrote a rebus story for a first grader whom they had interviewed to see what kind of story the child liked best. They wrote editorials on pending decisions by the school board and radio plays, some of which were read over the school intercom from the office and one of which was performed in the auditorium. There is no language arts textbook because, the teacher said, "The principal wants us to be creative." There is not much grammar, but there is punctuation. One morning when the observer arrived, the class was doing a punctuation ditto. The teacher later apologized for using the ditto. "It's just for review," she said. "I don't teach punctuation that way. We use their language." The ditto had three unambiguous rules for where to put commas in a sentence. As the teacher was going around to help the children with the ditto, she repeated several times, "Where you put commas depends on how you say the sentence; it depends on the situation and what you want to say." Several weeks later the observer saw another punctuation activity. The teacher had printed a five-paragraph story on an oak tag and then cut it into phrases. She read the whole story to the class from the book, then passed out the phrases. The group had to decide how the phrases could best be put together again. (They arranged the phrases on the floor.) The point was not to replicate the story, although that was not irrelevant, but to "decide what you think the best way is." Punctuation marks on cardboard pieces were then handed out, and the children discussed and then decided what mark was best at each place they thought one was needed. At the end of each paragraph the teacher asked, "Are you satisfied with the way the paragraphs are now? Read it to yourself and see how it sounds." Then she read the original story again, and they compared the two.

Describing her goals in science to the investigator, the teacher said, "We use ESS (Elementary Science Study). It's very good because it gives a hands-on experience—so they can make *sense* out of it. It doesn't matter whether it [what they find] is right or wrong. I bring them together and there's value in discussing their ideas."

The products of work in this class are often highly valued by the children and the teacher. In fact, this was the only school in which the investigator was not allowed to take original pieces of the children's work for her files. If the work was small enough, however, and was on paper, the investigator could duplicate it on the copying machine in the office.

The teacher's attempt to control the class involves constant nego- 35 tiation. She does not give direct orders unless she is angry because the children have been too noisy. Normally, she tries to get them to foresee the consequences of their actions and to decide accordingly. For example, lining them up to go see a play written by the sixth graders, she says, "I presume you're lined up by someone with whom you want to sit. I hope you're lined up by someone you won't get in trouble with." . . .

One of the few rules governing the children's movement is that no more than three children may be out of the room at once. There is a school rule that anyone can go to the library at any time to get a book. In the fifth grade I observed, they sign their name on the chalkboard and leave. There are no passes. Finally, the children have a fair amount of officially sanctioned say over what happens in the class. For example, they often negotiate what work is to be done. If the teacher wants to move on to the next subject, but the children say they are not ready, they want to work on their present projects some more, she very often lets them do it.

Executive Elite School

In the executive elite school, work is developing one's analytical intellectual powers. Children are continually asked to reason through a problem, to produce intellectual products that are both logically sound and of top academic quality. A primary goal of thought is to conceptualize rules by which elements may fit together in systems and then to apply these rules in solving a problem. Schoolwork helps one to achieve, to excel, to prepare for life.

The following are illustrative. The math teacher teaches area and perimeter by having the children derive formulas for each. First she helps them, through discussion at the board, to arrive at $A = W \times L$ as a formula (not *the* formula) for area. After discussing several, she says, "Can anyone make up a formula for perimeter? Can you figure that out yourselves? [pause] Knowing what we know, can we think of a formula?" She works out three children's suggestions at the board, saying to two, "Yes, that's a good one," and then asks the class if they can think of any more. No one volunteers. To prod them, she says, "If you use rules and good reasoning, you get many ways. Chris, can you think up a formula?"

She discusses two-digit division with the children as a decision-making process. Presenting a new type of problem to them, she asks, "What's the *first* decision you'd make if presented with this kind of example? What is the first thing you'd *think*? Craig?" Craig says, "To find my first partial quotient." She responds, "Yes, that would be your first decision. How would you do that?" Craig explains, and then the teacher says, "OK, we'll see how that works for you." The class tries his way. Subsequently, she comments on the merits and shortcomings of several other children's decisions. Later, she tells the investigator that her goals in math are to develop their reasoning and mathematical thinking and that, unfortunately, "there's no *time* for manipulables."

While right answers are important in math, they are not "given" by the book or by the teacher but may be challenged by the children. Going over some problems in late September the teacher says, "Raise your hand if you do not agree." A child says, "I don't agree with sixty-four." The teacher responds, "OK, there's a question about sixty-four. [to class] Please check it. Owen, they're disagreeing with you. Kristen, they're checking yours." The teacher emphasized this repeatedly during September and October with statements like "Don't be afraid to say you disagree. In the last [math] class, somebody disagreed, and they were right. Before you disagree, check yours, and if you still think we're wrong, then we'll check it out." By Thanksgiving, the children

40

did not often speak in terms of right and wrong math problems but of whether they agreed with the answer that had been given.

There are complicated math mimeos with many word problems. Whenever they go over the examples, they discuss how each child has set up the problem. The children must explain it precisely. On one occasion the teacher said, "I'm more—just as interested in *how* you set up the problem as in what answer you find. If you set up a problem in a good way, the answer is *easy* to find."

Social studies work is most often reading and discussion of concepts and independent research. There are only occasional artistic, expressive, or illustrative projects. Ancient Athens and Sumer are, rather, societies to analyze. The following questions are typical of those that guide the children's independent research. "What mistakes did Pericles make after the war?" "What mistakes did the citizens of Athens make?" "What are the elements of a civilization?" "How did Greece build an economic empire?" "Compare the way Athens chose its leaders with the way we choose ours." Occasionally the children are asked to make up sample questions for their social studies tests. On an occasion when the investigator was present, the social studies teacher rejected a child's question by saying, "That's just fact. If I asked you that question on a test, you'd complain it was just memory! Good questions ask for concepts."

In social studies—but also in reading, science, and health—the teachers initiate classroom discussions of current social issues and problems. These discussions occurred on every one of the investigator's visits, and a teacher told me, "These children's opinions are important— it's important that they learn to reason things through." The classroom discussions always struck the observer as quite realistic and analytical, dealing with concrete social issues like the following: "Why do workers strike?" "Is that right or wrong?" "Why do we have inflation, and what can be done to stop it?" "Why do companies put chemicals in food when the natural ingredients are available?" and so on. Usually the children did not have to be prodded to give their opinions. In fact, their statements and the interchanges between them struck the observer as quite sophisticated conceptually and verbally, and well-informed. Occasionally the teachers would prod with statements such as, "Even if you don't know [the answers], if you think logically about it, you can figure it out." And "I'm asking you [these] questions to help you think this through."

Language arts emphasizes language as a complex system, one that should be mastered. The children are asked to diagram sentences of complex grammatical construction, to memorize irregular verb conjugations (he lay, he has lain, and so on . . .), and to use the proper participles, conjunctions, and interjections in their speech. The teacher (the same one who teaches social studies) told them, "It is not enough to get these right on tests; you must use what you learn [in grammar classes] in your written and oral work. I will grade you on that."

Most writing assignments are either research reports and essays for social studies or experiment analyses and write-ups for science. There is only an occasional story or other "creative writing" assignment. On 45 the occasion observed by the investigator (the writing of a Halloween story), the points the teacher stressed in preparing the children to write involved the structural aspects of a story rather than the expression of feelings or other ideas. The teacher showed them a filmstrip, "The Seven Parts of a Story," and lectured them on plot development, mood setting, character development, consistency, and the use of a logical or appropriate ending. The stories they subsequently wrote were, in fact, well-structured, but many were also personal and expressive. The teacher's evaluative comments, however, did not refer to the expressiveness or artistry but were all directed toward whether they had "developed" the story well.

Language arts work also involved a large amount of practice in presentation of the self and in managing situations where the child was expected to be in charge. For example, there was a series of assignments in which each child had to be a "student teacher." The child had to plan a lesson in grammar, outlining, punctuation, or other language arts topic and explain the concept to the class. Each child was to prepare a worksheet or game and a homework assignment as well. After each presentation, the teacher and other children gave a critical appraisal of the "student teacher's" performance. Their criteria were: whether the student spoke clearly, whether the lesson was interesting, whether the student made any mistakes, and whether he or she kept control of the class. On an occasion when a child did not maintain control, the teacher said, "When you're up there, you have authority and you have to use it. I'll back you up." . . .

The executive elite school is the only school where bells do not demarcate the periods of time. The two fifth-grade teachers were very strict about changing classes on schedule, however, as specific plans for each session had been made. The teachers attempted to keep tight control over the children during lessons, and the children were sometimes flippant, boisterous, and occasionally rude. However, the children may be brought into line by reminding them that "It is up to you," "You must control yourself," "You are responsible for your work," you must "set your own priorities." One teacher told a child, "You are the only driver of your car—and only you can regulate your speed." A new teacher complained to the observer that she had thought "these children" would have more control.

While strict attention to the lesson at hand is required, the teachers make relatively little attempt to regulate the movement of the children at other times. For example, except for the kindergartners the children in this school do not have to wait for the bell to ring in the morning; they may go to their classroom when they arrive at school. Fifth graders often came early to read, to finish work, or to catch up. After the first two months of school, the fifth-grade teachers did not line the children up to change classes or to go to gym, and so on, but, when the children were ready and quiet, they were told they could go—sometimes without the teachers.

In the classroom, the children could get materials when they needed them and took what they needed from closets and from the teacher's desk. They were in charge of the office at lunchtime. During class they did not have to sign out or ask permission to leave the room; they just got up and left. Because of the pressure to get work done, however, they did not leave the room very often. The teachers were very polite to the children, and the investigator heard no sarcasm, no nasty remarks, and few direct orders. The teachers never called the children "honey" or "dear" but always called them by name. The teachers were expected to be available before school, after school, and for part of their lunch-time to provide extra help if needed. . . .

The foregoing analysis of differences in schoolwork in contrasting 50 social-class contexts suggests the following conclusion: the "hidden curriculum" of schoolwork is tacit preparation for relating to the process of production in a particular way. Differing curricular, pedagogical, and pupil evaluation practices emphasize different cognitive and behavioral skills in each social setting and thus contribute to the development in the children of certain potential relationships to physical and symbolic capital,[11] to authority, and to the process of work. School experience, in the sample of schools discussed here, differed qualitatively by social class. These differences may not only contribute to the development in the children in each social class of certain types of economically signif-icant relationships and not others but would thereby help to *reproduce* this system of relations in society. In the contribution to the reproduc-tion of unequal social relations lies a theoretical meaning and social consequence of classroom practice.

The identification of different emphases in classrooms in a sample of contrasting social-class contexts implies that further research should be conducted in a large number of schools to investigate the types of work tasks and interactions in each to see if they differ in the ways dis-cussed here and to see if similar potential relationships are uncovered. Such research could have as a product the further elucidation of com-plex but not readily apparent connections between everyday activity in schools and classrooms and the unequal structure of economic relation-ships in which we work and live.

ENGAGING THE TEXT

1. Examine the ways any single subject is taught in the four types of schools Anyon describes. What differences in teaching methods and in the student-teacher relationship do they reflect? What other differences do you

---

[11]**physical and symbolic capital:** Elsewhere Anyon defines *capital* as "property that is used to produce profit, interest, or rent"; she defines *symbolic capital* as the knowledge and skills that "may yield social and cultural power." [Eds.]

note in the schools? What schools in your geographic region would closely approximate the working-class, middle-class, affluent professional, and executive elite schools of her article?

2. What attitudes toward knowledge and work are the four types of schools teaching their students? What kinds of jobs are students being prepared to do? Do you see any evidence that the schools in your community are producing particular kinds of workers?

3. What is the "hidden curriculum" of Anyon's title? How is this curriculum taught, and what social, cultural, or political purposes does it serve?

EXPLORING CONNECTIONS

4. How might Anyon explain the boredom, absurdity, and childishness that John Taylor Gatto (p. 114) associates with compulsory public education? To what extent do Anyon and Gatto seem to agree about the relationship between school and social class?

5. Analyze the teaching styles that Mike Rose (p. 123) encounters at Our Lady of Mercy. Which of Anyon's categories would they fit best? Do Rose's experiences at his high school tend to confirm or complicate Anyon's analysis?

EXTENDING THE CRITICAL CONTEXT

6. Should all schools be run like professional or elite schools? What would be the advantages of making these schools models for all social classes? Do you see any possible disadvantages?

7. Choose a common elementary school task or skill that Anyon does not mention. Outline four ways it might be taught in the four types of schools.

CHOOSING A SCHOOL FOR MY DAUGHTER IN A SEGREGATED CITY*

NIKOLE HANNAH-JONES

Over half a century ago the U.S. Supreme Court declared an end to school segregation in its 1954 *Brown v. Board of Education* ruling. During the next two decades, school districts worked to integrate formerly "separate but equal" schools, often by busing black, Latino, and Asian students to white neighborhoods miles from their homes. Despite those efforts, thousands of public schools across the country remain heavily segregated today, and many Americans seem to have given up on the idea of integration. Instead of addressing the racial and economic inequities that have plagued American education since its inception, many families have pulled their kids out of local public schools and enrolled them in private, charter, or magnet schools that have more selective and more privileged student populations. Nikole Hannah-Jones represents a startling exception to this trend. When her daughter Najya was four, she and her husband Faraji resisted the private/charter/magnet school option, and enrolled her instead in the "intensely segregated" public elementary school that served their Brooklyn neighborhood. In this article, Hannah-Jones explains the reasoning behind their decision and offers a perspective on education and integration that challenges many of our assumptions about race and public schooling. Hannah-Jones (b. 1976) is an award-winning American journalist who focuses on issues of civil rights and a staff writer for the *New York Times*, the source of this selection.

IN THE SPRING OF 2014, when our daughter, Najya, was turning 4, my husband and I found ourselves facing our toughest decision since becoming parents. We live in Bedford-Stuyvesant, a low-income, heavily black, rapidly gentrifying neighborhood of brownstones in central Brooklyn. The nearby public schools are named after people intended to evoke black uplift, like Marcus Garvey, a prominent black nationalist in the 1920s, and Carter G. Woodson, the father of Black History Month, but the schools are a disturbing reflection of New York City's stark racial and socioeconomic divisions. In one of the most diverse cities in the world, the children who attend these schools learn in classrooms where all of their classmates—and I mean, in most cases, every single one—are black and Latino, and nearly every student is poor. Not surprisingly, the test scores of most of Bed-Stuy's schools reflect the marginalization of their students.

I didn't know any of our middle-class neighbors, black or white, who sent their children to one of these schools. They had managed to secure seats in the more diverse and economically advantaged magnet schools or gifted-and-talented programs outside our area, or opted to pay hefty tuition to progressive but largely white private institutions. I knew this because from the moment we arrived in New York with our 1-year-old, we had many conversations about where we would, should, and definitely should not send our daughter to school when the time came.

My husband Faraji and I wanted to send our daughter to public school. Faraji, the oldest child in a military family, went to public schools that served Army bases both in America and abroad. As a result, he had a highly unusual experience for a black American child: He never attended a segregated public school a day of his life. He can now walk into any room and instantly start a conversation with the people there, whether they are young mothers gathered at a housing-project tenants' meeting or executives eating from small plates at a ritzy cocktail reception.

I grew up in Waterloo, Iowa, on the wrong side of the river that divided white from black, opportunity from struggle, and started my education in a low-income school that my mother says was distressingly chaotic. I don't recall it being bad, but I do remember just one white child in my first-grade class, though there may have been more. That summer, my mom and dad enrolled my older sister and me in the school district's voluntary desegregation program, which allowed some black kids to leave their neighborhood schools for whiter, more well-off ones on the west side of town. This was 1982, nearly three decades after the Supreme Court ruled in *Brown v. Board of Education* that separate schools for black and white children were unconstitutional, and near the height of desegregation in this country. My parents chose one of the whitest, richest schools, thinking it would provide the best opportunities for us. Starting in second grade, I rode the bus an hour each morning across town to the "best" public school my town had to offer, Kingsley Elementary, where I was among the tiny number of working-class children and the even tinier number of black children. We did not walk to school or get dropped off by our parents on their way to work. We showed up in a yellow bus, visitors in someone else's neighborhood, and were whisked back across the bridge each day as soon as the bell rang.

I remember those years as emotionally and socially fraught, but 5 also as academically stimulating and world-expanding. Aside from the rigorous classes and quality instruction I received, this was the first time I'd shared dinners in the homes of kids whose parents were doctors and lawyers and scientists. My mom was a probation officer, and my dad drove a bus, and most of my family members on both sides worked in factories or meatpacking plants or did other manual labor. I understood, even then, in a way both intuitive and defensive, that my school friends' parents weren't better than my neighborhood friends' parents, who worked hard every day at hourly jobs. But this exposure helped me imagine possibilities, a course for myself that I had not considered before.

It's hard to say where any one person would have ended up if a single circumstance were different; our life trajectories are shaped by so many external and internal factors. But I have no doubt my parents' decision to pull me out of my segregated neighborhood school made the possibility of my getting from there to here—staff writer for the *New York Times Magazine*—more likely.

Integration was transformative for my husband and me. Yet the idea of placing our daughter in one of the small number of integrated schools troubled me. These schools are disproportionately white and serve the middle and upper middle classes, with a smattering of poor black and Latino students to create "diversity."

In a city where white children are only 15 percent of the more than one million public-school students, half of them are clustered in just 11 percent of the schools, which not coincidentally include many of the city's top performers. Part of what makes those schools desirable to white parents, aside from the academics, is that they have some students of color, but not too many. This carefully curated integration, the kind that allows many white parents to boast that their children's public schools look like the United Nations, comes at a steep cost for the rest of the city's black and Latino children.

The New York City public-school system is 41 percent Latino, 27 percent black, and 16 percent Asian. Three-quarters of all students are low-income. In 2014, the Civil Rights Project at the University of California, Los Angeles, released a report showing that New York City public schools are among the most segregated in the country. Black and Latino children here have become increasingly isolated, with 85 percent of black students and 75 percent of Latino students attending "intensely" segregated schools—schools that are less than 10 percent white.

This is not just New York's problem. I've spent much of my career 10 as a reporter chronicling rampant school segregation in every region of the country, and the ways that segregated schools harm black and Latino children. One study published in 2009 in the *Journal of Policy Analysis and Management* showed that the academic achievement gap for black children increased as they spent time in segregated schools. Schools with large numbers of black and Latino kids are less likely to have experienced teachers, advanced courses, instructional materials, and adequate facilities, according to the United States Department of Education's Office for Civil Rights. Most black and Latino students today are segregated by both race and class, a combination that wreaks havoc on the learning environment. Research stretching back 50 years shows that the socioeconomic makeup of a school can play a larger role in achievement than the poverty of an individual student's family. Getting Najya into one of the disproportionately white schools in the city felt like accepting the inevitability of this two-tiered system: one set of schools with excellent resources for white kids and some black and Latino middle-class kids, a second set of underresourced schools for the rest of the city's black and Latino kids.

When the New York City Public Schools catalog arrived in the mail one day that spring, with information about Mayor Bill de Blasio's new universal prekindergarten program, I told Faraji that I wanted to enroll Najya in a segregated, low-income school. Faraji's eyes widened as I explained that if we removed Najya, whose name we chose because it means "liberated" and "free" in Swahili, from the experience of most black and Latino children, we would be part of the problem. Saying my child deserved access to "good" public schools felt like implying that children in "bad" schools deserved the schools they got, too. I understood that so much of school segregation is structural—a result of decades of housing discrimination, of political calculations and the machinations of policy makers, of simple inertia. But I also believed that it is the choices of individual parents that uphold the system, and I was determined not to do what I'd seen so many others do when their values about integration collided with the reality of where to send their own children to school.

One family, or even a few families, cannot transform a segregated school, but if none of us were willing to go into them, nothing would change. Putting our child into a segregated school would not integrate it racially, but we are middle-class and would, at least, help to integrate it economically. As a reporter, I'd witnessed how the presence of even a handful of middle-class families made it less likely that a school would be neglected. I also knew that we would be able to make up for Najya anything the school was lacking.

As I told Faraji my plan, he slowly shook his head no. He wanted to look into parochial schools, or one of the "good" public schools, or even private schools. So we argued, pleading our cases from the living room, up the steps to our office lined with books on slavery and civil rights, and back down, before we came to an impasse and retreated to our respective corners. There is nothing harder than navigating our nation's racial legacy in this country, and the problem was that we each knew the other was right and wrong at the same time. Faraji couldn't believe that I was asking him to expose our child to the type of education that the two of us had managed to avoid. He worried that we would be hurting Najya if we put her in a high-poverty, all-black school. "Are we experimenting with our child based on our idealism about public schools?" he asked. "Are we putting her at a disadvantage?"

At the heart of Faraji's concern was a fear that grips black families like ours. We each came from working-class roots, fought our way into the middle class, and had no family wealth or safety net to fall back on. Faraji believed that our gains were too tenuous to risk putting our child in anything but a top-notch school. And he was right to be worried. In 2014, the Brookings Institution found that black children are particularly vulnerable to downward mobility—nearly seven of 10 black children born into middle-income families don't maintain that income level as adults. There was no margin for error, and we had to use our relative status to fight to give Najya every advantage. Hadn't we worked hard, he asked, frustration building in his voice, precisely so that she would not have to go to the types of schools that trapped so many black children?

Eventually I persuaded him to visit a few schools with me. Before 15 work, we peered into the classrooms of three neighborhood schools, and a fourth, Public School 307, located in the Vinegar Hill section of Brooklyn, near the East River waterfront and a few miles from our home.

P.S. 307's attendance zone was drawn snugly around five of the 10 buildings that make up the Farragut Houses, a public-housing project with 3,200 residents across from the Brooklyn Navy Yard. The school's population was 91 percent black and Latino. Nine of 10 students met federal poverty standards. But what went on inside the school was unlike what goes on in most schools serving the city's poorest children. This was in large part because of the efforts of a remarkable principal, Roberta Davenport. She grew up in Farragut, and her younger siblings attended P.S. 307. She became principal five decades later in 2003, to a low-performing school. Davenport commuted from Connecticut, but her car was usually the first one in the parking lot each morning, often because she worked so late into the night that, exhausted, she would sleep at a friend's nearby instead of making the long drive home. Soft of voice but steely in character, she rejected the spare educational orthodoxy often reserved for poor black and brown children that strips away everything that makes school joyous in order to focus solely on improving test scores. These children from the projects learned Mandarin, took violin lessons, and played chess. Thanks to her hard work, the school had recently received money from a federal magnet grant, which funded a science, engineering, and technology program aimed at drawing middle-class children from outside its attendance zone.

Faraji and I walked the bright halls of P.S. 307, taking in the reptiles in the science room and the students learning piano during music class. The walls were papered with the precocious musings of elementary children. While touring the schools, Faraji later told me, he started feeling guilty about his instinct to keep Najya out of them. Were these children, he asked himself, worthy of any less than his own child? "These are kids who look like you," he told me. "Kids like the ones you grew up with. I was being very selfish about it, thinking: I am going to get mine for my child, and that's it. And I am ashamed of that."

When it was time to submit our school choices to the city, we put down all four of the schools we visited. In May 2014, we learned Najya had gotten into our first choice, P.S. 307. We were excited but also nervous. I'd be lying if I said I didn't feel pulled in the way other parents with options feel pulled. I had moments when I couldn't ignore the nagging fear that in my quest for fairness, I was being unfair to my own daughter. I worried — I worry still — about whether I made the right decision for our little girl. But I knew I made the just one.

For many white Americans, millions of black and Latino children attending segregated schools may seem like a throwback to another era, a problem we solved long ago. And legally, we did. In 1954, the Supreme Court issued its landmark *Brown v. Board of Education* ruling, striking down laws that forced black and white children to attend separate schools. But while *Brown v. Board* targeted segregation by state law, we have proved largely unwilling to address segregation that is maintained by other means, resulting from the nation's long and racist history.

In the Supreme Court's decision, the justices responded unanimously to a group of five cases, including that of Linda Brown, a black 8-year-old who was not allowed to go to her white neighborhood school in Topeka, Kan., but was made to ride a bus to a black school much farther away. The court determined that separate schools, even if they had similar resources, were "inherently" — by their nature — unequal, causing profound damage to the children who attended them and hobbling their ability to live as full citizens of their country. The court's decision hinged on sociological research, including a key study by the psychologists Kenneth Clark and Mamie Phipps Clark, a husband-and-wife team who gave black children in segregated schools in the North and the South black and white dolls and asked questions about how they perceived them. Most students described the white dolls as good and smart and the black dolls as bad and stupid. (The Clarks also found that segregation hurt white children's development.) Chief Justice Earl Warren felt so passionate about the issue that he read the court's opinion aloud: "Does segregation of children in public schools solely on the basis of race, even though the physical facilities and other 'tangible' factors may be equal, deprive the children of the minority group of equal educational opportunities? We believe that it does." The ruling made clear that because this nation was founded on a racial caste system, black children would never become equals as long as they were separated from white children.

In New York City, home to the largest black population in the country, the decision was celebrated by many liberals as the final strike against school segregation in the "backward" South. But Kenneth Clark, the first black person to earn a doctorate in psychology at Columbia University and to hold a permanent professorship at City College of New York, was quick to dismiss Northern righteousness on race matters. At a meeting of the Urban League around the time of the decision, he charged that though New York had no law requiring segregation, it intentionally separated its students by assigning them to schools based on their race or building schools deep in segregated neighborhoods. In many cases, Clark said, black children were attending schools that were worse than those attended by their black counterparts in the South.

Clark's words shamed proudly progressive white New Yorkers and embarrassed those overseeing the nation's largest school system. The New York City Board of Education released a forceful statement promising to integrate its schools: "Segregated, racially homogeneous schools damage the personality of minority-group children. These schools decrease their motivation and thus impair their ability to learn. White children are also damaged. Public education in a racially homogeneous setting is socially unrealistic and blocks the attainment of the goals of democratic education, whether this segregation occurs by law or by fact." The head of the Board of Education undertook an investigation in 1955 that confirmed the widespread separation of black and Puerto Rican children in dilapidated buildings with the least-experienced and least-qualified teachers. Their schools were so overcrowded that some black children went to school for only part of the day to give others a turn.

The Board of Education appointed a commission to develop a city-wide integration plan. But when school officials took some token steps, they faced a wave of white opposition. "It was most intense in the white neighborhoods closest to African American neighborhoods, because they were the ones most likely to be affected by desegregation plans," says Thomas Sugrue, a historian at New York University and the author of *Sweet Land of Liberty: The Forgotten Struggle for Civil Rights in the North.* By the mid-'60s, there were few signs of integration in New York's schools. In fact, the number of segregated junior-high schools in the city had quadrupled by 1964. That February, civil rights leaders called for a major one-day boycott of the New York City schools. Some 460,000 black and Puerto Rican students stayed home to protest their segregation. It was the largest demonstration for civil rights in the nation's history. But the boycott upset many white liberals, who thought it was too aggressive, and as thousands of white families fled to the suburbs, the integration campaign collapsed.

Even as New York City was ending its only significant effort to desegregate, the Supreme Court was expanding the *Brown* ruling. Beginning in the mid-'60s, the court handed down a series of decisions that determined that not only did *Brown v. Board* allow the use of race to remedy the effects of long-segregated schools, it also *required* it. Assigning black students to white schools and vice versa was necessary to destroy a system built on racism—even if white families didn't like it. "All things being equal, with no history of discrimination, it might well be desirable to assign pupils to schools nearest their homes," the court wrote in its 1971 ruling in *Swann v. Charlotte-Mecklenburg Board of Education,* which upheld busing to desegregate schools in Charlotte, N.C. "But all things are not equal in a system that has been deliberately constructed and maintained to enforce racial segregation. The remedy for such segregation may be administratively awkward, inconvenient and even bizarre in some situations, and may impose burdens on some; but all awkwardness and inconvenience cannot be avoided."

In what would be an extremely rare and fleeting moment in American history, all three branches of the federal government aligned on the issue. Congress passed the 1964 Civil Rights Act, pushed by President Lyndon B. Johnson, which prohibited segregated lunch counters, buses, and parks and allowed the Department of Justice for the first time to sue school districts to force integration. It also gave the government the power to withhold federal funds if the districts did not comply. By 1973, 91 percent of black children in the former Confederate and border states attended school with white children.

But while Northern congressmen embraced efforts to force integration in the South, some balked at efforts to desegregate their own schools. They tucked a passage into the 1964 Civil Rights Act aiming to limit school desegregation in the North by prohibiting school systems

25

from assigning students to schools in order to integrate them unless ordered to do so by a court. Because Northern officials often practiced segregation without the cover of law, it was far less likely that judges would find them in violation of the Constitution.

Not long after, the nation began its retreat from integration. Richard Nixon was elected president in 1968, with the help of a coalition of white voters who opposed integration in housing and schools. He appointed four conservative justices to the Supreme Court and set the stage for a profound legal shift. Since 1974, when the *Milliken v. Bradley* decision struck down a lower court's order for a metro-area-wide desegregation program between nearly all-black Detroit city schools and the white suburbs surrounding the city, a series of major Supreme Court rulings on school desegregation have limited the reach of *Brown*.

When Ronald Reagan became president in 1981, he promoted the notion that using race to integrate schools was just as bad as using race to segregate them. He urged the nation to focus on improving segregated schools by holding them to strict standards, a tacit return to the "separate but equal" doctrine that was roundly rejected in *Brown*. His administration emphasized that busing and other desegregation programs discriminated against white students. Reagan eliminated federal dollars earmarked to help desegregation and pushed to end hundreds of school-desegregation court orders.

Yet this was the very period when the benefits of integration were becoming most apparent. By 1988, a year after Faraji and I entered middle school, school integration in the United States had reached its peak and the achievement gap between black and white students was at its lowest point since the government began collecting data. The difference in black and white reading scores fell to half what it was in 1971, according to data from the National Center for Education Statistics. (As schools have since resegregated, the test-score gap has only grown.) The improvements for black children did not come at the cost of white children. As black test scores rose, so did white ones.

Decades of studies have affirmed integration's power. A 2010 study released by the Century Foundation found that when children in public housing in Montgomery County, Md., enrolled in middle-class schools, the differences between their scores and those of their wealthier classmates decreased by half in math and a third in reading, and they pulled significantly ahead of their counterparts in poor schools. In fact, integration changes the entire trajectory of black students' lives. A 2015 longitudinal study by the economist Rucker Johnson at the University of California, Berkeley, followed black adults who had attended desegregated schools and showed that these adults, when compared with their counterparts or even their own siblings in segregated schools, were less likely to be poor, suffer health problems and go to jail, and more likely to go to college and reside in integrated neighborhoods. They even lived longer. Critically, these benefits were passed on to their children, while the children of adults who went to segregated schools were more likely to perform poorly in school or drop out.

But integration as a constitutional mandate, as justice for black and Latino children, as a moral righting of past wrongs, is no longer our country's stated goal. The Supreme Court has effectively sided with Reagan, requiring strict legal colorblindness even if it leaves segregation intact, and even striking down desegregation programs that ensured integration for thousands of black students if a single white child did not get into her school of choice. The most recent example was a 2007 case that came to be known as Parents Involved. White parents in Seattle and Jefferson County, Kentucky, challenged voluntary integration programs, claiming the districts discriminated against white children by considering race as a factor in apportioning students among schools in order to keep them racially balanced. Five conservative justices struck down these integration plans. In 1968, the court ruled in *Green v. County School Board of New Kent County* that we should no longer look across a city and see a "'white' school and a 'Negro' school, but just schools." In 2007, Chief Justice John Roberts Jr. wrote: "Before *Brown*, schoolchildren were told where they could and could not go to school based on the color of their skin. The school districts in these cases have not carried the heavy burden of demonstrating that we should allow this once again—even for very different reasons.... The way to stop discrimination on the basis of race is to stop discriminating on the basis of race."

Legally and culturally, we've come to accept segregation once again. Today, across the country, black children are more segregated than they have been at any point in nearly half a century. Except for a few remaining court-ordered desegregation programs, intentional integration almost never occurs unless it's in the interests of white students. This is even the case in New York City, under the stewardship of Mayor de Blasio, who campaigned by highlighting the city's racial and economic inequality. De Blasio and his schools chancellor, Carmen Fariña, have acknowledged that they don't believe their job is to force school integration. "I want to see diversity in schools organically," Fariña said at a town-hall meeting in Lower Manhattan in February. "I don't want to see mandates." The shift in language that trades the word "integration" for "diversity" is critical. Here in this city, as in many, diversity functions as a boutique offering for the children of the privileged but does little to ensure quality education for poor black and Latino children.

"The moral vision behind *Brown v. Board of Education* is dead," Ritchie Torres, a city councilman who represents the Bronx and has been pushing the city to address school segregation, told me. Integration, he says, is seen as "something that would be nice to have but not something we need to create a more equitable society. At the same time, we have an intensely segregated school system that is denying a generation of kids of color a fighting chance at a decent life."

Najya, of course, had no idea about any of this. She just knew she loved P.S. 307, waking up each morning excited to head to her pre-K class, where her two best friends were a little black girl named Imani from Farragut and a little white boy named Sam, one of a handful of white pre-K students at the school, with whom we car-pooled from our neighborhood. Four excellent teachers, all of them of color, guided Najya and her classmates with a professionalism and affection that belied the school's dismal test scores. Faraji and I threw ourselves into the school, joining the parent-teacher association and the school's leadership team, attending assemblies and chaperoning field trips. We found ourselves relieved at how well things were going. Internally, I started to exhale.

But in the spring of 2015, as Najya's first year was nearing its end, we read in the news that another elementary school, P.S. 8, less than a mile from P.S. 307 in affluent Brooklyn Heights, was plagued by overcrowding. Some students zoned for that school might be rerouted to ours. This made geographic sense. P.S. 8's zone was expansive, stretching across Brooklyn Heights under the Manhattan Bridge to the Dumbo neighborhood and Vinegar Hill, the neighborhood around P.S. 307. P.S. 8's lines were drawn when most of the development there consisted of factories and warehouses. But gentrification overtook Dumbo, which hugs the East River and provides breathtaking views of the skyline and a quick commute to Manhattan. The largely upper-middle-class and white and Asian children living directly across the street from P.S. 307 were zoned to the heavily white P.S. 8.

To accommodate the surging population, P.S. 8 had turned its drama and dance rooms into general classrooms and cut its pre-K, but it still had to place up to 28 kids in each class. Meanwhile, P.S. 307 sat at the center of the neighborhood population boom, half empty. Its attendance zone included only the Farragut Houses and was one of the tiniest in the city. Because Farragut residents were aging, with dwindling numbers of school-age children, P.S. 307 was underenrolled.

In early spring 2015, the city's Department of Education sent out notices telling 50 families that had applied to kindergarten at P.S. 8 that their children would be placed on the waiting list and instead guaranteed admission to P.S. 307. Distraught parents dashed off letters to school administrators and to their elected officials. They pleaded their case to the press. "We bought a home here, and one of the main reasons was because it was known that kindergarten admissions [at P.S. 8] were pretty much guaranteed," one parent told the New York Post, adding that he wouldn't send his child to P.S. 307. Another parent whose twins had secured coveted spots made the objections to P.S. 307 more plain: "I would be concerned about safety," he said. "I don't hear good things about that school."

That May, as I sat at a meeting that P.S. 8 parents arranged with school officials, I was struck by the sheer power these parents had drawn into that auditorium. This meeting about the overcrowding at P.S. 8, which involved 50 children in a system of more than one million, had summoned a state senator, a state assemblywoman, a City Council member, the city comptroller, and the staff members of several other elected officials. It had rarely been clearer to me how segregation and integration, at their core, are about power and who gets access to it. As the Rev. Dr. Martin Luther King Jr. wrote in 1967: "I cannot see how the Negro will totally be liberated from the crushing weight of poor education, squalid housing and economic strangulation until he is integrated, with power, into every level of American life."

As the politicians looked on, two white fathers gave an impassioned PowerPoint presentation in which they asked the Department of Education to place more children into already-teeming classrooms rather than send kids zoned to P.S. 8 to P.S. 307. Another speaker, whose child had been wait-listed, choked up as he talked about having to break it to his kindergarten-age son that he would not be able to go to school with the children with whom he'd shared play dates and Sunday dinners. "We haven't told him yet" that he didn't get into P.S. 8, the father said, as eyes in the crowd grew misty. "We hope to never have to tell him."

The meeting was emotional and at times angry, with parents shouting out their anxieties about safety and low test scores at P.S. 307. But the concerns they voiced may have also masked something else. While suburban parents, who are mostly white, say they are selecting schools based on test scores, the racial makeup of a school actually plays a larger role in their school decisions, according to a 2009 study published in the *American Journal of Education.* Amy Stuart Wells, a professor of sociology and education at Columbia University's Teachers College, found the same thing when she studied how white parents choose schools in New York City. "In a post-racial era, we don't have to say it's about race or the color of the kids in the building," Wells told me. "We can concentrate poverty and kids of color and then fail to provide the resources to support and sustain those schools, and then we can see a school full of black kids and then say, 'Oh, look at their test scores.' It's all very tidy now, this whole system."

I left that meeting upset about how P.S. 307 had been characterized, 40 but I didn't give it much thought again until the end of summer, when Najya was about to start kindergarten. I heard that the community education council was holding a meeting to discuss a potential rezoning of P.S. 8 and P.S. 307. The council, an elected group that oversees 28 public schools in District 13, including P.S. 8 and P.S. 307, is responsible for approving zoning decisions. School was still out for the summer, and almost no P.S. 307 parents knew plans were underway that could affect them. At the meeting, two men from the school system's Office of District Planning projected a rezoning map onto a screen. The plan would split the P.S. 8 zone roughly in half, divided by the Brooklyn Bridge. It would turn P.S. 8 into the exclusive neighborhood school for Brooklyn Heights and reroute Dumbo and Vinegar Hill students to P.S. 307. A tall, white man with brown hair that flopped over his forehead said he was from Concord Village, a complex that should have fallen on the 307 side of the line. He thanked the council for producing a plan that reflected his neighbors' concerns by keeping his complex in the P.S. 8 zone. It became clear that while parents in Farragut, Dumbo, and Vinegar Hill had not even known about the rezoning plan, some residents had organized and lobbied to influence how the lines were drawn.

The officials presented the rezoning plan, which would affect incoming kindergartners, as beneficial to everyone. If the children in the part of the zone newly assigned to P.S. 307 enrolled at the school, P.S. 8's overcrowding would be relieved at least temporarily. And P.S. 307, the officials' presentation showed, would fill its empty seats with white children and give all the school's students that most elusive thing: integration.

It was hard not to be skeptical about the department's plan. New York, like many deeply segregated cities, has a terrible track record of maintaining racial balance in formerly underenrolled segregated schools once white families come in. Schools like P.S. 321 in Brooklyn's Park Slope neighborhood and the Academy of Arts and Letters in Fort Greene tend to go through a brief period of transitional integration, in which significant numbers of white students enroll, and then the numbers of Latino and black students dwindle. In fact, that's exactly what happened at P.S. 8.

A decade ago, P.S. 8 was P.S. 307's mirror image. Predominantly filled with low-income black and Latino students from surrounding neighborhoods, P.S. 8, with its low test scores and low enrollment, languished amid a community of affluence because white parents in the neighborhood refused to send their children there. A group of parents worked hard with school administrators to turn the school around, writing grants to start programs for art and other enrichment activities. Then more white and Asian parents started to enroll their children. One of them was David Goldsmith, who later became president of the community education council tasked with considering the rezoning of P.S. 8 and P.S. 307. Goldsmith is white and, at the time, lived in Vinegar Hill with his Filipino wife and their daughter.

As P.S. 8 improved, more and more white families from Brooklyn Heights, Dumbo, and Vinegar Hill enrolled their children, and the classrooms in the lower grades became majority white. The whitening of the school had unintended consequences. Some of the black and Latino parents whose children had been in the school from the beginning felt as if they were being marginalized. The white parents were able to raise large sums at fund-raisers and could be dismissive of the much smaller fund-raising efforts that had come before. Then, Goldsmith says, the new parents started seeking to separate their children from their poorer classmates. "There were kids in the school that were really high-risk kids, kids who were homeless, living in temporary shelters, you know, poverty can be really brutal," Goldsmith says. "The school was really committed to helping all children, but we had white middle-class parents saying, 'I don't want my child in the same class with the kid who has emotional issues.'"

The parents who had helped build P.S. 8—black, Latino, white and Asian—feared they were losing something important, a truly diverse school that nurtured its neediest students, where families held equal value no matter the size of their paychecks. They asked for a plan to help the school maintain its black and Latino population by setting aside a percentage of seats for low-income children, but they didn't get approval.

P.S. 8's transformation to a school where only one in four students are black or Latino and only 14 percent are low income began during the administration of Mayor Michael Bloomberg, known for its indifference toward efforts to integrate schools. But integration advocates say that they've also been deeply disappointed by the de Blasio administration's stance on the issue. In October 2014, after the release of the U.C.L.A. study pointing to the extreme segregation in the city's schools, and nearly a year after de Blasio was elected, Councilmen Ritchie Torres and Brad Lander moved to force the administration to address segregation, introducing what became the School Diversity Accountability Act, which would require the Department of Education to release school-segregation figures and report what it was doing to alleviate the problem. "It was always right in front of our faces," says Lander, a representative from Brooklyn, whose own children attend heavily white public schools. "Then the U.C.L.A. report hit, and the segregation in the city became urgent."

Last June, de Blasio signed the School Diversity Accountability Act into law. But the law mandates only that the Department of Education report segregation numbers, not that it do anything to integrate schools. De Blasio declined to be interviewed, but when asked at a news conference in November why the city did not at least do what it could to redraw attendance lines, he defended the property rights of affluent parents who buy into neighborhoods to secure entry into heavily white schools. "You have to also respect families who have made a decision to live in a certain area," he said, because families have "made massive life decisions and investments because of which school their kid would go to." The mayor suggested there was little he could do because school segregation simply was a reflection of New York's stark housing segregation, entrenched by decades of discriminatory local and federal policy. "This is the history of America," he said.

Of course, de Blasio is right: Housing segregation and school segregation have always been entwined in America. But the opportunity to buy into "good" neighborhoods with "good" schools that de Blasio wants to protect has never been equally available to all.

P.S. 307 was a very different place from what it had been, but Najya was thriving. I watched as she and her classmates went from struggling to sound out three-letter words to reading entire books. She would surprise me in the car rides after school with her discussions of hypotheses and photosynthesis, words we hadn't taught her. And there was something almost breathtaking about witnessing an auditorium full of mostly low-income black and Latino children confidently singing in Mandarin and beating Chinese drums as they performed a fan dance to celebrate the Lunar New Year.

But I also knew how fragile success at a school like P.S. 307 could 50 be. The few segregated, high-poverty schools we hold up as exceptions are almost always headed by a singular principal like Roberta Davenport. But relying on one dynamic leader is a precarious means of ensuring a quality education. With all the resources Davenport was able to draw to the school, P.S. 307's test scores still dropped this year. The school suffers from the same chronic absenteeism that plagues other schools with large numbers of low-income families. And then Davenport retired last summer, just as the clashes over P.S. 307's integration were heating up, causing alarm among parents.

Najya and the other children at P.S. 307 were unaware of the turmoil and the battle lines adults were drawing outside the school's doors. Faraji, my husband, had been elected co-president of P.S. 307's P.T.A. along with Benjamin Greene, another black middle-class parent from Bed-Stuy, who also serves on the community education council. As the potential for rezoning loomed over the school, they were forced to turn their attention from fund-raising and planning events to working to prevent the city's plan from ultimately creating another mostly white school.

It was important to them that Farragut residents, who were largely unaware of the process, had a say over what happened. Faraji and I had found it hard to bridge the class divides between the Farragut families and the middle-class black families, like ours, from outside the neighborhood. We parents were all cordial toward one another. Outside the school, though, we mostly went our separate ways. But after the rezoning was proposed, Faraji and Benjamin worked with the Rev. Dr. Mark V. C. Taylor of the Church of the Open Door, which sits on the Farragut property, and canvassed the projects to talk to parents and inform them of the city's proposal. Not one P.S. 307 parent they spoke to knew anything about the plan, and they were immediately worried and fearful about what it would mean for their children. P.S. 307 was that rare example of a well-resourced segregated school, and these parents knew it.

The Farragut parents were also angry and hurt over how their school and their children had been talked about in public meetings and the press. Some white Dumbo parents had told Davenport that they'd be willing to enroll their children only if she agreed to put the new students all together in their own classroom. Farragut parents feared their children would be marginalized. If the school eventually filled up with children from high-income white families—the median income for Dumbo and Vinegar Hill residents is almost 10 times that of Farragut residents—the character of the school could change, and as had happened at other schools like P.S. 8, the results might not benefit the black and Latino students. Among other things, P.S. 307 might no longer qualify for federal funds for special programming, like free after-school care, to help low-income families.

"I don't have a problem with people coming in," Saaiba Coles, a Farragut mother with two children at P.S. 307, told those gathered at a community meeting about the rezoning. "I just don't want them to forget about the kids that were already here." Faraji and Benjamin collected and delivered to the education council a petition with more than 400 signatures of Farragut residents supporting the rezoning, but only under certain conditions, including that half of all the seats at P.S. 307 would be guaranteed for low-income children. That would ensure that the school remained truly integrated and that new higher-income parents would have to share power in deciding the direction of the school.

In January of this year, the education council held a meeting to vote on the rezoning. Nearly four dozen Farragut residents who'd taken two buses chartered by the church filed into the auditorium of a Brooklyn elementary school, sitting behind a cluster of anxious parents from Dumbo. Reporters lined up alongside them. In the months since the potential rezoning plan was announced, the spectacle of an integration fight in the progressive bastion of Brooklyn had attracted media attention. Coverage appeared in the *New York Times*, the *Wall Street Journal*, and on WNYC. "Brooklyn hipsters fight school desegregation," the news site Raw Story proclaimed. The meeting lasted more than three hours as parents spoke passionately, imploring the council to delay the vote so that the two communities could try to get to know each other and figure out how they could bridge their economic, racial, and cultural divides. Both Dumbo and Farragut parents asked the district for leadership, fearing integration that was not intentionally planned would fail.

In the end, the council proceeded with the vote, approving the rezoning with a 50 percent low-income set-aside, but children living in P.S. 307's attendance zone would receive priority. But that's not a guarantee. White children under the age of 5 outnumber black and Latino children of the same age in the new zone, according to census data. And the white population will only grow as new developments go on the market. Without holding seats for low-income children, it's not certain the school will achieve 50 percent low-income enrollment.

The decision felt more like a victory for the status quo. This rezoning did not occur because it was in the best interests of P.S. 307's black and Latino children, but because it served the interests of the wealthy, white parents of Brooklyn Heights. P.S. 8 will only get whiter and more exclusive: The council failed to mention at the meeting that the plan would send future students from the only three Farragut buildings that had been zoned for P.S. 8 to P.S. 307, ultimately removing almost all the low-income students from P.S. 8 and turning it into one of the most affluent schools in the city. The Department of Education projects that within six years, P.S. 8 could be three-quarters white in a school system where only one-seventh of the kids are white.

P.S. 307 may eventually look similar. Without seats guaranteed for low-income children, and with an increasing white population in the zone, the school may flip and become mostly white and overcrowded. Farragut parents worry that at that point, the project's children, like those at P.S. 8, could be zoned out of their own school. A decade from now, integration advocates could be lamenting how P.S. 307 went from nearly all black and Latino to being integrated for a period to heavily white.

That transition isn't going to happen immediately, so some Dumbo parents have threatened to move, or enroll their children in private schools. Others are struggling over what to do. By allowing such vast disparities between public schools—racially, socioeconomically, and academically—this city has made integration the hardest choice.

"You're not living in Brooklyn if you don't want to have a diverse 60 system around your kid," Michael Jones, who lives in Brooklyn Heights and considered sending his twins to P.S. 307 for pre-K because P.S. 8 no longer offered it, told me over coffee. "You want it to be multicultural. You know, if you didn't want that, you'd be in private school, or you would be in a different area. So, we're all living in Brooklyn because we want that to be part of the upbringing. But you can understand how a parent might look at it and go, 'While I want diversity, I don't want profound imbalance.' " He thought about what it would have meant for his boys to be among the few middle-class children in P.S. 307. "We could look at it and see there is probably going to be a clash of some kind," he said. "My kid's not an experiment." In the end, he felt that he could not take a chance on his children's education and sent them to private preschool; they now go to P.S. 8.

This sense of helplessness in the face of such entrenched segregation is what makes so alluring the notion, embraced by liberals and conservatives, that we can address school inequality not with integration but by giving poor, segregated schools more resources and demanding of them more accountability. True integration, true equality, requires a surrendering of advantage, and when it comes to our own children, that can feel almost unnatural. Najya's first two years in public school helped me understand this better than I ever had before. Even Kenneth Clark, the psychologist whose research showed the debilitating effects of segregation on black children, chose not to enroll his children in the segregated schools he was fighting against. "My children," he said, "only have one life." But so do the children relegated to this city's segregated schools. They have only one life, too.

ENGAGING THE TEXT

1. What kinds of schools did Hannah-Jones and her husband attend, and why were they important in their development? How racially and economically

integrated were the primary and secondary schools that you attended? How, for example, would they compare to the schools in the New York City public-school system that Hannah-Jones describes? How did the mix of students you encountered in school affect you?

2. Why is Hannah-Jones troubled by the prospect of sending her daughter to an integrated public school? What does she appear to like about P.S. 307, the segregated public school she eventually chooses for her daughter? Do you think she makes the right decision? Why or why not?

3. Why is segregation an important problem for black and Latino students, according to Hannah-Jones? How does it impact their academic performance and long-term life prospects, and what evidence does she offer to support her assertions? In your view, is the segregation of black and Latino students a problem if schools have equal economic resources? Why or why not?

4. What do you think of the statement by the New York City Board of Education: "Public education in a racially homogeneous setting is socially unrealistic and blocks the goals of democratic education" (para. 21)? What role should public schools play in preparing students to participate and live in a democracy? What kinds of skills and experiences should they have, and what do they need to know to become effective citizens in a democratic culture?

5. How did American attitudes toward integration and segregation change after the Reagan administration? What role has the emphasis on achievement test scores and gentrification played in the resegregation of urban schools?

6. Why is Hannah-Jones concerned about the "whitening" of P.S. 307 as the result of proposed rezoning efforts? How might an increase in the number of white students affect black and Latino students who attend the school? Overall, how would you explain her position on integration and segregation?

7. **Thinking Rhetorically**   What role does language play in the debate over school segregation? What, for example, are the connotations of terms like "integration" and "diversity"? What is the difference between talking about "intentional" and "forced" integration? To what extent would you agree that the word "diversity" is often used as a "boutique offering" to describe the educational experiences of privileged white students?

EXPLORING CONNECTIONS

8. How would you expect Hannah-Jones to respond to the list of functions that John Taylor Gatto associates with the "purpose of mandatory public education in this country" (p. 119)? For example, how might her view of the "adjustive or adaptive function" and the "integrative function" of public school differ from Gatto's? How likely is it that she would see students in public school as "deliberately dumbed down and declawed in order that government might

© Bendib, LLC.

proceed unchallenged"? How can you account for the differences in their views of public schools?

9. Given Jean Anyon's depiction of teaching and learning in working-class, middle-class, and elite schools (p. 136), is Hannah-Jones's husband Faraji right to be worried about the kind of education Najya will experience in P.S. 307? Why or why not? How does Hannah-Jones's experience of P.S. 307 challenge Anyon's description of working-class schools?

10. In "Theories and Constructs of Race" (p. 631), Linda Holtzman and Leon Sharpe discuss "implicit racism," the unconscious sense of superiority that whites often feel due to their position as the "societal norm" in the U.S. (para. 6). What role might this kind of "automatic" racism play in the school choice decisions of Hannah-Jones's middle-class neighbors? To what extent might misgivings about implicit bias and "backstage behavior" also factor into Hannah-Jones's concerns about the "whitening" of P.S. 307?

EXTENDING THE CRITICAL CONTEXT

11. Do some research to assess the level of segregation of the public schools in your home city, town, or state. What are the most recent demographics of

the public elementary and secondary schools in your area? How have the percentages of white, black, Latino, and Asian students enrolling changed over time? To what extent would you say that the schools in your area are segregated, and why?

12. Go online to learn more about the racial achievement gap in U.S. education. How have differences in the academic performance of white, black, Latino, and Asian secondary school students changed over time? What theories have been proposed to account for these differences, and which of these theories strike you as the most plausible? Why?

②

VISUAL PORTFOLIO

READING IMAGES OF EDUCATION AND EMPOWERMENT

Aaron Rubino/San Francisco Chronicle/Polaris

© Erik S. Lesser/The New York Times/Redux

Todd Anderson/The New York Times/Redux

Kristy Leibowitz/Splash News/Newscom

Sandy Kim/BeGood Studios/Little Big Man Agency

Jacquelyn Martin/AP Images

VISUAL PORTFOLIO
READING IMAGES OF EDUCATION
AND EMPOWERMENT

1. Compare the image of the 1950s San Francisco classroom on page 172 with the 1955 photograph of first graders reciting the Pledge of Allegiance on the opening page of this chapter (p. 107). What does each of these images of mid-twentieth-century classrooms tell us about the role and importance of education in the lives of young Americans? What does the Portfolio image suggest about the nature of schooling and the experience of learning? Which of these images do you identify with more, and why?

2. What does the sign on page 173 suggest about the real priorities of the North Georgia Falcons? How might John Taylor Gatto (p. 114) assess the sign and interpret what it says about contemporary American secondary education? Make a similar sign stating the priorities of the high school you attended. Share these in class and discuss what they reveal.

3. The students in the photo on page 174 are part of the "Bring Your Own Technology" to class program at New Smyrna Beach Middle School in Florida. What do you think these students are doing with their phones and tablets? At what age, in your opinion, should children start to work with technology in class on a regular basis? When did you? How did technology enhance or distract from your learning experience?

4. The first image on page 175 is a photo of Emma Sulkowicz, a fourth-year student at Columbia University who filed a complaint in 2013 asking for the expulsion of a fellow student for allegedly raping her in her dorm room. After the university declined to take action, Sulkowicz staged a work of protest-performance art called "Carry That Weight," which involved students carrying their dorm mattresses around campus throughout the 2014–15 school year. The second photo shows a mass protest at Columbia in support of Sulkowicz. How much have you heard about the issue of sexual assault on your campus? What, to the best of your knowledge, has your college or university done to reduce the risk of sexual harassment and assault?

5. What does the photo of an Occupy Wall Street protester on page 176 suggest about the myth of personal empowerment through educational success? Why do you think he calls himself a "superhero"? Go online to learn more about recent increases in college tuition and the debt accrued by college students as the result of student loans. How much debt would you be willing to assume to get your degree? How might being "shackled by debt" affect the values, attitudes, and choices of future American college grads? Would students and society benefit if public colleges were tuition free for all qualified students?

EDUCATION: ATTENTIONAL DISARRAY

SHERRY TURKLE

The invention of the smartphone and the development of social media have revolutionized our way of life. Smartphones and social networks have changed the way we work, the way we relate to our friends — even the way we fall in love. And as sociologist Sherry Turkle observes in this selection, technology is now disrupting the college classroom. A clinical psychologist and early critic of computer technology, Turkle is concerned that smartphones and social media are keeping students from developing the kind of attention span and social skills she believes are central to college-level learning. Turkle (b. 1948) holds an endowed chair at the Massachusetts Institute of Technology. She is also the founder of the MIT Initiative on Technology and the Self. Her many books include *The Second Self: Computers and the Human Spirit* (1984), *Life on the Screen: Identity in the Age of the Internet* (1995), *Alone Together: Why We Expect More from Technology and Less from Each Other* (2011), and *Reclaiming Conversation: The Power of Talk in a Digital Age* (2015), the source of this selection.

AT MIT, I TEACH A SEMINAR ON SCIENCE, TECHNOLOGY, AND MEMOIR. Enrollment is capped at twenty students. The atmosphere is intimate. We read memoirs by scientists, engineers, and designers (one student favorite is Oliver Sacks's[1] *Uncle Tungsten*) and then the students tell their own stories.

MIT students come from diverse backgrounds. Some have lived hardscrabble lives. During a recent fall semester, their stories were particularly poignant. One had escaped with his family from what was then the Soviet Union. Another had overcome deep poverty; there were many nights when he had no choice but to sleep in his car. And yet, through all of this, these students had found their way to science or engineering or design. Sometimes the inspiration had come from a teacher, parent, or friend. Sometimes it came from fascination with an object—a broken-down car, an old computer, a grandfather clock. The students seemed to understand each other, to find a rhythm. I thought the class was working.

And then, halfway through the semester, a group of students asks to see me. They want to say that they have been texting during class

---

[1] **Oliver Sacks**: (1933–2015), British neurologist, naturalist, historian of science, and author. [Eds.]

and feel bad because of the very personal material being discussed. They say that they text in all their classes, but here, well, it somehow seems wrong. We decide that this is something the class should discuss as a group.

In that discussion, more students admit that they, too, text in class. A small group says they are upset to hear this. They have been talking about the roughest times of their childhoods, about abuse and abandonment. But even they admit that they see checking for texts during class as the norm and have since high school. But why in *this* class? It's a small seminar. *They are talking about their lives.*

In the conversation that follows, my students portray constant connection as a necessity. These students don't feel they can be present unless they are also, in a way, absent. For some, three minutes is too long to go without checking their phones. Some say two minutes is their rule. Those who bring tablets to class point out that a "social check" is as simple as touching a Facebook icon on their screen. They want to see who is in touch with them, a comfort in itself.

We decide to try a device-free class with a short break to check phones. For me, something shifts. Conversations become more relaxed and cohesive. Students finish their thoughts, unrushed. What the students tell me is that they feel relief: When they are not tempted by their phones, they feel more in control of their attention. An irony emerges. For of course, on one level, we all see our phones as instruments for giving us greater control, not less.

My students became upset because, in this class, their usual split attention (looking at their phones; listening to their classmates) felt wrong. It devalued their classmates' life stories (and their own) and made them feel that they were crossing some moral line. They could imagine a day when people around you would be upset and you would still be pulled away to your phone.

A lot is at stake in attention. Where we put it is not only how we decide what we will learn; it is how we show what we value.

The Myth of Multitasking

These days, attention is in short supply—in college classrooms, its scarcity poses special problems because, after all, so much money, time, and effort has been spent to bring together these students, this professor, these educational resources. And yet here, like everywhere, if we have a device in our hands, we want to multitask.

But in this, we pursue an illusion. When we think we are multitasking, our brains are actually moving quickly from one thing to the next, and our performance degrades for each new task we add to the mix.[2]

[2]And if we don't do a worse job, it takes us longer. Carrie B. Fried, "Laptop Use and Its Effects on Student Learning," *Computers and Education* 50 (2008): 906–14, doi:10 .1016/j.compedu.2006.09.006.

Multitasking gives us a neurochemical high so we think we are doing better and better when actually we are doing worse and worse. We've seen that not only do multitaskers have trouble deciding how to organize their time, but over time, they "forget" how to read human emotions.[3] Students—for example, my students—think that texting during class does not interrupt their understanding of class conversation, but they are wrong. The myth of multitasking is just that: a myth.

And yet, multitasking is the norm in classrooms. By 2012, nine in ten college students said that they text in class.[4]

The widespread adoption of texting was a landmark in the unfolding of the multitasked life. For one group of high school seniors in Connecticut, getting a smartphone over the 2008 holiday break made the spring term that followed it a new kind of experience: When these students are at school, in class and out of class, they text continually. There is so much texting during school hours that their school put a "no texting in class" policy into effect, but the young men ignore it: Some claim to have never heard of it. Andrew says, "Most kids can text without looking, so...you'll just be looking at the teacher, and under the table you've got your thumbs going crazy."

One of the more studious boys in the group, Oliver, takes pains to insist that his teachers should not take it personally when he texts in class. Teachers put the notes online; he "gets" what is going on in class, so "I'm almost always bored and I want to be somewhere else and I'm almost always texting." He does admit that once he's texting, the possibilities for concentrating are pretty much gone: "You can't focus on the thing you are doing when you are sending the text...or waiting to receive a text...there is so much going on with other things you might want to receive on your phone."

Despite his new problem with focus, even in 2008, Oliver expects that what he has now is what he'll have in the future. He imagines that from now on, when he feels bored, he will immediately add a new layer of communication. So for him, "boredom is a thing of the past." Every generation, he says, had its own way of responding to being bored, especially during classes. Other generations passed notes, doodled, or zoned out. His generation can send texts and go to Facebook. He calls his generation "lucky": "We have the awesome new power to erase boredom."...

So, dropping out of a classroom conversation can begin with a 15 moment of boredom, because a friend reaches out to you, or because, as one student in my memoir class put it, "You just want to see who wants you." And once you are in that "circuit of apps," you want to stay with them.

[3]Eyal Ophir, Clifford Nass, and Anthony D. Wagner, "Cognitive Control in Media Multitaskers," *Proceedings of the National Academy of Sciences* (2009), doi:10.1073/pnas.0903620106.

[4]Deborah R. Tindell and Robert W. Bohlander, "The Use and Abuse of Cell Phones and Text Messaging in the Classroom: A Survey of College Students," *College Teaching* 60, no. 1 (January 2012): 1–9, doi:10.1080/87567555.2011.604 802.

In classrooms, the distracted are a distraction: Studies show that when students are in class multitasking on laptops, everyone around them learns less.[5] One college senior says, "I'll be in a great lecture and look over and see someone shopping for shoes and think to myself, 'Are you kidding me?' So I get mad at them, but then I get mad at myself for being self-righteous. But after I've gone through my cycle of indignation to self-hate, I realize that I have missed a minute of the lecture, and then I'm really mad."

It's easy to see how concentration would be disrupted in this crucible of emotion. But even for those who don't get stirred up, when you see someone in your class on Facebook or checking their email, two things cross your mind: Maybe this class is boring, and maybe I, too, should attend to some online business. Yet despite research that shows that multitasking is bad for learning, the myth of the moment is still that multitasking is a good idea. A series of ads for AT&T show a young man chatting with a group of schoolchildren about the things children know.[6] Or perhaps, the things children know that adults want to validate. One of the things that the children and the adult agree on is that faster is better. A second is that it is better to do more than one thing at a time. This is a myth that dies hard.

And we are not inclined to let it die because multitasking feels good. It is commonplace to talk about multitaskers as addicted. I don't like to talk about addiction in this context because I find that discussing the holding power of technology in these terms makes people feel helpless. It makes them feel they are facing something against which resistance seems almost futile. This is a fallacy. In this case, resistance is not futile but highly productive. Writers, artists, scientists, and literary scholars talk openly about disenabling the Wi-Fi on their computers in order to get creative work done. In the acknowledgments of her most recent book, the novelist Zadie Smith thanks Freedom and SelfControl, programs that shut off connectivity on her Mac.[7]

The analogy between screens and drugs breaks down for other reasons. There is only one thing that you should do if you are on heroin: Get off the heroin. Your life is at stake. But laptops and smartphones are not things to remove. *They are facts of life and part of our creative lives. The goal is to use them with greater intention.*

Instead of thinking about addiction, it makes sense to confront this reality: We are faced with technologies to which we are extremely vulnerable and we don't always respect that fact. The path forward is to learn more about our vulnerabilities. Then, we can design technology

20

---

[5]Faria Sana, Tina Weston, and Nicholas J. Cepeda, "Laptop Multitasking Hinders Classroom Learning for Both Users and Nearby Peers," *Computers and Education* 62 (March 2013): 24–31, doi:10.1016/j.compedu.2012.10.003.

[6]"AT&T Commercial—It's Not Complicated, 'Dizzy,'" YouTube video, posted by CommercialCow, February 4, 2013, https://www.youtube.com/watch?v=yYaSl_VgqbE.

[7]See the acknowledgments in Zadie Smith, *NW: A Novel* (New York: Penguin Press, 2013).

and the environments in which we use them with these insights in mind. For example, since we know that multitasking is seductive but not helpful to learning, it's up to us to promote "unitasking."

It's encouraging that it is often children who recognize their vulnerabilities to technology and come up with ways to deal with them, even when adults are pulling them in another direction. In fact, the critique of multitasking is a good example of where I've seen children take the lead. Reyna, fourteen, has been issued an iPad at school. The entire eighth-grade curriculum is on it. But so are her email and favorite games, including *Candy Crush.* In order to get work done, she prints out her reading assignments and puts aside the iPad. She learned to do this from her sister, who had experienced the same attention problems with a curriculum-on-a-tablet. Reyna describes the problem:

> People really liked [the iPad] because...they could look things up really quickly in class, but also...people were getting really distracted. Like, my sister had an iPad and she said that her and her friends' texts were blocked but they had school emails. And they would sit in class and pretend to be researching but really they were emailing back and forth just because they were bored—or they would take screenshots of a test practice sheet and send it out to their friends that hadn't had the class yet.
>
> But my sister also said that even when she and her friends were just trying to study for a test, "they would go and print everything that they had on their iPads," because studying was made a lot more difficult because of all the other distractions on the iPad, all the other apps they could download.

This student knows that it is hard to concentrate in class when you are holding a device that you associate with games and messaging—a device built to encourage doing one thing and then another and another. Reyna came to her experience with the iPad at school with many advantages: She had experienced school without it. She remembered that she used to be less distracted. She had a point of comparison and she had her sister as a mentor. But increasingly, students like Reyna are the exception. Children who begin school with an iPad won't know that you can "force" a state of greater concentration by using media that allow you to do only one thing at a time. It's up to a more experienced generation to teach them.

Students who print out their assignments in order to have time away from screens should give educators pause when they, with the best of intentions, try to make things more efficient by closing the library and declaring books obsolete.

The Opposite of Unitasking: Hyper Attention

Many educators begin with an accommodation: They note that students text and search the web in class, and they say, "Fine"—in previous days, students would find other ways to zone out, and this is the twenty-first-century equivalent. But some educators do more than accommodate the distractions of digital media. They see a new sensibility of fractured attention and they want to use it as an opportunity to teach in a new way.

So, literary theorist Katherine Hayles argues that fractured attention is the sensibility of the twenty-first century and that to look back to "deep attention" in the classroom is to be unhelpfully nostalgic.[8] (My skepticism begins here, as I think of Reyna and her sister, who print out their reading assignments so as not to be distracted on the iPad.) Students, says Hayles, think in a new mode, the mode of "hyper attention." Given the realities of the classroom, educators have a choice: "Change the students to fit the educational environment or change that environment to fit the students."[9]

In other words, for Hayles, there is no real choice. Education must embrace the culture of hyper attention. As an example of a constructive way to do this, Hayles points to experiments at the University of Southern California in a classroom outfitted with screens.

> One mode of interaction is "Google jockeying": While a speaker is making a presentation, participants search the web for appropriate content to display on the screens—for example, sites with examples, definitions, images, or opposing views. Another mode of interaction is "backchanneling," in which participants type in comments as the speaker talks, providing running commentary on the material being presented.[10]

There is no doubt that Google jockeying speaks to our moment. Students say that they want to turn away from class when there is a lull. Google jockeying implicitly says, all right, we will get rid of those lulls. Even experienced faculty start to ramp up their PowerPoint presentations in a spirit (not always acknowledged) of competing with students' screens. Or we tell them, as Hayles suggests, to go to the web during class time for opposing views, images, and comments. Or to make a comment of their own.

But there is another way to respond to students who complain that they need more stimulation than class conversation provides. It is to tell them that a moment of boredom can be an opportunity to go inward to your imagination, an opportunity for new thinking.

If a moment of boredom happens in a classroom, rather than competing for student attention with ever more extravagant technological fireworks (*Google jockeying!*), we should encourage our students to stay with their moment of silence or distraction. We can try to

---

[8]Katherine N. Hayles, "Hyper and Deep Attention," *Profession* (2007): 187–99.
[9]Ibid., 195.
[10]Ibid., 196.

build their confidence that such moments—when you stay with your thoughts—have a payoff. We can present classrooms as places where you can encounter a moment of boredom and "walk" toward its challenges. A chemistry professor puts it this way: "In my class I want students to daydream. They can go back to the text if they missed a key fact. But if they went off in thought...they might be making the private connection that pulls the course together for them."

When those who are fluent in both deep attention and hyper   30
attention—and certainly Hayles is in this group—look at hyper attention, it is tempting to see something exciting because it is new. But they still have a choice. They can switch between ways of knowing. But children who grow up in an all-multitasking environment may not have a choice.

A life of multitasking limits your options so that you cannot simply "pick up" deep attention. What is most enriching is having fluency in both deep and hyper attention. This is attentional pluralism and it should be our educational goal. You can choose multitasking. You can also focus on one thing at a time. And you know when you should.

But attentional pluralism is hard to achieve. Hyper attention feels good. And without practice, we can lose the ability to summon deep attention.

Eric Schmidt,[11] of Google, spoke to a college audience and expressed his own concern. He told the students that he used to read books on airplanes, the one place where there was no Wi-Fi. Now, with Wi-Fi on airplanes, things have changed: "Now I spend all my time being online, doing my emails, interacting and all that, and the book doesn't get read. I think we've got to work on that."[12] Schmidt made this comment while promoting a book he authored that celebrates, even in its subtitle, how technology will "reshape" people.[13] Schmidt isn't happy that he has exchanged books for email and messages, but he believes in the forward march of technology.

Elizabeth, a graduate student in economics, is not so sure about the forward march. She is convinced that the "natural multitasking" of her work life has left her with diminished cognitive capacity.

Before graduate school, Elizabeth worked as a consultant. It was a   35
job that led her to make multitasking a way of life. "For instance, I could be fielding emails from clients, looking up industry data to insert into a PowerPoint presentation for an urgent meeting, researching which restaurant to take my best friend to that night, while writing the actual requirements document I was supposed to be working on that day. My routine practice of multitasking led to another behavior—skimming."

---

[11]**Eric Schmidt:** (b. 1955), American software engineer, businessman, and former CEO of Google LLC. [Eds.]

[12]The Fletcher School, "Eric Schmidt and Jared Cohen on 'The New Digital Age,'" YouTube video, February 28, 2014, https://www.youtube.com/watch?v=NYGzB7uveh0.

[13]Eric Schmidt and Jared Cohen, *The New Digital Age: How Technology Is Reshaping the Future of People, Nations, and Business* (New York: Knopf, 2013).

It was only when Elizabeth returned to the university that she saw the full effect of years spent multitasking, a life lived in hyper attention. Now, as a graduate student, she has been assigned an excerpt of Plato's *Republic* for an ethics class.

> I had skimmed the chapter, as was my habit, then, realizing that I hadn't retained much, reread it again and even made a few notes. Unfortunately, on the day of the class, I did not have that notebook with me, and while I remembered the overall gist of the chapter (moderation—good; desire for luxury—bad), I struggled to recall specific ideas expressed in it. Without access to my cell phone to refer to the article or read up on Plato on Wikipedia, I wasn't able to participate in the class discussion. Having access to information is always wonderful, but without having at least some information retained in my brain, I am not able to build on those ideas or connect them together to form new ones.

As I speak with Elizabeth, it is clear that more is at stake than disappointment in her class performance. If she can't "build on ideas or connect them together to form new ones," she knows she won't be able to have certain kinds of conversations—in her view, probably the most important ones.

And attention is not a skill we learn for one domain. When you train your brain to multitask as your basic approach—when you embrace hyper attention—you won't be able to focus even when you want to. So, you're going to have trouble sitting and listening to your children tell you about their day at school. You're going to have trouble at work sitting in a meeting and listening to your colleagues. Their narrative will seem painfully slow. Just as middle school children don't acquire the skills for conversation because they lack practice, university students lose the capacity to sit in a class and follow a complex argument. Research shows that when college students watch online educational videos, they watch for six minutes no matter how long the video. So videos for online courses are being produced at six minutes.[14] But if you become accustomed to getting your information in six-minute bites, you will grow impatient with more extended presentations. One college senior describes her friends' taste for the short and terse: "If they had their choice, conversations would begin with a tweet and end in a tweet."

Maryanne Wolf, a cognitive neuroscientist at Tufts University, had long observed students' fractured attention spans but did not feel personally implicated until one evening when she sat down to read *The Glass Bead Game* by Hermann Hesse, one of her favorite authors.

---

[14]Philip J. Guo, Juho Kim, and Rob Rubin, "How Video Production Affects Student Engagement: An Empirical Study of MOOC Videos," *Proceedings of the First ACM Conference on Learning @ Scale Conference* (2014), doi:10.1145/2556325.2566239. See also Philip J. Guo, "Optimal Video Length for Student Engagement," edX (blog), November 13, 2013, https://www.edx.org/blog/optimal-video-length-student-engagement#.U71MsxZFFBW.

Wolf found it impossible to focus on the book. She panicked and wondered if her life on the web had cost her this ability. When Eric Schmidt noted his difficulty with sustained reading, he remarked, "We've got to work on that." Wolf immediately got to work. She began to study what skimming, scanning, and scrolling do to our ability to read with deep attention—what she calls "deep reading."[15] Her thesis is that a life lived online makes deep attention harder to summon. This happens because the brain is plastic—it is constantly in flux over a lifetime—so it "rewires" itself depending on how attention is allocated.[16]

Wolf, Hayles, and Schmidt have all diagnosed a problem with deep attention. But they turn in different directions when it comes to what to do next. Hayles argues for a conscious pedagogical accommodation to the new sensibility. Schmidt shrugs and says that in the end, technology will lead us in the right direction. Wolf's focus on the plasticity of the brain gives her a different perspective. For if the brain is plastic, this means that at any age, it can be set to work on deep attention. Put otherwise, if we decide that deep attention is a value, we can cultivate it. Indeed, that is what Wolf discovered for herself. She had trouble with the Hesse but kept at it. And she says that after two weeks of effort, she was once again able to focus sufficiently to immerse herself in deep reading. Wolf's experience suggests a pedagogy that supports unitasking and deep reading. But if we value these, we have to actively choose them.

---

[15]Michael S. Rosenwald, "Serious Reading Takes a Hit from Online Scanning and Skimming, Researchers Say," *Washington Post,* April 6, 2014, http://www.washingtonpost.com/local/serious-reading-takes-a-hit-from-online-scanning-and-skimming-researchers-say/2014/04/06/088028d2-bSd2-lle3-b899-20667de76985_story.html.

[16]Wolf has a developmental argument for how capacity can be lost: "The act of going beyond the text to analyze, infer and think new thoughts is the product of years of formation. It takes time, both in milliseconds and years, and effort to learn to read with deep, expanding comprehension and to execute all these processes as an adult expert reader. When it comes to building this reading circuit in a brain that has no preprogrammed set-up for it, there is no genetic guarantee that any individual novice reader will ever form the expert reading brain circuitry that most of us form. The reading circuit's very plasticity is also its Achilles' heel. It can be fully fashioned over time and fully implemented when we read, or it can be short-circuited—either early on in its formation period or later, after its formation, in the execution of only part of its potentially available cognitive resources. Because we literally and physiologically can read in multiple ways, how we read—and what we absorb from our reading—will be influenced by both the content of our reading and the medium we use." Maryanne Wolf, "Our 'Deep Reading' Brain: Its Digital Evolution Poses Questions," *Nieman Reports,* Summer 2010, http://www.nieman.harvard.edu/reports/article/102396/Our-Deep-Reading-Brain-Its-Digital-Evolution-Poses-Questions.aspx. And Wolf's argument for plasticity gives her a specific anxiety: "My major worry is that, confronted with a digital glut of immediate information that requires and receives less and less intellectual effort, many new (and many older) readers will have neither the time nor the motivation to think through the possible layers of meaning in what they read. The omnipresence of multiple distractions for attention—and the brain's own natural attraction to novelty—contribute to a mind-set toward reading that seeks to reduce information to its lowest conceptual denominator. Sound bites, text bites, and mind bites are a reflection of a culture that has forgotten or become too distracted by and too drawn to the next piece of new information to allow itself time to think." See Maryanne Wolf and Mirit Barzillai, "The Importance of Deep Reading," *Educational Leadership* 66, no. 6 (March 2009): 32–37, http://www.ascd.org/publications/educational-leadership/mar09/vol66/num06/The-Importance-of-Deep-Reading.aspx.

Seduced by Transcription:
Putting Machines Aside

Carol Steiker, a professor at Harvard Law School, is committed to a 40 particular form of unitasking: the unitasking that follows naturally when students take class notes *by hand.* Harvard, like so many other law schools, took great pride in having all classrooms "wired" over the past decade or so, and for many years, Steiker allowed her students to take notes on laptops.

I speak with Steiker and a group of other law professors. At one time they had all allowed their students to take class notes on laptops. It seemed natural. Coming out of college, students were accustomed to doing things this way. And the professors didn't want to be in the position of "thought police," checking if students were on Facebook during class time. The consensus: If a student couldn't pay attention in a law school class, that would soon become the student's problem. That student would fall behind.

Steiker explains why her position has changed, radically. She saw that students taking notes with computers suffered from more than inattention. They were losing the ability to take notes at all. She puts it this way: "Students taking notes on computers seemed compelled to type out the full record of what was said in class. They were trying to establish transcripts of the class."[17] To put it too simply: Students were putting themselves in the role of court stenographers. For Steiker, this was a problem in itself. She wants note taking to help students integrate the themes of her class. For her, note taking trains students to organize a subject in a personal way. It cultivates an art of listening and thinking that will be important to the future lawyer.

And Steiker says that the urge to "transcribe" had a curious side effect: *Her law students didn't want to be interrupted in class.* Steiker says, "They sometimes seemed annoyed if you called on them because it broke up their work on their transcriptions. If your notes are meant to capture the themes of the class, you remember your own participation and you make it part of the story. If you are trying to write a transcript of a class, class participation takes you away from your job."

Here is how Steiker describes a turning point in her understanding of how note taking on computers stands in the way of what she wants to accomplish in her classroom:

> One of the students in the first year had a serious illness that kept
> her out of class for several weeks. The students banded together

---

[17]Research on using computers to take notes supports this classroom experience. People who take notes on a computer turn into something close to transcribers. They have a hard time staying engaged with the content of the material. This suggests that there is a virtue in the "inefficiency" of taking notes by hand, a method that forces you to decide what to take down and what not. See Pam Mueller and Daniel M. Oppenheimer, "The Pen Is Mightier than the Keyboard," *Psychological Science* 25, no. 6 (2014), doi:10.1177/0956797614524581.

into teams that would take notes for her in every course. After one class, the young woman who had been responsible for note taking in my class on that day came up to me, upset. Could she please have my class notes to send to her absent classmate? Her computer had run out of power and she had no power cord. She hadn't been able to take notes in class. I asked the obvious: Why hadn't she taken notes with pen and paper? The student looked at me blankly. This simply had not occurred as a possibility. This simply was something she no longer could do.

There are at least two ironies here. First, behind our note taking on 45 computers was a fantasy: When the machines made it possible for us to take notes faster, we would take notes better. Instead, we don't take notes at all but behave like transcribing machines. Second, when the day comes that machines are able to take notes for us, it will not serve our purposes, because note taking is part of how we learn to think.

So now, Steiker allows no technology in any of her classes. She says, laughingly, that she came to this position in steps. She first told her students that they couldn't use computers in class. So they put their laptops away but kept checking their phones in class. "I found this amazing," she says. In fact, her students were thinking like lawyers, following the letter but not the spirit of her instructions. "So, then, I had to be explicit that I really meant no devices at all. This seemed surprising to them. They are so used to looking down at their phones—having a phone in class didn't seem to them like holding on to a technology." There is much talk about the advantage of our devices becoming so habitual and easy to use that they become invisible. It is usually assumed this is a good thing. But if we don't "see" our devices, we are less likely to register the effect they are having on us. We begin to think that the way we think when we have our devices in hand is the "natural" way to think.

Now, in a device-free class, Steiker says, "The students aren't annoyed when you call on them." She's optimistic, convinced that taking notes by hand is forcing her students to be better listeners. "They can't write fast enough to do a transcript, so they have to figure out what is most important." When she tells this story, I think back to a comment that an eleventh grader made to me a decade ago about why she likes to bring her laptop to class. "When I have my computer, I like it that I can write everything down." At the time, I didn't pursue the comment. Some costs take a while to become apparent.

A Love Letter to Collaboration

In a recent course, I required students to collaborate on a midterm project. I imagined my students in conversation, working together at long tables in a dining hall. I imagined late nights and cold coffee in Styrofoam cups. But there had been no late nights or long tables. All the collaboration had happened on Gchat and Google Docs, a program that allows several people to work on the same document at once. When my students handed in their projects, their work was good.

But when I gave out the assignment I was interested in more than the final product. I know that the alchemy of students sitting around a table can sometimes spark conversations that lead to a new idea. Instead, my students found an app that made presence unnecessary. They had a task; they accomplished it with efficiency. My experience in that course is a case study of why measurements of productivity in higher education are dicey. Gchat and Google Docs got the job done by classical "productivity" measures. But the value of what you produce, what you "make," in college is not just the final paper; it's the process of making it.

My students are unapologetic about not meeting in person. Jason, 50 a sophomore, says, "The majority of my studying in the past year has been that someone makes a Google Doc with the terms that need definitions, you fill in the ones you know, and then you work on it together. You have a chat session and you do that to collaborate." This joyless description made me rethink my fantasy of long tables, cold coffee, and late nights. My fantasy, from his point of view, asks for the unnecessary. But his reality allows little space to talk about a new idea.

Sometimes, students who collaborate with online chat and electronically shared documents work in the same building. They simply choose not to study in the same room at the same table. They go into online chat sessions rather than chat in person. Why? For one thing, they tell me, roles can be made clear and it is clear when someone falls behind. More important, when you collaborate online, everyone stays on point. People may drop out to text or do some online shopping, but when they are on the chat, they are on topic.

In a face-to-face meeting, you can see people's attention wander off to their phones. On Gchat, the inattention of your peers is invisible to you. Once you make the assumption that when people work, they will want to text and shop as well, it helps to collaborate on a medium that hides what Jason calls their "true absences." Gchat lets the simulation of focused attention seem like attention enough. Whenever you see them, your colleagues are working on the problem at hand. So, Jason says, "We take the route of technology whenever possible."

Gchat makes Jason's group seem "on topic" even as their minds wander. But it doesn't leave room for what I've said I want when my students collaborate. I'll call it intellectual serendipity. It may happen when someone tells a joke. Or daydreams and comes back with an idea that goes in a new direction. None of this is necessarily efficient. But so many of our best ideas are born this way, in conversations that take a turn. I want my students to have this experience.

But given an opportunity to collaborate, my students glide toward the virtual. Some tell me that anything else, regardless of the merits, is totally impractical in today's college environment. Everyone is too "busy." I can't help but think that talking in person is one of the things they should be busy with.

In my interviews with college students, most insist that they will 55 *know* when they have to schedule a face-to-face meeting. They will *know* if something comes up that they can't take care of over Gchat. But my experience is that you really don't know when you are going to have an important conversation. You have to show up for many conversations that feel inefficient or boring to be there for the conversation that changes your mind.

When the economist Daniel Kahneman won the Nobel Prize, he was, like every winner of the prize, asked to write an official Nobel biographical statement. One section of his biography is a tribute to his late colleague Amos Tversky. Kahneman explained that the ideas for which he won the prize grew out of their time spent working together. In the end, his Nobel biography amounted to a love letter to conversation.[18]

> We spent hours each day, just talking. When Amos's first son, Oren, then fifteen months old, was told that his father was at work, he volunteered the comment "Aba talk Danny." We were not only working, of course — we talked of everything under the sun, and got to know each other's mind almost as well as our own. We could (and often did) finish each other's sentences and complete the joke that the other had wanted to tell, but somehow we also kept surprising each other.

Here we see conversation as not only an intellectual engine but the means by which colleagues were able to cross boundaries that are usually only dissolved by love. Conversation led to intellectual communion. When I explain my current project, people often say, "You're so right to study conversation. For communication, it has the broadest bandwidth — it's the best way to exchange information." Kahneman and Tversky teach us that while this may be true, it is far from the whole story. Conversation is a kind of intimacy. You don't just get more information. You get different information. The bandwidth argument leaves out this essential.

What also is striking in Kahneman's Nobel address is his description of the pace of his work with Tversky. In 1974, Kahneman and Tversky wrote an article for *Science* that went on to be one of the founding documents of behavioral economics.[19] It took them a year, working four to six hours a day. Kahneman writes, "On a good day we would mark a net advance of a sentence or two." So the people who support conversation because they think it will make things go faster ("Don't email me, it's faster just to come to my desk and ask me!") are seeing only a small

[18]Daniel Kahneman and Vernon L. Smith, "Daniel Kahneman—Biographical," in *Les Prix Nobel (The Nobel Prizes), 2002*, Tore Fraängsmyr, ed. (Stockholm: Nobel Foundation, 2003). Full text available at: http://www.nobelprize.org/nobel_prizes/economic-sciences/laureates/2002/kahneman-bio.html.

[19]Amos Tversky and Daniel Kahneman, "Judgment Under Uncertainty: Heuristics and Biases," *Science* 185 (1974): 1124–31.

part of what makes face-to-face conversation powerful. For Kahneman and Tversky, conversation wasn't there to go faster, but to go deeper.

College should be a time to invest in teaching students about the long-term value of open-ended conversations, but in today's environment, it is hard to argue the value of conversation for learning because it is hard to measure its value with productivity metrics, especially in the short term.

GLASBERGEN

"I won't be impressed by technology in the classroom until you figure out how to install Google directly in my brain."

ENGAGING THE TEXT

1. Why do Turkle's students text during class? How common is texting in classes at your college or university? When do you think it's acceptable or necessary to text or go online in class?

2. Have you ever been in a class where cell phones and laptops were forbidden? Did the technology ban improve the class in your view? Why or why not?

3. What, in Turkle's view, is the "myth of multitasking" (para. 10)? To what extent would you agree that multitasking "feels good"? Have you ever tried to "unitask" deliberately as fourteen-year-old Reyna does when she studies

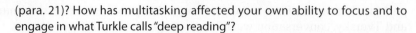
(para. 21)? How has multitasking affected your own ability to focus and to engage in what Turkle calls "deep reading"?

4. What has been your experience with technology in the classroom? How have instructors tried to integrate Google, Twitter, or other technologies in classes you've taken? Have you ever, for example, been in a class that involved "Google jockeying" or "backchanneling" (para. 26)? To what extent would you agree with Katherine Hayles that education today has to embrace new technologies that promote "hyper attention" (para. 30)?

5. How often do you take notes by hand in your classes? Would you agree that taking notes by hand helps you learn and retain more effectively than taking notes on a laptop? Why or why not?

6. Turkle sees a lot of value in collaborative learning and the face-to-face interactions it involves. To what extent do your current classes involve you in collaborative work? How valuable do you find collaborative learning experiences, and why? Would you agree that most students today tend to "glide toward the virtual" (para. 54) instead of working together face-to-face? Why or why not?

EXPLORING CONNECTIONS

7. How would you expect John Taylor Gatto (p. 114) to view the use of technology to engage students in the classroom? In your own experience, is technology typically used in the classroom in ways that foster the development of "leaders and adventurers" who "develop an inner life so that they'll never be bored" (p. 121, para. 19)? Or does technology in the classroom reinforce what Gatto sees as the worst aspects of schooling?

8. How might technology have changed the educational experiences of Mike Rose, Ted Richard, and Ken Harvey (p. 123)? How do you think Mr. MacFarland would have viewed using smart phones and social media in his classes?

9. How would you expect technology to be used in the four types of schools that Jean Anyon describes (p. 136)? What kinds of classroom technologies would you associate with the production of "workers," "managers," and "elite" decision makers?

EXTENDING THE CRITICAL CONTEXT

10. Survey your friends to learn more about their use of smartphones in class. How often do they consult their phones during a typical class period? Why do they feel the need? Are they bothered or distracted when other students use their phones in class? Do they think that phones should be banned or limited in classes at your college? Later, create a summary of your conclusions and discuss your findings in class.

11. Conduct your own experiment with device-free learning. Try to go for a week without checking your phone while in class. Keep a diary of your experience

to see how going device-free affects your ability to focus and engage with others in class.

12. Do some research to learn about the role technology plays in the schools Silicon Valley CEOs choose for their own children. To what extent did technology leaders like Bill Gates or Steve Jobs embrace or limit access to technology for their kids, and why?

BLURRED LINES, TAKE TWO
PEGGY ORENSTEIN

Before the #MeToo movement gained momentum following a series of high-profile sexual assault scandals in 2017, the issue of sexual assault on campus had been roiling colleges across the United States for more than a decade. Following several important governmental and independent reports in the early 2000s and a number of dramatic student protests, colleges and universities across the country began to address their role in the "campus rape crisis." In this selection, Peggy Orenstein explores the "blurred lines" that surround the issue of campus assault — the complex questions of guilt, innocence, and personal responsibility that have emerged as colleges have adopted policies of "affirmative consent." Orenstein (b. 1961) is a best-selling author, award-winning journalist, and internationally recognized speaker on issues affecting girls and women. She is the author of six books, including *Cinderella Ate My Daughter: Dispatches from the Front Lines of the New Girlie-Girl Culture* (2012), *Girls & Sex: Navigating the Complicated New Landscape* (2016), and *Don't Call Me Princess: Essays on Girls, Women, Sex, and Life* (2018), the source of this selection.

Rape by the Numbers

Throughout the 1990s and early 2000s, research on campus assault quietly continued to accrue, as did skepticism about the results. Using the narrowest definition of rape — as involving physical force — most studies found an annual incidence of between 3 and 5 percent.[1] That is not one in four or even the more recently asserted one in five. Still, given that according to the Census Bureau, there were 4.6 million female full-time undergraduates at four-year institutions in 2013, it would

[1]Jodi Raphael, *Rape Is Rape: How Denial, Distortion, and Victim Blaming are Fueling a Hidden Acquaintance Rape Crisis* (Chicago: Chicago Review Press, 2013).

mean that between 138,000 and 230,000 were raped each year—not so comforting.[2] What's more, that conservative definition is no longer employed by such notoriously radical feminist cabals as, say, the FBI, which as of 2013 defined rape as "penetration, no matter how slight, of the vagina or anus with any body part or object, or oral penetration by a sex organ of another person, without the consent of the victim." (That revised definition, incidentally, does not assume the victim is female.)

In 2015 two significant reports came out that should (but probably won't) put an end to all the squabbling. The Association of American Universities' Campus Climate Survey, comprised of over 150,000 students, found that a third of female undergraduate respondents had been victims of nonconsensual sexual contact.[3] Meanwhile, sociologists Jessie Ford and Paula England analyzed assault rates among seniors who had participated in the Online College Social Life Survey. Unlike the AAU report, Ford and England focused solely on acts of intercourse or attempted intercourse—they did not include the incidents of unwanted touching, oral sex, or psychological coercion that critics insist unfairly pad the numbers. Ten percent of the girls said they had been physically forced to have sex since starting college; 15 percent said that someone had tried to physically force them, but that they had escaped without having intercourse (the survey didn't ask whether they had been forced into other acts instead); 11 percent reported someone had unwanted intercourse with them while they were "drunk, passed out, asleep, drugged, or otherwise incapacitated"; and 25 percent reported at least one of these things had happened to them.[4] Including the types of assaults while intoxicated that Roiphe, Paglia, Sommers,[5] and their supporters (if not the criminal justice system) reject, that brings us back to one in four.[6]

---

[2]There was a total of more than 5.7 million female undergraduates at four-year institutions and more than 3.8 million at two-year institutions. U.S. Census Bureau, *School Enrollment in the United States 2013*, Washington, DC: U.S. Census Bureau, September 24, 2014.

[3]Cantor, Fisher, Chibnall, et al., *Report on the AAU Campus Climate Survey on Sexual Assault and Sexual Misconduct.*

[4]Ford and England, "What Percent of College Women Are Sexually Assaulted in College?" A third survey, released in 2015 by United Educators, which provides liability insurance to schools, found that 30 percent of rapes reported at its 104 client schools between 2011 and 2013 were committed through force or threat of force and 33 percent were committed while the victim was incapacitated. In another 13 percent of cases, the perpetrator didn't use force, but continued engaging in sexual contact after the victim hesitated or verbally refused. Eighteen percent of cases were labeled "failed consent": the perpetrator used no force, threat of force, or coercion but "ignored or misinterpreted cues or inferred consent from silence or lack of resistance." The remaining 7 percent of rapes involved the use of a knockout drug. Ninety-nine percent of perpetrators were male. Claire Gordon, "Study: College Athletes Are More Likely to Gang Rape," *Al Jazeera America*, February 26, 2015.

[5]**Roiphe, Paglia, Sommers:** Katie Roiphe (b. 1968), Camille Paglia (b. 1947), and Christina Hoff Sommers (b. 1950) are three noted American feminists who have raised concerns about the accuracy of campus rape statistics and have questioned the severity of the college rape crisis. [Eds.]

[6]Another 2015 study, of 483 students at an unnamed private university in upstate New York, found that 18.6 percent of freshman women were victims of rape or attempted rape. Carey, Durney, Shepardson, et al., "Incapacitated and Forcible Rape of College Women."

Since 1990, colleges and universities have been legally obliged to report to the Department of Education all crimes occurring on or near campus. Those that don't can lose federal financial aid funding, something few schools, no matter how well endowed, can afford. The impetus for that was the rape and murder of nineteen-year-old Jeanne Clery in her Lehigh University dorm room. Clery's parents later learned that there had been multiple violent crimes at the school over the previous three years, but with no consistent tracking policy, students were left oblivious, overestimating their safety on campus. Clery's attacker, who was not a student, had passed through three doors equipped with automatic locks, all of which had been propped open with boxes by dorm residents. Despite that, sanctions for fudging crime stats remained rare, and given that high rates of rape are not a big selling point for prospective students, it's probably not surprising that by 2006, 77 percent of campuses reported their number of sexual assaults at an implausible zero.[7]

That, however, will no longer cut it. In 2011, Russlynn Ali, Obama's new assistant secretary for civil rights, fired off a nineteen-page "Dear Colleague" letter reminding campus officials of their responsibility to uphold all aspects of Title IX, including those involving sexual harassment and violence. Along with a mandate to resolve cases quickly and ensure the physical and psychological safety of accusers (rearranging the class schedule of the accused or removing him from the alleged victim's dorm), the letter laid down a new, reduced burden of proof: "a preponderance of evidence," typically used in civil cases, rather than the more demanding "clear and convincing evidence" then being used on many campuses.[8] More controversy ensued, with conservative activists denouncing the standard as too low given the seriousness of the crime and the potential stigmatization of the accused. The thing is, though, as legal blogger Michael Dorf has written, the lower burden of proof in civil court is not based on either a crime's brutality or its potential to defame the perpetrator, but on the nature of the *punishment*: so someone such as O.J. Simpson could be found not guilty of murder by the standards of criminal court, where life in prison was at stake, but guilty in civil court where the penalty was solely to the pocketbook. Given, then, that colleges expel or suspend rather than jail rapists, "a preponderance of evidence" standard is, in fact, reasonable.

The Department of Education's warning roiled the academic world. 5 As with the right to sue for monetary damages in the 1990s, it also galvanized female students, who no longer needed traditional media to champion their cause: they had the Internet. In 2012, Angie Epifano,

---

[7]Kristen Lombardi, "Campus Sexual Assault Statistics Don't Add Up," Center for Public Integrity, December 2009. Between 2009 and 2014, over 40 percent of schools in a national sample had not conducted a single assault investigation. United States Senate, U.S. Senate Subcommittee on Financial and Contracting Oversight, *Sexual Violence on Campus*.

[8]Michael Dorf, "'Yes Means Yes' and Preponderance of the Evidence," *Dorf on Law* (blog), October 29, 2014.

a former student at Amherst, published a signed editorial in the school newspaper about college administrators' callous response to her rape allegations. The detailed description of a skeptical sexual assault counselor, her subsequent suicidal depression, a stint in a psych ward, and her ultimate withdrawal from school went viral, generating more than 750,000 page views. "Silence has the rusty taste of shame," she declared. "I will not be quiet." Soon a national movement began to form—activists, often assault survivors themselves, at Amherst, the University of North Carolina, Tufts, Yale, Berkeley—all connecting through social media. That caught the attention of the mainstream press. This round, the *New York Times* seemed all in: running, among other stories, front-page pieces on the student activists and on the White House initiatives; an account in the Sunday Review section by a University of Virginia rape survivor about the lax punishment meted out to her assailant; and numerous opinion pieces and online debates on institutional responsibility, alcohol abuse, the underreporting of assault, and the dubious culture of fraternities and sports teams. The paper also profiled Emma Sulkowicz, a senior at Columbia University who had vowed to lug a fifty-pound dormitory mattress on her back everywhere she went during the 2014/15 school year until the boy she accused of raping her—who had been found "not responsible" —was expelled. (He filed a suit against the university, claiming the administration's failure to protect him from Sulkowicz's accusations, which he said destroyed his college experience and reputation.) Some hailed Sulkowicz as a hero; others called her unhinged. Regardless, it is clear that public witness bearing—rejecting traditional anonymity with its attendant assumption of shame—had become girls' best weapon in the fight against rape.

By the spring of 2015 more than a hundred colleges were under investigation for possible mishandling of sexual assault cases. Among them were the most prestigious in the country: Amherst, Brandeis, Dartmouth, Emerson, Emory, Hampshire, Harvard (the college and the law school), Princeton, Sarah Lawrence, Stanford, Swarthmore, the University of California–Berkeley, the University of Chicago, the University of Michigan–Ann Arbor, the University of North Carolina at Chapel Hill, the University of Southern California, the University of Virginia, and Vanderbilt.[9] Will those inquiries make a difference? It's hard to say. The number of reported campus sexual assaults nearly doubled between 2009 and 2013, from 3,264 to 6,016. Although that wouldn't seem like good news, it is: rather than an increase in the incidence of rapes, the rise appears to reflect a new willingness of victims to step forward, a new belief that they will be heard.[10] The key may be to keep the bright light of public attention shining. According to a study by the American

[9]Edwin Rios, "The Feds Are Investigating 106 Colleges for Mishandling Sexual Assault. Is Yours One of Them?" *Mother Jones*, April 8, 2015.
[10]"New Education Department Data Shows Increase in Title IX Sexual Violence Complaints on College Campuses," Press release, May 5, 2015, Office of Barbara Boxer, U.S. Senator, California.

Psychological Association, the reported numbers of assaults increase an average of about 44 percent when campuses are under formal scrutiny. Afterward, though, they sink back to their original levels, indicating that some schools provide a more accurate picture of sexual assault only when forced to do so.[11]

In any case, I would argue that waiting to address rape until college is years too late. Sexual assault is even more common among secondary students; the difference is that their schools don't have the same duty to report it. Twenty-eight percent of female college freshmen in a 2015 survey of a large private university in upstate New York said they had been victims of either attempted or completed forcible or incapacitated rape *before* college—between the ages of fourteen and eighteen.[12] As in the early 1990s, many of the recent incidents that have shocked the nation also took place among younger kids. In the fall of 2012, Steubenville, Ohio, became the Glen Ridge[13] of its day after two football players hauled a drunk, insensible sixteen-year-old girl from party to party, taking turns sexually violating her, spitting on her, even urinating on her as classmates looked on, some cheering. Like the Glen Ridge jocks, who would, without asking their partners, Scotch tape photos to their high school's trophy case of themselves in flagrante delicto, these boys weren't content simply to assault their victim; they needed to document the "achievement." One member of the Steubenville "rape crew" tweeted such gems as "Song of the night is definitely Rape Me by Nirvana." Another boy posted a picture of the victim on Instagram, her head lolling back as the boys carried her by her wrists and ankles. In a YouTube video, a laughing young man calls her "deader than," respectively, Nicole Simpson, John F. Kennedy, Trayvon Martin, and the toddler Caylee Anthony.[14] Was online bragging about rape part of a new, ominous trend? A year earlier, a pair of boys in Louisville, Kentucky (fine students and athletes at a prestigious Catholic school), made news when they passed around cell phone pictures of themselves assaulting a sixteen-year-old who lay drunk and semiconscious in her kitchen. Audrie Pott, a fifteen-year-old from Saratoga, California, committed suicide after photos of

[11]Corey Rayburn Yung, "Concealing Campus Sexual Assault," *Psychology, Public Policy, and Law*, Vol. 21, No. 1, 2015.

[12]Unlike some other surveys, this one limited itself to the legal definition of rape; it did not include forced fondling or forced kissing. Carey et al., "Incapacitated and Forcible Rape of Women." The U.S. Justice Department has found that nearly one in five girls ages fourteen to seventeen had been the victims of attempted or completed assault. Finkelhor, Turner, and Ormrod, "Children's Exposure to Violence."

[13]**Glen Ridge:** In 1989, a mentally handicapped girl was raped with a broomstick and a baseball bat by members of the Glen Ridge High School football team in Glen Ridge, New Jersey. [Eds.]

[14]**Nicole Simpson... Trayvon Martin... Caylee Anthony:** In 1994, Nicole Brown Simpson, wife of retired football player and actor O.J. Simpson, was murdered outside her home; African American teenager Trayvon Martin was fatally shot by George Zimmerman, a neighborhood watch volunteer in 2012; in 2008, Casey Anthony was tried and acquitted for the murder of her two-year-old daughter, Caylee Anthony. [Eds.]

an assault perpetrated while she was passed out drunk were posted on the Internet. Ditto Rehtaeh Parsons, a seventeen-year-old girl from Nova Scotia, Canada, who was gang-raped while incapacitated.

Tracking those incidents, it struck me how often the words *funny* or, more commonly, *hilarious* came up among boys recounting stories of women's sexual degradation. When, during the Steubenville video an off-camera voice says rape isn't funny, Michael Nodianos, then a high school baseball player, responds, "It isn't funny. It's *hilarious!*" One of the Louisville boys told police he thought it would be "funny" to take pictures of himself assaulting his victim. A young woman I met at a California university told me how, freshman year, a male resident of her dorm invited her to watch a video he'd shot on his phone of a friend having sex with a girl who was out cold. "Come look at this," he had said. "It's *hilarious.*" A boy on a midwestern campus I visited, recalling the first time he saw hard-core porn, remembered thinking that was "hilarious," too; his classmate used the word while describing how the "ugly band girls" were the most sexually active in his high school. "Hilarious" seemed to be the default position for some boys—something like "awkward" for girls—when they were unsure of how to respond, particularly to something that was both sexually explicit and dehumanizing, something that perhaps actually upset them, offended them, unnerved them, repulsed them, confused them, or defied their ethics. "Hilarious" offered distance, allowing them to look without feeling, to subvert a more compassionate response that might be read as weak, overly sensitive, and unmasculine. "Hilarious" is particularly disturbing as a safe haven for bystanders—if assault is "hilarious," they don't have to take it seriously, they don't have to respond: there is no problem.

The photos shared by the assailants in Steubenville, Louisville, Nova Scotia, and Saratoga revictimized the girls—potentially in perpetuity, as the images could be endlessly copied, downloaded, and passed along. They also provided unique evidence that crimes had indeed been committed, though that made neither conviction inevitable nor punishments necessarily more severe. One of the Steubenville rapists was given a year in juvenile detention; the other got two years, including credit for time already served. The Louisville boys were ordered to perform fifty hours of community service, which, until the local newspaper intervened, they were fulfilling by putting away equipment after lacrosse practice. Two of Audrie Pott's assailants received thirty-day sentences in juvenile detention, to be served on weekends; a third served forty-five consecutive days. Rehtaeh Parsons's attackers were placed on probation. As in Glen Ridge, there was often a groundswell of sympathy for the boys in these cases: claims that their actions were unusual, a one-time mistake; anguish over the damage convictions would do to their bright futures; denunciations of the girl involved. One of the Louisville assailants took his appeal straight to his victim, texting her to ask that she stop pursuing her case against him. "There is another way to deal with this other than jeopardizing our lives forever. . . . I'm not a bad person just a dumb one."

"You don't think you ruined my life forever?" she shot back. . . .[15]   10

Don't Tell Girls Not to Drink; Tell Rapists Not to Rape

At the heart of the argument over consent is another argument over alcohol. How drunk is too drunk to mean yes? How drunk is too drunk to be unable to say no? Who bears responsibility for making that call? An estimated 80 percent of campus assaults involve alcohol, typically consumed voluntarily; often both victim and assailant (or assailants) have been drinking.[16] The party culture on college campuses (as well as in many high school communities) can act as cover for rapists, especially repeat rapists. Yet in 2013, when Emily Yoffe[17] wrote on *Slate DoubleX* that girls should be warned that heavy drinking increases their vulnerability to having sexual violence perpetrated against them, she was pilloried for victim-blaming.[18] *The Atlantic, New York Magazine, Jezebel, Salon, Huffington Post,* the *Daily Mail, Feminist-ing,* and even colleagues at *Slate DoubleX* itself labeled her a "rape apologist." During the ensuing furor, a generation gap emerged. Older women—that is, women the same age as Yoffe (a category that includes this author)—thought her advice sounded sensible. She wasn't, after all, saying that a drunk girl *deserved* to be raped or that it was her fault if she was. Nor was she saying that sobriety guaranteed protection against sexual assault. She only seemed to be voicing what most of us would tell our daughters: alcohol reduces your ability to recognize and escape a dangerous situation. Women metabolize liquor differently from men, too, reaching a higher blood alcohol level drink for drink and becoming more impaired than a guy the same size and weight.[19] Given the prevalence of binge drinking on campus, shouldn't they know that?

Many young women, though, countered with a stance similar to the one they held on dress codes: don't tell us not to drink, tell rapists not to rape. If you really want to reduce assault, they said, wouldn't it be equally, if not more, logical to target *boys'* alcohol abuse, especially

---

[15]Jason Riley and Andrew Wolfson, "Louisville Boys Sexually Assaulted Savannah Dietrich 'Cause We Thought It Would Be Funny,'" *Courier Journal,* August 30, 2012.

[16]Krebs, Lindquist, and Warner, *The Campus Sexual Assault (CSA) Study Final Report.*

[17]**Emily Yoffe:** (b. 1955), American journalist and contributing editor at the *Atlantic* magazine. [Eds.]

[18]Emily Yoffe, "College Women: Stop Getting Drunk," *Slate DoubleX,* October 15, 2013.

[19]Centers for Disease Control, "Binge Drinking: A Serious Under-Recognized Problem Among Women and Girls."

since perpetrators are about as likely to be drinking as victims?[20] Alcohol has proven to have a profound influence on would-be rapists' behavior. It lowers their inhibition; it allows them to disregard social cues or a partner's hesitation; it gives them the nerve they may not otherwise have to use force; and it offers a ready justification for misconduct.[21] The more that potential rapists drink, the more aggressive they are during an assault, and the less aware of their victims' distress. By contrast, sober guys not only are less sexually coercive but will more readily step up if they believe an alcohol-related assault is in the offing.[22]

Activists are correct in saying that the only thing that 100 percent of rapes have in common is a rapist. You can shroud women from head to toe, forbid them alcohol, imprison them in their homes—and there will still be rape. Plus, you will live in Afghanistan. To me, this seems like another of those both/and situations. I have a hard time defending *anyone's* inalienable right to get shit-faced, male or female, especially when they're underage. What's that, you say? Harmless collegiate rite of passage? Six hundred thousand students ages eighteen to twenty-four are unintentionally injured each year while under the influence; 1,825 die.[23] Teens who drink in high school, confident in their heightened alcohol tolerance, are at particular risk of harm in college.

I happen to live in Berkeley, California, the town where my state's best and brightest come for their education—the average high school grade point average of incoming freshmen here is 4.46. Yet, in the first two months of the 2013/14 school year, paramedics transported 107 of these smarty-pants students, all perilously intoxicated, to the hospital. During "move-in weekend" alone, the volume of calls about alcohol poisoning to 911 was so high that the city had to request ambulances from neighboring towns; the local ER was overrun with drunk students, forcing diversion of those vehicles elsewhere. (Heaven help the "townie" who happened to have a stroke or a heart attack on one of those nights.) In that same two-month period, incidentally, campus

---

[20]Gordon, "Study: College Athletes Are More Likely to Gang Rape"; Abbey, "Alcohol's Role in Sexual Violence Perpetration"; Davis, "The Influence of Alcohol Expectancies and Intoxication on Men's Aggressive Unprotected Sexual Intentions"; Foubert, Newberry, and Tatum, "Behavior Differences Seven Months Later"; Carr and VanDeusen, "Risk Factors for Male Sexual Aggression on College Campuses"; Abbey, Clinton-Sherrod, McAuslan, et al., "The Relationship Between the Quantity of Alcohol Consumed and Severity of Sexual Assaults Committed by College Men"; Norris, Davis, George, et al., "Alcohol's Direct and Indirect Effects on Men's Self-Reported Sexual Aggression Likelihood"; Abbey et al., "Alcohol and Sexual Assault"; Norris et al., "Alcohol and Hypermasculinity as Determinants of Men's Empathic Responses to Violent Pornography."

[21]Abbey, "Alcohol's Role in Sexual Violence Perpetration"; Davis, "The Influence of Alcohol Expectancies and Intoxication on Men's Aggressive Unprotected Sexual Intentions"; Abbey et al., "Alcohol and Sexual Assault."

[22]Abbey, "Alcohol's Role in Sexual Violence Perpetration"; Orchowski, Berkowitz, Boggis, et al., "Bystander Intervention Among College Men."

[23]Nicole Kosanake and Jeffrey Foote, "Binge Thinking: How to Stop College Kids from Majoring in Intoxication," *Observer*, January 21, 2015.

police cited exactly two kids for underage drinking.[24] And yet when binge drinking rises, so does sexual assault.[25] As part of an investigative story by the local ABC-TV affiliate, a paramedic who responded to some UC Berkeley calls, his face blurred and voice distorted to avoid reprisals, told a reporter that he had personally stopped a group of these top-tier college boys as they dragged an unconscious girl out of a party; one admitted he didn't even know her. "Who knows what their intentions were?"[26] the paramedic mused. Nine rapes were reported in the first three months of the 2014/15 school year; five on one night when members of a non-recognized fraternity allegedly slipped "roofies" into their female classmates' drinks, rendering them defenseless.

As a parent, I am all for harm reduction. So I will absolutely explain to my daughter the particular effects of alcohol on the female body. I will explain how predators leverage that difference by using liquor itself as a date rape drug, and how bingeing increases everyone's vulnerability to a variety of health and safety concerns. I know that getting loaded can seem an easy way to reduce social anxiety, help you feel like you fit in, quiet the nagging voice in your head of paralytic self-doubt. Still, knocking back six shots in an hour in order to have fun—or, for that matter, to prove *you* are fun—is, perhaps, overkill. Nor is it ideal to gin up courage to have sex that would otherwise feel too "awkward"—even if the results are consensual, the sex will probably suck. Two people who are lit may *both* behave in a manner they will later regret—or not fully remember, making consent difficult to determine. Should that constitute assault? Students themselves are divided. Nearly everyone in a 2015 *Washington Post*/Kaiser Family Foundation poll of current and former college students agreed that sex with someone who is incapacitated or passed out is rape (a huge and welcome cultural shift). But if *both* people are incapacitated? Only about one in five agree; roughly the same percentage say that is *not* assault, and nearly 60 percent are unsure.[27] That's understandable, given the paradox of students' sexual lives: drunkenness is obligatory for hookups, yet liquor negates consent. There are bright lines—lots of them—and they are too often crossed. But there are also situations that are confusing and complicated for everyone....

15

[24]Dan Noyes, "Binge Drinking at UC Berkeley Strains EMS System," *Eyewitness News*, ABC, November 7, 2013; Emilie Raguso, "Student Drinking at Cal Taxes Berkeley Paramedics," Berkeleyside.com, November 12, 2013; Nico Correia, "UCPD Responds to 8 Cases of Alcohol-Related Illness Monday Morning," *Daily Californian*, August 26, 2013. In 2012, twelve students were transported to the hospital during the first two weeks of school at UC Berkeley; in 2011 there were eleven incidents in the month of August alone. In 2014, however, the number of incidents during the first weekend of school dropped by half. *Daily Californian*, "Drinking Is a Responsibility," August 26, 2014.

[25]Mohler-Kuo, Dowdall, Koss, et al., "Correlates of Rape While Intoxicated in a National Sample of College Women." This is not, again, to say alcohol causes rape, but that rapists use alcohol in a variety of ways to abet their crimes.

[26]Noyes, "Binge Drinking at UC Berkeley Strains EMS System."

[27]"Poll: One in 5 Women Say They Have Been Sexually Assaulted in College," *Washington Post*, June 12, 2015.

So I'll tell my daughter that it's possible to make mistakes, that not all scenarios are as clear as we would like. That said, if, for whatever reason, she does get wasted — because it's part of the culture she's in or because she wants to see what it feels like or because the drink didn't taste strong — and, God forbid, is targeted for assault, it is positively, in no way, under any circumstances, her fault. I will tell her that nothing ever, ever, *ever* justifies rape. Victims are *never* responsible for an assailant's actions and need not feel shame or be silenced. If I had a son? I would be equally clear with him: drunk girls are not "easy pickings"; their poor choices are not your free pass to sex. I would tell him that heavy drinking, in addition to potential long-term physical harm, impairs boys' ability to detect or respect nonconsent. I would say that if there is *any* doubt about a girl's capacity to say yes — if the thought even flits across his mind — he should, for his own safety as well as hers, move along. There will be other opportunities to have sex (truly, there will be). So although I get why, for both parents and policy makers, focusing on girls' drinking is tempting, it is simply not enough....

What Yes Means

One of the Big Bads that conservatives warned of in the 1990s was that if alcohol-induced assaults were included in the definition of rape, college administrators would be swamped by vengeful girls who regretted their previous night's encounters. As if it's easy for a victim of sexual assault to come forward. As if girls have been readily believed. As if it weren't social suicide. As if they wouldn't be shunned, called sluts, blamed, harassed, and threatened. Consider the reaction in 2014 on CollegiateACB, a forum where students anonymously discuss campus issues, after a Vanderbilt University student's rape accusations resulted in the suspension of a fraternity. Forum users demanded to know the identity of "the girl who ratted" — a name was actually posted — and called her, among other things, "manic depressive," "a crazy bitch," "psycho," "NASTY AS SHIT," and, over and over, a "snitch." "This repeated use of the word 'snitching' in the thread," wrote André Rouillard, editor of the school's newspaper, "implies that the victim has revealed a secret that should have been kept hidden behind closed doors — under the rug and on floors that stick like flypaper and stink of old beer.... The OP [original poster] issues a rallying cry: 'we need to stick together and prevent shit like this from being ok.'"[28] By "shit like this" he didn't mean rape; he meant girls' reporting of it.

Those trying to prove that campuses are rife with psycho young women just itching to ruin their male classmates' lives were inadvertently handed an opportunity in the spring of 2015, when *Rolling Stone* magazine retracted an article on a gang rape at the University of Virginia that had fallen apart under scrutiny. I don't know if that scandal

[28]André Rouillard, "The Girl Who Ratted," *Vanderbilt Hustler*, April 16, 2014.

will become the cornerstone of a new suppression of activism—these are different times than the 1990s—but as a Columbia University Graduate School of Journalism investigation concluded, *Rolling Stone*'s editors "hoped their investigation would sound an alarm about campus sexual assault and would challenge Virginia and other universities to do better. Instead, the magazine's failure may have spread the idea that many women invent rape allegations."

There are, absolutely, false charges of rape. To say otherwise would be absurd. But they are rarer than alarmists would like you to believe. Legally, a "false report" is one in which it can be *demonstrably* proven that a rape was not committed. When investigators find that assault did not occur, that is something else: an unsubstantiated or inconclusive report. Conservative pundits such as Hoff Sommers, Cathy Young, and Wendy McElroy[29]—plus every troll ever on the Internet—assert that 40 to 50 percent of sexual assault accusations are actually *false*. (Although, oddly, as criminologist Jan Jordan has pointed out, while adamant that half of accusers lie, such critics believe women who recant are unfailingly truthful.)[30] In her book *Rape Is Rape*, Jody Raphael explains that this statistic comes from a 1994 report for which Eugene J. Kanin, a sociologist at Purdue University, compiled one police agency's characterizations of forty-five assault claims made over nine years in a small midwestern town—assessments that were not necessarily based on evidence or investigation. Kanin himself cautioned that his findings should not be generalized, and admitted, "Rape recantations could be the result of the complainants' desire to avoid a 'second assault' at the hands of the police."[31] More credible, Raphael wrote, are seven rigorous studies conducted in the United States and the United Kingdom over more than three decades. They place false claim rates at between 2 and 8 percent, a number, according to FBI statistics, that has been steadily dropping since 1990, when the controversy over acquaintance rape emerged.[32] Certainly it is important to bear in mind the potential for false claims, but our fear of them seems strangely disproportionate, especially given that most victims are not believed, that 80 percent of campus rapes are never even reported, and a mere 13 to 30 percent of assailants are found responsible among the sliver that are.[33]

---

[29]**Cathy Young... Wendy McElroy:** Catherine Young (b. 1963) is a Russian-born American journalist and feminist; Wendy McElroy (b. 1951) is a Canadian journalist and feminist. [Eds.]

[30]Raphael, *Rape Is Rape.*

[31]Additionally, victims were urged to take a polygraph test, a practice that has since been abandoned as adversely affecting their willingness to come forward. Rape victims asked to take a polygraph test believe they are being doubted from the get-go. Kanin, "False Rape Allegations."

[32]Raphael, *Rape Is Rape*; Lisak, Gardinier, Nicksa, et al., "False Allegations of Sexual Assault: An Analysis of Ten Years of Reported Cases."

[33]Sinozich and Langton, *Special Report: Rape and Sexual Assault Victimization Among College-Age Females, 1995–2013*; Tyler Kingkade, "Fewer Than One-Third of Campus Sexual Assault Cases Result in Expulsion," *Huffington Post*, September 29, 2014; Nick Anderson, "Colleges Often Reluctant to Expel for Sexual Violence," *Washington Post*, December 15, 2014.

Emily Yoffe, who also raises the specter of an "overcorrection" on [20] campus rape, has objected that lumping psychologically coerced or pressured sex into statistics risks "trivializing" assault.[34] She, too, fears it would tempt any girl who "regrets making out with a boy who has "persuaded' her" to file a complaint that could lead to his expulsion. "We may be teaching a generation of young men that pressuring a woman into sexual activity is never a good idea," she acknowledged, "but we are also teaching a generation of young women that they are malleable, weak, 'overwhelmed,' and helpless in the face of male persuasion."[35]

This is where she and I part ways. Most sexual interludes among high school or college students are, obviously, not violent: They are consensual and wanted, if not always reciprocal. That said, a sizable percentage is coerced; rather than "trivializing" rape, Yoffe risks "trivializing" the way such pressure is seen as a masculine right and how that shapes our understanding of consent—even of sex itself. Despite changing roles in other realms, boys continue to be seen as the proper initiators of sexual contact. (If you don't believe me, listen to the outrage of mothers of teen boys when discussing today's "aggressive" girls.) Boys' sex drive is considered natural, and their pleasure a given. They are supposed to be sexually confident, secure, and knowledgeable. Young women remain the gatekeepers of sex, the inertia that stops the velocity of the male libido.[36] Those dynamics create a haven for below-the-radar offenses that make a certain level of sexual manipulation, even violence, normal and acceptable. I don't know that such acts deserve expulsion, but they are worthy of serious discussion. As Lorelei Simpson Rowe, a clinical psychologist at Southern Methodist University who works with girls on refusal skills, explains, "The vast majority of sexual violence and coercion occurs in situations that are not obviously dangerous . . . so if nine times you go out with a boy and engage in consensual activity, and it's pleasant and you're excited to be developing a relationship, that doesn't prepare you for that one time when it switches."

While such transformations may be sudden, frequently, Simpson Rowe says, they're not. "Guys will start saying, 'Come on, let's go further' or 'Why not?' or 'I really like you. Don't you like me?' There's a lot of persuading and pleading and guilt-inducing tactics, along with a lot of complimenting and flattery. And because it's subtle, you see a lot of self-questioning among girls. They wonder, 'Am I reading this right?' 'Did he actually say that?' 'Did he actually mean that?'" Simpson Rowe and her colleagues have developed a training program that uses virtual

---

[34]Emily Yoffe, "The College Rape Overcorrection," *Slate DoubleX*, December 7, 2014.
[35]Emily Yoffe, "How *The Hunting Ground* Blurs the Truth," *Slate DoubleX*, February 27, 2015.
[36]See Tolman, Davis, and Bowman, "That's Just How It Is."

reality simulations to help girls recognize and resist those cues. In pilot trials of high school and college students, incoming participants generally rated themselves as confident that they could rebuff unwanted advances or escape threatening situations. Yet, when role-playing a range of increasingly fraught scenarios—from a male avatar who badgers girls for their phone numbers to one who threatens violence if they don't submit to sex—they would freeze. Simpson Rowe was quick to say that only perpetrators are responsible for assault, but assertiveness and self-advocacy are crucial defensive skills. "What we found is the importance of women being able to make quick, cognitive switches between normal sexual interaction and protecting their safety," she said. "And part of that involves being able to notice when something has gone from being a normal interaction to pressure."

The girls in her program worried that a direct rejection would hurt boys' feelings; they felt guilty and uncomfortable saying no. "Girls have all this modeling for being nice and polite and caring and compassionate about others' feelings," Simpson Rowe explained. "These are wonderful things—good characteristics. But because they're so ingrained, a lot of women think this is how they're supposed to be when faced with an unsafe situation, and they're afraid of being seen as rude. The word that comes up a lot is *bitchy*. So, it's kind of an 'aha' moment when they realize a guy who is pressuring and persuading and not stopping when you say you don't want to do something is not respecting you or your boundaries—and at that point, *you don't have to worry about hurting his feelings.* We emphasize how early the coercive process begins and help them respond to it before it ever gets to violence." Preliminary data showed that three months after completing the ninety-minute training, participants had experienced half the rate of sexual victimization than a control group. Another risk-reduction program piloted among more than four hundred fifty Canadian college freshmen had similar results: a year later, rates of rape among participants were half that of girls who had only received a brochure.[37] "We want to send the message that no one has the right to push or pressure you into what you don't want to do," Simpson Rowe said. "You have the right to stand up for yourself as loudly and physically as you want to and can."

Listening to Simpson Rowe, I thought about Megan, who told her rapist, "Thanks, I had fun." I thought about another girl I met, a freshman in college, who told me her high school boyfriend had raped her twice—once while they were together and once after they'd broken up, when he lured her into his car at a party to talk. Both times, she was drunk. Both times she told him no. Both times he ignored her. "I probably

---

[37]Senn, Eliasziw, Barata, et al., "Efficacy of a Sexual Assault Resistance Program for University Women." This is particularly important because rapists target freshman women. The resistance program involved four three-hour units in which skills were taught and practiced. The goal was for young women to be able to assess risk from acquaintances, overcome emotional barriers in acknowledging danger, and engage in effective verbal and physical self-defense.

could have pushed him off of me or rolled over or screamed loud enough so someone could hear," she said, "but something prevented me from doing it each time. I'm a very strong person. I have very strong morals. I'm not embarrassed about talking about anything. But I didn't do anything. It was kind of like being paralyzed." I recalled Simpson Rowe's words again in the summer of 2015, when I read the court testimony of a former student at St. Paul's prep school in New Hampshire. A popular senior boy had assaulted her in the spring of her freshman year, she recounted, during an end-of-year rite known as "the senior salute," in which graduating male students compete to have sexual encounters with as many younger female students as possible. Initially flattered by his attentions, she testified, she joined him in a dark maintenance room but was at a loss as to how to respond to his escalating aggression. "I said, 'No, no, no! Keep it up here,'" she told the jury, gesturing to the area above her waist. "I tried to be as polite as possible." Even as he groped, bit, and penetrated her, she said, "I wanted to not cause a conflict."[38]

Each of those girls could have used a session in Simpson Rowe's virtual reality simulator. At the same time, I also thought about a 2014 study in which nearly a third of college men agreed they would rape a woman if they could get away with it—though that percentage dropped to 13.6 percent when the word *rape* (as opposed to "force a woman to have sexual intercourse") was actually used in the question.[39] Teaching girls to self-advocate, to name and express their feelings in relationships, is important for all kinds of reasons, and it may indeed help some of them stop or escape an assault. Yet, just as focusing on girls' drinking disregards rapists' behavior, keeping the onus on victims to repel boys' advances leaves the prerogative to pressure in place; it also maintains sexual availability as a girl's default position even if, as feminist pundit Katha Pollitt has written, she "lies there like lox with tears running down her cheeks, too frozen or frightened or trapped by lifelong habits of demureness to utter the magic word." Even if that girl were to say no loud and clear, the boy might not hear it.[40]

"Affirmative consent" policies—versions of the one pioneered by Antioch[41]—have once again become the hope for change. In 2014, California was the first state to pass a "yes means yes" law directed at colleges and universities receiving state funds. Rather than requiring an accuser to prove she said no, it demands that an alleged assailant prove that there was "an affirmative, unambiguous, and conscious decision by each participant to engage in mutually agreed-upon sexual activity." In other words, that a clear, enthusiastic "you bet," either verbally or through body language, was given. Consent may also be revoked

25

[38]Bidgood, "In Girl's Account, Rite at St. Paul's Boarding School Turned into Rape."
[39]Edwards et al., "Denying Rape but Endorsing Forceful Intercourse."
[40]Katha Pollitt, "Why Is 'Yes Means Yes' So Misunderstood?" *Nation*, October 8, 2014.
[41]**Antioch:** Antioch College is a private, liberal arts college in Yellow Springs, Ohio. [Eds.]

anytime, and a person incapacitated due to drugs or alcohol is not legally able to give it. That's a fundamental shift in power relations, and twelve years after the "Is It Date Rape?"[42] *SNL* sketch, fewer people are laughing. New York passed affirmative consent legislation in 2015. New Hampshire, Maryland, and Colorado are all considering similar bills. Every Ivy League school except Harvard now has a version of "yes means yes" in place as well.

Conservatives have predictably warned that thousands of boys will soon be ejected from colleges for trying for a good-night kiss. But the policies have made liberals uneasy as well. Ezra Klein, editor in chief of Vox, wrote that he supported the law, though he believed it would "settle like a cold winter on college campuses, throwing everyday sexual practice into doubt and creating a haze of fear and confusion over what counts as consent." The anxiety on both sides reminded me of the 1993 fears about California's then-innovative law against peer-to-peer sexual harassment in schools, which allowed districts to expel offenders as young as nine years old. But you know what? Twenty-plus years later, no fourth-graders have been shipped off to San Quentin for hazarding a playground smooch. Nor have school districts been bankrupted by a deluge of frivolous lawsuits. At the same time, the legislation has not stopped sexual harassment. It has, however, provided a framework through which students can understand and discuss the issue, and the potential for recourse, on a number of levels, when it happens....

Increased awareness has also reduced tolerance for the winking acceptance of harassment and assault. Anheuser-Busch found that out in 2015, when the company unveiled a new tag line for Bud Light: "The perfect beer for removing 'no' from your vocabulary for the night." American sensibilities had changed since the 1990s, as had the targets of influential comedians' humor. So, rather than mocking overly sensitive women, John Oliver[43] drew cheers from his college-age studio audience by skewering the frat-boy mentality that allowed the slogan's approval: imagining Bud executives fist-pumping and shouting, "Sick idea, brah!" "That's what I'm talkin' about, *a'ight*," "No, no, no, no. That's what *I'm* talkin' about, son!" and a wordless, *"Blaaaaaaaaaaaaah!"* (The beer company had been forced several days prior to issue a public apology after news of the slogan had careened around Twitter.)

Will affirmative consent laws reduce campus assault? Will cases be more readily resolved? I can't say. As Pollitt pointed out, adjudication in many instances will still be based on he said/she said, with accused assailants replacing "She didn't say no" with "Dude, she said yes!" Among the students in the *Washington Post*/Kaiser Family Foundation poll, only 20 percent said the yes means yes standard was "very

---

[42]**"Is It Date Rape?":** In 1993, the late-night television variety show *Saturday Night Live* featured a skit lampooning the affirmative consent rules that had been recently adopted by Antioch College. [Eds.]

[43]**John Oliver:** (b. 1977), English comedian, writer, producer, political satirist, and host of the HBO series *Last Week Tonight*. [Eds.]

realistic" in practice, though an additional 49 percent considered it "somewhat realistic." What "yes means yes" may do, though, especially if states aim solid curricular efforts at younger students, as California plans to, is create a desperately needed reframing of the public conversation away from the negative — away from viewing boys as exclusively aggressive and girls as exclusively vulnerable, away from the embattled and the acrimonious — and toward what healthy, consensual, mutual encounters between young people ought to look like. Maybe it will allow girls to consider what they want—what they *really* want—sexually, and at last give them license to communicate it; maybe it will allow boys to more readily listen.

ENGAGING THE TEXT

1. How do you interpret the statistics Orenstein offers at the beginning of this selection? Based on these figures, would you agree that American colleges are facing a sexual assault crisis? How serious, in your view, is the problem of sexual assault at your college or university? Why do you think so?

2. Orenstein notes that following the Office for Civil Rights' "Dear Colleague" letter, a new, less rigorous burden of proof was established for college sexual assault hearings. What, according to Orenstein, was the rationale for this change? In 2017, after this selection was published, the Trump administration under Secretary of Education Betsy DeVos indicated that it would rescind the use of the lower standard of proof while it reviewed its sexual assault policy. What do you think might be the effect of rescinding these guidelines?

3. When should sexual assault training begin? In college? In high school? Earlier? What kind of sexual assault training did you receive in school? How effective was it?

4. How does Orenstein portray "boys" and "girls" throughout this selection? How does she describe the attitudes of boys toward sex and toward girls? How does she portray girls in relation to boys? How accurate and unbiased is her depiction of the genders?

5. What reasons does Orenstein offer to explain why college students indulge in binge drinking? Why, in your view, do college students drink so much, even when it makes them more susceptible to assault? Do you think that warning college women about the relationship between drinking and rape amounts to "blaming the victim"? Why or why not?

6. Orenstein explains what she would tell her own daughter and son about sexual assault. What, if anything, did your parents tell you about this issue during your teen years? What would you tell your own son and daughter about the dangers of drinking and sex on campus?

7. What are "affirmative consent" laws and policies, and how effective are they, in your opinion, as an approach to dealing with sexual assault? Would you agree

with some of the critics Orenstein cites that there has been an "overcorrection" in the way colleges address sexual assault? Why or why not? How would you reply to the assertion that colleges are "teaching a generation of young women that they are malleable, weak, 'overwhelmed,' and helpless…" (para. 20)?

EXPLORING CONNECTIONS

8. After reviewing the four types of schools described by Jean Anyon in "Social Class and the Hidden Curriculum of Work" (p. 136), discuss how the education offered in working-class, middle-class, affluent, and elite schools might prepare girls to say "No" to boys in college. What role, if any, might class background play in a young woman's ability to defend herself against sexual assault?

9. Look ahead to Noreen Malone's account of the online harassment Zoë Quinn suffered during the Gamergate controversy (p. 285). Drawing on both Orenstein and Malone, discuss the role that social media and the Internet have played in amplifying sexual harassment in school. In your view, does social media make it easier or more difficult for young women to deal with sexual assault and aggression? Why?

EXTENDING THE CRITICAL CONTEXT

10. Research the current state of sexual assault on U.S. college campuses. According to the most recent statistics you can find, how common is college sexual assault, and how have assault rates changed over the past decade? How effective do campus educational programs appear to be in addressing sexual assault?

11. Visit some of the websites dedicated to college sexual assault, including KnowyourIX.org, Endrapeoncampus.org, Survjustice.org, or Itsonus.org, and explore the kinds of information and support they offer. Which of these information clearinghouses strike you as being particularly interesting, effective, or valuable? Why? What resources related to sexual assault can you find online for men?

12. Explore the kinds of information and support offered at Heather Corinna's Scarleteen sex education website. How aware were you of resources like this when you were in secondary school? How well did your own early sex education training prepare you for the challenges you would encounter during and after high school?

13. Since this selection was published, the #MeToo movement has amplified the voices of assault victims in ways that Orenstein probably couldn't have imagined at the time of writing. As a class, discuss what you think have been the critical moments in the #MeToo movement and whether or not you think this and other recent developments signal the kind of real cultural change that Orenstein desires.

CITY OF BROKEN DREAMS

SARA GOLDRICK-RAB

Today, college students owe lenders $1.49 trillion — more than the total of all U.S. credit card debt. Generations of Americans have seen college as a road out of poverty for working-class students. But since state legislatures began cutting higher education budgets a few decades ago and colleges responded by increasing fees and tuition, many have come to view higher education as a financial trap. In 2008, Sara Goldrick-Rab and a team of researchers set out to study the impact of college costs on working-class students. Focusing on the University of Wisconsin system, Goldrick-Rab and her team documented the economic experiences of 3,000 students over a period of six years. What she discovered was a heartbreaking story of failed dreams and lives hobbled by debt. In this selection, Goldrick-Rab examines the fortunes of three students at the University of Wisconsin in Milwaukee, a place she describes as "one of the poorest and most segregated cities in America." Her account of what happens when José, Alicia, and Anne enroll in college suggests that instead of being a source of opportunity, colleges often reproduce social inequities that place a special burden on working-class students and students of color. Goldrick-Rab (b. 1977) is professor of Higher Education Policy and Sociology at Temple University. She is also the founder of the Wisconsin Hope Lab, a research center seeking ways to make college more affordable. Her publications include *Reinventing Financial Aid: Charting a New Course to College Affordability* (2014), coauthored with Andrew P. Kelly; *Putting Poor People to Work: How the Work-First Idea Eroded College Access for the Poor* (2006), coauthored with Kathleen M. Shaw; and *Paying the Price: College Costs, Financial Aid, and the Betrayal of the American Dream* (2017), the source of this selection.

FOR MOST STUDENTS, GOING TO COLLEGE IN AMERICA doesn't mean venturing far from home. More than three in four students attend colleges within fifty miles of their homes, continuing their relationships with families, neighbors, and nearby institutions as they pursue degrees.[1] Proximity to home is an especially important factor in the college decisions of low-income and race/ethnic minority students.[2] The college opportunities presented in a given home city or town, therefore,

---

[1]Author's calculations using the National Center for Education Statistics' *National Postsecondary Student Aid Study* of 2011–12, excluding students in solely online courses. [All notes are Goldrick-Rab's.]

[2]Turley, "College Proximity," 140; and Hillman, "Differential Impacts of College Ratings," 12–13.

help to determine what the college experience looks like. It also largely determines the price that students pay.

While there is a great deal of attention devoted to how much states contribute overall to their public colleges and universities, there is much less discussion about how funds are distributed among those institutions. The robust conversation about funding equity and adequacy in K–12 education has not yet taken place in higher education. Some colleges and universities are better positioned than others to draw on resources from diverse sources, including endowments and private funds, while others depend heavily on the state. When those resources are not forthcoming, students and families pay the price.[3]

In Wisconsin, the importance of location, community, and funding equity is nowhere more evident than in the city of Milwaukee. In 1936, Milwaukee was crowned "the best governed city in the U.S." Home to strong social services including excellent public parks, libraries and civic centers, and a notable work relief system, Wisconsin's major metropolitan city was in many respects a wonderful place to live and learn.[4] Consistent with the meaning of its Algonquian name, it was a beautiful and pleasant land.

Today Milwaukee is one of the poorest and most segregated cities in America. One-quarter of families live below the federal poverty level, nearly 27 percent of households are on food stamps, and over 36 percent of households take in $25,000 or less in annual income.[5] The level of black-white segregation in Milwaukee is the second highest in the nation. Some consider the city one of the worst places in the country to live for African Americans.[6] Its stock of college graduates lags behind nearly every other major central city in the country.[7]

Even though it is Wisconsin's largest and most diverse city—and only a ninety-minute drive from the state capitol in Madison—Milwaukee is often treated as an afterthought when it comes to state politics and policy. Reforms and budget cuts to social welfare programs like Badger Care and changes to public education, including the expansion of private school vouchers at public expense, and increased spending on corrections, disproportionally impact Milwaukee residents. Meanwhile, at the K–12 level, Wisconsin has the largest educational disparities between African American and white students in the country, and its schools suspend African American students at the highest rate in the country.[8]

Poverty and race are intertwined in cities across the United States, and the same is true in Milwaukee. While 13 percent of white households

[3]Goldrick-Rab and Kolbe, "Rethinking State Support for Higher Ed."
[4]Gurda, *The Making of Milwaukee*, 301–2 and 250–74.
[5]Author's calculations using U.S. Census Bureau, "American Community Survey."
[6]Logan and Stults, "The Persistence of Segregation in the Metropolis," 6.
[7]Milwaukee Department of City Development, *2000 City of Milwaukee Urban Atlas*, 54–55.
[8]Annie E. Casey Foundation, *Race for Results*, 13; and Richards, "Wisconsin Black Suspension Rate Highest in U.S. for High Schools."

fall below the poverty line in Milwaukee, the rate is 30 percent for Latinos and 39 percent of African Americans. That is to say, while only one in eight white residents live below the poverty line, three in ten Latinos and about two in five African Americans do.[9] The city isn't home to the widest racial disparities in poverty—Dane County, the home of Madison, holds that distinction—but the scope and scale of the challenge is far greater in Milwaukee.[10]

The concentration of poverty, coupled with what sociologist William Julius Wilson terms the "disappearance of work," has created extraordinarily difficult living conditions, creating challenges for pursuing educational opportunities.[11] It is hard to imagine how the city will ever get ahead when its residents are constrained in this way. As Mark Bittman, writing in the *New York Times*, noted: "When people are undereducated, impoverished, malnourished, un- or under-employed, or underpaid and working three jobs, their lives are diminished, as are their opportunities. As are the opportunities of their children."[12] With barely three in ten white Milwaukee residents over the age of twenty-five, and just one in ten African American residents, holding bachelor's degrees, the future of the city is in jeopardy.[13] Thirteen percent of African American men in Milwaukee are currently in prison, and half of all African American men in their thirties have been in prison, whereas just 9 percent hold bachelor's degrees.[14]

Political leaders at the state, county, and municipal levels are all trying to increase the percentage of college graduates among their constituents because people with higher education bring social and economic benefits. Graduates make higher wages and can spend more money. They contribute more to local tax bases, attract business investment, and are more likely to start their own enterprises. And they are less likely to need government public assistance services.[15] Falling behind in the competition to have a more educated workforce has dramatic consequences. One study estimated that if Wisconsin's educational attainment and incomes were equal to Minnesota's, Wisconsin residents would bring home $26 billion more every year.[16]

Milwaukee needs a college-educated workforce more than anywhere else in the state. Like other large, diverse cities in America, Milwaukee needs the educational and research enterprises of its higher

[9]Author's calculations using U.S. Census Bureau, "2009–2013 5-Year American Community Survey."

[10]In Dane County, the white poverty rate is 9 percent, while the black poverty rate is 54 percent. Wisconsin Council on Children and Families, *Race to Equity Report*, 12.

[11]For more on the economic state of Milwaukee, see Center for Economic Development, University of Wisconsin–Milwaukee, *The Economic State of Milwaukee*; and Wilson, *When Work Disappears*.

[12]Bittman, "No Justice, No...Anything."

[13]Author's calculations using U.S. Census Bureau, "American Community Survey."

[14]Pawasarat and Quinn, "Wisconsin's Mass Incarceration of African American Males."

[15]For more on the benefits of a college degree, see Oreopoulos and Petronijevic, "Making College Worth It"; and Hout, "Social and Economic Returns to College Education in the United States."

[16]Martin, "UW System's Growth Agenda for Wisconsin," 2.

education institutions to spur personal, community, and economic development. When higher education fails, Milwaukee loses out to other cities that offer expanding economic improvements and chances for equitable, inclusive futures. Some people and businesses have left Milwaukee, while others are choosing not to move there. As the old manufacturing base of the industrial Midwest continues to decline, those left behind have fewer and fewer opportunities.

Many of our students who were attending college in Milwaukee grew up under tougher circumstances than students from other parts of the state. They were more likely to come from single-parent families, and their parents earned less money. Life in the city often brought additional perils.... While Milwaukee students were not the only ones to voice concern about neighborhood violence, they did so more frequently than students from anywhere else.

The financial wager involved in attending college has higher stakes in Milwaukee, with some of Wisconsin's highest net prices and lowest graduation rates. Many students in this study attended the University of Wisconsin–Milwaukee (UW–Milwaukee), an institution that shares a research mission with UW–Madison but receives far less state support and has a much smaller endowment (Milwaukee's is just over $10 million while Madison's is close to $2.2 billion).[17] So even though many of the study's Pell recipients in Milwaukee needed a great deal of support to graduate, they were much less likely to find what they needed than students elsewhere in the state.

The Grinder

Alicia, an African American woman born in Milwaukee, graduated from a public high school and entered college with big ideas. She intended to earn a master's degree and become either a teacher or a social worker. Either of those careers, she thought, would pay about $30,000 a year. She felt that it was very important to get more education and a better job than her parents had—neither of them had finished college and both were struggling to hold onto their jobs. Alicia understood college was an important step toward her specific career goals and felt optimistic that education would pay off. Her daughter, two years old and born during her junior year of high school, was a strong source of motivation.

> I don't want to see myself where my mom is. I don't want to ever have to depend on a guy to take care of my daughter and me. It's all about us—everything I do is about us.... I look at people who don't go to college and I know I've got to do something. Without a college education you can't get a decent job anywhere.... I don't want to have to live paycheck to paycheck, struggling like I am

[17]The UWM Foundation, Inc., and Affiliates, *Consolidated Financial Statements and Supplementary Information*, 3; University of Wisconsin Foundation, "Connecting People, Inspiring Ideas," 26.

now. I just want me and my daughter to be happy and not worrying about anything. I've got to do it for us.

Alicia was determined. On her initial survey during the first few months of college, she said that there was no way she would drop out of college.

During that first semester, Alicia spent about 7.5 hours a day in class and studying and about four hours a day caring for her child. She was happy to have found affordable daycare at a program in the basement of her grandmother's church. Since she had no expected family contribution, she received the maximum Pell Grant and was chosen to get the Wisconsin Scholars Grant, too. But she still needed to pay more than $10,000 a year. "If you don't have the money, you have to find a way to get it or you can't go. They're not just going to let you in because, oh you have nice eyes, and you can go to college."

To pay the bills, Alicia took out a subsidized loan and worked thirty   15
hours a week. She worked both a work-study job and another job off campus, earning a total of $840 per month (about seven dollars per hour). She also used a credit card, carrying a balance between $500 and $1,000 per month. She slept about five hours a night.

Even though she had a busy schedule, she did not feel overwhelmed. When asked during our survey to rate her level of agreement with the statements "I'm having more problems affording college than I expected," and "I'm not as happy in college as I'd expected," Alicia strongly disagreed. She really liked the freedom of college life and found the classes interesting but difficult. She was only minimally concerned about money and paying for college. She wished, however, that she had the resources to concentrate her energy where it was most needed: "If I had more money, I wouldn't have to work as much, and I could spend more time with my daughter. That's one of my downfalls now—I'm so focused with school and work and then, I mean I do see her, but by the time we make it home it's like, 'Okay: eat dinner, bath, bed.'"

During that first semester, Alicia was only somewhat confident that if she faced financial problems, she could resolve them without dropping out of college. Like many other students who grew up in a persistently poor home, she was not sure she could get financial support from her family if she needed it, and she didn't feel strongly that they encouraged her to stay in college. But they did help her with childcare. Sometimes her father got off working the third shift and came right over in the morning to help Alicia get ready for school. This was important, because the childcare program at her university was greatly oversubscribed, as are the majority of such programs across the country.[18] In exchange for this help, she provided regular financial support to her family, especially to her mother who was unemployed.

Toward the end of that first year, however, things began to fall apart. Her daughter's daycare situation had grown unstable, her mother had

[18]Gault et al., "Campus Child Care Declining Even as Growing Numbers of Parents Attend College," 1–5.

begun staying with friends out of state because she could not pay rent, and she was no longer communicating with Alicia. Alicia managed to enroll for a second year of college but was able to spend very little time at school. Instead she spent most of her time taking care of her baby and working at a coffee shop off campus for thirty-nine hours per week at $8.25 an hour. Some days she worked from 8 A.M. to 6 P.M., other days, she worked 2 A.M. to 8 A.M. She slept just four hours a night, and she got up at 5:45 A.M. each day. She had to take sleeping pills at least three times a week and sometimes had trouble staying awake during the day. "School is a struggle," she said. "When I get stressed out my body just wants to shut down, but I can't let it because I have things to do."

Even with extensive work hours, Alicia had trouble regularly paying her rent and utilities and was very worried about having enough money to pay for things she needed. Her sister moved in with her but was not employed and received only a small amount of cash assistance from the state. They fought often.

At that point, Alicia was taking twelve credits and had a C average. 20 She was spending less time on school than she would have liked and was not doing as well as she wanted to despite trying hard. She met with professors during office hours and visited her adviser. She studied alone. She felt overwhelmed; she was not academically prepared for college work, she was exhausted, and she was now afraid of failing. Between work, her responsibilities to her daughter, and the demands of other family members, there was too much going on for her to focus on school. She wished she could simplify the situation and have more time for class. She still wanted that master's degree and now hoped that if she got it she would earn $55,000 a year. "Oh, I'm going to graduate—I don't have a choice. There ain't no stopping me," she told us.

Six months later, Alicia was still enrolled in college but had moved in with a man after her apartment was broken into while she was in class. She was now twenty years old. She still had difficulties with her mom, who came to visit from time to time and created "drama." Her boyfriend made her feel safe and helped take care of her daughter, and she felt better equipped to focus on school. She had less financial aid than in the past, likely because of her work earnings, but she felt it was easier to make ends meet with a partner.

That was the last time we saw Alicia. At the end of her sophomore year, she dropped out of touch. She was no longer enrolled in college and did not return phone calls. We were able to confirm through administrative records that though she spent eight semesters in school, by 2014 she had not earned a degree.

Big City, Big U

Improving educational attainment and economic conditions has been the driving force in public higher education in Milwaukee since its inception. The University of Wisconsin–Milwaukee began in 1956 when the Milwaukee State Teachers College was combined with a UW–Madison-run extension center in Milwaukee. This move redefined the scope and purpose of higher education for the region. Like many public urban universities, UW–Milwaukee affords much greater access to four-year higher education for working-class students throughout southeastern Wisconsin than would otherwise exist.[19] At the same time, it is a research university classified as having "high research activity," with thirty-two doctoral programs. Faculty and administrators often feel these dual missions are at cross-purposes. Students, however, speak only of the university's perceived "open door" policy—they know they can get in and research is not something they talk much about.

The major public two-year college in the city is Milwaukee Area Technical College (MATC), which began as a continuation school in 1912. Today it is one of the largest technical colleges in the Midwest, serving about 40,000 students with 170 degree, diploma, certificate, and apprentice programs. It has long focused on job training, but as the only two-year college in the area (the UW System does not have a two-year branch campus in the city), it is also tasked with providing open access for those who plan to transfer to the university to complete a four-year degree. Whether a transfer mission belongs in a technical college is an open question. Certainly, few students transfer out of MATC, especially when compared with the UW Colleges.

Most students of color who attend public higher education in Wisconsin are enrolled at either UW–Milwaukee or MATC, the former of which enrolls almost 40 percent of all students of color in the entire UW System. In 2014–15 this meant it educated 2,176 African Americans (8% of its total enrollment). In contrast, its sister research institution, UW–Madison, enrolled just 961 African American students that year—just 2 percent of total enrollment.[20] Students of color represent a little over 18 percent of all enrollment in the Wisconsin Technical Colleges statewide,[21] but at MATC, students of color make up 56 percent of the student body.[22]

The Milwaukee Public Schools (the city's K–12 public school system), which are the primary feeder for both UW–Milwaukee and MATC, like many urban school systems, are marked by low performance. The four-year high school graduation rate in Milwaukee Public Schools is 61 percent, compared to the statewide average of 88 percent. The graduation rate for black students in Milwaukee Public Schools is 58 percent and 57 percent for Hispanic students.[23]

Aspirations for college have increased among Milwaukee Public School students over time, such that by 2011, over three-fourths of Milwaukee Public School seniors said they planned to attend college.

[19]Zlotocha, "A 'Blue Shirt' UW for Milwaukee," 84–110.
[20]University of Wisconsin System, "University of Wisconsin Student Statistics, Fall 2014–15 Headcount Enrollment," 1.
[21]Wisconsin Technical College System Board, "An Overview of the Wisconsin Technical College System," 3.
[22]Milwaukee Area Technical College, "MATC Fast Facts," 1.
[23]Richards, "Wisconsin Graduation Rate Rises While MPS' Edges Down."

But far fewer than three-fourths seemed ready for higher education, given that the mean ACT composite score of the school system's seniors was just under seventeen and that only two-thirds of seniors planning to attend college completed the Free Application for Federal Student Aid (FAFSA). These seniors did not fare well: only 35 percent of high school graduates enrolled in college within a year and fewer than 13 percent received a postsecondary degree of any kind after six years.[24]

Over time, just as in the rest of the state, a growing number of Milwaukee students like Alicia have finished high school and enrolled in college. Moreover, faced with weak employment prospects, many adults across Milwaukee have returned to school. Over the past fifty years, enrollment in Milwaukee's public colleges and universities has grown substantially. Figure 1 shows this increase in enrollment at UW–Milwaukee. Between 1995 and 2010, the headcount expanded at a rate of several thousand students every five years. By contrast, UW–Madison enrollment grew at less than half that rate.[25]

Milwaukee Area Technical College is even larger than UW–Milwaukee, with a total headcount just over 40,000 students. Full-time equivalent enrollment grew more slowly at MATC and has leveled off since about 2004.[26] Many MATC students are part time (the full-time equivalency is about 13,000 students), but each and every student requires support services, regardless of how many courses she takes.[27]

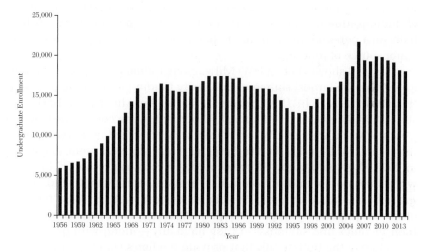

Figure 1.   Undergraduate enrollment at the University of Wisconsin–Milwaukee: 1956–2014.

Source: University of Wisconsin–Milwaukee Office of Assessment and Institutional Research, *Fact Book 2013–14.*

[24]Carl and Kappelman, "Post-Graduation Plans," 1.
[25]University of Wisconsin–Madison Academic Planning and Institutional Research, *Data Digest* 2014–2015, 1.
[26]Milwaukee Area Technical College, "College Enrollment," 2–3.
[27]Wisconsin Technical College System, "Fact Book 2014," 3.

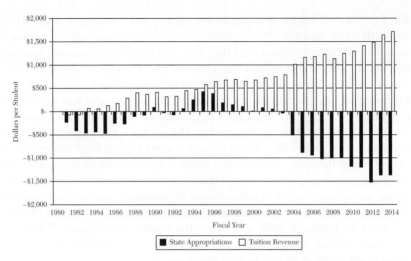

Figure 2.   Trends in state appropriations and tuition revenue per student at the University of Wisconsin–Milwaukee: 1980–2014. All figures are constant 1980 dollars.

Sources: Wisconsin State Appropriations and Tuition, Redbook Budget — Exhibit II and University of Wisconsin System, "Fact Book 13–14."

Funding for public higher education in Milwaukee has not kept   30
pace with enrollment growth. As state support has declined, tuition
has grown, practically in lock step (see fig. 2). As a result, the share
of undergraduate education funded by the state has dropped substantially on a per-student basis, to the point that tuition now constitutes the
major source of funding.

Figure 3 shows that, at UW–Milwaukee, tuition passed state support
to become the largest source of university funding around the time that
this study began. In 1990, when students like Alicia were born, the
state of Wisconsin covered almost 70 percent of the costs of instruction
for undergraduates at UW–Milwaukee, passing just 30 percent on in
the form of tuition. But by the time our study students went to college
in 2008, they paid about 60 percent of the costs via tuition.[28] In other
words, the public and private roles reversed, a trend reflected across
the nation. Once, going to UW–Milwaukee cost relatively little because
of the large state subsidy. Today, students and the families must use
their incomes and savings — if they have any — along with grants and
loans to pay the tuition bills that provide the lion's share of the school's
budget, which receives only a modest contribution from the state.

This funding switch flies in the face of what we know about expected
payoffs. The individual returns on higher education are more uncertain
than ever because students are far from assured that they will complete

[28]Calculations are based on inflation adjusted state appropriations per FTE (Full Time
Equivalent student) and tuition revenue per FTE at UW–Milwaukee over time, using data
provided by UW–Milwaukee.

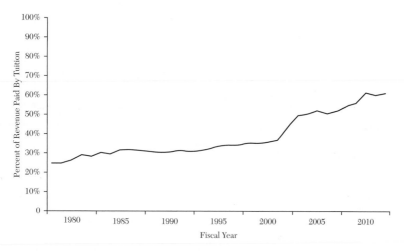

Figure 3.   Trends in percent of per-student revenue paid by tuition at University of Wisconsin–Milwaukee: 1980–2014.

Sources: University of Wisconsin System, "Wisconsin State Appropriations and Tuition, Redbook Budget — Exhibit II," and University of Wisconsin System, *Fact Book 13-14*.

a degree and are more likely to accumulate debt in the attempt. At the same time, we are more certain of the general benefits to the public of increasing the number of college graduates. The city of Milwaukee is struggling with economic growth partly because of inadequate human capital resources.

Similar trends in state support have occurred across Wisconsin public higher education but cuts to state support have not fallen equally on all institutions. As figure 4 (p. 220) shows, costs have been shifted far more quickly to students at UW–Milwaukee than to students attending the other universities throughout the state. Whereas in 1990 there was essentially parity among UW–Milwaukee, UW–Madison, and the rest of the eleven universities in the UW System, there are now clear disparities. Today, students at UW–Madison cover about 65 percent of their costs of instruction, while students at UW–Milwaukee shoulder more than 80 percent. Yet they are, on average, much less well off financially.

One in five applicants for financial aid in the UW System attend UW–Milwaukee. One in four applicants for financial aid in the Wisconsin Technical College System attend MATC. Together, the two institutions process about 45,000 FAFSAs annually. A huge concentration of the state's moderate and low-income students attend these two schools. Out of the forty-two public colleges and universities around the state, MATC and UW–Milwaukee together are home to 21 percent of all financial aid recipients. The result is de facto economic segregation in higher education.

Many familiar with Wisconsin higher education readily acknowledge that UW–Milwaukee has long been treated as a stepchild in the 35

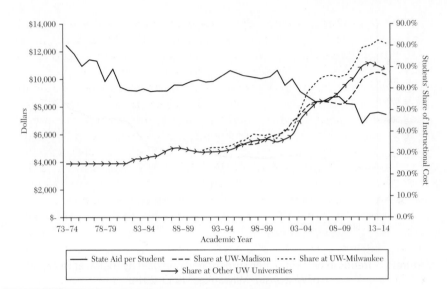

Figure 4.   Trends in Wisconsin state appropriations per student and student's share of instructional costs at UW–Milwaukee, UW–Madison, and the UW System comprehensive universities: 1973–2014. Instructional cost is simply the sum of state appropriations and tuition. This is a common practice throughout higher education — it is not the true cost of instruction. All figures are in constant 2014 dollars.

Source: Wisconsin Legislative Fiscal Bureau, "University of Wisconsin System Overview: [2015]."

UW System.[29] In fact, administrators at UW–Madison and the board of regents fought against the creation of a four-year institution in Milwaukee, believing it would undermine UW–Madison's prestige and compete for resources.[30] Today, the two research institutions are part of the same system but they are vastly different. Not only does the state appropriate more than twice as much per full-time equivalent student for UW–Madison than it does for UW–Milwaukee, but the institutions serve divergent populations. Ninety percent of UW–Milwaukee undergraduates come from Wisconsin, and 39 percent of them are first-generation students. At UW–Madison, just under 63 percent of undergraduates come from Wisconsin (and the school just eliminated any cap on out-of-state enrollment), and less than 20 percent are first-generation.[31] More than 33 percent of new freshman at UW–Milwaukee are students of color, while at UW–Madison, this figure is less than 10 percent.[32]

[29]Torinus, "Can Ray Cross Reposition the UW System?" Many familiar with Wisconsin higher education readily acknowledge that UW–Milwaukee has long been treated as a stepchild in the UW System, just as Milwaukee Area Technical College is treated as a stepchild in its region. See Day, Allen, and Henken, "Milwaukee Area Technical College's Fiscal Condition."

[30]Zlotocha, "A 'Blue Shirt' UW for Milwaukee," 93–95.

[31]Committee for Undergraduate Recruitment, Admissions, and Financial Aid, "CURAFA Report to the University Committee," 3–10; and Savidge, "Regents Give UW–Madison OK to Enroll More Out-of-State Students."

[32]University of Wisconsin System, "Student Statistics, Fall 2014–15."

At UW–Milwaukee, around 1,800 first-year students need math remediation each year, compared to fewer than fifty at UW–Madison.[33] Higher education scholar Estela Bensimon and her colleagues describe the UW–Milwaukee situation perfectly as "diversity without equity."[34]

The risk of dropping out for all students, including Pell recipients, is very high in Milwaukee. At UW–Milwaukee, about three in ten students do not return for a second year of college,[35] while only about 14 percent of entering students complete a bachelor's degree within four years. By six years, that rate rises to 43 percent. But these averages conceal sizable disparities. In fall 2012, 1,279 Pell recipients enrolled at UW–Milwaukee for the first time. One year later, 440 of them were no longer enrolled.[36] In contrast, all but forty-seven of 833 Pell recipients who enrolled at UW–Madison at the same time returned for a second year. While 44 percent of students who did not receive a Pell Grant at UW–Milwaukee graduated within six years, just 33 percent of Pell recipients did so. Pell recipients were more than twice as likely to earn a bachelor's degree at UW–Madison, where their graduation rate lagged behind that of other students, but was still 73 percent.

In fall 2012, 251 African American students enrolled at UW–Milwaukee for the first time. One year later, a hundred of them were no longer enrolled. By comparison, that same year UW–Milwaukee enrolled 2,403 white students and retained 1,723 for a second year of college (a retention rate of 72%, compared to 60% for African Americans).[37] Similarly, barely half of students who enter MATC for the first time and enroll full time return to the institution for a second year of schooling, and just 15 percent complete an associate degree within three years.[38]

The Milwaukee Price

The price of attending public higher education in Milwaukee is higher than it is elsewhere in Wisconsin in both absolute and relative terms (see table 1). Our students in Milwaukee had an average expected family contribution of $1,370, almost identical to the $1,372 average expected family contribution of students living in other parts of the state. Yet, the sticker price of attending college was about $2,300 more in Milwaukee, and the net price was about $1,600 more. There are two major reasons for this. First, the Milwaukee students faced higher tuition and

[33]University of Wisconsin System, "Report on Remedial Education in the UW System," 24.

[34]Center for Urban Education, "Partners in Achieving Equity."

[35]University of Wisconsin System, "Retention and Graduation: 2013–14," 5–25.

[36]In contrast, UW–Milwaukee enrolled 2,119 white students that year and retained 1,534 for a second year of college (for a retention rate of 72%, compared to 66% for Pell recipients). Ibid., 22–25.

[37]Ibid., 19–20.

[38]Milwaukee Area Technical College, "Student Retention Trends," 3; and Milwaukee Area Technical College, "Student Persistence," 2.

TABLE 1 College costs facing WSLS students for the first year of college, by location		
	MILWAUKEE	ALL OTHER LOCATIONS
Ability to pay:		
Expected family contribution	$1,370	$1,372
Percentage zero EFC	41	38
Percentage negative EFC	15	16
Average EFC among those with negative	−$7,986	−$11,005
Costs of attending college:		
Official cost of attendance	$16,901	$14,551
Tuition and fees	$6,411	$4,934
Nontuition costs	$10,490	$9,617
Grant aid:		
Total grants (not including WSG)	$6,810	$6,048
Pell amount	$3,390	$2,967
Percentage with state need-based grant	96	87
Average amount among recipients	$2,003	$1,899
Percentage with institutional grants	7	16
Average amount among recipients	$2,192	$862
Price students must pay:		
Net price	$10,091	$8,503
Net price as percentage of parent income	42	34

Source. WSLS data.

Note. Cost of attendance for four-year students includes housing on campus, and for two-year students it includes housing off campus not with family. Parent income and net price as percentage of parent income are reported at the median. All differences between columns are significant at $p < .05$, other than EFC differences, and state need-based grant "average amount among recipients." "Ability to pay" and "costs of attending college" include the entire sample. (Milwaukee, $n = 541$; other, $n = 2,459$.) "Grant aid" and "price students must pay" include subsample where financial aid is observed (Milwaukee, $n = 253$; other, $n = 1,185$.)

fees, largely due to the lower levels of state subsidies offered to UW–Milwaukee. Second, while students in Milwaukee were more likely to receive state grant aid (96% vs. 88% elsewhere), they were less likely to receive institutional aid (7% vs. 16%).

In 2012–13, Milwaukee Area Technical College awarded about $375,000 in institutional grants and emergency aid to a total of about 475 students. That was a substantial increase from 2008–9, the year our students began college, when just $100,000 of institutional grant support was distributed to about two hundred students.[39] Over at UW–Milwaukee, in 2012–13, just 217 first-year students received institutional support, totaling about $630,000.[40]

Thus, in 2008, Milwaukee students faced a net price about 19 percent higher than that of students enrolled elsewhere. That net price was 42 percent of family income in Milwaukee, compared to 34 percent elsewhere.

In order to cover the remaining price, students in Milwaukee were more likely than those in the rest of Wisconsin to take loans (see table 2). Seventy-four percent of students attending college in Milwaukee took loans for their first year of college, compared to 53 percent of students attending college elsewhere in Wisconsin. Among those who borrowed, students from Milwaukee took about $1,200 more than other Wisconsin students. Most importantly, not only were students in Milwaukee more likely to accept federal loans, but they were also much more likely to take out private loans — 15 percent of Milwaukee students made use of a private loan compared to just 1 percent of students outside of Milwaukee. In some cases, students in Milwaukee accepted private loans without first using federal loans. Nationally, about half of all private loan borrowers have not first taken all available federal loans, according to the Institute for College Access and Success.[41] Thirteen percent

TABLE 2 Strategies for covering college costs for the first year of college, by location

	MILWAUKEE	ALL OTHER LOCATIONS
Percentage with any loan	74	53
Average amount	$5,224	$3,973
Percentage with federal subsidized loan	63	62
Percentage with federal unsubsidized loan	46	25
Average amount	$2,363	$1,859
Percentage with nonfederal loans	15	1
Percentage employed (any job)	55	63
Percentage with work-study	2	13

Source. WSLS data.

Note. All differences between columns, except for subsidized loans, are significant at $p < .05$. Sample includes the subsample where financial aid is observed (Milwaukee, $n = 253$; other, $n = 1,185$). "Percentage employed" includes students who responded to first-year survey questions on employment (Milwaukee, $n = 376$; other, $n = 1,751$).

[39]Milwaukee Area Technical College, "Transforming Lives," 28.
[40]Author's calculations using U.S. Department of Education, "Integrated Postsecondary Education Data System Data Center."
[41]Institute for College Access and Success, "Private Loans," 1.

of students who enter loan repayment after leaving MATC default on their federal loan within two years, and 4 percent of students from UW–Milwaukee do as well....[42]

The Slow Road to Success

José went to college to pursue a degree in criminal justice and dreamed of joining the Milwaukee Police Department. He was a new father: his girlfriend had given birth to a baby girl shortly after he graduated from high school. He did not file as an independent student, which would have helped him qualify for about $2,500 more in grant aid, because he didn't know he could. (He did not learn about this important option until midway through his second year of college.) His father, the family's breadwinner, earned $45,000 during José's senior year of high school, and the family's expected contribution was $3,000 a year. After putting together his partial Pell Grant, state grants, a $3,500 subsidized loan, and the payment his father made, José still needed to come up with over $8,000. He worked to cover this amount and also tried to earn a bit more to save for his daughter's future. But it was not easy to secure steady employment. The first semester of college he worked at Sears, in a job he'd begun during the summer after high school. A few months later he reported, "Now they're giving me like twenty, twenty-five hours so as time goes on they are increasing. But they are also hiring other people—it's like, okay, you're barely starting to give me more hours and you're hiring more people now?" Within six months, he had to pick up a second job cleaning an office building because Sears was only offering him five hours a week. "I have a little girl," he said. "Five hours a week isn't going to help me at all."

José tried to balance out his uneven earnings by scrimping and saving his financial aid. Whenever he received a check for living expenses, he put most of it aside for a rainy day. He described in detail how he put together a budget and stuck to it, distinguishing between what was "a need situation versus just a want situation." José even opened a second savings account for his financial aid check, referring to it as separate from "my money," by which he meant his earnings from work.

He was grateful for the grants he received, which he said made college possible for him. He also explained how useful the financial aid administrators were in interpreting the aid rules and regulations. "They are really helpful.... They get everything straightened out. They tell you what exactly you need, what you need to do, or they tell you: 'Go do it online, go to the library and just come back and see me.' So every time I've gone there it's been, 'Do this, this, and this. Ok you're done.

---

[42]Twenty percent of students who enter loan repayment after leaving Milwaukee Area Technical College default on their federal loan within three years, and 5.6 percent of students from UW–Milwaukee do as well. Data from 2012 come from author's calculations using U.S. Department of Education, "Integrated Postsecondary Education Data System Data Center."

Just wait two or three weeks until you get your refund check, you can check it on the computer.' It's been real easy with financial aid to go through the process of it."

Midway through his third semester of college José dropped the second job, in part because the commuting time it required did not feel worthwhile, especially in the winter. Then a new challenge arrived: his father lost his job, a casualty of the recession. "He was earning $500 per week," José explained, "But with unemployment the most he can get is $360, and that's just barely putting us through with the bills. I try to help out whatever I can ... there is only so much you can do, you know, and I have my little daughter, too. It's like you're just sitting here feeling hopeless and saying, I wish I had a better job, or I wish I took a year off of school and worked at a real job."

Given that his parents no longer had any earnings, his family was no longer expected to contribute to college, and his grant aid increased by about $4,000. This helped, but the financial demands on José increased as well. His family needed his help to stay afloat more than ever. José responded by working more: during his first year of college he earned $9,500, and during his second, he earned more than $14,000. This meant he worked nearly full time, about thirty-five hours a week.

"Money has a lot to do with stress," he said. "You're worried about it—that's a lot of money, I don't know if I can pay for this. People obviously start thinking, should I just stop going to school? This is a lot of money I'm paying for classes, I shouldn't be here, and I'm going to go to work somewhere to make money."

The irregular hours of his job continued to frustrate him, especially when he needed more hours than his employer offered. He explained: "Right now, I would say anywhere from fifteen to twenty-five per week. Every week it's different. One week I might have ten and one week I have twenty-five, eighteen, twenty—they are pretty different. Before that I was getting twenty-five or thirty hours."

Despite this instability, José persisted in school because he was confident that over the long-term joining the police department would help his family. "If I can get ahead, I can help them out. That's one of a lot of things I think about. If I hit the lottery the first thing I would do is help my parents out, pay for whatever they have to pay.... They've helped me out so much, they support me going to school, they just keep pushing me and pushing me." He understood that his prospects for providing this support were slim if he did not finish his degree, and spoke of wanting to ensure that other people in his community knew that too. "High school is almost nothing nowadays. You *have* to get a degree.... There's a few people with college degrees and they have bigger and better jobs.... [Employers] see them as smarter people—they actually did their work, did their time in school and things like that." Even as he pursued his studies, José understood that not everyone had the opportunity to obtain a college degree. "There are people who just can't afford it. They can't go to school and do those things that people like me can do—for them it's really unfair." Drawing distinctions between his family (which at the time had no income other than unemployment benefits and his meager paycheck) and the families of his high school classmates, José noted that when college was not possible, most people went to a different institution, "the house of corrections." He aimed to join the police force in part because he wanted to address gang violence in the city, explaining, "I used to be with them... but there's no sense to it.... I used to be scared, wondering, 'Oh what if this happens?'... I know the streets, and I know where this stuff happens. Not many cops know that, and I do." After six semesters of attending school full time, José finally completed an associate degree. "It seems like it's been forever—a two-year degree is supposed to take two years," he noted. But he was "relieved, happy, and proud of myself" that he was finally done. He planned on going back to school to pursue a bachelor's degree if he didn't find a steady job within two years. He would need to finish that degree in no more than six semesters, since he was already halfway to using up his lifetime Pell Grant allotment.[43]

The sheer will exhibited by students like José, who grow up and 50 attend college in Milwaukee, is amazing given the obstacles they face. Writing in the *Washington Monthly*, journalist Jamaal Abdul-alim described what he learned from reporting on the situation facing African American students at UW–Milwaukee: "With remarkable consistency, the students I met... who were struggling or failing to graduate blamed themselves almost entirely for their fate. That willingness to take personal responsibility is admirable, and very American, and something to be encouraged, not undermined. But the truth is that the fault isn't all with them."[44] Abdul-alim described in detail the need that many Milwaukee students have for intensive advising to help them navigate their colleges and universities. Our data complement his and suggest that the advising needs to go further, to help students seeking degrees as they also traverse the many broken institutions in the city. Too often, researchers trying to understand problems in higher education fail to recognize that challenges created by the health and human services systems and the criminal justice system also affect college graduation rates. While researchers focus on what is happening inside school, critical parts of the undergraduate experience—parts that determine the success or failure of many students—occur outside.

No Full-Time Students Here

Anne went to college seeking the skills to find a good job and a better life for herself and her mom. She grew up in public housing, as her mom cycled on and off of assistance from the state, struggling to hold a job

[43]In 2011, shortly after José completed his associate degree, President Obama signed into law the Consolidated Appropriations Act, which limited students to twelve semesters of Pell Grant eligibility during their lifetime. This change affected all students regardless of when or where they received their first Pell Grant, and there were no exceptions.

[44]Abdul-alim, "Dropouts Tell No Tales."

while coping with lupus (a chronic inflammatory disease characterized by fatigue and fever, joint pain, a rash, and shortness of breath). Anne attended one of the city's better high schools where she completed an International Baccalaureate program. During high school she was focused and maintained good grades. When she finished, she chose the university closest to her: "I only had to catch one or two buses there and we were able to afford it," she said during our first interview with her, four months after she'd begun school.

What felt affordable to Anne? In her first year of college she received a Pell of almost $4,000 and a state grant of nearly $2,900. But that was the extent of the grants offered, so her net price was over $9,000—despite an expected family contribution of just $250. How would Anne and her family pay a price thirty-six times higher than what the federal needs analysis determined they could afford?

This price was only manageable for Anne because she lived at home, she and her mother did not pay for housing, and she received food stamps as well as support from the local energy company to cover the electric bill. She was very careful with her financial aid dollars, which she saved. "I put it up, in an envelope in a little area in my room where I know that it is," she said. With those supports in place, she was able to focus on school.

She had a strong, positive relationship with her mother and felt that she received a great deal of emotional support from her. During her first semester, she attended full time, taking math, English, German, and an economics of business class for a total of sixteen credits. She estimated that she spent six hours a day in class and two hours a day studying. The classes were interesting and she was making friends—life seemed to be going smoothly, and for this, she was grateful. But in contrast to many of her peers, she had some doubt that she would achieve her goals, estimating on a survey that it was only "somewhat likely" she would complete a bachelor's degree.

One day in November, there was a knock at her door. The manager 55 of the apartment building where she lived informed her that by enrolling in college full time, she had violated the terms of the family's subsidized housing. "The management says that if you're living at home and you're in college, you're not allowed to enroll full time. So I had to switch [to part time]."

Anne did not know what policy dictated this situation, but thought it might have to do with perceptions of undergraduate behavior. "I guess they're saying that they think if you're in college you might try and turn it into a dormitory, throwing parties or getting out of control. I don't really understand it. But if I didn't agree to go part time we would have to move. So I really didn't have a choice, we couldn't just up and move like that."

Anne had run up against her local public housing authority's definition of eligibility, which deprioritized full-time students. If the idea of this policy was to prevent people from taking advantage of public housing, it made little sense in Anne's case. She was not a student seeking a new, inexpensive place to live for a few years but, rather, a long-term resident who had lived in the building for years and who had very few assets of her own—and little ability to make significant money without a college degree. Public housing policies regarding college enrollment run the gamut. Ironically, had Anne's housing been funded by Section 8, she would have been pushed to remain enrolled full time—if she dropped to part time, she would no longer have been considered her mother's dependent and would not have been allowed to remain in the unit.[45]

Anne could see no recourse, so she switched to taking classes part time. Her adviser typed up a letter she gave her landlord to prove that she had done this. It seems that no one at Anne's school, including her academic adviser and financial aid counselor, called the housing authority in an effort to clarify the situation or intervene. But as a part-time student, Anne received much less grant aid. She was also concerned that by going part time and taking just three classes at a time, it would take longer to complete her degree. "I think it was going to take me five years anyway, and now maybe six." She spoke with her adviser about her concerns on several occasions but did not know whom else to turn to.

It became increasingly difficult for Anne and her mom to make ends meet. She had been helping to pay for household expenses with her financial aid, contributing half the grocery costs not covered by food stamps. Anne had few options. If she worked, her income could disqualify them from receiving the housing subsidy. She did not want to take student loans. They were not truly a form of financial aid, she said, and they felt risky. She did not have a credit card and said, "I'm not really sure if I want one." She did not feel that debt was an acceptable way to get funds or that it was appropriate to take out a loan to enjoy a better life. She also worried that it would be hard to get out of debt.

At the same time, she knew college was worth the investment. By the time she was thirty, Anne planned to have a master's degree and work in accounting or finance. She thought that this path would mean she would earn about $50,000 a year. "I really like working with numbers and math," she said, "This will mean I am able to support myself and my mom." In contrast, if she left school without a degree, she estimated that she would earn just $20,000 a year. 60

She continued to try to focus on school: "I just keep trying to bring my GPA up higher each semester and stay focused, working harder." But then midway through her second year of college her mom grew very ill and went into the hospital. "It was all at once, everything was coming at me, and I didn't know what to do," she said.

---

[45]U.S. Department of Housing and Urban Development, *Barriers to Success*, 6.

I mean, it's one thing when you're prepared for a situation but when it comes out of nowhere as far as the bills and food and then still going to school, well, I just didn't know what to do. When she got out of the hospital she needed someone with her twenty-four hours a day. I was like, what am I gonna do for school? Because I didn't want to miss something. I would rather miss school than miss being at home, but what was I going to do at home all day? My aunts and uncles would help out, too, but they needed to take care of their families too. I was just like, what am I gonna do, with everything coming at me at once?

After a few weeks of supporting her mom, the stress took its toll. "I get a lot of headaches," she said, also noting that though she felt hungry she was too sick to eat. On a survey she indicated that she often felt blue and bothered by things that didn't used to bother her. She was depressed and lonely. Yet she was trying to make things work at school. In the midst of these difficulties, she reassessed the likelihood that she would complete the bachelor's degree and decided that it was now "extremely likely."

Low-income families face a different situation than middle- and upper-income families when a family member becomes sick, because the family can't pay someone to help out. Hiring a home health aide is not affordable.

Anne's teachers seem to have had little indication that she was facing troubles at home, and she was having difficulty telling them about it. "I don't really have time to go and see them because I have to go home.... They [professors that she needed to talk to] have office hours from 3 to 5 P.M. on Tuesdays but I have to go home every day. I've been wanting to go but every time I plan on going, I have to go talk with a doctor about what's wrong with my mom. So I'm never able to go."

While her mom was in the hospital Anne took an exam she had not studied for, having been with her mom all night before. "I wanted to tell him [the professor] but I just didn't. I didn't want people to keep feeling sorry for me. It was a thing for myself—to not really want to put it out there.... So I just took the exam and went back to the hospital and that was it."

As her mom began to feel better, Anne focused again on school. She began doing her homework long before it was due and got tutoring for her accounting and statistics courses. Her grades began to improve. The apartment manager had returned to tell her that she could now enroll full time, but Anne did not trust this information. It seemed to her like some kind of "loophole," and she did not want to go through the paperwork and hassle to switch again. "I'll just stay part time and go from there, because I have a feeling that if I do go back to full time she will come with something else where I have to go back down again. She's like that—she will just find something else to bother you with. I will just keep everything calm and stay part time and I can deal with it."

Anne's feelings of confusion and distrust were neither uncommon nor unusual, but they had significant implications. For each additional semester she stayed in school, the costs mounted and the odds of completing a degree diminished. Many researchers have found that low-income people are subject to rules that are not explained to them and that are often inconsistent.[46]

The last time we saw Anne was at the start of her third year of college. She'd taken a job working at a local retailer called the Boston Store, completed her midterm exams, and said that her mom was feeling better. She was trying to work a little, but not too much, since she needed money to pay the bills but did not want to make too much and be disqualified from her housing. Half of her earnings went to help her mom with the bills and half went into savings, which she now kept in a bank rather than in an envelope. She seemed on track with school, and administrative records indicate that she remained continuously enrolled until spring 2014. But then she left, without a degree in hand. After six years of attending college we don't know why she gave up.

No End in Sight

The low degree-completion rates of our students in Milwaukee stand in stark contrast to the rest of the students in this study, but they are generally consistent with the pattern observed for Milwaukee college students overall, and students of color in particular. Six years after beginning college, just 41 percent of Milwaukee students in our study had completed a credential of any kind, compared to 52 percent of students in the rest of the state (table 3, p. 231). They were far less likely to have completed an associate degree, whether in two years (2% in Milwaukee vs. almost 11% elsewhere) or six years (7% in Milwaukee vs. almost 24% elsewhere). Bachelor's degree completion rates in Milwaukee lagged as well, though not by nearly as much. Students in Milwaukee were more likely to still be enrolled in college but not yet have a degree as of spring 2014. But most importantly, students in Milwaukee who left college without a credential were much more likely to be in debt (66% vs. 47% elsewhere) and held on average $1,500 more debt (from the first year of college) than their peers in the rest of the state. They carried these incomplete college experiences and compromised financial circumstances back into a community already full of financial hardship.

---

[46]For further reading, see Levine, *Ain't No Trust*; Edin and Lein, *Making Ends Meet*; and Soss, Fording, and Schram, *Disciplining the Poor.*

TABLE 3   Degree attainment rates for WSLS students, by location

	MILWAUKEE	ALL OTHER LOCATIONS	DIFFERENCE TEST
Completed any certificate or degree within six years	41%	52%	• • •
Completed certificate or associate degree:			
Within 2 years	2%	11%	
Within 3 years	4%	17%	• • •
Within 6 years	7%	24%	• • •
Completed bachelor's degree:			
Within 4 years	11%	15%	
Within 5 years	33%	41%	• • •
Within 6 years	44%	50%	
No degree, still enrolled in 2014:	18%	11%	• • •
Number of terms enrolled over six years	10	9	• • •
No degree, not enrolled	41%	37%	
Percentage who borrowed during first year of college	66%	47%	• •
Amount borrowed among borrowers' first year of college	$5,123	$3,762	• • •

Source. WSLS data.

Note. Numbers are weighted averages and may not sum to 100 percent. Associate degrees and certificates are combined because National Student Clearinghouse data doesn't make it possible to distinguish between the two. Completion and enrollment include the entire sample (Milwaukee, $n = 541$; other, $n = 2,459$). "Percentage who took loans during the first year" and "average amount borrowed" use the subsample where financial aid is observed (Milwaukee, $n = 253$; other, $n = 1,185$).
• • $p < .05$
• • • $p < .01$

ENGAGING THE TEXT

1. What challenges does the Milwaukee area create for students, according to Goldrick-Rab? How does the city or town your college is located in compare economically, socially, and demographically with Milwaukee? Why might areas like Milwaukee have a special need for the benefits of higher education?

2. Which of the three students Goldrick-Rab describes faces the most significant obstacles, in your opinion? Why? What could Alicia and Anne have done differently to reach their educational goals?

Ted Rall/Dist. by Andrews McMeel Syndication

3. How does your own economic situation compare with those of Alicia, José, and Anne? How much do you have to pay to cover tuition, books, and other related living expenses once you have deducted all the scholarships, grants, and loans you receive? How do you make up the difference? Write a journal entry about how the cost of your college education affects you.

4. What, according to Goldrick-Rab, is "the Milwaukee price" (p. 221)? Is Goldrick-Rab suggesting that the Wisconsin system of higher education is intentionally discriminatory, and if so, would you agree?

5. Given the outcomes of the three students Goldrick-Rab profiles in this selection and the data that she offers on college completion rates and student debt, what advice would you give a low-income high school senior trying to decide whether or not she should go to college? Why?

6. **Thinking Rhetorically** Assess Goldrick-Rab's use of statistical and anecdotal evidence. Why do you think she chose to mix these two different forms of support? Which form of substantiation seems more persuasive or informative to you, and why?

EXPLORING CONNECTIONS

7. How might Jean Anyon (p. 136) explain the inequities that Goldrick-Rab observes in Wisconsin's system of higher education? Why do you think such dramatic disparities exist between the campuses discussed in this selection?

8. Drawing on Goldrick-Rab's examination of how college costs affect low-income students and Peggy Orenstein's discussion of campus sexual assault (p. 193), write a journal entry or a brief essay about the myths and realities of college life. How much guidance did your college give you about sexual harassment and the economic challenges that students face? Were these issues adequately addressed during admission and orientation?

EXTENDING THE CRITICAL CONTEXT

9. Explore the racial and economic inequities in the higher education system of your state. How do the demographics and budgets of the "elite" public colleges and universities compare with those that serve primarily working-class students? Should all public colleges in your state receive the same funding per student? Why or why not?

10. Poll your class to find out how your fellow students cover the costs of college. How many receive Pell grants and college scholarships? How many have taken out loans or have jobs? Who pays a relatively low "price" for their education? Who pays the most? Then discuss what you think could or should be done to make this situation more equitable.

11. Research the student debt crisis. How many students leave college today in debt, and what is the average debt that students carry? How long does it take to repay? What has the government done to address this situation, and, in your view, what else should be done?

FURTHER CONNECTIONS

1. In the United States, the notion of schooling as the road to success has always been balanced by a pervasive distrust of education. This phenomenon, known as "American anti-intellectualism," grew out of the first settlers' suspicion of anything that reminded them of the "corrupting" influences of European sophistication. American anti-intellectualism shows up in pop-cultural portrayals of school, students, and teachers. It also emerges in political attacks on the value of formal schooling and the college degree. In groups, discuss current cultural attitudes toward schooling. How are schools, teachers, and students portrayed in recent films and television series? What have you heard recently from political and business leaders about the value of a college education? How powerful does anti-intellectualism seem to be in American culture today, and who might benefit from this tendency to belittle or mistrust education?

2. Go online to review the latest results of the Program for International Student Assessment (PISA), the most respected worldwide comparative evaluation of student learning (http://www.oecd.org/pisa/keyfindings/pisa-2012-results.htm). Where does the United States stand in relation to other nations in terms of student performance in mathematics, reading, and science? How can you explain the fact that despite thirty years of educational reform efforts, U.S. scores trail those of nations like Slovenia, Vietnam, Italy, Spain, and Russia?

3. Educational researchers estimate that 25 percent to 60 percent of the ninth graders in America's urban public schools will drop out before graduation. Do additional research on the "dropout crisis" to learn more about the scope and causes of this problem. Why are so many Americans opting out of school today? Which groups are most in danger of leaving school before graduation? What can be done to encourage young Americans to stay in school?

4. Over the past few years, educational critics across the political spectrum have voiced concern about declining success rates for males in America's schools and colleges. During the last decade, for example, the number of women in America's colleges and universities has steadily increased until, today, women outnumber men in almost every academic field outside the so-called hard sciences. Research this issue to learn more about how males are faring in America's schools. Do you think, as some critics claim, that school is particularly hostile to boys? What other reasons might explain declines in male educational achievement over the past two decades?

THE WILD WIRED WEST
Myths of Progress on the Tech Frontier

Library of Congress/Getty Images

Museum of Science & Industry, Chicago/Getty Images

FAST FACTS

1. In 1984, women accounted for 37% of computer science majors in the United States. Since 2010, the percentage of women studying computer science has held steady at just 18%.

2. Four out of ten Americans have personally experienced harassment or abusive behavior online, and two-thirds have witnessed online harassment of others. A quarter of African Americans report harassment online because of their race.

3. 34% of all American students and 55% of LGBTQ students have experienced cyberbullying. Two-thirds of those affected say it hurt their ability to learn and made them feel unsafe at school.

4. 91% of Americans feel they have lost control of how personal information is collected and used by companies; technology experts generally agree that few individuals have the time, energy, or resources to protect themselves from corporate surveillance.

5. Roughly three quarters of Americans say they are worried about robots replacing human workers in the future. They anticipate that the economy won't create new jobs to replace those lost to automation, and they worry that automation will worsen economic inequality.

6. Following the 2016 presidential election, 64% of Americans said that fake news stories online had left the nation confused about basic facts. However, 84% also feel either "very confident" or "somewhat confident" that they can recognize fake news when they see it.

7. Between 2002 and 2015, traffic at the white supremacist website Stormfront grew from 5,000 to 300,000 registered users. In July of 2016, the alt-right site Daily Stormer surpassed Stormfront with double that number of users. In 2014, the Southern Poverty Law Center documented that nearly 100 murders had been committed by Stormfront followers.

Data from (1) "Disturbing Drop of Women in Computing Field," *Fortune*, March 26, 2015, http://fortune.com/2015/03/26/report-the-number-of-women-entering-computing-took-a-nosedive/; (2) "Online Harassment 2017," Pew Research Center, 2017, http://www.pewinternet.org/2017/07/11/online-harassment-2017/; (3) Cyberbullying Research Center, https://cyberbullying.org/new-national-bullying-cyberbullying-data; stopbullying.gov, https://www.stopbullying.gov/media/facts/index.html#ftn17; (4) "The State of Privacy in Post-Snowden America," Pew Research Center, 2016, http://www.pewresearch.org/fact-tank/2016/09/21/the-state-of-privacy-in-america/; (5) "Automation in Everyday Life," Pew Research Center, 2017, http://assets.pewresearch.org/wp-content/uploads/sites/14/2017/10/03151500/PI_2017.10.04_Automation_FINAL.pdf; (6) "Many Americans Believe Fake News Is Sowing Confusion," Pew Research Center, 2016, http://www.journalism.org/2016/12/15/many-americans-believe-fake-news-is-sowing-confusion/; (7) "Eye of the Stormer," Southern Poverty Law Center, https://www.splcenter.org/fighting-hate/intelligence-report/2017/eye-stormer.

A LITTLE OVER A CENTURY AGO, two of America's most powerful cultural myths crossed paths at the Chicago World's Fair. Officially known as the World's Columbian Exposition, the fair celebrated the 400th anniversary of Christopher Columbus's "discovery" of the Americas and served as a showcase for the cultural and economic achievements of the United States. By any measure, it was an astonishing event. The exposition included 200 temporary buildings spread over 635 acres on Chicago's South Side, and during its brief six-month run it attracted over 27 million visitors — more than half the U.S. population in 1893. Dubbed the "White City" because of the elaborate stucco buildings that lined its central court, the exposition featured 65,000 exhibits. It also witnessed a number of notable firsts. Americans drank their first carbonated sodas and ate their first hamburgers at the fair; they also got their first taste of Aunt Jemima's Pancake Mix and Pabst Blue Ribbon beer. Visitors lined up to take rides on the world's first Ferris wheel, a 265-foot-high behemoth that accommodated 2,160 passengers in 36 closed gondolas. They also had the chance to stroll along the "Midway Plaisance," the nation's first modern amusement park, which included rides along with food concessions, sideshow attractions, and corporate-sponsored exhibits. Over the next century, the World's Exposition would have an enduring influence on American pop culture. The "Midway" would inspire a series of theme parks across the country, from Coney Island to Disneyland, and the charms of the White City itself would echo in Chicagoan L. Frank Baum's depiction of the Emerald City in his 1899 classic *The Wonderful Wizard of Oz*.

But the fair had a more telling legacy. During a meeting of the American Historical Association held on fair grounds, a young University of Wisconsin professor delivered a scholarly paper that would influence American politics and culture for decades to come. In "The Significance of the Frontier in American History," Frederick Jackson Turner argued that life on the western frontier — and not the influence of Europe — had left an indelible impression on American society. According to Turner's famous "Frontier Thesis," life on the untamed, ever-advancing western edge of the United States had freed Americans from the old subservient traditions and authoritarian ways of Europe's feudal past. The western frontier had transformed Americans into fiercely independent, freedom-loving individualists who had a

PF-(bygone1)/Alamy Stock Photo

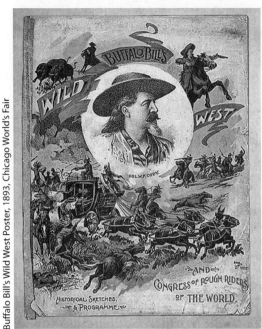

Buffalo Bill's Wild West Poster, 1893, Chicago World's Fair

"practical, inventive turn of mind" and who were "full of restless nervous energy." According to Turner, the demands of frontier life had toughened American settlers and endowed them with the kind of self-reliance citizens needed in a democratic society. Turner's optimistic vision of the West as a purifying and liberating force reassured generations of Americans that their nation was indeed the "land of the free and the home of the brave." It also provided a ready-made explanation for America's growing sense of its superiority and national destiny as it moved into the new century.

Ironically, while Turner was explaining that the real American Frontier had "closed," or ceased to exist, because civilization had finally overwhelmed the last traces of open prairie in 1890, the myth of the "Old West" was just getting started. As Turner finished delivering his paper, William Frederick Cody was selling tickets to the first "Buffalo Bill's Wild West Show" just outside the Exposition's gates. The frontier may have "closed" in 1890, but the national fantasy of cowboy independence and heroism was just taking hold of America. Buffalo Bill's traveling Wild West show offered melodramatic dime-novel reenactments of famous Western scenes and cowboy exploits, from the "Great Train Robbery" to "Custer's Last Stand" at the Battle of Little Bighorn. It popularized mythic American figures like Annie Oakley, Calamity Jane, Wild Bill Hickok, and Sitting Bull. Thanks to Buffalo Bill's theatrics, the glamor of the untamed Old West and the rough

PF-(bygone1)/Alamy Stock Photo

virtues of the cowboy hero would have a lasting impact on American culture.

Yet, as we know today, the future didn't belong to the cowboy. Technology was the real star of the 1893 World Exposition. Almost every exhibit featured some type of technological innovation calculated to awe the visiting public. At night, the fair's main buildings were illuminated by 100,000 incandescent lights in a stunning demonstration of how electrification would transform American cities in the coming century. The Machinery Hall proudly displayed the 127 dynamos that powered the fair's exhibits and mechanical attractions. In the Electricity Hall, Thomas Edison demonstrated his newly invented phonograph, gave rides in electric horseless carriages, and introduced visitors to the kinetoscope and the prospect of moving pictures. There was even an exhibit showcasing the "Kitchen of the Future," complete with electric stove, refrigerator, and dishwasher.

Since then, Americans have never stopped dreaming about the promise of technology. After the turn of the twentieth century, it seemed as if electricity and the innovations it made possible would solve every problem and satisfy every need. In his book *The Big Switch*, author Nicholas Carr describes the impact of the American cult of technology in the early twentieth century:

> Electrification, people were told, would cleanse the earth of disease and strife, turning it into a pristine new Eden. "We are soon to have everywhere," wrote one futurist, "smoke annihilators, dust absorbers, ozonators, sterilizers of water, air, food, and clothing, and accident preventers on the streets, elevated roads, and subways. It will become next to impossible to contract disease germs or get hurt in the city."
>
> People expected emerging technologies to "eliminate blizzards, droughts, and other climatic extremes." They believed that new forms of transportation would "practically eliminate distances" and that under the sway of technical expertise, we would all live in harmony like "cogs" in a "wonderful mechanism . . . acting in response to the will of a corporate mind . . ."

Technology, then, and not the Wild West, fueled the myths of progress and perfection that drove American dreams in the twentieth century. For our models of heroism and the promise of a better life, we began to look forward to the frontier of technological innovation and not backward to the dusty past of buffalo hunters and cowboy roundups. And modern science didn't disappoint. The incandescent light was followed by the automobile, the airplane, television, antibiotics, the X-ray, space flight, nuclear power, the laser, and the digital computer. Every new technology spawned a new batch of inflated expectations. Television would put an end to ignorance. Antibiotics would eliminate disease. Nuclear energy would free us from dependence on coal and oil. Space travel would lead to colonies on the moon by the year 2001.

Of course, the myth of technology also has its dark side. Every dream of technological utopia has inspired a corresponding nightmare vision of tech-driven apocalypse. Today, in the new digital age of social media and increasingly intelligent machines, most of us are well-versed in high-tech fantasies and fears. We all know how scientists can accidentally unleash deadly microbes — or resurrected dinosaurs — and how computers designed to help us do the impossible might someday turn a glowing eye against us when the chips are down. Yet, as a nation, we're still hooked on the idea that technology can solve our problems and that innovations like the cell phone and the Internet have changed our lives for the better.

In this chapter, you'll have the chance to explore the myth of technological progress and reflect on how emerging technologies are changing our society and our sense of self. We begin with a selection by two committed techno-dreamers. In "Our Future Selves," Google's Eric Schmidt and Jared Cohen invite us to contemplate what life will be like in a "connected" world of super smartphones, household robots, and intelligent apartments that anticipate our every need. The next group of four selections highlights the impact of social media and the Internet on our daily lives. In "Has the Smartphone Destroyed a Generation?" Jean M. Twenge explores how the lives of American teens have changed, often for the worse, since the introduction of the iPhone. Next, in "Let's Get Lost," poet and professor Kenneth Goldsmith encourages us to ignore the critics and to embrace our smartphones, video games, and favorite social networking sites. A proponent of all things tech, Goldsmith is fascinated by the Internet's power to make us more creative, connected, and self-aware. The two selections that follow offer a darker view of the Internet and social media. In "Zoë and the Trolls," Noreen Malone examines the misogynist underbelly of the Internet as she relates the story of video game developer Zoë Quinn and her experience of online sexual harassment during the Gamergate incident of 2014. Jessie Daniels brings the first half of the chapter to a close by examining the growth of online racism and its connection with American politics in "Twitter and White Supremacy, A Love Story."

The chapter's Visual Portfolio presents images that invite further thinking about American attitudes toward technology. Here you'll find photos dramatizing the impact of smartphones and social media, screenshots of websites that raise questions about Internet culture, and even an image of Sophia, the first humanoid robot to be granted citizenship.

The last section of the chapter takes a more focused look at future challenges posed by our relationship with technology. In "How We Sold Our Souls — and More — to the Internet Giants," security expert Bruce Schneier explains that we now live in a world of "mass surveillance" and warns that we have become dangerously dependent on a handful of Internet "overlords." In "You Will Lose Your Job to a Robot — And Sooner Than You Think," Kevin Drum wonders how we will cope in a world where most workers have been replaced by self-educating Artificial Intelligence systems and most humans have little or nothing to do. Historian and best-selling author Yuval Noah Harari rounds off the chapter by challenging us to consider whether "Dataism" is replacing both religion and humanism as the dominant belief system of our time.

In the chapter's Further Connections section, you'll find more ideas for research projects on the impact of the Internet and the role it may have played in the 2016 presidential election. This section also includes activities related to the role of technology in policing and "transhumanism"— the idea of using emerging technologies to transcend normal human limitations.

Sources

Carr, Nicholas. *The Big Switch: Rewiring the World from Edison to Google*. New York: W. W. Norton & Company, 2008. Print.

Hine, Robert H., and John Mack Faragher. *The American West: A New Interpretive History*. New Haven, CT: Yale University Press, 2000. Print.

Turner, Frederick Jackson. "The Significance of the Frontier in American History." *An American Primer*, edited by Daniel Boorstin. Chicago: University of Chicago Press, 1966. Print.

"The World's Columbian Exposition: Idea, Experience, Aftermath." American Studies at the University of Virginia Hypertexts. 1 August 1996. 24 June 2015.

BEFORE READING

- In groups, discuss your own expectations about technology and the future. How, in your view, will technology change your life in the next twenty years? How will expanding access to the Internet and emerging technologies affect the way we learn, work, and socialize? What inventions or technological breakthroughs are you looking forward to, and why?

- Inventory the different types of technology you use every day. What kinds of technology do you use most frequently? Which technologies could you live without if you had to? On a scale of 1 to 10, how would you rate your technology dependence?

OUR FUTURE SELVES

ERIC SCHMIDT AND JARED COHEN

What will the technological future look like? It may come as no surprise that to former Google CEO Eric Schmidt it seems pretty bright. Since Thomas Edison ushered in the age of electricity from his lab in Menlo Park, Americans have dreamed of future technological utopias where all material needs are satisfied and all social problems solved. Today, the invention of the computer and the development of the Internet have inspired a new generation of high-tech dreamers. In this selection from their best-selling 2013 book, *The New Digital Age: Reshaping the Future of People, Nations, and Business*, Eric Schmidt and Jared Cohen offer their vision of how technology will change the world and revolutionize our lives. Trained as an electrical engineer, Eric Schmidt (b. 1955) joined Google founders Sergey Brin and Larry Page in 2001 as the company's CEO. In 2011 he left that position to become Google's first Executive Chairman, a post he held until stepping down in 2017. Jared Cohen (b. 1981) has served as an adviser to former Secretaries of State Condoleezza Rice and Hillary Clinton. Currently, he is the CEO of Jigsaw, a subsidiary of Google's parent company, Alphabet Inc., dedicated to finding technological solutions to global problems. Cohen is also an adjunct senior fellow at the Council on Foreign Relations. Eric Schmidt's most recent publication, coauthored with Jonathan Rosenberg, is *How Google Works* (2014).

SOON EVERYONE ON EARTH WILL BE CONNECTED. With five billion more people[1] set to join the virtual world, the boom in digital connectivity will bring gains in productivity, health, education, quality of life and myriad other avenues in the physical world—and this will be true for everyone, from the most elite users to those at the base of the economic pyramid. But being "connected" will mean very different things to different people, largely because the problems they have to solve differ so dramatically. What might seem like a small jump forward for some—like a smartphone priced under $20—may be as profound for one group as commuting to work in a driverless car is for another. People will find that being connected virtually makes us feel more equal—with access to the same basic platforms, information and online resources—while significant differences persist in the physical world. Connectivity will not solve income inequality, though it will alleviate some of its more intractable causes, like lack of available education and economic opportunity. So we must recognize and celebrate innovation in its own context. Everyone will benefit from connectivity, but not equally, and how those differences manifest themselves in the daily lives of people is our focus here.

Increased Efficiency

Being able to do more in the virtual world will make the mechanics of our physical world more efficient. As digital connectivity reaches the far corners of the globe, new users will employ it to improve a wide range of inefficient markets, systems and behaviors, in both the most and least advanced societies. The resulting gains in efficiency and productivity will be profound, particularly in developing countries where technological isolation and bad policies have stymied growth and progress for years, and people will do more with less.

The accessibility of affordable smart devices, including phones and tablets, will be transformative in these countries. Consider the impact of basic mobile phones[2] for a group of Congolese fisherwomen today. Whereas they used to bring their daily catch to the market and watch it slowly spoil as the day progressed, now they keep it on the line, in the river, and wait for calls from customers. Once an order is placed, a fish is brought out of the water and prepared for the buyer. There is no need for an expensive refrigerator, no need for someone to guard it at night, no danger of spoiled fish losing their value (or poisoning customers), and there is no unnecessary overfishing. The size of these women's

---

[1]*The World in 2011: ICT Facts and Figures,* International Telecommunication Union (ITU), accessed October 10, 2012, http://www.itu.int/ITUD/ict/facts/2011/material/ICTFactsFigures2011.pdf. The above source shows that as of 2011 35 percent of the world's population is online. We factored in population increase projections to estimate five billion set to join the virtual world. [All notes are Schmidt and Cohen's, except 13 and 17.]

[2]This fisherwomen thought experiment came out of a conversation with Rebecca Cohen, and while we put it in the context of the Congo, the example belongs to her.

market can even expand as other fishermen in surrounding areas coordinate with them over their own phones. As a substitute for a formal market economy (which would take years to develop), that's not a bad work-around, for these women or the community at large.

Mobile phones are transforming how people in the developing world access and use information, and adoption rates are soaring. There are already more than 650 million mobile-phone users in Africa,[3] and close to 3 billion across Asia.[4] The majority of these people are using basic-feature phones[5] — voice calls and text messages only — because the cost of data service in their countries is often prohibitively expensive, so that even those who can buy Web-enabled phones or smartphones cannot use them affordably. This will change, and when it does, the smartphone revolution will profoundly benefit these populations.

Hundreds of millions of people today are living the lives of their grandparents, in countries where life expectancy is less than sixty years, or even fifty in some places,[6] and there is no guarantee that their political and macroeconomic circumstances will improve dramatically anytime soon. What is new in their lives and their futures is connectivity. Critically, they have the chance to bypass earlier technologies, like dial-up modems, and go directly to high-speed wireless connections, which means the transformations that connectivity brings will occur even more quickly than they did in the developed world. The introduction of mobile phones is far more transformative than most people in modern countries realize. As people come online, they will quite suddenly have access to almost all the world's information in one place in their own language. This will even be true for an illiterate Maasai cattle herder in the Serengeti, whose native tongue, Maa, is not written[7] — he'll be able to verbally inquire about the day's market prices and crowd-source the whereabouts of any nearby predators, receiving a spoken answer from his device in reply. Mobile phones will allow formerly isolated people to connect with others very far away and very different from themselves. On the economic front, they'll find ways to use the new tools at their disposal to enlarge their businesses, make them more efficient and maximize their profits, as the fisherwomen did much more locally with their basic phones.

[3]"Africa's Mobile Phone Industry 'Booming,'" BBC, November 9, 2011, http://www.bbc.co.uk/news/world-africa-15659983.

[4]See mobile cellular subscriptions, Asia & Pacific, year 2011, in "Key ICT Indicators for the ITU/BDT Regions (Totals and Penetration Rates)," International Telecommunication Union (ITU), ICT Data and Statistics (IDS), updated November 16, 2011, http://www.itu.int/ITU-D/ict/statistics/at_glance/KeyTelecom.html.

[5]Ibid. Compare mobile cellular subscriptions to active mobile broadband subscriptions for 2011.

[6]"Country Comparison: Life Expectancy at Birth," CIA, World Fact Book, accessed October 11, 2012, https://www.cia.gov/library/publications/the-world-factbook/rankorder/2102rank.html#top.

[7]One of the authors spent the summer of 2001 in this remote village, without electricity, running water, or a single cell phone or landline. During a return trip in the fall of 2010, many of the Maasai women had crafted beautiful beaded pouches to store their cell phones in.

What connectivity also brings, beyond mobile phones, is the ability to collect and use data. Data itself is a tool, and in places where unreliable statistics about health, education, economics and the population's needs have stalled growth and development, the chance to gather data effectively is a game-changer. Everyone in society benefits from digital data, as governments can better measure the success of their programs, and media and other nongovernmental organizations can use data to support their work and check facts. For example, Amazon is able to take its data on merchants and, using algorithms, develop customized bank loans to offer them—in some cases when traditional banks have completely shut their doors. Larger markets and better metrics can help create healthier and more productive economies.

And the developing world will not be left out of the advances in gadgetry and other high-tech machinery. Even if the prices for sophisticated smartphones and robots to perform household tasks like vacuuming remain high, illicit markets like China's expansive *"shanzhai"* network[8] for knock-off consumer electronics will produce and distribute imitations that bridge the gap. And technologies that emerged in first-world contexts will find renewed purpose in developing countries. In "additive manufacturing," or 3-D printing, machines can actually "print" physical objects by taking three-dimensional data about an object and tracing the contours of its shape, ultra-thin layer by ultra-thin layer, with liquid plastic or other material, until the whole object materializes.[9] Such printers have produced a huge range of objects, including customized mobile phones, machine parts and a full-sized replica motorcycle.[10] These machines will definitely have an impact on the developing world. Communal 3-D printers in poor countries would allow people to make whatever tool or item they require from open-source templates—digital information that is freely available in its edited source—rather than waiting on laborious or iffy delivery routes for higher-priced premade goods.

In wealthier countries 3-D printing will be the perfect partner for advanced manufacturing. New materials and products will all be built uniquely to a specification from the Internet and on demand by a machine run by a sophisticated, trained operator. This will not replace the acres of high-volume, lowest-cost manufacturing present in many industries, but it will bring an unprecedented variety to the products used in the developed world.

As for life's small daily tasks, information systems will streamline many of them for people living in those countries, such as integrated

---

[8]Nicholas Schmidle, "Inside the Knockoff-Tennis-Shoe Factory," *New York Times Magazine*, August 19, 2010, Global edition, http://www.nytimes.com/2010/08/22/magazine/22fake-t.html?pagewanted=all.

[9]"The Printed World: Three-Dimensional Printing from Digital Designs Will Transform Manufacturing and Allow More People to Start Making Things," *Economist*, February 10, 2011, http://www.economist.com/node/18114221.

[10]Patrick Collinson, "Hi-Tech Shares Take US for a Walk on the High Side," *Guardian* (Manchester), March 16, 2012, http://www.guardian.co.uk/money/2012/mar/16/hi-tech-shares-us.

clothing machines (washing, drying, folding, pressing and sorting) that keep an inventory of clean clothes and algorithmically suggest outfits based on the user's daily schedule. Haircuts will finally be automated and machine-precise. And cell phones, tablets and laptops will have wireless recharging capabilities, rendering the need to fiddle with charging cables an obsolete nuisance. Centralizing the many moving parts of one's life into an easy-to-use, almost intuitive system of information management and decision making will give our interactions with technology an effortless feel. As long as safeguards are in place to protect privacy and prevent data loss, these systems will free us of many small burdens — including errands, to-do lists and assorted "monitoring" tasks — that today add stress and chip away at our mental focus throughout the day. Our own neurological limits, which lead us to forgetfulness and oversights, will be supplemented by information systems designed to support our needs. Two such examples are memory prosthetics — calendar reminders and to-do lists — and social prosthetics, which instantly connect you with your friend who has relevant expertise in whatever task you are facing.

By relying on these integrated systems, which will encompass both 10 the professional and the personal sides of our lives, we'll be able to use our time more effectively each day — whether that means having the time to have a "deep think," spending more time preparing for an important presentation or guaranteeing that a parent can attend his or her child's soccer game without distraction. Suggestion engines that offer alternative terms to help a user find what she is looking for will be a particularly useful aid in efficiency by consistently stimulating our thinking processes, ultimately enhancing our creativity, not pre-empting it. Of course, the world will be filled with gadgets, holograms that allow a virtual version of you to be somewhere else, and endless amounts of content, so there will be plenty of ways to procrastinate, too — but the point is that when you choose to be productive, you can do so with greater capacity.

Other advances in the pipeline in areas like robotics, artificial intelligence and voice recognition will introduce efficiency into our lives by providing more seamless forms of engagement with the technology in our daily routines. Fully automated human-like robots with superb AI [artificial intelligence] abilities will probably be out of most people's price range for some time, but the average American consumer will find it affordable to own a handful of different multipurpose robots fairly soon. The technology in iRobot's Roomba vacuum cleaner, the progenitor of this field of consumer "home" robots (first introduced in 2002), will only become more sophisticated and multipurpose in time. Future varieties of home robots should be able to handle other household duties, electrical work and even plumbing issues with relative ease.

We also can't discount the impact that superior voice-recognition software will have on our daily lives. Beyond searching for information online and issuing commands to your robots (both of which are possible today), better voice recognition will mean instant transcription of any-thing you produce: e-mails, notes, speeches, term papers. Most people speak much faster than they type, so this technology will surely save many of us time in our daily affairs—not to mention helping us avoid cases of carpal tunnel syndrome. A shift toward voice-initiated writing may well change our world of written material. Will we learn to speak in paragraphs, or will our writing begin to mirror speech patterns?

Everyday use of gesture-recognition technology is also closer than we think. Microsoft's Kinect, a hands-free sensor device for the Xbox 360 video-game console that captures and integrates a player's motion, set a world record in 2011 as the fastest selling consumer-electronics device in history, with more than eight million devices sold in the first sixty days on the market. Gestural interfaces will soon move beyond gaming and entertainment into more functional areas; the futuristic information screens displayed so prominently in the film *Minority Report*—in which Tom Cruise used gesture technology and holographic images to solve crimes on a computer—are just the beginning. In fact, we've already moved beyond that—the really interesting work today is building "social robots" that can recognize human gestures and respond to them in kind, such as a toy dog that sits when a child makes a command gesture.[11]

And, looking further down the line, we might not need to move physically to manipulate those robots. There have been a series of excit-ing breakthroughs in thought-controlled motion technology—directing motion by thinking alone—in the past few years. In 2012, a team at a robotics laboratory in Japan demonstrated successfully that a person lying in an fMRI machine (which takes continuous scans of the brain to measure changes in blood flow) could control a robot hundreds of miles away just by imagining moving different parts of his body.[12] The subject could see from the robot's perspective, thanks to a camera on its head, and when he thought about moving his arm or his legs, the robot would move correspondingly almost instantaneously. The possibilities of thought-controlled motion, not only for "surrogates" like separate robots but also for prosthetic limbs, are particularly exciting in what they portend for mobility-challenged or "locked in" individuals—spinal-cord-injury patients, amputees and others who cannot communicate or move in their current physical state.

More Innovation, More Opportunity

That the steady march of globalization will continue apace, even 15 accelerate, as connectivity spreads will come as no surprise. But what might surprise you is how small some of the advances in technology,

[11]Sarah Constantin, "Gesture Recognition, Mind-Reading Machines, and Social Robotics," *H+ Magazine*, February 8, 2011, http://hplusmagazine.com/2011/02/08/gesture-recognition-mind-reading-machines-and-social-robotics/.

[12]Helen Thomson, "Robot Avatar Body Controlled by Thought Alone," *New Scientist*, July 2012, 19–20.

when paired with increased connection and interdependence across countries, will make your world feel. Instant language translation, virtual-reality interactions and real-time collective editing—most easily understood today as wikis—will reshape how firms and organizations interact with partners, clients and employees in other places. While certain differences will perhaps never be fully overcome—like cultural nuance and time zones—the ability to engage with people in disparate locations, with near-total comprehension and on shared platforms, will make such interactions feel incredibly familiar.

Supply chains for corporations and other organizations will become increasingly disaggregated, not just on the production side but also with respect to people. More effective communication across borders and languages will build trust and create opportunities for hardworking and talented individuals around the world. It will not be unusual for a French technology company to operate its sales team from Southeast Asia, while locating its human-resources people in Canada and its engineers in Israel. Bureaucratic obstacles that prevent this level of decentralized operation today, like visa restrictions and regulations around money transfers, will either become irrelevant or be circumvented as digital solutions are discovered. Perhaps a human-rights organization with staff living in a country under heavy diplomatic sanctions will pay its employees in mobile money credits, or in an entirely digital currency.

As fewer jobs require a physical presence, talented individuals will have more options available to them. Skilled young adults in Uruguay will find themselves competing for certain types of jobs against their counterparts in Orange County. Of course, just as not all jobs can or will be automated in the future, not every job can be conducted from a distance—but more can than you might think. And for those living on a few dollars per day, there will be endless opportunities to increase their earnings. In fact, Amazon Mechanical Turk,[13] which is a digital task-distribution platform, offers a present-day example of a company outsourcing small tasks that can be performed for a few cents by anyone with an Internet connection. As the quality of virtual interactions continues to improve, a range of vocations can expand the platform's client base; you might retain a lawyer from one continent and use a Realtor from another. Globalization's critics will decry this erosion of local monopolies, but it should be embraced, because this is how our societies will move forward and continue to innovate. Indeed, rising connectivity should *help* countries discover their competitive advantage—it could be that the world's best graphic designers come from Botswana, and the world just doesn't know it yet.

[13] **Amazon Mechanical Turk:** A crowd-sourcing Internet marketplace that allows individuals to earn money doing tasks inside computer applications that computers are currently unable to do by themselves. The original Mechanical Turk was a chess-playing "robot" that created a sensation when it toured Europe in the eighteenth century defeating famous opponents like Napoleon Bonaparte and Benjamin Franklin. Not really a robot at all, the "Turk" actually contained a live chess master hidden behind a mechanical façade. [Eds.]

This leveling of the playing field for talent extends to the world of ideas, and innovation will increasingly come from the margins, outside traditional bastions of growth, as people begin to make new connections and apply unique perspectives to difficult problems, driving change. New levels of collaboration and cross-pollination across different sectors internationally will ensure that many of the best ideas and solutions will have a chance to rise to the top and be seen, considered, explored, funded, adopted and celebrated. Perhaps an aspiring Russian programmer currently working as a teacher in Novosibirsk will discover a new application of the technology behind the popular mobile game Angry Birds, realizing how its game framework could be used to improve the educational tools he is building to teach physics to local students. He finds similar gaming software that is open source and then he builds on it. As the open-source movement around the world continues to gain speed (for governments and companies it is low cost, and for contributors the benefits are in recognition and economic opportunities to improve and enlarge the support ecosystems), the Russian teacher-programmer will have an enormous cache of technical plans to learn from and use in his own work. In a fully connected world, he is increasingly likely to catch the eyes of the right people, to be offered jobs or fellowships, or to sell his creation to a major multinational company. At a minimum, he can get his foot in the door.

Innovation can come from the ground up, but not all local innovation will work on a larger scale, because some entrepreneurs and inventors will be building for different audiences, solving very specific problems. This is true today as well. Consider the twenty-four-year-old Kenyan inventor Anthony Mutua, who unveiled at a 2012 Nairobi science fair an ultrathin crystal chip he developed that can generate electricity when put under pressure.[14] He placed the chip in the sole of a tennis shoe and demonstrated how, just by walking, a person can charge his mobile phone.[15] (It's a reminder of how bad the problems of reliable and affordable electricity, and to a lesser extent short battery life, are for many people—and how some governments are not rushing to fix the electricity grids—that innovators like Mutua are designing microchips that turn people into portable charging stations.) Mutua's chip is now set to go into mass production,[16] and if that successfully brings down the cost, he will have invented one of the cleverest designs that no one outside the developing world will ever use, simply because they'll never need to. Unfortunately, the level of a population's access to technology is often determined by external factors, and even if power and electricity problems are eventually solved (by the government or by citizens), there is no telling what new roadblocks will prevent certain groups from reaching the same level of connectivity and opportunity as others.

[14]"Shoe Technology to Charge Cell Phones," *Daily Nation*, May 2012, http://www.nation.co.ke/News/Shoe+technology+to+charge+cell+phones++/-/1056/1401998/-/view/printVersion/-/sur34lz/-/index.html.
[15]Ibid.
[16]Ibid.

The most important pillar behind innovation and opportunity — education — will see tremendous positive change in the coming decades as rising connectivity reshapes traditional routines and offers new paths for learning. Most students will be highly technologically literate, as schools continue to integrate technology into lesson plans and, in some cases, replace traditional lessons with more interactive workshops. Education will be a more flexible experience, adapting itself to children's learning styles and pace instead of the other way around. Kids will still go to physical schools, to socialize and be guided by teachers, but as much, if not more, learning will take place employing carefully designed educational tools in the spirit of today's Khan Academy,[17] a nonprofit organization that produces thousands of short videos (the majority in science and math) and shares them online for free. With hundreds of millions of views on the Khan Academy's YouTube channel already, educators in the United States are increasingly adopting its materials and integrating the approach of its founder, Salman Khan — modular learning tailored to a student's needs. Some are even "flipping" their classrooms, replacing lectures with videos watched at home (as homework) and using school time for traditional homework, such as filling out a problem set for math class.[18] Critical thinking and problem-solving skills will become the focus in many school systems as ubiquitous digital-knowledge tools, like the more accurate sections of Wikipedia, reduce the importance of rote memorization.

For children in poor countries, future connectivity promises new access to educational tools, though clearly not at the level described above. Physical classrooms will remain dilapidated; teachers will continue to take paychecks and not show up for class; and books and supplies will still be scarce. But what's new in this equation — connectivity — promises that kids with access to mobile devices and the Internet will be able to experience school physically *and* virtually, even if the latter is informal and on their own time.

In places where basic needs are poorly met by the government, or in insecure areas, basic digital technologies like mobile phones will offer safe and inexpensive options for families looking to educate their children. A child who cannot attend school due to distance, lack of security or school fees will have a lifeline to the world of learning if she has access to a mobile phone. Even for those children without access to data plans or the mobile Web, basic mobile services, like text messages and IVR (interactive voice response, a form of voice-recognition technology), can provide educational outlets. Loading tablets and mobile phones with high-quality education applications and entertainment content before they are sold will ensure that the "bandwidth poor,"

[17] **Khan Academy:** A nonprofit, online educational organization that provides micro lectures on thousands of academic topics via YouTube videos. [Eds.]

[18] Clive Thompson, "How Khan Academy Is Changing the Rules of Education," *Wired Magazine*, August 2011, posted online July 15, 2011, http://www.wired.com/magazine/2011/07/ff_khan/.

who lack reliable connectivity, will still benefit from access to these devices. And for children whose classrooms are overcrowded or under-staffed, or whose national curriculum is dubiously narrow, connectivity through mobile devices will supplement their education and help them reach their full potential, regardless of their origins. Today numerous pilot projects exist in developing countries that leverage mobile tech-nology to teach a wide range of topics and skills, including basic liter-acy for children and adults, second languages and advanced courses from universities. In 2012, the MIT Media Lab tested this approach in Ethiopia[19] by distributing preloaded tablets to primary-age kids without instructions or accompanying teachers.[20] The results were extraordi-nary: within months the kids were reciting the entire alphabet and writ-ing complete sentences in English. Without the connectivity that will be ubiquitous in the future, there are limits to what any of these efforts can accomplish today.

Just imagine the implications of these burgeoning mobile or tablet-based learning platforms for a country like Afghanistan, which has one of the lowest rates of literacy in the world.[21] Digital platforms, whether presented in simple mobile form or in more sophisticated ways online, will eventually be able to withstand any environmental turbulence (political instability, economic collapse, perhaps even bad weather) and continue to serve the needs of users. So while the educational expe-rience in the physical world will remain volatile for many, the virtual experience will increasingly become the more important and predict-able option. And students stuck in school systems that teach narrow curriculums or only rote memorization will have access to a virtual world that encourages independent exploration and critical thinking.

A Better Quality of Life

In tandem with the wide variety of functional improvements in your daily life, future connectivity promises a dazzling array of "quality of life" improvements: things that make you healthier, safer and more engaged. As with other gains, there remains a sliding scale of access here, but that doesn't make them any less meaningful.

The devices, screens and various machines in your future apart-   25 ment will serve a purpose beyond utility—they will offer entertainment, wanted distraction, intellectual and cultural enrichment, relaxation and opportunities to share things with others. The key advance ahead is per-sonalization. You'll be able to customize your devices—indeed, much of

[19] Nicholas Negroponte, "EmTech Preview: Another Way to Think About Learning," *Technology Review*, September 13, 2012, http://www.technologyreview.com/view/429206/emtech-preview-another-way-to-think-about/.

[20] David Talbot, "Given Tablets but No Teachers, Ethiopian Children Teach Themselves," *Technology Review*, October 29, 2012, http://www.technologyreview.com/news/506466/given-tablets-but-no-teachers-ethiopian-children-teach-themselves/.

[21] "Field Listing: Literacy," CIA, World Fact Book, accessed October 11, 2012, https://www.cia.gov/library/publications/the-world-factbook/fields/2103.html#af.

the technology around you—to fit your needs, so that your environment reflects your preferences. People will have a better way to curate their life stories and will no longer have to rely on physical or online photo albums, although both will still exist. Future videography and photography will allow you to project any still or moving image you've captured as a three-dimensional holograph. Even more remarkable, you will be able to integrate any photos, videos and geographic settings that you choose to save into a single holographic device that you will place on the floor of your living room, instantaneously transforming the space into a memory room. A couple will be able to re-create their wedding ceremony for grandparents who were too ill to attend.

What you can watch on your various displays (high-quality LCD—liquid crystal display—screens, holographic projections or a handheld mobile device) will be determined by you, not by network-television schedules. At your fingertips will be an entire world's worth of digital content, constantly updated, ranked and categorized to help you find the music, movies, shows, books, magazines, blogs and art you like. Individual agency over entertainment and information channels will be greater than ever, as content producers shift from balkanized protectiveness to more unified and open models, since a different business model will be necessary in order to keep the audience. Contemporary services like Spotify, which offers a large catalog of live-streaming music for free, give us a sense of what the future will look like: an endless amount of content, available anytime, on almost any device, and at little or no cost to users, with copyrights and revenue streams preserved. Long-standing barriers to entry for content creators are being flattened as well; just as YouTube can be said to launch careers today[22] (or at least offer fleeting fame), in the future, even more platforms will offer artists, writers, directors, musicians and others in every country the chance to reach a wider audience. It will still require skill to create quality content, but it will also be easier to assemble a team with the requisite skills to do this—say, an animator from South Korea, a voice actor from the Philippines, a storyboarder from Mexico and a musician from Kenya—and the finished product may have the potential to reach as wide an audience as any Hollywood blockbuster.

Entertainment will become a more immersive and personalized experience in the future. Integrated tie-ins will make today's product placements seem passive and even clumsy. If while watching a television show you spot a sweater you want or a dish you think you'd like to cook, information including recipes or purchasing details will be readily available, as will every other fact about the show, its story lines, actors and locations. If you're feeling bored and want to take an hour-long holiday, why not turn on your holograph box and visit Carnival in Rio? Stressed? Go spend some time on a beach in the Maldives. Worried

---

[22]The Korean K-pop star Psy's fame reached global proportions almost overnight as the video he created for his song "Gangnam Style" became the most-watched YouTube video ever within a span of three months.

your kids are becoming spoiled? Have them spend some time wandering around the Dharavi slum in Mumbai. Frustrated by the media's coverage of the Olympics in a different time zone? Purchase a holographic pass for a reasonable price and watch the women's gymnastics team compete right in front of you, live. Through virtual-reality interfaces and holographic-projection capabilities, you'll be able to "join" these activities as they happen and experience them as if you were truly there. Nothing beats the real thing, but this will be a very close second. And if nothing else, it will certainly be more affordable. Thanks to these new technologies, you can be more stimulated, or more relaxed, than ever before.

You'll be safer, too, at least on the road. While some of the very exciting new possibilities in transportation, like supersonic tube commutes and suborbital space travel, are still far in the distance, ubiquitous self-driving cars are imminent. Google's fleet of driverless cars, built by a team of Google and Stanford University engineers, has logged hundreds of thousands of miles without incident, and other models will soon join it on the road. Rather than replacing drivers altogether, the liminal step will be a "driver-assist" approach, where the self-driving option can be turned on, just as an airline captain turns on the autopilot. Government authorities are already well versed on self-driving cars and their potential — in 2012, Nevada became the first state to issue licenses to driverless cars,[23] and later that same year California also affirmed their legality.[24] Imagine the possibilities for long-haul truck-driving. Rather than testing the biological limits of human drivers with thirty-hour trips, the computer can take over primary responsibility and drive the truck for stretches as the driver rests.

The advances in health and medicine in our near future will be among the most significant of all the new game-changing developments. And thanks to rising connectivity, an even wider range of people will benefit than at any other time in history. Improvements in disease detection and treatment, the management of medical records and personal-health monitoring promise more equitable access to health care and health information for potentially billions more people when we factor in the spread of digital technology.

The diagnostic capability of your mobile phone will be old news. 30
(*Of course* you will be able to scan body parts the way you do bar codes.) But soon you will be benefiting from a slew of physical augmentations designed to monitor your well-being, such as microscopic robots in your circulatory system that keep track of your blood pressure,

[23] Chris Gaylord, "Ready for a Self-Driving Car? Check Your Driveway," *Christian Science Monitor*, June 25, 2012, http://www.csmonitor.com/Innovation/Tech/2012/0625/Ready-for-a-self-driving-car-Check-your-driveway.

[24] James Temple, "California Affirms Legality of Driverless Cars," *The Tech Chronicles* (blog), *San Francisco Chronicle*, September 25, 2012, http://blog.sfgate.com/techron/2012/09/25/california-legalizes-driverless-cars/; Florida has passed a similar law. See Joann Muller, "With Driverless Cars, Once Again It Is California Leading the Way," *Forbes*, September 26, 2012, http://www.forbes.com/sites/joannmuller/2012/09/26/with-driverless-cars-once-again-it-is-california-leading-the-way/.

detect nascent heart disease and identify early-stage cancer. Inside your grandfather's new titanium hip there will be a chip that can act as a pedometer, monitor his insulin levels to check for the early stages of diabetes, and even trigger an automated phone call to an emergency contact if he takes a particularly hard fall and might need assistance. A tiny nasal implant will be available to you that will alert you to airborne toxins and early signs of a cold.

Eventually these accoutrements will be as uncontroversial as artificial pacemakers (the first of which was implanted in the 1950s). They are the logical extensions of today's personal-health-tracking applications, which allow people to use their smartphones to log their exercise, track their metabolic rates and chart their cholesterol levels. Indeed, ingestible health technology already exists — the Food and Drug Administration (FDA) approved the first electronic pill in 2012. Made by a California-based biomedical firm called Proteus Digital Health, the pill carries a tiny sensor one square millimeter in size, and once the pill is swallowed, stomach acid activates the circuit and sends a signal to a small patch worn outside the body (which then sends its data to a mobile phone). The patch can collect information about a patient's response to a drug (monitoring body temperature, heart rate and other indicators), relay data about regular usage to doctors and even track what a person eats. For sufferers of chronic illnesses and the elderly particularly, this technology will allow for significant improvements: automatic reminders to take various medications, the ability to measure directly how drugs are reacting in a person's body and the creation of an instant digital feedback loop with doctors that is personalized and data-driven. Not everyone will want to actively oversee their health to this degree, let alone the even more detailed version of the future, but they probably will want their doctor to have access to such data. "Intelligent pills" and nasal implants will be sufficiently affordable so as to be as accessible as vitamins and supplements. In short order, we will have access to personal health-care systems run off of our mobile devices that will automatically detect if something is wrong with us based on data collected from some of the above-mentioned augmentations, prompt us with appointment options for a nearby doctor and subsequently (with consent) send all of the relevant data about our symptoms and health indicators to the doctor being consulted.

Tissue engineers will be able to grow new organs to replace patients' old or diseased ones, using either synthetic materials or a person's own cells. At the outset, affordability will limit the use. Synthetic skin grafts, which exist today, will give way to grafts made from burn victims' own cells. Inside hospitals, robots will take on more responsibilities, as surgeons increasingly let sophisticated machines handle difficult parts of certain procedures, where delicate or tedious work is involved or a wider range of motion is required.[25]

---

[25] Robotic surgical suites are already in operation in hospitals in the United States and Europe.

Advances in genetic testing will usher in the era of personalized medicine. Through targeted tests and genome sequencing (decoding a person's full DNA), doctors and disease specialists will have more information about patients, and what might help them, than ever before. Despite steady scientific progress, severe negative reactions to prescribed drugs remain a leading cause of hospitalization and death. Pharmaceutical companies traditionally pursue a "one-size-fits-all" approach to drug development, but this is due to change as the burgeoning field of pharmacogenetics continues to develop. Better genetic testing will reduce the likelihood of negative reactions, improve patients' chances and provide doctors and medical researchers with more data to analyze and use. Eventually, and initially only for the wealthy, it will be possible to design pharmaceutical drugs tailored to an individual's genetic structure. But this too will change as the cost of DNA sequencing drops below $100 and almost everything biological is sequenced, making it possible for a much broader segment of the world's population to benefit from highly specific, personalized diagnoses. . . .

The Upper Band

Connectivity benefits everyone. Those who have none will have some, and those who have a lot will have even more. To demonstrate that, imagine you are a young urban professional living in an American city a few decades from now. An average morning might look something like this:

There will be no alarm clock in your wake-up routine—at least, not in the traditional sense. Instead, you'll be roused by the aroma of freshly brewed coffee, by light entering your room as curtains open automatically, and by a gentle back massage administered by your high-tech bed. You're more likely to awake refreshed, because inside your mattress there's a special sensor that monitors your sleeping rhythms, determining precisely when to wake you so as not to interrupt a REM cycle. 35

Your apartment is an electronic orchestra, and you are the conductor. With simple flicks of the wrist and spoken instructions, you can control temperature, humidity, ambient music and lighting. You are able to skim through the day's news on translucent screens while a freshly cleaned suit is retrieved from your automated closet because your calendar indicates an important meeting today. You head to the kitchen for breakfast and the translucent news display follows, as a projected hologram hovering just in front of you, using motion detection, as you walk down the hallway. You grab a mug of coffee and a fresh pastry, cooked to perfection in your humidity-controlled oven—and skim new e-mails on a holographic "tablet" projected in front of you. Your central computer system suggests a list of chores your housekeeping robots should tackle today, all of which you approve. It further suggests that, since your coffee supply is projected to run out next Wednesday, you consider purchasing a certain larger-size container that it noticed currently on sale online. Alternatively, it offers a few recent reviews of other coffee blends your friends enjoy.

As you mull this over, you pull up your notes for a presentation you'll give later that day to important new clients abroad. All of your data—from your personal and professional life—is accessible through all of your various devices, as it's stored in the cloud, a remote digital-storage system with near limitless capacity. You own a few different and interchangeable digital devices; one is the size of a tablet, another the size of a pocket watch, while others might be flexible or wearable. All will be lightweight, incredibly fast and will use more powerful processors than anything available today.

You take another sip of coffee, feeling confident that you'll impress your clients. You already feel as if you know them, though you've never met in person, since your meetings have been conducted in a virtual-reality interface. You interact with holographic "avatars" that exactly capture your clients' movements and speech. You understand them and their needs well, not least because autonomous language-translation software reproduces the speech of both parties in perfect translations almost instantly. Real-time virtual interactions like these, as well as the ability to edit and collaborate on documents and other projects, makes the actual distance between you seem negligible.

As you move about your kitchen, you stub your toe, hard, on the edge of a cabinet—ouch! You grab your mobile device and open the diagnostics app. Inside your device there is a tiny microchip that uses low-radiation submillimeter waves to scan your body, like an X-ray. A quick scan reveals that your toe is just bruised, not broken. You decline the invitation your device suggests to get a second opinion at a nearby doctor's office.

There's a bit of time left before you need to leave for work—which 40 you'll get to by driverless car, of course. Your car knows what time you need to be in the office each morning based on your calendar and, after factoring in traffic data, it communicates with your wristwatch to give you a sixty-minute countdown to when you need to leave the house. Your commute will be as productive or relaxing as you desire.

Before you head out, your device reminds you to buy a gift for your nephew's upcoming birthday. You scan the system's proposed gift ideas, derived from anonymous, aggregated data on other nine-year-old boys with his profile and interests, but none of the suggestions inspire you. Then you remember a story his parents told you that had everyone forty and older laughing: Your nephew hadn't understood a reference to the old excuse "A dog ate my homework"; how could a dog eat his cloud storage drive? He had never gone to school before digital textbooks and online lesson plans, and he had used paper to do his homework so rarely—and used cloud storage so routinely—that the notion that he would somehow "forget" his homework *and* come up with an excuse like that struck him as absurd. You do a quick search for a robotic dog and buy one with a single click, after adding a few special touches he might like, such as a reinforced titanium skeleton so that he can ride on it. In the card input, you type: "Just in case." It will arrive at his house within a five-minute window of your selected delivery time.

You think about having another cup of coffee, but then a haptic device ("haptic" refers to technology that involves touch and feeling) that is embedded in the heel of your shoe gives you a gentle pinch—a signal that you'll be late for your morning meeting if you linger any longer. Perhaps you grab an apple on the way out, to eat in the backseat of your car as it chauffeurs you to your office.

If you are a part of the world's upper band of income earners (as most residents of wealthy Western countries are), you will have access to many of these new technologies directly, as owners or as friends of those who own them. You probably recognize from this morning routine a few things you have already imagined or experienced. Of course, there will always be the super-wealthy people whose access to technology will be even greater—they'll probably eschew cars altogether and travel to work in motion-stabilized automated helicopters, for example.

We will continue to encounter challenges in the physical world, but the expansion of the virtual world and what is possible online—as well as the inclusion of five billion more minds—means we will have new ways of getting information and moving resources to solve those problems, even if the solutions are imperfect. While there will remain significant differences between us, more opportunities to interact and better policy can help blur the edges.

ENGAGING THE TEXT

1. How do Schmidt and Cohen portray the impact of technology on the future? Which of the innovations they mention would you particularly look forward to, and why? Which of their predictions seem problematic or overly optimistic?

2. How do the authors see technology changing global human relations? Do you think that greater "connectivity" will necessarily make the world politically, culturally, and economically a better place? What other effects might it have?

3. What role has technology played in your own education? For example, how much experience have you had with technological "tools" like the Kahn Academy or concepts like the "flipped classroom"? Do you agree with Schmidt and Cohen that more technology in the classroom will increase critical thinking and problem solving?

4. How do you think new technologies like personalized devices, immersive virtual reality, holographic TV, driverless cars, genetic testing, and electronic memory aids will change human beings in the future? Would you like to live in the "upper band" world Schmidt and Cohen envision at the end of this selection?

EXPLORING CONNECTIONS

5. How might Sherry Turkle (p. 178) respond to Schmidt and Cohen's predictions about the impact of technology on the classroom? Why might she be less than optimistic about their vision of a coming educational revolution?

Bill Watterson/Andrews McMeel Syndication

6. Schmidt and Cohen conclude this selection by imagining what a day will be like in the future for someone who is in the "upper band" of technology users. How do you think technology will change the worlds of poor or working-class people, like those described by Barbara Ehrenreich (p. 368) or Mehrsa Baradaran (p. 391)? Explain why you think technology will either equalize or exacerbate class divisions.

EXTENDING THE CRITICAL CONTEXT

7. Research the impact of new technologies on the developing world today. How, for example, are things like inexpensive cell phones, tablet computers, and alternative energy sources changing lives in Africa and Latin America? For more information, visit the website of Kopernik or of any other nongovernmental organization dedicated to bringing modern technologies to developing nations.

8. As a class, watch a film about artificial intelligence, like *Ex Machina*, *Chappie*, or *Her*, or view an episode of the AMC television series *Humans*, and then discuss what it suggests about the future of human–robot relations. How is the impact of artificial intelligence on humans portrayed, and what questions are raised about the ethics of artificial intelligence? Do you think that in the future people and machines will have "relationships"?

HAS THE SMARTPHONE DESTROYED A GENERATION?

JEAN M. TWENGE

Are you a member of iGen? If you spend more than an hour a day texting, started driving after you were seventeen, didn't work during high school, and spent a lot of time in your bedroom as a teen, there's a good chance you are, according to Jean Twenge. There's also a good chance you're addicted to your smartphone and that your mental health is at risk. A professor of psychology at San Diego State University, Twenge (b. 1957) began studying generational differences more than twenty-five years ago, comparing the development and personality traits of Baby Boomers, Gen Xers, and Millennials. Sometime in 2012, she noted a sharp change in attitudes and behaviors among teens, a change that coincided with the advent of the iPhone. As Twenge sees it, the smartphone has changed today's teenagers in ways that separate them from prior generations. It has also made them profoundly unhappy. Over her career, Twenge has authored more than 120 scientific publications and three books, including *The Narcissism Epidemic: Living in the Age of Entitlement* (2010); *Generation Me: Why Today's Young Americans Are More Confident, Assertive, Entitled — and More Miserable Than Ever Before* (2014); and *iGen: Why Today's Super-Connected Kids Are Growing Up Less Rebellious, More Tolerant, Less Happy — and Completely Unprepared for Adulthood — and What That Means for the Rest of Us* (2017). This article originally appeared in the *Atlantic*.

ONE DAY LAST SUMMER, AROUND NOON, I called Athena, a 13-year-old who lives in Houston, Texas. She answered her phone — she's had an iPhone since she was 11 — sounding as if she'd just woken up. We chatted about her favorite songs and TV shows, and I asked her what she likes to do with her friends. "We go to the mall," she said. "Do your parents drop you off?," I asked, recalling my own middle-school days, in the 1980s, when I'd enjoy a few parent-free hours shopping with my friends. "No—I go with my family," she replied. "We'll go with my mom and brothers and walk a little behind them. I just have to tell my mom where we're going. I have to check in every hour or every 30 minutes."

Those mall trips are infrequent — about once a month. More often, Athena and her friends spend time together on their phones, unchaperoned. Unlike the teens of my generation, who might have spent an evening tying up the family landline with gossip, they talk on Snapchat, the smartphone app that allows users to send pictures and videos that quickly disappear. They make sure to keep up their Snapstreaks, which show how many days in a row they have Snapchatted with each other. Sometimes they save screenshots of particularly ridiculous pictures of friends. "It's good blackmail," Athena said. (Because she's a minor, I'm not using her real name.) She told me she'd spent most of the summer hanging out alone in her room with her phone. That's just the way her generation is, she said. "We didn't have a choice to know any life without iPads or iPhones. I think we like our phones more than we like actual people."

I've been researching generational differences for 25 years, starting when I was a 22-year-old doctoral student in psychology. Typically, the characteristics that come to define a generation appear gradually, and along a continuum. Beliefs and behaviors that were already rising simply continue to do so. Millennials, for instance, are a highly individualistic generation, but individualism had been increasing since the Baby Boomers turned on, tuned in, and dropped out. I had grown accustomed to line graphs of trends that looked like modest hills and valleys. Then I began studying Athena's generation.

Around 2012, I noticed abrupt shifts in teen behaviors and emotional states. The gentle slopes of the line graphs became steep mountains and sheer cliffs, and many of the distinctive characteristics of the Millennial generation began to disappear. In all my analyses of generational data — some reaching back to the 1930s — I had never seen anything like it.

At first I presumed these might be blips, but the trends persisted, across several years and a series of national surveys. The changes weren't just in degree, but in kind. The biggest difference between the Millennials and their predecessors was in how they viewed the world; teens today differ from the Millennials not just in their views but in how they spend their time. The experiences they have every day are radically different from those of the generation that came of age just a few years before them.

What happened in 2012 to cause such dramatic shifts in behavior? It was after the Great Recession, which officially lasted from 2007 to 2009 and had a starker effect on Millennials trying to find a place in a sputtering economy. But it was exactly the moment when the proportion of Americans who owned a smartphone surpassed 50 percent.

The more I pored over yearly surveys of teen attitudes and behaviors, and the more I talked with young people like Athena, the clearer it became that theirs is a generation shaped by the smartphone and by the concomitant rise of social media. I call them iGen. Born between 1995 and 2012, members of this generation are growing up with smartphones, have an Instagram account before they start high school, and do not remember a time before the Internet. The Millennials grew up with the Web as well, but it wasn't ever-present in their lives, at hand at all times, day and night. iGen's oldest members were early adolescents when the iPhone was introduced, in 2007, and high-school students when the iPad entered the scene, in 2010. A 2017 survey of more than 5,000 American teens found that three out of four owned an iPhone.

The advent of the smartphone and its cousin the tablet was followed quickly by hand-wringing about the deleterious effects of "screen time." But the impact of these devices has not been fully appreciated, and goes far beyond the usual concerns about curtailed attention spans. The arrival of the smartphone has radically changed every aspect of teenagers' lives, from the nature of their social interactions to their mental health. These changes have affected young people in every corner of the nation and in every type of household. The trends appear among teens poor and rich; of every ethnic background; in cities, suburbs, and small towns. Where there are cell towers, there are teens living their lives on their smartphone.

To those of us who fondly recall a more analog adolescence, this may seem foreign and troubling. The aim of generational study, however, is not to succumb to nostalgia for the way things used to be; it's to understand how they are now. Some generational changes are positive, some are negative, and many are both. More comfortable in their bedrooms than in a car or at a party, today's teens are physically safer than teens have ever been. They're markedly less likely to get into a car accident and, having less of a taste for alcohol than their predecessors, are less susceptible to drinking's attendant ills.

Psychologically, however, they are more vulnerable than Millennial were: Rates of teen depression and suicide have skyrocketed since 2011. It's not an exaggeration to describe iGen as being on the brink of the worst mental-health crisis in decades. Much of this deterioration can be traced to their phones.

Even when a seismic event—a war, a technological leap, a free concert in the mud[1]—plays an outsize role in shaping a group of young people, no single factor ever defines a generation. Parenting styles continue to change, as do school curricula and culture, and these things matter. But the twin rise of the smartphone and social media has caused an earthquake of a magnitude we've not seen in a very long time, if ever. There is compelling evidence that the devices we've placed in young people's hands are having profound effects on their lives—and making them seriously unhappy.

In the early 1970s, the photographer Bill Yates shot a series of portraits at the Sweetheart Roller Skating Rink in Tampa, Florida. In one, a shirtless teen stands with a large bottle of peppermint schnapps stuck in the waistband of his jeans. In another, a boy who looks no older than 12 poses with a cigarette in his mouth. The rink was a place where kids could get away from their parents and inhabit a world of their own, a world where they could drink, smoke, and make out in the backs of their cars. In stark black-and-white, the adolescent Boomers gaze at Yates's camera with the self-confidence born of making your own choices—even if, perhaps especially if, your parents wouldn't think they were the right ones.

Fifteen years later, during my own teenage years as a member of Generation X, smoking had lost some of its romance, but independence was definitely still in. My friends and I plotted to get our driver's license as soon as we could, making DMV appointments for the day we turned 16 and using our newfound freedom to escape the confines of our suburban neighborhood. Asked by our parents, "When will you be home?," we replied, "When do I have to be?"

---

[1] **a free concert in the mud:** An allusion to the 1969 Woodstock Music & Art Festival, considered a defining event for the countercultural Baby Boomer generation. [Eds.]

But the allure of independence, so powerful to previous generations, holds less sway over today's teens, who are less likely to leave the house without their parents. The shift is stunning: 12th-graders in 2015 were going out less often than *eighth-graders* did as recently as 2009.

Today's teens are also less likely to date. The initial stage of court-15 ship, which Gen Xers called "liking" (as in "Ooh, he likes you!"), kids now call "talking"—an ironic choice for a generation that prefers text-ing to actual conversation. After two teens have "talked" for a while, they might start dating. But only about 56 percent of high-school seniors in 2015 went out on dates; for Boomers and Gen Xers, the number was about 85 percent.

The decline in dating tracks with a decline in sexual activity. The drop is the sharpest for ninth-graders, among whom the number of sexually active teens has been cut by almost 40 percent since 1991. The average teen now has had sex for the first time by the spring of 11th grade, a full year later than the average Gen Xer. Fewer teens having sex has contributed to what many see as one of the most positive youth trends in recent years: The teen birth rate hit an all-time low in 2016, down 67 percent since its modern peak, in 1991.

Even driving, a symbol of adolescent freedom inscribed in Amer-ican popular culture, from *Rebel Without a Cause* to *Ferris Bueller's Day Off*, has lost its appeal for today's teens. Nearly all Boomer high-school students had their driver's license by the spring of their senior year; more than one in four teens today still lack one at the end of high school. For some, Mom and Dad are such good chauffeurs that there's no urgent need to drive. "My parents drove me everywhere and never complained, so I always had rides," a 21-year-old student in San Diego told me. "I didn't get my license until my mom told me I had to because she could not keep driving me to school." She finally got her license six months after her 18th birthday. In conversation after conversation, teens described getting their license as something to be nagged into by their parents—a notion that would have been unthinkable to previous generations.

Independence isn't free—you need some money in your pocket to pay for gas, or for that bottle of schnapps. In earlier eras, kids worked in great numbers, eager to finance their freedom or prodded by their parents to learn the value of a dollar. But iGen teens aren't working (or managing their own money) as much. In the late 1970s, 77 percent of high-school seniors worked for pay during the school year; by the mid-2010s, only 55 percent did. The number of eighth-graders who work for pay has been cut in half. These declines accelerated during the Great Recession, but teen employment has not bounced back, even though job availability has.

Of course, putting off the responsibilities of adulthood is not an iGen innovation. Gen Xers, in the 1990s, were the first to postpone the traditional markers of adulthood. Young Gen Xers were just about as likely to drive, drink alcohol, and date as young Boomers had been, and more likely to have sex and get pregnant as teens. But as they left their teenage years behind, Gen Xers married and started careers later than their Boomer predecessors had.

Gen X managed to stretch adolescence beyond all previous lim- 20 its: Its members started becoming adults earlier and finished becoming adults later. Beginning with Millennials and continuing with iGen, adolescence is contracting again—but only because its onset is being delayed. Across a range of behaviors—drinking, dating, spending time unsupervised—18-year-olds now act more like 15-year-olds used to, and 15-year-olds more like 13-year-olds. Childhood now stretches well into high school.

Why are today's teens waiting longer to take on both the responsibilities and the pleasures of adulthood? Shifts in the economy, and parenting, certainly play a role. In an information economy that rewards higher education more than early work history, parents may be inclined to encourage their kids to stay home and study rather than to get a part-time job. Teens, in turn, seem to be content with this homebody arrangement—not because they're so studious, but because their social life is lived on their phone. They don't need to leave home to spend time with their friends.

If today's teens were a generation of grinds, we'd see that in the data. But eighth-, 10th-, and 12th-graders in the 2010s actually spend less time on homework than Gen X teens did in the early 1990s. (High-school seniors headed for four-year colleges spend about the same amount of time on homework as their predecessors did.) The time that seniors spend on activities such as student clubs and sports and exercise has changed little in recent years. Combined with the decline in working for pay, this means iGen teens have more leisure time than Gen X teens did, not less.

So what are they doing with all that time? They are on their phone, in their room, alone and often distressed.

One of the ironies of iGen life is that despite spending far more time under the same roof as their parents, today's teens can hardly be said to be closer to their mothers and fathers than their predecessors were. "I've seen my friends with their families—they don't talk to them," Athena told me. "They just say 'Okay, okay, whatever' while they're on their phones. They don't pay attention to their family." Like her peers, Athena is an expert at tuning out her parents so she can focus on her phone. She spent much of her summer keeping up with friends, but nearly all of it was over text or Snapchat. "I've been on my phone more than I've been with actual people," she said. "My bed has, like, an imprint of my body."

In this, too, she is typical. The number of teens who get together 25 with their friends nearly every day dropped by more than 40 percent from 2000 to 2015; the decline has been especially steep recently. It's not only a matter of fewer kids partying; fewer kids are spending time simply hanging out. That's something most teens used to do: nerds and jocks, poor kids and rich kids, C students and A students. The roller rink, the basketball court, the town pool, the local necking spot — they've all been replaced by virtual spaces accessed through apps and the Web.

You might expect that teens spend so much time in these new spaces because it makes them happy, but most data suggest that it does not. The Monitoring the Future survey, funded by the National Institute on Drug Abuse and designed to be nationally representative, has asked 12th-graders more than 1,000 questions every year since 1975 and queried eighth- and 10th-graders since 1991. The survey asks teens how happy they are and also how much of their leisure time they spend on various activities, including nonscreen activities such as in-person social interaction and exercise, and, in recent years, screen activities such as using social media, texting, and browsing the Web. The results could not be clearer: Teens who spend more time than average on screen activities are more likely to be unhappy, and those who spend more time than average on non-screen activities are more likely to be happy.

There's not a single exception. All screen activities are linked to less happiness, and all nonscreen activities are linked to more happiness. Eighth-graders who spend 10 or more hours a week on social media are 56 percent more likely to say they're unhappy than those who devote less time to social media. Admittedly, 10 hours a week is a lot. But those who spend six to nine hours a week on social media are still 47 percent more likely to say they are unhappy than those who use social media even less. The opposite is true of in-person interactions. Those who spend an above-average amount of time with their friends in person are 20 percent less likely to say they're unhappy than those who hang out for a below-average amount of time.

If you were going to give advice for a happy adolescence based on this survey, it would be straightforward: Put down the phone, turn off the laptop, and do something — anything — that does not involve a screen. Of course, these analyses don't unequivocally prove that screen time *causes* unhappiness; it's possible that unhappy teens spend more time online. But recent research suggests that screen time, in particular social-media use, does indeed cause unhappiness. One study asked college students with a Facebook page to complete short surveys on their phone over the course of two weeks. They'd get a text message with a link five times a day, and report on their mood and how much they'd used Facebook. The more they'd used Facebook, the unhappier they felt, but feeling unhappy did not subsequently lead to more Facebook use.

Social-networking sites like Facebook promise to connect us to friends. But the portrait of iGen teens emerging from the data is one of a lonely, dislocated generation. Teens who visit social-networking sites every day but see their friends in person less frequently are the most likely to agree with the statements "A lot of times I feel lonely," "I often feel left out of things," and "I often wish I had more good friends." Teens' feelings of loneliness spiked in 2013 and have remained high since.

This doesn't always mean that, on an individual level, kids who spend more time online are lonelier than kids who spend less time online. Teens who spend more time on social media also spend more time with their friends in person, on average — highly social teens are more social in both venues, and less social teens are less so. But at the generational level, when teens spend more time on smartphones and less time on in-person social interactions, loneliness is more common.

So is depression. Once again, the effect of screen activities is unmistakable: The more time teens spend looking at screens, the more likely they are to report symptoms of depression. Eighth-graders who are heavy users of social media increase their risk of depression by 27 percent, while those who play sports, go to religious services, or even do homework more than the average teen cut their risk significantly.

Teens who spend three hours a day or more on electronic devices are 35 percent more likely to have a risk factor for suicide, such as making a suicide plan. (That's much more than the risk related to, say, watching TV.) One piece of data that indirectly but stunningly captures kids' growing isolation, for good and for bad: Since 2007, the homicide rate among teens has declined, but the suicide rate has increased. As teens have started spending less time together, they have become less likely to kill one another, and more likely to kill themselves. In 2011, for the first time in 24 years, the teen suicide rate was higher than the teen homicide rate.

Depression and suicide have many causes; too much technology is clearly not the only one. And the teen suicide rate was even higher in the 1990s, long before smartphones existed. Then again, about four times as many Americans now take antidepressants, which are often effective in treating severe depression, the type most strongly linked to suicide.

What's the connection between smartphones and the apparent psychological distress this generation is experiencing? For all their power to link kids day and night, social media also exacerbate the age-old teen concern about being left out. Today's teens may go to fewer parties and spend less time together in person, but when they do congregate, they document their hangouts relentlessly — on Snapchat, Instagram, Facebook. Those not invited to come along are keenly aware of it. Accordingly, the number of teens who feel left out has reached all-time highs across age groups. Like the increase in loneliness, the upswing in feeling left out has been swift and significant.

This trend has been especially steep among girls. Forty-eight percent more girls said they often felt left out in 2015 than in 2010, compared with 27 percent more boys. Girls use social media more often, giving them additional opportunities to feel excluded and lonely when they see their friends or classmates getting together without them. Social media levy a psychic tax on the teen doing the posting as well, as she anxiously awaits the affirmation of comments and likes. When Athena posts pictures to Instagram, she told me, "I'm nervous about what people think and are going to say. It sometimes bugs me when I don't get a certain amount of likes on a picture."

Girls have also borne the brunt of the rise in depressive symptoms among today's teens. Boys' depressive symptoms increased by 21 percent from 2012 to 2015, while girls' increased by 50 percent—more than twice as much. The rise in suicide, too, is more pronounced among girls. Although the rate increased for both sexes, three times as many 12-to-14-year-old girls killed themselves in 2015 as in 2007, compared with twice as many boys. The suicide rate is still higher for boys, in part because they use more-lethal methods, but girls are beginning to close the gap.

These more dire consequences for teenage girls could also be rooted in the fact that they're more likely to experience cyberbullying. Boys tend to bully one another physically, while girls are more likely to do so by undermining a victim's social status or relationships. Social media give middle- and high-school girls a platform on which to carry out the style of aggression they favor, ostracizing and excluding other girls around the clock.

Social-media companies are of course aware of these problems, and to one degree or another have endeavored to prevent cyberbullying. But their various motivations are, to say the least, complex. A recently leaked Facebook document indicated that the company had been touting to advertisers its ability to determine teens' emotional state based on their on-site behavior, and even to pinpoint "moments when young people need a confidence boost." Facebook acknowledged that the document was real, but denied that it offers "tools to target people based on their emotional state."

In July 2014, a 13-year-old girl in North Texas woke to the smell of something burning. Her phone had overheated and melted into the sheets. National news outlets picked up the story, stoking readers' fears that their cellphone might spontaneously combust. To me, however, the flaming cellphone wasn't the only surprising aspect of the story. *Why*, I wondered, *would anyone sleep with her phone beside her in bed*? It's not as though you can surf the Web while you're sleeping. And who could slumber deeply inches from a buzzing phone?

Curious, I asked my undergraduate students at San Diego State 40 University what they do with their phone while they sleep. Their answers were a profile in obsession. Nearly all slept with their phone, putting it under their pillow, on the mattress, or at the very least within arm's reach of the bed. They checked social media right before they went to sleep, and reached for their phone as soon as they woke up in the morning (they had to—all of them used it as their alarm clock). Their phone was the last thing they saw before they went to sleep and the first thing they saw when they woke up. If they woke in the middle of the night, they often ended up looking at their phone. Some used the language of addiction. "I know I shouldn't, but I just can't help it," one said about looking at her phone while in bed. Others saw their phone as an extension of their body—or even like a lover: "Having my phone closer to me while I'm sleeping is a comfort."

It may be a comfort, but the smartphone is cutting into teens' sleep: Many now sleep less than seven hours most nights. Sleep experts say that teens should get about nine hours of sleep a night; a teen who is getting less than seven hours a night is significantly sleep deprived. Fifty-seven percent more teens were sleep deprived in 2015 than in 1991. In just the four years from 2012 to 2015, 22 percent more teens failed to get seven hours of sleep.

The increase is suspiciously timed, once again starting around when most teens got a smartphone. Two national surveys show that teens who spend three or more hours a day on electronic devices are 28 percent more likely to get less than seven hours of sleep than those who spend fewer than three hours, and teens who visit social-media sites every day are 19 percent more likely to be sleep deprived. A meta-analysis of studies on electronic-device use among children found similar results: Children who use a media device right before bed are more likely to sleep less than they should, more likely to sleep poorly, and more than twice as likely to be sleepy during the day.

Electronic devices and social media seem to have an especially strong ability to disrupt sleep. Teens who read books and magazines more often than the average are actually slightly less likely to be sleep deprived—either reading lulls them to sleep, or they can put the book down at bedtime. Watching TV for several hours a day is only weakly linked to sleeping less. But the allure of the smartphone is often too much to resist.

Sleep deprivation is linked to myriad issues, including compromised thinking and reasoning, susceptibility to illness, weight gain, and high blood pressure. It also affects mood: People who don't sleep enough are prone to depression and anxiety. Again, it's difficult to trace the precise paths of causation. Smartphones could be causing lack of sleep, which leads to depression, or the phones could be causing depression, which leads to lack of sleep. Or some other factor could be causing both depression and sleep deprivation to rise. But the smartphone, its blue light glowing in the dark, is likely playing a nefarious role.

The correlations between depression and smartphone use are strong [45] enough to suggest that more parents should be telling their kids to put down their phone. As the technology writer Nick Bilton has reported, it's a policy some Silicon Valley executives follow. Even Steve Jobs limited his kids' use of the devices he brought into the world.

What's at stake isn't just how kids experience adolescence. The constant presence of smartphones is likely to affect them well into adulthood. Among people who suffer an episode of depression, at least half become depressed again later in life. Adolescence is a key time for developing social skills; as teens spend less time with their friends face-to-face, they have fewer opportunities to practice them. In the next decade, we may see more adults who know just the right emoji for a situation, but not the right facial expression.

I realize that restricting technology might be an unrealistic demand to impose on a generation of kids so accustomed to being wired at all times. My three daughters were born in 2006, 2009, and 2012. They're not yet old enough to display the traits of iGen teens, but I have already witnessed firsthand just how ingrained new media are in their young lives. I've observed my toddler, barely old enough to walk, confidently swiping her way through an iPad. I've experienced my 6-year-old asking for her own cellphone. I've overheard my 9-year-old discussing the latest app to sweep the fourth grade. Prying the phone out of our kids' hands will be difficult, even more so than the quixotic efforts of my parents' generation to get their kids to turn off MTV and get some fresh air. But more seems to be at stake in urging teens to use their phone responsibly, and there are benefits to be gained even if all we instill in our children is the importance of moderation. Significant effects on both mental health and sleep time appear after two or more hours a day on electronic devices. The average teen spends about two and a half hours a day on electronic devices. Some mild boundary-setting could keep kids from falling into harmful habits.

In my conversations with teens, I saw hopeful signs that kids themselves are beginning to link some of their troubles to their ever-present phone. Athena told me that when she does spend time with her friends in person, they are often looking at their device instead of at her. "I'm trying to talk to them about something, and they don't actually look at my face," she said. "They're looking at their phone, or they're looking at their Apple Watch." "What does that feel like, when you're trying to talk to somebody face-to-face and they're not looking at you?," I asked. "It kind of hurts," she said. "It hurts. I know my parents' generation didn't do that. I could be talking about something super important to me, and they wouldn't even be listening."

Once, she told me, she was hanging out with a friend who was texting her boyfriend. "I was trying to talk to her about my family, and what was going on, and she was like, 'Uh-huh, yeah, whatever.' So I took her phone out of her hands and I threw it at my wall."

I couldn't help laughing. "You play volleyball," I said. "Do you have 50 a pretty good arm?" "Yep," she replied.

Liam Francis Walsh/The New Yorker Collection/The Cartoon Bank

"It keeps me from looking at my phone every two seconds."

ENGAGING THE TEXT

1. What, according to Twenge, are the major differences between iGen and earlier generations of Americans? What evidence, if any, have you seen that iGen is "on the brink of the worst mental-health crisis in decades" (para. 10)?

2. Twenge claims that social media use among teens makes them unhappy because of their "concern about being left out" (para. 34). How widespread is this fear among your friends? What other reasons might explain why heavy social media use makes young people unhappy?

3. Why, according to Twenge, is social media use more toxic for girls than for boys? What differences do you see, if any, in the ways that young males and females use and relate to social media?

4. What other factors besides technology might explain the trends Twenge notes among iGen teens? What other reasons, for example, might explain why today's teens spend more time at home, work less, get less sleep, or learn to drive later than earlier generations? Does Twenge, in your view, overstate the case for technology's influence? Why or why not?

5. How realistic is Twenge's suggestion that it's time for parents to tell kids "to put down their phone" (para. 45)? To what extent did your parents try to limit

or control your use of smartphones or social media? In general, how successful are such efforts, and why?

6. How do iGen teens view their smartphones, according to Twenge? Do you agree that young people today are becoming "addicted" to their phones? How would you describe your own relationship with your phone?

7. **Thinking Rhetorically**   Twenge takes pains to address counterarguments to her claims and alternative interpretations of the data she presents. Find several passages where she offers and replies to alternative points of view. How well does she represent opposing positions, and how persuasive do you find her responses?

EXPLORING CONNECTIONS

8. How might Twenge respond to the positive vision of our technological future offered by Eric Schmidt and Jared Cohen (p. 241)? Would a future of "greater connectivity" filled with apps that anticipate your every desire appeal to her? Why or why not?

9. How might Twenge's análysis of the smartphone's impact on young adults explain why Sherry Turkle's students prefer online communication to face-to-face contact (p. 178)? How realistic is it to expect members of iGen to put their phones down and stop multitasking in class?

EXTENDING THE CRITICAL CONTEXT

10. Survey students outside your class to learn about their attitudes toward their smartphones. How many of them feel that their phones are a source of stress, anxiety, or sleeplessness? How many think that dependence on their phones makes them feel isolated and lonely? How many would say that they are "addicted" to their phones? Share your results in class and then work together to create a list of guidelines for parents who are thinking about buying a smartphone for a child. What tips would you include to help kids avoid some of the negative consequences Twenge describes?

11. Do some research to learn more about smartphone and social media addiction. Why do some experts resist categorizing heavy smartphone and social media use as addiction? What signs suggest that someone is addicted to smartphone technology? What studies can you find documenting serious negative effects of heavy social media and smartphone use? What are the most commonly recommended approaches for coping with technology addiction?

12. Research how technology companies deliberately design smartphones and social media apps to create dependency. What features of these technologies are particularly addictive, and why? How do our high-tech devices "program" us to respond to them? What, if anything, should be done to keep tech companies from manipulating their customers?

3

LET'S GET LOST

KENNETH GOLDSMITH

> In 2014, Kenneth Goldsmith announced on Twitter that he'd be offering
> a new class at the University of Pennsylvania called "Wasting Time on
> the Internet." In the course description, he challenged students to see
> the Internet as "the greatest poem ever written" and noted that stu-
> dents would be required to interact "only through chat rooms, bots,
> social media, and LISTSERVs." Within hours of posting, Goldsmith's
> Twitter account blew up, and by the time the class convened he had a
> waiting list of more than 100 students for a classroom with only fifteen
> seats. While critics have bewailed the horrors of digital technology
> since the Internet was created, Goldsmith clearly understands that any-
> one under the age of twenty-five feels right at home living online. In
> this selection, he examines some of our assumptions about the Internet
> and its effects and concludes by wondering if life online might actually
> be changing us for the better. Appointed the Museum of Modern Art's
> first Poet Laureate in 2013, Goldsmith is a conceptual artist and the
> author of ten books of poetry. He has also written several other books,
> including *Uncreative Writing: Managing Language in the Digital Age*
> (2011), *Seven American Deaths and Disasters* (2013), and *Wasting Time*
> *on the Internet* (2016), the source of this selection.

I'M WASTING TIME ON THE INTERNET. I click to the *New York Times*
front page to see the latest headlines and today a major nuclear deal
with Iran was signed. The banner headline screams HISTORY and even
though I haven't really been following the story, I click on it. I'm taken
to a page with an embedded video that features Thomas Friedman[1]
asking Obama to explain what he thinks the United States gained from
the nuclear deal with Iran.[2] I check the time on the video—three and
a half minutes—and figure that's not too long to listen to the president
speak. He speaks; I watch. He continues to speak; I scroll through my
Twitter feed but I still listen. I click back on the *Times* window and
watch again. Somewhere about the three-minute mark, I start to think,
Am I really wasting time on the Internet? This is important stuff that I've
stumbled on to. I'm struggling to see what's so shameful about this. The
video ends and, impressed by what the president was saying, I start to
read Freidman's lengthy article about this beneath the video. I read the

---

[1]**Thomas Friedman:** American journalist and author (b. 1953) specializing in global
issues. [All notes are the editors', except for 2, 4, 5, 7, 9, 10, 11, 13, and 14.]

[2]http://www.nytimes.com/2015/07/15/opinion/thomas-friedman-obama-makes-his-
case-on-iran-nuclear-deal.html, August 17, 2015.

first few paragraphs carefully, then scroll down and read some more. It's starting to get too granular for me. But my interest is piqued. Although I'm not going to read this piece to the end, I'm going to start following this story as it unfurls over the next few days. I stumbled on it and got hooked. Is my engagement deep? Not right now. But judging by the way these things tend to go, as I start to follow the story, my appetite for the topic will most likely become voracious. I can't see this event—one that happens several times a day—as being anything other than good. Because of it, I'm better informed, more engaged, and perhaps even a bit smarter.

After I finish with this article, I click over to Facebook and find myself watching a video of Keith Richards[3] discussing how he gets ideas for his songs. He says that when he's in restaurants and overhears conversation coming from the next table, he simply writes down what they're saying. "Give me a napkin and a pen," he says, smiling. "You feel that one phrase could be a song." Although the video is only a minute long, it's packed with wisdom. Really? Could his process be that simple, that pure? After listening to Keith, I feel inspired. After all, I feel like I spend tons of time eavesdropping on Facebook conversations. Might I be able to wring a song or a poem out of those as well?

I'm back on Facebook, and the next thing I know I'm looking at this incredible black-and-white photo from 1917 of a full-size battleship being built in New York's Union Square. The picture is huge and brimming with details. I click on it and I'm taken to a website. As I scroll down, there's a short explanatory text about how this came to be, followed by a dozen more giant, rich photos of the ship being built in progress. It's fascinating. I just wrote a book about New York City and I'm floored that I somehow missed this but grateful to know about it. I bookmark the page and move on.

What is wasting time on the Internet? It's not so easy to say. It strikes me that it can't be simply defined. When I was clicking around, was I wasting time because I should've been working instead? But I had spent hours working—in front of the same screen—and quite frankly I needed a break. I needed to stop thinking about work and do a bit of drifting. But, unlike the common perception of what we do when we waste time on the Internet, I wasn't watching cat videos—well, maybe one or two. I was actually interested in the things that I stumbled on: the president, the rock star, and the battleship. I had the choice not to click on these things, but I chose to do so. They seemed to me to be genuinely interesting. There were many more things that I didn't click on.

Listening to Internet pundits tell it, you'd think we stare for three hours at clickbait—those Web pages with hypersensational headlines that beg you to click on them—the way we once sat down and watched

5

---

[3]**Keith Richards:** English rock musician and songwriter (b. 1943) best known as a founding member of the Rolling Stones.

three hours of cartoons on Saturday morning TV. But the truth is most of us don't do any one thing on the Internet for three hours. Instead, we do many things during that time, some of it frivolous, some of it heavy. Our time spent in front of the computer is a mixed time, a time that reflects our desires — as opposed to the glazed-eyed stare we got from sitting in front of the television where we were fed something we ultimately weren't much interested in. TV gave us few choices. Naturally, we became "couch potatoes" and many of us truly did feel like we wasted our time — as our parents so often chided us — "rotting away" in front of the TV.

I'm reading these days — ironically, on the Web — that we don't read anymore. People often confess this same thing to me when they hear I'm a poet. The other day, I was opening up a bank account and the associate working at the bank, when he found out what I did, sighed and admitted that he doesn't read as much as he used to. I asked him whether he had a Facebook account, which he did, and a Twitter, which he also did. I asked him whether he sent and received e-mails. Yes, he said, many every day. I told him that he was, in fact, reading and writing a lot. We're reading and writing more than we have in a generation, but we are doing it differently — skimming, parsing, grazing, bookmarking, forwarding, and spamming language — in ways that aren't yet recognized as literary, but with a panoply of writers using the raw material of the Web as the basis for their works it's only a matter of time until it is.

I keep reading that in the age of screens we've lost our ability to concentrate, that we've become distracted, unable to focus. But when I look around me and see people riveted to their devices, I've never seen such a great wealth of concentration, focus, and engagement. I find it ironic that those who say we have no concentration are most bothered by how addicted people are to their devices. I find it equally ironic that most of the places I read about how addicted we are to the Web is on the Web itself, scattered across numerous websites, blog posts, tweets, and Facebook pages.

On those blogs, I read how the Internet has made us antisocial, how we've lost the ability to have a conversation. But when I see people with their devices, all I see is people communicating with one another: texting, chatting, IM'ing. And I have to wonder, in what way is this not social? A conversation broken up into short bursts and quick emoticons is still a conversation. Watch someone's face while they're in the midst of a rapid-fire text message exchange: it's full of human emotion and expression — anticipation, laughter, affect. Critics claim that even having a device present acts to inhibit conversation, and that the best antidote to our technological addiction is a return to good old-fashioned face-to-face conversation. They say, "Conversation is there for us to reclaim. For the failing connections of our digital world, it is the talking cure."[4]

---

[4]http://www.nytimes.com/2015/09/27/opinion/sunday/stop-googling-lets-talk.html, October 12, 2015.

But this seems to ignore the fact that smartphones are indeed phones: two-way devices for human-to-human conversations, replete with expressive vocal cadence and warmth. Is conversation over the telephone still—140 years after the phone was invented—somehow not considered "intimate" enough, lessened because it is mediated by technology?

But beyond that, life is still full of attentive, engaged face-to-face conversations and close listening, be it at the many conferences, lectures, or readings I attend where large audiences hang on every word the speakers say, or my own therapy sessions—nothing more than two people in a room—the tenor and intensity of which hasn't changed in decades despite several technological revolutions. When a student comes and finds me during office hours, that student—normally tethered to their device—can still go deep without one. Even my seventeen-year-old son, awash in social media, still demands that we "talk" in the darkness of his bedroom each night before he goes to sleep, just as we have done his entire life. It's a ritual that neither of us are willing to forgo in spite of our love of gadgets. Everywhere I look—on the street, in restaurants and cafés, in classrooms, or waiting in line for a movie—in spite of dire predictions, people still seem to know how to converse.

Our devices, if anything, tend to amplify our sociability. Sometimes 10 we converse face-to-face, other times over our devices, but often, it's a combination of the two. I'm in a hotel lobby and I'm watching two fashionable women in their twenties sitting next to each other on a modernist sofa. They are parallel with one another: their shoulders are touching; their legs are extended with their feet resting on a table in front of them. They're both cradling their devices, each in their own world. From time to time, they hold their phones up and share something on-screen before retreating into their respective zones. While they peck away at their keyboards, shards of conversation pass between them, accompanied by laughter, head nods, and pointing. Then, at once, they put their phones in their purses, straighten up their bodies, angle toward one another, and launch into a fully attentive face-to-face conversation. They're now very animated, gesticulating with their hands; you can feel the words being absorbed into their bodies, which are vehicles for augmenting what they're saying. It's fascinating: just a moment ago it was parallel play; now it's fully interactive. They continue this way for several more minutes until, as if again on cue, they both reach into their purses, take out their phones, and resume their previous postures, shoulders once again touching and legs outstretched. They're no longer conversing with each other, but are now conversing with someone unseen. Our devices might be changing us, but to say that they're dehumanizing us is simply wrong.

The Internet has been accused of making us shallow. We're skimming, not reading. We lack the ability to engage deeply with a subject anymore. That's both true and not true: we skim and browse certain types of content, and read others carefully. Oftentimes, we'll save a long form journalism article and read it later offline, perhaps on the train home from work. Accusations like those tend to assume we're all using our devices the same way. But looking over the shoulders of people absorbed in their devices on the subway, I see many people reading newspapers and books on their phones and many others playing *Candy Crush Saga*. Sometimes someone will be glancing at a newspaper one moment and playing a game the next. There's a slew of blogs I've seen recently which exhaustively document photos of people reading paper books on the subway. One photographer nostalgically claims that he wanted to capture a fading moment when "books are vanishing and are being replaced by characterless iPads and Kindles."[5] But that's too simple, literally judging a book by its cover. Who's to say what they're reading? Often we assume that just because someone is reading a book on a device that it's trashy. Sometimes it is; sometimes it isn't. Last night I walked into the living room and my wife was glued to her iPad, reading the *Narrative of the Life of Frederick Douglass*. Hours later, when I headed to bed she hadn't moved an inch, still transfixed by this 171-year-old narrative on her twenty-first-century device. When I said good night, she didn't even look up.

And while these critics tell us time and again that our brains are being rewired, I'm not so sure that's all bad. Every new media requires new ways of thinking. How strange it would be if in the midst of this digital revolution we were still expected to use our brains in the same way we read books or watched TV? The resistance to the Internet shouldn't surprise us: cultural reactionaries defending the status quo have been around as long as media has. Marshall McLuhan[6] tells us that television was written off by people invested in literature as merely "mass entertainment" just as the printed book was met with the same skepticism in the sixteenth century by scholastic philosophers. McLuhan says that "the vested interests of acquired knowledge and conventional wisdom have always been by-passed and engulfed by new media. . . . The student of media soon comes to expect the new media of any period whatever to be classed as pseudo by those who have acquired the patterns of earlier media, whatever they may happen to be."[7]

I'm told that our children are most at risk, that the excessive use of computers has led our kids to view the real world as fake. But I'm not so sure that even I can distinguish "real" from "fake" in my own life. How is my life on Facebook any less "real" than what happens in my day-to-day life? In fact, much of what does happen in my day-to-day life comes through Facebook—work opportunities, invitations to dinner parties,

[5]http://www.slate.com/blogs/be-hold/2015/01/09/reinier_gerritsen_photographs_readers_on_the_subway_in_his_series_the_last.html, March 15, 2016.

[6]**Marshall McLuhan:** Herbert Marshall McLuhan (1911–1980) was a Canadian professor and philosopher famous for his work on media theory.

[7]Marshall McLuhan, *Understanding Media* (New York: McGraw-Hill, 1965), unpaginated, iBooks.

and even the topics I discuss at those dinner parties often comes from stuff I've found out about on Facebook. It's also likely that I met more than a few of my dinner companions via social media.

I'm reading that screen time makes kids antisocial and withdrawn, but when I see my kids in front of screens, they remind me of those women on the couch, fading in and out, as they deftly negotiate the space of the room with the space of the Web. And when they're, say, gaming, they tend to get along beautifully, deeply engaged with what is happening on the screen while being highly sensitive to each other; not a move of their body or expression of emotion gets overlooked. Gaming ripples through their entire bodies: they kick their feet, jump for joy, and scream in anger. It's hard for me to see in what way this could be considered disconnected. It's when they leave the screens that trouble starts: they start fighting over food or who gets to sit where in the car. And, honestly, after a while they get bored of screens. There's nothing like a media-soaked Sunday morning to make them beg me to take them out to the park to throw a football or to go on a bike ride.

It's Friday night and my teenage son has invited about a dozen of 15 his buddies—boys and girls—over to the house. They're sprawled out on the couch, mostly separated by gender, glued to their smartphones. Over by the TV, a few kids are playing video games that along with their yelps and whoops are providing the soundtrack for the evening. The group on the couch are close, emotionally and physically; they form a long human chain, shoulders snuggled up against their neighbor's. Some of the girls are leaning into the other girls, using them as pillows. The boys are physical with each other, but differently: they reach out occasionally to fist bump or high-five. One couple, a boyfriend and girl-friend, are clumped in the middle of the couch, draped on top of one another, while at the same time pressed up against the others.

There's an electric teenage energy to the group. They're function-ing as a group, yet they're all independent. They spend long periods in silence; the only noises emanating from the gang are the occasional sounds that are emitted from their devices—pings, plonks, chimes, and tinny songs from YouTube pages. Bursts of laughter are frequent, start-ing with one person and spreading like wildfire to the others. As they turn their devices toward one another, I hear them saying, "Have you seen this?" and shrieking, "Oh my god!" Laughter ripples again, dying out quickly. Then they plunge back into concentrated silence. Out of the blue, one of the kids on the couch playfully says to the other, "You jerk! I can't believe you just sent me that!" And it's then that I realize that as much as they're texting and status updating elsewhere on the Web, a large part of their digital communication is happening between these kids seated on the same couch.

They're constantly taking pictures of themselves and of each other. Some are shooting videos, directing their friends to make faces, to say outrageous things to the camera, or to wave hello. And then, it's right back to the devices, where those images are uploaded to social media and shared among the group, as links are blasted out—all within a minute. Suddenly, the girls shriek, "I look so ugly!" or "You look so pretty!" and "We need to take this one again." I hear someone say, "That was so funny! Let's watch it again." They count likes and favorites as they pile up and read comments that are instantly appearing from both inside and outside the room. This goes on for hours. In a sense, this is as much about creativity as it is about communication. Each photo, posed and styled, is considered with a public response in mind. They are excited by the idea of themselves as images. But why wouldn't they be? From before the moment they were born, my kids have been awash in images of themselves, beginning with the fuzzy in utero sonograms that they now have pinned to their bedroom walls. Since then, our cameras—first clumsy digital cameras and now smartphones—have been a constant presence in their life, documenting their every move. We never took just one picture of them but took dozens in rapid-fire fashion, offloaded them to the computer, and never deleted a single one. Now, when I open my iPhoto album to show them their baby pictures, the albums look like Andy Warhol[8] paintings, with the same images in slight variations repeated over and over, as we documented them second by second. Clearly we have created this situation.

There is no road map for this territory. They are making it up as they go along. But there's no way that this evening could be considered asocial or antisocial. Their imaginations are on full throttle and are wildly engaged in what they're doing. They are highly connected and interacting with each other, but in ways that are pretty much unrecognizable to me. I'm struggling to figure out what's so bad about this. I'm reading that screen addiction is taking a terrible toll on our children, but in their world it's not so much an addiction as a necessity. Many key aspects of our children's lives are in some way funneled through their devices. From online homework assignments to research prompts, right on down to where and when soccer practice is going to be held, the information comes to them via their devices. (And yes, my kids love their screens and love soccer.)

After reading one of these hysterical "devices are ruining your child" articles, my sister-in-law decided to take action. She imposed a system whereby, after dinner, the children were to "turn in" their devices—computers, smartphones, and tablets—to her. They could "check them out" over the course of the evening, but only if they could explain exactly what they needed them for, which had to be for "educational purposes." But if there was no reason to check them out, the devices stayed with my sister-in-law until they were given back the next day for their allotted after-school screen time, which she also monitors. Upon confiscating my nephew's cell phone one Friday night, she

---

[8]**Andy Warhol:** Born Andrew Warhola (1928–1987), an American artist, director, and producer who was a leading figure in the pop art movement and famous for his repetitive prints of household products and celebrities.

asked him on Saturday morning, "What plans do you have with your friends today?" "None," he responded. "You took away my phone."

On a family vacation, after a full day of outdoor activities that included seeing the Grand Canyon and hiking, my friend and her family settled into the hotel for the evening. Her twelve-year-old daughter is a fan of preteen goth girl crafting videos on YouTube, where she learns how to bedazzle black skull T-shirts and make perfectly ripped punk leggings and home-brewed perfumes. That evening, the girl selected some of her favorite videos to share with her mother. After agreeing to watch a few, her mother grew impatient. "This is nice, but I don't want to spend the whole night clicking around." The daughter indignantly responded that she wasn't just "clicking around." She was connecting with a community of girls her own age who shared similar interests. Her mother was forced to reconsider her premise that her daughter wasn't just wasting time on the Internet; instead, she was fully engaged, fostering an aesthetic, feeding her imagination, indulging in her creative proclivities, and hanging out with her friends, all from the comfort of a remote hotel room perched on the edge of the Grand Canyon.

In theorizing or discussing our time spent online, we tend to oversimplify what is an extraordinarily nuanced experience, full of complexity and contradiction. The way we speak about technology belies our monolithic thinking about it. During his recent run for president, a number of Donald Trump's legal depositions were scrutinized by the *New York Times*, which intended to show how Trump spoke when he wasn't in the spotlight. During a series of questions about the ways he used technology, he was asked about television, to which he replied, "I don't have a lot of time for listening to television."[9] I was struck by the phrase "listening to television." You don't really listen to television; you watch it. You listen exclusively to radio. Born in 1946, it's safe to assume that Trump spent his formative years listening to radio. My father, roughly the same age as Trump, says similar things. Growing up, he used to berate us kids for watching TV, saying that it took no imagination. Waxing nostalgic, he'd say, "When I was a boy listening to radio, you had to make up everything in your mind. You kids have it all there for you." For my father—and I can imagine Trump, too—although they watched television, I don't think they really understood it. Certainly, Trump's statement belies a basic misapprehension of the medium.

Trump's comment is a textbook example of Marshall McLuhan's theory which states that the content of any medium is always another medium: "The content of writing is speech, just as the written word is the content of print, and print is the content of the telegraph."[10] For Trump, the content of TV is radio. It's common for people to pick up everything they know about a previous medium and throw it at a newer one.

[9] Michael Barbaro and Steve Eder. "Under Oath, Donald Trump Shows His Raw Side." *New York Times*, July 28, 2015, p. Al.
[10] McLuhan, *Understanding Media*.

I'm often reminded of Trump's comment when I hear complaints about how we're wasting time on the Internet. To them, television is the content of the Web. What they seem to be missing is that the Web is not monolithic, but instead is multiple, diverse, fractured, contradictory, high, and low, all at the same time in ways that television rarely was.

It's a Sunday morning and I go downstairs to get the *New York Times.* In the travel section is a piece entitled "Going Off the Grid on a Swedish Island." It's about a woman who takes a digital detox on a remote island as a reminder that she is not, in fact, "merely the sum of my posts and tweets and filter-enhanced iPhone photos."[11] She checks herself into a "hermit hut"—an isolated cabin without electricity or running water—and gives her phone to her husband who locks it with a pass code. As she settles into the hut, bereft of her technology, she suddenly discovers herself connected to nature, listening to the sound of waves folding by the nearby shore. She also rediscovers the pleasure of reading books. She becomes introspective, remarking, "Now, disconnected from the imposed (or imagined) pressures from followers and friends loitering unseen in the ether of the Web, I found myself reaching for a more authentic, balanced existence for myself, online and off."

She takes long walks. But each natural experience she has is filtered through the lens of technology. While listening to the sounds of nature, she muses, "Without a Spotify playlist to lose myself in. . . . What else had I been blind to while distracted by electronics, I wondered?" She sees marvelous things: towering wind turbines, whose "graceful blades whoosh audibly overhead," and congratulates herself when she resists the urge to record and share the scene on social media. She conveniently forgets the fact that these turbines are wholly designed and driven by digital interfaces. She nostalgically finds older, pre-digital technologies—ironically littering the landscape—charming. Seeing an upturned rotting car that "looks like a bug," she can't resist: "I pulled out my camera and took a photo, one that I knew would never get a single 'like' from anyone but me. And that was just fine." On these sojourns, she mechanizes nature, describing it with tech metaphors: "Along the way, the only tweets I encountered were from birds." On her final evening on the island, she has a cosmic epiphany whilst musing on the stars in the night sky, one that is served with a dose of self-flagellation for her previous misdeeds: "Those spellbinding heavens are always hiding in plain sight above us, if only we would unplug long enough to notice."

Even in such lighthearted Sunday morning fare, her words are laced with an all-too-pervasive, unquestioning guilt about technology. Try as she might, the writer is enmeshed with technology to the point that she is unable to experience nature without technological mediation. She may have left her devices at home, but she's still seeing the world entirely

25

---

[11] http://www.nytimes.com/2015/07/12/travel/going-off-the-grid-on-a-swedish-island.html, July 12, 2015.

through them. Her brain, indeed, has become differently wired and all the nature in the world on a weekend digital detox won't change that. What was accomplished by this trip? Not much. Far away from her devices, all she did was think obsessively about them. Returning from her trip, it's hard to imagine that much changed. I can't imagine that in the spirit of her adventure she wrote her piece out longhand in number 2 pencils on legal pads by candlelight, only to sit down at a Remington typewriter bashing out the final draft, and filing it via carrier pigeon. No. Instead, the morning her piece appeared, she retweeted a link to the article: "@ingridkwilliams goes off the grid on a charming Swedish island."

What these types of articles tend to ignore is the fact that technology has been entwined with nature for as long as humans have been depicting it. French landscape painters such as Claude Lorrain (1600–1682) often painted what they called ideal landscapes, which rendered nature in pitch-perfect states that never existed. So you get classical ruins nestled in dense, thick jungles that couldn't possibly grow in the rocky Greek soil. These painters claimed that architecture was a kind of technology, one that either represented the spoiling of nature or its conquest by man. Even Thoreau's cabin on Walden Pond[12] was within earshot of the rattle and hum of a busy East Coast railroad line that ran about a kilometer away from his "hermit hut."

Another article in this morning's newspaper—this time in the business section—sends an identical message. It's called "Put Down the Phone." The piece focuses on various types of software and apps that monitor and restrict the time you spend on social media. These technologies include wearable clothing—with a sweep of an arm you can silence your phone—and suggests twelve-step-style parlor games you can play with your friends: the winner is the one who looks at their phone the least. There's also a review of an app that turns your smartphone back into a "dumb phone" circa 1999 that does nothing more than make and receive calls.

But the highlight of the article is a plastic facsimile of a smartphone that is a piece of plastic that does absolutely nothing. It's touted as "a security blanket for people who want to curb their phone addiction but are afraid to leave home without something to hold on to."[13] And yet in psychoanalytic theory, a security blanket is known as a transitional object, one that represents "me" and "not me" simultaneously.[14] That definition—me and not me simultaneously—seems to be a more realistic assessment of our online lives than the tirade of pleas for a return to

[12] **Thoreau's cabin on Walden Pond:** In 1845, American essayist, philosopher, and naturalist Henry David Thoreau (1817–1862) moved into a small hand-built cabin on the banks of Walden Pond outside of Concord, Massachusetts, to conduct a two-year long experiment in "simple living" and self-reliance, which he documented in *Walden; or, Life in the Woods* (1854).

[13] http://www.nytimes.com/2015/07/12/sunday-review/addicted-to-your-phone-theres-help-for-that.html, July 12, 2015.

[14] https://thinkingthoughts-dotorg.wordpress.com/2013/05/14/d-w-winnicott-on-transitional-object-and-transitional-space/, July 12, 2015.

some long-lost, unified "authentic" self. Online, I am me and not me at the same time. Surely, the way I portray myself on Facebook isn't really me; it's an image of myself as I wish to project it to the world. Sometimes that image is true. Other times it's a complete lie.

The article concludes with a quote from a psychology professor at the University of Kansas, who disparagingly says, "Smartphones are a potent delivery mechanism for two fundamental human impulses: our quest to find new and interesting distractions, and our desire to feel that we have checked off a task." But I find that to be positive. That quote sums up the complex balancing act we perform with our devices. We're productive—we're checking off tasks—and we're distracted in new and interesting ways. (Since when are *new* and *interesting* pejorative?) It's that frisson of opposites—bacon-infused chocolate or salted caramel ice cream—that makes it zing. The professor goes on to bemoan the fact that "with these devices you can get that sense of accomplishment multiple times a minute. The brain gets literally rewired to switch—to constantly seek out novelty, which makes putting the phone down difficult." It sounds great to me. Novelty *and* accomplishment. They work together.

When I used to watch TV, "likes" weren't really part of the game. 30 Sure, I liked one show better than another, but I was forced to choose from a tiny set of options, seven channels, to be specific. Today, "like" has come to mean something very different. We can support something, expressing ourselves by clicking Like or we can download something we like. In this way, we build a rich ecosystem of artifacts around us based on our proclivities and desires. What sits in my download folder—piles of books to be read, dozens of movies to be watched, and hundreds of albums to be heard—constitutes a sort of self-portrait of both who I am in this particular point in time, and who I was in earlier parts of my life. In fact, you'll find nestled among the Truffaut films[15] several episodes of *The Brady Bunch*, a show I really "liked" back in the day. Sometimes I'm in the mood to watch Truffaut; other times I'm in the mood to watch *The Brady Bunch*. Somehow those impulses don't contradict one another; instead, they illuminate the complexities of being me. I'm rarely just one way: I like high art sometimes and crap others.

While I could discuss any number of musical epiphanies I've personally experienced over the past half century, all of them would pale in comparison to the epiphany of seeing Napster for the first time in 1999. Although prior to Napster I had been a member of several file-sharing communities, the sheer scope, variety, and seeming endlessness of Napster was mind-boggling: you never knew what you were going to find and how much of it was going to be there. It was as if every record store, flea market, and thrift shop in the world had been connected by a searchable database and flung their doors open, begging you to walk away with as much as you could carry for free. But it was even better

---

[15] **Truffaut films:** François Roland Truffaut (1932–1984) was a French film director and a founder of the revolutionary French New Wave movement of filmmaking.

because the supply never exhausted; the coolest record you've ever dug up could now be shared with all your friends. Of course this has been exacerbated many times over with the advent of torrents and MP3 blogs.

But the most eye-opening thing about Napster was the idea that you could browse other people's shared files. It was as if a little private corner of everyone's world was now publicly available for all to see. It was fascinating — perhaps even a bit voyeuristic — to see what music other people had in their folders and how they organized it. One of the first things that struck me about Napster was how impure and eclectic people's tastes were. Whilst browsing another user's files, I was stunned to find John Cage[16] MP3s alphabetically snuggled up next to, say, Mariah Carey files in the same directory. It boggled the mind: how could a fan of thorny avant-garde music also like the sugary pop of Mariah Carey? And yet it's true. Everyone has guilty pleasures. But never before have they been so exposed — and celebrated — this publicly. To me, this was a great relief. It showed that online — and by extension in real life — we never have been just one way, all the time. That's too simple. Instead, we're a complex mix, full of contradictions.

The Web is what Stanford professor Sianne Ngai calls "*stuplime*," a combination of the stupid and the sublime. That cat video on Buzz-Feed is so stupid, but its delivery mechanism — Facebook — is so mind-bogglingly sublime. Inversely, that dashboard cam of the meteor striking Russia[17] is so cosmically sublime, but its delivery mechanism — Facebook — is so mind-bogglingly stupid. It's this tension that keeps us glued to the Web. Were it entirely stupid or were it entirely sublime, we would've gotten bored long ago. A befuddling mix of logic and nonsense, the Web by its nature is surrealist: a shattered, contradictory, and fragmented medium. What if, instead of furiously trying to stitch together these various shards into something unified and coherent — something many have been desperately trying to do — we explore the opposite: embracing the disjunctive as a more organic way of framing what is, in essence, a medium that defies singularity? . . .

When futurist poet F. T. Marinetti[18] famously wrote in a 1909 manifesto that "we will destroy the museums, libraries, academies of every kind," he could not have foreseen the double-edged sword of web-based structures. On one hand, artists are embracing the meme's infinitesimal life span as a new metric (think: short attention span as a new avant-garde), constructing works not for eternity but only for long enough to ripple across the networks, vanishing as quickly as they appear, replaced by new ones tomorrow. On the other hand, our every gesture is archived by

---

[16] **John Cage:** American composer and musical theorist (1912–1992) who pioneered avant-garde compositional style that featured improvisation, chance, nonstandard instruments, and silence.

[17] **meteor striking Russia:** On February 15, 2013, a meteorite was filmed exploding over Russia's Ural Mountains.

[18] **F. T. Marinetti:** Filippo Tommaso Emilio Marinetti (1876–1944) was an Italian poet and founder of futurism, an avant-garde social and aesthetic movement that celebrated technology, speed, youth, and violence.

search engines and cemented into eternally recallable databases. Unlike Marinetti's call to erase history, on the Web everything is forever. The Internet itself is a giant museum, library, and academy all in one, comprised of everything from wispy status updates to repositories of dense classical texts. And every moment you spend wasting time on the Internet contributes to the pile—even your clicks, favorites, and likes. Read through a literary lens, could we think of our web sojourns as epic tales effortlessly and unconsciously written, etched into our browser histories as a sort of new memoir? Beyond that, in all its glory and hideousness, Facebook is the greatest collective autobiography that a culture has ever produced, a boon to future sociologists, historians, and artists.

This accretion of data is turning us into curators, librarians, and [35] amateur archivists, custodians of our own vast collections. The web's complex ecosystem of economies—both paid and pirated—offer us more cultural artifacts than we can consume: There are more movies on Netflix than I will ever be able to see, not to mention all the movies I've simultaneously downloaded from file-sharing which languish unwatched on my hard drive. The fruits of what's known as "free culture"—the idea that the Web should be a place for an open exchange of ideas and intellectual materials, bereft of over-restrictive copyright laws—create a double-edged sword. Abundance is a lovely problem to have, but it produces a condition whereby the management of my cultural artifacts—their acquisition, filing, redundancy, archiving, and redistribution—is overwhelming their actual content. I tend to shift my artifacts around more than I tend to use them.... I've happily swapped quality for quantity, uniqueness for reproduction, strength for weakness, and high resolution for super compression in order to participate in the global cornucopia of file sharing and social media. And what of consumption? I've outsourced much of it. While I might only be able to read a fraction of what I've downloaded, web spiders—indexing automatons—have read it all. While part of me laments this, another part is thrilled at the rare opportunity to live in one's own time, able to reimagine the status of the cultural object in the twenty-first century where context is the new content.

The Web ecology runs on quantity. Quantity is what drove the vast data leaks of Julian Assange, Aaron Swartz, Chelsea Manning, and Edward Snowden,[19] leaks so absurdly large they could never be read in their entirety, only parsed, leaks so frighteningly huge they were derided by the mainstream media as "information vandalism," a critique that

---

[19] **Julian Assange, Aaron Swartz, Chelsea Manning, and Edward Snowden:** Julian Assange (b. 1971) is an Australian Internet activist and the founder of Wikileaks, a website dedicated to publishing secret information. Aaron Swartz (1986–2013) was an American entrepreneur, writer, and Internet activist who committed suicide while under federal indictment for stealing and publishing journal articles written by faculty at the Massachusetts Institute of Technology. Chelsea Manning (born Bradley Manning in 1987) is an American activist, who was convicted by court-martial in 2013 after she provided nearly 750,000 pages of classified material to Wikileaks for publication. Edward Snowden (b. 1983) is a former Central Intelligence Agency employee who leaked thousands of classified National Security Agency files to the press in 2013.

mistook the leak's form for function—or malfunction—as if to say the gesture of liberating information is as important as what's actually being moved. To Assange, Swartz, Manning, and Snowden, what was being moved *was* important—a matter of life and death. But then again to many of us, our devices are a matter of life and death. The ubiquity of smartphones and dashboard and body cams, combined with the ability to distribute these images virally, have shed light on injustices that previously went unnoticed. When critics insist we put down our devices because they are making us less connected to one another, I have to wonder how the families of Tamir Rice or Laquan McDonald[20] might react to that....

Scrawled across the walls of Paris in May 1968,[21] the slogan "live without dead time" became a rallying cry for a way of reclaiming spaces and bureaucracies that suck the life from you. I'd like to think our web experience can be nearly bereft of dead time if only we had the lens through which to see it that way. I don't mean to paint too rosy a picture. The downsides of the Web are well known: trolling, hate, flame wars, spam, and rampant stupidity. Still, there's something perverse about how well we use the Web yet how poorly we theorize our time spent on it. I'm hearing a lot of complaints, but I'm not getting too many answers, which makes me think perhaps our one-dimensional approach has been wrongheaded. Befitting a complex medium, one that is resistant to singularities, let's consider a panoply of ideas, methods, and inspirations. The word "rhizomatic" has been used to describe the Web to the point of cliché, but I still find it useful. The rhizome, a root form that grows unpredictably in all directions, offers many paths rather than one. The genie will not be put back in the bottle. Walking away is not an option. We are not unplugging anytime soon. Digital detoxes last as long as grapefruit diets do; transitional objects are just that. I'm convinced that learning, interaction, conversation, and engagement continues as it always has, but it's taking new and different forms. I think it's time to drop the simplistic guilt about wasting time on the Internet and instead begin to explore—and perhaps even celebrate—the complex possibilities that lay before us.

ENGAGING THE TEXT

1. How do you waste time on the Internet? Keep a log for a day or two of the sites you visit; your posts, likes, and shares; and the things you read, graze, or skim. How does your use of the Internet compare with Goldsmith's? Would you agree that your time online is well spent?

[20] **Tamir Rice or Laquan McDonald:** In 2014, Tamir Rice, an unarmed 12-year-old African American, was shot and killed by two Cleveland police officers. In 2014, Laquan McDonald, an unarmed 17-year-old African American, was shot and killed by a Chicago police officer. Both cases ignited protests when cell phone videos of the killings were made public.

[21] **the walls of Paris in May 1968:** In May 1968, a series of massive student-led demonstrations and strikes were staged across France protesting against capitalism, consumerism, and American imperialism.

2. What common criticisms of the Internet does Goldsmith explore and reject in this selection? Which of them seem valid to you? Which strike you as overreactions, and why?

3. How has the Internet affected the way you read? How often do you read novels or book-length works of nonfiction? How much time do you spend reading blogs or articles online? To what extent, if any, has your online life harmed your ability to read "deeply"?

4. Based on your experience, how realistic is the image of teenagers and technology that Goldsmith presents? To what extent would you agree that smartphones and social media have made today's kids more sociable and creative than ever before?

5. Overall, how does Goldsmith see the Internet changing us? What is it doing to the world we live in, and how is it transforming us? How do you see it changing people and the world around you?

6. **Thinking Rhetorically**   Review several of the personal anecdotes that Goldsmith offers to support his view of the Internet and its impact. How persuasive do you find these personal experiences? Why do you think he chose not to include statistics or research results to back up his claims? How would you describe his purpose and audience?

EXPLORING CONNECTIONS

7. How might Sherry Turkle (p. 178) respond to Goldsmith's claim that "Our devices, if anything, tend to amplify our sociability" (para. 10)? How do Turkle's observations of her students challenge Goldsmith's optimistic view of smartphones? Has your smartphone made you more or less able to sustain relationships? Why do you think so?

8. Compare Goldsmith's view of technology's impact on teens with that offered by Jean Twenge (p. 257). How does Goldsmith respond to the idea that smartphones and social media are addictive and that they have made teenagers antisocial and depressed? Whose position on this issue do you find more persuasive, and why?

EXTENDING THE CRITICAL CONTEXT

9. Goldsmith's book, the source of this selection, offers hundreds of suggestions for how to waste time on the Internet. Working in groups, examine a sampling of the ideas he offers below. Which of these suggestions for class activities strike you as being potentially problematic, and why? Which, if any, would you like to try in class?

   • Connect a computer to a large screen or monitor and have volunteers waste a few minutes on the Internet publicly for the class to see. Later, vote on who wasted time the best.

- As a class, attack a social media site and try to clog it with as many postings as you can.

- Try to create a meme and make it go viral.

- Have everyone open their laptops, log onto Facebook, and walk away from their computers. For the next fifteen minutes, everyone in class is free to roam from computer to computer and type whatever they want into the user's status window. Later, have volunteers read what others wrote.

- Sit in a circle with laptops open and plug your headphones into the computer of your neighbor to the right. Play music for the student on your left that fits the vibe of the music being played for you. Keep changing songs until you sense the circle reaches equilibrium.

- Sit in a circle and do a background check on the person to your left. Collect as much information as you can from any source, create a profile of what you learn, and send it to them.

- Find a piece of audio that you think summarizes the Internet. Share these in class and discuss why you chose them.

- Have everyone in class put their addresses in a bowl. After drawing an address, each person goes on eBay and buys a gift costing under a dollar to send to the person they've drawn. Later discuss your choice of gifts.

10. Over the period of a week or two, create a class website where you collectively build an album of artifacts that expresses what the Internet is or does. Feel free to post photos, images, GIFs, audio clips, memes, rants, or anything else you find online.

ZOË AND THE TROLLS
NOREEN MALONE

Before there were #MeToo and #TimesUp, there was Gamergate. In 2013, Eron Gjoni, an ex-boyfriend of video game developer Zoë Quinn, published a 9,425-word online manifesto attacking her for breaking up with him. Linked to 4chan, a message/image board website often recognized as the birthplace of trolling, Gjoni's blog post went viral, and Quinn and her family soon found themselves under assault, on- and offline, by an organized mob of misogynist harassers. Within a year, the attacks spread to other women associated with the gaming industry, including developer Brianna Wu and gaming critic Anita Sarkeesian.

Of course, it's not surprising that gaming would spawn a venomous backlash against women. As Noreen Malone, the author of this selection, notes, sexism and misogyny have been the stock and trade of the video gaming industry since the birth of the GameBoy in 1984. Beyond raising questions about the male-centric culture of video gaming, Malone's retelling of Quinn's experience also traces the links between gaming and the racism and sexism we've come to accept as the new normal in American politics. Noreen Malone (b. 1984) is the features editor at *New York* magazine. In 2015, she won the George Polk and News Women's Club Awards for "Cosby: The Women, An Unwelcome Sisterhood," a *New York* magazine feature story detailing the accounts of thirty-five women accusing comedian Bill Cosby of sexual assault.

ONE DAY IN 2014, THE VIDEO-GAME DESIGNER Zoë Quinn decided to make herself a cyborg. And so, this being the modern world, she simply ordered a kit from the Internet that would allow her, via a large sterilized syringe that she plunged into the webbing between her left thumb and index finger, to implant a microchip the size of a Tic Tac under her skin.

For a while, Quinn programmed the chip, which has a short-range radio transmitter that lets it send code to compatible devices, to do useful things, like call up a link to a game onto anyone's phone that she touched, or make a new friend's phone automatically text her contact information, which particularly came in handy at video-game conventions. But nowadays, she says, "I like the idea of using cool cyberpunk stuff to tell really stupid jokes." The only script she currently runs on it pops up a notification window on the target phone that says, simply, "dicks."

Quinn (who already had a magnet under the skin of her index finger, which she says allows her to "feel electromagnetic fields, like an additional sense," as well as pick up anything magnetic as a party trick) originally installed the chip to promote a comedy video game she had begun building called *It's Not OK, Cupid*. The game was inspired by her attempt to meet someone on the dating website, and, like many of Quinn's projects, it was high concept: Set in a reality where people find love via an artificial intelligence, the game asks characters to scan a chip to verify that they are who they say they are. The joke, in part, is that authentication like that is unimaginable, really. "You'd have to be totally honest online," she explains. And as everyone knows, the Internet isn't built for accountability.

She never actually finished the game, however, and in the end, the chip wasn't even vaguely the most dystopian OkCupid-related event in Quinn's life. The previous December, while living in Boston, she went out with Eron Gjoni, a programmer she'd met on the site, with whom she had a 98 percent match. The first date involved drinks at a dive bar in Cambridge, sneaking into Harvard Stadium, a sleepover. They started a relationship that was intense at first, then off and on as the spring wound down. It was not an unusual course of events for a

20-something romance. But what followed was extraordinary, an act of revenge on an ex that became about much more than the two of them, that rippled across the video-game industry and far beyond. As Quinn writes in her memoir, *Crash Override*, "My breakup required the intervention of the United Nations."

The broad strokes of the episode — Gamergate, as it came to be called — go something like this: In August 2014, Gjoni published an extensive blog post accusing Quinn of various infidelities, including, he said, sleeping with a journalist at the gaming site Kotaku. The post was explosive, particularly on certain Internet forums like 4chan,[1] where it was suggested that she'd cheated on Gjoni in order to get a positive review of a game she'd built. In fact, no such review exists, but Quinn was an appealing target: She was already known for her work as a designer whose most famous game seemed built more to provoke an argument than to be enjoyable, and for her outspokenness on gender inequities in the industry.

Almost instantly, Quinn began receiving messages like "If I ever see you are doing a pannel [*sic*] at an event I am going to, I will literally kill you. You are lower than shit and deserve to be hurt, maimed, killed." The slurs were constant, and deeply personal. But the participants — anonymous or pseudonymous commenters posting on 4chan, on ever-multiplying Reddit message boards like r/quinnspiracy, or even under their real names on Twitter — framed their attacks as just retribution for a moral lapse on Quinn's part that was larger than what Quinn had "done" to her boyfriend. It was, in the phrase that became a joke almost as quickly as it became a rallying cry, "about ethics in gaming journalism." Somehow, one woman's fidelity in a relatively casual relationship was imagined to matter a huge amount, as if it were the epitome of everything wrong with not just gamer or Internet culture but culture in general and even politics.

And then, horrifically, that all became true. Gamergate went on for months and months, taking on a life of its own. Milo Yiannopoulos,[2] then a relatively anonymous blogger for Breitbart,[3] made a specialty of targeting Quinn, raising his own profile and moving the fight into the right-wing pockets of Internet culture, by publishing pieces like "Feminist Bullies Tearing the Video Game Industry Apart." The argument shifted away from video games to how "social-justice warriors" like Quinn and her defenders (in other words, anyone who suggested the harassment was caused by sexism and prejudice) were intent on bending the culture to their politically correct will. Free speech — even masculinity in general — was under attack. A lawyer named Mike

---

[1]**4chan:** An anonymous Internet imageboard forum associated with trolling, hacking, and alt-right subcultures. [All notes are the editors'.]

[2]**Milo Yiannopolos:** Pen name of Milo Hanrahan (b. 1984), a conservative British political commentator and writer who is known for his critiques of feminism, Islam, social justice, and political correctness.

[3]**Breitbart:** Founded in 2007 by Andrew Breitbart, Breitbart News Network is a far-right American news website that features conspiracy theories, misleading stories, and content that has been considered misogynist, racist, and xenophobic.

Cernovich[4] became obsessed with the case and volunteered advice to Gjoni and his supporters when Quinn eventually sought a restraining order against her ex. "Young men have it rough," he wrote on his blog about the wider cultural significance of Gamergate. By late 2015, Yiannopoulos and Cernovich had become Internet-famous, with virtual armies of acolytes who shared a distinct sensibility. And they had found a new source of inspiration, something else at which to throw their frustrations, their nihilism, the identity-politics-obsessed rage that they'd honed during Gamergate: supporting the candidacy of our now-president.

All from the lashing out of one young man against one young woman.

Quinn, who is 29, cultivates a self-presentation that can make her seem a little bit like a video-game character, the heroine of her own mythological rendering. She swears a lot, rides a Harley, colors her hair silver-blonde with a blue streak that matches her silver-blue eye shadow, and dresses her anime curves dramatically: The first time we met, in New York, she was wearing tall black boots and a black-and-white striped dress under a double-breasted coat that dipped down in the back like a Renaissance Faire costume. She carried a studded Alexander McQueen backpack she was quick to tell me was a gift, not a purchase. "The first thing I ever heard about McQueen was he wanted the women he dresses to be somebody people are afraid of," she explained. Everywhere else, too, she has worked to make herself seem tough, with gauges in her ears and tattoos on both arms, a lip ring and the just-visible marks of its disappeared eyebrow twin. She scowls in pictures, but in person there is an essential teenage softness to Quinn: She picks nervously at her glittery gold nail polish, confides easily.

As we began to talk, Quinn put down her phone, holstered in a   10
case of her own design that's decorated as a pink butt—the charging plug between the cheeks—and swallowed a pill. She has been diagnosed with complex PTSD, the result of prolonged, repeated exposure to trauma. Her eyes get red when she talks about "the troubles," as she calls it, or when she talks about Gjoni, whom she refers to only as "the ex." She is ambivalent about the degree to which identity politics has become the thing everyone associates with her. "My big thing was *please stop sending me rape threats*," Quinn said of Gamergate. "It's hard to call that feminist criticism."

Quinn, like many adult gamers, was a child gamer first, finding some escape from the part of upstate New York where she grew up, which she calls "shit-kicker country." Her father worked on motorcycles; bikers were their community. Quinn played on a 3DO, a failed early-'90s console that her father had picked up at a garage sale, and

---

[4]**Mike Cernovich:** Alt-right social media personality and writer (b. 1977) infamous for spreading conspiracy theories.

so her canon of formative games is full of "weird" ones no one else really played. Depression came on young; she tried to kill herself in early adolescence. In high school, she skewed goth, sang in a ska band, and lost her virginity to an older girl who then told the whole school. She didn't have many friends her own age, but she did have dial-up Internet. Online, she found thrills and comfort: tips on her favorite games; women talking about wanting other women; Rotten.com's pictures of autopsies; Erowid's suggestions for how to safely do drugs; and chat rooms filled with other depressed people who became her support system and stopped her from trying suicide again. "My circle of online friends helped steer me away from potentially stupid decisions with really scary consequences," she writes in *Crash Override.*

She was a creature of message boards, in other words. Some of her online friends were the kind of grown men who were happy to let 15-year-old girls pretend to be 22. She traveled to meet a handful of them, doing exactly the thing every parent in that era was terrified their daughter might do. The farthest she went was bus-hopping to Alberta, Canada, to see a man she'd struck up a correspondence with on VampireFreaks ("like Facebook, for goths"). At 17, she broke up with a man who knocked out part of one of her molars in anger. "I fucking come from circumstances," she says.

After high school, Quinn worked at a series of dead-end jobs and did some nude pinup modeling; her glasses and tattoos got her labeled in the fetish category. She tried stripping but found it didn't mesh well with her shyness. She married, at 19, the roommate of a blue-haired tollbooth worker she'd become friends with during her many trips out of town to meet Internet acquaintances. Quinn says it was "mostly for car insurance" that the couple made it legal.

Her husband didn't do much for work: For a while, his primary source of income was as a "gold farmer" in the video game *EverQuest,* which meant that he'd sell the digital currency he racked up to other players looking for shortcuts. The couple wound up homeless, couch-surfing and occasionally sleeping in their car, until Quinn got a job as a rent-a-cop in Albany. Meanwhile, her online friendships deepened, especially the ones she made in an Internet Relay Chat room, a technology that attracts some of the most hard-core, deep-web users—the same kind of people who'd later become Gamergaters. "Years passed in that IRC room," she writes. "I spent my 21st birthday chatting with my online friends because my husband had little interest in celebrating with me, and there was no other group of people I'd rather spend time with, even if they weren't there with me in person."

When the marriage ended, in 2010, Quinn moved to Toronto, where she had another friend from the Internet. She decided to apply for one of six spots in a short seminar for women on making video games, put on by programmers concerned about the lack of women in the industry. At the informational session, Quinn raised her hand and asked whether the class discussion could extend to an online forum accessible to all the women who didn't get in. She believes the question is why she won a spot in the course, which changed her career, and her life.

She began to make weird, often comic games that had almost no relationship to what we think of as video games. One is called *Waiting for Godot: The Game*[5] (it never loads); another, called *Jeff Goldblum Staring Contest*, challenges players not to blink before his photo does. Money was tight, and she couldn't land a full-time job at a studio, but she had made enough friends online that when her laptop broke, donors on a GoFundMe page paid for a new one.

Then, in a two-week binge, with the help of the writer Patrick Lindsey, Quinn finished a free, text-based game called *Depression Quest*, a choose-your-own-adventure-style journey in which the player struggles to make the minor decisions of daily life and, as the game progresses, finds that the healthy option—seeing friends, exercising rather than staying in bed, even seeking treatment—isn't always available to her. It was the kind of idea-driven experimentation that excites indie design- ers and a certain kind of liberal-artsy video-game critic ("Writers liked it because it turns out a lot of writers have depression," she told me), but which the majority of the video-game community doesn't like at all. *Depression Quest* isn't fun to play, and while that might be exactly the point Quinn was trying to make, for many, gaming is meant to be an escape from the difficulties of the real world, not a meditation on it.

When Quinn and Lindsey released *Depression Quest* in February 2014, it was a minor hit. It also occasioned a rape threat directed at Quinn, and a discussion on Wizardchan, a message board for adult male vir- gins, of how much the game "sucked" and how a woman could never really know true depression. Some of those users found Quinn's phone number—she had entered it on a spreadsheet for volunteers after the Boston bombing—and began to call her.

Quinn doesn't believe it was an accident that the brunt of the criti- cism was directed at her and not at her male co-writer. She saw friends on Twitter arguing that the gaming community didn't have a problem with women, that "these are all lone wolves," she said. "Motherfucker, then there's a pack somewhere." She posted the screenshots of the harassment she'd gotten. This mostly served as an invitation to escalate the attacks.

But it also helped her to cultivate a reputation as someone who   20 spoke out on issues of inclusion and misogyny in the industry. She was chosen as one of two women on *Game_Jam*, a reality-TV show Maker Studios was trying to mount about indie game designers. Quinn helped incite a rebellion on the first day of filming when, among other things, the producer asked a male competitor if he thought his team was at a disadvantage because there was a "pretty woman" on it. Production

---

[5] ***Waiting for Godot***: A famous 1953 play by avant-garde playwright Samuel Beckett (1906–1989) in which two characters wait for a mysterious person named Godot who never arrives.

shut down, costing Maker Studios hundreds of thousands of dollars. Quinn also flew out to San Francisco, with her then-boyfriend Gjoni, to give a talk at a gaming conference about the harassment she'd experienced.

Video games weren't always such a male-dominated world. In the early days, they were so simple that there weren't really ways to gender the games themselves (think *Space Invaders*). A successful 1970s game called *King's Quest* was both designed by a woman and mostly played by a core audience of women in their 30s; female protagonists weren't remarkable.

But in 1983, the industry experienced a severe recession — precipitated by a glut of low-quality games, and especially by the massive flop that was the Atari *E.T.* game, designed quickly at Steven Spielberg's behest. (Fewer than a third of the 5 million copies produced were sold, resulting in a disaster so complete the company buried and cemented-over copies in a landfill in the New Mexico desert.)

The industry languished until Nintendo broke through in 1985, in part by marketing its consoles as toys, not just games — and thus launching itself into the gender-binary world of toy stores. (Its most famous product was Game Boy.) Research showed that more boys than girls were playing, which only reinforced the marketing strategies, which in turn reshaped the industry. To hook the adolescent-and-beyond segment, sex was introduced, at least in a theoretical way. Women were depicted on game covers as panting onlookers. Female protagonists, like Lara Croft, had builds that would give Barbie a crisis of confidence. Games like *Myst* and the *Sims* still had largely female playerships, but shooter games began to dominate the public conception of what a video game was.

And "gamer" matured into an identity — a distinctly modern, if not forward-looking, version of escapist masculinity. "Live in Your World. Play in Ours," went the Sony PlayStation slogan. To observers, it could be hard to understand why a community of demographically advantaged young people would feel the need to protect their community from interlopers like Quinn, or the few female gamers before her who talked about gender in gaming. But any accommodations to diversity, or signals among journalists or developers that perhaps this might be valuable, did seem to provoke a hostile backlash. On 4chan and other sites, young men "policed the purity of games — the boundaries of what was a real game and what was not," says Anita Sarkeesian, who, in 2012, came under attack from a proto-Gamergate horde for her video series called *Tropes vs. Women in Video Games.* She explains the intensity of harassment directed to women gamers with some sympathy. "When you have been told as a boy that games are for you, you have this deep sense of entitlement," she told me. "Then they're told they deserve fancy cars and hot women. When they don't have that, they're like, *At least we have games.* And then they see women saying, no, we're here too."

In June 2014, Gjoni and Quinn saw each other for a coda to their rela-   25
tionship, back in San Francisco once more. Even though they were in
the same place, he communicated with her mostly via Facebook Mes-
senger, from a library, trying to get her to confess to cheating, and
asked for access to her accounts for proof. Gjoni had begun to compile
a dossier of all their communications and of hers with others on public
platforms.

According to Quinn's account, they had sex one last time in San
Francisco, and she says Gjoni became "violent" during the encounter.
(Gjoni strongly denies this characterization.) She left with bruises on
her arm, she says, and later found out she was pregnant. They went
back and forth, in a series of emotional texts, about whether to keep
the baby. She considered it, then thought about what she would be giving up. She had an abortion, stopped talking to Gjoni, blocked him on
several forms of communication, and didn't speak to him until the "Zoe
Post," as he titled it, went live. He wrote it, he told me, "as a cautionary
tale for those who stood to be harmed by Zoë."...

Quinn was at a bar with friends and her new boyfriend of a week,
Alex Lifschitz, celebrating her 27th birthday, when she got a text from
a friend: "You just got helldumped something fierce," it said. "I tried to
focus on the conversation at the table, but the agitated rattling of my
phone was the only thing I could hear," she writes in her book. "It was
like counting the seconds between thunderclaps to see how far away
the storm is and knowing it's getting closer."

As they stood outside the bar, one friend showed Quinn that her
Wikipedia page had been changed to say she was going to die "soon";
it was then edited to show her date of death as her next public appearance. Nudes from her time modeling circulated. She and Lifschitz
stayed up all night fielding messages and texting with friends who were
working to get the posts deleted, taking screenshots of everything.
(Quinn keeps the documentation of her harassment in a file called "Just
Another Day at the Office.")

Quinn can be analytical when talking about what happened to her:
She believes that abusing her turned into a game in which participants
tried to outdo one another with their vitriol; upvotes and retweets on
social media showed them they'd scored. She also believes that Gjoni
knew exactly the kind of situation he would create when he posted in
the gamer forums. "Look at Elliot Rodger,"[6] she told me, referring to the
man who, in 2014, went on a killing spree at UC Santa Barbara. "He
posted in the same places. Look at Dylann Roof.[7] It's like you're playing

[6] **Elliot Rodger:** In 2014, Elliot Oliver Robertson Rodger (b. 1991) posted a racist,
misogynist manifesto online before killing six people and injuring fourteen near the campus of the University of California, Santa Barbara.
[7] **Dylann Roof:** In 2015, the white supremacist Dylann Storm Roof (b. 1994) killed nine
African Americans during a prayer service at the Emanuel African Methodist Episcopal
Church in Charleston, South Carolina.

Schrödinger's murderer[8] with all these people. Are they a shitty fucking edgelord"—a 4chan term of art for a certain kind of nihilist omnipresent on the site—"or are they actually going to kill me?" She also believes that he was taking advantage of his knowledge of her mental-health history. "Imagine all of the shitty tapes that play in the mind of a depressed person, externalized and with Twitter accounts blasting at you constantly."

Quinn had displayed and lived so much of her life online that, with diligent searching, it was possible to burrow deeply into her psyche and personal history and friendships. Once her personal information had been exposed—her address and phone number were published, her Tumblr and other accounts were hacked into—she and Lifschitz began staying with friends. When her father's address was posted, he began getting photographs in the mail of his daughter covered in a stranger's actual semen. When Quinn's grandfather died, she watched as posters in the forums boasted about combing his obituary for additional family members they could harass. Rather than try to reset her accounts, she deleted many of them. It was, she writes, "wrenching," like burning photographs that don't have negatives. Anyone who defended Quinn or the idea of a more diverse industry—Sarkeesian, developers like Brianna Wu and Phil Fish—also became targets....

When people would call Quinn's phone, she said, they wouldn't know what to do upon hearing her voice. "I'm a stand-in for other bullshit they've got going on," she said. "They are the hero of their own story, and when you think you're the good guy, you can get away with doing anything. If you think your enemy is a symbol and not a person, suddenly there's a bunch of inhuman shit you have the emotional bandwidth to do, and I know, because I've been an asshole. If Gamergate had happened to somebody else, years earlier, I probably would've been on the wrong side. As a shitty teenager with mental illness that had a misogynist streak and loved video games? Yeah."

On a sunny L.A. morning in April, just past the churning muscles of the USC[9] swimmers hard at practice, a quiet stream of young people with tattoos or My Little Pony–colored hair—dusty rose, soft tangerine, one especially dreamy mane of bright turquoise and '80s hot pink—walked into a classroom building, for the annual Queerness and Games conference. Attendees, a fair number of whom were women, people of color, or trans, were asked to write their preferred pronouns on a name tag; many scribbled down the gender-neutral "they." Quinn wrote, "Any work for me:)."

---

[8]**Schrödinger's murderer:** In 1935, Austrian physicist Erwin Schrödinger proposed a "thought experiment" to test the idea of indeterminacy in theoretical physics. He proposed that if a cat were placed in sealed box with a radioactive atom that might or might not kill it, one wouldn't know if the cat were alive or dead until the box was opened; hence, the cat would be, indeterminately, both "alive and dead" inside the box. Here, the notion is that someone randomly may or may not be a murderer.

[9]**USC:** The University of Southern California.

This was as far as you could get from conferences like E3,[10] where triple-A studios (the Hollywood-studio equivalent) showcase their wares. Here, there were panels on "Unruly Bodies: The Queer Physics of Fumblecore"[11] and "Cute Games: Using Icelandic Krútt Music to Understand Revolution and Resistance in Alt/Queer Games." Booths displayed games designed by attendees, many meant as social learning as much as play, like one on "emotional labor and otherness."

Stephen Totilo, the editor of Kotaku, told me that one of the reasons Gamergate exploded when it did is that it coincided with the rise of indie game culture, in which newly powerful laptops and cheaper technology meant that outside studios, more people could make games about whatever seemed interesting to them, with any kind of protagonist they wanted. But gaming is a culture obsessed with delineation and hierarchies; Totilo points to the '90s, when politicians began to blame video games for violence, as the moment when, in a defensive crouch, there arose the "sensibility that there is real gaming and there is the people outside who don't get it." And that any criticism of gaming culture, even from inside of it, amounted to an attack. As I listened to the conference's keynote speaker, John Epler, answer questions from the audience about why he designed the hit game *Dragon Age* without "romanceable" queer or fat or dwarf characters, I began to think about how all anyone wanted in that room was to be able to imagine themselves in these imaginary worlds. A refuge from the more difficult one was what both sides of this intra-gaming war wanted, and yet it was so hard for each to see that in the other....

Gamergate's harassment of Quinn slowed as 2015 began. It didn't end—"A lot of what was happening in Gamergate was happening before it and has been happening since," says Totilo. "The wounds are still more open than people realize"—but there were new targets: the actor Leslie Jones, supposedly ruining *Ghostbusters* by her mere presence in its reboot; John Boyega, doing the same with *Star Wars*; the new, more diverse Spider-Man comics—the list of villains went on and on. Gamergaters had not only created a whole new set of celebrities, like Yiannopoulos and Cernovich; it had solidified their methods (message-board-coordinated harassment on public-facing platforms, publishing personal information, creating memes about the target that made the whole thing seem fun) and their grudges had calcified into a worldview, one in which a cabal of identity-politics-obsessed feminists were nagging, whining, and guilting the world into watering down and ruining everything good that might have been.

The movement also had a new hero: Donald Trump, who didn't have much to say about video games but had plenty to dog-whistle

[10] **E3:** The Electronic Entertainment Expo is the largest trade event for the video game industry.

[11] **Fumblecore:** A type of video game that involves controls that are deliberately difficult to manipulate.

about identity politics. Steve Bannon, the former Breitbart chairman who served as the connection between the alt-right and the White House, has said that he was struck by the power of "rootless white males" on websites about *World of Warcraft* (which he'd learned about by investing in a firm that sought to profit off the kind of "gold farming" that Quinn's ex-husband had done) and actively thought about how to co-opt their potential. Gradually, many of the accounts that had been obsessed with Quinn and ethics in video-game journalism changed their avatars to Pepe the Frog,[12] tweeted about #MAGA,[13] and explored white nationalism.

Quinn didn't move on as quickly. She kept lurking in the chat rooms where her abuse had originated. She and Lifschitz had spent the past year becoming experts in documenting and reporting online harassment, and they decided to start an organization, Crash Override, that took on those tasks for others targeted by similar mobs. (The non-profit is funded through Anita Sarkeesian's Feminist Frequency.) Quinn became a figurehead for the movement; she and Sarkeesian were invited to speak before the U.N. about how to combat a "rising tide of online violence against women and girls.". . .

Quinn is nearly done building a new game, crowdfunded with $85,000 of Kickstarter contributions, to be released this fall. It's a satiri-cal full-motion video project about the campy erotic-fiction icon Chuck Tingle (known for titles like *Buttageddon*). A team of around ten built the game, but according to John Warren, her business partner on the project, Quinn is responsible for the majority of the programming, in addition to writing the narrative. "A lot of people are quick to assume she isn't the one doing the technical stuff," he says, in the same way "women at E3 always get asked if they're in marketing." It's by far the most complex project she's made.

Warren met Quinn when he tried to hire her to work on a game; he knew who she was from Gamergate but had also played *Depression Quest*. He liked her ear for dialogue and facility with branching narra-tives. The rest of his team ultimately vetoed Quinn's hiring — "She was an attention magnet in a way they weren't comfortable with," Warren says — but Quinn and Warren kept talking and, eventually, she told him about *Fail State*, a game she'd been dreaming of making for a while.

The premise of *Fail State*, a meta one, is that players find them-[40] selves inside an imaginary, multiplayer, web-enabled game that was so disastrously built and incoherent that its creators will shut it down soon — a dying world that, it turns out, players love anyway. It's a "microapocalypse," in Warren's words, in which "everyone is facing the end of this thing that's really important to them."

---

[12] **Pepe the Frog:** Originally appearing in *Boy's Club*, a comic by Matt Furie, Pepe the Frog became a popular racist meme after it was appropriated by the alt-right in 2015.

[13] **#MAGA:** "Make America Great Again," the slogan of Donald Trump's 2016 presi-dential campaign.

SOCIAL MEDIA BINGO

WRITE SOMETHING ABOUT FEMINISM ON SOCIAL MEDIA. MARK THE SQUARE WHEN YOU SEE THE COMMENT. PLAY ALONE OR WITH FRIENDS! *SO MUCH FUN!*

"what about INTERNATIONAL MENS DAY?"	[RAPE THREATS]	"... BUT WOMEN DO THAT TOO!"	YOU'RE JUST BITTER 'CUZ NOBODY WANTS TO FUCK YOU.	I'm more of an egalitarian really
YOU'RE A FEMINAZI	"CAN'T YOU TAKE A Joke?"	You're too Sensitive	IS IT THAT TIME OF THE MONTH	[completely IRRELEVANT analogy]
DON'T YOU HAVE MORE IMPORTANT THINGS TO WORRY ABOUT	"I'm a woman and I don't feel discriminated against!"	FREE SPACE	STOP PLAYING THE VICTIM	SEXISM DOESN'T EXIST ANYMORE!
"YOU'RE Hysterical"	"Men are biologically SUPERIOR" #Science	#NOT ALL MEN	"YOU'RE JUST LOOKING FOR THINGS TO BE OFFENDED BY!"	[MANSPLAINING]
[bad statistics]	I don't NEED FEMINISM because	"BUT MEN ARE OBJECTIFIED BY WOMEN"	THE "WAGE GAP" is A MYTH!	[link to bullshit article]

I thought about why Quinn might have been drawn to build a world like that, fallen and imploding and yet treasured, full of surprising joy and possibilities. During one of the hearings for the legal action against Gjoni, a judge who saw no grounds for criminal harassment charges suggested that Quinn get a job that didn't involve the Internet, if the Internet had been so bad to her. She told him that there was no offline version of what she did. "You're a smart kid," he replied. "Find a different career."

To Quinn, this was one of the most coldhearted moments of the whole ordeal. Because for all that the Web has taken from her, she still believes it has given her far more. In her book, she writes, "The Internet was my home," as it is all of ours now.

ENGAGING THE TEXT

1. What do we learn about Zoë Quinn as a person from the details Malone provides throughout this article? For example, what does the fact that she wanted to "make herself a cyborg" by implanting a microchip in her hand suggest about her (para. 1)? What other details help us understand who Quinn is?

2. What does Malone mean when she talks about "gamer culture"? What behaviors, beliefs, and values do you associate with gamers and the world of video games? What kind of person, in your view, is the typical gamer?

3. Briefly summarize the Gamergate controversy. In what sense might this incident be seen as "the epitome of everything wrong with not just gamer or internet culture but culture in general and even politics" (para. 6)? How, specifically, does Gamergate connect to American culture and politics?

4. To what extent do video games exploit sex and violence? Can you think of any games that still portray women as "panting onlookers" or feature female protagonists with "builds that would give Barbie a crisis of confidence" (para. 23)? How have video games evolved since the early days of *Grand Theft Auto* or *World of Warcraft*?

5. Why would a group of "demographically advantaged young people" lash out against someone like Zoë Quinn (para. 24)? If, as Quinn suggests, they think of themselves as the "hero of their own story" (para. 31), what story are they telling themselves, and what roles do they and Quinn play in it?

6. Does Malone go too far when she links Donald Trump to Gamergate and the underground world of online white nationalism? Why or why not?

7. **Thinking Rhetorically**   To what extent does Malone convey her own opinion of Zoë Quinn in this article? How does she view Quinn? What passages give you a sense of Malone's position on Quinn, and what choices of language or emphasis does Malone make as a writer to give you this impression?

EXPLORING CONNECTIONS

8. How does Malone's examination of male-dominated gamer culture augment Jean Twenge's depiction of the impact of smartphones and social media on teenagers (p. 257)? To what extent do gamers, in your view, suffer from the same psychological issues that are common among heavy social media users?

9. How does Malone's depiction of gamer culture complicate Kenneth Goldsmith's (p. 270) relatively positive view of the Internet? How does Zoë Quinn's Gamergate experience challenge Goldsmith's assertion that the Internet is making kids more creative and sociable than ever before? How might it be possible to reconcile these very different views of life online?

EXTENDING THE CRITICAL CONTEXT

10. Visit Anita Sarkeesian's Feminist Frequency website, and sample a few of the videos in her *Tropes vs. Women in Video Games* series. What audience is Sarkeesian trying to reach with these videos? What is she trying to achieve? Which of the videos you sampled strike you as being particularly interesting, informative, or effective? Why?

11. Explore Quinn's Crash Override Network antitrolling website. How is online abuse defined on the site? Which of the tools and suggestions on the site seem particularly useful, and why?

12. Research the topic of gender bias in the video game industry. What are the demographics of game designers, developers, and programmers? To what extent do male and female game developers enjoy equal wages and opportunities? How common are sexual assault and harassment among industry employees? What evidence do you see to suggest that the video game industry is changing?

TWITTER AND WHITE SUPREMACY, A LOVE STORY

JESSIE DANIELS

Many were shocked when hundreds of white supremacists gathered in Charlottesville, Virginia, in the summer of 2016 to protest the removal of a statue of Robert E. Lee. The public display of swastikas, Confederate battle flags, and anti-Muslim banners caught many Americans off guard, but perhaps not as much as President did when he appeared to excuse the racist marchers by saying that there were "very fine people on both sides." Public displays of bigotry began to go out of style in the United States after the civil rights movement. But online, racism and bigotry have flourished in cyberspace. As Jessie Daniels explains in this selection, the Internet has fostered the resurgence of hate and intolerance in America and has made attitudes and behaviors that were unthinkable a generation ago part of our daily discourse. It has also given rise to a new group of alt-right national figures, like Milo Yiannopoulos, Richard Spencer, and Andew Anglin, who exploit the web's reach and anonymity to spread their gospel of hate. Jessie Daniels (b. 1961) is Professor of Sociology at Hunter College and the Graduate Center of the City University of New York. She is a nationally recognized expert on racism and technology. Her publications include *Cyber Racism: White*

Supremacy Online and the New Attack on Civil Rights (2009) and *Digital Sociologies* (2016), which she edited with Karen Gregory and Tressie McMillan Cottom. This selection originally appeared in *DAME* magazine.

THE INTERNET HAS BEEN THE BIGGEST ADVANCE for white supremacy since the end of Jim Crow.[1]

"I believe that the Internet will begin a chain reaction of racial enlightenment that will shake the world by the speed of its intellectual conquest," former KKK Grand Wizard David Duke wrote on his website in 1998. White supremacists like Duke and Don Black, who started Stormfront—the largest and longest running portal for white supremacy online—saw the potential of the Internet for spreading their message early on.

"Pioneering white nationalism on the Web was my dad's goal. That was what drove him from the early '90s, from the beginning of the Web," Don Black's son, Derek (and Duke's godson), explained in a recent interview.[2] "We had the latest computers, we were the first people in the neighborhood to have broadband because we had to keep Stormfront running, and so technology and connecting people on the website, long before social media." Stormfront provided a hub for connections among white supremacists globally, even for children. "When I was a little kid, I would get on chat rooms in the evening . . . and I had friends in Australia who I would talk to at a certain hour . . . I had friends in Serbia I would talk to at a certain hour," Derek said.

While Derek would leave the movement behind as an adult, his father's quest to make Stormfront into the gathering place for racial grievance-sharing and conspiracy-theory-spinning forged a set of connections among white nationalists that positioned them well to make the most of social media. Their opportunistic agenda converged with tech companies' approach to all content as value-neutral. Then, both of these synced up with the peculiarly American anything-goes-approach to free speech. It's this constellation of factors that prompted legal scholar Peter Breckheimer to refer to the U.S. as a "haven for hate" online as early as 2002.[3]

When Twitter launched in 2006, it unwittingly gave white supremacists an ideal venue for their hatred. Social media experts like to talk about the "design affordances" of a platform, meaning the built-in clues that suggest how a platform is meant to be used. Twitter gained a reputation among some users for its use of hashtags for breaking news and

---

[1]**Jim Crow:** Jim Crow laws enforced racial segregation in the South from the end of the Civil War until the civil rights movement of the 1960s. [All notes are the editors', except for 2, 3, 9, 15, 20, 21, 22, 23, and 24.]

[2]Michael Barbaro, "Interview with Former White Nationalist Derek Black," *The Daily* (podcast), *New York Times*, August 22, 2017.

[3]Peter J. Breckheimer II, "A Haven for Hate: The Foreign and Domestic Implications of Protecting Internet Hate Speech Under the First Amendment," *HeinOnline*, 2001–2002.

for organizing, as in the Arab Spring in 2010[4] and Black Lives Matter in 2013.[5] For ideologically committed white supremacists, the affordances of Twitter pointed to new mechanisms for the furtive spread of propaganda and for vicious harassment with little accountability.

The rise of social media platforms like Twitter, 4chan, and Reddit,[6] meant that white nationalists had many places to go online besides Stormfront. It also meant that the spread of white nationalist symbols and ideas could be accelerated and amplified by algorithms.

Take Pepe the Frog,[7] for example, an innocuous cartoon character that has so thoroughly changed meaning that in September 2016, the Anti-Defamation League[8] added Pepe the Frog to its database of online hate symbols. It was a transformation that began on 4chan and culminated on Twitter. "Turning Pepe into a white nationalist icon was one of our original goals," an anonymous white supremacist on Twitter told a reporter for the Daily Beast in 2016.[9]

The move to remake Pepe began on /r9k/, a 4chan board where a wide variety of users, including hackers, tech guys (and they were mostly guys), libertarians, and white supremacists who migrated from Stormfront, gathered online. The content at 4chan is eclectic, or, as one writer put it, "a jumble of content, hosting anything from pictures of cute kittens to wildly disturbing images and language." It's also one of the most popular websites ever, with 20 million unique visitors a month, according to founder Christopher ("Moot") Poole. "We basically mixed Pepe in with Nazi propaganda, etc. We built that association [on 4chan]," a white nationalist who goes by @JaredTSwift said. Once the connection between them got mentioned on Twitter by a journalist, white nationalists scored a victory. The mention of the 4chan meme by a "normie"[10] on Twitter was a prank with a big pay-off: it got them attention.

"In a sense, we've managed to push white nationalism into a very mainstream position," @JaredTSwift said. "Now, we've pushed the Overton window,"[11] referring to the range of ideas tolerated in public discourse. Twitter is the key platform for shaping that discourse. "People have adopted our rhetoric, sometimes without even realizing it. We're setting up

---

[4]**Arab Spring in 2010:** Refers to a series of peaceful and violent revolutions that spread across North Africa and the Middle East beginning in December 2010.

[5]**Black Lives Matter:** An international movement that began following the killing of Trayvon Martin by George Zimmerman in 2013 and that campaigns against violence, racism, and police brutality directed at African Americans.

[6]**4chan and Reddit:** Popular anonymous Internet message/image boards that are frequented by alt-right extremists, hackers, and trolls.

[7]**Pepe the Frog:** Originally appearing in *Boy's Club*, a comic by Matt Furie, Pepe the Frog became a popular racist meme after it was appropriated by the alt-right in 2015.

[8]**Anti-Defamation League:** Also known as the ADL, an international Jewish nongovernmental organization that fights anti-Semitism and bigotry.

[9]Olivia Nuzzi, "How Pepe the Frog Became a Nazi Trump Supporter and Alt-Right Symbol," *Daily Beast*, May 26, 2016.

[10] **"normie":** A derogatory term for a boring "normal" person, originally popularized by trolls and members of Internet subcultures on sites like 4chan and Reddit.

[11]**Overton window:** Created by conservative activist Joseph P. Overton (1960–2003), a technique for categorizing the public acceptability of an idea along a range of six degrees or levels: Unthinkable, Radical, Acceptable, Sensible, Popular, and Policy.

for a massive cultural shift," @JaredTSwift said. The thinking goes among white supremacists, if today we can get "normies" talking about Pepe the Frog, then tomorrow we can get them to ask the other questions on our agenda: "Are Jews people?" or "What about black on white crime?"

"You can't understate 4chan's role," says Keegan Hankes, a research analyst at the Southern Poverty Law Center's[12] Intelligence Project. Hankes sees the more tech-savvy guys in the white nationalist movement "getting their content from 4chan." Even with 4chan's influence, for Hankes, who has been observing white nationalists online for several years now, it's Reddit that's become the go-to venue for those seeking the most violent and explicit racism online. The typical user at Reddit, like at 4chan, is young, white, and male. Twitter users, on the other hand, are more likely to be black or Latinx. For white supremacists that want to make sport out of harassing people of color, Twitter is a "target rich" environment.

These platforms are driven by different economic imperatives. While 4chan is a low-budget, sole proprietor operation with no paid employees, Reddit and Twitter are both companies with an interest in turning a profit. And both face similar dilemmas. Twitter is valued at $13 billion and Reddit at $500 million, but both struggle to attract buyers and advertisers because of their toxic, racist, sexist content. For Twitter, the decision to allow white supremacists a place on their platform is one that seems to be good for their bottom line, at least in the short term. And for white supremacists, there are two things Twitter offers that 4chan and Reddit do not: an outsize influence on the news cycle and lots of people of color to target.

Today, Richard Spencer,[13] one of the organizers of the lethal tiki-torch rally in Charlottesville, tweets from a blue-check-verified account[14] with more than 75,000 followers. And he is not alone. Twitter accounts such as @SageGang_ and @WhiteGenocide post violent racism and anti-Semitism on the platform with impunity. When a promoted tweet appeared from a white supremacist website blaring the headline, "United States founded as a White People's Republic," Twitter co-founder Jack Dorsey apologized, claiming it was a "mistake." But, the apology was meaningless; white supremacists are still using the platform to advertise their message in ways both subtle and overt.

One study by J. M. Berger at George Washington University found that "white nationalist movements on Twitter added about 22,000 followers since 2012, an increase of about 600%."[15] Reliable data on the overall number or percentage of white supremacists on Twitter are hard

---

[12] **Southern Poverty Law Center:** Also known as the SPLC, an American nonprofit legal advocacy organization supporting civil rights litigation and antiracist research.

[13] **Richard Spencer:** American white supremacist (b. 1978) who was a featured speaker at the Unite the Right rally in Charlottesville, Virginia, which resulted in the death of one and the injury of nineteen when a white nationalist sympathizer drove his car into a crowd of antiracist counterprotesters.

[14] **blue-check-verified account:** On Twitter, a blue checkmark next to an account's name indicates that it is authentic.

[15] J. M. Berger, "Nazis vs. ISIS on Twitter: A Comparative Study of What Nationalist and ISIS Online Social Media Networks," George Washington University Program on Extremism, September 2016.

to come by. Berger's study includes a network analysis of 4,000 individual white nationalist accounts, but there's no way of knowing how much of this universe he's captured with his analysis. Still, even a small handful of white supremacists can create a lot of noise. One of the white nationalists involved in the memeing of Pepe, for example, said that it only took ten core people with another thirty or so helping occasionally to make that meme take hold. These are tiny numbers given Twitter's 328 million monthly active users overall.

Targeted Abuse and "Fake" Accounts

Men's rights activists had been mad about the all-female reboot of *Ghostbusters* for at least a year before it was released in July 2016. Still, few would have anticipated that it would become the focus of white supremacist invective, but it did. The movie featured a black woman, Leslie Jones, in a prominent role and it appears that her presence alone was enough to enrage white supremacist instigator Milo Yiannopoulos.[16] He posted a negative review of *Ghostbusters* on Breitbart[17] that dissed Jones's "flat-as-a-pancake black stylings."

Then all hell broke loose on Twitter. Taking Milo's lead, white   15 supremacists began to bombard Jones's timeline with sexist and racist comments and hateful memes. These tweets threatened rape and death, and hurled vile epithets at her. The abuse escalated when Milo began tweeting at Jones directly, and this amped up his followers into a frenzied mob, driving Jones off of Twitter. It was at this point that public pressure and bad press finally convinced Jack Dorsey to personally intervene and permanently ban Milo from the site, and Jones returned.

It often seems arbitrary how and when Twitter removes someone from the site or locks their account. Most recently, these puzzling standards got applied to Rose McGowan[18] who had her account locked after tweeting about Harvey Weinstein's sexual abuse. The reality is that there aren't effective platform-wide solutions for those who are targeted for abuse, especially if they're not celebrities. Users who are targeted can "block" offensive accounts, but as Yonatan Zunger, former Google engineer, pointed out recently: "Twitter chose to optimize for traffic at the expense of user experience. That's why Gamergate,[19] that's why Trump, that's why Nazis."

---

[16] **Milo Yiannopolos:** Pen name of Milo Hanrahan (b. 1984), a conservative British political commentator and writer who is known for his critiques of feminism, Islam, social justice, and political correctness.

[17] **Breitbart:** Founded in 2007 by Andrew Breitbart, Breitbart News Network is a far-right American news website that features conspiracy theories, misleading stories, and content that has been considered misogynist, racist, and xenophobic.

[18] **Rose McGowan:** American actress, model, singer, and author (b. 1973) who, in 2017, alleged that movie producer Harvey Weinstein had raped her in 1997 and who subsequently became a leading figure in the #MeToo anti-sexual assault movement.

[19] **Gamergate:** Often interpreted as a misogynist backlash against women working in technology, the Gamergate controversy involved a coordinated online group harassment campaign in 2014 directed against video game developers Zoë Quinn and Briana Wu and feminist media critic Anita Sarkeesian.

Because the platform puts the burden on the user who is being harassed to block people (a process that takes several clicks), it creates a differential cost to the Leslie Joneses of the world relative to the white supremacists. For the latter, there's very little cost to using the platform and they get to enjoy one of their favorite pastimes: harassing and intimidating others from the safe distance of their keyboard.

Indeed, the kind of harassment Leslie Jones faced is exactly what black women have had to deal with on Twitter, day-in, and day-out, for years. But without the prominence of being Leslie Jones, one doesn't get the benefit of personal intervention from Jack Dorsey.

"It's the gamificiation of hate," says author Mikki Kendall. "I was going to leave Twitter at one point. It just wasn't usable for me. I would log on and have 2,500 negative comments. One guy who seemed to have an inexhaustible energy would Photoshop my image on top of lynching pictures and tell me I should be 'raped by dogs,' that kind of thing."

When Kendall was living in Tennessee, she says she received a picture of her and her family in a photo that "looked like it had been sighted through a rifle." She was also doxxed—that is, had her address posted online. She moved shortly thereafter. "I had two minor children in my home then. I had to do something different." She lives on the southside of Chicago now and says she feels much safer. "No one's going to come for me here. If they do, I'd like to watch them try." [20]

Kendall has been deft at figuring out tech-savvy ways to both document and battle online harassment. She did a "race swap" experiment with a white guy—they traded Twitter avatars. "For me, it was like, *Oh my God, it's so quiet!* People told me how smart I was and perceptive," she says. Kendall has also figured out how to turn the tables on the algorithms by coding her own auto-blockers that sniff out potentially harmful Twitter accounts and blocks them.

When I asked her why she thought Twitter wasn't more responsive to reports of abuse on the site, she said, "Being a white guy on Twitter is a whole other world. I think that what's happening with Jack and Biz (Twitter executives) is they're experiencing a whole other Twitter."

White supremacists have used Twitter to target Jews, as well, in ways both banal and life-threatening. In June 2016 several highly visible Jewish political reporters began to report a barrage of online harassment that involved a symbolic gesture: triple parentheses placed around their names, like (((this))). The ADL added the triple parentheses to their catalog of hateful symbols. One report called them "the digital equivalent of a yellow star," intended to separate Jews from the rest of the population and pave the way for worse.

Part of what made the symbols effective is that they were hard to track on Twitter. The search tool built into Twitter didn't reveal the parentheses (most search tools omit punctuation). Without a search function, the use of the symbols as slur goes undetected. If it wanted to, Twitter could specifically monitor the (((echoes))) symbol, and shut down accounts that were using it. Twitter could also make the term searchable. But it has done neither.

Reporter Kurt Eichenwald, who has epilepsy, was targeted by a 25
Twitter account that sent him a GIF containing a strobe light. When he
clicked on it, the flashing light sent him into a seizure. The FBI began
investigating and someone was arrested in the case, but few details
have been released. What's clear is that Twitter hasn't made substantive
changes to the platform since this happened. Eichenwald says he has
received at least forty more strobe light images since the first attack.

A favorite tactic of propagandists is to disguise themselves online.
Twitter is particularly appealing for those who want to hide their identities because, unlike Facebook, it doesn't have a "real-name" policy (requiring a name that appears on a government-issued ID) and it
doesn't prohibit automated accounts (also known as bots). The attacks
on Jones and Eichenwald, for instance, involved Twitter accounts that
disguised the identity of the perps. And, white supremacists on Twitter
have discovered a way to make this an orchestrated campaign of racism
through the systematic creation of "fake black people" accounts.

"When you have time, create a fake black person account," wrote
Andrew Anglin, at his virulently racist website the Daily Stormer in
November 2016. "Just go on black Twitter and see what they look like,
copy that model. Start filling it with rap videos and booty-shaking or
whatever else these blacks post," Anglin said. He claimed there were
already over 1,000 such accounts at the time.

Love Triangle with an 800-Pound Gorilla

White supremacists fell in love with Donald J. Trump in early 2016.
Until then, they'd been suspicious of him and his run for the presidency,
chiefly due to his "globalist" (a.k.a. Jewish) son-in-law Jared Kushner.
They quickly set aside those concerns after a few opportune retweets
from the Donald.

Bob Whitaker, a committed white supremacist according to the
SPLC, worked for years to promulgate the racist meme "white genocide." Whitaker's two-word tagline conveys a key tenet of contemporary
white supremacist ideology: that immigration, multiculturalism, interracial marriage, and feminism are excuses to not only dilute the influence of white culture, but to get rid of white people entirely. (Hence,
the Charlottesville ralliers' chant, "You will not replace us.") Whitaker began posting the phrase "white genocide" on various forums like
4chan and Reddit in 2015, and then moved to Twitter where he would
sometimes tweet directly to @realDonaldTrump.

In late January 2016, Trump recirculated a tweet from Whitaker's 30
"@WhiteGenocideTM" account that insulted his opponent Jeb Bush. The
common disclaimer that "RT's are not endorsements" might have held
sway, except that he did it again. Within a few days, Trump had retweeted
@WhiteGenocideTM a second time, then a third. Although his campaign
tried to dismiss these as "accidents" or "mistakes," those on the far right
were convinced that he was acknowledging support for their ideas.

Andrew Anglin of the Daily Stormer read the retweets as endorsements. "Obviously, most people will be like 'obvious accident, no harm done.' Meanwhile, we here at the Daily Stormer will be all like 'wink wink wink wink wink,'" Anglin wrote.[20]

Clearly, white supremacist Twitter loves Donald Trump. Following his initial retweets of the Whitaker account, by mid-March 2016 an analysis of the key influencers using the hashtag #WhiteGenocide found that 67.5 percent of them were following @realDonaldTrump.[21]

And, Trump loves white supremacist Twitter. According to social media expert Marshall Kirkpatrick, who analyzed Trump's retweets during early 2016, "It turns out that Donald Trump mostly retweets white supremacists saying nice things about him."[22] Of the twenty-one people retweeted in one particular week, Kirkpatrick found that six follow major white-nationalist accounts and thirteen of them follow multiple accounts that have used the #whitegenocide hashtag.

Unfortunately for everyone of goodwill, candidate Trump became president. He continues to tweet from the White House, the golf course, his residence, anywhere he can. When asked recently about the president's Twitter feed, a panel of three *New York Times* journalists covering the White House agreed that it offers a "remarkably transparent window" into his thinking.[23] "Oh, come on," *New York Times* White House correspondent Peter Baker responded when asked if it was possible to ignore the president's tweets. "So, if we didn't write about the tweets, the 40 million people reading them—and the other millions more who would be retweeting—would suddenly not pay attention, or not care?" Baker said. It's not just the *New York Times*, all the cable news networks now routinely report on his tweets. There are occasional calls to ban Trump for violating their Terms of Service agreement, but it's little more than a thought experiment because Twitter can't afford to ban him.

The minute-by-minute updates create a feedback loop that amplifies both Trump's power and Twitter's influence.   35

Jemele Hill, an on-air personality for ESPN, recently used her Twitter account to say "Donald Trump is a white supremacist that largely surrounds himself w/ other white supremacists." As black feminist scholar Brittney Cooper asked about Hill's tweet, "Where is the lie?"[24] denials came rushing from the White House, along with a call for Hill to be fired from ESPN for the tweet. She has since been suspended for a tweet about the #TakeAKnee protests, with Trump congratulating the move from the Twitter peanut gallery.

[20] J. M. Berber, "How White Nationalists Learned to Love Donald Trump," *Politico Magazine*, October 25, 2016.

[21] Ben Kharakh and Dan Primack, "Donald Trump's Social Media Ties to White Supremacists," *Fortune*, March 22, 2016.

[22] Jay Hathaway, "More Than Half of Trump's Retweets are White Supremacists Praising Him," *New York Magazine*, January 27, 2016.

[23] Stephen Hiltner, "Seven Takeaways from the Times Journalists Who Cover Trump," *The New York Times*, October 13, 2017.

[24] Brittney Cooper, "Jemel Hill Called Donald Trump a White Supremacist. Where's the Lie?", *Cosmopolitan*, September 15, 2017.

On Twitter, Trump and white supremacists are in a racists-loving-each-other-feedback-loop through retweets while they simultaneously use the platform to bully, harass, and threaten black women, Jews, and anyone else who opposes them. With each retweet they push the window of acceptable political discourse further along the path from hate speech to violence. Meanwhile, Twitter dithers.

The company's sporadic, impartial effort to systematically deal with white supremacists (and other harassers, including Trump) is revealing. It's rooted in Twitter's decision to prioritize driving traffic and its investors' returns over everything else. For white supremacists, that hands-off approach is all they need to exploit the platform for their own ends. And, it pays dividends for them in attention, in followers, and in entertainment value.

Simply put, white supremacists love Twitter because it loves them back.

ENGAGING THE TEXT

1. How has the Internet fostered the popularity of white supremacist groups, according to Daniels? How often have you encountered racist propaganda on social media sites like Facebook and Twitter or social messaging platforms like 4chan or Reddit? In general, would you agree that sites like Twitter and Reddit have offered racists a "haven for hate" (para. 4)?

2. Why are memes like Pepe the Frog effective tools for spreading hate online? What other memes have you encountered that appear to be associated with racism, sexism, anti-Semitism, or other forms of bigotry?

3. Why has racism taken root on sites like Twitter, Reddit, and 4chan? What steps have social media platforms like Facebook and YouTube taken to limit racist postings? What do you think should be done, if anything, to discourage the growth of racism on the Internet?

4. Daniels refers to the concept of the Overton window, which offers a method for ranking the social acceptability of ideas and opinions in public discourse according to six categories: Unthinkable, Radical, Acceptable, Sensible, Popular, and Policy. Using this technique, how would you rank the ideas listed below in terms of their acceptability in public discourse today? Which of these ideas have become more acceptable over the past ten or twenty years? Which have become less acceptable? What role, if any, might the Internet have played in these changes?

   • Marijuana is a relatively safe recreational drug

   • All drugs should be legalized

   • Gay people have the right to marry

   • Immigrants are a source of strength

- Immigrants are a threat to the United States

- Global warming is a hoax

- Animals have rights

- Assault weapons should be banned

- American Christians are the victims of discrimination

- Health care is a right

- Welfare recipients are lazy

- The Civil War was about states' rights

- The U.S. government poses a threat to individual liberty

- Women can do any job under any circumstances

- Islam is at war with the West

- The white race faces extinction

5. Noting that President Trump has repeatedly retweeted well-known white racists and that he enjoys a large racist following, Daniels suggests that the president has helped to "push the window of acceptable political discourse further along the path from hate speech to violence" (para. 37). To what extent would you hold Trump personally responsible for legitimizing racist thinking since the beginning of his 2016 presidential campaign?

EXPLORING CONNECTIONS

6. How does Daniels's examination of racism and social media complicate the optimistic picture of our technological future offered by Eric Schmidt and Jared Cohen (p. 241)? How might Schmidt and Cohen respond to the idea that the Internet is fueling the growth of racism? Overall, how optimistic are you about the long-term effects of the Internet on public discourse, and why?

7. Drawing on Daniels's discussion of sites like 4chan, Reddit, and Twitter, and on Noreen Malone's account of Zoë Quinn and the Gamergate incident (p. 285), write a journal entry or short essay on the Internet's impact on civility. How does the Internet seem to be changing our attitudes about people with differing backgrounds and beliefs? What is it doing to gender relations and political discourse?

EXTENDING THE CRITICAL CONTEXT

8. In 2017, Harvard University rescinded the admission of at least ten students because they had posted racist, sexist, or anti-Semitic memes on social media sites. Go online to learn more about Harvard's decision and other examples of

colleges monitoring or limiting student self-expression on the Internet. Did Harvard make the right decision? How involved do you think colleges should be in policing the online activities of their students?

9. Visit Richard Spencer's Twitter page and explore the site's "Who to Follow" feature to see how easy it is to connect with white supremacists online. Should extremists like Spencer be banned from social media, or is there some value in allowing them to speak freely?

10. Research how social media sites like Facebook, YouTube, Twitter, Instagram, and Reddit have responded to the growth of online extremism. What policies have these and other social media companies adopted to combat hatred on the web? What else, if anything, do you think they should be doing to curb online intolerance?

VISUAL PORTFOLIO

READING IMAGES OF WIRED CULTURE

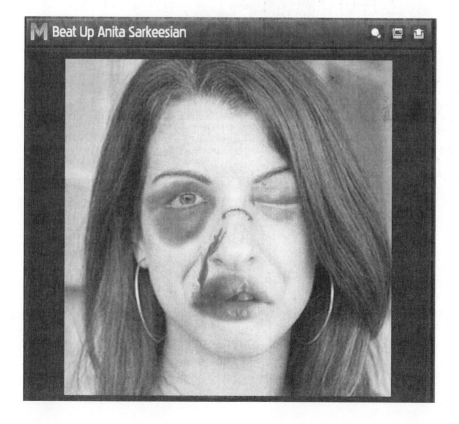

Steve Burns, WTIU News

VISUAL PORTFOLIO
READING IMAGES OF WIRED CULTURE

1. What does the photo of two toddlers with smartphones on page 309 say to you? When did you get your first cell phone, and how did it change your life? When, in general, do you think children should have their own phones or access to social media, and why?

2. The staged photo on page 310 is one of Eric Pickergall's "Removed" series: photos of people without their smartphones and electronic devices. What does this image say to you about families in the digital age? To what extent has our growing dependence on technology hurt or improved human relationships? Do you think that there are places (kitchens, restaurants, college classrooms, etc.) where access to technology should be restricted? Why, and under what circumstances?

3. The first image on page 311 comes from Anita Sarkeesian's *Feminist Frequency* website, which is devoted to analyzing representations of women in video games and gamer culture. The second image comes from a video game called *Beat Up Anita Sarkeesian*, which was posted online in 2012 in response to a Kickstarter campaign to fund her *Tropes vs. Women in Video Games* YouTube series. Do some Internet research to learn more about the harassment Sarkeesian faced in response to her websites and about the 2014 Gamergate controversy, which involved a series of misogynistic attacks on female game developers like Zoë Quinn and Brianna Wu. Working in groups, compare notes on your own online experiences. To what extent would you agree that the culture of video games and, more generally, of social media is misogynist and unwelcoming for women? What, in your view, could or should be done to address the problem?

4. The screenshot on page 312 shows the Internet homepage of the Westboro Baptist Church in late 2014. An unaffiliated Baptist congregation, Westboro is infamous for hate speech campaigns directed against LGBT people, Jews, the Pope, the U.S. military, and liberal politicians. This site is only one of thousands of online sites that promote hate, violence, and terrorist activity. To what extent does the existence of sites like this complicate the idea that the Internet can help bridge the differences between races, cultures, and counties? Should sites like this be shut down? Why or why not?

5. Described as a social humanoid robot, Sophia (p. 313) was first activated by Hong Kong–based Hanson Robotics on April 19, 2015. Equipped with general artificial intelligence, which allows her to learn from experience, Sophia has been interviewed on *60 Minutes* and *The Tonight Show Starring Jimmy Fallon* and has appeared in several music videos. In October 2017, she was granted citizenship by Saudi Arabia before appearing at a global investment summit in Riyahd. Hanson Robotics, the company that developed Sophia, says that she has seven "siblings." How long do you think it will be before robots with human levels of intelligence will become commonplace? What questions arise when a machine is granted citizenship? What concerns do you have about the development of machines like Sophia, and why?

HOW WE SOLD OUR SOULS — AND MORE — TO THE INTERNET GIANTS

BRUCE SCHNEIER

> If you've ever suspected that someone is watching you, you'll feel right at home with the author of this selection. Bruce Schneier is a nationally recognized expert on surveillance who has been writing about the impact of technology on privacy for more than three decades. In this essay, which originally appeared in the *Guardian*, Schneier argues that we live under a state of mass surveillance thanks to modern technological devices that we increasingly take for granted. As Schneier sees it, we've bartered away our privacy for convenience and kitty videos. Schneier (b. 1952) is a fellow at the Berkman Klein Center for the Internet and Society at Harvard University, a Lecturer in Public Policy at the Harvard Kennedy School, and the Chief Technology Officer at IBM Resilient. He has written hundreds of academic papers, articles, and essays, and he is also the author of thirteen books, including *Liars and Outliers: Enabling the Trust That Society Needs to Thrive* (2012), *Carry On: Sound Advice from Schneier on Security* (2013), and *Data and Goliath: The Hidden Battles to Collect Your Data and Control Your World* (2015).

LAST YEAR, WHEN MY REFRIGERATOR BROKE, the repair man replaced the computer that controls it. I realised that I had been thinking about the refrigerator backwards: it's not a refrigerator with a computer, it's a computer that keeps food cold. Just like that, everything is turning into a computer. Your phone is a computer that makes calls. Your car is a computer with wheels and an engine. Your oven is a computer that cooks lasagne. Your camera is a computer that takes pictures. Even our pets and livestock are now regularly chipped; my cat could be considered a computer that sleeps in the sun all day.

Computers are being embedded into all sort of products that connect to the Internet. Nest, which Google purchased last year for more than $3 billion, makes an Internet-enabled thermostat. You can buy a smart air conditioner that learns your preferences and maximises energy efficiency. Fitness tracking devices, such as Fitbit or Jawbone, collect information about your movements, awake and asleep, and use that to analyse both your exercise and sleep habits. Many medical devices are starting to be Internet-enabled, collecting and reporting a variety of biometric data. There are — or will be soon — devices that continually measure our vital signs, moods, and brain activity.

This year, we have had two surprising stories of technology monitoring our activity: Samsung televisions that listen to conversations in the room and send them elsewhere for transcription — just in case someone is telling the TV to change the channel—and a Barbie that records your child's questions and sells them to third parties.

All these computers produce data about what they're doing and a lot of it is surveillance data. It's the location of your phone, who you're talking to and what you're saying, what you're searching and writing. It's your heart rate. Corporations gather, store, and analyze this data, often without our knowledge, and typically without our consent. Based on this data, they draw conclusions about us that we might disagree with or object to and that can affect our lives in profound ways. We may not like to admit it, but we are under mass surveillance.

Internet surveillance has evolved into a shockingly extensive,   5 robust, and profitable surveillance architecture. You are being tracked pretty much everywhere you go, by many companies and data brokers: ten different companies on one website, a dozen on another. Facebook tracks you on every site with a Facebook Like button (whether you're logged in to Facebook or not), while Google tracks you on every site that has a Google Plus g+ button or that uses Google Analytics to monitor its own Web traffic.

Most of the companies tracking you have names you've never heard of: Rubicon Project, AdSonar, Quantcast, Undertone, Traffic Marketplace. If you want to see who's tracking you, install one of the browser plug-ins that let you monitor cookies.[1] I guarantee you will be startled. One reporter discovered that 105 different companies tracked his Internet use during one 36-hour period. In 2010, the seemingly innocuous site Dictionary.com installed more than 200 tracking cookies on your browser when you visited.

It's no different on your smartphone. The apps there track you as well. They track your location and sometimes download your address book, calendar, bookmarks, and search history. In 2013, the rapper Jay-Z and Samsung teamed up to offer people who downloaded an app the ability to hear the new Jay-Z album before release. The app required that users give Samsung consent to view all accounts on the phone, track its location and who the user was talking to. The *Angry Birds* game even collects location data when you're not playing. It's less Big Brother[2] and more hundreds of tittletattle little brothers.

Most Internet surveillance data is inherently anonymous, but companies are increasingly able to correlate the information gathered with other information that positively identifies us. You identify yourself willingly to lots of Internet services. Often you do this with only a username, but increasingly usernames can be tied to your real name. Google tried to enforce this with its "real name policy," which required users

---

[1]**cookies:** A small bit of data sent from a website and stored on a user's computer. Cookies allow websites to remember users' identities and record their browser activity. [All notes are the editors'.]

[2]**Big Brother:** In George Orwell's dystopic novel *Nineteen Eighty-Four* (1949), Big Brother is the mysterious unseen leader of a totalitarian state who keeps all citizens under constant surveillance.

register for Google Plus with their legal names, until it rescinded that policy in 2014. Facebook pretty much demands real names. Whenever you use your credit card number to buy something, your real identity is tied to any cookies set by companies involved in that transaction. And any browsing you do on your smartphone is tied to you as the phone's owner, although the website might not know it.

Surveillance is the business model of the Internet for two primary reasons: people like free and people like convenient. The truth is, though, that people aren't given much of a choice. It's either surveillance or nothing and the surveillance is conveniently invisible so you don't have to think about it. And it's all possible because laws have failed to keep up with changes in business practices.

In general, privacy is something people tend to undervalue until they 10 don't have it anymore. Arguments such as "I have nothing to hide" are common, but aren't really true. People living under constant surveillance quickly realise that privacy isn't about having something to hide. It's about individuality and personal autonomy. It's about being able to decide who to reveal yourself to and under what terms. It's about being free to be an individual and not having to constantly justify yourself to some overseer.

This tendency to undervalue privacy is exacerbated by companies deliberately making sure that privacy is not salient to users. When you log on to Facebook, you don't think about how much personal information you're revealing to the company; you chat with your friends. When you wake up in the morning, you don't think about how you're going to allow a bunch of companies to track you throughout the day; you just put your cell phone in your pocket.

But by accepting surveillance-based business models, we hand over even more power to the powerful. Google controls two-thirds of the US search market. Almost three-quarters of all Internet users have Facebook accounts. Amazon controls about 30 percent of the US book market and 70 percent of the e-book market. Comcast owns about 25 percent of the US broadband market. These companies have enormous power and control over us simply because of their economic position.

Our relationship with many of the Internet companies we rely on is not a traditional company–customer relationship. That's primarily because we're not customers — we're products those companies sell to their real customers. The companies are analogous to feudal lords[3] and we are their vassals, peasants, and — on a bad day — serfs. We are tenant farmers for these companies, working on their land by producing data that they in turn sell for profit.

Yes, it's a metaphor, but it often really feels like that. Some people have pledged allegiance to Google. They have Gmail accounts, use Google Calendar and Google Docs, and have Android phones. Others

[3]**feudal lords:** The social system that dominated Europe between the ninth and fifteenth centuries, feudalism was built on pledges of loyalty which established reciprocal obligations between a warrior caste of aristocratic lords and a laboring caste of dependent vassals and peasants.

have pledged similar allegiance to Apple. They have iMacs, iPhones, and iPads and let iCloud automatically synchronize and back up everything. Still others let Microsoft do it all. Some of us have pretty much abandoned e-mail altogether for Facebook, Twitter, and Instagram. We might prefer one feudal lord to the others. We might distribute our allegiance among several of these companies or studiously avoid a particular one we don't like. Regardless, it's becoming increasingly difficult to avoid pledging allegiance to at least one of them.

After all, customers get a lot of value out of having feudal lords. It's 15
simply easier and safer for someone else to hold our data and manage our devices. We like having someone else take care of our device configurations, software management, and data storage. We like it when we can access our e-mail anywhere, from any computer, and we like it that Facebook just works, from any device, anywhere. We want our calendar entries to appear automatically on all our devices. Cloud storage sites do a better job of backing up our photos and files than we can manage by ourselves; Apple has done a great job of keeping malware out of its iPhone app store. We like automatic security updates and automatic backups; the companies do a better job of protecting our devices than we ever did. And we're really happy when, after we lose a smartphone and buy a new one, all of our data reappears on it at the push of a button.

In this new world of computing, we're no longer expected to manage our computing environment. We trust the feudal lords to treat us well and protect us from harm. It's all a result of two technological trends.

The first is the rise of cloud computing. Basically, our data is no longer stored and processed on our computers. That all happens on servers owned by many different companies. The result is that we no longer control our data. These companies access our data—both content and metadata[4]—for whatever profitable purpose they want. They have carefully crafted terms of service that dictate what sorts of data we can store on their systems, and can delete our entire accounts if they believe we violate them. And they turn our data over to law enforcement without our knowledge or consent. Potentially even worse, our data might be stored on computers in a country whose data protection laws are less than rigorous.

The second trend is the rise of user devices that are managed closely by their vendors: iPhones, iPads, Android phones, Kindles, ChromeBooks, and the like. The result is that we no longer control our computing environment. We have ceded control over what we can see, what we can do, and what we can use. Apple has rules about what software can be installed on iOS devices. You can load your own documents onto your Kindle, but Amazon is able to delete books it has already sold

---

[4]**metadata:** Data that provides essential information about other data such as the time, duration, location, and destination of phone calls, e-mails, or text messages.

you. In 2009, Amazon automatically deleted some editions of George Orwell's[5] *Nineteen Eighty-Four* from users' Kindles because of a copyright issue. I know, you just couldn't write this stuff any more ironically.

It's not just hardware. It's getting hard to just buy a piece of software and use it on your computer in any way you like. Increasingly, vendors are moving to a subscription model—Adobe did that with Creative Cloud in 2013—that gives the vendor much more control. Microsoft hasn't yet given up on a purchase model but is making its MS Office subscription very attractive. And Office 365's option of storing your documents in the Microsoft cloud is hard to turn off. Companies are pushing us in this direction because it makes us more profitable as customers or users.

Given current laws, trust is our only option. There are no consistent or predictable rules. We have no control over the actions of these companies. I can't negotiate the rules regarding when Yahoo! will access my photos on Flickr. I can't demand greater security for my presentations on Prezi or my task list on Trello. I don't even know the cloud providers to whom those companies have outsourced their infrastructures. If any of those companies delete my data, I don't have the right to demand it back. If any of those companies give the government access to my data, I have no recourse. And if I decide to abandon those services, chances are I can't easily take my data with me.

Political scientist Henry Farrell observed: "Much of our life is conducted online, which is another way of saying that much of our life is conducted under rules set by large private businesses, which are subject neither to much regulation nor much real market competition."

The common defence is something like "business is business." No one is forced to join Facebook or use Google search or buy an iPhone. Potential customers are choosing to enter into these quasi-feudal user relationships because of the enormous value they receive from them. If they don't like it, goes the argument, they shouldn't do it.

This advice is not practical. It's not reasonable to tell people that if they don't like their data being collected, they shouldn't e-mail, shop online, use Facebook, or have a mobile phone. I can't imagine students getting through school anymore without an Internet search or Wikipedia, much less finding a job afterward. These are the tools of modern life. They're necessary to a career and a social life. Opting out just isn't a viable choice for most of us, most of the time; it violates what have become very real norms of contemporary life.

Right now, choosing among providers is not a choice between surveillance or no surveillance, but only a choice of which feudal lords get to spy on you. This won't change until we have laws to protect both us and our data from these sorts of relationships. Data is power and those that have our data have power over us. It's time for government to step in and balance things out.

---

[5]**George Orwell:** Pen name of Eric Arthur Blair (1903–1950), English novelist, essayist, journalist, and critic, and author of the dystopic novel *Nineteen Eighty-Four*.

ENGAGING THE TEXT

1. What kinds of personal and household devices create information about us that can be stored and accessed on the Internet? What kinds of information could your car, Fitbit, or home assistant be generating about you?

2. What information could be derived about you from your Internet searches and your social media posts, "likes," and shares over the past year? Using this information, what could a company like Google or any company that buys your information predict about your race, class, gender, politics, religious beliefs, relationships, interests, goals, plans, fears, and health? How comfortable are you with the idea that we live "under mass surveillance"?

3. How often do you think about the information that your phone is gathering about you? Should law-abiding citizens be concerned because smartphones can track a user's location, calls, contacts, and calendar? Why or why not?

4. To what extent would you agree that most people tend to undervalue their privacy? What do you do to protect the privacy of your information when you use your phone or browse the Internet? Why does Schneier think privacy should be important to everyone?

5. Do you consider yourself a "serf" who has "pledged allegiance" to a group of electronic "feudal lords" (paras. 13–14)? Which technology and Internet companies do you use regularly without question? Would you describe your relationship with them in terms of dependency? Why or why not?

6. What does Schneier mean when he says that "surveillance is the business model of the Internet" and that we are the "product" for Internet companies and not their customers (para. 9)? What deal have we made with companies like Google, Facebook, and Amazon? Is there any way to regain control of our data without literally giving up smartphones, social media, and the Internet?

7. **Thinking Rhetorically**   Schneier uses the term "surveillance" throughout this essay to refer to the collection of personal information during interaction with online apps and companies. What are the connotations of this word, and what does it imply about the motives and methods of Internet companies? How would the tone of this essay change if the word "surveillance" were replaced or deleted?

EXPLORING CONNECTIONS

8. How do Schneier's views on mass surveillance complicate or challenge Eric Schmidt and Jared Cohen's explanation of how technology will change our lives in the future (p. 241)? How might Schneier rewrite Schmidt and Cohen's version of what the future will be like for people in the "upper band"?

9. What might Schneier make of Kenneth Goldsmith's celebration of the Internet (p. 270)? How, for example, might Schneier view Goldsmith's claim that when we register our "likes" online "we build a rich ecosystem of artifacts around us based on our proclivities and desires" (para. 30)? How might he view Goldsmith's notion that our online activities constitute "a sort of self-portrait of both who I am in this particular moment, and who I was in earlier parts of my life" (para. 30)? Given Schneier's concerns about corporate surveillance, how dangerous is it to view the Internet as a means of self-expression or as a tool for gaining self-knowledge?

10. Revisit the selections about online harassment by Noreen Malone (p. 285) and about Internet racism by Jessie Daniels (p. 298). How might Zoë Quinn, Leslie Jones, or Rose McGowan respond to Schneier's concerns about online privacy? In your view, which is the bigger problem on the Internet — surveillance or anonymity? Why?

EXTENDING THE CRITICAL CONTEXT

11. Go online to learn more about cookies and how they facilitate Internet surveillance. To what extent were you aware that cookies are frequently planted by music downloads, multiplayer video games, and almost all online commercial sites? How often do you monitor the cookies on your computer or your phone?

12. Do some research to learn about data and privacy protections in the European Union. What laws or directives protect an individual's online data in the EU? What kinds of protections do these laws and regulations provide? What

privacy protections are in place in the United States? How would you explain why attitudes toward privacy and data ownership are so different in Europe and the U.S.?

13. Research the ways that technological innovations such as body cameras, license plate scanners, GPS tracking devices, RFID tags, closed circuit TV, drones, and facial recognition technology are changing police work today. In class, discuss whether you think emerging technologies are making law enforcement more or less effective and accountable to the public. What problems do you see associated with police use of such technological innovations?

YOU WILL LOSE YOUR JOB TO A ROBOT — AND SOONER THAN YOU THINK*

KEVIN DRUM

We humans have a weird relationship with robots. We've been dreaming about having mechanical servants since the ancient Greek poet Homer featured them in the *Iliad* nearly three thousand years ago. We've also feared them: our misgivings about intelligent machines go back long before the supercomputer HAL tried to murder his human charges in Stanley Kubrik's film *2001: A Space Odyssey*. And it turns out that our doubts have always been well founded. Robots, it seems, are here to replace us, first by taking away our jobs and, eventually, by taking away our reason for being. In this selection, Kevin Drum sounds the alarm: within a generation or two most of us will lose our work and our livelihoods to artificial intelligence systems and intelligent machines. The question, according to Drum, isn't whether we can retrain ourselves or learn to compete with our mechanical rivals; instead, we should be thinking about how we'll adapt to a world without work. Drum (b. 1958) is a political blogger and columnist who currently writes for *Mother Jones* magazine, the source of this selection.

I WANT TO TELL YOU STRAIGHT OFF what this story is about: Sometime in the next 40 years, robots are going to take your job.

I don't care what your job is. If you dig ditches, a robot will dig them better. If you're a magazine writer, a robot will write your articles better. If you're a doctor, IBM's Watson will no longer "assist" you in finding the right diagnosis from its database of millions of case studies and journal articles. It will just be a better doctor than you.

And CEOs? Sorry. Robots will run companies better than you do. Artistic types? Robots will paint and write and sculpt better than you. Think you have social skills that no robot can match? Yes, they can. Within twenty years, maybe half of you will be out of jobs. A couple of decades after that, most of the rest of you will be out of jobs.

In one sense, this all sounds great. Let the robots have the damn jobs! No more dragging yourself out of bed at 6 A.M. or spending long days on your feet. We'll be free to read or write poetry or play video games or whatever we want to do. And a century from now, this is most likely how things will turn out. Humanity will enter a golden age.

But what about twenty years from now? Or thirty? We won't *all* be   5 out of jobs by then, but a lot of us will—and it will be no golden age. Until we figure out how to fairly distribute the fruits of robot labor, it will be an era of mass joblessness and mass poverty. Working-class job losses played a big role in the 2016 election, and if we don't want a long succession of demagogues blustering their way into office because machines are taking away people's livelihoods, this needs to change, and fast. Along with global warming, the transition to a workless future is the biggest challenge by far that progressive politics—not to mention all of humanity—faces. And yet it's barely on our radar.

That's kind of a buzzkill, isn't it? Luckily, it's traditional that stories about difficult or technical subjects open with an entertaining or provocative anecdote. The idea is that this allows readers to ease slowly into daunting material. So here's one for you: Last year at Christmas, I was over at my mother's house and mentioned that I had recently read an article about Google Translate.[1] It turns out that a few weeks previously, without telling anyone, Google had switched over to a new machine-learning algorithm. Almost overnight, the quality of its translations skyrocketed. I had noticed some improvement myself but had chalked it up to the usual incremental progress these kinds of things go through. I hadn't realized it was due to a quantum leap in software.

But if Google's translation algorithm was better, did that mean its voice recognition was better too? And its ability to answer queries? Hmm. How could we test that? We decided to open presents instead of cogitating over this.

But after that was over, the subject of erasers somehow came up. Which ones are best? Clear? Black? Traditional pink? Come to think of it, why *are* erasers traditionally pink? "I'll ask Google!" I told everyone. So I pulled out my phone and said, "Why are erasers pink?" Half a second later, Google told me.

[1]Gideon Lewis-Kraus, "The Great A.I. Awakening," *New York Times Magazine*, December 14, 2016. [All notes are Drum's, except for 2, 3, 4, 5, 7, and 13.]

Not impressed? You should be. We all know that phones can recognize voices tolerably well these days. And we know they can find the nearest café or the trendiest recipe for coq au vin.[2] But what about something entirely random? And not a simple who, where, or when question. This was a *why* question, and it wasn't about why the singer Pink uses erasers or why erasers are jinxed. Google has to be smart enough to figure out in context that I said *pink* and that I'm asking about the historical reason for the color of erasers, not their health or the way they're shaped. And it did. In less than a second. With nothing more than a cheap little microprocessor and a slow link to the Internet.

(In case you're curious, Google got the answer from Design* Sponge: 10 "The eraser was originally produced by the Eberhard Faber Company. . . . The erasers featured pumice, a volcanic ash from Italy that gave them their abrasive quality, along with their distinctive color and smell.")

Still not impressed? When Watson[3] famously won a round of *Jeopardy!* against the two best human players of all time, it needed a computer the size of a bedroom to answer questions like this. *That was only seven years ago.*

What do pink erasers have to do with the fact that we're all going to be out of a job in a few decades? Consider: Last October, an Uber trucking subsidiary named Otto delivered 2,000 cases of Budweiser 120 miles from Fort Collins, Colorado, to Colorado Springs—without a driver at the wheel. Within a few years, this technology will go from prototype to full production, and that means millions of truck drivers will be out of a job.

Automated trucking doesn't rely on newfangled machines, like the powered looms and steam shovels that drove the Industrial Revolution of the nineteenth century. Instead, like Google's ability to recognize spoken words and answer questions, self-driving trucks—and cars and buses and ships—rely primarily on software that mimics human intelligence. By now everyone's heard the predictions that self-driving cars could lead to 5 million jobs being lost, but few people understand that once artificial-intelligence software is good enough to drive a car, it will be good enough to do a lot of other things too. It won't be millions of people out of work; it will be tens of millions.

This is what we mean when we talk about "robots." We're talking about cognitive abilities, not the fact that they're made of metal instead of flesh and powered by electricity instead of chicken nuggets.

In other words, the advances to focus on aren't those in robotic 15 engineering—though they are happening, too—but the way we're hurtling toward artificial intelligence, or AI. While we're nowhere near human-level AI yet, the progress of the past couple of decades has been stunning. After many years of nothing much happening, suddenly robots can play chess better than the best grandmaster. They can play

---

[2]**coq au vin:** A French dish of chicken stewed in wine.
[3]**Watson:** Since the supercomputer Watson won first place on the television game show *Jeopardy!* in 2011, IBM has adapted it for use in making management decisions in cases of lung cancer treatment.

Jeopardy! better than the best humans. They can drive cars around San Francisco—and they're getting better at it every year. They can recognize faces well enough that Welsh police recently made the first-ever arrest in the United Kingdom using facial recognition software. After years of plodding progress in voice recognition, Google announced earlier this year that it had reduced its word error rate from 8.5 percent to 4.9 percent *in 10 months.*

All of this is a sign that AI is improving exponentially, a product of both better computer hardware and software. Hardware has historically followed a growth curve called Moore's law, in which power and efficiency double every couple of years, and recent improvements in software algorithms have been even more explosive. For a long time, these advances didn't seem very impressive: Going from the brainpower of a bacterium to the brainpower of a nematode[4] might technically represent an enormous leap, but on a practical level it doesn't get us that much closer to true artificial intelligence. However, if you keep up the doubling for a while, eventually one of those doubling cycles takes you from the brainpower of a lizard (who cares?) to the brainpower of a mouse and then a monkey (wow!). Once that happens, human-level AI is just a short step away.

Are we really this close to true AI? Here's a yardstick to think about. Even with all this doubling going on, until recently computer scientists thought we were still years away from machines being able to win at the ancient game of Go, usually regarded as the most complex human game in existence. But last year, a computer beat a Korean grandmaster considered one of the best of all time, and earlier this year it beat the highest-ranked Go player in the world. Far from slowing down, progress in artificial intelligence is now outstripping even the wildest hopes of the most dedicated AI cheerleaders. Unfortunately, for those of us worried about robots taking away our jobs, these advances mean that mass unemployment is a lot closer than we feared—so close, in fact, that it may be starting already. But you'd never know that from the virtual silence about solutions in policy and political circles.

I'm hardly alone in thinking we're on the verge of an AI Revolution. Many who work in the software industry—people like Bill Gates and Elon Musk[5]—have been sounding the alarm for years. But their concerns are largely ignored by policymakers and, until recently, often ridiculed by writers tasked with interpreting technology or economics. So let's take a look at some of the most common doubts of the AI skeptics.

#1: We'll never get true AI because computing power won't keep doubling forever. We're going to hit the limits of physics before long. There are several pretty good reasons to dismiss this claim as a roadblock. To start, hardware designers will invent faster, more specialized chips.

---

[4]**nematode:** A species of roundworm.
[5]**Bill Gates and Elon Musk:** William Gates III (b. 1955) is the principal founder of the Microsoft Corporation; Elon Musk (b. 1971) is the founder and CEO of SpaceX aerospace company and the cofounder and CEO of Tesla, Inc. automobile and energy company.

Google, for example, announced last spring that it had created a microchip called a Tensor Processing Unit, which it claimed was up to 30 times faster and 80 times more power efficient than an Intel processor for machine learning tasks.[6] A huge array of those chips are now available to researchers who use Google's cloud services. Other chips specialized for specific aspects of AI (image recognition, neural networking, language processing, etc.) either exist already or are certain to follow.

#2: Even if computing power keeps doubling, it has already been dou- [20] **bling for decades. You guys keep predicting full-on AI, but it never happens.** It's true that during the early years of computing there was a lot of naive optimism about how quickly we'd be able to build intelligent machines. But those rosy predictions died in the '70s, as computer scientists came to realize that even the fastest mainframes of the day produced only about a billionth of the processing power of the human brain. It was a humbling realization, and the entire field has been almost painfully realistic about its progress ever since.

We've finally built computers with roughly the raw processing power of the human brain—although only at a cost of more than $100 million and with an internal architecture that may or may not work well for emulating the human mind. But in another ten years, this level of power will likely be available for less than $1 million, and thousands of teams will be testing AI software on a platform that's actually capable of competing with humans.

#3: Okay, maybe we will get full AI. But it only means that robots will act intelligent, not that they'll really be intelligent. This is just a tedious philosophical debating point. For the purposes of employment, we don't really care if a smart computer has a soul—or if it can feel love and pain and loyalty. We only care if it can act like a human being well enough to do anything we can do. When that day comes, we'll all be out of jobs even if the computers taking our places aren't "really" intelligent.

#4: Fine. But waves of automation—steam engines, electricity, computers—always lead to predictions of mass unemployment. Instead they just make us more efficient. The AI Revolution will be no different. This is a popular argument. It's also catastrophically wrong.

The Industrial Revolution was all about mechanical power: Trains were more powerful than horses, and mechanical looms were more efficient than human muscle. At first, this *did* put people out of work: Those loom-smashing weavers in Yorkshire—the original Luddites[7]— really did lose their livelihoods. This caused massive social upheaval

---

[6]Norm Jouppi, "Quantifying the Performance of the TPU, Our First Machine Learning Chip," *Google Cloud Platform Blog*, April 7, 2017.
[7]**Luddites:** A group of English textile workers in the nineteenth century who destroyed weaving looms to protest mechanization.

for decades until the entire economy adapted to the machine age. When that finally happened, there were as many jobs tending the new machines as there used to be doing manual labor. The eventual result was a huge increase in productivity: A single person could churn out a lot more cloth than she could before. In the end, not only were as many people still employed, but they were employed at jobs tending machines that produced vastly more wealth than anyone had thought possible 100 years before. Once labor unions began demanding a piece of this pie, everyone benefited.

The AI Revolution will be nothing like that. When robots become as smart and capable as human beings, there will be nothing left for people to do because machines will be both stronger *and* smarter than humans. Even if AI creates lots of new jobs, it's of no consequence. *No matter what job you name, robots will be able to do it.* They will manufacture themselves, program themselves, repair themselves, and manage themselves. If you don't appreciate this, then you don't appreciate what's barreling toward us.

In fact, it's even worse. In addition to doing our jobs at least as well as we do them, intelligent robots will be cheaper, faster, and far more reliable than humans. And they can work 168 hours a week, not just forty. No capitalist in her right mind would continue to employ humans. They're expensive, they show up late, they complain whenever something changes, and they spend half their time gossiping. Let's face it: We humans make lousy laborers.

If you want to look at this through a utopian lens, the AI Revolution has the potential to free humanity forever from drudgery. In the best-case scenario, a combination of intelligent robots and green energy will provide everyone on Earth with everything they need. But just as the Industrial Revolution caused a lot of short-term pain, so will intelligent robots. While we're on the road to our *Star Trek* future, but before we finally get there, the rich are going to get richer—because they own the robots—and the rest of us are going to get poorer because we'll be out of jobs. Unless we figure out what we're going to do about that, the misery of workers over the next few decades will be far worse than anything the Industrial Revolution produced.

So let's talk about which jobs are in danger first. Economists generally break employment into cognitive versus physical jobs and routine versus nonroutine jobs. This gives us four basic categories of work:

Routine physical: digging ditches, driving trucks

Routine cognitive: accounts-payable clerk, telephone sales

Nonroutine physical: short-order cook, home health aide

Nonroutine cognitive: teacher, doctor, CEO

Routine tasks will be the first to go—and thanks to advances in robotics engineering, both physical and cognitive tasks will be affected. In a recent paper, a team from Oxford and Yale surveyed a large number of machine-learning researchers to produce a "wisdom of crowds" estimate of when computers would be able to take over various human jobs.[8] Two-thirds said progress in machine learning had accelerated in recent years, with Asian researchers even more optimistic than North American researchers about the advent of full AI within forty years.

But we don't need full AI for everything. The machine-learning researchers estimate that speech transcribers, translators, commercial drivers, retail sales, and similar jobs could be fully automated during the 2020s. Within a decade after that, all routine jobs could be gone.

Nonroutine jobs will be next: surgeons, novelists, construction workers, police officers, and so forth. These jobs could all be fully automated during the 2040s. By 2060, AI will be capable of performing any task currently done by humans. This doesn't mean that literally every human being on the planet will be jobless by then — in fact, the researchers suggest it could take another century before that happens — but that's hardly any solace. By 2060 or thereabouts, we'll have AI that can do anything a normal human can do, which means that nearly all normal jobs will be gone. And normal jobs are what almost all of us have.

2060 seems a long way off, but if the Oxford-Yale survey is right, we'll face an employment apocalypse far sooner than that: the disappearance of routine work of all kinds by the mid-2030s. That represents nearly half the US labor force. The consulting firm Pricewaterhouse-Coopers recently released a study[9] saying much the same. It predicts that 38 percent of all jobs in the United States are "at high risk of automation" by the early 2030s, most of them in routine occupations. In the even nearer term, the World Economic Forum predicts[10] that the rich world will lose 5 million jobs to robots by 2020, while a group of AI experts, writing in *Scientific American*, figures that 40 percent of the 500 biggest companies will vanish within a decade.[11]

Not scared yet? Kai-Fu Lee, a former Microsoft and Google executive who is now a prominent investor in Chinese AI startups, thinks artificial intelligence "will probably replace 50 percent of human jobs." When? Within ten years. *Ten years!* Maybe it's time to really start thinking hard about AI.

And forget about putting the genie back in the bottle. AI is coming whether we like it or not. The rewards are just too great. Even if America did somehow stop AI research, it would only mean that the Chinese or the French or the Brazilians would get there first. Russian President Vladimir Putin agrees. "Artificial intelligence is the future,

[8]Katja Grace, John Salvatier, Allan Dafoe, Baobao Zhang, and Owain Evans, "When Will AI Exceed Human Performance? Evidence from AI Experts," arxiv.org, May 30, 2017.

[9]Richard Berriman and John Hawksworth, "Will Robots Steal Our Jobs? The Potential Impact of Automation on the UK and Other Major Economies," UK *Economic Outlook*, Price Waterhouse Cooper, March 2017.

[10]Alex Grey, "5 Million Jobs to Be Lost by 2020," World Economic Forum, January 19, 2016.

[11]Dirk Helbing, "Will Democracy Survive Big Data and Artificial Intelligence?" *Scientific American*, February 25, 2017.

not only for Russia but for all humankind," he announced in September.[12] "Whoever becomes the leader in this sphere will become the ruler of the world." There's just no way around it: For the vast majority of jobs, work as we know it will come steadily to an end between about 2025 and 2060.

So who benefits? The answer is obvious: the owners of capital, who will control most of the robots. Who suffers? That's obvious too: the rest of us, who currently trade work for money. No work means no money.

But things won't actually be quite that grim. After all, fully automated farms and factories will produce much cheaper goods, and competition will then force down prices. Basic material comfort will be cheap as dirt.

Still not free, though. And capitalists can only make money if they have someone to sell their goods to. This means that even the business class will eventually realize that ubiquitous automation doesn't really benefit them after all. They need customers with money if they want to be rich themselves.

One way or another, then, the answer to the mass unemployment of the AI Revolution has to involve some kind of sweeping redistribution of income that decouples it from work. Or a total rethinking of what "work" is. Or a total rethinking of what wealth is. Let's consider a few of the possibilities.

The welfare state writ large: This is the simplest to think about. It's basically what we have now, but more extensive. Unemployment insurance will be more generous and come with no time limits. National health care will be free for all. Anyone without a job will qualify for some basic amount of food and housing. Higher taxes will pay for it, but we'll still operate under the assumption that gainful employment is expected from anyone able to work.

This is essentially the "bury our heads in the sand" option. We refuse to accept that work is truly going away, so we continue to punish people who aren't employed. Jobless benefits remain stingy so that people are motivated to find work — even though there aren't enough jobs to go around. We continue to believe that eventually the economy will find a new equilibrium.

This can't last for too long, and millions will suffer during the years we continue to delude ourselves. But it will protect the rich for a while.

Universal basic income #1: This is a step further down the road. Everyone would qualify for a certain level of income from the state, but the level of guaranteed income would be fairly modest because we would still want people to work. Unemployment wouldn't be as stigmatized as it is in today's welfare state, but neither would widespread joblessness be truly accepted as a permanent fact of life. Some European countries are moving toward a welfare state with cash assistance for everyone.

---

[12] "'Whoever Leads in AI Will Rule the World': Putin to Russian Children on Knowledge Day," RT, September 1, 2017.

Universal basic income #2: This is UBI on steroids. It's available to everyone, and the income level is substantial enough to provide a satisfying standard of living. This is what we'll most likely get once we accept that mass unemployment isn't a sign of lazy workers and social decay, but the inevitable result of improving technology. Since there's no personal stigma attached to joblessness and no special reason that the rich should reap all the rewards of artificial intelligence, there's also no reason to keep the universal income level low. After all, we aren't trying to prod people back into the workforce. In fact, the time will probably come when we actively want to do just the opposite: provide an income large enough to motivate people to leave the workforce and let robots do the job better.

Silicon Valley—perhaps unsurprisingly—is fast becoming a hotbed of UBI enthusiasm. Tech executives understand what's coming, and that their own businesses risk a backlash unless we take care of its victims. Uber has shown an interest in UBI. Facebook CEO Mark Zuckerberg supports it. Ditto for Tesla CEO Elon Musk and Slack CEO Stewart Butterfield. A startup incubator called Y Combinator is running a pilot program to find out what happens if you give people a guaranteed income.

There are even some countries that are now trying it. Switzerland rejected a UBI proposal in 2016, but Finland is experimenting with a small-scale UBI that pays the unemployed about $700 per month even after they find work. UBI is also getting limited tryouts by cities in Italy and Canada. Right now these are all pilot projects aimed at learning more about how to best run a UBI program and how well it works. But as large-scale job losses from automation start to become real, we should expect the idea to spread rapidly.

Despite the amount of media attention that both robots and AI have gotten over the past few years, it's difficult to get people to take them seriously. But start to pay attention and you see the signs: An Uber car can drive itself. A computer can write simple sports stories. SoftBank's Pepper robot[13] already works in more than 140 cellphone stores in Japan and is starting to get tryouts in America too. Alexa can order replacement Pop-Tarts before you know you need them. A Carnegie Mellon computer that seems to have figured out human bluffing beat four different online-poker pros earlier this year. California, suffering from a lack of Mexican workers, is ground zero for the development of robotic crop pickers. Sony is promising a robot that will form an emotional bond with its owner.

These are all harbingers, the way a dropping barometer signals a coming storm—not the possibility of a storm, but the inexorable reality. The two most important problems facing the human race right now are the need for widespread deployment of renewable energy and figuring out how to deal with the end of work. Everything else pales in comparison. Renewable energy already gets plenty of attention, even if half the country still denies that we really need it. It's time for the end of work to start getting the same attention.

---

[13] **SoftBank's Pepper robot:** Pepper is a humanoid robot that has the ability to read emotions and respond accordingly.

ENGAGING THE TEXT

1. Why does Drum believe that we will all be replaced by machines in the next twenty to forty years? What breakthrough has made this possible, and why are most people unaware of it?

2. What evidence does Drum offer to support his claims about automation and AI? Which of the many examples he offers strikes you as particularly impressive or convincing? Why?

3. What types of jobs are most likely to be replaced by AI systems? Which are the least likely? Make a list of the jobs or careers you think have the best chances of surviving the wave of automation that Drum predicts. Then compare them in class and discuss how automation might affect the career you've chosen to pursue.

4. How does Drum address counterarguments to his claims? Which of these counterarguments strikes you as the strongest or most important, and why? How does he respond to each of them, and how persuasive are the points that he makes?

5. Which of the scenarios Drum offers for surviving mass unemployment seems most realistic or attractive to you, and why? Discuss in class the pros and cons of his second, more generous universal basic income proposal. Do you think the UBI could ever become a reality in the United States? Would you agree that some day we might enter a "new golden age" when "we'll be free to read or write poetry or play video games" (para. 4)? What do you think people would do to give their lives a sense of purpose and meaning — or simply to pass time — when work disappears?

6. **Thinking Rhetorically**   How would you describe the tone of this selection? Find several lines or passages that illustrate Drum's style, and explain why you think he chose to include so much informal language. Do constructions like "That's kind of a buzzkill, isn't it?" (para. 6) detract from the seriousness of his message?

EXPLORING CONNECTIONS

7. Review Sherry Turkle's discussion of technology in the classroom (p. 178). How might Turkle respond to the idea that professors will someday be replaced by digital teachers? Would you want to have an intelligent robot or an AI system teach your classes and monitor your progress? Why or why not?

8. Revisit Eric Schmidt and Jared Cohen's "Our Future Selves" (p. 241) to assess how they present the impact of artificial intelligence and automation on society. How do they generally portray advances in AI? How do Drum's claims about mass unemployment complicate their vision of our technological future?

9. Drawing on Drum's analysis of automation and Bruce Schneier's examination of Internet surveillance, write a journal entry or a short essay about technology's impact on society. How optimistic do you feel about what the Internet and the AI revolution are doing to the world, and why?

EXTENDING THE CRITICAL CONTEXT

10. Go online to sample the warnings about AI that have been issued by famous technologists such as Tesla and SpaceX founder Elon Musk, former Microsoft CEO Bill Gates, and theoretical physicist Stephen Hawking. Why are these and other important scientists and technological innovators concerned about the rapid development of intelligent machines? What do they think we should do to protect ourselves from our own future inventions?

11. Visit the websites of the University of Oxford's Future of Humanity Institute, Cambridge University's Centre for the Study of Existential Risk, or Boston's Future of Life Institute. Learn about the purposes and goals of these organizations, and explore the resources they offer related to the risks of AI. How serious a threat does AI development appear to be in comparison to other existential challenges, like climate change and the spread of nuclear weapons?

12. Research the history of the universal basic income movement in the United States and other nations, like Canada, Finland, Scotland, and Italy. Where have UBI pilot programs been attempted, and how successful do they appear to have been? What problems or issues have arisen when people receive a guaranteed minimal income from the government? How likely is it, in your opinion, that the UBI will be the solution to the problems posed by a world without work?

BIG DATA, GOOGLE, AND THE END OF FREE WILL[*]

YUVAL NOAH HARARI

We tend to think of our tech devices as things that are helpful. Like Rosie the robot maid on the old *Jetsons* television show or R2D2 in *Star Wars*, our technological gadgets are designed to be both cute and convenient. We rarely think about how technology is changing us and altering the way we think about ourselves. This selection challenges us to consider whether technology is turning all of us into "Dataists"—people who have gotten used to thinking of themselves in terms of numbers and algorithms—and, as a result, whether we are giving up on "humanist" ideas like individuality and free will. Yuval Noah Harari (b. 1976) is no stranger to big ideas. A lecturer in history at the Hebrew University of Jerusalem, he is the author of the best-selling *Sapiens: A Brief History of Humankind* (2014) and *Homo Deus: A Brief History of Tomorrow* (2016). This selection originally appeared in the *Financial Times*.

FOR THOUSANDS OF YEARS HUMANS BELIEVED that authority came from the gods. Then, during the modern era, humanism gradually shifted authority from deities to people. Jean-Jacques Rousseau[1] summed up this revolution in *Emile*, his 1762 treatise on education. When looking for the rules of conduct in life, Rousseau found them "in the depths of my heart, traced by nature in characters which nothing can efface. I need only consult myself with regard to what I wish to do; what I feel to be good is good, what I feel to be bad is bad."[2] Humanist thinkers such as Rousseau convinced us that our own feelings and desires were the ultimate source of meaning, and that our free will was, therefore, the highest authority of all.

Now, a fresh shift is taking place. Just as divine authority was legitimized by religious mythologies, and human authority was legitimized by humanist ideologies, so high-tech gurus and Silicon Valley prophets are creating a new universal narrative that legitimizes the authority of algorithms and Big Data. This novel creed may be called "Dataism." In its extreme form, proponents of the Dataist worldview perceive the entire universe as a flow of data, see organisms as little more than biochemical algorithms, and believe that humanity's cosmic vocation is to create an all-encompassing data-processing system—and then merge into it.

We are already becoming tiny chips inside a giant system that nobody really understands. Every day I absorb countless data bits through e-mails, phone calls, and articles; process the data; and transmit back new bits through more e-mails, phone calls, and articles. I don't really know where I fit into the great scheme of things, and how my bits of data connect with the bits produced by billions of other humans and computers. I don't have time to find out, because I am too busy answering e-mails. This relentless dataflow sparks new inventions and disruptions that nobody plans, controls, or comprehends.

But no one needs to understand. All you need to do is answer your e-mails faster. Just as free-market capitalists believe in the invisible hand of the market,[3] so Dataists believe in the invisible hand of the dataflow. As the global data-processing system becomes all-knowing and all-powerful, so connecting to the system becomes the source of all meaning. The new motto says: "If you experience something—record it. If you record something—upload it. If you upload something—share it."

Dataists further believe that given enough biometric data and computing power, this all-encompassing system could understand humans much better than we understand ourselves. Once that happens, humans will lose their authority, and humanist practices such as democratic elections will become as obsolete as rain dances and flint knives.

[1]**Jean-Jacques Rousseau:** (1712–1778), a French philosopher, writer, and composer whose political philosophy and ideas about the self influenced the European Enlightenment. [All notes are the editors', except 2.]

[2]Jean-Jacques Rousseau, *Emile, or On Education*. Trans. Allan Bloom. New York: Basic Books, 1979.

[3]**the invisible hand of the market:** As used by Scottish economist Adam Smith (1723–1790), an unobservable force in free markets that guides the supply and demand of goods until they reach equilibrium.

For the past few centuries humanism has seen the human heart as the supreme source of authority not merely in politics but in every other field of activity. From infancy we are bombarded with a barrage of humanist slogans counselling us: "Listen to yourself, be true to yourself, trust yourself, follow your heart, do what feels good."

In politics, we believe that authority depends on the free choices of ordinary voters. In market economics, we maintain that the customer is always right. Humanist art thinks that beauty is in the eye of the beholder; humanist education teaches us to think for ourselves; and humanist ethics advise us that if it feels good, we should go ahead and do it.

Of course, humanist ethics often run into difficulties in situations when something that makes *me* feel good makes *you* feel bad. For example, every year for the past decade the Israeli LGBT community has held a gay parade in the streets of Jerusalem. It is a unique day of harmony in this conflict-riven city, because it is the one occasion when religious Jews, Muslims, and Christians suddenly find a common cause — they all fume in accord against the gay parade. What's really interesting, though, is the argument the religious fanatics use. They don't say: "You shouldn't hold a gay parade because God forbids homosexuality." Rather, they explain to every available microphone and TV camera that "seeing a gay parade passing through the holy city of Jerusalem hurts our feelings. Just as gay people want us to respect their feelings, they should respect ours." It doesn't matter what you think about this particular conundrum; it is far more important to understand that in a humanist society, ethical and political debates are conducted in the name of conflicting human feelings, rather than in the name of divine commandments.

Yet humanism is now facing an existential challenge and the idea of "free will" is under threat. Scientific insights into the way our brains and bodies work suggest that our feelings are not some uniquely human spiritual quality. Rather, they are biochemical mechanisms that all mammals and birds use in order to make decisions by quickly calculating probabilities of survival and reproduction.

Contrary to popular opinion, feelings aren't the opposite of rationality; they are evolutionary rationality made flesh. When a baboon, giraffe, or human sees a lion, fear arises because a biochemical algorithm calculates the relevant data and concludes that the probability of death is high. Similarly, feelings of sexual attraction arise when other biochemical algorithms calculate that a nearby individual offers a high probability for successful mating. These biochemical algorithms have evolved and improved through millions of years of evolution. If the feelings of some ancient ancestor made a mistake, the genes shaping these feelings did not pass on to the next generation. 10

Even though humanists were wrong to think that our feelings reflected some mysterious "free will," up until now humanism still made very good practical sense. For although there was nothing magical about our feelings, they were nevertheless the best method in the universe for making decisions — and no outside system could hope to understand my feelings better than me. Even if the Catholic Church or the Soviet KGB[4] spied on me every minute of every day, they lacked the biological knowledge and the computing power necessary to calculate the biochemical processes shaping my desires and choices. Hence, humanism was correct in telling people to follow their own heart. If you had to choose between listening to the Bible and listening to your feelings, it was much better to listen to your feelings. The Bible represented the opinions and biases of a few priests in ancient Jerusalem. Your feelings, in contrast, represented the accumulated wisdom of millions of years of evolution that have passed the most rigorous quality-control tests of natural selection.

However, as the Church and the KGB give way to Google and Facebook, humanism loses its practical advantages. For we are now at the confluence of two scientific tidal waves. On the one hand, biologists are deciphering the mysteries of the human body and, in particular, of the brain and of human feelings. At the same time, computer scientists are giving us unprecedented data-processing power. When you put the two together, you get external systems that can monitor and understand my feelings much better than I can. Once Big Data systems know me better than I know myself, authority will shift from humans to algorithms. Big Data could then empower Big Brother.[5]

This has already happened in the field of medicine. The most important medical decisions in your life are increasingly based not on your feelings of illness or wellness, or even on the informed predictions of your doctor — but on the calculations of computers who know you better than you know yourself. A recent example of this process is the case of the actress Angelina Jolie. In 2013, Jolie took a genetic test that proved she was carrying a dangerous mutation of the BRCA1 gene. According to statistical databases, women carrying this mutation have an 87 percent probability of developing breast cancer. Although at the time Jolie did not have cancer, she decided to pre-empt the disease and undergo a double mastectomy. She didn't feel ill but she wisely decided to listen to the computer algorithms. "You may not feel anything is wrong," said the algorithms, "but there is a time bomb ticking in your DNA. Do something about it — now!"

What is already happening in medicine is likely to take place in more and more fields. It starts with simple things, like which book to buy and read. How do humanists choose a book? They go to a bookstore, wander between the aisles, flip through one book and read the first few sentences of another, until some gut feeling connects them to a particular tome. Dataists use Amazon. As I enter the Amazon virtual store, a

[4]**KGB:** The main intelligence agency of the former Soviet Union.
[5]**Big Brother:** In George Orwell's dystopic novel *Nineteen Eighty-Four* (1949), Big Brother is the mysterious unseen leader of a totalitarian state who keeps all citizens under constant surveillance.

message pops up and tells me: "I know which books you liked in the past. People with similar tastes also tend to love this or that new book."

This is just the beginning. Devices such as Amazon's Kindle are able 15 constantly to collect data on their users while they are reading books. Your Kindle can monitor which parts of a book you read quickly, and which slowly; on which page you took a break, and on which sentence you abandoned the book, never to pick it up again. If Kindle were to be upgraded with facial recognition software and biometric sensors, it would know how each sentence influenced your heart rate and blood pressure. It would know what made you laugh, what made you sad, what made you angry. Soon, books will read you while you are reading them. And whereas you quickly forget most of what you read, computer programs need never forget. Such data should eventually enable Amazon to choose books for you with uncanny precision. It will also allow Amazon to know exactly who you are, and how to press your emotional buttons.

Take this to its logical conclusion, and eventually people may give algorithms the authority to make the most important decisions in their lives, such as who to marry. In medieval Europe, priests and parents had the authority to choose your mate for you. In humanist societies we give this authority to our feelings. In a Dataist society I will ask Google to choose. "Listen, Google," I will say, "both John and Paul are courting me. I like both of them, but in a different way, and it's so hard to make up my mind. Given everything you know, what do you advise me to do?"

And Google will answer: "Well, I know you from the day you were born. I have read all your e-mails, recorded all your phone calls, and know your favorite films, your DNA, and the entire biometric history of your heart. I have exact data about each date you went on, and I can show you second-by-second graphs of your heart rate, blood pressure, and sugar levels whenever you went on a date with John or Paul. And, naturally enough, I know them as well as I know you. Based on all this information, on my superb algorithms, and on decades' worth of statistics about millions of relationships—I advise you to go with John, with an 87 percent probability of being more satisfied with him in the long run.

"Indeed, I know you so well that I even know you don't like this answer. Paul is much more handsome than John and, because you give external appearances too much weight, you secretly wanted me to say 'Paul.' Looks matter, of course, but not as much as you think. Your biochemical algorithms—which evolved tens of thousands of years ago in the African savannah—give external beauty a weight of 35 percent in their overall rating of potential mates. My algorithms—which are based on the most up-to-date studies and statistics—say that looks have only a 14 percent impact on the long-term success of romantic relationships. So, even though I took Paul's beauty into account, I still tell you that you would be better off with John."

Google won't have to be perfect. It won't have to be correct all the time. It will just have to be better on average than me. And that is not so difficult, because most people don't know themselves very well, and most people often make terrible mistakes in the most important decisions of their lives.

The Dataist worldview is very attractive to politicians, business people, and ordinary consumers because it offers groundbreaking technologies and immense new powers. For all the fear of missing our privacy and our free choice, when consumers have to choose between keeping their privacy and having access to far superior healthcare—most will choose health.

For scholars and intellectuals, Dataism promises to provide the scientific Holy Grail that has eluded us for centuries: a single overarching theory that unifies all the scientific disciplines from musicology through economics, all the way to biology. According to Dataism, Beethoven's *Fifth Symphony*, a stock-exchange bubble, and the flu virus are just three patterns of dataflow that can be analysed using the same basic concepts and tools. This idea is extremely attractive. It gives all scientists a common language, builds bridges over academic rifts, and easily exports insights across disciplinary borders.

Of course, like previous all-encompassing dogmas, Dataism, too, may be founded on a misunderstanding of life. In particular, Dataism has no answer to the notorious "hard problem of consciousness." At present we are very far from explaining consciousness in terms of data-processing. Why is it that when billions of neurons in the brain fire particular signals to one another, a subjective feeling of love or fear or anger appears? We don't have a clue.

But even if Dataism is wrong about life, it may still conquer the world. Many previous creeds gained enormous popularity and power despite their factual mistakes. If Christianity and communism could do it, why not Dataism? Dataism has especially good prospects, because it is currently spreading across all scientific disciplines. A unified scientific paradigm may easily become an unassailable dogma.

If you don't like this, and you want to stay beyond the reach of the algorithms, there is probably just one piece of advice to give you, the oldest in the book: know thyself. In the end, it's a simple empirical question. As long as you have greater insight and self-knowledge than the algorithms, your choices will still be superior and you will keep at least some authority in your hands. If the algorithms nevertheless seem poised to take over, it is mainly because most human beings hardly know themselves at all.

ENGAGING THE TEXT

1. How does Harari define Dataism? What are the primary beliefs and values that make up this emerging worldview? How does it differ from traditional religions and humanism in terms of its understanding of authority and the individual self?

2. Would you agree that people today "are already becoming tiny chips inside a giant system that nobody really understands" (para. 3)? How often do you feel this way in relation to modern technology, and why?

3. Harari suggests that we are at a turning point in history when humanist ideas are giving way to Dataism. To what extent do you feel the tension between these two very different worldviews? Do you believe, for example, that feelings are "some uniquely human spiritual quality" (para. 9) or the result of complex "biochemical mechanisms"? Do you think our actions are controlled by our own desires, by divine will, or by "biochemical algorithms [that] have evolved and improved through millions of years of evolution" (para. 10)?

4. Harari claims that Dataism might eventually threaten "humanist practices" such as democratic elections. Why might our growing dependence on data and technology undermine democracy? What evidence do you see, if any, to suggest that this process is already underway?

5. How much of a Dataist are you? Do you believe that you need to record and share your experiences for them to have value? How frequently do you turn to algorithms for guidance on decisions about books, about where to eat, where to go, what to do, or who to date? How much of your own free will have you ceded to the Internet?

6. At the end of this essay, Harari suggests that the only way to resist Dataism is to "know thyself." How might self-knowledge help you resist the temptations of social networks and smart algorithms? What else could you do, alone and with others, to make sure that the Internet doesn't compromise or replace your ability to make your own choices and decisions?

7. **Thinking Rhetorically**   While he admits that Dataism might be "founded on a misunderstanding" (para. 22), Harari generally presents the idea as if it were an inevitable reality beyond the understanding or control of any individual or group of human beings. Why does he take this deterministic approach to his topic? Who benefits when we feel that nothing can be done to protect our privacy — or that we have no choice but to cede our agency to "the system"?

EXPLORING CONNECTIONS

8. Compare Harari's vision of the future with that offered by Eric Schmidt and Jared Cohen (p. 241). How would you explain the differences in their views about the future benefits of technology?

9. How might Harari's analysis of technology's impact on free will help explain the negative effects of technology that Jean Twenge documents in "Has the Smartphone Destroyed a Generation?" (p. 257)? To what extent does Twenge's account of smartphones and depression challenge Harari's idea that feelings can be seen as "biochemical mechanisms" (para. 9)?

10. How might Bruce Schneier (p. 315) respond to Harari's concept of Dataism? Would Schneier be likely to accept Harari's claim that we are becoming part of a system "that nobody really understands" (para. 3)? Why or why not?

11. Drawing on Kevin Drum's examination of artificial intelligence and mass unemployment (p. 322) and Harari's exploration of Dataism, write a journal entry or short essay about how technology threatens to change us. What will we be like when we depend on machines to make decisions for us and no longer need to work? How will technology change what it means to be human?

EXTENDING THE CRITICAL CONTEXT

12. Research the Quantified Self movement to learn about its goals, techniques, and principles. How do the members of this movement see themselves? What technologies do they use? What do they hope to achieve by "self tracking"? Do you see "self-surveillance" as a viable method of self-improvement, or does the idea strike you as narcissistic? To what extent have "self-trackers" embraced the idea that human beings are really just a collection of "biochemical mechanisms" (para. 9)?

FURTHER CONNECTIONS

1. Working in groups, do additional research on the impact of the Internet and social media on adolescents. First, go online to identify a selection of scholarly articles reporting the results of studies conducted by psychologists or social science researchers. You may want to focus your efforts on a single topic, like Internet addiction, or the effect of Internet use on friendship, peer pressure, stress, depression, or sexual attitudes. After sampling a few of the most promising of these studies, share their conclusions with your group members. Later in class, debate whether the Internet should be viewed as a useful tool or as a source of serious problems for most teens.

2. Do some research to learn more about the role that social media played in the 2016 presidential election. What kinds of false stories were spread on social media accounts during the 2016 campaign, and how many Americans viewed and shared them? How many bots were involved in making these stories go viral? What impact, if any, do you think these stories had on the outcome of the election? What has already been done to curb the spread of fake news online? What more, if anything, should be done?

3. Research the growth of mass surveillance in modern American society. How has government surveillance of the general population increased in response to terrorist threats and the development of new crime-fighting technologies? How have federal and local agencies used any of the following innovations to monitor the activities of U.S. citizens?

- Tracking cell phone and social media site use

- Data-mining bank and bookstore records

- Closed-circuit TV cameras

- Facial recognition systems

- GPS tracking

- DNA databases

- Surveillance drones

- RFID tagging

To what extent do you think these activities and technologies threaten the privacy and personal freedom of American citizens? Why?

4. In 2014 Facebook admitted that, along with professors from Cornell University and the University of California, it had participated in a controversial study that involved manipulating the news feeds of nearly 700,000 users. Go online to learn more about what came to be known as the "Facebook newsfeed scandal" and about Facebook's response to it. What ethical questions are raised when social media companies like Facebook or online dating services participate in social science research? To what extent should social media sites — including dating services — be free to use or market the information they collect for other purposes?

5. Go online to learn more about "transhumanism" and the human enhancement movement. What are the goals and expectations of advocates of transhumanism and human enhancement? How do they believe technologies like smart prosthetics, neural supplements, neural implants, nanotechnology, genetic engineering, and gene therapy will change human beings in the future? What are some of the ethical and moral questions raised by the desire for technological human enhancement? Do you think that it's part of our destiny as a species to become "posthuman"? Why or why not?

MONEY AND SUCCESS
The Myth of Individual Opportunity

Image Source/Getty Images

FAST FACTS

1. A 2017 report from the Institute for Policy Studies shows that America's three richest men — Bill Gates, Jeff Bezos, and Warren Buffett — hold more wealth than the poorer half of all Americans.

2. According to a Census Bureau Current Population survey, for every $100 in income earned by white families, black families earn only $57.30, and for every $100 of wealth held by white families, black families have only $5.04. Americans' perceptions of this wealth gap are wildly inaccurate: survey respondents estimated that black family wealth was more than 80% of white family wealth.

3. According to a World Bank estimate, 97 of 149 nations have greater income equality than the United States. Ukraine is the most equal, South Africa the least. The U.S. is comparable to Turkey, Jamaica, Uganda, Haiti, El Salvador, and Morocco.

4. American children born into households in the bottom 20% of earnings have a lower chance of upward mobility than their counterparts in Sweden, Italy, France, or Britain. The probability of these children moving from the bottom quintile to the top quintile is 7.8%.

5. According to a 2018 study conducted by Temple University and the Wisconsin Hope Lab, 36% of university students and 42% of community college students can't afford to eat regular meals; 9% of university students and 12% of community college students report having been homeless at some point during the academic year.

6. According to the *Washington Post*, the GOP tax bill that passed in December 2017 will produce these changes ten years later: those with an income below $28,100 will save $30; those between $154,900 and $225,400 will pay $100 more; those with incomes over $912,100 will get a tax break of $20,660.

7. Women who work full time in the U.S. are paid only 80 cents for every dollar paid to their male counterparts. For each dollar paid to white, non-Hispanic men, Asian women are paid 87 cents, black women 63 cents, Native American women 57 cents, and Latina women 54 cents.

Data from (1) "Bill Gates, Jeff Bezos, and Warren Buffett are wealthier than poorest half of US," *Guardian*, November 8, 2017; (2) Emily Badger, "Whites Have Huge Wealth Edge Over Blacks (but Don't Know It)," *New York Times*, September 18, 2017; (3) Jason Beaubien, "The Country with the World's Worst Inequality Is . . . ," NPR, *Goats and Soda: Stories of Life in a Changing World*, April 2, 2018; (4) "Americans overestimate social mobility in their country," *Economist*, https://www.economist.com/blogs/graphicdetail/2018/02/daily-chart-9; (5) Caitlin Dewey, "The hidden crisis on college campuses: 36 percent of students don't have enough to eat,"

Washington Post, Wonkblog, April 3, 2018; (6) "Republicans say it's a tax cut for the middle class. The biggest winners are the rich," *Washington Post*, January 30, 2018 https://www.washingtonpost.com/graphics/2017/business/what-republican-tax-plans-could-mean-for-you/?utm_term=.643ac4f89c5c; (7) "FAQs About the Wage Gap," National Women's Law Center, September 2017, https://nwlc-ciw49tixgw5lbab.stackpathdns.com/wp-content/uploads/2017/09/FAQ-About-the-Wage-Gap-2017.pdf.

THE AMERICAN DREAM — OUR SENSE OF THE UNITED STATES as a land of unique opportunities and individual achievement — is at the very heart of our cultural narrative; it would seem to be a defining, unshakable premise about who we are as a people and a nation. Its roots can be traced back to the earliest European explorers who crossed the Atlantic in search of legendary "New World" cities like Eldorado, where the streets were paved with gold. By the time the colonies declared their independence, the national myth of success was fully formed. Early immigrants like J. Hector St. John de Crèvecoeur, for example, extolled the freedom and opportunity to be found in this new land. Crèvecoeur's glowing descriptions of a classless society where anyone could attain success through honesty and hard work fired the imaginations of many European readers: in *Letters from an American Farmer* (1782) he wrote, "We are all animated with the spirit of an industry which is unfettered and unrestrained, because each person works for himself.... We have no princes, for whom we toil, starve, and bleed: we are the most perfect society now existing in the world." The promise of a land where hard work seemed to guarantee success drew poor immigrants from Europe and fueled national expansion into the western territories.

If Crèvecoeur was the most effective early advocate of the American Dream, the emerging nation's ultimate success story was Benjamin Franklin, the self-educated printer who rose from modest origins to become a renowned scientist, philosopher, and statesman. While it's clear to us that Franklin was a genius, he often attributed his success to practicing the virtues of honesty, hard work, and thrift, as in this passage from "Advice to a Young Tradesman": "Without industry and frugality nothing will do, and with them every thing. He that gets all he can honestly, and saves all he gets ... will certainly become RICH." Although Franklin was no Puritan, his advice — including its moral dimension — was in perfect harmony with the Puritan work ethic of the earliest colonists.

This version of the American Dream survived for at least a century after Franklin. In the decades after the Civil War, Horatio Alger, a writer of pulp fiction for young boys, became America's best-selling author, publishing more than a hundred rags-to-riches tales like *Ragged Dick* (1868), *Struggling Upward* (1886), and *Bound to Rise* (1873). Alger's name has become synonymous with the notion that anyone can succeed, even to generations of Americans who have never read any of his works. Like Franklin, Alger's heroes were concerned with moral rectitude as well as financial gain: a benefactor advises Ragged Dick, "If you'll try to be somebody, and grow up into a respectable member of society, you will. You may not become rich, — it isn't everybody that becomes rich, you know, — but you can obtain a good position and be respected." In retrospect it's easy to see how limited Alger's promises really were; none of his enterprising young people were women, for example, and none were black. Contemporary scholar Harlon Dalton has analyzed the pernicious effects of the Alger myth for people of color, concluding that its blindness to racial bias "serves to maintain the racial pecking order [and] trivialize, if not erase, the social meaning of race."

The myth grew increasingly complicated in the twentieth century, as we can see in the dramatic shift from Alger's wholehearted optimism to F. Scott Fitzgerald's nuanced treatment of the American Dream in *The Great Gatsby*, which chronicles one man's attempt to gain everything the Roaring Twenties had to offer. If Alger's *Ragged Dick* is a sunny fairy tale for boys, *Gatsby* is a tragic fairy tale for the nation. One reason for *Gatsby*'s enduring power is surely that Fitzgerald captures the deep allure of the dream — ambition, wealth, the golden girl whose voice "is full of money" — while simultaneously undermining Gatsby's romantic quest with crime, infidelity, and violence, the "foul dust" that "floated in the wake of his dreams."

The myth faced its greatest challenge when the prosperity and energy of the Roaring Twenties collapsed into the Great Depression of the 1930s, but a booming postwar economy and our status as a global superpower restored many people's faith. As detailed in "What We Really Miss About the 1950s" by Stephanie Coontz, the postwar era did bring stability and economic opportunity to some Americans but meant "racism, sexism, and repression" for others (p. 26). Even in good times, the mood of the myth had changed. In the 1970s, Robert Ringer's enormously popular *Looking Out for Number One* urged readers to "forget foundationless traditions, forget the 'moral' standards others may have tried to cram down your throat ... and, most important, think of yourself — Number One.... You and you alone will be responsible for your success or failure."

Ringer's strong emphasis on individual striving is just one element of the American Dream that feminist writers have more recently critiqued. In brief, the myth strikes them as "masculinist" — that is, reflecting the attitudes, behaviors, and values traditionally associated with men. Whether they are explorers, cowboys, inventors, oil barons, or presidents, our mythic heroes have most often been male; their masculine characteristics include physical prowess (Babe Ruth, Teddy Roosevelt, the Terminator, Muhammad Ali), self-sufficiency or isolation (Henry David Thoreau, the Marlboro Man, private detectives), and excellence in hunting or fighting (Buffalo Bill, Robert E. Lee, Wyatt Earp, Luke Skywalker). The myth's heavy emphasis on masculinity means that cultural values such as family, community, collaboration, and tradition end up undervalued, as do the myriad contributions of ordinary people who supported the supposedly "self-made" men.

Despite these complications, the notion of success clearly continues to haunt us: we spend millions every year reading about the rich and famous and learning how to "make a fortune in real estate with no money down." We become engrossed in status symbols, trying to live in the "right" neighborhoods and wear the "right" clothes. We follow the diets of movie stars and the fitness regimens of Olympic athletes. Trying to boost our chances at a good career and a comfortable life, we take out student loans that might take decades to pay off. The myth of success has even invaded our personal relationships: we tally Facebook friends and Twitter followers, and aspire to be as "successful" in marriage or parenthood as in business.

Unfortunately our dreams can easily turn into nightmares. Every American who hopes to "make it" also knows the fear of failure, because the myth of success inevitably implies comparison between the haves and the have-nots, the achievers and the drones, the stars and the anonymous crowd. It's also hard to square the myth with some brutal contemporary realities, including entrenched poverty, wage stagnation, a shrinking middle class, the extreme concentration of wealth in the hands of billionaires, and even modern forms of slavery. Upward mobility, a key promise of the American Dream, turns out to be no easier here than in England and France with their well-defined class structures, and harder here than in Canada and some Scandinavian countries. Moreover, it is almost impossible for Americans to escape poverty: 95 percent of children born to poor parents will themselves be poor all their lives. Sociologist Robert Putnam, professor of public policy at Harvard, worries that the "opportunity gap" between rich and poor is so large that children may soon simply inherit their rank in a two-caste system of privileged and poor. Even for fortunate Americans, the recession that battered world economies in 2008 made maintaining the comfortable lifestyle of the middle class seem dependent less on hard work than on global economic forces like the price of crude oil and the migration of American jobs overseas.

The chapter opens with Gregory Mantsios's "Class in America," an essay that replaces the rosy, mythical view of a middle-class nation with a portrait of an economic system that serves the powerful and wealthy. From the broad canvas of "Class in America" we move to personal narrative — Barbara Ehrenreich's "Serving in Florida," which makes vivid the daily grind of working-class life as Ehrenreich struggles to make ends meet on waitressing wages. Next, Alan Aja and his fellow researchers explore connections between class and race in "From a Tangle of Pathology to a Race-Fair America," laying out the structural barriers faced by people of color, including discriminatory hiring practices, racially segregated occupations, and a wealth gap that impedes self-employment and entrepreneurship among minorities. The opening cluster of readings concludes with an excerpt from *How the Other Half Banks*, a compassionate examination of how challenging life can be for those whom financial institutions exploit or ignore altogether.

Midway through the chapter, the Visual Portfolio, "Reading Images of Individual Opportunity," explores dreams of success, the cost of failure, the struggle for economic justice, and the relationship of opportunity to race, gender, and education. Continuing a look at visual media, Diana Kendall's "Framing Class, Vicarious Living, and Conspicuous Consumption" reveals how TV distorts our view of economic inequalities — by treating poverty as individual misfortune, for example, rather than systematic oppression.

Because the American Dream says success is built on hard work, the chapter includes two pieces that deal with work environments. In the excerpt from *Reset: My Fight for Inclusion and Lasting Change*, Ellen K. Pao describes misogynistic practices at a prestigious venture capital firm, complete with a predatory man in a bathrobe. In "Thank God It's Monday," Kate Aronoff gives us a glimpse of future work — a flexible, entrepreneurial environment where espresso shots, craft beers, and perhaps a sense of community compensate workers for the crushing hours and nonstop pressure.

The chapter concludes with an essay about what all of us would welcome — free money. Perhaps surprisingly, Rutger Bregman's "Why We Should Give Free Money to Everyone" is not satiric or fanciful, but rather a fact-based analysis of why the best way to combat poverty may in fact be to throw money at all of us, no strings attached.

Sources

Baida, Peter. *Poor Richard's Legacy: American Business Values from Benjamin Franklin to Donald Trump*. New York: William Morrow, 1990. Print.

Correspondents of the *New York Times*. *Class Matters*. New York: Times Books/Henry Holt, 2005. Print.

Dalton, Harlon L. *Racial Healing: Confronting the Fear Between Blacks and Whites*. New York: Doubleday, 1995. Print.

Fitzgerald, F. Scott. *The Great Gatsby*. New York: Scribner's, 1925. Print.

McNamee, Stephen J., and Robert K. Miller Jr. *The Meritocracy Myth*. New York: Rowman & Littlefield, 2004. Print.

Putnam, Robert. "*Bowling Alone* — Author Robert Putnam Takes on America's Opportunity Gap." *Forum with Michael Krasny*, National Public Radio, July 3, 2015. Web.

St. John de Crèvecoeur, J. Hector. *Letters from an American Farmer*. New York: Dolphin Books, 1961. First published in London, 1782. Print.

BEFORE READING

- Working alone or in groups, make a list of people who best represent your idea of success. (You may want to consider leaders in government, sports, entertainment, education, science, business, or other fields.) List the specific qualities or accomplishments that make these people successful. Compare notes with your classmates, then freewrite about the meaning of success: What does it mean to you? To the class as a whole?

- Write an imaginative profile of the man pictured in the frontispiece for this chapter (p. 341). For example, where was he born, what do you imagine his parents did for a living, and where was he educated? What do his clothes, his posture, his facial expression, and the limousine say about him today? Where does he live, what is his current job or profession, and how much money does he make? Compare your profile with those of classmates to see shared or divergent ideas about some of the issues explored throughout *Rereading America* — the "American Dream," certainly, but also cultural myths of family, education, gender, and ethnicity.

- Write down the job and salary you expect to have in the next 10–15 years. Share with classmates and keep the guesstimate in mind as you read this chapter, adjusting up or down as you gain new information.

CLASS IN AMERICA

GREGORY MANTSIOS

Which of these gifts might a high school graduate in your family receive — a new dress, a $500 savings bond, or a BMW? The answer hints at your social class, a key factor in American lives that runs counter to the more comfortable notion that the United States is essentially a middle-class nation. The selection below makes it hard to deny class distinctions and their nearly universal influence on our lives. The essay juxtaposes myths and realities as Mantsios outlines four widely held beliefs about class in the United States and then systematically refutes them with statistical evidence. Even if you already recognize the importance of social class, some of the numbers the author cites are likely to surprise you. Mantsios is founder and director of the Joseph S. Murphy Institute for Worker Education and Labor Studies in the School of Professional Studies at CUNY (City University of New York) and editor of *A New Labor Movement for the New Century* (1998). In 2017 City & State New York honored him with their Corporate Social Responsibility Award for Labor and Law. The essay reprinted below appeared in *Race, Class, and Gender in the United States: An Integrated Study*, edited by Paula S. Rothenberg (2016).

THERE WASN'T MUCH ATTENTION GIVEN to America's class divide, at least not until a band of mostly young activists decided to occupy Wall Street in the fall of 2011 and in the process capture the media spotlight, add the word "99 percenters" to our lexicon, and change the national—and in many ways, the international—discourse. While there has been recent interest in the rising level of inequality, the class divide is anything but recent and its consequences remain severely understated in the mass media. Perhaps most importantly, the point that is missed is that inequality is persistent and structural—and it manifests itself in a multitude of cultural and social ways.

Americans, in general, don't like to talk about class. Or so it would seem. We don't speak about class privileges, or class oppression, or the class nature of society. These terms are not part of our everyday vocabulary, and in most circles this language is associated with the language of the rhetorical fringe. Unlike people in most other parts of the world, we shrink from using words that classify along economic lines or that point to class distinctions: Phrases like "working class," "upper class," "capitalist class," and "ruling class" are rarely uttered by Americans.

For the most part, avoidance of class-laden vocabulary crosses class boundaries. There are few among the poor who speak of themselves as lower class; instead, they refer to their race, ethnic group, or geographic location. Workers are more likely to identify with their employer, industry, or occupational group than with other workers, or with the working class. Neither are those at the upper end of the economic spectrum likely to use the word "class."[1] In her study of thirty-eight wealthy and socially prominent women, Susan Ostrander asked participants if they considered themselves members of the upper class. One participant responded, "I hate to use the word 'class.' We are responsible, fortunate people, old families, the people who have something." Another said, "I hate [the term] upper class. It is so non-upper class to use it. I just call it 'all of us'—those who are well-born."[2]

It is not that Americans, rich or poor, aren't keenly aware of class differences—those quoted above obviously are; it is that class is usually not in the domain of public conversation. Class is not discussed or debated in public because class identity has been stripped from popular culture. The institutions that shape mass culture and define the parameters of public debate have avoided class issues. In politics, in primary and secondary education, and in the mass media, formulating issues in terms of class has been considered culturally unacceptable, unnecessarily combative, and even un-American.

There are, however, two notable exceptions to this phenomenon. 5 First, it is acceptable in the United States to talk about "the middle class." Interestingly enough, the term middle class appears to be acceptable precisely because it mutes class differences. References to the middle class by politicians, for example, are designed to encompass and attract the broadest possible constituency. Not only do references to the middle class gloss over differences, but they also avoid any suggestion of conflict or injustice.

This leads us to a second exception to the class-avoidance phenomenon. We are, on occasion, presented with glimpses of the upper class and the lower class (the language used is "the wealthy" and "the poor"). In the media, these presentations are designed to satisfy some real or imagined voyeuristic need of "the ordinary person." As curiosities, the ground-level view of street life and trailer parks and the inside look at the rich and the famous serve as unique models, one to avoid and one to emulate. In either case, the two sets of lifestyles are presented as

The author wishes to thank Maya Pinto for her assistance in updating this article. © Gregory Mantsios, 2012. Reprinted by permission of the author.

[1]See Jay MacLead, *Ain't No Makin' It: Aspirations and Attainment in a Lower-Income Neighborhood* (Boulder, CO: Westview Press, 1995); Benjamin DeMott, *The Imperial Middle: Why Americans Can't Think Straight About Class* (New York: Morrow, 1990); Ira Katznelson, *City Trenches: Urban Politics and Patterning of Class in the United States* (New York: Pantheon Books, 1981); Charles W. Tucker, "A Comparative Analysis of Subjective Social Class: 1945–1963," *Social Forces*, no. 46 (June 1968): 508–14; Robert Nisbet, "The Decline and Fall of Social Class," *Pacific Sociological Review* 2 (Spring 1959): 11–17; and Oscar Glantz, "Class Consciousness and Political Solidarity," *American Sociological Review* 23 (August 1958): 375–82. [All notes are Mantsios's.]

[2]Susan Ostrander, "Upper-Class Women: Class Consciousness as Conduct and Meaning," in *Power Structure Research*, ed. G. William Domhoff (Beverly Hills, CA: Sage Publications, 1980), 78–79. Also see Stephen Birmingham, *America's Secret Aristocracy* (Boston: Little, Brown, 1987).

though they have no causal relation to each other: There is nothing to suggest that our economic system allows people to grow wealthy *at the expense of* those who are not.

Similarly, when politicians and social commentators draw attention to the plight of the poor, they do so in a manner that obscures the class structure and denies any sense of exploitation. Wealth and poverty are viewed as one of several natural and inevitable states of being: Differences are only differences. One may even say differences are the American way, a reflection of American social diversity.

We are left with one of two possible explanations for why Americans usually don't talk about class: Either class distinctions are not relevant to U.S. society, or we mistakenly hold a set of beliefs that obscure the reality of class differences and their impact on people's lives.

Let's look at four common, albeit contradictory, beliefs about class in America that have persisted over time.

Myth 1: We are a middle-class nation. Despite some variations in economic status, most Americans have achieved relative affluence in what is widely recognized as a consumer society.

Myth 2: Class really doesn't matter in the United States. Whatever differences do exist in economic standing, they are — for the most part — irrelevant. Our democracy provides for all regardless of economic class: Rich or poor, we are all equal in the eyes of the law.

Myth 3: We live in a land of upward mobility. The American public as a whole is steadily moving up the economic ladder and each generation propels itself to greater economic well-being.

Myth 4: Everyone has an equal chance to succeed. Success in the United States requires no more than hard work, sacrifice, and perseverance: "In America, anyone can become a billionaire; it's just a matter of being in the right place at the right time."

In trying to assess the legitimacy of these beliefs, we want to ask 10 several important questions. Are there significant class differences among Americans? If these differences do exist, are they getting bigger or smaller? Do class differences have a significant impact on the way we live? How much upward mobility is there in the United States? Finally, does everyone in the United States really have an equal opportunity to succeed and an equal voice in our democracy?

The Economic Spectrum

For starters, let's look at difference. An examination of available data reveals that variations in economic well-being are, in fact, dramatic. Consider the following:

- The richest 20 percent of Americans hold nearly 90 percent of the total household wealth in the country. The wealthiest 1 percent of the American population holds 36 percent of the total national wealth. That is, the top 1 percent own over one-third of all the consumer durables (such as houses, cars, televisions, and computers) and financial assets (such as stocks, bonds, property, and bank savings).[3]

- There are 323,067 Americans—approximately 1 percent of the adult population—who earn more than $1 million annually.[4] There are over 1,000 billionaires in the United States today, more than 70 of them worth over $10 billion each.[5] It would take the typical American earning $49,445 (the median income in the United States)—and spending absolutely nothing at all—a total of 202,240 years (or over 2,500 lifetimes) to earn $10 billion.

Affluence and prosperity are clearly alive and well in certain segments of the U.S. population. However, this abundance is in sharp contrast to the poverty that persists in America. At the other end of the spectrum:

- More than 15 percent of the American population—that is, 1 of every 7 people in this country—live below the official poverty line (calculated at $11,139 for an individual and $22,314 for a family of four).[6] In 2010, there were 42 million poor people in the United States—the largest number since the Census Bureau began publishing poverty statistics more than 50 years ago.[7]

- An estimated 3.5 million people—of whom nearly 1.4 million are children—are homeless.[8]

- The 2010 U.S. Census reported that more than 1 out of every 5 children under the age of 18 lives in poverty.[9]

[3]Economic Policy Institute, "Wealth Holdings Remain Unequal in Good and Bad Times," *The State of Working America* (Washington, DC: Economic Policy Institute, 2011), accessed September 25, 2011, http://www.stateofworkingamerica.org/files/files/Figure%20B_wealth_dis_byclass.xlsx.

[4]The number of individuals filing tax returns that had a gross adjusted income of $1 million or more in 2008 was 323,067 ("Tax Stats at a Glance," Internal Revenue Service, U.S. Treasury Department, available at http://www.irs.gov/pub/irs-soi/10taxstatscard.pdf). The adult population (18 years and over) of the United States in 2008 was 229,945,000, according to U.S. Census figures, U.S. Census Bureau, *Current Population Survey, Annual Social and Economic Supplement 2010*, available at http://www.census.gov/compendia/statab/2012/tables/12s0007.pdf.

[5]*Forbes*, "The World's Billionaires List: United States," accessed September 25, 2011, http://www.forbes.com/wealth/billionaires#p_l_s_arank_-l__225.

[6]Based on 2010 census figures. Carmen DeNavas-Walt, Bernadette D. Proctor, and Jessica C. Smith, U.S. Census Bureau, Current Population Reports, P60–239, *Income, Poverty, and Health Insurance Coverage in the United States: 2010* (Washington, DC: U.S. Government Printing Office).

[7]U.S. Census Bureau, "Poverty," available at http://www.census.gov/hhes/www/poverty/about/overview/index.html.

[8]National Coalition for the Homeless, "How Many People Experience Homelessness?" NCH Fact Sheet #2, July 2009, http://www.nationalhomeless.org/factsheets/How_Many.html?.

[9]See U.S. Census Bureau, "Poverty," available at http://www.census.gov/hhes/www/poverty/about/overview/index.html.

Reality 1: The contrast between rich and poor is sharp, and with one-third of the American population living at one extreme or the other, it is difficult to argue that we live in a classless society.

While those at the bottom of the economic ladder have fared poorly relative to those at the top, so too have those in the middle—and their standing relative to the top has been declining as well.

- The middle fifth of the population holds less than 4 percent of the national *wealth*.[10]

- The share of wealth held by the middle fifth thirty years ago was 5.2 percent of the total. Today's share held by the middle sector is 23 percent less than what it was three decades ago.[11]

Reality 2: The middle class in the United States holds a very small 15 share of the nation's wealth and that share has declined steadily.

The gap between rich and poor—and between the rich and the middle class—leaves the vast majority of the American population at a distinct disadvantage.

- Eighty percent of the population—that is, four out of every five Americans—is left sharing a little more than 10 percent of the nation's wealth.[12]

- The income gap between the very rich (top 1 percent) and everyone else (the 99 percent) more than tripled over the past three decades, creating the greatest concentration of income since 1928.[13]

This level of inequality is neither inevitable nor universal. The income gap between rich and poor in a country is generally measured by a statistic called the Gini coefficient, which provides a mathematical ratio and scale that allows comparisons between countries of the world. The U.S. government's own reports using the Gini coefficient show that the United States ranked number 95 out of 134 countries studied—that is, 94 countries (including almost all the industrialized nations of the world) had a more equal distribution of income than the United States.[14]

The numbers and percentages associated with economic inequality are difficult to fully comprehend. To help his students visualize the

---

[10]Economic Policy Institute, *The State of Working America*, accessed September 25, 2011, http://www.stateofworkingamerica.org/files/files/Figure%20B_wealth_dis_byclass.xlsx.

[11]Edward N. Wolff, "Recent Trends in Household Wealth in the U.S." Levy Economics Institute of Bard College Working Paper no. 502, Levy Economics Institute, Annandale-on-Hudson, NY, March 2010.

[12]Economic Policy Institute, "Wealth Holdings Remain Unequal in Good and Bad Times," *The State of Working America* (Washington, DC: Economic Policy Institute, 2001), accessed September 25, 2011, http://www.stateofworkingamerica.org/files/files/Figure%20B_wealth_dis_byclass.xlsx.

[13]Arloc Sherman and Chad Stone, "Income Gaps Between Very Rich and Everyone Else More Than Tripled in Last Three Decades, New Data Show," Center for Budget and Policy Studies, June 26, 2010.

[14]See the CIA report *The World Factbook*, https://www.cia.gov/library/publications/the-world-factbook/rankorder/2172rank.html.

distribution of income, the well-known economist Paul Samuelson asked them to picture an income pyramid made of children's blocks, with each layer of blocks representing $1,000. If we were to construct Samuelson's pyramid today, the peak of the pyramid would be much higher than the Eiffel Tower, yet almost all of us would be within 6 feet of the ground.[15] In other words, a small minority of families takes the lion's share of the national income, and the remaining income is distributed among the vast majority of middle-income and low-income families. Keep in mind that Samuelson's pyramid represents the distribution of income, not wealth (accumulated resources). The distribution of wealth is skewed even further. Ten billion dollars of wealth would reach more than 1,000 times the height of the Eiffel Tower.[16]

Reality 3: Middle- and lower-income earners—what many in other parts of the world would refer to as the working class—share a minuscule portion of the nation's wealth. For the most part, the real class divide in the United States is between the very wealthy and everyone else—and it is a divide that is staggering.

American Lifestyles

The late political theorist/activist Michael Harrington once commented, "America has the best-dressed poverty the world has ever known."[17] Clothing disguises much of the poverty in the United States, and this may explain, in part, the country's middle-class image. With increased mass marketing of "designer" clothing and with shifts in the nation's economy from blue-collar (and often better-paying) manufacturing jobs to white-collar and pink-collar jobs in the service sector, it is becoming increasingly difficult to distinguish class differences based on appearance.[18] The dress-down environment prevalent in the high-tech industry (what American Studies scholar Andrew Ross refers to as the "no-collar movement") has reduced superficial distinctions even further.[19]

Beneath the surface, there is another reality. Let's look at some "typical" and not-so-typical lifestyles.

20

American Profile

Name: Harold S. Browning

Father: Manufacturer, industrialist

Mother: Prominent social figure in the community

---

[15]Paul Samuelson, *Economics*, 10th ed. (New York: McGraw-Hill, 1976), 84.

[16]Calculated at 1.5 inches per children's block and 1,050 feet for the height of the Eiffel Tower.

[17]Michael Harrington, *The Other America* (New York: Macmillan, 1962), 12–13.

[18]Stuart Ewen and Elizabeth Ewen, *Channels of Desire: Mass Images and the Shaping of American Consciousness* (New York: McGraw-Hill, 1982).

[19]Andrew Ross, *No-Collar: The Humane Workplace and Its Hidden Costs* (New York: Basic Books, 2002).

Principal child-rearer:	Governess
Primary education:	An exclusive private school on Manhattan's Upper East Side *Note:* A small, well-respected primary school where teachers and administrators have a reputation for nurturing student creativity and for providing the finest educational preparation *Ambition:* "To become President"
Supplemental tutoring:	Tutors in French and mathematics
Summer camp:	Sleep-away camp in northern Connecticut *Note:* Camp provides instruction in the creative arts, athletics, and the natural sciences
Secondary education:	A prestigious preparatory school in Westchester County *Note:* Classmates included the sons of ambassadors, doctors, attorneys, television personalities, and well-known business leaders *Supplemental education:* Private SAT tutor *After-school activities:* Private riding lessons *Ambition:* "To take over my father's business" *High-school graduation gift:* BMW
Family activities:	Theater, recitals, museums, summer vacations in Europe, occasional winter trips to the Caribbean *Note:* As members of and donors to the local art museum, the Brownings and their children attend private receptions and exhibit openings at the invitation of the museum director
Higher education:	An Ivy League liberal arts college in Massachusetts *Major:* Economics and political science *After-class activities:* Debating club, college newspaper, swim team *Ambition:* "To become a leader in business"
First full-time job (age 23):	Assistant manager of operations, Browning Tool and Die, Inc. (family enterprise)

Subsequent employment:	3 years—Executive assistant to the president, Browning Tool and Die *Responsibilities included:* Purchasing (materials and equipment), personnel, and distribution networks 4 years—Advertising manager, Lackheed Manufacturing (home appliances) 3 years—Director of marketing and sales, Comerex, Inc. (business machines)
Current employment (age 38):	Executive vice president, SmithBond and Co. (digital instruments) *Typical daily activities:* Review financial reports and computer printouts, dictate memoranda, lunch with clients, initiate conference calls, meet with assistants, plan business trips, meet with associates *Transportation to and from work:* Chauffeured company limousine *Annual salary:* $324,000 *Ambition:* "To become chief executive officer of the firm, or one like it, within the next five to ten years"
Current residence:	Eighteenth-floor condominium on Manhattan's Upper West Side, eleven rooms, including five spacious bedrooms and terrace overlooking river *Interior:* Professionally decorated and accented with elegant furnishings, valuable antiques, and expensive artwork *Note:* Building management provides doorman and elevator attendant; family employs au pair for children and maid for other domestic chores
Second residence:	Farm in northwestern Connecticut, used for weekend retreats and for horse breeding (investment/hobby) *Note:* To maintain the farm and cater to the family when they are there, the Brownings employ a part-time maid, groundskeeper, and horse breeder

Harold Browning was born into a world of nurses, maids, and governesses. His world today is one of airplanes and limousines, five-star restaurants, and luxurious living accommodations. The life and lifestyle of Harold Browning is in sharp contrast to that of Bob Farrell.

American Profile

Name:	Bob Farrell
Father:	Machinist
Mother:	Retail clerk
Principal child-rearer:	Mother and sitter
Primary education:	A medium-size public school in Queens, New York, characterized by large class size, outmoded physical facilities, and an educational philosophy emphasizing basic skills and student discipline *Ambition:* "To become President"
Supplemental tutoring:	None
Summer camp:	YMCA day camp *Note:* Emphasis on team sports, arts and crafts
Secondary education:	Large regional high school in Queens *Note:* Classmates included the sons and daughters of carpenters, postal clerks, teachers, nurses, shopkeepers, mechanics, bus drivers, police officers, salespersons *Supplemental education:* SAT prep course offered by national chain *After-school activities:* Basketball and handball in school park *Ambition:* "To make it through college" *High-school graduation gift:* $500 savings bond
Family activities:	Family gatherings around television set, softball, an occasional trip to the movie theater, summer Sundays at the public beach
Higher education:	A two-year community college with a technical orientation *Major:* Electrical technology *After-school activities:* Employed as a part-time bagger in local supermarket *Ambition:* "To become an electrical engineer"
First full-time job (age 19):	Service-station attendant *Note:* Continued to take college classes in the evening

Subsequent employment:	Mail clerk at large insurance firm; manager trainee, large retail chain
Present employment (age 38):	Assistant sales manager, building supply firm *Typical daily activities:* Demonstrate products, write up product orders, handle customer complaints, check inventory *Transportation to and from work:* City subway *Annual salary:* $45,261 *Additional income:* $6,100 in commissions from evening and weekend work as salesman in local men's clothing store *Ambition:* "To open up my own business"
Current residence:	The Farrells own their own home in a working-class neighborhood in Queens, New York

Bob Farrell and Harold Browning live very differently: One is very privileged, the other much less so. The differences are class differences, which have a profound impact on the way they live. They are differences between playing a game of handball in the park and taking riding lessons at a private stable; watching a movie on television and going to the theater; and taking the subway to work and being driven in a limousine. More important, the difference in class determines where they live, who their friends are, how well they are educated, what they do for a living, and what they come to expect from life.

Yet, as dissimilar as their lifestyles are, Harold Browning and Bob Farrell have some things in common: they live in the same city, they work long hours, and they are highly motivated. More importantly, they are both white males.

Let's look at someone else who works long and hard and is highly motivated. This person, however, is black and female.

American Profile	
Name:	Cheryl Mitchell
Father:	Janitor
Mother:	Waitress
Principal child-rearer:	Grandmother

Primary education:	Large public school in Ocean Hill-Brownsville, Brooklyn, New York *Note:* Rote teaching of basic skills and emphasis on conveying the importance of good attendance, good manners, and good work habits; school patrolled by security guards *Ambition:* "To be a teacher"
Supplemental tutoring:	None
Summer camp:	None
Secondary education:	Large public school in Ocean Hill-Brownsville *Note*: Classmates included sons and daughters of hairdressers, grounds-keepers, painters, dressmakers, dishwashers, domestics *Supplemental education:* None *After-school activities:* Domestic chores, part-time employment as babysitter and housekeeper *Ambition:* "To be a social worker" *High-school graduation gift:* new dress
Family activities:	Church-sponsored socials
Higher education:	One semester of local community college *Note*: Dropped out of school for financial reasons
First full-time job (age 17):	Counter clerk, local bakery
Subsequent employment:	File clerk with temporary-service agency, supermarket checker
Current employment (age 38):	Nurse's aide at a municipal hospital *Typical daily activities:* Make up hospital beds, clean out bedpans, weigh patients and assist them to the bathroom, take temperature readings, pass out and collect food trays, feed patients who need help, bathe patients, and change dressings *Annual salary:* $17,850 *Ambition:* "To get out of the ghetto"
Current residence:	Three-room apartment in the South Bronx, needs painting, has poor ventilation, is in a high-crime area *Note*: Cheryl Mitchell lives with her four-year-old son and her elderly mother

When we look at Cheryl Mitchell, Bob Farrell, and Harold Browning, 25
we see three very different lifestyles. We are not looking, however, at
economic extremes. Cheryl Mitchell's income as a nurse's aide puts her
above the government's official poverty line.[20] Below her on the income
pyramid are 42 million poverty-stricken Americans. Far from being poor,
Bob Farrell has an annual income ($51,361) as an assistant sales manager
that puts him above the median income level — that is, more than 50
percent of the U.S. population earns less money than Bob Farrell.[21] And
while Harold Browning's income puts him in a high-income bracket, he
stands only a fraction of the way up Samuelson's income pyramid. Well
above him are the 323,067 Americans whose annual incomes exceed
$1 million. Yet Harold Browning spends more money on his horses than
Cheryl Mitchell earns in a year.

Reality 4: Even ignoring the extreme poles of the economic spectrum, we find enormous class differences in the lifestyles among the
haves, the have-nots, and the have-littles.

Class affects more than lifestyle and material well-being. It has a significant impact on our physical and mental well-being as well. Researchers have found an inverse relationship between social class and health.
Lower-class standing is correlated with higher rates of infant mortality,
eye and ear disease, arthritis, physical disability, diabetes, nutritional deficiency, respiratory disease, mental illness, and heart disease.[22] In all areas
of health, poor people do not share the same life chances as those in the
social class above them. Furthermore, low income correlates with a lower
quality of treatment for illness and disease. The results of poor health and
poor treatment are borne out in the life expectancy rates within each class.
Researchers have found that the higher one's class standing is, the higher
one's life expectancy is. Conversely, they have also found that within each
age group, the lower one's class standing, the higher the death rate; in
some age groups, the figures are as much as two and three times higher.[23]

---

[20]Based on a poverty threshold for a three-person household in 2007 of $16,650
(DeNavas-Walt et al., p. 1).

[21]The median income in 2007 was $45,113 for men working full time, year round;
$35,102 for women, and $50,233 for households (DeNavas-Walt et al., p. 6).

[22]U.S. Government Accountability Office, *Poverty in America: Economic Research
Shows Adverse Impacts on Health Status and Other Social Conditions* (Washington, DC:
U.S. Government Accountability Office, 2007), 9–16; see also E. Pamuk, D. Makuc, K.
Heck, C. Reuben, and K. Lochner, *Health, United States, 1998: Socioeconomic Status and
Health Chartbook* (Hyattsville, MD: National Center for Health Statistics, 1998), 145–59;
Vincente Navarro, "Class, Race, and Health Care in the United States," in *Critical Perspec-
tives in Sociology*, 2nd ed., ed. Bersh Berberoglu (Dubuque, IA: Kendall/Hunt, 1993), 148–
56; Melvin Krasner, *Poverty and Health in New York City* (New York: United Hospital Fund
of New York, 1989). See also U.S. Department of Health and Human Services, "Health
Status of Minorities and Low Income Groups, 1985"; and Dan Hughes, Kay Johnson, Sara
Rosenbaum, Elizabeth Butler, and Janet Simons, *The Health of America's Children* (The
Children's Defense Fund, 1988).

[23]Pamuk et al., *Health, United States, 1998*; Kenneth Neubeck and Davita Glassberg,
Sociology: A Critical Approach (New York: McGraw-Hill, 1996), 436–38; Aaron Antonovsky,
"Social Class, Life Expectancy, and Overall Mortality," in *The Impact of Social Class* (New
York: Thomas Crowell, 1972), 467–91. See also Harriet Duleep, "Measuring the Effect of
Income on Adult Mortality Using Longitudinal Administrative Record Data," *Journal of
Human Resources* 21, no. 2 (Spring 1986); and Paul Farmer, *Pathologies of Power: Health,
Human Rights, and the New War on the Poor* (Berkeley: University of California Press, 2005).

It's not just physical and mental health that is so largely determined by class. The lower a person's class standing is, the more difficult it is to secure housing; the more time is spent on the routine tasks of everyday life; the greater is the percentage of income that goes to pay for food, healthcare (which accounts for 23 percent of spending for low-income families)[24] and other basic necessities; and the greater is the likelihood of crime victimization.[25]

Class and Educational Attainment

School performance (grades and test scores) and educational attainment (level of schooling completed) also correlate strongly with economic class. Furthermore, despite some efforts to make testing fairer and schooling more accessible, current data suggest that the level of inequity is staying the same or getting worse.

In his study for the Carnegie Council on Children in 1978, Richard 30 De Lone examined the test scores of over half a million students who took the College Board exams (SATs). His findings were consistent with earlier studies that showed a relationship between class and scores on standardized tests; his conclusion: "the higher the student's social status, the higher the probability that he or she will get higher grades."[26] Today, more than thirty years after the release of the Carnegie report, College Board surveys reveal data that are no different: test scores still correlate with family income.

Average Combined Scores by Income (400 to 1600 scale)[27]

FAMILY INCOME	MEDIAN SCORE
More than $200,000	1721
$160,000 to $200,000	1636
$140,000 to $160,000	1619
$120,000 to $140,000	1594
$100,000 to $120,000	1580
$80,000 to $100,000	1545
$60,000 to $80,000	1503
$40,000 to $60,000	1461
$20,000 to $40,000	1398
Less than $20,000	1323

These figures are based on the test results of 1,647,123 SAT takers in 2010–2011.

[24]Patricia Ketsche, Sally Wallace, and Kathleen Adams, "Hidden Health Care Costs Hit Low-Income Families the Hardest," Georgia State University, September 21, 2011, http://www.gsu.edu/news/54728.html.

[25]Pamuk et al., Health, United States, 1998, figure 20; Dennis W. Roncek, "Dangerous Places: Crime and Residential Environment," Social Forces 60, no. 1 (September 1981), 74–96. See also Steven D. Levitt, "The Changing Relationship Between Income and Crime Victimization," Economic Policy Review 5, no. 3 (September 1999).

[26]Richard De Lone, Small Futures (New York: Harcourt Brace Jovanovich, 1978), 14–19.

[27]College Board, "2011 College-Bound Seniors Total Group Profile Report," available at http://professionals.collegeboard.com/profdownload/cbs2011_total_group_report.pdf.

In another study conducted thirty years ago, researcher William Sewell showed a positive correlation between class and overall educational achievement. In comparing the top quartile (25 percent) of his sample to the bottom quartile, he found that students from upper-class families were twice as likely to obtain training beyond high school and four times as likely to attain a postgraduate degree. Sewell concluded: "Socioeconomic background ... operates independently of academic ability at every stage in the process of educational attainment."[28]

Today, the pattern persists. There are, however, two significant changes. On the one hand, the odds of getting into college have improved for the bottom quartile of the population, although they still remain relatively low compared to the top. On the other hand, the chances of completing a four-year college degree for those who are poor are extraordinarily low compared to the chances for those who are rich. Researchers estimate college completion is ten times more likely for the top 25 percent of the population than it is for the bottom 25 percent.[29]

Reality 5: From cradle to grave, class position has a significant impact on our well-being. Class accurately predicts chances for survival, educational achievement, and economic success.

Media-induced excitement over big-payoff reality shows, celebrity salaries, and multimillion-dollar lotteries suggests that we in the United States live in a "rags to riches" society. So too does news about dot-com acquisitions and initial public offerings (IPOs) that provide enormous windfalls to young company founders. But rags-to-riches stories notwithstanding, the evidence suggests that "striking it rich" is extremely rare and that class mobility in general is uncommon and becoming increasingly so.

One study showed that 79 percent of families remained in the same 35 quintile (fifth) of income earners or moved up or down only one quintile. (Of this group, most families did not move at all.)[30] Another study showed that fewer than one in five men surpass the economic status of their fathers.[31] Several recent studies have shown that there is less class mobility in the United States than in most industrialized democracies in the world. One such study placed the United States in a virtual tie for last place.[32] Why does the United States occupy such a low

[28]William H. Sewell, "Inequality of Opportunity for Higher Education," *American Sociological Review* 36, no. 5 (1971): 793–809.

[29]Thomas G. Mortenson, "Family Income and Educational Attainment, 1970 to 2009," *Postsecondary Education Opportunity*, no. 221 (November 2010).

[30]Derived from David Leonhardt, "A Closer Look at Income Mobility," *New York Times*, May 14, 2005; and Katharine Bradbury and Jane Katz, "Trends in U.S. Family Income Mobility 1969–2006," Federal Reserve Bank of Boston, 2009.

[31]De Lone, *Small Futures*, 14–19. See also Daniel McMurrer, Mark Condon, and Isabel Sawhill, "Intergenerational Mobility in the United States" (Washington DC: Urban Institute, 1997), http://www.urban.org/publications/406796.html?; and Bhashkar Mazumder, "Earnings Mobility in the U.S.: A New Look at Intergenerational Inequality," Federal Reserve Bank of Chicago Working Paper no. 2001–18, March 21, 2001. doi: 10.2139/ssrn.295559.

[32]Miles Corak, "Do Poor Children Become Poor Adults? Lessons from a Cross-Country Comparison of Generational Earnings Mobility" (Bonn, Germany: IZA, 2006). Available at http://repec.iza.org/dpl993.pdf.

position on the mobility scale? Several explanations have been offered: The gap between rich and poor in the United States is greater; the poor are poorer in the United States and have farther to go to get out of poverty; and the United States has a lower rate of unionization than other industrialized nations.

The bottom line is that very affluent families transmit their advantages to the next generation and poor families stay trapped.[33] For those whose annual income is in six figures, economic success is due in large part to the wealth and privileges bestowed on them at birth. Over 66 percent of the consumer units with incomes of $100,000 or more have inherited assets. Of these units, over 86 percent reported that inheritances constituted a substantial portion of their total assets.[34]

Economist Howard Wachtel likens inheritance to a series of Monopoly games in which the winner of the first game refuses to relinquish his or her cash and commercial property for the second game. "After all," argues the winner, "I accumulated my wealth and income by my own wits." With such an arrangement, it is not difficult to predict the outcome of subsequent games.[35]

Reality 6: All Americans do not have an equal opportunity to succeed, and class mobility in the United States is lower than that of the rest of the industrialized world. Inheritance laws provide built-in privileges to the offspring of the wealthy and add to the likelihood of their economic success while handicapping the chances for everyone else.

One would think that increases in worker productivity or a booming economy would reduce the level of inequality and increase class mobility. While the wages of workers *may* increase during good times—that is, relative to what they were in the past—the economic advantages of higher productivity and a booming economy go disproportionately to the wealthy, a factor that adds still further to the level of inequality. For example, during the period 2001 to 2007, the U.S. economy expanded and productivity (output per hours worked) increased by more than 15 percent. During that same period, however, the top 1 percent of U.S. households took two-thirds of the nation's income gains, their inflation-adjusted income grew more than ten times faster than the income of the bottom 90 percent, and their share of the national income

---

[33]Jason DeParle, "Harder for Americans to Rise from Lower Rungs," *New York Times*, January 4, 2012.

[34]Howard Tuchman, *Economics of the Rich* (New York: Random House, 1973), 15. See also Greg Duncan, Ariel Kalil, Susan Mayer, Robin Tepper, and Monique Payne, "The Apple Does Not Fall Far From the Tree," in *Unequal Chances: Family Background and Economic Success*, ed. Samuel Bowles, Herbert Gintis, and Melissa Groves (Princeton, NJ: Princeton University Press, 2008), 23–79; Bhashkar Mazumder, "The Apple Falls Even Closer to the Tree Than We Thought," in Bowles et al., 80–99. For more information on inheritance, see Samuel Bowles and Herbert Gintis, "The Inheritance of Inequality," *Journal of Economic Perspectives* 16, no. 3 (Summer 2002): 2–30; and Tom Hertz, *Understanding Mobility in America*, Center for American Progress, available at http://www.americanprogress.org/wp-content/uploads/kf/hertz_mobility_analysis.pdf?.

[35]Howard Wachtel, *Labor and the Economy* (Orlando, FL: Academic Press, 1984), 161–62.

reached its highest peak. At the same time, the inflation-adjusted weekly salary of the average American during that six-year economic expansion declined by 2.3 percent.[36] Observing similar patterns in U.S. economic history, one prominent economist described economic growth in the United States as a "spectator sport for the majority of American families."[37] Economic decline, on the other hand, is much more "participatory," with layoffs and cuts in public services hitting middle- and lower-income families hardest—families that rely on public services (e.g., public schools, transportation) and have fewer resources to fall back on during difficult economic times.

Reality 7: Inequality in the United States is persistent in good times and bad.

While most Americans rely on their wages or salaries to make ends meet, the rich derive most of their wealth from such income-producing assets as stocks, bonds, business equity, and non-home real estate. This type of wealth is even more highly concentrated than wealth in general. Over 89 percent of all stocks in the United States for example, are owned by the wealthiest 10 percent of Americans.[38] This makes the fortunes of the wealthy (whether they are corporate executives, investment bankers, or not) closely tied to the fortunes of corporate America and the world of finance. While defenders of capitalism and the capitalist class argue that what's good for corporate America is good for all of America, recent economic experience has raised more doubts than ever about this. Putting aside illegal manipulation of the financial system, the drive to maximize corporate profit has led to job destruction (as companies seek cheaper labor in other parts of the world and transfer investments off shore); deregulation (e.g., so environmental protections don't inhibit corporate profit); and changes in tax policy that favor corporations (through loopholes) and those who rely on corporate profit for their wealth (by taxing their capital gains at lower rates).

Reality 8: The privileges that accrue to the wealthy are tied to the worlds of capital and finance—worlds whose good fortune are often the misfortune of the rest of the population.

Government is often portrayed as the spoiler of Wall Street—and at times it is. There are certainly examples of the government imposing fines for environmental violations, establishing regulations that protect consumers and workers, restrict corporate conduct, etc. But government as the "great equalizer" often isn't what it appears to be. In 2010, for

---

[36]See Hannah Shaw and Chad Stone, "Incomes at the Top Rebounded in First Full Year of Recovery, New Analysis of Tax Data Shows," Center on Budget and Policy Priorities, March 7, 2011, http://www.cbpp.org/files/3-7-12inc.pdf. Also see Andrew Fieldhouse and Ethan Pollack, "Tenth Anniversary of the Bush-Era Tax Cuts," Economic Policy Institute, June 1, 2011, http://www.epi.org/publication/tenth_anniversary_of_the_bush-era_tax_cuts/.

[37]Alan Blinder, quoted by Paul Krugman, in "Disparity and Despair," *U.S. News and World Report*, March 23, 1992, 54.

[38]Derived from Edward N. Wolff, "Recent Trends in Household Wealth in the U.S." Levy Economics Institute at Bard College, March 2010, table 9. Available at http://www.levyinstitute.org/pubs/wp_589.pdf.

example, when the federal government concluded a fraud case against a major investment bank (Goldman Sachs), it touted the case as one of the largest settlements in U.S. history — a whopping $550 million. It turns out that $550 million was less than 4 percent of what the bank paid its executives in bonuses that year.

Similarly, changes in policy that reduce taxes are often touted as vehicles for leveling the playing field and bringing economic relief to the middle class. But at best, these do little or nothing to help middle- and low-income families. More often than not, they increase the level of inequality by providing disproportionate tax benefits to the wealthy while reducing public budgets and increasing the costs of such public services as transportation and college tuition. For example, changes in tax policy over the last five decades — especially those during the 1980s — have favored the wealthy: Federal taxes for the wealthiest 0.1 percent have fallen from 51 to 26 percent over the last fifty years, while the rate for middle income earners has risen from 14 to 16 percent.[39]

It's not just that economic resources are concentrated in the hands 45 of a few; so too are political resources. And it is the connection between wealth and political power that allows economic inequality to persist and grow. Moreover, as the costs of political influence rise, so does the influence of the "monied" class. Running for public office has always been an expensive proposition, but it's become increasingly so: It now costs, on average, $1.4 million in campaign funds to win a seat in the House of Representatives and $7 million to win a seat in the U.S. Senate.[40] Most politicians rely on wealthy donors to finance their campaigns. Alternatively, wealthy individuals who want to make public policy often underwrite their own campaigns.* The average wealth of U.S. senators, for example, is $12.6 million.[41]

High-priced lobbyists also ensure that the interests of the wealthy and of corporate America are well represented in the halls of government. Not surprisingly, organizations that track the connection between political contributions and votes cast by public officials find a strong correlation between money and voting.[42] It's not that the power of the

*Over the course of three elections, Michael Bloomberg spent more than $261 million of his own money to become mayor of New York City. He spent $102 million in his last mayoral election alone — more than $172 per vote.

[39]The National Economic Council, "The Buffett Rule: A Basic Principle of Tax Fairness," White House, April 2012, citing Internal Revenue System Statistics of Income 2005 Public Use File, National Bureau of Economic Research TAXISM, and CEA calculations. Available at http://www.whitehouse.gov/sites/default/files/Buffett_Rule_Report_Final.pdf. Also cited in the *New York Times* editorial "Mr. Obama and the 'Buffett Rule,'" April 10, 2012. Available at http://www.nytimes.com/2012/04/ll/opinion/mr-obama-and-the-buffett-rule.html?_r=0.

[40]Campaign Finance Institute, "2010 Federal Election," accessed March 22, 2011, http://cfinst.org/federal/election2010.aspx.

[41]2009 figures from the Center for Responsive Politics, "Average Wealth of Members of Congress," available at http://www.opensecrets.org/pfds/averages.php.

[42]See Larry Bartels, *Unequal Democracy: The Political Economy of the New Gilded Age* (Princeton, NJ: Princeton University Press, 2008), chapter 9; see also MAPLight.org (MAPLight tracks political contributions and their impact on the votes of public officials).

economic elite is absolute; it's not. The power of the wealthy is often miti-gated by social movements and by grassroots organizations that advocate on behalf of the poor and working class. The Occupy Wall Street move-ment—like movements that came before it—changed not only the public debate, but led to policy reforms as well. The power of the rich, however, remains so disproportionate that it severely undermines our democracy. Over three-quarters of a century ago, such an assault on democratic prin-ciples led Supreme Court Justice Louis Brandeis to observe, "We can have democracy in this country or we can have great wealth concen-trated in the hands of a few, but we can't have both." Talking about the power elite or the ruling class may put people off, but there is no doubt that the interests of the wealthy predominate in American politics.

Reality 9: Wealth and power are closely linked. The economic elite have a grossly disproportionate amount of political power—more than enough power to ensure that the system that provides them such extraordinary privileges perpetuates itself.

Spheres of Power and Oppression

When we look at society and try to determine what it is that keeps most people down—what holds them back from realizing their potential as healthy, creative, productive individuals—we find institutional forces that are largely beyond individual control. Class domination is one of these forces. People do not choose to be poor or working class; instead, they are limited and confined by the opportunities afforded or denied them by a social and economic system. The class structure in the United States is a function of its economic system: capitalism, a system that is based on private rather than public ownership and con-trol of commercial enterprises. Under capitalism, these enterprises are governed by the need to produce a profit for the owners, rather than to fulfill societal needs. Class divisions arise from the differences between those who own and control corporate enterprise and those who do not.

Racial and gender domination are other forces that hold people down. Although there are significant differences in the way capitalism, racism, and sexism affect our lives, there are also a multitude of paral-lels. And although class, race, and gender act independently of each other, they are at the same time very much interrelated.

On the one hand, issues of race and gender cut across class lines. 50
Women experience the effects of sexism whether they are well-paid professionals or poorly paid clerks. As women, they are not only sub-jected to stereotyping and sexual harassment, they face discrimination and are denied opportunities and privileges that men have. Similarly, a wealthy black man faces racial oppression, is subjected to racial slurs, and is denied opportunities because of his color. Regardless of their class standing, women and members of minority races are constantly dealing with institutional forces that hold them down precisely because of their gender, the color of their skin, or both.

Chances of Being Poor in America[43]

WHITE MALE/ FEMALE	WHITE FEMALE HEAD*	HISPANIC MALE/ FEMALE	HISPANIC FEMALE HEAD*	BLACK MALE/ FEMALE	BLACK FEMALE HEAD*
1 in 14	1 in 4	1 in 4	1 in 2	1 in 4	1 in 2

*Persons in families with female householder, no husband present.

On the other hand, the experiences of women and minorities are differentiated along class lines. Although they are in subordinate positions vis-à-vis white men, the particular issues that confront women and people of color may be quite different, depending on their position in the class structure.

Power is incremental and class privileges can accrue to individual women and to individual members of a racial minority. While power is incremental, oppression is cumulative, and those who are poor, black, and female are often subject to all of the forces of class, race, and gender discrimination simultaneously. This cumulative situation is what is sometimes referred to as the double and triple jeopardy of women and people of color.

Furthermore, oppression in one sphere is related to the likelihood of oppression in another. If you are black and female, for example, you are much more likely to be poor or working class than you would be as a white male. Census figures show that the incidence of poverty varies greatly by race and gender.

In other words, being female and being nonwhite are attributes in our society that increase the chances of poverty and of lower-class standing.

Reality 10: Racism and sexism significantly compound the effects of class in society. 55

None of this makes for a very pretty picture of our country. Despite what we like to think about ourselves as a nation, the truth is that the qualities of our lives and the opportunities for success are highly circumscribed by our race, our gender, and the class we are born into. As individuals, we feel hurt and angry when someone is treating us unfairly; yet as a society we tolerate unconscionable injustice. A more just society will require a radical redistribution of wealth and power. We can start by reversing the current trends that polarize us as a people and adapt policies and practices that narrow the gaps in income, wealth, power, and privilege. That will only come about with pressure from below: strong organizations and mass movements advocating for a more just and equitable society.

[43]DeNavas-Walt et al., *Income, Poverty, and Health Insurance Coverage in the United States: 2010.*

ENGAGING THE TEXT

1. Reexamine the four myths Mantsios identifies (para. 9). What does he say is wrong about each myth, and what evidence does he provide to critique each? How persuasive do you find his evidence and reasoning?

2. Does the essay make a case that the wealthy are exploiting the poor? Does it simply assume this? Are there other possible interpretations of the data Mantsios provides? Explain your position, taking into account the information in "Class in America."

3. Work out a rough budget for a family of four with an annual income of $25,100, the poverty guideline for 2018. Be sure to include costs for food, clothing, housing, transportation, healthcare, and other unavoidable expenses. Do you think this is a reasonable poverty level, or is it too high or too low?

4. Imagine that you are Harold S. Browning, Bob Farrell, or Cheryl Mitchell. Write an entry for this person's journal after a tough day on the job. Compare and contrast your entry with those written by other students.

5. In his final paragraph, Mantsios calls for "a radical redistribution of wealth and power" and "policies and practices that narrow the gaps in income, wealth,

power, and privilege." What specific changes do you imagine Mantsios would like to see? What changes, if any, would you recommend?

EXPLORING CONNECTIONS

6. Choose three or four figures from the list below. Working in small groups, discuss the specific ways that social class shapes their lives:

   Gary Soto in "Looking for Work" (p. 20)

   Mercedes in "When Should a Child Be Taken from His Parents?" (p. 51)

   Mike Rose in "I Just Wanna Be Average" (p. 123)

   George in "Serving in Florida" (p. 368)

   Clyde Ross in "The Case for Reparations" (p. 604)

   The narrator of "Gentrification" (p. 646)

7. Mantsios describes how "spheres of oppression" often overlap: for example, racial discrimination and sexism can multiply the challenges of working-class life. For more detailed analyses of how sexism and racism work as systems of oppression (not just individual prejudice), read either Allan Johnson's "The Gender Knot" (p. 527) or Ta-Nehisi Coates's "The Case for Reparations" (p. 604) — or both. To what extent do these authors call attention to overlapping injustices based on gender, sexual orientation, race, economic class, education, or media representations?

8. Discuss Tom Tomorrow's "Poverty eliminated" cartoon on page 366 in terms of Mantsios's analysis of class in America. To what extent does the cartoon have a basis in actual American ideas about money, success, wealth, and poverty?

EXTENDING THE CRITICAL CONTEXT

9. Mantsios points out that "inheritance laws provide built-in privileges to the offspring of the wealthy and add to the likelihood of their economic success while handicapping the chances for everyone else" (para. 38). Explain why you think this is or is not a serious problem. Keeping in mind the difference between wealth and income, discuss how society might attempt to remedy this problem and what policies you would endorse.

10. Skim through a few recent issues of a financial magazine like *Forbes* or *Money*. Who is the audience for these publications? What kind of advice is offered? What kinds of products and services are advertised? What levels of income and investment are discussed?

11. Study the employment listings in your location at an online source such as Monster.com. Roughly what percentage of the openings would you consider upper class, middle class, and lower class? On what basis do you make your distinctions? What do the available jobs suggest about the current levels of affluence in your area?

SERVING IN FLORIDA
BARBARA EHRENREICH

What's it like to live on minimum wage? As a journalist preparing to write about working-class life, Barbara Ehrenreich decided to take a series of unglamorous jobs — waitressing, housecleaning, retail sales — and to live on the meager wages these jobs paid. In this account of her experiences, Ehrenreich describes trying to make ends meet by adding a second waitressing job at "Jerry's" to her eight-hour shift at "The Hearthside," having discovered that $2.43 an hour plus tips doesn't add up as fast as her rent and other bills. The full account of Ehrenreich's "plunge into poverty" may be found in the New York Times best-seller *Nickel and Dimed: On (Not) Getting By in America* (2001). Barbara Ehrenreich (b. 1941) has published articles in many of America's leading magazines and newspapers and has authored more than a dozen books. Recent works include *Living with a Wild God: A Nonbeliever's Search for the Truth About Everything* (2014) and *Natural Causes: An Epidemic of Wellness, the Certainty of Dying, and Killing Ourselves to Live Longer* (2018).

PICTURE A FAT PERSON'S HELL, and I don't mean a place with no food. Instead there is everything you might eat if eating had no bodily consequences — the cheese fries, the chicken-fried steaks, the fudge-laden desserts — only here every bite must be paid for, one way or another, in human discomfort. The kitchen is a cavern, a stomach leading to the lower intestine that is the garbage and dishwashing area, from which issue bizarre smells combining the edible and the offal: creamy carrion, pizza barf, and that unique and enigmatic Jerry's[1] scent, citrus fart. The floor is slick with spills, forcing us to walk through the kitchen with tiny steps, like Susan McDougal in leg irons.[2] Sinks everywhere are clogged with scraps of lettuce, decomposing lemon wedges, water-logged toast crusts. Put your hand down on any counter and you risk being stuck to it by the film of ancient syrup spills, and this is unfortunate because hands are utensils here, used for scooping up lettuce onto the salad plates, lifting out pie slices, and even moving hash browns from one plate to another. The regulation poster in the single unisex rest room admonishes us to wash our hands thoroughly, and even

---

[1]**Jerry's:** Not the real name of the restaurant where Ehrenreich worked; the restaurant was part of a "well-known national chain." [All notes are the editors', except 6, 9, 12, and 13.]

[2]**Susan McDougal in leg irons:** McDougal refused to testify against President Bill Clinton and Hillary Clinton before the Whitewater grand jury in 1996; she spent almost twenty-two months in various prisons and eventually received a presidential pardon in 2001.

offers instructions for doing so, but there is always some vital substance missing—soap, paper towels, toilet paper—and I never found all three at once. You learn to stuff your pockets with napkins before going in there, and too bad about the customers, who must eat, although they don't realize it, almost literally out of our hands.

The break room summarizes the whole situation: there is none, because there are no breaks at Jerry's. For six to eight hours in a row, you never sit except to pee. Actually, there are three folding chairs at a table immediately adjacent to the bathroom, but hardly anyone ever sits in this, the very rectum of the gastroarchitectural system. Rather, the function of the peri-toilet area is to house the ashtrays in which servers and dishwashers leave their cigarettes burning at all times, like votive candles, so they don't have to waste time lighting up again when they dash back here for a puff. Almost everyone smokes as if their pulmonary well-being depended on it—the multinational mélange of cooks; the dishwashers, who are all Czechs here; the servers, who are American natives—creating an atmosphere in which oxygen is only an occasional pollutant. My first morning at Jerry's, when the hypoglycemic shakes set in, I complain to one of my fellow servers that I don't understand how she can go so long without food. "Well, I don't understand how *you* can go so long without a cigarette," she responds in a tone of reproach. Because work is what you do for others; smoking is what you do for yourself. I don't know why the antismoking crusaders have never grasped the element of defiant self-nurturance that makes the habit so endearing to its victims—as if, in the American workplace, the only thing people have to call their own is the tumors they are nourishing and the spare moments they devote to feeding them.

Now, the Industrial Revolution is not an easy transition, especially, in my experience, when you have to zip through it in just a couple of days. I have gone from craft work straight into the factory, from the air-conditioned morgue of the Hearthside[3] directly into the flames. Customers arrive in human waves, sometimes disgorged fifty at a time from their tour buses, puckish and whiny. Instead of two "girls" on the floor at once, there can be as many as six of us running around in our brilliant pink-and-orange Hawaiian shirts. Conversations, either with customers or with fellow employees, seldom last more than twenty seconds at a time. On my first day, in fact, I am hurt by my sister servers' coldness. My mentor for the day is a supremely competent, emotionally uninflected twenty-three-year-old, and the others, who gossip a little among themselves about the real reason someone is out sick today and the size of the bail bond someone else has had to pay, ignore me completely. On my second day, I find out why. "Well, it's good to see *you* again," one of them says in greeting. "Hardly anyone comes back after the first day." I feel powerfully vindicated—a survivor—but it would take a long time, probably months, before I could hope to be accepted into this sorority.

---

[3]**Hearthside:** The other restaurant where Ehrenreich worked.

I start out with the beautiful, heroic idea of handling the two jobs at once, and for two days I almost do it: working the breakfast/lunch shift at Jerry's from 8:00 till 2:00, arriving at the Hearthside a few minutes late, at 2:10, and attempting to hold out until 10:00. In the few minutes I have between jobs, I pick up a spicy chicken sandwich at the Wendy's drive-through window, gobble it down in the car, and change from khaki slacks to black, from Hawaiian to rust-colored polo. There is a problem, though. When, during the 3:00–4:00 o'clock dead time, I finally sit down to wrap silver, my flesh seems to bond to the seat. I try to refuel with a purloined cup of clam chowder, as I've seen Gail and Joan do dozens of times, but Stu[4] catches me and hisses "No *eating*!" although there's not a customer around to be offended by the sight of food making contact with a server's lips. So I tell Gail I'm going to quit, and she hugs me and says she might just follow me to Jerry's herself.

But the chances of this are minuscule. She has left the flophouse   5 and her annoying roommate and is back to living in her truck. But, guess what, she reports to me excitedly later that evening, Phillip has given her permission to park overnight in the hotel parking lot, as long as she keeps out of sight, and the parking lot should be totally safe since it's patrolled by a hotel security guard! With the Hearthside offering benefits like that, how could anyone think of leaving? This must be Phillip's theory, anyway. He accepts my resignation with a shrug, his main concern being that I return my two polo shirts and aprons.

Gail would have triumphed at Jerry's, I'm sure, but for me it's a crash course in exhaustion management. Years ago, the kindly fry cook who trained me to waitress at a Los Angeles truck stop used to say: Never make an unnecessary trip; if you don't have to walk fast, walk slow; if you don't have to walk, stand. But at Jerry's the effort of distinguishing necessary from unnecessary and urgent from whenever would itself be too much of an energy drain. The only thing to do is to treat each shift as a one-time-only emergency: you've got fifty starving people out there, lying scattered on the battlefield, so get out there and feed them! Forget that you will have to do this again tomorrow, forget that you will have to be alert enough to dodge the drunks on the drive home tonight—just burn, burn, burn! Ideally, at some point you enter what servers call a "rhythm" and psychologists term a "flow state," where signals pass from the sense organs directly to the muscles, bypassing the cerebral cortex, and a Zen-like emptiness sets in. I'm on a 2:00–10:00 P.M. shift now, and a male server from the morning shift tells me about the time he "pulled a triple"—three shifts in a row, all the way around the clock—and then got off and had a drink and met this girl, and maybe he shouldn't tell me this, but they had sex right then and there and it was like *beautiful*.

---

[4]**Gail, Joan, Stu:** Waitress, hostess, and assistant manager at the Hearthside restaurant. Phillip, mentioned in the subsequent paragraph, is the top manager.

But there's another capacity of the neuromuscular system, which is pain. I start tossing back drugstore-brand ibuprofens as if they were vitamin C, four before each shift, because an old mouse-related repetitive-stress injury in my upper back has come back to full-spasm strength, thanks to the tray carrying. In my ordinary life, this level of disability might justify a day of ice packs and stretching. Here I comfort myself with the Aleve commercial where the cute blue-collar guy asks: If you quit after working four hours, what would your boss say? And the not-so-cute blue-collar guy, who's lugging a metal beam on his back, answers: He'd fire me, that's what. But fortunately, the commercial tells us, we workers can exert the same kind of authority over our painkillers that our bosses exert over us. If Tylenol doesn't want to work for more than four hours, you just fire its ass and switch to Aleve.

True, I take occasional breaks from this life, going home now and then to catch up on e-mail and for conjugal visits (though I am careful to "pay" for everything I eat here, at $5 for a dinner, which I put in a jar), seeing *The Truman Show*[5] with friends and letting them buy my ticket. And I still have those what-am-I-doing-here moments at work, when I get so homesick for the printed word that I obsessively reread the six-page menu. But as the days go by, my old life is beginning to look exceedingly strange. The e-mails and phone messages addressed to my former self come from a distant race of people with exotic concerns and far too much time on their hands. The neighborly market I used to cruise for produce now looks forbiddingly like a Manhattan yuppie emporium. And when I sit down one morning in my real home to pay bills from my past life, I am dazzled by the two- and three-figure sums owed to outfits like Club Body Tech and Amazon.com.

Management at Jerry's is generally calmer and more "professional" than at the Hearthside, with two exceptions. One is Joy, a plump, blowsy woman in her early thirties who once kindly devoted several minutes of her time to instructing me in the correct one-handed method of tray carrying but whose moods change disconcertingly from shift to shift and even within one. The other is B.J., aka B.J. the Bitch, whose contribution is to stand by the kitchen counter and yell, "Nita, your order's up, move it!" or "Barbara, didn't you see you've got another table out there? Come *on*, girl!" Among other things, she is hated for having replaced the whipped cream squirt cans with big plastic whipped-cream-filled baggies that have to be squeezed with both hands—because, reportedly, she saw or thought she saw employees trying to inhale the propellant gas from the squirt cans, in the hope that it might be nitrous oxide. On my third night, she pulls me aside abruptly and brings her face so close that it looks like she's planning to butt me with her forehead. But instead of saying "You're fired," she says, "You're doing fine." The only trouble is I'm spending time chatting with customers:

[5]***The Truman Show:*** 1998 film (directed by Peter Weir and starring Jim Carrey) about a man who discovers his whole life is actually a TV show.

"That's how they're getting you." Furthermore I am letting them "run me," which means harassment by sequential demands: you bring the catsup and they decide they want extra Thousand Island; you bring that and they announce they now need a side of fries, and so on into distraction. Finally she tells me not to take her wrong. She tries to say things in a nice way, but "you get into a mode, you know, because everything has to move so fast."[6]

I mumble thanks for the advice, feeling like I've just been stripped   10 naked by the crazed enforcer of some ancient sumptuary law:[7] No chatting for *you*, girl. No fancy service ethic allowed for the serfs. Chatting with customers is for the good-looking young college-educated servers in the downtown carpaccio and ceviche joints, the kids who can make $70–$100 a night. What had I been thinking? My job is to move orders from tables to kitchen and then trays from kitchen to tables. Customers are in fact the major obstacle to the smooth transformation of information into food and food into money—they are, in short, the enemy. And the painful thing is that I'm beginning to see it this way myself. There are the traditional asshole types—frat boys who down multiple Buds and then make a fuss because the steaks are so emaciated and the fries so sparse—as well as the variously impaired—due to age, diabetes, or literacy issues—who require patient nutritional counseling. The worst, for some reason, are the Visible Christians—like the ten-person table, all jolly and sanctified after Sunday night service, who run me mercilessly and then leave me $1 on a $92 bill. Or the guy with the crucifixion T-shirt (someone to look up to) who complains that his baked potato is too hard and his iced tea too icy (I cheerfully fix both) and leaves no tip at all. As a general rule, people wearing crosses or wwjd? ("What Would Jesus Do?") buttons look at us disapprovingly no matter what we do, as if they were confusing waitressing with Mary Magdalene's[8] original profession.

I make friends, over time, with the other "girls" who work my shift: Nita, the tattooed twenty-something who taunts us by going around saying brightly, "Have we started making money yet?" Ellen, whose teenage son cooks on the graveyard shift and who once managed a restaurant in Massachusetts but won't try out for management here because she prefers being a "common worker" and not "ordering

---

[6]In *Workers in a Lean World: Unions in the International Economy* (Verso, 1997), Kim Moody cites studies finding an increase in stress-related workplace injuries and illness between the mid-1980s and the early 1990s. He argues that rising stress levels reflect a new system of "management by stress" in which workers in a variety of industries are being squeezed to extract maximum productivity, to the detriment of their health. [Ehrenreich's note.]

[7]**sumptuary laws:** Laws that regulate personal behavior on moral or religious grounds.

[8]**Mary Magdalene:** A figure in the New Testament gospels whom popular culture has often painted as a prostitute. Contemporary scholars dispute that view, some offering characterizations of Mary as a saint, an apostle, or a rabbi. See, for example, *Mary Magdalene in Medieval Culture: Conflicted Roles*, ed. Peter V. Loewen and Robin Waugh (New York: Routledge, 2014).

people around." Easygoing fiftyish Lucy, with the raucous laugh, who limps toward the end of the shift because of something that has gone wrong with her leg, the exact nature of which cannot be determined without health insurance. We talk about the usual girl things—men, children, and the sinister allure of Jerry's chocolate peanut-butter cream pie—though no one, I notice, ever brings up anything potentially expensive, like shopping or movies. As at the Hearthside, the only recreation ever referred to is partying, which requires little more than some beer, a joint, and a few close friends. Still, no one is homeless, or cops to it anyway, thanks usually to a working husband or boyfriend. All in all, we form a reliable mutual-support group: if one of us is feeling sick or overwhelmed, another one will "bev" a table or even carry trays for her. If one of us is off sneaking a cigarette or a pee, the others will do their best to conceal her absence from the enforcers of corporate rationality.[9]

But my saving human connection—my oxytocin receptor, as it were—is George, the nineteen-year-old Czech dishwasher who has been in this country exactly one week. We get talking when he asks me, tortuously, how much cigarettes cost at Jerry's. I do my best to explain that they cost over a dollar more here than at a regular store and suggest that he just take one from the half-filled packs that are always lying around on the break table. But that would be unthinkable. Except for the one tiny earring signaling his allegiance to some vaguely alternative point of view, George is a perfect straight arrow—crew-cut, hardworking, and hungry for eye contact. "Czech Republic," I ask, "or Slovakia?" and he seems delighted that I know the difference. "Vaclav Havel," I try, "Velvet Revolution, Frank Zappa?" "Yes, yes, 1989," he says, and I realize that for him this is already history.

My project is to teach George English. "How are you today, George?" I say at the start of each shift. "I am good, and how are you today, Barbara?" I learn that he is not paid by Jerry's but by the "agent" who shipped him over—$5 an hour, with the agent getting the dollar or so difference between that and what Jerry's pays dishwashers. I learn also that he shares an apartment with a crowd of other Czech "dishers," as he calls them, and that he cannot sleep until one of them goes off for his shift, leaving a vacant bed. We are having one of our ESL [English as a Second Language] sessions late one afternoon when B.J. catches

[9]Until April 1998, there was no federally mandated right to bathroom breaks. According to Marc Linder and Ingrid Nygaard, authors of *Void Where Prohibited: Rest Breaks and the Right to Urinate on Company Time* (Cornell University Press, 1997), "The right to rest and void at work is not high on the list of social or political causes supported by professional or executive employees, who enjoy personal workplace liberties that millions of factory workers can only dream about.... While we were dismayed to discover that workers lacked an acknowledged right to void at work, [the workers] were amazed by outsiders' naïve belief that their employers would permit them to perform this basic bodily function when necessary.... A factory worker, not allowed a break for six-hour stretches, voided into pads worn inside her uniform; and a kindergarten teacher in a school without aides had to take all twenty children with her to the bathroom and line them up outside the stall door while she voided." [Ehrenreich's note.]

us at it and orders "Joseph" to take up the rubber mats on the floor near the dishwashing sinks and mop underneath. "I thought your name was George," I say loud enough for B.J. to hear as she strides off back to the counter. Is she embarrassed? Maybe a little, because she greets me back at the counter with "George, Joseph—there are so many of them!" I say nothing, neither nodding nor smiling, and for this I am punished later, when I think I am ready to go and she announces that I need to roll fifty more sets of silverware, and isn't it time I mixed up a fresh four-gallon batch of blue-cheese dressing? May you grow old in this place, B.J., is the curse I beam out at her when I am finally permitted to leave. May the syrup spills glue your feet to the floor.

I make the decision to move closer to Key West. First, because of the drive. Second and third, also because of the drive: gas is eating up $4–$5 a day, and although Jerry's is as high-volume as you can get, the tips average only 10 percent, and not just for a newbie like me. Between the base pay of $2.15 an hour and the obligation to share tips with the busboys and dishwashers, we're averaging only about $7.50 an hour. Then there is the $30 I had to spend on the regulation tan slacks worn by Jerry's servers—a setback it could take weeks to absorb. (I had combed the town's two downscale department stores hoping for something cheaper but decided in the end that these marked-down Dockers, originally $49, were more likely to survive a daily washing.) Of my fellow servers, everyone who lacks a working husband or boyfriend seems to have a second job: Nita does something at a computer eight hours a day; another welds. Without the forty-five-minute commute, I can picture myself working two jobs and still having the time to shower between them.

So I take the $500 deposit I have coming from my landlord, the $400 15 I have earned toward the next month's rent, plus the $200 reserved for emergencies, and use the $1,100 to pay the rent and deposit on trailer number 46 in the Overseas Trailer Park, a mile from the cluster of budget hotels that constitute Key West's version of an industrial park. Number 46 is about eight feet in width and shaped like a barbell inside, with a narrow region—because of the sink and the stove—separating the bedroom from what might optimistically be called the "living" area, with its two-person table and half-sized couch. The bathroom is so small my knees rub against the shower stall when I sit on the toilet, and you can't just leap out of the bed, you have to climb down to the foot of it in order to find a patch of floor space to stand on. Outside, I am within a few yards of a liquor store, a bar that advertises "free beer tomorrow," a convenience store, and a Burger King—but no supermarket or, alas, Laundromat. By reputation, the Overseas park is a nest of crime and crack, and I am hoping at least for some vibrant multicultural street life. But desolation rules night and day, except for a thin stream of pedestrians heading for their jobs at the Sheraton or the 7-Eleven. There are not exactly people here but what amounts to canned labor, being preserved between shifts from the heat.

In line with my reduced living conditions, a new form of ugliness arises at Jerry's. First we are confronted—via an announcement on the computers through which we input orders—with the new rule that the hotel bar, the Driftwood, is henceforth off-limits to restaurant employees. The culprit, I learn through the grapevine, is the ultraefficient twenty-three-year-old who trained me—another trailer home dweller and a mother of three. Something had set her off one morning, so she slipped out for a nip and returned to the floor impaired. The restriction mostly hurts Ellen, whose habit it is to free her hair from its rubber band and drop by the Driftwood for a couple of Zins[10] before heading home at the end of her shift, but all of us feel the chill. Then the next day, when I go for straws, I find the dry-storage room locked. It's never been locked before; we go in and out of it all day—for napkins, jelly containers, Styrofoam cups for takeout. Vic, the portly assistant manager who opens it for me, explains that he caught one of the dishwashers attempting to steal something and, unfortunately, the miscreant will be with us until a replacement can be found—hence the locked door. I neglect to ask what he had been trying to steal but Vic tells me who he is—the kid with the buzz cut and the earring, you know, he's back there right now.

I wish I could say I rushed back and confronted George to get his side of the story. I wish I could say I stood up to Vic and insisted that George be given a translator and allowed to defend himself or announced that I'd find a lawyer who'd handle the case pro bono.[11] At the very least I should have testified as to the kid's honesty. The mystery to me is that there's not much worth stealing in the dry-storage room, at least not in any fenceable quantity: "Is Gyorgi here, and am having 200—maybe 250—catsup packets. What do you say?" My guess is that he had taken—if he had taken anything at all—some Saltines or a can of cherry pie mix and that the motive for taking it was hunger.

So why didn't I intervene? Certainly not because I was held back by the kind of moral paralysis that can mask as journalistic objectivity. On the contrary, something new—something loathsome and servile—had infected me, along with the kitchen odors that I could still sniff on my bra when I finally undressed at night. In real life I am moderately brave, but plenty of brave people shed their courage in POW camps, and maybe something similar goes on in the infinitely more congenial milieu of the low-wage American workplace. Maybe, in a month or two more at Jerry's, I might have regained my crusading spirit. Then again, in a month or two I might have turned into a different person altogether—say, the kind of person who would have turned George in.

But this is not something I was slated to find out. When my month-long plunge into poverty was almost over, I finally landed my dream job—housekeeping. I did this by walking into the personnel office of the only place I figured I might have some credibility, the hotel attached

---

[10]**Zins:** Glasses of zinfandel wine.
[11]**pro bono:** Free of charge.

to Jerry's, and confiding urgently that I had to have a second job if I was to pay my rent and, no, it couldn't be front-desk clerk. "All *right*," the personnel lady fairly spits, "so it's *housekeeping*," and marches me back to meet Millie, the housekeeping manager, a tiny, frenetic Hispanic woman who greets me as "babe" and hands me a pamphlet emphasizing the need for a positive attitude. The pay is $6.10 an hour and the hours are nine in the morning till "whenever," which I am hoping can be defined as a little before two. I don't have to ask about health insurance once I meet Carlotta, the middle-aged African American woman who will be training me. Carlie, as she tells me to call her, is missing all of her top front teeth.

On that first day of housekeeping and last day—although I don't yet know it's the last—of my life as a low-wage worker in Key West, Carlie is in a foul mood. We have been given nineteen rooms to clean, most of them "checkouts," as opposed to "stay-overs," and requiring the whole enchilada of bed stripping, vacuuming, and bathroom scrubbing. When one of the rooms that had been listed as a stay-over turns out to be a checkout, she calls Millie to complain, but of course to no avail. "So make up the motherfucker," she orders me, and I do the beds while she sloshes around the bathroom. For four hours without a break I strip and remake beds, taking about four and a half minutes per queen-sized bed, which I could get down to three if there were any reason to. We try to avoid vacuuming by picking up the larger specks by hand, but often there is nothing to do but drag the monstrous vacuum cleaner—it weighs about thirty pounds—off our cart and try to wrestle it around the floor. Sometimes Carlie hands me the squirt bottle of "Bam" (an acronym for something that begins, ominously, with "butyric"—the rest of it has been worn off the label) and lets me do the bathrooms. No service ethic challenges me here to new heights of performance. I just concentrate on removing the pubic hairs from the bathtubs, or at least the dark ones that I can see.

I had looked forward to the breaking-and-entering aspect of cleaning the stay-overs, the chance to examine the secret physical existence of strangers. But the contents of the rooms are always banal and surprisingly neat—zipped-up shaving kits, shoes lined up against the wall (there are no closets), flyers for snorkeling trips, maybe an empty wine bottle or two. It is the TV that keeps us going, from Jerry to Sally to *Hawaii Five-O* and then on to the soaps. If there's something especially arresting, like "Won't Take No for an Answer" on Jerry, we sit down on the edge of a bed and giggle for a moment, as if this were a pajama party instead of a terminally dead-end job. The soaps are the best, and Carlie turns the volume up full blast so she won't miss anything from the bathroom or while the vacuum is on. In Room 503, Marcia confronts Jeff about Lauren. In 505, Lauren taunts poor cheated-on Marcia. In 511, Helen offers Amanda $10,000 to stop seeing Eric, prompting Carlie to emerge from the bathroom to study Amanda's troubled face. "You take it, girl," she advises. "I would for sure."

The tourists' rooms that we clean and, beyond them, the far more expensively appointed interiors in the soaps begin after a while to merge. We have entered a better world — a world of comfort where every day is a day off, waiting to be filled with sexual intrigue. We are only gate-crashers in this fantasy, however, forced to pay for our presence with backaches and perpetual thirst. The mirrors, and there are far too many of them in hotel rooms, contain the kind of person you would normally find pushing a shopping cart down a city street — bedraggled, dressed in a damp hotel polo shirt two sizes too large, and with sweat dribbling down her chin like drool. I am enormously relieved when Carlie announces a half-hour meal break, but my appetite fades when I see that the bag of hot dog rolls she has been carrying around on our cart is not trash salvaged from a checkout but what she has brought for her lunch.

Between the TV and the fact that I'm in no position, as a first dayer, to launch new topics of conversation, I don't learn much about Carlie except that she hurts, and in more than one way. She moves slowly about her work, muttering something about joint pain, and this is probably going to doom her, since the young immigrant housekeepers — Polish and Salvadoran — like to polish off their rooms by two in the afternoon, while she drags the work out till six. It doesn't make any sense to hurry, she observes, when you're being paid by the hour. Already, management has brought in a woman to do what sounds like time-motion studies and there's talk about switching to paying by the room.[12] She broods, too, about all the little evidences of disrespect that come her way, and not only from management. "They don't care about us," she tells me of the hotel guests; in fact, they don't notice us at all unless something gets stolen from a room — "then they're all over you." We're eating our lunch side by side in the break room when a white guy in a maintenance uniform walks by and Carlie calls out, "Hey you," in a friendly way, "what's your name?"

"Peter Pan," he says, his back already to us.

"That wasn't funny," Carlie says, turning to me. "That was no kind 25 of answer. Why did he have to be funny like that?" I venture that he has an attitude, and she nods as if that were an acute diagnosis. "Yeah, he got a attitude all right."

"Maybe he's having a bad day," I elaborate, not because I feel any obligation to defend the white race but because her face is so twisted with hurt.

When I request permission to leave at about 3:30, another housekeeper warns me that no one has so far succeeded in combining housekeeping with serving at Jerry's: "Some kid did it once for five days, and you're no kid." With that helpful information in mind, I rush back

---

[12]A few weeks after I left, I heard ads on the radio for housekeeping jobs at this hotel at the amazing rate of "up to $9 an hour." When I inquired, I found out that the hotel had indeed started paying by the room, and I suspect that Carlie, if she lasted, was still making the equivalent of $6 an hour or quite a bit less. [Ehrenreich's note]

to number 46, down four Advils (the name brand this time), shower, stooping to fit into the stall, and attempt to compose myself for the oncoming shift. So much for what Marx termed the "reproduction of labor power," meaning the things a worker has to do just so she'll be ready to labor again. The only unforeseen obstacle to the smooth transition from job to job is that my tan Jerry's slacks, which had looked reasonably clean by 40-watt bulb last night when I hand washed my Hawaiian shirt, prove by daylight to be mottled with catsup and ranch-dressing stains. I spend most of my hour-long break between jobs attempting to remove the edible portions of the slacks with a sponge and then drying them over the hood of my car in the sun.

I can do this two-job thing, is my theory, if I can drink enough caffeine and avoid getting distracted by George's ever more obvious suffering.[13] The first few days after the alleged theft, he seemed not to understand the trouble he was in, and our chirpy little conversations had continued. But the last couple of shifts he's been listless and unshaven, and tonight he looks like the ghost we all know him to be, with dark half-moons hanging from his eyes. At one point, when I am briefly immobilized by the task of filling little paper cups with sour cream for baked potatoes, he comes over and looks as if he'd like to explore the limits of our shared vocabulary, but I am called to the floor for a table. I resolve to give him all my tips that night, and to hell with the experiment in low-wage money management. At eight, Ellen and I grab a snack together standing at the mephitic end of the kitchen counter, but I can only manage two or three mozzarella sticks, and lunch had been a mere handful of McNuggets. I am not tired at all, I assure myself, though it may be that there is simply no more "I" left to do the tiredness monitoring. What I would see if I were more alert to the situation is that the forces of destruction are already massing against me. There is only one cook on duty, a young man named Jesus ("Hay-Sue," that is), and he is new to the job. And there is Joy, who shows up to take over in the middle of the shift dressed in high heels and a long, clingy white dress and fuming as if she'd just been stood up in some cocktail bar.

Then it comes, the perfect storm. Four of my tables fill up at once. Four tables is nothing for me now, but only so long as they are obligingly staggered. As I bev table 27, tables 25, 28, and 24 are watching enviously. As I bev 25, 24 glowers because their bevs haven't even been ordered. Twenty-eight is four yuppyish types, meaning everything on the side and agonizing instructions as to the chicken Caesars. Twenty-five is a middle-aged black couple who complain, with some justice, that the iced tea isn't fresh and the tabletop is sticky.

[13]In 1996 the number of persons holding two or more jobs averaged 7.8 million, or 6.2 percent of the work force. It was about the same rate for men and for women (6.1 versus 6.2). About two-thirds of multiple jobholders work one job full-time and the other part-time. Only a heroic minority—4 percent of men and 2 percent of women—work two full-time jobs simultaneously (John F. Stinson Jr., "New Data on Multiple Jobholding Available from the CPS," *Monthly Labor Review*, March 1997). [Ehrenreich's note]

But table 24 is the meteorological event of the century: ten British tourists who seem to have made the decision to absorb the American experience entirely by mouth. Here everyone has at least two drinks—iced tea *and* milk shake, Michelob *and* water (with lemon slice in the water, please)—and a huge, promiscuous orgy of breakfast specials, mozz sticks, chicken strips, quesadillas, burgers with cheese and without, sides of hash browns with cheddar, with onions, with gravy, seasoned fries, plain fries, banana splits. Poor Jesus! Poor me! Because when I arrive with their first tray of food—after three prior trips just to refill bevs—Princess Di refuses to eat her chicken strips with her pancake and sausage special since, as she now reveals, the strips were meant to be an appetizer. Maybe the others would have accepted their meals, but Di, who is deep into her third Michelob, insists that everything else go back while they work on their starters. Meanwhile, the yuppies are waving me down for more decaf and the black couple looks ready to summon the NAACP.

Much of what happens next is lost in the fog of war. Jesus starts 30 going under. The little printer in front of him is spewing out orders faster than he can rip them off, much less produce the meals. A menacing restlessness rises from the tables, all of which are full. Even the invincible Ellen is ashen from stress. I take table 24 their reheated main courses, which they immediately reject as either too cold or fossilized by the microwave. When I return to the kitchen with their trays (three trays in three trips) Joy confronts me with arms akimbo: "What *is* this?" She means the food—the plates of rejected pancakes, hash browns in assorted flavors, toasts, burgers, sausages, eggs. "Uh, scrambled with cheddar," I try, "and that's—" "*No*," she screams in my face, "is it a traditional, a super-scramble, an eye-opener?" I pretend to study my check for a clue, but entropy has been up to its tricks, not only on the plates but in my head, and I have to admit that the original order is beyond reconstruction. "You don't know an eye-opener from a traditional?" she demands in outrage. All I know, in fact, is that my legs have lost interest in the current venture and have announced their intention to fold. I am saved by a yuppie (mercifully not one of mine) who chooses this moment to charge into the kitchen to bellow that his food is twenty-five minutes late. Joy screams at him to get the hell out of her kitchen, *please*, and then turns on Jesus in a fury, hurling an empty tray across the room for emphasis.

I leave. I don't walk out, I just leave. I don't finish my side work or pick up my credit card tips, if any, at the cash register or, of course, ask Joy's permission to go. And the surprising thing is that you *can* walk out without permission, that the door opens, that the thick tropical night air parts to let me pass, that my car is still parked where I left it. There is no vindication in this exit, no fuck-you surge of relief, just an overwhelming dank sense of failure pressing down on me and the entire parking lot. I had gone into this venture in the spirit of science, to test a mathematical proposition, but somewhere along the line, in the tunnel vision imposed by long shifts and relentless concentration, it became a test of myself, and clearly I have failed. Not only had I flamed out as a housekeeper/server, I had forgotten to give George my tips, and, for reasons perhaps best known to hardworking, generous people like Gail and Ellen, this hurts. I don't cry, but I am in a position to realize, for the first time in many years, that the tear ducts are still there and still capable of doing their job.

When I moved out of the trailer park, I gave the key to number 46 to Gail and arranged for my deposit to be transferred to her. She told me that Joan was still living in her van and that Stu had been fired from the Hearthside. According to the most up-to-date rumors, the drug he ordered from the restaurant was crack and he was caught dipping into the cash register to pay for it. I never found out what happened to George.

ENGAGING THE TEXT

1. What's the point of Ehrenreich's experiment? What do you think she was hoping to learn by stepping down the economic ladder, and what can you learn from her experience? Explain why you find her approach more or less effective than one that emphasizes economic data and analysis.

2. Ehrenreich ordinarily lives much more comfortably than she did as a waitress, and of course she had an escape hatch from her experiment — she would not serve food or clean rooms forever and could have gone back to her usual life if necessary at any time. Explain the effect her status as a "tourist" in working-class culture has on you as a reader.

3. Write a journal entry about your worst job. How did your experience of being "nickeled and dimed" compare with Ehrenreich's? What was the worst aspect of this work experience for you? What, if anything, did you learn from this job — about work, about success, and about yourself?

4. **Thinking Rhetorically** Throughout this selection Ehrenreich seeks not merely to narrate facts but to elicit emotional responses from her readers. Explain how you react to one or more of the passages listed below and identify specific details in the text that help shape your responses:

   The opening description of Jerry's (paras. 1–2)

   The description of customers (para. 10)

   George's story (paras. 12–13, 16–18)

   The description of trailer number 46 (para. 15)

   Ehrenreich's footnotes throughout the narrative

EXPLORING CONNECTIONS

5. In "City of Broken Dreams" (p. 210) Sara Goldrick-Rab describes the decision to attend college as a "financial wager" (para. 11), a bet that the long-term benefits will outweigh short-term costs and risks. Do you think that Gail, Ellen, or George in Ehrenreich's narrative should make this wager? Taking into account Goldrick-Rab's profiles of Alicia, José, and Anne, how might the situations of Gail, Ellen, and George change if they began taking college classes? Conversely, how does Ehrenreich's narrative help explain the stress Alicia, José, and Anne experience balancing work and school?

6. Imagine that Gail, Ellen, or George participated in the "Fight for $15 Day of Disruption" (pages 409 and 413 in the Visual Portfolio). Write a journal entry from their point of view about the experience of that day.

7. In "You Will Lose Your Job to a Robot — and Sooner Than You Think" (p. 322), Kevin Drum suggests that robots will soon do virtually all of the work currently done by humans. What effects would you expect automation to have on workers like Gail, Ellen, and George over the next decade? Might their jobs actually survive because their wages are so low?

EXTENDING THE CRITICAL CONTEXT

8. Ehrenreich made $6.10 per hour as a housekeeper. Working in groups, sketch out a monthly budget based on this salary for (a) an individual, (b) a single parent with a preteen child, and (c) a family of four in which one adult is ill or has been laid off. Be sure to include money for basics like rent, utilities, food, clothing, transportation, and medical care.

9. Research the *least* promising job prospects in your community. Talk to potential employers and learn as much as you can about such issues as wages, working conditions, hours, drug screening, and healthcare, retirement, or other benefits.

10. Order a meal at whichever restaurant in your community is most like "Jerry's." Study the working conditions in the restaurant, paying special attention to the kinds of problems Ehrenreich faced on her shifts. Write up an informal journal entry from the imagined point of view of a server at the restaurant.

11. Research recent efforts to increase the state and federal minimum wage and the concept of a "sustainable" or a "living wage." What arguments are made for and against raising minimum income guarantees? How have experiments with sustainable wages in cities like San Francisco, New York, or Washington, DC, affected workers and businesses? In class, debate whether your own state should implement a sustainable wage program.

④

FROM A TANGLE OF PATHOLOGY
TO A RACE-FAIR AMERICA
ALAN AJA, DANIEL BUSTILLO,
WILLIAM DARITY JR., AND DARRICK HAMILTON

Some Americans saw the election of President Barack Obama as a sign that the nation had entered a new postracial era in which the problems of racism and discrimination had been largely solved. This essay challenges that view by analyzing how race and money are intertwined in contemporary America. The authors point to continuing patterns of bias in hiring practices and unemployment rates and present dramatic data on the "racial wealth gap" between blacks and whites. Arguing that deep-rooted structural problems continue to hold back African Americans, they propose two new federal policies to support a "race-fair" America. Alan Aja is professor of Puerto Rican and Latino studies at Brooklyn College. Daniel Bustillo is a doctoral student in the School of Social Work at Columbia University. William Darity Jr. is professor of economics and the Samuel DuBois Cook Professor of Public Policy at Duke University's Sanford School of Public Policy. Darrick Hamilton is professor of economics and urban policy at The New School's Milano School of International Affairs, Management, and Urban Policy. The essay appeared in *Dissent: A Quarterly of Politics and Culture* (2014).

WHEN PRESIDENT LYNDON JOHNSON gave his June 4, 1965, commencement address at Howard University, he invoked a symbolic language that would both seize the political moment and serve as a foundation for subsequent policy. The Civil Rights Act had passed only a year earlier, and Johnson, noting that it is "not enough just to open the gates of opportunity," told the black graduating class that America needed "not just equality as a right and a theory but equality as a fact and as a result." This call for "results" was a precursor to Johnson's Executive Order 11246, a mandate for the enforcement of positive anti-discrimination measures in preferred positions of society, or "affirmative action."

But later in the speech, Johnson moved away from his point of departure, abruptly arguing that "perhaps most important—its influence radiating to every part of life—is the breakdown of the Negro family structure." This "rhetorical sleight of hand," as sociologist Stephen Steinberg aptly calls it, would reverberate in public discussion for years to come. By defining the central problem facing the black community as not the deep-seated structures that perpetuate racism but rather deficiencies internal to blacks themselves, the focus of policy would become the rehabilitation of the black family.

The roots of this ideology can be traced to Oscar Lewis's[1] notion of a "culture of poverty" and the 1965 Moynihan Report,[2] in which black families were characterized as being caught up in a "tangle of pathology." The contemporary version of this thesis is the "postracial" narrative in which America has largely transcended its racial divides. The narrative of grand racial progress is coupled with the claim that whatever racial disparities remain are overwhelmingly the result of actions (or inactions) on the part of subaltern[3] groups themselves. If blacks (and other subaltern communities, including Native Americans, Mexicans, Filipinos, Puerto Ricans, and Vietnamese) simply would reverse their self-sabotaging attitudes and behaviors, this argument goes, full equality could be achieved. Herein lies much of the rationale for austerity policies.[4] If behavioral modification is the central issue, why fund government agencies and programs, which, at best, misallocate resources to irresponsible individuals and, at worst, create dependencies that further fuel irresponsible behavior?

Post-racialists often confirm their perspective by pointing to black and minority appointments to the nation's elite positions, including the election of Barack Obama to the highest office in the land. Indeed, the president himself often perpetuates this "postracial" trope. In his speech marking the fiftieth anniversary of the March on Washington for Jobs and Freedom, Obama described how "legitimate grievances" had "tipped into excuse-making" and "the transformative message of unity and brotherhood was drowned out by the language of recrimination." "And what had once been a call for equality of opportunity," he continued, "the chance for all Americans to work hard and get ahead, was too often framed as a mere desire for government support, as if we had no agency in our own liberation, as if poverty was an excuse for not raising your child and the bigotry of others was reason to give up on yourself."

The president's rhetoric on race is consistent with the following premises: 5

1. The civil rights era has virtually ended structural barriers to black equality; remaining barriers are due to the legacy of past discrimination, the residual effects of concentrated poverty, and black folks'

---

[1]**Oscar Lewis:** American anthropologist (1914–1970) who theorized that poor and marginalized groups may create a self-perpetuating subculture of poverty, "especially because of what happens to the worldview, aspirations, and character of the children who grow up in it." [All notes are the editors'.]

[2]**Moynihan Report:** "The Negro Family: The Case for National Action," a controversial report by sociologist and Assistant Secretary of Labor (later U.S. Senator) Daniel Patrick Moynihan that pointed to the relative scarcity of traditional nuclear families in black communities as a primary cause of African American poverty.

[3]**subaltern:** Outside the dominant power structure.

[4]**austerity policies:** Government policies that would reduce spending on programs like Head Start, Aid to Families with Dependent Children, Temporary Assistance for Needy Families, and the Supplemental Nutrition Assistance Program (food stamps).

own behaviors. After all, virtually all groups of Americans have faced some form of discrimination but managed to "get ahead" anyway.

2. Blacks need to cease making particularistic claims on America and begin, in the president's words, to "[bind] our grievances to the larger aspirations of all Americans."

3. Blacks need to recognize their own complicity in the continuation of racial inequality, as well as their own responsibility for directly changing their disparate position.

But if structural factors are largely artifacts of the past, what explains the marked and persistent racial gaps in employment and wealth? Is discrimination genuinely of only marginal importance in America today? Has America really transcended the racial divide, and can the enormous racial wealth gap be explained on the basis of dysfunctional behaviors?

The Racial Employment Gap

In marked contrast to incremental gains in relative educational attainment and income, the racial gap in mass long-term unemployment continues to remain intolerably high, with black Americans bearing a disproportionate burden. In the spring of 2014 the black unemployment rate was estimated at 12.0 percent, compared to 5.8 percent for whites. This continues a structural trend where the black rate remains roughly twice as high as the white rate. In fact, over the past forty years there has been only one year, 2000, in which the black unemployment rate has been below 8.0 percent. In contrast, there have only been four years in which the white rate has reached that level. Blacks are in a perpetual state of employment crisis.

At every rung of the educational ladder, the black unemployment rate is twice the white rate. In 2012 the unemployment rate for whites with less than a high school diploma was 11.4 percent, but for blacks with the same educational level the rate was 20.4 percent. Most telling as an indication of ongoing discrimination in U.S. labor markets is that the unemployment rate for adult white high school dropouts (11.4 percent) was less than the rate for blacks with some college education or an associate's degree (11.6 percent).

Field experiments of employment audits provide powerful evidence that employer discrimination remains a plausible explanation for racial labor market disparity. Economists Marianne Bertrand and Sendhil Mullainathan found a 50 percent higher callback rate for résumés with "white-sounding names" than for comparable résumés with "African American–sounding names." Even more telling, the "better"-quality résumés with African American–sounding names received fewer callbacks than "lower"-quality résumés with white-sounding names.

Princeton sociologist Devah Pager conducted another employment study in Milwaukee, Wisconsin, that revealed the difficulties for stigmatized populations in finding a job. Wisconsin has outlawed employer use of criminal background checks for most jobs, yet among young males of comparable race, experience, and education, audit testers with a criminal record received half as many employment callbacks as testers without a record. Nonetheless, race was found to be even more stigmatizing than incarceration. White testers with criminal records had a slightly higher callback rate than black testers without criminal records.

Racial disparities persist even for those employed. Nearly 87 percent of U.S. occupations can be classified as racially segregated even after accounting for educational differences. Black males experience the most severe underrepresentation in construction, extraction, and maintenance occupations.[5] These occupations tend to require low educational credentials but offer relatively high wages. At the other extreme, service occupations have the highest concentrations of black males; these are also low-credentialed occupations but, in contrast to construction, tend to offer relatively low pay. This distinction is noteworthy given the widely held view that the lack of "soft skills" on the part of blacks is a major factor in explaining their labor market difficulties.

The "soft skills" explanation fits neatly within the "post-racial" narrative. For example, Harvard sociologist William Julius Wilson argues that employers in service industries fail to hire black men because they "lack the soft skills that their jobs require: the tendency to maintain eye contact, the ability to carry on polite and friendly conversations with consumers, the inclination to smile and be responsive to consumer requests." Yet the hard fact remains that blacks are "crowded in" to the service sector, which typically requires customer and coworker interactions, and "crowded out" of the construction sector, which primarily involves not soft skills but working with materials and machinery. This contradicts the notion that soft-skills differentials explain the racial labor market disparity.

The Racial Wealth Gap

Wealth is of paramount importance as a pool of resources, beyond income, that individuals or families can use as a sustained mechanism for provision of support for their offspring. Wealth represents long-term resource accumulation and provides the economic security to take risks, shield against financial loss, and cope with emergencies.

Wealth is also the economic indicator in which blacks and whites are farthest apart. Prior to the Great Recession, white households had a median net worth of approximately $135,000 and black households a median net worth of a little over $12,000. Thus, the typical black family

---

[5]**extraction ... occupations:** Industries that extract resources from the natural environment, such as mining, oil drilling, and timber harvesting.

had less than 9 cents for every dollar in wealth of the typical white family. According to the Pew Hispanic Center, this gap nearly doubled after the Great Recession, with the typical black family having about a nickel for every dollar in wealth held by the typical white family; in 2009 the typical black household had less than $6,000 in net worth.

Regardless of age, household structure, education, occupation, or income, black families typically have less than a quarter of the wealth of otherwise comparable white families. Perhaps even more disturbing, the median wealth of black families whose head graduated from college is less than the median wealth of white families whose head dropped out of high school, and high-earning married black households typically have less wealth than low-earning married white households.

Wealth provides, perhaps, the best evidence to dispel the myth of a postracial society. It also provides the best evidence to dispel the parallel and reinforcing myth that the vestiges of racial inequality are the result of poor choices on the part of blacks themselves. The conventional wisdom explains the persistence of this massive racial wealth gap across all levels of income by invoking allegedly poor savings behavior or inferior portfolio management on the part of blacks. For example, when asked at an April 2009 lecture at Morehouse College about the racial wealth gap, then Federal Reserve Chair Ben Bernanke attributed the gap to a lack of "financial literacy" on the part of blacks, particularly with respect to savings behavior.

But greater financial literacy will do next to nothing to close the racial wealth gap in the absence of finances to manage; nor does it provide insulation against heavy hits to one's investment portfolio. The massive loss in wealth experienced by shareholders on Wall Street in 2008 was not due to their financial illiteracy; it was due to the stock market crash. Most of the individuals defrauded in Bernie Madoff's pyramid scheme could hardly be described as "financially illiterate." Presumably, all Americans may benefit from improved knowledge about management of their personal financial resources, but racial differences in knowledge about management of personal financial resources do not explain the racial gulf in wealth. Maury Gittleman and Ed Wolff reinforced this in an analysis of data predating the mortgage market crisis that finds no significant racial advantage in asset appreciation rates for white families with positive assets after controlling for household income. They also find no meaningful difference in savings by race after controlling for household income — a conclusion that economists as ideologically disparate as Milton Friedman and Marcus Alexis (a founding member of Black Enterprise's Board of Economists) have reached.

Most of the racial wealth gap is explained by inheritances, bequests, and intrafamily transfers — transfers largely based on the economic position of the family into which an individual is born. Indeed, inheritances and intrafamily transfers are far more important considerations in explaining the racial wealth gap than education, income, and household structure. Moreover, intrafamilial shifts of resources are transfers made on a nonmerit basis. The continued structural barriers that inhibit blacks from amassing resources and making intergenerational transfers provide strong opposition to the postracial narrative. Past, present, and prospective racial exploitation and discrimination provide a sounder basis for understanding the vast material disparities between blacks and whites in the United States. There is a long history of structural impediments to black wealth accumulation. Beginning with the period of chattel slavery, when blacks were literally the property of white slave owners, and continuing through the use of restrictive covenants, redlining, general housing and lending discrimination—policies that generated a white asset-based middle class—and the foreclosure crisis (which was characterized by predation and racially disparate impacts), blacks have faced structural barriers to wealth accumulation.

The Racial Self-Employment Gap

Substantial attention has been given to black business development as a means of closing the racial wealth gap. This confuses cause and effect: the racial wealth gap would have to be closed as a prelude to closing the racial self-employment gap. Business formation, success, and survival depend heavily on the initial level of financial capital available to the entrepreneur, and black firms start with much less initial capital than white firms. Policy has often reinforced this initial disadvantage. [Sociologist] Tamara Nopper has documented specific changes in Small Business Administration policy—such as more aggregate targeting of women and other minority groups, and a shift to private-sector lenders with more stringent collateral and credit requirements—that accounted for a substantial reduction in loans directed to black business. Nopper also noted that the tendency for ethnic banks to service co-ethnics coupled with a relative paucity of black-owned banks and undercapitalization of these banks negatively affected black business access to finance. For example, in 2008 the Federal Deposit Insurance Corporation identified a total of ninety-six Asian- and Pacific Islander–owned banks with a total of $53 billion in assets in contrast to only forty-four black-owned banks with $7.5 billion in assets. The business success of certain immigrant groups relative to blacks is a consequence of greater initial wealth upon entry into the United States, the selectivity of immigration, and the support of the Small Business Administration, rather than a "deficient" entrepreneurial spirit or cultural orientation toward business among blacks.

What Can Be Done?

The most parsimonious policy approach would be carefully targeted 20 race-based policies. However, if such policies are becoming politically unfeasible, then we need bold policies that lead to economic security, mobility, and sustainability for all Americans, or what john a. powell[6] has labeled "targeted universalism."

Child Trust Accounts (Baby Bonds).   These accounts are designed to provide an opportunity for asset development for all newborns regardless of the financial position in which they are born. The baby bonds would set up trusts for all newborns with an average account of $20,000 that progressively rise to $60,000 for babies born into the poorest families. The accounts would be federally managed and grow at a federally guaranteed annual interest rate of 1.5–2 percent to be accessed when the child becomes an adult and used for asset-enhancing endeavors, such as purchasing a home or starting a new business. With approximately four million infants born each year, and an average endowment of around $20,000, we estimate the cost of the program to be $80 billion. In relative proportional costs, this would constitute only 2.2 percent of 2012 federal expenditures.

These accounts could be paid for by a more equitable allocation of what the federal government already spends on asset development. A 2010 report by the Corporation for Enterprise Development and the Annie E. Casey Foundation estimates that the federal government allocated $400 billion of its 2009 budget in the form of tax subsidies and savings to promote asset-development policies, with more than half of the benefits going to the top 5 percent of earners—those with incomes higher than $160,000. In contrast, the bottom 60 percent of taxpayers received only 4 percent of the benefits. If the federal asset-promotion budget were allocated in a more progressive manner, federal policies could be transformative for low-income Americans. For example, repealing the mortgage interest deduction—which primarily benefits middle- and upper-income households—would be an important first step in creating a tax code that is fairer for all and treats renters and homeowners alike.

A Federal Job Guarantee.   This would provide economic security, mobility, and sustainability for all Americans, while also addressing the longstanding pattern of racial inequality in employment. We estimate that the average cost per job directly created by the employment corps—including salary, benefits, training, and equipment—would be $50,000, with the total compensation package amounting to $750 billion, which is less than the first $787 billion stimulus package[7] and considerably less than the first phase of the bailout of the investment banks[8] estimated at $1.3 trillion. The net expenses of the job-guarantee

[6]**john a. powell:** Professor of law, African American studies, and ethnic studies at UC Berkeley and executive director of the Haas Institute for a Fair and Inclusive Society.

[7]**stimulus package:** The American Recovery and Investment Act of 2009, signed into law to stimulate the economy as the Great Recession began.

[8]**bailout of the investment banks:** The Emergency Economic Stabilization Act of 2008 and the Troubled Asset Relief Program created by that act.

program would be reduced because of a wide array of cost savings from other social programs; in 2011 alone, federal antipoverty programs (Medicaid, unemployment insurance, and so on) cost approximately $746 billion.

While liberal leaders, whether they be Lyndon Johnson or Barack Obama, may rhetorically acknowledge the legacies of racism, they often support policies that are based on conservative notions of a culture of poverty. Policies that emphasize deficient norms, values, and behaviors on the part of blacks and other subaltern groups amount to what William Ryan categorized over forty years ago as simply "blaming the victim." These include efforts to encourage small business development without first addressing the racial maldistribution of wealth and the current White House initiative, "My Brother's Keeper," which is aimed at transforming the motivation and behaviors of "defective" black male youths to make them more "employable" without addressing their lack of job opportunities and labor market discrimination. Addressing the racial employment and wealth gaps will require not paternalistic policy, but policies providing access to jobs and asset building for all Americans.

ENGAGING THE TEXT

1. Review the three premises of "postracialism" in paragraph 5. How has reading this article influenced your ideas about each of these premises? What specific ideas or information in the article challenged or reinforced your existing beliefs?

2. Do you agree that President Obama's words in paragraph 4 are indeed consistent with the three premises of postracialism the authors articulate? Why or why not?

3. At the end of their article, the authors propose two policy initiatives — "Child Trust Accounts" and a "Federal Job Guarantee" — to move the United States closer to racial equality. What do you think would be the impact of these initiatives? What arguments could be made against them, and how might those arguments be addressed?

4. In paragraphs 11–12, the authors try to discredit the notion that a lack of "soft skills" limits blacks' opportunities in the labor market. How important do you think soft skills are for workers? What soft skills should CEOs be required to have? To what extent might "soft skills" be a cover term that obscures deeper issues such as racial discrimination, gender bias, or preferences for a particular dialect or accent?

5. **Thinking Rhetorically** What is the thesis of this article? Is it implied or directly stated? Using the article's subheadings as cues, outline the organization of the article and assess the strength of the evidence in each section.

EXPLORING CONNECTIONS

6. Read or review Nikole Hannah-Jones's "Choosing a School for My Daughter in a Segregated City" (p. 152). Explain how a postracialist might view PS 307; then detail how you think Hannah-Jones and Aja et al. would challenge such a perspective.

7. Critiquing President Lyndon Johnson's commencement address, Aja and his colleagues write that "by defining the central problems facing the black community as not the deep-seated structures that perpetuate racism but rather deficiencies internal to blacks themselves, the focus of policy would become the rehabilitation of the black family" (para. 2). Use Hannah-Jones's "Choosing a School for My Daughter in a Segregated City" (p. 152) to craft a rebuttal of Johnson's views on "the breakdown of the Negro family structure."

8. In paragraph 18 the authors provide a quick snapshot of the "history of structural impediments to black wealth accumulation." Look ahead to "The Case for Reparations" by Ta-Nehisi Coates (p. 604); identify relevant examples of impediments in Coates's essay and explain how they have limited black accumulation of wealth.

EXTENDING THE CRITICAL CONTEXT

9. The quotations from President Obama in paragraph 4 come from "Remarks by the President at the 'Let Freedom Ring' Ceremony Commemorating the 59th Anniversary of the March on Washington," a speech delivered at the Lincoln Memorial on August 28, 2013. Find and read the full speech online. Discuss whether the quotations selected by Aja and his coauthors accurately represent the speech as a whole. For example, to what extent does the speech seem to support a "postracial trope" or valorize the American Dream, and to what extent does the president identify the kinds of structural changes that Aja and his colleagues consider necessary?

10. The authors note that "affirmative action" dates back to President Lyndon B. Johnson's Executive Order 11246 (para. 1). Research the contentious history of affirmative action over the past half century. How effective has the program been as a means of addressing racial inequities? What does the history of affirmative action suggest about the likelihood of implementing the kinds of initiatives favored by the authors?

FROM *HOW THE OTHER HALF BANKS*

MEHRSA BARADARAN

Does your bank need you more than you need them? If so, you are fortunate to have enough assets that a financial institution is willing to serve you (at a price, of course). More than 70 million Americans, however, are "unbanked" — they have no relationship with a bank, credit union, or brokerage house, usually because they lack the wealth to make such a relationship worthwhile to the financial institution. Ironically, being unbanked is expensive: working exclusively with cash wastes time and often involves fees for check cashing or other services. And if you need to borrow money in an emergency, you can quickly find yourself in a spiral of debt, paying triple-digit interest rates. This excerpt from *How the Other Half Banks* explores the causes and effects of living outside the world of credit cards, car loans, automatic deposits, and online shopping that many of us take for granted. Mehrsa Baradaran (b. 1978) is Associate Dean for Strategic Initiatives and a J. Alton Hosch Associate Professor at the University of Georgia School of Law. In addition to numerous publications in legal journals and reviews, she has authored two books, *The Color of Money: Black Banks and the Racial Wealth Gap* (2017) and *How the Other Half Banks: Exclusion, Exploitation, and the Threat to Democracy* (2015), the source of this reading.

Unbanked and Unwanted

A lawyer once wrote that "poverty creates an abrasive interface with society; the poor are always bumping into sharp legal things."[1] They are also constantly bumping into sharp financial things. Without a financial cushion, every mistake, unexpected problem, or minor life change can quickly turn into a financial disaster. This is why those who live paycheck to paycheck often rely on fringe lenders.[2] But the high cost of borrowing money to avoid small or large disasters is just one dimension of what it means to live without access to banking.

Michael Barr noted that not having a bank account reduces take-home pay and makes it difficult for families to save and establish a credit history.[3] When an unbanked person gets her paycheck, she must

---

[1]Stephen Wexler, "Practicing Law for Poor People," *Yale Law Journal* 79 (1970): 1049, 1053.

[2]**fringe lenders:** Payday lenders, pawn shops, and other non-bank lenders. [Eds.]

[3]Michael S. Barr, "An Inclusive, Progressive National Savings and Financial Services Policy," *Harvard Law and Policy Review* 1 (2007): 164, 164.

go to a check casher; in the process, she loses up to 10 percent of her paycheck.[4] She must then pay her bills, and because most institutions will not take cash for bill payments, she must purchase money orders, which can cost anywhere from five to twenty dollars. To be clear, that is one payment in order to convert an article of commercial paper (a paycheck) into cash and then several payments in order to turn that cash back into commercial paper (money orders) in order to pay bills. Some institutions will accept cash for bill payments but never by mail, and so paying by cash requires possibly missing work, which is stressful, to show up at their office during business hours and wait in line every time the bill is due.

Most Americans and nearly all U.S. businesses operate in an electronic currency economy. Only those left out of the banking sector must operate in a cash economy—at a great cost. These people do not have access to credit and debit cards, which are the primary payment methods most of the population uses. For everyday purchases, the unbanked use either cash or a fee-based prepaid card. (Cash is much easier to lose and more likely to be stolen than an electronic transfer.) In addition to these expenses, if the unbanked need to send money to anyone, they must pay a significant fee—anywhere from ten dollars to eighty dollars— depending on the size of the transfer. These charges, which are only borne by the poor, pile additional expenses and stresses on top of their already strained lives.

In fact, the average unbanked family with an annual income of around $25,000 spends about $2,400 per year, *almost 10 percent of its income*, on financial transactions. This is more money than these families spend on food.[5] In 2012, the unbanked spent a total of $89 billion on financial transactions alone.[6] And these expenses can mean the difference between a family's financial survival and its failure. For example, on average, families who filed for bankruptcy in 2012 were just $26 short per month on meeting their expenses.[7] Saving $2,400 per year, or $200 per month, could save many families from the devastation of bankruptcy. The fact that so much money is being spent by the poor to pay for simple financial services that the nonpoor get for free is a tragedy.

Nor are we talking about a small group of people. Approximately 70 million Americans do not have a bank account or access to traditional

---

[4]Michael S. Barr, *No Slack: The Financial Lives of Low-Income Americans* (Washington, DC: Brookings Institution, 2012), 3.

[5]USPS, Office of the Inspector General, "Providing Non-Bank Financial Services for the Underserved," White Paper Report Number: RARC-WP-14-007 January 27, 2014, accessed March 17, 2015, www.uspsoig.gov/sites/default/files/document-library-files/2014/rarc-wp-14-007.pdf. Based on 34 million households earning an average of $25,500 per year, spending a total of $82 billion in 2011; KPMG, "Serving the Underserved Market, 2011," 1, accessed September 29, 2014, www.kpmg.com/US/en/IssuesAndInsights/ArticlesPublications/Documents/serving-underserved-market.pdf; Center for Financial Services Innovation (CFSI), "2012 Financially Underserved Market Size Study," December 2013, 1, www.cfsinnovation.com/content/2012-financially-underserved-market-sizing-study.

[6]CFSI, "2012 Financially Underserved Market Size Study," 1.

[7]Ibid.

financial services. That is more people than live in California, New York, and Maryland combined. It is more than the total number of people who voted for Barack Obama (or Mitt Romney) in the 2012 election.[8] The term "unbanked" or "underbanked" describes a group of people who rely on fringe lenders, but these terms underestimate the problem. An even larger and less quantifiable number of people do have bank accounts but rely primarily on alternative banking services for a variety of reasons.[9] In fact, you must have a bank account in order to use a pay-day lender. We are talking about anywhere from 30 to 50 percent of the population—the 30 to 50 percent at the bottom of the income ladder.[10]

* * *

What are the simple economic realities of banking for the poor? Several barriers keep mainstream banks from serving the poor—the most important is simple math. Banks can make much higher profits elsewhere. The poor may need banks, but banks most definitely do not need the poor. Banks' transaction and overhead costs are much the same whether they lend $500 or $500,000, but of course, the larger loan yields a much higher profit. The American poet Ogden Nash put it this way: "One rule which woe betides the banker who fails to heed it; Never lend any money to anybody unless they don't need it."

Maintaining simple checking or savings accounts costs banks money. They must hire staff, pay for buildings, update technology, build automated teller machines (ATMs), send monthly statements, and more. Different estimates say that each deposit account costs a bank between $48 and $200 every year.[11] They can make up these costs by lending customer deposits. To a bank, customer deposits are microloans from the customer to the bank (notably, relatively interest-free loans) that the institution can use to make profit and create income-paying assets: customer loans. And of course, the more deposits invested, the more loan volume and the higher the profits. Thus, when a bank is considering whether or not to open a new account, it must determine whether the

[8]Derek Thompson, "When You're Poor, Money is Expensive," *Atlantic*, July 14, 2014, accessed March 17, 2015, m.theatlantic.com/business/archive/2014/07/its-expensive-to-be-poor-money/374361/.

[9]Barr, *No Slack*, 120.

[10]FDIC, "2013 FDIC National Survey of Unbanked and Underbanked Households," October 2014, accessed March 17, 2015, www.fdic.gov/householdsurvey/2013report.pdf; University Neighborhood Housing Program, "Banking in the Bronx: Assessing Options in a Historically Redlined and Underbanked Borough," April 2012, accessed March 17, 2015, www.unhp.org/pdf/BankingInTheBronx.pdf.

[11]"In fact, the ABA says, the annual cost of a checking account is actually $250 to $300." The American Bankers Association (ABA) claims that the cost of opening an account runs between $150 and $200, and the annual cost of maintaining an account runs between $250 and $300. The American Bankers Association catalogs the costs of maintaining an account: "These costs reflect the expense of processing transactions, providing monthly statements, investing in payment system technology and software, paying the cost of tellers, ATMs, and online banking, staffing call centers, complying with countless regulations, ensuring privacy and data protection, and preventing fraud and covering fraud losses." Marcie Geffner, "Bank Account Costs $250," *Bankrate*, July 26, 2010, accessed March 17, 2015, www.bankrate.com/financing/banking/bank-account-costs-250/.

profits made from the new customer's deposits will outweigh the costs associated with providing that customer services.

If an account contains too little money, the profits will be low or nonexistent. Simple business math suggests that if a product (like a small account) is not profitable, it should be avoided—which is exactly what banks do. But the logic is not so straightforward when applied to banks. Although it is true that these accounts do not yield profits, it is also true that banks do not necessarily lose money by providing these services; the infrastructure is already in place. Sophisticated technology has made it easy and virtually risk-free to cash most checks, create money orders, or transfer funds. If banks were to offer these products to small-account holders, their wealthier clients would essentially be subsidizing the services, which is how community banks were able to serve the poor for much of the nation's history. And importantly, because government support and protection guaranteed banks healthy profits, they did so willingly.

Although the state support is still there, the onus of serving the public has been lifted from banks. Most banks, especially the financial giants, no longer see their role as serving a community at large but view each customer as a potential source of profit. And those deemed unprofitable are either rejected outright or repelled by punishing fees. The most prevalent fee on small accounts are overdraft fees, which make up 75 percent of all bank fees.[12] These costs are borne primarily by the poor—90 percent of the fees are paid by 10 percent of the customers. A 2014 report studied the annual costs of checking accounts at large banks among five categories of spenders and found that by far, the people in the lowest category, the "cash-strapped," paid the most to use a checking account.[13] Comedian Louis C. K. quipped: "You ever get so broke that the bank starts charging you money . . . for not having enough money? The bank called me up, they said, 'Hi, we're calling you because you don't have enough money.' I said, I know! They said, 'You have insufficient funds,' and I said, well, I agree with that. I find my funds to be grossly insufficient! So they charged me $15, that's how much it costs to only have $20. But here is the f***ed-up part, now I only have $5! What am I paying the $15 for if I don't get to have the $20 ... that I paid to have!"[14]

These fees are used both as a way to repel and punish low balances and as a significant source of revenue.[15] When a bank customer writes a   10

[12]Mark Maremont and Tom McGinty, "Why Banks at Wal-Mart Are among America's Top Fee Collectors," *Wall Street Journal*, May 11, 2014, accessed March 17, 2015, www.wsj.com/news/articles/SB10001424052702304734304579515730198367754?KEYWORDS=maremont&mg=reno64-wsj.

[13]Anna Bernasek, "In Checking Accounts, the Less You Have, the More You Pay," *New York Times*, September 20, 2014, accessed March 17, 2015, www.nytimes.com/2014/09/21/your-money/in-checking-accounts-the-less-you-have-the-more-you-pay.html.

[14]www.youtube.com/watch?v=J0rSXjVuJVg. Accessed March 17, 2015.

[15]Annamaria Andriotis, "Overdraft Fees at Banks Hit a High, Despite Curbs," *Wall Street Journal*, April 1, 2014, accessed March 17, 2015, www.wsj.com/news/articles/SB10001424052702304157204579475573602576630.

check and there isn't enough money in the account to fulfill the check, the bank can still clear it. This would effectively be a loan to the customer who has overdrawn her account. Or the bank could just freeze the account without allowing the transaction to go through. The bank risks no loss at all by not covering the transaction for the customer. Instead, the bank issues a fee right away. These fees can be quite high; up to thirty-five dollars for the first overdraw and repeated every day — or every few days if the account remains overdrawn.[16] If you consider the fee as a payment the customer makes for the extension of credit for the overdrawn amount, a 2008 Federal Deposit Insurance Corporation (FDIC) study showed that these fees carry an effective APR[17] in excess of 3,500 percent![18]

These draconian fees haven't gone unnoticed, and in recent years bank regulators, perhaps spurred by lawsuits, have tried to rein in some of the large banks' most egregious practices.[19] For example, Bank of America entered a settlement in Florida for its "unfair and unconscionable assessment and collection of excessive overdraft fees." The civil court settlement explained the problem and its roots succinctly: "For years, banks covered customers who occasionally bounced checks and even did so for a time for customers using debit cards without charging their customers. Since the early 1990's, however, banks have devised methods to provide overdraft 'protection' for customers and charge them in each instance."[20] In this particular case, Bank of America charged a twenty-five-dollar fee for each transaction on the first day and a thirty-five-dollar fee for the second day and all subsequent days the account had an "occurrence," defined as "a day with at least one overdraft item or one returned item."[21] . . .

Banks simply deny bank accounts to those who may have a history of overdrawing. The majority of banks, credit unions, and thrifts use a

[16]Justin Lutz, "Overdrawn and Underwhelmed: A College Student's Tale of Bank of America," *Roosevelt Institute*, accessed March 17, 2015, www.rooseveltinstitute.org/new-roosevelt/overdrawn-and-underwhelmed-college-student-s-tale-bank-america.

[17]**APR:** Annual percentage rate. [Eds.]

[18]FDIC, *FDIC Study of Bank Overdraft Programs*, November 2008, 79, accessed March 17, 2015, www.fdic.gov/bank/analytical/overdraft/FDIC138_Report_Final_v508 .pdf. Banks collected 32 billion in overdraft fees in 2012. Maremont and McGinty, "Why Banks at Wal-Mart."

[19]The Federal Reserve has issued regulation on requirements for overdraft services for electronic funds transfers like ATM transactions (12 CFR 205.17). Generally speaking, the financial institution needs to provide consumers notice of the fees, and the consumer must opt-in. The Consumer Financial Protection Bureau's regulations on overdraft services can be found in 12 CFR 1030.11. This regulation requires financial institutions to disclose, in each periodic statement, the total amount of overdraft fees and the total amount of fees for returning unpaid items. 12 CFR 1030.11(a)(1). Additionally, advertisements promoting overdraft fee services must clearly, and in a conspicuous manner, state the fees charged for each overdraft, the types of transactions covered by the overdraft fee, the time period over which a consumer needs to repay or cover the overdraft, and the circumstances under which the institution will not pay the overdraft. 12 CFR 1030.11(b)(1).

[20]In re: Checking Account Overdraft Litigation, Third Amended Consolidated Class Action Complaint, Case No. 1: 09-MD-02036-JLK (S.D. FL.), accessed March 17, 2015, bofaoverdraftsettlement.com/LinkClick.aspx?fileticket=pSsSlbBGB6s%3D&tabid=67&mid=415.

[21]Ibid.

database called ChexSystems, which allows them to screen potential account holders.[22] A blemished ChexSystems screening is the number one reason banks give for declining account applications.[23] Banks that use the database, and the company itself, claim that the system's primary purpose is to weed out fraud, but only 2 percent of the accounts in the system are placed there because of fraudulent activity.[24] Of the activities used to permanently block people from the banking system, 97.5 percent were overdraft, or "account mishandling," activities.[25] But unlike a credit score, ChexSystems information is not available to customers (even though they stay in the database for five years).[26]

The *New York Times* reported the story of one would-be credit union customer, Tiffany Murrell of Brooklyn, who despite holding down a steady job as a secretary, was denied an account because of a ChexSystems report. Two years earlier, Tiffany had an overdraft of roughly forty dollars. Even though she had already repaid the amount plus interest and fees, she was "barred from opening an account at nearly every bank she has tried, an experience she called 'insulting and frustrating.'"[27] Tiffany lamented that "the sting of being rejected... can make lower-income individuals feel like second-class citizens." Twenty-three-year-old David Korzeniowski, blocked out of the banking system for seven years, acknowledged that "he made a mistake" but that "the fees he pays for cashing checks, paying bills and wiring money cannibalize the paycheck he gets from part-time construction work ... 'Everything is more expensive,' he said."[28]

Banks have no need for small accounts because they do not yield high profits. Therefore, they have employed a variety of tactics to slough off their low-yield customers. High fees and barriers to entry have accomplished their desired result: those with small savings have weighed the costs and have decided to leave the banking system entirely.

[22]The majority of banks, 87 percent, require a third-party screen before they will open checking accounts, and 81 percent of banks require third-party screens to open savings accounts. FDIC, "Banks' Efforts to Serve the Unbanked and Underbanked," December 2008, 11, accessed March 17, 2015, www.fdic.gov/unbankedsurveys/2008survey/index.html.

[23]Ibid., 193. The number of individuals currently on record is unknown since the 2007 acquisition of ChexSystems by Fidelity National Information Services.

[24]Jessica Silver-Greenberg, "Over a Million Are Denied Bank Accounts for Past Errors," *New York Times Deal Book*, July 30, 2013, accessed March 17, 2015, dealbook.nytimes.com/2013/07/30/over-a-million-are-denied-bank-accounts-for-past-errors/.

[25]Dennis Campbell, Asis Martinez-Jerez, and Peter Tufano, "Bouncing Out of the Banking System: An Empirical Analysis of Involuntary Bank Account Closures," *Boston Federal Reserve*, June 6, 2008 (draft) 6, accessed March 17, 2015, www.bostonfed.org/economic/cprc/conferences/2008/payment-choice/papers/campbell_jerez_tufano.pdf.

[26]James Perez, "Blacklisted: The Unwarranted Divestment of Access to Bank Accounts," *New York University Law Review* 80 (2005): 1586; ChexSystems' website states that "each report submitted to ChexSystems remains on our files for five years, unless the source of the information requests its removal or ChexSystems becomes obligated to remove it under applicable law." ChexSystems, Consumer Assistance, "Frequently Asked Questions," accessed September 30, 2014, www.consumerdebit.com/consumerinfo/us/en/chexsystems/faqs.htm#FAQ_01. In 2006, the database had a record of 22 million "closed for cause accounts" at 8,900 institutions. An account is considered closed-for-cause when, for example, a consumer refuses to pay the account fee and the bank closes the account. Ibid.

[27]Silver-Greenberg, "Over a Million."

[28]Ibid.

How the Other Half Borrows

Today, American society not only accepts credit as a way of life, we ⁵ embrace it. The average American has $15,000 in credit card debt, $33,000 in student loan debt, and $156,000 in mortgage debt.[29] Not only do the majority of the American public borrow their way up the income ladder, but federal mortgage and student loan markets and loose credit policies led to the creation of the American middle class. We, the people, have decided (through laws and policies enacted by our elected representatives) that as a society, we want access to affordable credit for both big wealth-building items like homes, education, and businesses and day-to-day smooth-out-the-bumps sorts of things via credit cards and car loans that would have even higher interest rates if not for government policies. However, in a society built on credit as a means to wealth, a large proportion of people at the bottom are currently left out. If the state enables the banking system (and therefore, the credit markets), the provision of credit certainly becomes a matter of political and social concern, and we, as a society, must determine what we will and will not accept.[30] We cannot tolerate such heavy state involvement in providing credit to the banks while leaving the less well-to-do at the mercy of the modern day sharks.

This is a weighty and consequential issue because equality in the credit market leads to a more fair and just society. Leveling the credit playing field extends to the poor the possibility of improving their lives, as well. But inexpensive credit will not cure or even reduce poverty. The causes of poverty are varied and complex and its cures, elusive. Even so, insofar as policy initiatives can provide ladders out of poverty, we need to understand the chutes that affect the poor—financial setbacks from which it takes years (or lifetimes) to recover: job loss, unexpected healthcare costs, and other minor and major pitfalls that are a part of

[29]Federal Reserve Bank of New York, "Total Household Debts," *The Center for Microeconomic Data*, accessed September 29, 2014, www.newyorkfed.org/microeconomics/hhdc.html; Tim Chen, "American Household Credit Card Debt Statistics: 2014," *NerdWallet Finance*, accessed September 29, 2014, www.nerdwallet.com/blog/credit-card-data/average-credit-card-debt-household/; Over 60 percent of small businesses are funded through loans and over 90 percent use credit cards, even though 20 percent of them fail within the first year. Federal Reserve Board of Governors, *Report to the Congress on the Availability of Credit to Small Businesses* (September 2012), 2, 17, accessed March 17, 2015, www.federalreserve.gov/publications/other-reports/files/sbfreport2012.pdf; The average large commercial firm had $650 billion in debt in 2014. Federal Reserve Board of Governors, *Assets and Liabilities of Commercial Banks in the United States*, accessed January 18, 2015, www.federalreserve.gov/releases/h8/current/default.htm#fn1; In 2008, Lehman brothers buckled under approximately that much debt without anyone accusing these high level bankers of not understanding basic finance. Sam Mamudi, "Lehman Folds with Record $613 Billion Debt," *MarketWatch*, September 15, 2008, accessed March 17, 2015, www.marketwatch.com/story/lehman-folds-with-record-613-billion-debt.

[30]I have limited the scope of state control to the banking sphere, where state support is obvious and tangible. Others would extend it further, claiming that the state enables all markets. Anthropologist David Graeber highlights the compelling case that credit and debt markets have always been enabled by states. Graeber, *Debt*, 54–55. And, that there are no markets independent of state control and that debt and credit, therefore, are only possible through state control.

life. Fringe banks are the market response that fill this void. We must understand them to see how wide the divide is to bridge; how deep the wound is to dress. Only after fully appreciating the moral perversion of such lending can we find the urgency to act.

The Sharks

When banks sloughed off their low and moderate income customers and opted out of lending to the poor, a new "fringe lending" industry popped up to meet their needs and has grown ever since. There are a variety of fringe loans across the country. The most common are payday loans, which are currently permitted in thirty-eight states.[31] A payday loan is so-called because the borrower must have a regular paycheck against which she borrows, usually up to $500, with a typical term of anywhere from a week to a month. The borrower gives the lender access to her bank account in the form of either a postdated check or permission for direct withdrawal. The lender then deducts the outstanding payment when it becomes due, typically, the next payday. Consider these staggering statistics about the payday lending sector:

> The average payday lending customer is indebted for 199 days, "or roughly 55% of the year. A quarter of consumers were indebted for 92 days or less over the 12-month study period, while another quarter was indebted for more than 300 days."[32]
>
> Over 80 percent of payday loans are rolled over or followed by another loan within fourteen days (i.e., renewed).[33]
>
> Of the loans that are rolled over, *half* are made in a sequence of *at least ten loans,* and the majority, 62 percent, are in sequences of seven or more loans.[34] The payday industry relies on the constant renewal of these loans. One large payday lender even instructs its employees on how to perpetuate the loans with a circle diagram that reflects the need for constant renewal.
>
> A staggering 90 percent of payday lending business is generated by borrowers with five or more loans per year, and over 60 percent of business is generated by borrowers with twelve or more loans per year. Fees on these loans quickly add up. If a typical payday loan of $325 is flipped eight times—this usually takes just four months—the borrower will have paid $468 in interest. In order to fully repay the loan and principal, the borrower will need to pay $793 for the original $325. Most borrowers pay even more than that.[35]

[31]Heather Morton, "NCSL Payday Lending State Statutes," September 12, 2013, accessed March 17, 2015, www.ncsl.org/research/financial-services-and-commerce/payday-lending-state-statutes.aspx; Consumer Federation of America, "Payday Loan Consumer Information: Legal Status of Payday Loans by State," accessed September 29, 2014, www.paydayloaninfo.org/state-information.

[32]The CFPB sample size was 12 million loans in 2013. "Payday Loans and Deposit Advance Products," *CFPB White Paper*, 23, April 24, 2013, accessed March 17, 2015, files.consumerfinance.gov/f/201304_cfpb_payday-dap-whitepaper.pdf.

[33]Kathleen Burke et al., "CFPB Data Point: Payday Lending," March 25, 2014, accessed March 17, 2015, files.consumerfinance.gov/f/201403_cfpb_report_payday-lending.pdf.

[34]Ibid., 12.

[35]Center for Responsible Lending, "Fast Facts: Payday Loans," accessed September 29, 2014, www.responsiblelending.org/payday-lending/tools-resources/fast-facts.html.

Few borrowers amortize, or have reductions in principal, between the first and last loan of a sequence. For more than 80 percent of the loan sequences longer than one loan, the final loan in the sequence is the same size or larger than the first. Loan size is likely to go up in larger loan sequences, and principal increases are associated with higher default rates.

The average borrower pays an average of between $500 to $600 in interest.[36] One quarter of borrowers pay $781 or more in fees.

A Pew report also found that a payday loan takes 36 percent of a borrower's pretax paycheck.[37] That is, once a loan is made, a person uses more than one-third of their income just to pay it off.

Crushing debt is, after all, the business model for the industry. The Consumer Financial Protection Bureau (CFPB) director has stated that "the payday lending industry depends on people becoming stuck in these loans for the long term, since almost half their business comes from people who are basically paying high-cost rent on the amount of the original loan."[38]

Payday lending requires no credit report. In most cases, a borrower only needs a bank account (which they allow their lender to access) and a paystub to verify income. Over half of payday borrowers end up overdrawing their bank accounts (and incurring bank fees), usually a direct result of payday lenders taking money from their accounts. The fees and interest generally range between $10 to $30 for every $100 borrowed.[39] A typical two-week payday loan with a $15 per $100 fee equates to an annual percentage rate (APR) of about 400 percent. By comparison, APRs on credit cards can range from about 12 percent to 30 percent.[40] But APR vastly underestimates the costs of these loans because they are short-term, and the interest compounds quickly and exponentially if they are held for a year. Because most of these loans are rolled over, the interest is much higher than what the APR reflects. For example, say a borrower takes out a $300 loan. When she is unable to pay the loan at the end of the payday cycle, she pays $50 to extend the loan term, a "rollover," for another two weeks. The borrower still owes the original amount of the loan, the principal. Until she can come up with that amount, she continues to make a $50 payment every two

[36]Pew Charitable Trusts, "Payday Lending in America: Who Borrows, Where They Borrow, and Why," July 2012, 4, accessed March 17, 2015, www.pewtrusts.org/~/media/legacy/uploadedfiles/pcs_assets/2012/PewPaydayLendingReportpdf.pdf. The CFPB found that the average consumer had over ten transactions over a twelve-month period and paid a total of $574 in fees, which does not include the loan principal.

[37]"On average, a payday loan takes 36 percent of a person's pre-tax paycheck, Bourke [project director at Pew] said." "States with Highest, Lowest Payday Loan Rates," *USA Today*, April 20, 2014, accessed March 17, 2015, www.usatoday.com/story/money/personalfinance/2014/04/20/id-nv-ut-have-among-highest-payday-loan-rates/7943519/.

[38]Richard Cordray, "Remarks at the Payday Field Hearing," March 25, 2014, accessed March 17, 2015, www.consumerfinance.gov/newsroom/director-richard-cordray-remarks-at-the-payday-field-hearing/.

[39]CFPB, "Ask CFPB: What Is a Payday Loan?," accessed September 29, 2014, www.consumerfinance.gov/askcfpb/1567/what-payday-loan.html.

[40]Ibid.

weeks to avoid default. As demonstrated above, this can and usually does go on for months and years, with the borrower paying $50 in fees every two weeks just for the original loan amount. If continued for a year, the borrower will have paid $1,300 in interest in exchange for the use of $300 in cash.

In those states where payday lending is prohibited, title loans take 20 their place. Title loans emerged in the 1990s and are essentially payday loans secured by collateral—the title to the borrower's car. (The loans are often configured this way in order to avoid prohibitions on payday lending.) With title loans, not only do borrowers pay extremely high interest rates, but they also stand to lose what is perhaps their most valuable asset: their car. In other words, despite being a "secured" loan that fully protects the lender, the cost is still exorbitant. A typical borrower receives a cash loan equal to about 26 percent of a car's value and pays 300 percent APR.[41] This means that borrowers are paying very high interest for loans that are carrying significant excess collateral. One in six borrowers also faces repossession, and repossession fees average half of the outstanding loan balance. Title loans have grown into a massive industry. Approximately 8,138 car title lenders operate in twenty-one states and generate nearly $2 billion in loans annually, with borrowers paying more than $4 billion in fees.[42] In states where they are not expressly authorized, lenders are able to operate through loopholes in the law.[43]

Because title lenders can rely on the threat of repossession, the majority of borrowers repeatedly renew their loans, turning what is described as a short-term loan into long-term, high-cost debt requiring borrowers to pay more than twice in interest than what they received in credit. The average amount of a title loan is $1,000, much higher than what can be borrowed from payday lenders.[44] Much like a payday loan borrower, the average car title borrower renews a loan eight times, paying $2,142 in interest for $951 of credit.[45] Title lenders have recently taken a more high-tech approach to ensuring repayment. Rather than

[41]According to a study done by the Center for Responsible Lending, the median loan-to-value ratio among borrowers is 26 percent. In other words, the loan received is worth less than a third of the collateral. Susanna Montezemolo, "The State of Lending in America and its Impact on U.S. Households: Car-Title Lending," *Center for Responsible Lending*, July 2013, 3, accessed March 17, 2015, www.responsiblelending.org/state-of-lending/reports/7-Car-Title-Loans.pdf.

[42]Ibid., 16 (explaining the difference between title and payday loans). See also Delvin Davis et al., "Driven to Disaster: Car-Title Lending and Its Impact on Consumers," *Center for Responsible Lending*, February 28, 2013, 2, accessed March 17, 2015, www.responsiblelending.org/other-consumer-loans/car-title-loans/research-analysis/CRL-Car-Title-Report-FINAL.pdf (with similar but not identical figures).

[43]Ibid.; States that allow car-title lending include Alabama, Arizona, California, Delaware, Georgia, Kansas, Louisiana, Idaho, Illinois, Mississippi, Missouri, Nevada, New Mexico, South Carolina, South Dakota, Tennessee, Texas, Utah, Virginia, and Wisconsin. Center for Responsible Lending, "Car Title Lending by State," accessed March 17, 2015, www.responsiblelending.org/other-consumer-loans/car-title-loans/tools-resources/car-title-lending-by-state.html.

[44]Jim Hawkins, "Credit on Wheels: The Law and Business of Auto-Title Lending," *Washington and Lee Law Review 69* (2012): 535, 536, accessed March 17, 2015, scholarly-commons.law.wlu.edu/cgi/viewcontent.cgi?article=4272&context=wlulr.

[45]Davis et al., "Driven to Disaster," 2.

having to undergo the costs associated with finding and repossessing a car, many lenders, at the time of borrowing, now install chips in borrowers' vehicles that will remotely disable them.[46] This happened to one borrower whose car was disabled while she was at a shelter hiding from her abusive husband, as well as others whose cars have shut down in dangerous neighborhoods or even on the way to pick up their children from school.

Even pawn loans, the oldest and perhaps least financially ruinous form of fringe loans, exact a high price. The Catholic Church created the first pawnshops in the 1300s in Italy and Spain as a philanthropic venture to lend to the poor. They were motivated to eradicate usury but also had the more sinister goal of eradicating Jewish moneylenders. As such, they extracted involuntary "contributions" from the Jewish lenders to fund the pawn lenders.[47] Today, the borrower takes something of value to the pawnshop and gets a loan worth much less than the value of the item, usually around 20 percent of the value. There is a flat interest on the loan, around 30 percent, which the borrower must pay to retrieve the item within a predetermined period of time—typically, two weeks to one month. The borrower can pay another 30 percent to take out another loan if he or she cannot pay at the end of the term. If a borrower chooses not to pay back the loan principal, the borrower loses the pawned item. Although these loans have very high interest rates, they are not as punishing as other fringe loans because the loss to the borrower is capped at the interest paid each time and the value of the collateral offered. Pawn lenders do not require any credit check or bank account information, as all loans are secured by an item that can be seized.

Many also rely on their future tax returns as a source of credit. These loans, called Refund Anticipation Loans, are high-cost loans secured by a taxpayer's expected refund. The usual term is two weeks, and the average loan is for a few hundred dollars. The borrower pays about 300 percent APR for the ability to receive the tax refund a few weeks early.[48] The tax preparer files the return and collects the refund when it is issued. The borrower walks away with a tax refund reduced by a hefty interest payment, preparation, filing, and finance fees. These fees can be

---

[46]Michael Corkery and Jessica Silver-Greenberg. "Miss a Payment? Good Luck Moving that Car," *New York Times Dealbook*, September 24, 2014, accessed March 17, 2015, dealbook.nytimes.com/2014/09/24/miss-a-payment-good-luck-moving-that-car/.

[47]The United States also had charitable pawn institutions: The Provident Loan Society, established in 1894 with $100,000 provided by the richest men in New York City, was a charitable organization that aimed to "relieve distress through enlightened and liberal lending but also, through competition, to force lower margins on profit-making pawnbrokers." By 1919, it was making more loans than any domestic savings bank with a policy "first, to make small and costly loans and, only second, to make large and profitable ones. It made loans of as little as one dollar [that required minimal collateral]." The fund's humanity was in stark contrast to the pawnbrokers at the time, but due to the nature of the bank's loans, "the truly indigent, almost by definition, were excluded, as they had nothing to pawn." James Grant, *Money of the Mind: How the 1980s Got That Way* (New York: Farrar, Straus and Giroux, 1992), 77, 85, 87.

[48]David K. Randall, "Taxes: Why 'Rapid Refunds' Are Rip-Offs," *Forbes*, February 9, 2010, accessed March 17, 2015, www.forbes.com/2010/02/09/taxes-rapid-refund-personal-finance-refund-anticipation-loans.html.

quite high, anywhere from $150 to $500 per transaction, depending on the lender. Banks provided many of these loans for years, but new laws prohibit them from offering these loans. They are now primarily offered by a few fringe lenders and are unregulated in most states.

The Borrowers

Just who borrows these usurious loans? Studies conducted by the Consumer Financial Protection Bureau, the Federal Deposit Insurance Corporation, the Federal Reserve, and the Pew Charitable Trusts reveal the characteristics of the population that must rely on the fringe-banking industry.[49] To take out a loan, consumers generally provide a paystub, deposit account statement, or other information to document income as part of the application process. Payday borrowers usually have a steady job and must have a bank account. The average payday borrower profile is a white woman who is divorced or separated, does not have a college degree, and is between twenty-five and forty-four years old. Single parents, blacks, Hispanics, and recent immigrants were more likely to use payday loans than other groups. Payday advance customers are also relatively educated, according to one survey (74.4 percent had a high school diploma or some college), with incomes that most would describe as middle class (over half had incomes between $25,000 and $49,999, with an average income of $40,000).[50] The studies clearly indicate that the customer base is not the destitute but those households with low to moderate income.[51] The average loan this borrower needs is only $350, but because none of the high-interest payments on these loans goes toward the principal, the debt can quickly compound.[52]

Payday borrowers are not, as is often assumed, financially illiterate 25 or casual about borrowing under such demanding terms. The reality is that for many of the poor, these loans represent their only access to credit, and they go to them reluctantly. A Pew study found that

[49]Consumer Financial Protection Bureau, "Nashville, TN: Field Hearing on Payday Loans," March 2014, accessed March 17, 2015, youtube/ZpnXG0UdeoQ; CFPB, "Payday Loans and Deposit Advance Products," April 24, 2013, 15; *CFPB White Paper of Initial Data Findings*, accessed March 17, 2015, files.consumerfinance.gov/f/201304_cfpb_payday-dap-whitepaper. pdf; Susan Urahn et al., "Payday Lending in America: Who Borrows, Where They Borrow, and Why," *Pew Charitable Trust*, 2012, 32, accessed March 17, 2015, www.pewtrusts.org/~/media/legacy/uploadedfiles/pcs_assets/2012/PewPaydayLendingReportpdf.pdf.

[50]FDIC, "National Survey of Unbanked and Underbanked Households," *Executive Summary*, September 2012, 5, accessed March 17, 2015, www.fdic.gov/householdsurvey/2012_unbankedreport_execsumm.pdf; Gregory Elliehausen and Edward C. Lawrence, "Payday Advance Credit in America: An Analysis of Consumer Demand," Georgetown University McDonough School of Business Credit Research, monograph no. 35, 2001, 28, 33, accessed March 17, 2015, www.fdic.gov/bank/analytical/cfr/2005/jan/CFRSS_2005_elliehausen.pdf.

[51]John P. Caskey, "Payday Lending: New Research and the Big Question" (working paper no. 10–32, Federal Reserve Bank of Philadelphia, October 2010), accessed March 17, 2015, www.philadelphiafed.org/research-and-data/publications/working-papers/2010/wpl0–32.pdf; Financial Service Centers of America, "Consumer Financial Services Fact Sheet," cited in Christopher S. Fowler et al., "The Geography of Fringe Banking," *Journal of Regional Science* 54 (2014): 690.

[52]Pew Charitable Trusts, "Payday Lending in America, Report 2: How Borrowers Choose and Repay Payday Loans," February 2013, 6, accessed March 17, 2015, www.pewtrusts.org/~/media/Assets/2013/02/20/Pew_Choosing_Borrowing_Payday_Feb2013-(l).pdf.

desperation often influenced the choice to borrow, as 37 percent of borrowers said they have been in such a difficult financial situation that they have taken out a payday loan on any terms offered. To pay off their loans, many of these borrowers (40 percent) turned to friends or family, sold or pawned personal possessions, or took out another type of loan. One in six has used a tax refund to eliminate payday loan debt.[53]

Nor is the borrowing frivolous. Surveys reveal that loans are used to pay for food or rent, but the budget shortfalls are likely due to a variety of setbacks, such as medical emergencies, car repairs, or other unexpected life expenses.[54] Most Americans do not have savings large enough to cover unplanned expenses. Government studies show that over half the households in the United States could not come up with just $400 to cover a medical emergency without having to borrow, and 60 percent lacked enough money to get by for three months.[55] People just do not have a financial buffer large enough to deal with even small emergencies, as shown by the fact that unexpected medical expenses are the number one cause of bankruptcy in the United States.[56]

And for many, incomes have gotten less predictable, as well. Since the 1970s, household incomes have become much more volatile and yet household bills have remained constant. "More than 30 percent of Americans reported spikes and dips in their incomes. Among that group, 42 percent cited an irregular work schedule; an additional 27 percent blamed a span of joblessness or seasonal work."[57]

Financial education has been embraced by policymakers as a way of turning the poor into "responsible" and "empowered" consumers who can use these tools to increase their own welfare. The thinking goes that if consumers would only learn to avoid financial land mines, the poor could ably maneuver through various credit options and avoid harmful products. If they only knew how to manage their money, they would not be so poor!

[53]Ibid., 7.

[54]The Pew survey found that "sixty-nine percent of first-time payday borrowers used the loan to cover a recurring expense, such as utilities, credit card bills, rent or mortgage payments, or food, while 16 percent dealt with an unexpected expense, such as a car repair or emergency medical expense." Ibid., 8. However, the loan may have gone to pay for basics that would have been met by funds diverted to pay for such unexpected events. Thus, these potentially are not loans that people subsist on.

[55]Federal Reserve System, Board of Governors, "Supplemental Appendix to the Report on the Economic Well-Being of U.S. Households in 2013," July 2014, 5, accessed March 17, 2015, www.federalreserve.gov/econresdata/2013-report-economic-well-being-us-households-supplemental-appendix-201407.pdf; A 2011 National Bureau of Economic Research study showed about half of households surveyed reported that they couldn't come up with $2,000 within thirty days in a pinch, even if they turned to relatives for help. Annamaria Lusardi et al., "Financially Fragile Households: Evidence and Implications," (NBER working paper no. 17072, May 2011), accessed March 17, 2015, www.nber.org/papers/w17072; A 2011 FDIC survey put 29.3 percent of households without a savings account. FDIC, "Unbanked and Underbanked Households," 3.

[56]Dan Mangan, "Medical Bills Are the Biggest Cause of U.S. Bankruptcies: Study," CNBC, June 25, 2013, accessed March 17, 2015, www.cnbc.com/id/100840148.

[57]Federal Reserve Board of Governors, "Report on the Economic Well-Being of U.S. Households in 2013," accessed March 17, 2015, www.federalreserve.gov/econresdata/2013-report-economic-well-being-us-households-201407.pdf; www.nytimes.com/2014/12/04/business/unsteady-incomes-keep-millions-of-workers-behind-on-bills-.html, accessed March 17, 2015.

It is not stupidity but rather necessity that drives people to borrow. If lower-cost credit options were available to the poor, wouldn't they use them? A study of payday borrowing showed that payday loan customers searched extensively for preferred credit before deciding on a payday loan. Loan applicants had an average of over five credit inquiries during the twelve months leading up to their initial payday loan application.[58] Research shows that the poor understand debt and the costs of the loans they take out—they weigh options when in need and they choose these loans.[59] In a 2007 California survey, 92 percent of respondents said that they were aware of the fees on their loans before taking them out.[60]

According to the research, financial education simply does not work   30
to discourage this borrowing.[61] This seems obvious. Educating the poor to choose better options must mean that better options exist. Although more education and financial savvy would certainly help all of us make the most of our money, financial education is not what separates the poor and the middle class. Contrast, for example, the financial literacy required by an average middle- to high-income family who puts money into the local bank and perhaps invests any extra money in a 401(k) provided by an employer with someone who is poor and must manage several loans at a time while making small payments on each. Factor in the costs and fees on this person's simple financial transactions, such as cashing a paycheck. Managing multiple loans and fees shows a level of financial literacy that many in the middle class don't have and frankly, don't need. The middle class juggles too—transferring credit card debt from one card to a new one that offers 0 percent APR for six months in the hopes of paying less than 16 percent interest for a while.[62] But in comparison, the middle class seems to be juggling with beanbags, and the poor are juggling with knives. Dipped in poison.

If anything, the pervasive usage of payday lending does not show irresponsibility or ignorance. It just shows that many people need small loans. . . . They borrow to pay for things that are widely considered essential. They borrow with forethought and with care. They are mainstream, ordinary people forced to borrow at the fringe. And fringe lenders are the only ones meeting this large market demand because banks, credit unions, and other mainstream lenders have chosen not to.

[58]Neil Bhutta, Paige Marta Skiba, and Jeremy Tobacman, "Payday Loan Choices and Consequences," *Journal of Money, Credit, and Banking* (forthcoming), 14, accessed March 17, 2015, http://assets.wharton.upenn.edu/~tobacman/papers/Payday%20Loan%20 Choices%20 and%20Consequences.pdf.

[59]Caskey, "Payday Lending"; Elliehausen, "Payday Advance Credit," 45–46.

[60]Applied Management and Planning Group, *2007 Department of Corporations Payday Loan Study*, Report Submitted to California Department of Corporations, December 2007, 57.

[61]For discussion of the muddled empirical evidence, see Annamaria Lusardi and Olivia S. Mitchell, "The Economic Importance of Financial Literacy: Theory and Evidence," *Journal of Economic Literature* 52 (2014): 5, accessed March 17, 2015, www.umass.edu/preferen/You%20Must%20Read%20This/Financial%20Literacy%20JEP%20 2014.pdf.

[62]For example, see Discover's balance transfer offers, www.discover.com/credit-cards/member-benefits/balance-transfer.html, accessed March 17, 2015.

ENGAGING THE TEXT

1. What expenses do you pay by check or credit/debit card, and when do you use cash? How difficult would it be to shift to using only cash or money orders, and why?

2. Using information from this reading selection, draw a financial flow chart for an unbanked person with a minimum-wage job. How might income from the job flow to expenditures like rent, food, healthcare, check cashing, and loan payments? Where and how often would the worker incur the direct or indirect costs of being unbanked?

3. Baradaran claims that banking should be a matter of "political and social concern." She also critiques the way banks have abandoned the idea of serving a community in favor of a model based primarily on profits (para. 9). To what extent do you agree with the notion that banks have a civic duty in addition to a profit motive? Explain why you would or would not support legislation to cap interest rates on credit cards or payday loans, and at what annual percentage rate. What about breaking up sprawling financial institutions that are "too big to fail"?

4. Review the figures in paragraph 15 on the average American's debt. Write a journal entry describing where you stand now in relation to these averages, where you expect to be when you graduate college, and where you expect to be ten years after that. Do you see borrowing as a ladder toward wealth and financial security, or perhaps as a chute of downward mobility?

EXPLORING CONNECTIONS

5. Look ahead to Rutger Bregman's "Why We Should Give Free Money to Everyone" (p. 456). How do you think Bregman might respond to Baradaran's comment that "inexpensive credit will not cure or even reduce poverty" (para. 16)?

6. Read or review Bruce Schneier's "How We Sold Our Souls — and More — to the Internet Giants" (p. 315), which discusses the ways Americans are surveilled by contemporary technology. Explain whether you consider ChexSystems as described by Baradaran a form of surveillance, and discuss whether citizens should have access to ChexSystems data about them.

7. Take a close look at the Troubletown comic on page 405, especially the two panels devoted to banking. How many of the issues Baradaran raises does cartoonist Lloyd Dangle portray? Explain the significance of each detail in these cells, including the facial expressions, the signs, the line of people, the dog, the litter, and the guitar in the window.

EXTENDING THE CRITICAL CONTEXT

8. Research current offers for checking accounts from local banks, noting all requirements and fees. Where do you think these banks expect to turn a profit? Do their requirements and fees offer substantial barriers to low-income citizens?

9. What would it cost in your state to borrow $5,000 in an emergency using a "fringe lender"? Are the annual percentage rates for payday or title loans roughly in line with those Baradaran cites?

10. Search online to identify bank locations and ATMs in your region. Can you find significant differences in how convenient or inconvenient they are in different areas? Does the data you find suggest a geography of social class?

11. Watch "Payday," an episode from the Netflix investigatory series *Dirty Money* (Episode 2, Season 1, 2018). Compare the practices Baradaran describes to those revealed in "Payday" and discuss the film's portrayals of lenders, borrowers, shell companies, race car driving, and social class.

VISUAL PORTFOLIO

READING IMAGES OF INDIVIDUAL OPPORTUNITY

Copyright © Paul D'Amato. Used by permission.

AP Photo/Jacquelyn Martin

a katz/Shutterstock

LUCY NICHOLSON/REUTERS/Newscom

Aaron McCoy/Getty Images

4

Aaron McCoy/Getty Images

David McNew/Getty Images

VISUAL PORTFOLIO
READING IMAGES OF INDIVIDUAL OPPORTUNITY

1. In the photograph of a man repairing novelty items during vocational training (p. 407), what else is going on? What is the man thinking? What is his relationship to his work, to the toys, and to his coworkers? What do you make of the slogan on his T-shirt, "Freedom by any means necessary"?

2. The photo on page 408 shows Treasury Secretary Steven Mnuchin and his wife Louise Linton displaying a sheet of $1 bills bearing his signature. Why do you think this photo went viral in November 2017? How do you interpret the setting and the couple's facial expressions, hair styles, and clothing? What did comedian Andy Richter tweet about the photo? What other responses to this image can you find on the Internet, and what do they suggest about contemporary attitudes toward wealthy people?

3. How do you think the protesters on page 409 would answer the questions posed on their signs? How might Steven Mnuchin (p. 408) answer them? And you?

4. Who are the men waiting for work on page 410, and what life histories do you imagine have brought them to this place? What kinds of work are they are hoping for? Could you find a scene like this in or near your community, and if so, what kind of wages would such workers earn? Which worker do you think is most likely to get hired, and why?

5. Describe your reactions to the photo on page 411 of a homeless man outside a pawn shop. What emotions does it trigger, and what point do you think photographer Aaron McCoy is making in this image? Discuss the low-angle perspective of the photo as well as details like the passersby and the pawn shop's name.

6. Any photo of a child sleeping in a car is likely to be unsettling, but what makes the image on page 412 particularly powerful? What do parents, community, schools, or government agencies "owe" the boy to give him a chance to escape poverty?

7. On November 29, 2016, workers across the United States staged protests on the "Fight for $15 Day of Disruption"—part of a campaign to raise the minimum wage and guarantee union rights. The young woman pictured on page 413 was one of some forty McDonald's restaurant employees arrested for sitting in a Los Angeles intersection after walking off the job. What do you see in her face? What about in the expressions of the arresting officers? What message does the photo send to customers of fast-food chains?

FRAMING CLASS, VICARIOUS LIVING, AND CONSPICUOUS CONSUMPTION

DIANA KENDALL

Diana Kendall, a professor of sociology at Baylor University, has performed an extensive study of how newspapers and TV have portrayed social class in the last half-century. She concludes that the media shape public opinions about the upper, middle, working, and poverty classes by "framing" their stories and their programming in a relatively small number of patterned, predictable, and misleading ways. For example, "the media glorify the upper classes, even when they are accused of wrongdoing." In this excerpt from her award-winning book *Framing Class: Media Representations of Wealth and Poverty in America* (2005), Kendall analyzes how several common media frames communicate cultural messages about social class. Her recent books include *Members Only: Elite Clubs and the Process of Exclusion* (2008) and *Sociology in Our Times: The Essentials* (2015).

> *"The Simple Life 2"—the second season of the reality show, on which the celebutante Paris Hilton and her Best Friend Forever, the professional pop-star-daughter Nicole Richie, are set on a cross-country road trip—once again takes the heaviest of topics and makes them as weightless as a social X-ray.*[1]

THIS STATEMENT BY TELEVISION CRITIC CHOIRE SICHA, in [his] review of FOX TV's reality-based entertainment show *The Simple Life*, sums up a recurring theme of *Framing Class*: The media typically take "the heaviest of topics," such as class and social inequality, and trivialize it. Rather than providing a meaningful analysis of inequality and showing realistic portrayals of life in various social classes, the media either play class differences for laughs or sweep the issue of class under the rug so that important distinctions are rendered invisible. By ignoring class or trivializing it, the media involve themselves in a social construction of reality that rewards the affluent and penalizes the working class and the poor. In real life, Paris Hilton and Nicole Richie are among the richest young women in the world; however, in the world of *The Simple Life*, they can routinely show up somewhere in the city or the country, pretend they are needy, and rely on the kindness of strangers who have few economic resources.

---

[1]Choire Sicha, "They'll Always Have Paris," *New York Times*, June 13, 2004, AR31 [emphasis added]. [All notes are Kendall's, except 26.]

The Simple Life is only one example of many that demonstrate how class is minimized or played for laughs by the media. [Below] I have provided many examples of how class is framed in the media and what messages those framing devices might convey to audiences.... I will look at the sociological implications of how framing contributes to our understanding of class and how it leads to vicarious living and excessive consumerism by many people. I will also discuss reasons why prospects for change in how journalists and television writers portray the various classes are limited. First, we look at two questions: How do media audiences understand and act upon popular culture images or frames? Is class understood differently today because of these frames?

Media Framing and the Performance of Class in Everyday Life

In a mass-mediated culture such as ours, the media do not simply mirror society; rather, they help to shape it and to create cultural perceptions.[2] The blurring between what is real and what is not real encourages people to emulate the upper classes and shun the working class and the poor. Television shows, magazines, and newspapers sell the idea that the only way to get ahead is to identify with the rich and powerful and to live vicariously through them. From sitcoms to reality shows, the media encourage ordinary people to believe that they may rise to fame and fortune; they too can be the next American Idol. Constantly bombarded by stories about the lifestyles of the rich and famous, viewers feel a sense of intimacy with elites, with whom they have little or no contact in their daily lives.[3] According to the social critic bell hooks, we overidentify with the wealthy, because the media socialize us to believe that people in the upper classes are better than we are. The media also suggest that we need have no allegiance to people in our own class or to those who are less fortunate.[4]

Vicarious living — watching how other individuals live rather than experiencing life for ourselves — through media representations of wealth and success is reflected in many people's reading and viewing habits and in their patterns of consumption. According to hooks, television promotes hedonistic consumerism:

> Largely through marketing and advertising, television promoted the myth of the classless society, offering on one hand images of an American dream fulfilled wherein any and everyone can become rich and on the other suggesting that the lived experience of this lack of class hierarchy was expressed by our *equal right to purchase anything we could afford.*[5]

[2]Tim Delaney and Allene Wilcox, "Sports and the Role of the Media," in *Values, Society and Evolution*, ed. Harry Birx and Tim Delaney, 199–215 (Auburn, NY: Legend, 2002).

[3]bell hooks [Gloria Watkins], *Where We Stand: Class Matters* (New York: Routledge, 2000), 73.

[4]hooks, *Where We Stand*, 77.

[5]hooks, *Where We Stand*, 71 [emphasis added].

As hooks suggests, equality does not exist in contemporary society, but media audiences are encouraged to view themselves as having an "equal right" to purchase items that somehow will make them equal to people above them in the social class hierarchy. However, the catch is that we must actually be able to afford these purchases. Manufacturers and the media have dealt with this problem by offering relatively cheap products marketed by wealthy celebrities. Paris Hilton, an heir to the Hilton Hotel fortune, has made millions of dollars by marketing products that give her fans a small "slice" of the good life she enjoys. Middle- and working-class people can purchase jewelry from the Paris Hilton Collection — sterling silver and Swarovski crystal jewelry ranging in price from fifteen to a hundred dollars — and have something that is "like Paris wears." For less than twenty dollars per item, admirers can purchase the Paris Hilton Wall Calendar; a "Paris the Heiress" Paper Doll Book; Hilton's autobiography, *Confessions of an Heiress*; and even her dog's story, *The Tinkerbell Hilton Diaries: My Life Tailing Paris Hilton.* But Hilton is only one of thousands of celebrities who make money by encouraging unnecessary consumerism among people who are inspired by media portrayals of the luxurious and supposedly happy lives of rich celebrities. The title of Hilton's television show, *The Simple Life*, appropriates the image of simple people, such as the working class and poor, who might live happy, meaningful lives, and transfers this image to women whose lives are anything but simple as they flaunt designer clothing and spend collectively millions of dollars on entertainment, travel, and luxuries that can be afforded only by the very wealthy.[6]

How the media frame stories about class *does* make a difference in what we think about other people and how we spend our money. Media frames constitute a mental shortcut (schema) that helps us formulate our thoughts.

The Upper Classes: Affluence and Consumerism for All

Although some media frames show the rich and famous in a negative manner, they still glorify the material possessions and lifestyles of the upper classes. Research has found that people who extensively watch television have exaggerated views of how wealthy most Americans are and what material possessions they own. Studies have also found that extensive television viewing leads to higher rates of spending and to lower savings, presumably because television stimulates consumer desires.[7]

For many years, most media framing of stories about the upper classes has been positive, ranging from *consensus framing* that depicts members of the upper class as being like everyone else, to *admiration*

---

[6]hooks, *Where We Stand*, 72.

[7]Juliet B. Schor, *Born to Buy: The Commercialized Child and the New Consumer Culture* (New York: Scribner, 2004).

framing that portrays them as generous, caring individuals. The frame most closely associated with rampant consumerism is *emulation framing*, which suggests that people in all classes should reward themselves with a few of the perks of the wealthy, such as buying a piece of Paris's line of jewelry. The writers of television shows such as ABC's *Life of Luxury*, E!'s *It's Good to Be . . .* [a wealthy celebrity, such as Nicole Kidman], and VH1's *The Fabulous Life* rely heavily on admiration and price-tag framing, by which the worth of a person is measured by what he or she owns and how many assistants constantly cater to that person's whims. On programs like FOX's *The O.C.* and *North Shore* and NBC's *Las Vegas*, the people with the most expensive limousines, yachts, and jet aircraft are declared the winners in life. Reality shows like *American Idol*, *The Billionaire*, *For Love or Money*, and *The Apprentice* suggest that anyone can move up the class ladder and live like the rich if he or she displays the best looks, greatest talent, or sharpest entrepreneurial skills. It is no wonder that the economist Juliet B. Schor finds that the overriding goal of children age ten to thirteen is to get rich. In response to the statement "I want to make a lot of money when I grow up," 63 percent of the children in Schor's study agreed, whereas only 7 percent disagreed.[8]

Many adults who hope to live the good life simply plunge farther into debt. Many reports show that middle- and working-class American consumers are incurring massive consumer debts as they purchase larger houses, more expensive vehicles, and many other items that are beyond their means. According to one analyst, media portrayals of excessive consumer spending and a bombardment of advertisements by credit-card companies encourage people to load up on debt.[9] With the average U.S. household now spending 13 percent of its after-tax income to *service* debts (not pay off the principal!), people with average incomes who continue to aspire to lives of luxury like those of the upper classes instead may find themselves spending their way into the "poorhouse" with members of the poverty class.

The Poor and Homeless: "Not Me!" — Negative Role Models in the Media

The sharpest contrasts in media portrayals are between depictions of people in the upper classes and depictions of people at the bottom of the class structure. At best, the poor and homeless are portrayed as deserving of our sympathy on holidays or when disaster strikes. In these situations, those in the bottom classes are depicted as being temporarily down on their luck or as working hard to get out of their current situation but in need of public assistance. At worst, however, the poor are blamed for their own problems; stereotypes of the homeless as bums, alcoholics, and drug addicts, caught in a hopeless downward spiral

10

[8]Schor, *Born to Buy*.
[9]Joseph Nocera, *A Piece of the Action: How the Middle Class Joined the Money Class* (New York: Simon and Schuster, 1994).

because of their *individual* pathological behavior, are omnipresent in the media.

For the most part, people at the bottom of the class structure remain out of sight and out of mind for most media audiences. *Thematic framing* depicts the poor and homeless as "faceless" statistics in reports on poverty. *Episodic framing* highlights some problems of the poor but typically does not link their personal situations [and] concerns to such larger societal problems as limited educational opportunities, high rates of unemployment, and jobs that pay depressingly low wages.

The poor do not fare well on television entertainment shows, where writers typically represent them with one-dimensional, bedraggled characters standing on a street corner holding cardboard signs that read "Need money for food." When television writers tackle the issue of homelessness, they often portray the lead characters (who usually are white and relatively affluent) as helpful people, while the poor and homeless are depicted as deviants who might harm themselves or others. Hospital and crime dramas like *E.R.*, *C.S.I.*, and *Law & Order* frequently portray the poor and homeless as "crazy," inebriated in public, or incompetent to provide key information to officials. Television reality shows like *Cops* go so far as to advertise that they provide "footage of debris from the bottom tiers of the urban social order."[10] Statements such as this say a lot about the extent to which television producers, directors, and writers view (or would have us view) the lower classes.

From a sociological perspective, framing of stories about the poor and homeless stands in stark contrast to framing of stories about those in the upper classes, and it suggests that we should distance ourselves from "those people." We are encouraged to view the poor and homeless as the *Other*, the outsider; in the media we find little commonality between our lives and the experiences of people at the bottom of the class hierarchy. As a result, it is easy for us to buy into the dominant ideological construction that views poverty as a problem of individuals, not of the society as a whole, and we may feel justified in our rejection of such people.[11]

The Working Class: Historical Relics and Jokes

The working class and the working poor do not fare much better than the poor and homeless in media representations. The working class is described as "labor," and people in this class are usually nothing more

[10]Karen De Coster and Brad Edmonds, "TV Nation: The Killing of American Brain Cells," Lewrockwell.com, 2004, www.lewrockwell.com/decoster/decoster78.html (accessed July 7, 2004).

[11]Judith Butler ("Performative Acts and Gender Constitution: An Essay in Phenomenology and Feminist Theory," in *Performing Feminisms: Feminist Critical Theory and Theatre*, ed. Sue-Ellen Case [Baltimore: Johns Hopkins University Press, 1990], 270) has described gender identity as performative, noting that social reality is not a given but is continually created as an illusion "through language, gesture, and all manner of symbolic social sign." In this sense, class might also be seen as performative, in that people act out their perceived class location not only in terms of their own class-related identity but in regard to how they treat other people, based on their perceived class position.

than faces in a crowd on television shows. The media portray people who *produce* goods and services as much less interesting than those who *excessively consume* them, and this problem can only grow worse as more of the workers who produce the products are thousands of miles away from us, in nations like China, very remote from the typical American consumer.[12]

Contemporary media coverage carries little information about the working class or its problems. Low wages, lack of benefits, and hazardous working conditions are considered boring and uninteresting topics, except on the public broadcasting networks or an occasional television "news show" such as *60 Minutes* or *20/20*, when some major case of worker abuse has recently been revealed. The most popular portrayal of the working class is *caricature framing*, which depicts people in negative ways, such as being dumb, white trash, buffoons, bigots, or slobs. Many television shows featuring working-class characters play on the idea that the clothing, manners, and speech patterns of the working class are not as good as those of the middle or upper classes. For example, working-class characters (such as Roseanne, the animated Homer Simpson, and *The King of Queens'* Doug) may compare themselves to the middle and upper classes by saying that they are not as "fancy as the rich people." Situation comedy writers have perpetuated working-class stereotypes, and now a number of reality shows, such as *The Swan* and *Extreme Makeover*, try to take "ordinary" working-class people and "improve" them through cosmetic surgery, new clothing, and different hairstyles.

Like their upper-class celebrity counterparts, so-called working-class comedians like Jeff Foxworthy have ridiculed the blue-collar lifestyle. They also have marketed products that make fun of the working class. Foxworthy's website, for example, includes figurines ("little statues for *inside* the house"), redneck cookbooks, Games Rednecks Play, and calendars that make fun of the working class generally. Although some people see these items as humorous ("where's yore sense of humor?"), the real message is that people in the lower classes lack good taste, socially acceptable manners, and above all, middle-class values. If you purchase "redneck" merchandise, you too can make fun of the working class and clearly distance yourself from it.

Middle-Class Framing and Kiddy-Consumerism

Media framing of stories about the middle class tells us that this economic group is the value center and backbone of the nation. *Middle-class values framing* focuses on the values of this class and suggests that they

---

[12]See Thomas Ginsberg, "Union Hopes to Win Over Starbucks Shop Workers," *Austin American-Statesman*, July 2, 2004, D6.

hold the nation together. Early television writers were aware that their shows needed to appeal to middle-class audiences, who were the targeted consumers for the advertisers' products, and middle-class values of honesty, integrity, and hard work were integral ingredients of early sitcoms. However, some contemporary television writers spoof the middle class and poke fun at values supposedly associated with people in this category. The writers of FOX's *Malcolm in the Middle* and *Arrested Development*, for example, focus on the dysfunctions in a fictional middle-class family, including conflicts between husband and wife, between parents and children, and between members of the family and outsiders.

Why do these shows make fun of the middle class? Because corporations that pay for the advertisements want to capture the attention of males between ages eighteen and thirty-nine, and individuals in this category are believed to enjoy laughing at the uptight customs of conventional middle-class families. In other shows, as well, advertisers realize the influence that their programs have on families. That is why they are happy to spend billions of dollars on product placements (such as a Diet Coke can sitting on a person's desk) in the shows and on ads during commercial breaks. In recent research, Schor examined why very young children buy into the consumerism culture and concluded that extensive media exposure to products was a key reason. According to Schor, "More children [in the United States] than anywhere else believe that their clothes and brands describe who they are and define their social status. American kids display more brand affinity than their counterparts anywhere else in the world; indeed, experts describe them as increasingly 'bonded to brands.'"[13]

Part of this bonding occurs through constant television watching and Internet use, as a steady stream of ads targets children and young people. Schor concludes that we face a greater problem than just excessive consumerism. A child's well-being is undermined by the consumer culture: "High consumer involvement is a significant cause of depression, anxiety, low self-esteem, and psychosomatic complaints."[14] Although no similar studies have been conducted to determine the effects of the media's emphasis on wealth and excessive consumerism among adults, it is likely that today's children will take these values with them into adulthood if our society does not first reach the breaking point with respect to consumer debt.

The issue of class in the United States is portrayed in the media 20 not through a realistic assessment of wealth, poverty, or inequality but instead through its patterns of rampant consumerism. The general message remains, one article stated, "We pledge allegiance to the mall."[15]

---

[13]Schor, *Born to Buy*, 13.
[14]Schor, *Born to Buy*, 167.
[15]Louis Uchitelle, "We Pledge Allegiance to the Mall," *New York Times*, December 6, 2004, C12.

Media Framing and Our Distorted View of Inequality

Class clearly permeates media culture and influences our thinking on social inequality. How the media frame stories involving class constitutes a *socially constructed reality* that is not necessarily an accurate reflection of the United States. Because of their pervasive nature, the media have the symbolic capacity to define the world for other people. In turn, readers and viewers gain information from the media that they use to construct a picture of class and inequality—a picture that becomes, at least to them, a realistic representation of where they stand in the class structure, what they should (or should not) aspire to achieve, and whether and why they should view other people as superior, equal, or inferior to themselves.

Because of the media's power to socially construct reality, we must make an effort to find out about the objective nature of class and evaluate social inequality on our own terms. Although postmodern thinkers believe that it is impossible to distinguish between real life and the fictionalized version of reality that is presented by the media, some sociologists argue that we can learn the difference between media images of reality and the actual facts pertaining to wealth, poverty, and inequality. The more we become aware that we are not receiving "raw" information or "just" entertainment from the media, the more we are capable of rationally thinking about how we are represented in media portrayals and what we are being encouraged to do (engage in hedonistic consumerism, for example) by these depictions. The print and electronic media have become extremely adept at framing issues of class in a certain manner, but we still have the ability to develop alternative frames that better explain who we are and what our nation is truly like in regard to class divisions.

The Realities of Class

What are the realities of inequality? The truth is that the rich are getting richer and that the gulf between the rich and the poor continues to widen in the United States. Since the 1990s, the poor have been more likely to stay poor, and the affluent have been more likely to stay affluent. How do we know this? Between 1991 and 2001, the income of the top one-fifth of U.S. families increased by 31 percent; during the same period, the income of the bottom one-fifth of families increased by only 10 percent.[16] The chasm is even wider across racial and ethnic categories; African Americans and Latinos/Latinas are overrepresented among those in the bottom income levels. Over one-half of African American and Latino/Latina households fall within the lowest income categories.

[16]Carmen DeNavas-Walt and Robert W. Cleveland, "Income in the United States: 2002," *U.S. Census Bureau: Current Population Reports*, P60–221 (Washington, DC: U.S. Government Printing Office, 2003).

Wealth inequality is even more pronounced. The super-rich (the top 0.5 percent of U.S. households) own 35 percent of the nation's wealth, with net assets averaging almost nine million dollars. The very rich (the next 0.5 percent of households) own about 7 percent of the nation's wealth, with net assets ranging from $1.4 million to $2.5 million. The rich (9 percent of households) own 30 percent of the wealth, with net assets of a little over four hundred thousand dollars. Meanwhile, everybody else (the bottom 90 percent of households) owns only 28 percent of the nation's wealth. Like income, wealth disparities are greatest across racial and ethnic categories. According to the Census Bureau, the net worth of the average white household in 2000 was more than ten times that of the average African American household and more than eight times that of the average Latino/Latina household. Moreover, in 2002, almost thirty-five million people lived below the official government poverty level of $18,556 for a family of four, an increase of more than one million people in poverty since 2001.[17]

The Realities of Hedonistic Consumerism

Consumerism is a normal part of life; we purchase the things that we 25 need to live. However, hedonistic consumerism goes beyond all necessary and meaningful boundaries. As the word *hedonism* suggests, some people are so caught up in consumerism that this becomes the main reason for their existence, the primary thing that brings them happiness. Such people engage in the self-indulgent pursuit of happiness through what they buy. An example of this extreme was recently reported in the media. When Antoinette Millard was sued by American Express for an allegedly past-due account, she filed a counterclaim against American Express for having provided her with a big-spender's credit card that allowed her to run up bills of nearly a million dollars in luxury stores in New York.[18] Using the "victim defense," Millard claimed that, based on her income, the company should not have solicited her to sign up for the card. Although this appears to be a far-fetched defense (especially in light of some of the facts),[19] it may be characteristic of the lopsided

---

[17]Bernadette D. Proctor and Joseph Dalaker, "Poverty in the United States: 2002," *U.S. Census Bureau: Current Population Reports*, P60–222 (Washington, DC: U.S. Government Printing Office, 2003).

[18]Antoinette Millard, also known as Lisa Walker, allegedly was so caught up in hedonistic consumerism that she created a series of false identities (ranging from being a Saudi princess to being a lawyer, a model, and a wealthy divorcee) and engaged in illegal behavior (such as trying to steal $250,000 from an insurance company by reporting that certain jewelry had been stolen, when she actually had sold it). See Vanessa Grigoriadis, "Her Royal Lie-ness: The So-Called Saudi Princess Was Only One of the Many Identities Lisa Walker Tried On Like Jewelry," *New York Metro*, www.newyorkmetro.com/nymetro/news /people/columns/intelligencer/n_10418 (accessed December 18, 2004); Samuel Maull, "Antoinette Millard Countersues American Express for $2 Million for Allowing Her to Charge $951,000," creditsuit.org/credit.php/blog/comments/antoinette_millard_countersues _american_express_for_2_million_for_allowing (accessed December 18, 2004).

[19]Steve Lohr, "Maybe It's Not All Your Fault," *New York Times*, December 5, 2004, WR1.

thinking of many people who spend much more money than they can hope to earn. Recent studies have shown that the average American household is carrying more than eight thousand dollars in credit-card debt and that (statistically speaking) every fifteen seconds a person in the United States goes bankrupt.[20] Although fixed costs (such as housing, food, and gasoline) have gone up for most families over the past thirty years, these debt-and-bankruptcy statistics in fact result from more people buying items that are beyond their means and cannot properly use anyway. Our consumer expectations for ourselves and our children have risen as the media have continued to attractively portray the "good life" and to bombard us with ads for something else that we *must* have.

Are we Americans actually interested in learning about class and inequality? Do we want to know where we really stand in the U.S. class structure? Although some people may prefer to operate in a climate of denial, media critics believe that more people are finally awakening to biases in the media, particularly when they see vast inconsistencies between media portrayals of class and their everyday lives. According to the sociologists Robert Perrucci and Earl Wysong, "It is apparent that increasing experiences with and knowledge about class-based inequalities among the nonprivileged is fostering a growing awareness of and concerns about the nature and extent of superclass interests, motives, and power in the economic and political arenas."[21] Some individuals are becoming aware of the effect that media biases can have on what they read, see, and hear. A recent Pew Research Center poll, for example, reflects that people in the working class do not unquestioningly accept media information and commentary that preponderantly support the status quo.[22]

Similarly, Perrucci and Wysong note that television can have a paradoxical effect on viewers: It can serve both as a pacifier and as a source of heightened class consciousness. Programs that focus on how much money the very wealthy have may be a source of entertainment for nonelites, but they may also produce antagonism among people who work hard and earn comparatively little, when they see people being paid so much for doing so little work (e.g., the actress who earns seventeen million dollars per film or the sports star who signs a hundred-million-dollar multiyear contract). Even more egregious are individuals who do not work at all but are born into the "right family" and inherit billions of dollars.

Although affluent audiences might prefer that the media industry work to "reinforce and disguise privileged-class interests,"[23] there is a good chance that the United States will become more class conscious and that people will demand more accurate assessments of the

[20]Lohr, "Maybe It's Not All Your Fault."

[21]Robert Perrucci and Earl Wysong, *The New Class Society*, 2nd ed. (Lanham, MD.: Rowman & Littlefield, 2003), 199.

[22]Perrucci and Wysong, *The New Class Society*.

[23]Perrucci and Wysong, *The New Class Society*, 284.

problems we face if more middle- and working-class families see their lifestyles continue to deteriorate in the twenty-first century.

Is Change Likely? Media Realities Support the Status Quo

Will journalists and entertainment writers become more cognizant of class-related issues in news and in television shows? Will they more accurately portray those issues in the future? It is possible that the media will become more aware of class as an important subject to address, but several trends do not bode well for more accurate stories and portrayals of class. Among these are the issues of media ownership and control.

Media Ownership and Senior Management

Media ownership has become increasingly concentrated in recent decades. Massive mergers and acquisitions involving the three major television networks (ABC, CBS, and NBC) have created three media "behemoths" — Viacom, Disney, and General Electric — and the news and entertainment divisions of these networks now constitute only small elements of much larger, more highly diversified corporate structures. Today, these media giants control most of that industry, and a television network is viewed as "just another contributor to the bottom line."[24] As the media scholar Shirley Biagi states, "The central force driving the media business in America is the desire to make money. American media are businesses, vast businesses. The products of these businesses are information and entertainment.... But American media are, above all, profit-centered."[25]

Concentration of media ownership through chains, broadcast networks, cross-media ownership, conglomerates, and vertical integration (when one company controls several related aspects of the same business) are major limitations to change in how class is represented in the news and entertainment industry. Social analysts like Greg Mantsios[26] are pessimistic about the prospects for change, because of the upper-class-based loyalties of media corporate elites:

> It is no wonder Americans cannot think straight about class. The mass media is neither objective, balanced, independent, nor neutral. Those who own and direct the mass media are themselves part of the upper class, and neither they nor the ruling class in general have to conspire to manipulate public opinion. Their interest is in preserving the status quo, and their view of society as fair and equitable comes naturally to them. But their ideology dominates our

[24]Committee of Concerned Journalists, "The State of the News Media 2004," www.journalism.org (accessed June 17, 2004).

[25]Shirley Biagi, *Media Impact: An Introduction to Mass Media* (Belmont, CA.: Wadsworth, 2003), 21.

[26]**Mantsios:** See "Class in America" (p. 347). [Eds.]

society and justifies what is in reality a perverse social order—one
that perpetuates unprecedented elite privilege and power on the
one hand and widespread deprivation on the other.[27]

According to Mantsios, wealthy media shareholders, corporate executives, and political leaders have a vested interest in obscuring class
relations not only because these elites are primarily concerned about
profits but because—being among the "haves" themselves—they do
not see any reason to stir up class-related animosities. Why should they
call attention to the real causes of poverty and inequality and risk the
possibility of causing friction among the classes?

Media executives do not particularly care if the general public criticizes the *content* of popular culture as long as audiences do not begin to
question the superstructure of media ownership and the benefits these
corporations derive from corporate-friendly public policies. According
to the sociologist Karen Sternheimer,

> Media conglomerates have a lot to gain by keeping us focused on
> the popular culture "problem," lest we decide to close some of the
> corporate tax loopholes to fund more social programs.... In short,
> the news media promote media phobia because it doesn't threaten
> the bottom line. Calling for social programs to reduce inequality
> and poverty would.[28]

Although the corporate culture of the media industry may be set
by shareholders and individuals in the top corporate ranks, day-to-day
decisions often rest in the hands of the editor-in-chief (or a person in a
similar role) at a newspaper or a television executive at a local station.
Typically, the goals of these individuals reflect the profit-driven missions of their parent companies and the continual need to generate the
right audiences (often young males between eighteen and thirty-five
years of age) for advertisers. Television commentator Jeff Greenfield
acknowledges this reality: "The most common misconception most
people have about television concerns its product. To the viewer, the
product is the programming. To the television executive, the product is
the audience."[29] The profits of television networks and stations come
from selling advertising, not from producing programs that are accurate
reflections of social life.

Recent trends in the media industry—including concentration of
ownership, a focus on increasing profits, and a move toward less regulation of the media by the federal government—do not offer reassurance
that media representations of class (along with race, gender, age, and
sexual orientation) will be of much concern to corporate shareholders or

---

[27]Gregory Mantsios, "Media Magic: Making Class Invisible," in *Privilege: A Reader*,
ed. Michael S. Kimmel and Abby L. Ferber, 99–109 (Boulder, CO: Westview, 2003), 108.

[28]Karen Sternheimer, *It's Not the Media: The Truth About Pop Culture's Influence on
Children* (Boulder, CO: Westview, 2003), 211.

[29]Quoted in Biagi, *Media Impact*, 170.

executives at the top media giants—unless, of course, this issue becomes related to the bottom line or there is public demand for change, neither of which seems likely. However, it does appear that there is a possibility for change among some journalists and entertainment writers.

Journalists: Constraints and Opportunities

Some analysts divide journalists into the "big time" players—reporters and journalists who are rich, having earned media salaries in the millions and by writing best-selling books (e.g., ABC's Peter Jennings)—and the "everyday" players, who are primarily known in their local or regional media markets.[30] Elite journalists in the first category typically are employed by major television networks (ABC, CBS, and NBC), popular cable news channels (such as CNN and FOX News), or major national newspapers such as the *Wall Street Journal*, *New York Times*, or *USA Today*. These journalists may be influential in national media agenda-setting, whereas the everyday media players, beat reporters, journalists, and middle- to upper-level managers at local newspapers or television stations at best can influence local markets.

Some of these individuals — at either level — are deeply concerned about the state of journalism in this country, as one recent Pew Research Center for the People and the Press study of 547 national and local reporters, editors, and executives found.[31] One of the major concerns among these journalists was that the economic behavior of their companies was eroding the quality of journalism in the United States. By way of example, some journalists believe that business pressures in the media industry are making the news "thinner and shallower."[32] Journalists are also concerned that the news media pay "too little attention ... to complex issues."[33] However, a disturbing finding in the Pew study was that some journalists believe that news content is becoming more shallow because that is what the public *wants*. This cynical view may become a self-fulfilling prophecy that leads journalists to produce a shallower product, based on the mistaken belief that the public cannot handle anything else.[34]

---

[30]One study identified the "typical journalist" as "a white Protestant male who has a bachelor's degree from a public college, is married, 36 years old, earns about $31,000 a year, has worked in journalism for about 12 years, does not belong to a journalism association, and works for a medium-sized (42 journalists), group-owned daily newspaper" (Weaver and Wilhoit 1996). Of course, many journalists today are white women, people of color, non-Protestants, and individuals who are between the ages of 45 and 54 (Committee of Concerned Journalists, "The State of the News Media 2004").

[31]Pew Center for Civic Journalism, "Finding Third Places: Other Voices, Different Stories," 2004, www.pewcenter.org/doingcj/videos/thirdplaces.html (accessed July 6, 2004).

[32]Bill Kovach, Tom Rosenstiel, and Amy Mitchell, "A Crisis of Confidence: A Commentary on the Findings," Pew Research Center for the People and the Press, 2004, www. stateofthenewsmedia.org/prc.pdf (accessed July 6, 2004), 27.

[33]Kovach, Rosenstiel, and Mitchell, "A Crisis of Confidence," 29.

[34]Kovach, Rosenstiel, and Mitchell, "A Crisis of Confidence."

Despite all this, some opportunities do exist in the local and national news for *civic journalism*— "a belief that journalism has an obligation to public life — an obligation that goes beyond just telling the news or unloading lots of facts."[35] Civic journalism is rooted in the assumption that journalism has the ability either to empower a community or to help disable it. Based on a civic journalism perspective, a news reporter gathering information for a story has an opportunity to introduce other voices beyond those of the typical mainstream spokesperson called upon to discuss a specific issue such as the loss of jobs in a community or the growing problem of homelessness. Just as more journalists have become aware of the importance of fair and accurate representations of people based on race, gender, age, disability, and sexual orientation, it may be possible to improve media representations of class. Rather than pitting the middle class against the working class and the poor, for example, the media might frame stories in such a way as to increase people's awareness of their shared concerns in a nation where the upper class typically is portrayed as more important and more deserving than the average citizen.

The process of civic journalism encourages journalists to rethink their use of frames. Choosing a specific frame for a story is "the most powerful decision a journalist will make."[36] As journalists become more aware that the media are more than neutral storytelling devices, perhaps more of them will develop alternative frames that look deeply into a community of interest (which might include the class-based realities of neighborhoods) to see "how the community interacts with, interrelates to, and potentially solves a pressing community problem." By asking "What is the essence of this story?" rather than "What is the conflict value of this story?" journalists might be less intent, for example, on pitting the indigenous U.S. working class against more recent immigrants or confronting unionized workers with their nonunionized counterparts. Stories that stress conflict have winners and losers, victors and villains; they suggest that people must compete, rather than cooperate, across class lines.[37] An exploration of other types of framing devices might produce better results in showing how social mobility does or does not work in the U.S. stratification system — highlighting, for example, what an individual's real chances are for moving up the class ladder (as is promised in much of the jargon about the rich and famous).

Advocates of civic journalism suggest that two practices might help journalists do a better job of framing in the public interest: *public listening* and *civic mapping*. Public listening refers to "the ability of

[35]Pew Center for Civic Journalism, "Finding Third Places."

[36]Steve Smith, "Developing New Reflexes in Framing Stories," Pew Center for Civic Journalism, 1997, www.pewcenter.org/doingcj/civiccat/displayCivcat.php?id=97 (accessed July 3, 2004).

[37]Richard Harwood, "Framing a Story: What's It About?" Pew Center for Civic Journalism, 2004, www.pewcenter.org/doingcj/videos/framing.html (accessed July 3, 2004).

journalists to listen with open minds and open ears; to understand what people are really saying."[38] Journalists engaged in public listening would be less interested in getting "superficial quotes or sound bites" and instead would move more deeply into the conversations that are actually taking place. Journalists would use open-ended questions in their interviews, by which they could look more deeply into people's hopes, fears, and values, rather than asking closed-ended questions to which the only allowable response choices are "yes/no" or "agree/disagree"—answers that in effect quickly (and superficially) gauge an individual's opinion on a topic. When journalists use civic mapping, they seek out underlying community concerns through discussions with people. They attempt to look beneath the surface of current public discourse on an issue. Mapping helps journalists learn about the ideas, attitudes, and opinions that really exist among diverse groups of people, not just "public opinion" or politicians' views of what is happening.

By seeking out *third places* where they can find "other voices" and hear "different stories," journalists may learn more about people from diverse backgrounds and find out what they are actually thinking and experiencing.[39] A "third place" is a location where people gather and often end up talking about things that are important to them. According to the sociologist Ray Oldenburg, the third place is "a great variety of public places that host the regular, voluntary, informal, and happily anticipated gatherings of individuals beyond the realms of home and work."[40] If the first place is the home, and the second place is the work setting, then the third place includes such locations as churches, community centers, cafes, coffee shops, bookstores, bars, and other places where people informally gather. As journalists join in the conversation, they can learn what everyday people are thinking about a social issue such as tax cuts for the wealthy. They can also find out what concerns people have and what they think contributes to such problems as neighborhood deterioration.

In addition to listening to other voices and seeking out different stories in third places, journalists might look more systematically at how changes in public policies—such as in tax laws, welfare initiatives, or policies that affect publicly funded child care or public housing—might affect people in various class locations. What are the political and business pressures behind key policy decisions like these? How do policies affect the middle class? The working class? Others? For example, what part does class play in perceptions about local law enforcement agencies? How are police officers viewed in small, affluent incorporated cities that have their own police departments, as compared to low-income neighborhoods of the bigger cities? While wealthy residents in the smaller cities may view police officers as "employees" who do their

---

[38]Smith, "Developing New Reflexes in Framing Stories."
[39]Pew Center for Civic Journalism, "Finding Third Places."
[40]Ray Oldenburg, *The Great Good Place: Cafés, Coffee Shops, Bookstores, Bars, Hair Salons and Other Hangouts at the Heart of a Community* (New York: Marlowe, 1999), 16.

bidding (such as prohibiting the "wrong kind of people" from entering their city limits at night), in some low-income sectors of larger cities the police may be viewed as "oppressors" or as "racists" who contribute to, rather than reduce, problems of lawlessness and crime in the community. Journalists who practice civic journalism might look beyond typical framing devices to tell a more compelling story about how the intersections of race *and* class produce a unique chemistry between citizens and law enforcement officials. In this way, journalists would not be using taken-for-granted framing devices that have previously been employed to "explain" what is happening in these communities.

Given current constraints on the media, including the fact that much of the new investment in journalism today is being spent on disseminating the news rather than on collecting it,[41] there is room for only cautious optimism that some journalists will break out of the standard reflexive mode to explore the microscopic realities of class at the level where people live, and at the macroscopic level of society, where corporate and governmental elites make important decisions that affect everyone else.

Some media analysts believe that greater awareness of class-related realities in the media would strengthen the democratic process in the United States. According to Mantsios, "A mass media that did not have its own class interests in preserving the status quo would acknowledge that inordinate wealth and power undermine democracy and that a 'free market' economy can ravage a people and their communities."[42] It remains to be seen, however, whether organizations like the Project for Excellence in Journalism and the Committee of Concerned Journalists will be successful in their efforts to encourage journalists to move beyond the standard reflexive mode so that they will use new frames that more accurately reflect class-based realities.

Like journalists, many television entertainment writers could look for better ways to frame stories. However, these writers are also beleaguered by changes in the media environment, including new threats to their economic security from reality shows that typically do not employ in-house or freelance writers like continuing series do. As a result, it has become increasingly difficult for entertainment writers to stay gainfully employed, let alone bring new ideas into television entertainment.[43]

We cannot assume that most journalists and television writers are in a position to change media portrayals of class and inequality; however, in the final analysis, the responsibility rests with each of us to evaluate the media and to treat it as only one, limited, source of information and entertainment in our lives. For the sake of our children and grandchildren, we must balance the perspectives we gain from the media with our own lived experiences and use a wider sociological lens to look at

45

[41]Committee of Concerned Journalists, "The State of the News Media 2004."

[42]Mantsios, "Media Magic," 108.

[43]"So You Wanna Be a Sitcom Writer?" soyouwanna.com, 2004, www.soyouwanna.com/site/syws/sitcom/sitcom.html (accessed July 7, 2004).

what is going on around us in everyday life. Some analysts believe that the media amuse and lull audiences rather than stimulating them to think, but we must not become complacent, thinking that everything is all right as our society and world become increasingly divided between the "haves" and the "have nots."[44] If the media industry persists in retaining the same old frames for class, it will behoove each of us as readers and viewers to break out of those frames and more thoroughly explore these issues on our own.

Bibliography

Biagi, Shirley. *Media Impact: An Introduction to Mass Media.* Belmont, CA: Wadsworth, 2003.

Butler, Judith. "Performative Acts and Gender Constitution: An Essay in Phenomenology and Feminist Theory." In *Performing Feminisms: Feminist Critical Theory and Theatre.* Edited by Sue-Ellen Case. Baltimore: Johns Hopkins University Press, 1990.

Committee of Concerned Journalists. "The State of the News Media 2004." www.journalism.org (accessed June 17, 2004).

De Coster, Karen, and Brad Edmonds. Lewrockwell.com, 2003. "TV Nation: The Killing of American Brain Cells." www.lewrockwell.com/decoster/decoster78.html (accessed July 7, 2004).

Delaney, Tim, and Allene Wilcox. "Sports and the Role of the Media." In *Values, Society and Evolution,* edited by Harry Birx and Tim Delaney, 199–215. Auburn, NY: Legend, 2002.

DeNavas-Walt, Carmen, and Robert W. Cleveland. "Income in the United States: 2002." *U.S. Census Bureau: Current Population Reports,* P60–221. Washington, DC: U.S. Government Printing Office, 2003.

Ginsberg, Thomas. "Union Hopes to Win Over Starbucks Shop Workers." *Austin American-Statesman,* July 2, 2004, D6.

Grigoriadis, Vanessa. "Her Royal Lie-ness: The So-Called Saudi Princess Was Only One of the Many Identities Lisa Walker Tried On Like Jewelry." *New York Metro.* www.newyorkmetro.com/nymetro/news/people/columns/intelligencer/n_10418 (accessed December 18, 2004).

Harwood, Richard. "Framing a Story: What's It Really About?" Pew Center for Civic Journalism, 2004. www.pewcenter.org/doingcj/videos/framing.html (accessed July 3, 2004).

hooks, bell [Gloria Watkins]. *Where We Stand: Class Matters.* New York: Routledge, 2000.

Kovach, Bill, Tom Rosenstiel, and Amy Mitchell. "A Crisis of Confidence: A Commentary on the Findings." Pew Research Center for the People and the Press, 2004. www.stateofthenewsmedia.org/prc.pdf (accessed July 6, 2004).

Mantsios, Gregory. "Media Magic: Making Class Invisible." In *Privilege: A Reader,* edited by Michael S. Kimmel and Abby L. Ferber, 99–109. Boulder, CO: Westview, 2003.

Maull, Samuel. "Antoinette Millard Countersues American Express for $2 Million for Allowing Her to Charge $951,000." creditsuit.org/credit.php/blog/comments/antoinette_millard_countersues_american_express_for_2_million_for_allowing (accessed December 18, 2004).

[44]Sternheimer, *It's Not the Media.*

Nocera, Joseph. *A Piece of the Action: How the Middle Class Joined the Money Class.* New York: Simon and Schuster, 1994.

Oldenburg, Ray. *The Great Good Place: Cafés, Coffee Shops, Bookstores, Bars Hair Salons and Other Hangouts at the Heart of a Community.* New York: Marlowe, 1999.

Perrucci, Robert, and Earl Wysong. *The New Class Society.* 2nd edition. Lanham, MD: Rowman & Littlefield, 2003.

Pew Center for Civic Journalism. 2004, "Finding Third Places: Other Voices, Different Stories." www.pewcenter.org/doingcj/videos/thirdplaces.html (accessed July 6, 2004).

Proctor, Bernadette D., and Joseph Dalaker. "Poverty in the United States: 2002." *U.S. Census Bureau: Current Population Reports*, P60–22. Washington, DC: U.S. Government Printing Office, 2003.

Schor, Juliet B. *Born to Buy: The Commercialized Child and the New Consumer Culture.* New York: Scribner, 2004.

Sicha, Choire. "They'll Always Have Paris." *New York Times*, June 13, 2004, AR31, AR41.

Smith, Steve. "Developing New Reflexes in Framing Stories." Pew Center for Civic Journalism, 1997. www.pewcenter.org/doingcj/civiccat/displayCivcat.php?id=97 (accessed July 3, 2004).

"So You Wanna Be a Sitcom Writer?" soyouwanna.com, 2004. www.soyouwanna.com/site/syws/sitcom/sitcom.html (accessed July 7, 2004).

Sternheimer, Karen. *It's Not the Media: The Truth About Pop Culture's Influence on Children.* Boulder, CO: Westview, 2003.

Uchitelle, Louis. "We Pledge Allegiance to the Mall." *New York Times*, December 6, 2004, C12.

Weaver, David H., and G. Cleveland Wilhoit. *The American Journalist in the 1990s.* Mahwah, NJ: Lawrence Erlbaum, 1996.

ENGAGING THE TEXT

1. Debate Kendall's assertion that "the media do not simply mirror society; rather, they help to shape it and to create cultural perceptions" (para. 3). Do you agree with Kendall's claim that the media distort our perceptions of social inequality? Do you think that watching TV inclines Americans to run up credit card debt?

2. Review Kendall's explanation of why middle- and working-class people sometimes buy items beyond their means, particularly items associated with wealthy celebrities. Do you agree that this behavior is best understood as "vicarious living" and "unnecessary consumerism"? In small groups, brainstorm lists of purchases you think exemplify hedonistic or unnecessary consumerism. What does hedonistic consumerism look like in a college setting?

3. Kendall says the media use "thematic framing" and "episodic framing" in portraying poor Americans. Define these terms in your own words and discuss whether the media typically portray the poor as "deviant" or "other."

4. According to Kendall, how do media representations of the working class and the middle class differ? Do you see evidence of this difference in the shows she mentions or in others you are familiar with?

5. What does Kendall mean by "civic journalism" (para. 37)? Why is she pessimistic about the future of civic journalism in national news organizations? Do you see any evidence of such journalism in your local news outlets?

EXPLORING CONNECTIONS

6. Imagine what "Looking for Work" (p. 20) might look like if it were turned into a TV episode. Keeping Kendall's observations in mind, how do you think TV might frame Gary Soto's narrative about social class?

7. Review the Visual Portfolio (pp. 407–413) and discuss each image in terms of frames — both the literal framing of the photograph and the interpretive framing of the settings, events, and people pictured. To what extent do the photos endorse or challenge common media images or assumptions?

EXTENDING THE CRITICAL CONTEXT

8. Review Kendall's definitions of consensus framing, admiration framing, emulation framing, and price-tag framing. Then watch one of the TV shows she mentions in paragraph 8 or a similar current show and look for evidence of these framing devices. Discuss with classmates how prominent these frames seem to be in contemporary TV programs.

9. Study the design of several social media sites such as Facebook, Instagram, Twitter, Reddit, Tumblr, Pinterest, LinkedIn and Ello — how they look, what they promise, and what users they seem to be targeting. Do these sites seem neutral in terms of class, or do they reproduce the kinds of media bias that Kendall discusses in her essay?

FROM *RESET: MY FIGHT FOR INCLUSION AND LASTING CHANGE*

ELLEN K. PAO

The subtitle of *Reset* identifies the themes of this reading. Ellen Pao is fighting for the inclusion and fair treatment of women at the highest levels of business, finance, and tech. This means diversity in hiring, a genuine chance at promotion, equitable compensation, and a work environment free of sexual harassment. Pao recounts the experiences that eventually led her to file a gender discrimination suit against Kleiner Perkins, one of Silicon Valley's most prominent venture capital (VC) firms. These firms are, in Pao's words, "the cash engine that fuels the tech industry"—they supply entrepreneurs with the money and guidance needed to turn an idea into a profitable company. As an early investor in Amazon, Google, Sun Microsystems, Genentech, Airbnb, and many other companies, Kleiner Perkins was a prestigious and lucrative place to work, but Pao found the environment distinctly unfriendly to women. Pao (b. 1970) holds a degree in electrical engineering from Princeton and business and law degrees from Harvard. She is the former CEO of Reddit, cofounder of the nonprofit Project Include, and Chief Diversity and Inclusion Officer at the Kapor Center for Social Impact. *Reset* was shortlisted for the 2017 *Financial Times* and McKinsey Business Book of the Year.

THE YEAR 2008 WAS A GREAT ONE for me personally. Right around the anniversary of when we met, Buddy and I had a beautiful daughter. I worked through the day on Friday, played tennis on Saturday, and our baby was born on Monday. She was everything I'd ever hoped for.

Becoming a mother changed me forever. I was also blessed with an astoundingly easy baby. She ate, she slept, she was happy. I avoided first-time-parent jitters by asking advice only from people who had two or more kids (and were thus more mellow—and more efficient). We found two great nannies who were careful and loving—thank goodness, because my job had no flexibility and Buddy's travel schedule was unpredictable, so we needed round-the-clock backup care in place. I was lucky to be able to afford them, but between the childcare and eventually preschool tuition, child-related costs would take up a huge portion of my post-tax salary.

Some partners at work treated my taking maternity leave as the equivalent of abandoning a ship in the middle of a typhoon to get a manicure, so I was nervous about what being a mother would mean for me at the office. . . . I'd arranged to take four months off, but after three I felt pressure to cut my leave short. I missed my baby horribly, but I also felt motivated to work harder than ever to get back to the office and to improve the world my baby would be inheriting.

As happy as I was in my personal life during 2008, it was a terrible year for the tech industry. When I'd first arrived, Silicon Valley was driven by creative techies fueled by love of technology, products, and hard problems. But just a few years later, it was dominated by money guys. When the crash happened in 2008, during my maternity leave, things seemed to change for the worse—even more so than during the crash in 2000. Shortly after, the press was calling Goldman Sachs[1] "a great vampire squid wrapped around the face of humanity," and a few years after that saw the start of the Occupy Wall Street movement.

[1]**Goldman Sachs:** A prominent global banking, investment, and financial management firm. [All notes are the editors'.]

And so ambitious, money-hungry people began turning their attention away from Wall Street and toward the tech sector, idolizing the rapid ascent to billionaire status of the Google founders. Almost overnight, it seemed to me, the amount of money and money types pouring in changed the vibe. Even the new rich people were different. Famous rich guy of the earlier era Bill Gates was known for working hard and then for doing good with his money. His goal was a PC on every desktop. Famous rich guy of the new era Mark Zuckerberg was known for spitefully attending a VC[2] meeting in his pajamas. His goal was making it easier to find women to date. The newest crop of billionaire boys included Evan Spiegel,[3] who sent crude emails about trying to get "sorori-sluts" drunk enough to have sex with his frat brothers, and about peeing on a classmate. His goal was to enable nude selfies with self-deleting photos.

A friend in New York told me that financial types were building out their homes to feature—and I am not exaggerating—panic rooms stocked with automatic weapons and millions of dollars in cash. The New Zealand escape-route stories came a year later, but it seemed like apocalypse fever was spreading. We even created a $200 million Pandemic and Bio Defense Fund to try to prevent it. I kept having more and more conversations like this one:

Very rich VC: *The avian flu is going to kill everyone! We need to stockpile Tamiflu for the managing partners and their families!*

Me *[Laughing]: Only for the managing partners? You do know I'm in the room, right? Where's my hypothetical Tamiflu?*

As a non-managing partner, I would presumably be left to die, flu-ravaged face pressed against the window of the conference room. I also pointed out that it wasn't so cool to hoard Tamiflu, because there was a shortage, and a lot of people who needed it right then, including sick kids, weren't able to get it.

Very rich VC: *Says who?*

Me: *Says my sister.*

VRVC: *Who's your sister?*

Me: *An MD/PhD pediatric oncologist at Memorial Sloan Kettering.*

VRVC: *Whatever. I forgot you come from a family of overachievers. We have to be prepared!*

So many super-rich people I encountered in the corridors of power believed that the rules didn't, or shouldn't, apply to them. Any of the rules. Even back when I was working at Cravath,[4] a trusts-and-estates lawyer told me that one of her clients, a famous public company CEO, said on his deathbed, "Why do *I* have to die?"

---

[2]**VC:** Venture Capital/Venture Capitalist.
[3]**Evan Spiegel:** Internet entrepreneur and cofounder of Snapchat. In 2016 Forbes estimated the twenty-six-year-old's wealth at $4 billion.
[4]**Cravath:** The U.S. law firm Cravath, Swaine, and Moore.

Out in the rest of the world, inclusion seemed to be on the march. Gay marriage was becoming legal in more and more states. But in Silicon Valley, the culture seemed to be getting worse and worse. Maybe I was more sensitive to it because now I had a daughter, but also I saw a shamelessness about the way they left people out, as if they knew no one would ever object or ask them to change. Their arrogance began to grate on me, and every change that came to the office seemed to make it harder for me to do my job. And I was starting to notice that it wasn't just me—it was happening to the other women partners, too.

After a while, the few women left were all treading water, just trying   10 to get by as our ranks thinned and progress got harder. The attrition I had seen in engineering school was even greater in tech and greatest in VC. We were wondering: *Is it just me? Is it possible that I am really too ambitious while being too quiet while being too aggressive while being unlikable? Are my elbows too sharp? Am I not promoting myself enough, or am I too self-promotional? Am I not funny enough or not serious enough? Am I not working hard enough? Do I belong?*

* * *

In the spring of 2011, I started voicing concerns again. I told Juliet[5] I was not given opportunities to succeed. She responded that the growing firm was not a great fit for my "quiet thoughtfulness"—or, unfortunately, she added, for women in general. When I shared my concerns with John,[6] including about the all-male dinners and women's exclusion from interviewing partner candidates, I got a meager response.

The last interviews I had been involved in had been for a search led by an outside recruiter for another junior partner in 2009, and the interview spreadsheet confirmed the firm's bias: Only three out of the approximately thirty-seven candidates on the list were women, and only two women were invited to interview. The notes contained information regarding the candidates' gender, age, marital status, race, and ethnicity. The Kleiner partners' written feedback on one candidate indicated that she was very strong and had important skills and knowledge missing from the team, but added that she was rejected because of her age. She wasn't much older than me, but was a lot older than the firm's coveted twenty-six-year-old target hire. The reasons for passing on the second woman were equally troubling; she was very much liked by the team, but "too Eastern European."

At around the same time, I was interviewing CEO candidates for one of John's companies. There was some vagueness about why one otherwise strong candidate had left his last role. We were trying to dig in, with little success. It seemed as if the candidate may have been involved in some form of harassment at the firm, but it wasn't clear how.

---

[5]**Juliet:** Juliet de Baubigny, a corporate recruiter who helped bring Pao to Kleiner.
[6]**John:** John Doerr, a managing partner at Kleiner who oversaw the firm's investments in Genentech, Intuit, Amazon, Netscape, and Google, among others.

I had a good relationship with the other VC involved in the search, and so I asked him how he thought about it. He told me that in all the years he'd been a CEO, only two employees had raised discrimination or harassment issues at his company.

"It was interesting," he said, "because the two incidents were reported only a week apart. The first person, it was clear it was true. She had told two other people in the company, which *obviously* you would do if you were harassed. We got rid of the guy. But the second one? It came after a bad performance review. She had never told anybody she worked with before that. So it was clearly false."

I just about had a heart attack. *Holy shit,* I thought. *I haven't told any of my peers about Ajit*[7] *blackballing me after we broke up, and my experiences were true, so maybe I should go tell some people.* I ended up telling two women partners and Randy.[8] The first woman was super supportive. I liked her because she was always direct and straight with me, and she had shared helpful advice since I started at Kleiner, ranging from explanations on how Kleiner worked to parenting advice and even book recommendations when I had my daughter. Talking about Ajit was awkward, but afterward I actually felt better that I had told someone in the office. The second person was Randy, the culture guru and my mentor. He told me he didn't have any advice for me and not to mention it again: "I never heard this," he said as he folded his arms and pursed his lips. So I went to fellow junior partner Trae Vassallo. Telling her opened up a longer conversation.

Trae had been a gymnast and was very hard-working; she was enthusiastic about everything, cheerful and willing to do everything asked of her — well, almost. We often were the last to leave the office at night, so we'd chat about our projects, our families, our health, our struggles in the office. She and I commiserated about how difficult it was to work with Randy — his need to take credit and companies, his difficulty connecting with CEOs, his my-way-or-the-highway approach to compromise, and his political nature. . . .

Those conversations made me feel like I could trust Trae. When I told her about Ajit, she grew uncharacteristically quiet. Then she said something I never expected: She had been harassed by Ajit, too. She had fretted that it was her fault, and she was still very upset more than a year later. When Ajit had asked her out for drinks to talk shop, she had been happily pregnant though hadn't announced it yet, but in the course of the evening he started touching her with his leg under the table. Then I said something I still feel bad about. I recommended that she shouldn't report it, because I'd reported and had a hard time ever since — and they didn't do anything, anyway.

---

[7]**Ajit:** Ajit Nazre, a Kleiner partner with whom Pao had a "short-lived, sporadic fling" when both were junior partners — and when she did not know he was still living with his wife. In *Reset* Pao describes an increasingly adversarial relationship with Nazre, who was promoted to senior partner in 2007.

[8]**Randy:** Randy Komisar, a managing partner.

Fortunately, Trae didn't take my advice. She reported Ajit's behavior soon after, when she found out Ajit was about to do her review. He had stacked the review with people who didn't know her work well. She also saw what he'd been doing to me since I'd rejected him. She'd rebuffed Ajit and was concerned that he would take revenge on her via her review. . . .

In that round of summer reviews, Kleiner had six junior partners who had worked there for four or more years. The women (Trae, Risa Stack, and I) had twice as many years at Kleiner and twice as much total work experience as the men (Wen, Chi-Hua, and Amol Deshpande). The men were all promoted and none of the women were even considered for promotion, though Trae and I continued to work hard and to hold out hope that things would turn around.

Then, around the end of November, Ajit told Trae that he needed her   20
to go to New York with him for a big due-diligence[9] trip. He sent emails about a dinner with a well-known CEO who might be able to help one of Trae's companies. But when they arrived in New York, Trae saw that the table was set for two at dinner. She learned that no CEO was coming—the trip was just her and Ajit, in a hotel together for the weekend. When she realized what he had planned, she left the restaurant.

Later that night he came to her hotel room in his bathrobe and banged on the door, asking to be let in. Aghast, she eventually had to physically push him out the door. She still seemed traumatized when she told me about her experience a month later, after our December offsite. She said she thought he might be a sociopath. I felt terrible guilt that I had told her not to report him in the first place, and I was glad she'd ignored my advice and spoken up about it. I also felt guilty that I hadn't pushed the firm to get rid of him when I'd realized what kind of guy he was. . . .

When Trae had first reported her concerns about Ajit to Kleiner a year earlier, they told her, just as they told me, that if he did anything more he would be out. So she went to them and disclosed the fake New York trip. Far from its being the final straw, one of the managing partners suggested, "You should feel flattered."

After that conversation, I finally had clarity on the whole situation. For years, partners had promised to build a better culture, to prevent Ajit from harassing women, to help everyone succeed, and to live up to their goal of Kleiner being a meritocracy. I had come to believe that they were unwilling to have the conversations and take the difficult actions to fix these problems. Instead they made promises to mollify us, promises I'm not sure they ever intended to keep. . . .

On January 4, 2012, I sent an email to the COO[10] and managing partners to try to reach a solution, even if that meant my leaving the

---

[9]**due diligence:** The process of vetting a company to assess its strengths and weaknesses before finalizing an investment.

[10]**COO:** The chief operating officer of a company, responsible for its daily operations.

firm. . . . I concluded with a request for an open dialogue on solutions, and for either protection from further ostracism or help with an exit.

I was wrong in assuming Kleiner would take immediate action. After more than a month, the company responded to Trae's and my complaints by putting Ajit on leave, but he continued to participate in meetings, anyway, as if he were still there. The managing partners didn't do anything about it. I learned that Ajit was negotiating for a gigantic severance package. Ultimately, after two tense months, he did leave.

He was able to negotiate for compensation while being kicked out, but my experience as an ongoing employee had been so different. In 2009, I had mentioned to John that I was unhappy that my compensation wasn't in line with what the men around me were getting. I'd been promised the world when he hired me, and again when I'd tried to quit in 2007, but it hadn't happened. I'd thought my request to John was professional and reasoned.

John didn't agree. In fact, he yelled at me in person. He told me that asking for more compensation wasn't a good look. He punctuated his message with an email:

> I strongly recommend you stop complaining about your compensation. Just drop it. . . . It clearly still bugs you, and that attitude of yours is a) no secret and b) damaging to your standing among [our firm's leaders].

That was in 2009. For almost three years, his response had intimidated and shamed me into silence—to the point where I said nothing even when I was denied any share of profits in our next fund, while all the men working on the fund were allocated carry[11] worth at least several million dollars.

It was 2012. I was sick of being patient. Not only weren't things changing, the arrogance seemed to be at a new high: I found out the partners had taken some CEOs and founders on an all-male ski trip, a total boondoggle. They spent $50,000 on the private jet back and forth to Vail, several hundred dollars per person on ski condos, at least three hundred dollars for each ski jacket, not including lift tickets, private ski instructors, meals, drinks, and massages. Chi-Hua[12] later explained that they didn't invite any women, because women probably wouldn't want to share a condo with men. I wondered what other all-male events had taken place that I hadn't even heard about. . . .

Still, there was no sexual-harassment or discrimination policy or training at Kleiner. Still no effort to make the culture more diverse or inclusive. Still I felt like years of my life had been wasted. I thought of Sheryl Sandberg's[13] speech encouraging women in the business world

[11]**carry:** Kleiner's share of any increase in the value of a company it invested in, typically 20 percent to 30 percent of that gain.

[12]**Chi-Hua:** Chi-Hua Chien, a junior partner.

[13]**Sheryl Sandberg:** Chief operating officer of Facebook and author of the best-seller *Lean In: Women, Work, and the Will to Lead.* Pao refers here to Sandberg's 2010 TED talk, "Why We Have Too Few Women Leaders."

to demand our place at the table and to ask for pay equity. The strategy hadn't gone well for me so far in VC, but I was determined to keep trying.

When I spoke to the COO again, he asked how much I wanted in order to quietly leave. I suspected it would take around $10 million to wake up the firm and prevent future problems, and I imagined that was in the ballpark of what Ajit would be given. And I knew that amount wouldn't break them but would hurt. They were billionaires and routinely loaned out amounts like $18 million. That's the equivalent of $1,800 if you have $100,000, or $180 if you have $10,000. It's annoying, but it won't wreck you.

"I want no less than what Ajit gets," I said. The COO gasped. . . .

Finally, after weeks had passed with no news of any changes, I told John I was filing a claim with the California Department of Fair Employment and Housing, based on the lack of responsiveness of the firm to my years of claims, the poor quality of the investigation into the serial harassment and related retaliation, the lack of a response in the form of any kind of sexual-harassment policy, and the bigger issues of culture and inclusion that were being ignored. That was in March 2012.

I quietly filed a lawsuit directly against Kleiner in May; I saw the lawsuit described in the press several days later. I suspected that Chi-Hua, who had just been on a conference panel with the reporter, leaked the story himself. . . .

In response to my suit, Kleiner hired a powerful crisis-management PR firm. Companies hire them when the shit hits the fan. These firms can be paid to do things that you don't want to do—and Brunswick[14] was known for it. On their website, they bragged about having troll farms— "integrated networks of influence" used in part for "reputation management" —and I believe they enlisted one to defame me online. Dozens, then thousands, of messages a day derided me as bad at my job, crazy, an embarrassment. This company that I had given years of my life to, that I had made millions for, was crucifying me publicly. Repeatedly, Kleiner was quoted as calling me a "poor performer"; on their website they said I was making "false allegations" and "unfounded claims," and they went out of their way to criticize me to the press, leading to a slew of negative publicity that would culminate in an online *Vanity Fair* hit piece insinuating that Buddy was gay, a fraud, and a fake husband.

Everywhere I looked, strangers on the Internet were calling me a bad employee. *Look at the praise I got before I complained*, I imagined telling them. They were calling my marriage a sham. *Tell that to our baby*, I thought. Even in the sonogram she looked like Buddy. They said I was money-grubbing. *Can you name anyone in the venture capital industry who is less money-grubbing than I am?* I wanted to ask these writers.

---

[14]**Brunswick:** The Brunswick Group, a global partnership that advises businesses about such issues as mergers and acquisitions, public relations, and crisis management.

I work almost every waking minute, and I can't even remember the last time I bought anything for myself. Everyone I work for has multiple jets!

I tried to stay focused on my personal life. Buddy and I were over the moon that our daughter was so happy and healthy and that, after a lot of trying, I was pregnant with our second child.

Still, the negativity wore me down. I was so tired, and the barrage of anger was so relentless that I began to sleep even less than usual. I barely ate. I kept going to work day after day, even though I knew most of the partners didn't want me there. I was invited to fewer and fewer meetings and sent fewer and fewer emails. I spent almost all my time in the office alone, except for Monday meetings and occasional visits from people outside Kleiner. . . .

Partners would not greet me when we crossed paths, much less make eye contact. Hallway conversations would pause until I passed. When I sat down near coworkers, they would sometimes get up, gather their notebooks and coffee mugs, and move to other chairs. Trae and I moved our chats outside the office; we would leave five minutes apart so no one would know. Eventually even that got too uncomfortable. That feeling of being unwanted, unwelcomed, and excluded was exceedingly painful.

Then in June, during a regular pregnancy checkup, my doctor looked at the sonogram and I could tell something was wrong. He called me into his office and leaned across his big wooden desk to gently let me know that I'd had a miscarriage.

"When I saw all the horrible things being said about you, I was traveling in Russia, and I was worried about you and the baby," my doctor said, referring to an article in *The New York Times* earlier that month. The article harkened back to the dark ages: An expert was quoted saying he was skeptical about my claims because he hadn't ever heard of mistreatment of women in Silicon Valley, and anonymous sources asked why I didn't leave after such poor treatment. "Stress can be a correlating factor, and you've certainly had plenty of that. I'm so sorry."

I felt, in that moment, that Kleiner had taken everything from me: They had taken all my time and energy for seven years. They had taken my dignity by refusing to listen to me. They had championed a man who had sexually harassed me and at least one or two other women and had promoted him over us. Now I felt they had taken my chance to have another child. I wanted more than anything to leave that terrible place. Crumpled in my doctor's office, I also felt more determined to make things better for other women.

* * *

For all the talk about how Kleiner was a family, women never seemed to succeed there. For all the company's pride about the women they'd brought in, very few of them were happy, and almost none of them stayed.

The Kleiner higher-ups acted as if the dearth of women was a huge mystery. Some people passed it off as biological. Others said it had something to do with maternal clocks, a burning desire to "opt out." But I was in those rooms for nearly a decade and I could have told them, if they had asked, why the women never lasted. It wasn't a mystery and it had nothing to do with our unbridled desire for babies.

The real reason was: The system is designed to keep us out. These 45 are rooms full of white heterosexual men who want to keep acting like rooms full of white heterosexual men, and so either they continue to do so, creating a squirm-inducing experience for the rest of us, or they shut down when people of color or women enter the room and resent having to change their behavior.

We are either silenced or we are seen as buzzkills. We are either left out of the social network that leads to power—the strip clubs and the steak dinners and the all-male ski trips—and so we don't fit in, or our presence leads to changes in the way things are done, and that causes anger, which means we *still* don't fit in. If you talk, you talk too much. If you don't talk, you're too quiet. You don't own the room. If you want to protect your work, you're not a team player. Your elbows are too sharp. You're too aggressive. If you don't protect your work, you should be leaning in. If you don't negotiate, you're underpaid. If you do negotiate, you're complaining. If you want a promotion, you're overreaching. If you don't ask for a promotion, you get assigned all the unwanted tasks. The same goes when asking for a raise.

There is no way to win, and you're subject to constant gaslighting.[15] When you stand up for yourself, there are fifteen reasons why you don't deserve what you're asking for. You're whining. You don't appreciate what you have. There is this steady drumbeat of: *We let you in here even though you don't belong! Be grateful. Just drop it.*

The internal bias was also directed externally. One woman partner told me that she was reluctant to bring women CEOs in to pitch to Kleiner partners, because she knew they faced much higher bars for investment. Two outsiders—including one male founder—complained to me about how Kleiner talked about women in a sexist way. Unfortunately, they're not the only ones. I've heard too many stories from women CEOs about their struggles to be treated fairly when asking VCs for funding. They get talked over, interrupted, ignored, leered at, and propositioned. And I've heard too many stories from men in those rooms—one of whom declared himself a feminist after watching his CEO beaten down in those conversations. One VC asked an entrepreneur to babysit his kids—and I am positive he's not the one in charge of childcare in his family.

I felt confident that if anyone asked, I could suggest how to dismantle this Catch-22-based system, how to create an inclusive workplace,

---

[15]**gaslighting:** Psychological manipulation whose goal is to undermine another person's memory, perception, or even sanity.

NEXT CHAPTER: THE PERV STAGES HIS "COMEBACK"

how to make it a real family. I would say that there has to be a path to victory for every kind of person, not just guys who like golf and skiing and good scotch, who all went to the same schools. I would say that you do business during business hours, you listen to each other, and you find ways to work as a team rather than as cutthroat competitors; you don't get rewarded for screwing over other people, especially the quietest or least connected people. And I would say that, at the bare minimum, when you have a man who is behaving in a predatory, manipulative fashion toward multiple women in your "family," and you're hearing worrisome things about him over the course of several years, by God, you don't tolerate it.

ENGAGING THE TEXT

1. To what extent do you think Pao's career was blocked by a "glass ceiling"? What injurious workplace policies, incidents, and comments does Pao describe? Which of these seem most important to you, and why?

2. Most of us will never own multiple private jets or make million-dollar deals. Does the simple fact of the venture capitalists' extreme wealth prompt an emotional or political reaction in you? Explain.

3. Review paragraphs 10 and 46–47. Would you agree with Pao that women face more difficult balancing acts at work than most men? What experiences from your own employment and education support or challenge Pao's perspective?

4. Review Pao's description of Kleiner's hiring practices in paragraph 12. What, if anything, do you consider problematic here? Do you see any practices that you think might be (or should be) illegal? What would a rejected candidate learn about why she was rejected, and should she have the right to know more? Who inside a company has an obligation to report biased hiring practices?

5. In paragraph 14, what do you make of the CEO's observation concerning the two women who reported sexual harassment at another company — that is, that a woman would "obviously" report such a thing, and that the second woman was lying? Why might someone not report harassment? How closely does the CEO's logic resemble arguments made by supporters of President Trump or Judge Roy Moore when they were accused of sexual misconduct?

6. Review the solutions that Pao offers in her concluding paragraph. To what extent would you endorse her goals, and do you think we are making progress toward the equitable treatment of working women?

7. Pao lost her gender discrimination lawsuit against Kleiner in 2015, before the #MeToo movement went viral and before accusations of harassment were made against numerous powerful men including Hollywood mogul Harvey Weinstein, Alabama Judge Roy Moore, President Donald Trump, and television hosts Charlie Rose and Matt Lauer. Explain whether you think jurors today might decide Pao's case differently. What role, if any, do you think public awareness of an issue should have in the administration of justice?

EXPLORING CONNECTIONS

8. Read "The Gender Knot" by Allan Johnson (p. 527), paying close attention to its analysis of patriarchy as a *kind of society* (not just a group of sexist men) and to its various descriptions of careers, money, power, and highly successful women. What parts of Pao's story could be used to illustrate the points Johnson makes, and where can you apply his theoretical framework to explain the world of Kleiner Perkins?

9. In the cartoon on page 443, what real-life person seems to be the model for Sorensen's man in a bathrobe, and how does the cartoonist make this clear without naming him? In what ways does the cartoon mirror the incidences of harassment Pao describes, the decision-making processes of the women targeted, and the assumptions and behavior of the men involved?

10. Read or review Noreen Malone's "Zoë and the Trolls" (p. 285) and compare Pao's experience in an elite Silicon Valley venture capital firm with Zoë Quinn's experience during the Gamergate incident. How does misogyny operate in Pao's and Quinn's different environments, and what do you think can be done to combat it?

EXTENDING THE CRITICAL CONTEXT

11. Research and report on Reddit, where Pao was formerly CEO, or one of the organizations she is currently involved in — Project Include or the Kapor Center for Social Impact. For example, did Pao's leadership at Reddit make its corporate culture or its media site more welcoming to women? How have Project Include and the Kapor Center tried to foster inclusivity and diversity in the tech world, and with what degree of success?

THANK GOD IT'S MONDAY
KATE ARONOFF

There are still jobs where folks punch the clock, put in their forty hours a week, stick with one employer for decades, and maintain a clear divide between work and the rest of life, but they are increasingly rare. "Put in your time" has been replaced by "innovate," "leverage," "network," "disrupt," and "hustle." If the upside is unprecedented opportunities for interesting careers and financial success, the downside includes high stress, little job security, no pension, and soul-crushing work weeks of sixty, seventy, or sometimes a hundred hours. In this article Kate Aronoff takes a critical look at WeWork, a "co-working" company that's redefining work environments and erasing lines between work and life. Aronoff is a writing fellow at *In These Times* and, according to her Twitter profile, an Aspiring Mistress of Economics; her work on climate change and politics has appeared in such publications as the *Intercept*, the *Nation*, the *Guardian*, and *Dissent*, the source of this selection.

THE ORIGIN STORY OF WEWORK, the co-working company, might be as big a part of its image as the office space it rents out. Its co-founder and CEO Adam Neumann was raised on a kibbutz,[1] an Israeli cooperative built

---

[1]**kibbutz:** A communal settlement in Israel, usually a farm. [All notes are the editors'.]

in the mold of the early twentieth-century socialist Zionists who sought a "conquest of labor"[2] (*kibbush avodah*) in establishing a homeland for Jews in Palestine. Speaking at a tech conference in New York in 2015, Neumann reflected fondly on his childhood, going to school, eating dinner, and doing homework with the same kids each day. But there was a flaw.

"In a kibbutz everyone makes the same amount of money," Neumann lamented. "I always remember thinking that it's not fair that someone's effort is not being rewarded based on what he puts in." In starting WeWork, Neumann—a tall thirty-six-year-old, usually sporting a blazer thrown over a WeWork T-shirt—set out to correct the imbalance. He calls his company "a capitalistic kibbutz: On the one hand, community. On the other hand, you eat what you kill."

Since opening up shop in 2010, Neumann has certainly been eating well. In the wake of the housing crisis, he and his co-founder, Miguel McKelvey, have built WeWork into a company worth tens of billions by following a simple business model: buy large chunks of space in huge metropolitan office buildings, deck them out with desks, walls, and kegs, and then sublet to freelancers, mid-sized companies, and start-up founders at a premium on month-to-month contracts. Don't sell space, though; sell community, in the form of single-origin coffee and craft beer, a company-wide social networking app, and an office environment that plays as hard as it works. WeWork doesn't have tenants. It has "members," of WeWork and of the WeGeneration.

The average WeWork member—a millennial, to be sure—is an almost Platonic ideal of what the journalist Paul Mason describes in his book *Postcapitalism: A Guide to Our Future* as "the T-shirted techno-bourgeoisie...their information stored in the Cloud and their ultra-liberal attitudes to sexuality, ecology and philanthropy." They represent a "new normal" of office life and life in general: where work and play are increasingly indistinguishable, and both hinge on access to vast networks and limitless streams of information.

WeWork's network-first approach to work is reflected in its cosmopolitan, creative-class aesthetic. Locations around the world are virtually identical, from San Francisco to the Negev:[3] they all feature the same oak floors, clean lines, and hand-worn metal and wood furniture. Walls throughout the building are plastered with multi-colored, productivity-themed aphorisms like "Hustle" and "Thank God It's Monday."

Reverence for hard work is not simply a decorative gimmick, but core to the WeWork philosophy. The imperative to hustle reflects the way the founders see (and wish to shape) the future of work. Meanwhile, WeWork's popularity is driven—in part—by the increasing

[2]**socialist Zionists who sought a "conquest of labor":** Early supporters of a Jewish nation in what is now Israel; they urged Jewish landowners to favor Jewish workers over Arabs in order to establish a Jewish working class and a connection to the land.
[3]**the Negev:** An arid region in southern Israel.

atomization of labor[4], across income brackets. By offering workers an alternative to days spent alone behind a computer, Neumann and McKelvey discovered they could turn a profit by exploiting one of the defining features of work's so-called future: isolation.

Sharing Looks a Lot Like Paying Rent

Despite the fact that WeWork has been around for years and is currently valued at $16 billion, the company is still commonly referred to as a "start-up," a misidentification the founders are keen to perpetuate. To hear Neumann tell it, WeWork is disrupting work itself, revolutionizing the economy by applying a sharing economy ethos to drab office life. "We are a community of creators," he told *Bloomberg*[5] when asked about the company in May 2015. "We create an environment for entrepreneurs and freelancers and we leverage technology to connect people. . . . It's a new way of working. Just like Uber is the sharing economy for cars . . . we're the sharing economy for space."

But sharing, in WeWork's vision, looks a lot like paying rent. Joining the WeGeneration doesn't come cheap. A $45 "We Membership" buys access to WeWork's online community and the ability to work at a location anywhere in the world for two days a month. Dedicated desks in Manhattan range anywhere from $450 to $800, with single occupancy private offices stretching up to $2,100 per month. By square footage, space tends to be more expensive than that in the surrounding neighborhood. Aside from the beer and office services (one year of Amazon Web Services credits, discounted payment processing, lunch delivery, and so on), the price point is said to derive from all the immaterial benefits of being surrounded by young, driven professionals who "do what they love"—a slogan stamped on the coffee cups that line each floor. In April 2016 WeWork opened its flagship WeLive location on Wall Street, offering fully furnished, dorm-like accommodations complete with extracurriculars like yoga, "family dinners," and building-wide karaoke. Another WeLive, in the D.C. suburb of Arlington, Virginia, opened shortly thereafter. Members—at work, home, and play—can now lead their whole lives within the WeWork bubble, so long as they can cough up a few grand a month.

Company founders have repeatedly denied that their brainchild is in the real-estate business—in large part through clever branding. Senior staff hold titles like "Head of Community," and Neumann seldom makes it through an interview or press event without rattling off stories about his childhood in Israel, first years in New York, failed early business ventures, or relationship with his muse-turned-wife. Such

---

[4]**atomization of labor:** The breaking up of work and production into small parts. This can mean outsourcing tasks to individual freelancers or building complex networks of contractors, subcontractors, franchises, and suppliers.

[5]***Bloomberg:*** *Bloomberg Businessweek,* a weekly magazine.

tales, too, are why investors and consumers both treat WeWork more like a unicorn[6] than a multinational corporation.

If there is sharing happening, it's between WeWork and major 10 developers. According to WeWork Real Estate Head Mark Lapidus, the company has built close relationships over the years with real-estate giants like Rudin Management and Boston Properties to negotiate favorable leasing terms. Lapidus calls their landlords "partners," and notes that "60 percent of our deals probably come through either land-lords with existing relationships, where we have other locations, or landlord referrals, or just landlords reaching out to us and saying, 'Hey, before I put this on the market. . . .'"

Do What You Love — Or Else

What happens inside the walls of WeWork is as old-fashioned as the process through which the company acquires its space. Referring to employees as family members has a long tradition in the corporate world as a means to rebuff organizing drives and calls for higher wages. In the case of WeWork, talking points about community and family have come in handy when deflecting the many labor complaints it has fielded over the last several years.

Building trade unions placed an inflatable Scabby the Rat[7] outside of WeWork's Wall Street location last year, to protest the company's decision to work with notoriously anti-union builder Gilbane on their new development on the Brooklyn waterfront. In 2015, after contracted WeWork cleaning staff in New York tried to unionize with SEIU 32BJ,[8] WeWork president and COO Arthur Minson sent members and other employees a company-wide email:

> To be clear, employees always have a right to unionize. However, we don't think having a union at WeWork makes sense. Similar to the way many of you run your businesses, we take great pride in the fact that every WeWork employee is part of the WeWork family. Having an independent voice representing a portion of our employees goes against our fundamental belief that all of the WeWork employees should be treated the same, and all jobs at WeWork are equally valued.

The cleaners, paid just $10 an hour, were employed by Commercial Building Maintenance Corporation (CBM). After the unionization drive WeWork cancelled its contract with the company. With the union's help, workers led a campaign called "We Work Here Too," demanding that

---

[6]**unicorn:** In business jargon, a successful startup whose valuation reaches $1 billion.
[7]**Scabby the Rat:** A symbol used by organized labor to protest unfair business prac-tices; "scab" is a derogatory term for someone who works despite an ongoing labor strike.
[8]**SEIU 32BJ:** An affiliate of the Service Employees International Union, SEIU 32BJ represents more than 150,000 cleaners, doormen, security officers, food service employees, and other workers.

fired cleaners be brought back as WeWork staff at higher wages. In replacing the workers, WeWork "invited" janitorial staff to apply for their old jobs, though many of the now-unionized staff didn't receive calls back. The company eventually settled after months of protests, agreeing to hire some workers as staff at wages between $15 to $18 an hour, and to give priority to fired CBM employees. WeWork now uses a mix of in-house and contracted cleaners. Contracted cleaning staff in New York and Boston are now members of SEIU 32BJ, according to a spokesperson for the union, and talks are ongoing to establish collective bargaining agreements at locations in other cities.

Ironically, as of 2015, cleaners were the only WeWork employees mandated to wear shirts that said "Do What You Love." For Community Managers—the company's frontline staff, responsible for changing kegs and keeping WeWork locations running—the shirts are optional. As are—some employees allege—breaks for meals, overtime pay, and (until recently) their legally guaranteed right to unionize.

WeWork's page on Glassdoor, a Yelp-like ratings site for employ- 15 ees to anonymously rate their employers, offers a window into what it's like to work there. Community Managers are typically college grads making upwards of $40,000 a year. Reading their reviews, a few trends surface: a near-total collapse of work-life balance, marathon working days, unclear job descriptions, a cult-like enforcement of the company's mission, and a senior management that's as demanding and raucous as it is disorganized. Of his time at WeWork, one reviewer wrote that he "would rather rub salt on [an] open wound than work here again."

According to former Associate Community Manager Tara Zoumer, negative reviews aren't just angry exceptions. She worked at the company from March until November 2015 for a $42,000 per annum salary. Zoumer reported that she and other employees regularly worked fifty- and sixty-hour weeks without overtime, with some weeks pushing a hundred hours on end. "You're not getting a single dollar extra for any of that time but you're made to be responsible, and punished if you aren't keeping pace," she told me. "You're given a goofy title and fed three shots, but you can't pay your rent with that."

In her training, she recalled that one of the first mantras she and her colleagues were fed was, "Work hard, hustle harder, everyone does everything." Staff were required to give out their personal cell phone numbers to members, without receiving either company phones or reimbursement.

"They blurred the work-life balance to such a point where WeWork really does become your life," Zoumer said. Rebekah Paltrow Neumann— WeWork founding partner, Chief Brand Officer, and Adam Neumann's wife—went a step farther in an interview with *Fast Company*. "We don't have a line at all between work and life. It's not even a blurred line. There is no line."

When Zoumer started voicing her concerns to management and fellow coworkers, she was called into a meeting with her supervisor and one of WeWork's West Coast managers. They told her to back off, and she was asked if she wanted to resign. In another meeting, Zoumer alleges, one manager chalked the company's flexible relationship to labor standards up to its status as a start-up.

Compliance was still a long way off, but WeWork made moves [20] shortly thereafter to protect itself from employee complaints. Several weeks after Zoumer's meeting, all the employees at her location were called into a conference room, one by one, and asked to sign a non-disclosure agreement and enroll in an Employee Dispute Resolution Program (EDRP)—or, as Zoumer calls it, "a really cute name for a program that completely strips you of your rights." EDRPs are contracts that prevent workers and consumers from joining class-action lawsuits and taking other forms of legal action against their employers, directing them instead toward out-of-court arbitration processes paid for by the company.

As a *New York Times* investigation into arbitration found, the tool—traditionally wielded by major corporations—is increasingly being used by tech companies and start-ups. Drivers in ride-sharing apps like Lyft and Uber, for instance (each of which have offices in WeWork locations), have long existed in a legal grey area between contractors and full-time employees, allowing companies to pick and choose the protections they extend to their employees; an arbitration agreement prevents workers from banding together to take Uber to court.

With one suit already filed against WeWork, Zoumer told her manager she would need a few days to look over the EDRP paperwork, which was dozens of pages long. She sent an email to 150 of her coworkers with links to the *Times* investigation, and informed them of their right to a trial by jury. The next Monday, Zoumer found her email account suddenly disabled. Minutes later she was called into another meeting with her supervisor, told she was being fired for refusing to sign the documents, and escorted out of the building.

Zoumer currently has two ongoing claims against WeWork. One is over what she alleges was a misclassification of her employment status, which will enter into arbitration this spring thanks to a stipulation in the contract she signed when she was hired. The second is a complaint filed by the NLRB in response to Zoumer's claims, in which it alleges that WeWork unlawfully restricted the concerted activities of its employees, and that it specifically retaliated against Zoumer for her efforts to organize with her colleagues. That case could end up in front of the Supreme Court, setting a precedent not just for how WeWork treats employees but for how workers should be treated in the sharing economy as a whole.

From Scrip to Start-ups

Meanwhile, the WeWork founders like to encourage a lax attitude to the distinctions between life and livelihood for their members as well as their workers. On top of its dealings in real estate, WeWork is a full-fledged lifestyle brand. Neumann hopes the company will one day swell to include a "WeStreet" and "WeNeighborhood"—reminiscent of Uber's ambition to "evolve the way the world moves," on every front from mass transit to logistics. At WeWork's core is a utopian vision, based on having life itself revolve around a passion for what pays the bills.

A high rise in New York City's Financial District is the home of the first WeLive, a "coliving" complex that opened in early 2016. Inside, it looks and feels like a college dorm—albeit an expensive one. The company's two ventures are stylistically seamless, bringing the shabby-chic minimalism of WeWork to the shared kitchens and lounges, or "neighborhoods" (sets of residential floors), of WeLive. Many WeLive residents commute to *other* WeWork offices around New York, rather than descend several floors to the one at 110 Wall Street. But it isn't only twenty-something WeWorkers yearning for dorm life that move into WeLive. The oldest tenants are a couple in their mid-sixties, my tour guide at WeLive (a Community Manager and WeLive resident herself, who preferred to remain anonymous) told me. The couple, she said, had wanted to downsize from their apartment on the Upper East Side and house in Westchester. There are also young families and divorcees punctuating the building's majority-millennial population. "It's a great place for people who are in a period of transition in their life," my tour guide explained.

Long before WeLive, co-living helped provide the start-up capital for America's own transition into industrial capitalism. Most infamous in this vein were the Lowell Mill Girls, teenagers shipped off from the countryside to make textiles in Northern Massachusetts during the early nineteenth century. Loosely inspired by Robert Owen's utopian socialist experiment in New Lanark, Scotland, company towns like Lowell were intended, on one hand, to shelter the poor from the "Satanic Mills" of early industrial capitalism, providing decent food, shelter, and a paid day's work. On another, less altruistic hand, company towns were a means for cost cutting and control. Having workers centralized, living yards away from their bosses, was an obvious boon to productivity. That they had their basic needs already met was a justification for lower wages, since employees wouldn't have to shop for homes and meat on the open market.

Just as important for employers was constructing a world for their workers that was dependent at every level on the company's success. If profits were down, after all, there might be less food in the company store. In places like Appalachia, coal camps—maybe the most brutal example of the company-town model—were the only industry for miles around. Company stores, by extension, were the only stores for buying necessities like grains and cloth. Whole families could be raised on the company scrip[9] and goods doled out by coal bosses. And as waged work became the norm in America, both the productive and

---

[9]**company scrip:** A substitute for government currency which employees can use only at company stores.

reproductive labor necessary to eke out profit could be housed in the same compound. If proximity to work eased the transition from feudalism, several of the early company towns in the United States began to resemble fiefdoms. Considering that the company-town model predominated in capital-intensive extractive industries (coal and lumber, especially), it quite literally fueled the United States' rise as an industrial superpower.

By design, the bosses' interests fused with those of their workers, who didn't have an ideological motivation for a fatter bottom line so much as a material one to put food on the table and wood in the stove. Community, in a company town, meant everyone: from foreman to chimney sweep, with some benevolent industrialist sitting atop a familial hierarchy. As unions entered the coal camps, in battles like Matewan[10] and the one for Blair Mountain,[11] it wasn't only the coal barons beating them back. In addition to private agencies like the Pinkertons, companies regularly used locals to suppress organizing efforts. In Butte, Montana, for instance, the sheriff's office deputized mine guards — employees of the Anaconda Copper Mining Company — to break a 1920 strike, sparking the bloody conflict that became known as the Anaconda Road Massacre.

As the company-town model started to fade, though, automation brought with it Fordism[12] and a wage theoretically big enough to pay for both a car and a middle-class life — backed at least partially by a moderately functional social safety net.

WeWork invites us to imagine another kind of transition. Neumann   30
may not be creating a new regime of labor for the twenty-first century so much as capitalizing on one already in the works. Programmers at companies like Google and Facebook are well accustomed to having employers meet their every need, such as meals from five-star chefs and fully equipped gyms in exchange for ten- and twelve-hour workdays. One of the labor movement's hallmark victories — an eight-hour workday — is now being eroded on each end of the economic spectrum: by start-up wunderkinder[13] toiling late into the night as well as by low-wage service workers juggling multiple jobs just to make rent, one of which might happen to be as an Uber driver. Where one might walk away with millions in venture-capital funding, another could be making less than $7 an hour, as Uber drivers did during the Republican National Convention. Though it's not happening on a large scale yet, it's not inconceivable to imagine an expanded version of the WeLive accommodations used to house the company's cleaners and Community

---

[10]**Matewan:** A West Virginia town where a 1920 shootout between coal miners and a private detective agency left seven detectives and three townspeople dead.
[11]**Blair Mountain:** West Virginia site of a battle between approximately 10,000 armed coal miners and 3,000 lawmen and strikebreakers.
[12]**Fordism:** The system of mass production pioneered by the Ford Motor Company.
[13]**wunderkinder:** [German] Child prodigies.

Managers as well as the employees of members who run their own start-ups and small businesses, crafting a totalizing "WeLife" for members and employees alike.

WeWork, WeLive, We Fight

WeWork's embrace of the idea of boundless workdays ignores the psychic toll they can take, though it grasps their appeal. Life under capitalism is getting increasingly lonely, anxious, and depressing—especially for the millennials who form the core of WeWork's customer base. (A study from 2014 found that eighteen- to twenty-four-year-olds were four times as likely to be lonely as people over seventy.) We humans are social creatures, too, and our endless, solitary workdays might—literally—be killing us, raising the risk of early death by 26 percent. A physiological study of social animals—dogs, monkeys, and other species—found that our non-human brethren are more likely to choose physical pain than isolation. As George Monbiot has pointed out, too, the

Jen Sorensen

poor are far more likely to suffer from loneliness. Living with the stigma of poverty and eviction can be just as deadly. Following the housing crisis, suicide rates in austerity-pummeled Spain[14] shot up by 20 percent. In the first two years of Greece implementing its austerity programs, that country's suicide rate climbed by a full 35 percent.

Unlike livable wages, the isolation of neoliberalism in the twenty-first century cuts across class—though its burden is shared unequally. So while WeWork's business runs, in part, off old-fashioned labor exploitation, it also serves a need that's become more pressing in an economy defined by both inequality and alienation: community, but only for those who can afford a few thousand dollars a month.

In the left's quest to beat back inequality, bread-and-butter demands—for things like a $15 minimum wage and paid family leave—sometimes neglect the emotional pain of suffering under capitalism. Reaching beyond more individualized concepts of "selfcare," what would it look like for movements to foreground a vision of a better society free not just from fossil fuels and poverty wages, but also from loneliness?

ENGAGING THE TEXT

1. Aronoff reports that WeWork members include "freelancers, mid-sized companies, and start-up founders" (para. 3). Why might WeWork be a good fit for these clients, and what kinds of businesses do you think would be a poor fit for a "capitalist kibbutz" environment?

2. Explain the ways in which WeWork is selling community, not space. Which of these are most and least attractive to you, and why? To extend the assignment, write a brief account of one worker's day in a WeWork office, portraying it either as an ideal environment or as an intolerable dystopia. Share stories with classmates and discuss what they tell you about WeWork and about your own ideas about jobs and careers.

3. Unpack Paul Mason's description of millennial workers in paragraph 4. What does "techno-bourgeoisie" mean, for example, and what "ultra-liberal" attitudes about sexuality, ecology, and philanthropy might Mason have in mind? To what extent do you agree with this description of millennials, and how well does it apply to your own generation?

4. Rebekah Paltrow Neumann says "we don't have a line at all between life and work" at WeWork (para. 18). What are your own aspirations in terms of life/work balance? What percentage of your time and energy would you happily

[14]**housing crisis...austerity-pummeled Spain:** The global financial crisis hit Spain's housing market especially hard; its subsequent austerity program (including a salary freeze, a raised retirement age, and a reduction of benefits to families with children) plunged the nation into recession.

devote to work, and what are your realistic expectations? What goals, if any, would motivate you to work sixty or seventy hours a week?

5. If you have any experience living in a dorm or other communal environment, what sense of community or joint purpose did it provide? Could you be happy living in a very nice dorm or WeLive building for a decade or more? Why or why not?

6. **Thinking Rhetorically** In discussing WeWork's confrontations with unions, Aronoff reminds us of mill towns and coal mining companies — two infamous examples of the systematic exploitation of workers. Is it reasonable — or rhetorically effective — to imply comparisons between WeWork and armed conflicts that historians call "battles" and "massacres"? What can you infer about Aronoff's politics from her accounts of labor disputes?

EXPLORING CONNECTIONS

7. Read "The Gender Knot" by Allan Johnson (p. 527), paying special attention to the section on "male identification" (paras. 531–534). What aspects of WeWork might lead Johnson to consider it a "male-identified model" of work, and to what extent does WeWork also promote qualities that he labels stereotypically feminine?

8. Whether she is writing about mill towns, the mining industry, or WeWork, Aronoff highlights problems such as the exploitation of workers, job insecurity, and cutthroat competition. Compare her perspective to the Utopian vision in Rutger Bregman's "Why We Should Give Free Money to Everyone" (p. 456). Whose vision do you think will prove more accurate over the next twenty years, and why?

9. Read or review Kevin Drum's "You Will Lose Your Job to a Robot — And Sooner Than You Think" (p. 322) for another vision of the future of work. Discuss how the prospects of automation and artificial intelligence might impact the WeWork model. If you have a career goal in mind, how would you assess the likelihood of these risks — losing work/life balance, having your job outsourced to another country, and being replaced by a robot or AI program?

EXTENDING THE CRITICAL CONTEXT

10. Research how WeWork has fared since 2017, the year this essay was published. Has the company expanded into new cities? Has its value increased or declined? Has the company gone public with an initial public offering of stock (IPO) — a move that many analysts predicted for 2018? What is the status of Tara Zoumer's lawsuit, and how has WeWork handled the "many labor complaints" (para. 11) that Aronoff mentions? Taking into account what you learn about these issues, discuss whether you expect WeWork's "capitalistic kibbutz" model to be successful in the long term.

④

WHY WE SHOULD GIVE
FREE MONEY TO EVERYONE

RUTGER BREGMAN

Battling poverty by giving people money, no strings attached, is the kind of idea you might expect from a nine-year-old: it sounds simplistic, ignoring issues like who would get the cash, how we would motivate them to keep working despite the handout, and how to make sure they don't spend it on booze or weed. It's striking, then, that proposals for a Universal Basic Income, or UBI, are gaining traction among professional economists, sociologists, and politicians. In their view, UBI is not simplistic but elegantly simple, sidestepping rules and bureaucracies to give the poor what they most need — money. This selection describes several successful trials of UBI and argues that "it's an idea whose time has come." Rutger Bregman (b. 1988) is a prizewinning journalist and the author of four books on economics, philosophy, and history. His *History of Progress* (2013) won the Belgian Liberales prize for best nonfiction book, and in 2017 he was recognized by *Forbes* as one of Europe's most prominent young intellectuals. The selection below comes from his international best-seller *Utopia for Realists: How We Can Build the Ideal World* (2017).

LONDON, MAY 2009 — AN EXPERIMENT is under way. Its subjects: thirteen homeless men. They are veterans of the street. Some have been sleeping on the cold pavement of the Square Mile, Europe's financial center, for going on forty years. Between the police expenses, court costs, and social services, these thirteen troublemakers have racked up a bill estimated at £400,000 ($650,000) or more.[1] Per year.

The strain on city services and local charities is too great for things to go on this way. So Broadway, a London-based aid organization, makes a radical decision: From now on, the city's thirteen consummate drifters will be getting VIP treatment. It's *adiós* to the daily helpings of food stamps, soup kitchens, and shelters. They're getting a drastic and instantaneous bailout.

From now on, these rough sleepers will receive free money.

---

[1]This is a very conservative estimate. A study conducted by the British government put the amount at £30,000 per homeless person per year (for social services, police, legal costs, etc.). In this case the amount would have been much higher as they were the most notorious vagrants. The study cites sums as high as £400,000 for a single homeless person per year. See: Department for Communities and Local Government, "Evidence Review of the Costs of Homelessness" (August 2012). https://www.gov.uk/government/uploads/system/uploads/attachment_data/file/7596/2200485.pdf.

To be exact, they're getting £3,000 in spending money, and they don't have to do a thing in return.[2] How they spend it is up to them. They can opt to make use of an advisor if they'd like—or not. There are no strings attached, no questions to trip them up.[3]

The only thing they're asked is: What do *you* think you need? 5

Gardening Classes

"I didn't have enormous expectations," one social worker later recalled.[4] But the drifters' desires proved eminently modest. A telephone, a dictionary, a hearing aid—each had his own ideas about what he needed. In fact, most were downright thrifty. After one year, they had spent an average of just £800.

Take Simon, who had been strung out on heroin for twenty years. The money turned his life around. Simon got clean and started taking gardening classes. "For some reason, for the first time in my life, everything just clicked," he said later. "I'm starting to look after myself, wash and shave. Now I'm thinking of going back home. I've got two kids."

A year and a half after the experiment began, seven of the thirteen rough sleepers had a roof over their heads. Two more were about to move into their own apartments. All thirteen had taken critical steps toward solvency and personal growth. They were enrolled in classes, learning to cook, going through rehab, visiting their families, and making plans for the future.

"It empowers people," one of the social workers said about the personalized budget. "It gives choices. I think it can make a difference." After decades of fruitless pushing, pulling, pampering, penalizing, prosecuting, and protecting, nine notorious vagrants had finally been brought in from the streets. The cost? Some £50,000 a year, including the social workers' wages. In other words, not only did the project help thirteen people, it also cut costs considerably.[5] Even the *Economist* had

---

[2]The recipients were generally not told the exact amount of money in their "personalised budget," according to the Broadway report; however, as the report goes on to say that one of the homeless suggested lowering it from £3,000 to £2,000, he obviously did know.

[3]The homeless were not given the money directly. All their expenditures had to be approved first by the "street population manager," which he always did "promptly." That this scrutiny was limited was also affirmed by one of the social workers in an interview with the *Economist* (see footnote 6): "We just said, 'It's your life and up to you to do what you want with it, but we are here to help if you want.'" The report also states that "Throughout the interviews, many people used the phrases 'I chose' or 'I made the decision' when discussing their accommodation and the use of their personalised budget, emphasising their sense of choice and control."

[4]The Joseph Rowntree Foundation published an extensive report on the experiment, which is the source of all the quotes cited here. See: Juliette Hough and Becky Rice, *Providing Personalised Support to Rough Sleepers. An Evaluation of the City of London Pilot* (2010). http://www.jrf.org.uk/publications/support-rough-sleepers-london.

For another evaluation, see: Liz Blackender and Jo Prestidge, "Pan London Personalised Budgets for Rough Sleepers," *Journal of Integrated Care* (January 2014). http://www.emeraldinsight.com/journals.htm?articleid=17104939&.

[5]In 2013, the project was expanded to twenty-eight rough sleepers in London's City, of whom twenty already had a roof over their heads.

to conclude that the "most efficient way to spend money on the home-less might be to give it to them."[6]

Hard Data

Poor people can't handle money. This seems to be the prevailing sen- 10
timent, almost a truism. After all, if they knew how to manage money,
how could they be poor in the first place? We assume that they must
spend it on fast food and soda instead of on fresh fruit and books. So
to "help," we've rigged up a myriad of ingenious assistance programs,
with reams of paperwork, registration systems, and an army of inspectors, all revolving around the biblical principle that "those unwilling to
work will not get to eat" (2 Thessalonians 3:10). In recent years, government assistance has become increasingly anchored in employment,
with recipients required to apply for jobs, enroll in return-to-work programs, and do mandatory "volunteer" work. Touted as a shift "from
welfare to work-fare," the underlying message is clear: Free money
makes people lazy.

Except that, according to the evidence, it doesn't.

Meet Bernard Omondi. For years he earned $2 a day working in
a stone quarry in an impoverished part of western Kenya. Then, one
morning, he received a rather peculiar text message. "When I saw the
message, I jumped up," Bernard later recalled. A sum of $500 had just
been deposited in his bank account. For Bernard, this was almost a
year's wages.

Several months later a journalist from the *New York Times* visited
Bernard's village. It was as though the entire population had won the
lottery: The village was flush with cash. Yet no one was drinking their
money away. Instead, homes had been repaired and small businesses
started. Bernard invested his money in a brand-new Bajaj Boxer motorcycle from India and was making $6–$9 a day ferrying people around as
a taxi driver. His income had more than tripled.

"This puts the choice in the hands of the poor," says Michael Faye,
founder of GiveDirectly, the organization behind Bernard's windfall.
"And the truth is, I don't think I have a very good sense of what the
poor need."[7] Faye doesn't give people fish, or even teach them to fish.
He gives them cash, in the conviction that the real experts on what poor
people need are the poor people themselves. . . .

[6]"Cutting out the middle men," *Economist* (November 4, 2010). http://www.economist.com/node/17420321.
[7]Quoted in: Jacob Goldstein, "Is It Nuts to Give to the Poor Without Strings Attached?" *New York Times* (August 13, 2013). http://www.nytimes.com/2013/08/18/magazine/ is-it-nuts-to-give-to-the-poor-without-strings-attached.html.

A Southerly Revolution

Studies from all over the world offer proof positive: Free money works. 15

Already, research has correlated unconditional cash disbursements with reductions in crime, child mortality, malnutrition, teenage pregnancy, and truancy, and with improved school performance, economic growth, and gender equality.[8] "The big reason poor people are poor is because they don't have enough money," notes economist Charles Kenny, "and it shouldn't come as a huge surprise that giving them money is a great way to reduce that problem."[9]

In their book *Just Give Money to the Poor* (2010), scholars at the University of Manchester furnish countless examples of cases where cash handouts with few or no strings attached have worked. In Namibia, figures for malnutrition took a nosedive (from 42% to 10%), as did those for truancy (from 40% to virtually nothing) and crime (by 42%). In Malawi, school attendance among girls and women surged 40%, regardless of whether the cash came with or without conditions. Time and again, the ones to profit most are children. They suffer less hunger and disease, grow taller, perform better at school, and are less likely to be forced into child labor.[10]

From Brazil to India, from Mexico to South Africa, cash-transfer programs have become all the rage across the Global South. When the United Nations formulated its Millennium Development Goals in 2000, these programs weren't even on the radar. Yet by 2010, they were already reaching more than 110 million families in forty-five countries.

Back at the University of Manchester, the researchers summed up these programs' benefits: (1) households put the money to good use, (2) poverty declines, (3) there can be diverse long-term benefits for income, health, and tax revenues, and (4) the programs cost less than the alternatives. . . .[11]

The great thing about money is that people can use it to buy things 20 they need instead of things that self-appointed experts think they need. And, as it happens, there is one category of product which poor people

---

[8]The following is a selection of studies on the effects of conditional and unconditional "cash grants." In South Africa: Jorge M. Agüero and Michael R. Carter, "The Impact of Unconditional Cash Transfers on Nutrition: The South African Child Support Grant," University of Cape Town (August 2006). http://www.ipc-undp.org/pub/IPCWorkingPaper39.pdf.

In Malawi: W. K. Luseno et al., "A multilevel analysis of the effect of Malawi's Social Cash Transfer Pilot Scheme on school-age children's health," *Health Policy Plan* (May 2013). http://www.ncbi.nlm.nih.gov/pmc/articles/PMC4110449/.

Also in Malawi: Sarah Baird et al., "The Short-Term Impacts of a Schooling Conditional Cash Transfer Program on the Sexual Behavior of Young Women." http://cega .berkeley.edu/assets/cega_research_projects/40/Short_Term_Impacts_of_a_Schooling_CCT_on_Sexual_Behavior.pdf.

[9]Charles Kenny, "For Fighting Poverty, Cash Is Surprisingly Effective," *Bloomberg Businessweek* (June 3, 2013). http://www.bloomberg.com/bw/articles/2013-06-03/for-fighting-poverty-cash-is-surprisingly-effective.

[10]Joseph Hanlon et al., *Just Give Money to the Poor* (2010), p. 6.

[11]Armando Barrientos and David Hulme, "Just Give Money to the Poor. The Development Revolution from the Global South," Presentation for the OECD. http://www.oecd.org/dev/pgd/46240619.pdf.

do *not* spend their free money on, and that's alcohol and tobacco. In fact, a major study by the World Bank demonstrated that in 82% of all researched cases in Africa, Latin America, and Asia, alcohol and tobacco consumption actually *declined*.[12]

But it gets even stranger. In Liberia, an experiment was conducted to see what would happen if you give $200 to the shiftiest of the poor. Alcoholics, addicts, and petty criminals were rounded up from the slums. Three years later, what had they spent the money on? Food, clothing, medicine, and small businesses. "If these men didn't throw away free money," one of the researchers wondered, "who would?"[13] . . .

Utopia

Free money: It's a notion already proposed by some of history's leading thinkers. Thomas More dreamed about it in his book *Utopia* in 1516. Countless economists and philosophers—Nobel Prize winners among them—would follow.[14] Its proponents have spanned the spectrum from left to right, all the way to the founders of neoliberal thought, Friedrich Hayek and Milton Friedman.[15] And Article 25 of the Universal Declaration of Human Rights (1948) promises that, one day, it will come.

A universal basic income.

And not merely for a few years, or in developing countries alone, or only for the poor, but just what it says on the box: free money for everyone. Not as a favor, but as a right. Call it the "capitalist road to communism."[16] A monthly allowance, enough to live on, without having to lift a finger. The only condition, as such, is that you "have a pulse."[17] No inspectors looking over your shoulder to see if you've spent it wisely, nobody questioning if it's really deserved. No more special benefit and assistance programs; at most an additional allowance for seniors, the unemployed, and those unable to work.

Basic income: It's an idea whose time has come. . . .   25

---

[12]It should be noted that this decline was not statistically significant, so in most cases cash transfers have no effect on the level of tobacco and alcohol consumption. See: David K. Evans and Anna Popova, "Cash Transfers and Temptation Goods. A Review of Global Evidence," World Bank Policy Research Working Papers (May 2014). http://documents.worldbank.org/curated/en/2014/05/19546774/cash-transfers-temptation-goods-review-global-evidence.

[13]Christopher Blattman and Paul Niehaus, "Show Them the Money. Why Giving Cash Helps Alleviate Poverty," *Foreign Affairs* (May/June 2014).

[14]Including Thomas Paine, John Stuart Mill, H. G. Wells, George Bernard Shaw, John Kenneth Galbraith, Jan Tinbergen, Martin Luther King, and Bertrand Russell.

[15]See, for example: Matt Zwolinski, "Why Did Hayek Support a Basic Income?" *Libertarianism.org* (December 23, 2013). http://www.libertarianism.org/columns/why-did-hayek-support-basic-income.

[16]Robert van der Veen and Philippe van Parijs, "A Capitalist Road to Communism," *Theory & Society* (1986). https://www.ssc.wisc.edu/~wright/ERU_files/PVP-cap-road.pdf.

[17]A quote by the conservative proponent of basic income, Charles Murray, in: Annie Lowrey, "Switzerland's Proposal to Pay People for Being Alive," *New York Times* (November 12, 2013). http://www.nytimes.com/2013/11/17/magazine/switzerlands-proposal-to-pay-people-for-being-alive.html.

From Experiment to Law

. . . Few people today are aware that the U.S. was just a hair's breadth from realizing a social safety net at least as extensive as those in most Western European countries. When President Lyndon B. Johnson declared his "War on Poverty" in 1964, Democrats and Republicans alike rallied behind fundamental welfare reforms.

First, however, some trial runs were needed. Tens of millions of dollars were budgeted to provide a basic income for more than 8,500 Americans in New Jersey, Pennsylvania, Iowa, North Carolina, Indiana, Seattle, and Denver in what were also the first-ever large-scale social experiments to distinguish experimental and control groups. The researchers wanted answers to three questions: (1) Would people work significantly less if they receive a guaranteed income? (2) Would the program be too expensive? (3) Would it prove politically unfeasible?

The answers were no, no, and yes.

Declines in working hours were limited across the board. "The 'laziness' contention is just not supported by our findings," the chief data analyst of the Denver experiment said. "There is not anywhere near the mass defection the prophets of doom predicted." The reduction in paid work averaged 9% per family, and in every state it was mostly the twentysomethings and women with young children who worked less.[18]

Later research showed that even 9% was probably exaggerated. In the original study, this was calculated on the basis of self-reported income, but when the data was compared with official government records, it turned out that a significant portion of earnings had gone unreported. After correcting for this discrepancy, the researchers discovered that the number of hours worked had scarcely decreased at all.[19]

"[The] declines in hours of paid work were undoubtedly compensated in part by other useful activities, such as search for better jobs or work in the home," noted the Seattle experiment's concluding report. For example, one mother who had dropped out of high school worked less in order to earn a degree in psychology and get a job as a researcher. Another woman took acting classes; her husband began composing music. "We're now self-sufficient, income-earning artists," she told the researchers.[20] Among youth included in the experiment, almost all the

30

---

[18]Allan Sheahen, *Basic Income Guarantee. Your Right to Economic Security* (2012), p. 108.

[19]Dylan Matthews, "A Guaranteed Income for Every American Would Eliminate Poverty—And It Wouldn't Destroy the Economy," *Vox.com* (July 23, 2014). http://www.vox.com/2014/7/23/5925041/guaranteed-income-basic-poverty-gobry-labor-supply.

[20]Quoted in: Allan Sheahen, "Why Not Guarantee Everyone a Job? Why the Negative Income Tax Experiments of the 1970s Were Successful." USBIG Discussion Paper (February 2002). http://www.usbig.net/papers/013-Sheahen.doc.

The researchers thought people might eventually even work *more*, provided the government created additional jobs. "Any reduction in work effort caused by cash assistance would be more than offset by the increased employment opportunities provided in public service jobs."

hours not spent on paid work went into more education. Among the New Jersey subjects, the rate of high-school graduations rose 30%.[21]

And thus, in the revolutionary year of 1968, when young demonstrators the world over were taking to the streets, five famous economists — John Kenneth Galbraith, Harold Watts, James Tobin, Paul Samuelson, and Robert Lampman — wrote an open letter to Congress. "The country will not have met its responsibility until everyone in the nation is assured an income no less than the officially recognized definition of poverty," they said in an article published on the front page of the *New York Times*. According to the economists, the costs would be "substantial, but well within the nation's economic and fiscal capacity."[22]

The letter was signed by 1,200 fellow economists.

And their appeal did not fall on deaf ears. The following August, President Nixon presented a bill providing for a modest basic income, calling it "the most significant piece of social legislation in our nation's history." According to Nixon, the baby boomers would do two things deemed impossible by earlier generations. Besides putting a man on the moon (which had happened the month before), their generation would also, finally, eradicate poverty.

A White House poll found 90% of all newspapers enthusiastically receptive to the plan.[23] The *Chicago Sun-Times* called it "A Giant Leap Forward," the *Los Angeles Times* "A bold new blueprint."[24] The National Council of Churches was in favor, and so were the labor unions and even the corporate sector.[25] At the White House, a telegram arrived declaring, "Two upper middle class Republicans who will pay for the program say bravo."[26] Pundits were even going around quoting Victor Hugo — "Nothing is stronger than an idea whose time has come."

It seemed that the time for a basic income had well and truly arrived.

"WELFARE PLAN PASSES HOUSE . . . A BATTLE WON IN CRUSADE FOR REFORM," headlined the *New York Times* on April 16, 1970. With 243 votes for and 155 against, President Nixon's Family Assistance Plan (FAP) was approved by an overwhelming majority. Most pundits expected the plan to pass the Senate, too, with a membership even more progressive than that of the House of Representatives. But in the Senate Finance Committee, doubts reared up. "This bill represents the most extensive, expensive, and expansive welfare legislation ever handled," one

[21]Matthews, "A Guaranteed Income for Every American Would Eliminate Poverty."

[22]Economists Urge Assured Income," *New York Times* (May 28, 1968).

[23]Brian Steensland, *The Failed Welfare Revolution. America's Struggle over Guaranteed Income Policy* (2008), p. 123.

[24]Quoted in: Sheahen, *Basic Income Guarantee*, p. 8.

[25]Steensland, *The Failed Welfare Revolution*, p. 69.

[26]Quoted in: Peter Passell and Leonard Ross, "Daniel Moynihan and President-Elect Nixon: How Charity Didn't Begin at Home," *New York Times* (January 14, 1973). http://www.nytimes.com/books/98/10/04/specials/moynihan-income.html.

Republican senator said.[27] Most vehemently opposed, however, were the Democrats. They felt the FAP didn't go far enough, and pushed for an even higher basic income.[28] After months of being batted back and forth between the Senate and the White House, the bill was finally canned.

In the following year, Nixon presented a slightly tweaked proposal to Congress. Once again, the bill was accepted by the House, now as part of a larger package of reforms. This time, 288 voted in favor, 132 against. In his 1971 State of the Union address, Nixon considered his plan to "place a floor under the income of every family with children in America" the most important item of legislation on his agenda.[29]

But once again, the bill foundered in the Senate.

Not until 1978 was the plan for a basic income shelved once and for all, however, following a fatal discovery upon publication of the final results of the Seattle experiment. One finding in particular grabbed everybody's attention: The number of divorces had jumped more than 50%. Interest in this statistic quickly overshadowed all the other outcomes, such as better school performance and improvements in health. A basic income, evidently, gave women too much independence.

Ten years later, a reanalysis of the data revealed that a statistical error had been made; in reality, there had been no change in the divorce rate at all.[30]

Futile, Dangerous, and Perverse

"It Can Be Done! Conquering Poverty in America by 1976," Nobel Prize winner James Tobin confidently wrote in 1967. At that time, almost 80% of Americans supported a guaranteed basic income.[31] Years later, Ronald Reagan would famously sneer, "In the sixties we waged a war on poverty, and poverty won."

The great milestones of civilization always have the whiff of utopia about them at first. According to renowned sociologist Albert Hirschman, Utopias are initially attacked on three grounds: futility (it's not possible), danger (the risks are too great), and perversity (it will degenerate into dystopia). But Hirschman also wrote that almost as soon as a Utopia becomes a reality, it often comes to be seen as utterly commonplace.

[27]Quoted in: Leland G. Neuberg, "Emergence and Defeat of Nixon's Family Assistance Plan," USBIG Discussion Paper (January 2004). http://www.usbig.net/papers/066-Neuberg-FAP2.doc.

[28]Bruce Bartlett, "Rethinking the Idea of a Basic Income for All," *New York Times Economix* (December 10, 2013). http://economix.blogs.nytimes.com/2013/12/10/rethinking-the-idea-of-a-basic-income-for-all.

[29]Steensland, *The Failed Welfare Revolution,* p. 157.

[30]Glen G. Cain and Douglas Wissoker, "A Reanalysis of Marital Stability in the Seattle-Denver Income Maintenance Experiment," Institute for Research on Poverty (January 1988). http://www.irp.wisc.edu/publications/dps/pdfs/dp85788.pdf.

[31]According to a poll conducted by Harris in 1969. Mike Alberti and Kevin C. Brown, "Guaranteed Income's Moment in the Sun," *Remapping Debate.* http://www.remappingdebate.org/article/guaranteed-income's-moment-sun.

Not so very long ago, democracy still seemed a glorious Utopia. Many a great mind, from the philosopher Plato (427–347 B.C.) to the statesman Edmund Burke (1729–97), warned that democracy was futile (the masses were too foolish to handle it), dangerous (majority rule would be akin to playing with fire), and perverse (the "general interest" would soon be corrupted by the interests of some crafty general or other). Compare this with the arguments against basic income. It's supposedly futile because we can't pay for it, dangerous because people would quit working, and perverse because ultimately a minority would end up having to toil harder to support the majority.

But . . . hold on a minute.

Futile? For the first time in history, we are actually rich enough to finance a sizable basic income. We can get rid of the whole bureaucratic rigmarole designed to force assistance recipients into low-productivity jobs at any cost, and we can help finance the new simplified system by chucking the maze of tax credits and deductions, too. Any further necessary funds can be raised by taxing assets, waste, raw materials, and consumption.

Let's look at the numbers. Eradicating poverty in the U.S. would cost only $175 billion, less than 1% of GDP.[32] That's roughly a quarter of U.S. military spending. Winning the war on poverty would be a bargain compared to the wars in Afghanistan and Iraq, which a Harvard study estimated have cost us a staggering $4–$6 trillion.[33] As a matter of fact, all the world's developed countries had it within their means to wipe out poverty years ago.[34]

And yet, a system that helps solely the poor only drives a deeper wedge between them and the rest of society. "A policy for the poor is a poor policy," observed Richard Titmuss, the great theoretician of the British welfare state. It's an ingrained reflex among those on the left to make every plan, every credit, and every benefit income dependent. The problem is, that tendency is counter-productive.

In a now famous article published in the late 1990s, two Swedish sociologists showed that the countries with the most universal government programs have been the most successful at reducing poverty.[35] Basically, people are more open to solidarity if it benefits them personally.

45

---

[32]Matt Bruenig, "How a Universal Basic Income Would Affect Poverty," *Demos* (October 3, 2013). http://www.demos.org/blog/10/3/13/how-universal-basic-income-would-affect-poverty.

[33]Linda J. Bilmes, "The Financial Legacy of Iraq and Afghanistan: How Wartime Spending Decisions Will Constrain Future National Security Budgets," Faculty Research Working Paper Series (March 2013). https://research.hks.harvard.edu/publications/getFile.aspx?Id=923.

[34]Try this for a thought experiment: A basic income of $1.25 a day for everyone on Earth would cost an annual $3 trillion, or 3.5% of global GDP. The same cash assistance to the world's 1.3 billion poorest inhabitants would require less than $600 billion, or approximately 0.7% of global GDP, and would completely eliminate extreme poverty.

[35]Walter Korpi and Joakim Palme, "The Paradox of Redistribution and Strategies of Equality: Welfare State Institutions, Inequality and Poverty in the Western Countries," *American Sociological Review* (October 1998). http://citeseerx.ist.psu.edu/viewdoc/download?doi= 10.1.1.111.2584&rep=rep1&type=pdf.

The more we, our family, and our friends stand to gain through the welfare state, the more we're willing to contribute.[36] Logically, therefore, a universal, unconditional basic income would also enjoy the broadest base of support. After all, everyone stands to benefit.[37]

Dangerous? Certainly, some people may opt to work less, but then that's precisely the point. A handful of artists and writers ("all those whom society despises while they are alive and honors when they are dead" — Bertrand Russell) might actually stop doing paid work altogether. There is overwhelming evidence to suggest that the vast majority of people actually want to work, whether they need to or not.[38] In fact, not having a job makes us deeply unhappy.[39]

One of the perks of a basic income is that it would free the poor from the welfare trap and spur them to seek a paid job with true opportunities for growth and advancement. Since basic income is unconditional, and will not be taken away or reduced in the event of gainful employment, their circumstances can only improve.

Perverse? On the contrary, it is the welfare system that has devolved into a perverse behemoth of control and humiliation. Officials keep tabs on public assistance recipients via Facebook to check whether they're spending their money wisely — and woe betide anyone who dares to do unapproved volunteer work. An army of social services workers is needed to guide people through the jungle of eligibility, application, approval, and recapture procedures. And then the corps of inspectors has to be mobilized to sift through the paperwork.

The welfare state, which should foster people's sense of security and pride, has degenerated into a system of suspicion and shame. It is a grotesque pact between right and left. "The political right is afraid people will stop working," laments Professor Forget in Canada, "and the left doesn't trust them to make their own choices."[40] A basic income

---

[36]Wim van Oorschot, "Globalization, the European Welfare State, and Protection of the Poor," in: A. Suszycki and I. Karolewski (eds), *Citizenship and Identity in the Welfare State* (2013), pp. 37–50.

[37]Alaska is the best example of this, as the only political entity to have a universal, unconditional basic income (just over $ 1,000 a year), financed by oil revenues. Support is virtually unanimous. According to University of Alaska in Anchorage professor Scott Goldsmith, for a politician to question this program would be political suicide. It is thanks in part to this small basic income that Alaska has the lowest inequality of any U.S. state. See: Scott Goldsmith, "The Alaska Permanent Fund Dividend: An Experiment in Wealth Distribution," 9th International Congress BIEN (September 12, 2002). http://www.basicincome .org/bien/pdf/2002Goldsmith.pdf.

[38]Studies of the behavior of lottery winners shows that even hitting the jackpot rarely makes people quit their jobs, and if they do it's to spend more time with their children or find other work. See this famous study: Roy Kaplan, "Lottery Winners: The Myth and Reality," *Journal of Gambling Behavior* (Fall 1987), pp. 168–78.

[39]Prison inmates are a good example. Given food and a roof over their heads, they can just enjoy kicking back, you might think. Yet in prison the withholding of work is actually used as a punishment. If an inmate misbehaves, he's barred from the shop floor or kitchen. Almost everyone wants to make some sort of contribution, though what we mean by "work" and "unemployment" is subject to change. Indeed, we place far too little emphasis on the huge amount of unpaid work that people already do.

[40]She said this on Canadian TV. Watch the clip here: https://youtube/EPRTUZsiDYw?t= 45m30s.

system would be a better compromise. In terms of redistribution, it would meet the left's demands for fairness; where the regime of interference and humiliation are concerned, it would give the right a more limited government than ever.

Talk Different, Think Different

It's been said before.

We're saddled with a welfare state from a bygone era when the breadwinners were still mostly men and people spent their whole lives working at the same company. The pension system and employment protection rules are still keyed to those fortunate enough to have a steady job, public assistance is rooted in the misconception that we can rely on the economy to generate enough jobs, and welfare benefits are often not a trampoline, but a trap.

Never before has the time been so ripe for the introduction of a universal, unconditional basic income. Look around. Greater flexibility in the workplace demands that we also create greater security. Globalization is eroding the wages of the middle class. The growing rift between those with and those without a college degree makes it essential to give the have-nots a leg-up. And the development of ever-smarter robots could cost even the haves their jobs.

In recent decades the middle class has retained its spending power by borrowing itself into ever-deeper debt. But this model isn't viable, as we now know. The old adage of "those unwilling to work will not get to eat" is now abused as a license for inequality.

Don't get me wrong, capitalism is a fantastic engine for prosperity. "It has accomplished wonders far surpassing Egyptian pyramids, Roman aqueducts, and Gothic cathedrals," as Karl Marx and Friedrich Engels wrote in their *Communist Manifesto*. Yet it's precisely because we're richer than ever that it is now within our means to take the next step in the history of progress: to give each and every person the security of a basic income. It's what capitalism ought to have been striving for all along. See it as a dividend on progress, made possible by the blood, sweat, and tears of past generations. In the end, only a fraction of our prosperity is due to our own exertions. We, the inhabitants of the Land of Plenty, are rich thanks to the institutions, the knowledge, and the social capital amassed for us by our forebears. This wealth belongs to us all. And a basic income allows all of us to share it.

Of course, this is not to say we should implement this dream without forethought. That could be disastrous. Utopias always start out small, with experiments that ever so slowly change the world. It happened just a few years ago on the streets of London, when thirteen street sleepers got £3,000, no questions asked. As one of the aid workers said, "It's quite hard to just change overnight the way you've always approached this problem. These pilots give us the opportunity to talk differently, think differently, describe the problem differently...."

And that's how all progress begins.

ENGAGING THE TEXT

1. What were the most significant results of the experiment in London that Bregman describes at the beginning of this reading? What assumptions about homelessness and poverty did the project challenge, and why do you think it worked as well as it did?

2. Bregman describes U.S. efforts in the 1960s and 1970s to eradicate poverty by establishing a Universal Basic Income (UBI). What can we learn from his history lesson, and what do you consider the most daunting challenges today in moving toward UBI?

3. Bregman reports on UBI experiments in Namibia, Malawi, Liberia, and several other countries. Do you consider the data from these studies relevant to the United States? Why or why not? If you see complications in extrapolating from foreign experiments, do they result more from economic differences or from cultural ideas such as America's "Protestant work ethic"?

4. Referring to the title of an essay by Robert van der Veen and Philippe van Parijs, Bregman briefly frames UBI as a "capitalist road to communism" (para. 24). Explain whether you think UBI reflects a communist ideology and whether the characterization of UBI as a step toward communism makes its broad adoption in the United States unlikely.

5. Two key results in the trial runs of UBI in the 1960s were that "declines in working hours were limited" and that "it was mainly twentysomethings and women with young children who worked less" (para. 29). If you are now a teen or "twentysomething," write a journal entry or short essay imagining what role a UBI might play in your own life in the first few years after you graduate from college.

6. **Thinking Rhetorically** Throughout this excerpt Bregman balances scholarship with the success stories of particular individuals (for example, the Kenyan man who became a taxi driver, or the woman who earned her psychology degree). Study a few passages that include descriptions of individuals, and discuss what these descriptions add to the logical or emotional impact of Bregman's prose.

7. The American Dream has always rested on the premise that individual success comes from hard work and dedication. Discuss the potential impact of UBI on this foundational myth. Do you think UBI would serve primarily as a safety net, or might it radically alter our notions of what it means to succeed?

EXPLORING CONNECTIONS

8. Consider some of the disadvantaged people described elsewhere in *Rereading America* — Mercedes in "When Should a Child Be Taken from His Parents?" (p. 51); the Milwaukee students in "City of Broken Dreams" (p. 210); or the food service workers in "Serving in Florida" (p. 368). Discuss the specific ways in which a UBI might have helped these people improve their lives.

9. Read or review Kevin Drum's discussion of UBI in "You Will Lose Your Job to a Robot — and Sooner Than You Think" (p. 322). Which of Drum's scenarios — "the welfare state writ large," "Universal basic income #1," or "Universal basic income #2"— seems closest to Bregman's utopian vision? Of all these approaches, which seems most sensible (or least problematic) to you, and why?

10. Bregman explains that the death blow to UBI legislation in 1978 was the reaction to a statistical error — the inaccurate finding that Seattle's divorce rate rose after a UBI trial (paras. 40–41). How would you expect Stephanie Coontz, author of "What We Really Miss about the 1950s" (p. 26), to interpret this chain of events? What about Allan Johnson, author of "The Gender Knot" (p. 527)?

EXTENDING THE CRITICAL CONTEXT

11. Using a $1 million grant, Stockton, California, has initiated a UBI experiment that will give $500 a month to 100 Stockton families, no strings attached, for up to 18 months. Do some Internet research to learn more about the plan, its supporters, its skeptics, and the involvement of Silicon Valley tech firms in funding the trial.

12. Organize small research teams to begin exploring the scope and cost of services provided to poor people in your area. Look for data in key areas such as food, shelter, clothing, healthcare, unemployment benefits, and emergency services; time permitting, include services provided by nonprofits, local governments, and federal programs like SNAP (Supplemental Nutrition Assistance Program) and TANF (Temporary Assistance for Needy Families). Pool your information and discuss what effects free money for everyone might have in your area.

FURTHER CONNECTIONS

1. How would you expect your county to compare with other counties in your state in terms of wealth? How would you expect your state to compare with other states? Research state and county data from the U.S. Census Bureau website (www.census.gov) and present or write up your findings. To what extent do you think you have had advantages or disadvantages because of where you were born or grew up?

2. Working in groups, discuss recent movies or television series that you associate with the spirit of the American Dream. What aspects of the Dream do you see in these films or TV shows? What do they tell us about the state of the Dream today and about contemporary attitudes toward wealth and success?

3. As an individual or a class project, make a video reflecting your vision of the American Dream.

4. This chapter of *Rereading America* has been criticized by conservatives for undermining the work ethic of American college students. Rush Limbaugh, for example, claimed that the chapter "presents America as a stacked deck," thus "robbing people of the ability to see the enormous opportunities directly in front of them." Do you agree? Write a journal entry or an essay in which you explain how these readings have influenced your attitudes toward work and success.

TRUE WOMEN AND REAL MEN
Myths of Gender

FAST FACTS

1. 63% of women 15–34 years old believe that women face substantial discrimination in the United States today, while only 43% of men in that age range agree.

2. 75% of 15–34-year-olds agree that there is some social pressure for men to act in traditionally masculine ways; young women are more likely to believe that this pressure encourages men's sexual aggression, violent behavior, and homophobic attitudes.

3. 54% of American women have experienced unwanted and inappropriate sexual advances. Of those who experienced sexual harassment at work, nearly all (95%) reported that male harassers seldom faced punishment, close to two-thirds felt intimidated by the experience, and fewer than half reported it to a supervisor.

4. According to a January 2018 survey, nearly 75% of Americans think that sexual harassment is a serious problem, up 8 percentage points since news of the Harvey Weinstein scandal broke in October 2017. 62% believe that debate about the issue will create lasting change.

5. The 2015 School Climate Survey found that over 95% of LGBTQ students heard homophobic remarks or negative comments about gender expression, and about 60% heard them frequently. Over two-thirds experienced discriminatory policies or practices at school, reported higher levels of depression, and missed school three times more often than others.

6. Nearly half of transgender people (47%) have been sexually assaulted during their lifetimes, and transgender people with disabilities were over 60% more likely to experience sexual assault. Of 52 reported anti-LGBTQ homicides in 2017, nearly half of the victims were transgender women of color.

7. Almost two-thirds of LGBTQ Americans feel less safe since the election of Donald Trump. In an earlier poll following the 2015 Supreme Court decision on gay marriage, 54% predicted that social acceptance of LGBTQ people would improve a lot in the next decade; that percentage has dropped 20 points since then.

Data from (1), (2) MTV/Public Religion Research Institute survey: "Diversity, Division, Discrimination: The State of Young America" 1/10/2018; (3) ABC/*Washington Post* survey: "Unwanted Sexual Advances: Not Just a Hollywood Story" 10/17/2017; (4) ABC/*Washington Post* survey: "Six in Ten Have Hope for Lasting Change on Sexual Harassment" 1/24/2018; (5) Gay, Lesbian and Straight Education Network: "The 2015 School Climate Survey"; (6) National Center for Transgender Equality: "2015 U.S. Transgender Survey Report"; National Coalition of Anti-Violence Programs Report: "A Crisis of Hate: Lesbian, Gay, Bisexual, Transgender and Queer Hate Violence Homicides in 2017"; (7) Survey Monkey/TIME: "LGBTQ Americans Say They Feel Less Safe Under President Trump" 6/21–24/2016.

COMMON SENSE TELLS US that there are obvious differences between females and males: after all, biology, not culture, determines whether you're able to bear children. But culture and cultural myths do shape the roles men and women play in our public and private relationships: we may be born female and male, but we are made women and men. Sociologists distinguish between sex and gender — between one's biological identity and the conventional patterns of behavior we learn to associate with each sex. While biological sex remains relatively stable, gendered behavior varies dramatically from one cultural group or historical period to the next.

European colonists to America adhered to a patriarchal culture — one in which men were dominant: ancestry was traced through the male line, and men were the explorers, traders, and leaders of the colonies. Women were subservient first to their fathers and then to their husbands; once married, all their property, and even their children, legally belonged to their husbands. By contrast, American Indian cultural beliefs led to very different gender roles. For example, Choctaw/Cherokee scholar Kay Givens McGowan writes that indigenous civilizations of the Southeast (Cherokee, Choctaw, Chickasaw, Muskogee, and Seminole) were matriarchal societies. Women held considerable social, economic, and political power: ancestry was traced through the mother; women farmed, controlled the distribution of crops, and often served as traders; and women held leadership positions on the Women's Council. McGowan notes that "When a woman married, she worked and bore children for her own lineage, not her husband's"; she also points out that unlike colonial women, Southeastern women "had sexual freedom . . . including the right to have sex with anyone they chose." Colonists could scarcely begin to understand native gender norms, and certainly had no interest in adopting them. When these two cultures came into conflict, the Southeastern civilizations were brutally suppressed, and patriarchy prevailed.

French aristocrat Alexis de Tocqueville noted the enduring impact of patriarchy on American gender roles when he published *Democracy in America* (1835). He recognized that democratic government would inevitably "raise woman, and make her more and more the equal of man." But Tocqueville maintained that complete equality would violate the natural order. In Europe, while revolutionary thinkers were beginning to view man and woman as "beings not only equal, but alike," he warned that "by thus attempting to make one sex equal to the other, both are degraded; and from so preposterous a medley of the works of nature, nothing could ever result but weak men and disorderly women."

In the United States, by contrast, Tocqueville saw men's and women's roles as entirely distinct and separate. Men's "natural" sphere encompassed business, politics, and labor, whereas women's was "the quiet circle of domestic employments," where, despite their intelligence, their chief duty was to be attractive and refined:

> American women never manage the outward concerns of the family, or conduct a business, or take a part in political life; nor are they, on the other hand, ever compelled to perform the rough labor of the fields, or to make any of those laborious exertions which demand the exertion of physical strength. No families are so poor as to form an exception to this rule. . . . Hence it is, that the women of America, who often exhibit a masculine strength of understanding and a manly energy, generally preserve great delicacy of personal appearance, and always retain the manners of women.

As an aristocrat and conservative, Tocqueville was uninterested in the hard physical labor routinely performed by many women, and he entirely discounted the roles played by working-class and slave women. American women, he continued, knew their place, and submitted willingly to their husbands' authority — that is, if they were virtuous:

> They hold that every association must have a head in order to accomplish its object and that the natural head of the conjugal association is man. . . . [T]hey attach a sort of pride to the voluntary surrender of their own will and make it their boast to bend themselves to the yoke, — not to shake it off. Such, at least, is the feeling expressed by the most virtuous of their sex.

According to Tocqueville, Americans considered male dominance "natural" in government as well as in marriage: "The object of democracy is to regulate and legalize the powers which are necessary, and not to subvert all power."

History is replete with examples of how the apparent "naturalness" of gender has been used to regulate political, economic, and personal relations between the sexes. Many nineteenth-century scientists argued that it was "unnatural" for women to attend college; rigorous intellectual activity, they asserted, would draw vital energy away from a woman's reproductive organs and make her sterile. According to this line of reasoning, women who sought higher education threatened the natural order by jeopardizing their ability to bear children and perpetuate the species. Arguments based on nature were likewise used to justify women's exclusion from political life. In his classic 1832 treatise on American democracy, James Fenimore Cooper remarked that women's domestic role and "necessary" subordination to men made them unsuitable for participation in public affairs. Thus, denying women the right to vote was perfectly consistent with the principles of American democracy and did "not very materially affect the principle of political equality."

Resistance to gender equality has been remarkably persistent in the United States. It took more than seventy years of hard political work by both black and white women's organizations to win the right to vote. But while feminists gained the vote for women in 1920 and the legal right to equal educational and employment opportunities in the 1970s, attitudes change even more slowly than laws. Contemporary antifeminist campaigns voice some of the same anxieties as their nineteenth-century counterparts over the "loss" of femininity and domesticity.

Women continue to suffer economic inequities based on cultural assumptions about gender. What's defined as "women's work" — nurturing, feeding, caring for family and home — is devalued and pays low wages or none at all. When women enter jobs traditionally held by men, they often encounter discrimination, harassment, or "glass ceilings" that limit their advancement. In fact, the United States ranked forty-ninth out of 144 countries on the World Economic Forum's 2017 Global Gender Gap Report, trailing Slovenia (#7), Namibia (#13), Bolivia (#17), and Burundi (#22). The report measures gender equality in four areas: economic participation and opportunity, educational attainment, political empowerment, and health and survival. While the United States has virtually eliminated the gender gap in education, it ranks nineteenth in "wage equality for similar work." And despite the growing number of women holding political positions, the United States placed ninety-sixth in political empowerment.

But men, too, pay a high price for their culturally imposed roles. Psychological research shows higher rates of depression among people of both sexes who adhere closely to traditional roles than among those who do not. Moreover, studies of men's mental and physical health suggest that social pressure to "be a man" (that is, to be emotionally controlled, powerful, and successful) can contribute to isolation, anxiety, stress, and illness, and may be partially responsible for men's shorter life spans. As sociologist Margaret Andersen observes, "Traditional gender roles limit the psychological and social possibilities for human beings."

Even our assumption that there are "naturally" only two genders is a cultural invention that fails to accommodate the diversity of human experience. Some cultures have three or more gender categories. One of the best-known third genders is the American Indian *berdache*, or two-spirit, a role that was found in over 150 North American tribes. The two-spirit was a biological male who took the social role of a woman and did women's work (or in some cases both women's and men's work) or a biological female who adopted the identities of warrior and hunter, roles that were typically male. In general, they engaged in same-sex relationships, and in many tribes, two-spirits performed important work as healers, shamans, or "bridge-makers" between the natural and spiritual worlds. Today, Native Americans use "two-spirit" to refer to lesbian, gay, and transgender people.

Euro-American culture, by contrast, offers few socially acceptable alternative gender roles. Just as many Americans in the past considered it "unnatural" and socially destructive for women to vote or go to college, some now consider it "unnatural" and socially destructive for gays and lesbians to marry or for individuals to express a gender identity that violates conventional notions of masculinity or femininity. Cultural conflict over gender is ongoing and intense: a number of right-wing groups are fighting to reverse the Supreme Court's decision to legalize gay marriage. When the U.S. military announced that it would begin accepting transgender applicants, conservatives called the concern for trans rights "social pathology." In 2017, the president signed an executive order banning transgender troops from serving in the military, an order that was quickly overturned as unconstitutional. He then issued a revised transgender ban, which is still in litigation.

This chapter focuses on cultural myths of gender and the influence they wield over human development and personal identity. The first four selections examine how dominant American culture defines female and male gender roles — and how those roles both define and constrain us. Jamaica Kincaid's "Girl," a story framed as a mother's advice to her daughter, presents a contemporary take on what it means to be raised a woman. "How to Do Gender," by Lisa Wade and Myra Marx Ferree, examines gender as a culturally constructed category and discusses ways that we negotiate the "rules" to shape our gender identity. In "Guys' Club: No Faggots, Bitches, or Pussies Allowed," Carlos Andrés Gómez describes his own changing perceptions of gender, from his childhood encounters with homophobia and "enforced masculinity" to his adult understanding that "there is a fluid, changing spectrum of sexuality and gender, where actions aren't prescribed and roles aren't all but scripted." Ruth Padawer's "Sisterhood Is Complicated," explores some of that fluidity through the experiences of transmasculine students, analyzing how Wellesley, a women's college, has responded to their demands for recognition.

The second half of the chapter opens with a Visual Portfolio, which presents conventional and unconventional images of women and men, providing an opportunity to think about the ways that we "read" gender visually. Next, in a selection from *The Gender Knot*, "Patriarchy," Allan G. Johnson explores what it means to live in a society that promotes men and male privilege, while it devalues and oppresses women. Johnson provides many examples of the economic and political inequality of women and claims that patriarchy "encourages women to accept and adapt to their oppressed position even to the extent of undermining movements to bring about change." The next two readings give us a closer look at patriarchy in action. Jean Kilbourne's "'Two Ways a Woman Can Get Hurt': Advertising and Violence" argues that the objectification of women in ads constitutes a form of cultural abuse. "The Longest War" by Rebecca Solnit offers a furious exposé of the "pattern of violence against women that's broad and deep and horrific and incessantly overlooked." The chapter concludes with a provocative essay by Jackson Katz, "From Rush Limbaugh to Donald Trump: Conservative Talk Radio and the Defiant Reassertion of White Male Authority." Katz contends that conservative "outrage media"— with their misogyny, over-the-top rhetoric, and hatred of "soft" liberals — paved the way for the rise of Donald Trump.

Sources

Cooper, James Fenimore. *The American Democrat*. N.p.: Minerva Press, 1969. Print.

Foss, Sonia H., Mary E. Domenico, and Karen A. Foss. *Gender Stories: Negotiating Identity in a Binary World*. Long Grove, IL: Waveland Press, 2013. Print.

French, Marilyn. *Beyond Power: On Women, Men, and Morals*. New York: Ballantine Books, 1985. Print.

Giddings, Paula. *When and Where I Enter: The Impact of Black Women on Race and Sex in America*. New York: Bantam Books, 1984. Print.

Hubbard, Ruth. *The Politics of Women's Biology*. New Brunswick, NJ: Rutgers University Press, 1990. Print.

Lorber, Judith. *Paradoxes of Gender*. New Haven and London: Yale University Press, 1994. Print.

McGowan, Kay Givens. "Weeping for the Lost Matriarchy." *Daughters of Mother Earth*. Ed. Barbara Alice Mann and Winona LaDuke. Westport, CT: Praeger, 2006. Print.

Ross, Janell. "Mike Huckabee Says the Military's Job Is to 'Kill People and Break Things.' Well, Not Quite." *The Washington Post*. 7 August 2015. Web.

Tocqueville, Alexis de. *Democracy in America*. Trans. Henry Reeve, Esq. Vol. 2. 2nd ed. Cambridge: Sever and Francis, 1863. Print.

Wilson, Alex. "How We Find Ourselves: Identity Development and Two-Spirit People." *Race, Gender, Sexuality, and Social Class*. Ed. Susan J. Ferguson. Los Angeles: Sage, 2013. Print.

World Economic Forum. The Global Gender Gap Report 2017. www3.weforum.org/docs/WEF_GGGR_2017.pdf.

BEFORE READING

- Imagine for a moment that you were born a different sex. How would your life be changed? Would any of your interests and activities differ?

How about your relationships with other people? Write a journal entry describing your past, present, and possible future in this alternate identity.

- Collect and bring to class gender images taken from popular magazines and newspapers. Working in groups, make a collage of male, female, and transgender images; then compare and discuss your results. What do these media images tell you about what it means to be gendered in this culture?

- The woman in the frontispiece to this chapter is attending the 365 Empress Movement march in Baltimore; one of the organizers of the movement explained that women work for change 365 days a year, and that "Empress" signifies the value of black women. The march was held to demand an end to police violence, promote change in the community, and unify black women. Do a freewrite about the woman as you see her: What do you imagine that she does for a living? Is she a feminist? What role do you think she plays in the 365 Empress Movement — is she a leader, a follower involved with the group, or someone who heard about the march and just decided to show up? To support your views, refer to details of dress, makeup, hairstyle, body art, and attitude, as well as to what she's holding in her hands. How do you interpret the sign that she's carrying?

GIRL

JAMAICA KINCAID

Although she now lives in New England, Jamaica Kincaid (b. 1949) retains strong ties, including citizenship, to her birthplace — the island of Antigua in the West Indies. After immigrating to the United States to attend college, she ended up educating herself instead, eventually becoming a staff writer for *The New Yorker*, the author of several critically acclaimed books, and an instructor at Harvard University. About the influence of parents on children she says, "The magic is they carry so much you don't know about. They know you in a way you don't know yourself." Some of that magic is exercised in the story "Girl," which was first published in *The New Yorker* and later appeared in Kincaid's award-winning collection *At the Bottom of the River* (1983). She has written and edited many volumes of nonfiction on subjects ranging from colonialism to gardening and travel. She has published five novels: *Annie John* (1985), *Lucy* (1990), *The Autobiography of My Mother* (1996), *Mr. Potter* (2002), and *See Now Then* (2013).

WASH THE WHITE CLOTHES ON MONDAY and put them on the stone heap; wash the color clothes on Tuesday and put them on the clothesline to dry; don't walk barehead in the hot sun; cook pumpkin fritters[1] in very hot sweet oil; soak your little clothes right after you take them off; when buying cotton to make yourself a nice blouse, be sure that it doesn't have gum[2] on it, because that way it won't hold up well after a wash; soak salt fish overnight before you cook it; is it true that you sing benna[3] in Sunday school?; always eat your food in such a way that it won't turn someone else's stomach; on Sundays try to walk like a lady and not like the slut you are so bent on becoming; don't sing benna in Sunday school; you mustn't speak to wharf-rat boys, not even to give directions; don't eat fruits on the street—flies will follow you; *but I don't sing benna on Sundays at all and never in Sunday school*; this is how to sew on a button; this is how to make a buttonhole for the button you have just sewed on; this is how to hem a dress when you see the hem coming down and so to prevent yourself from looking like the slut I know you are so bent on becoming; this is how you iron your father's khaki shirt so that it doesn't have a crease; this is how you iron your father's khaki pants so that they don't have a crease; this is how you grow okra[4]—far from the house, because okra tree harbors red ants; when you are growing dasheen,[5] make sure it gets plenty of water or else it makes your throat itch when you are eating it; this is how you sweep a corner; this is how you sweep a whole house; this is how you sweep a yard; this is how you smile to someone you don't like too much; this is how you smile to someone you don't like at all; this is how you smile to someone you like completely; this is how you set a table for tea; this is how you set a table for dinner; this is how you set a table for dinner with an important guest; this is how you set a table for lunch; this is how you set a table for breakfast; this is how to behave in the presence of men who don't know you very well, and this way they won't recognize immediately the slut I have warned you against becoming; be sure to wash every day, even if it is with your own spit; don't squat down to play marbles—you are not a boy, you know; don't pick people's flowers—you might catch something; don't throw stones at blackbirds, because it might not be a blackbird at all; this is how to make a bread pudding; this is how to make doukona;[6] this is how to make pepper pot;[7] this is how to make a good medicine for a cold; this is how to make a good medicine to throw away a child before it even becomes a child; this is how to catch a fish; this is how to throw back a fish you don't like, and that way something bad won't fall on you; this is how to bully a man; this is how a man bullies you; this is how to love

---

[1]**fritters:** Small fried cakes of batter, often containing vegetables, fruit, or other fillings. [All notes are the editors'.]

[2]**gum:** Plant residue on cotton.

[3]**sing benna:** Sing popular music (not appropriate for Sunday school).

[4]**okra:** A shrub whose pods are used in soups, stews, and gumbo.

[5]**dasheen:** The taro plant, cultivated, like the potato, for its edible tuber.

[6]**doukona:** Plantain pudding; the plantain fruit is similar to the banana.

[7]**pepper pot:** A spicy West Indian stew.

a man, and if this doesn't work there are other ways, and if they don't work don't feel too bad about giving up; this is how to spit up in the air if you feel like it, and this is how to move quick so that it doesn't fall on you; this is how to make ends meet; always squeeze bread to make sure it's fresh; *but what if the baker won't let me feel the bread?*; you mean to say that after all you are really going to be the kind of woman who the baker won't let near the bread?

ENGAGING THE TEXT

1. What are your best guesses as to the time and place of the story? Who is telling the story? What does this dialogue tell you about the relationship between the characters, their values and attitudes? What else can you surmise about these people (for instance, ages, occupation, social status)? On what evidence in the story do you base these conclusions?

2. Why does the story juxtapose advice on cooking and sewing, for example, with the repeated warning not to act like a slut?

3. Explain the meaning of the last line of the story: "you mean to say that after all you are really going to be the kind of woman who the baker won't let near the bread?"

4. What does the story tell us about male–female relationships? According to the speaker, what roles are women and men expected to play? What kinds of power, if any, does the speaker suggest that women may have?

EXPLORING CONNECTIONS

5. How would Lisa Wade and Myra Marx Ferree (p. 480) interpret the behaviors and attitudes that the mother is trying to teach her daughter in this selection?

6. What does it mean to be a successful mother in "Girl"? How does this compare to being a good mother in Gary Soto's "Looking for Work" (p. 20)? Which mother do you consider more successful, and why?

EXTENDING THE CRITICAL CONTEXT

7. Write an imitation of the story. If you are a woman, record some of the advice or lessons your mother or another woman gave you; if you are a man, put down advice received from your father or from another male. Read what you have written aloud in class, alternating between male and female speakers, and discuss the results: How does parental guidance vary according to gender?

8. Write a page or two recording what the daughter might be thinking as she listens to her mother's advice; then compare notes with classmates.

HOW TO DO GENDER
LISA WADE AND MYRA MARX FERREE

While gender roles may appear straightforward, according to Lisa Wade and Myra Marx Ferree they're actually "complicated, constantly shifting, and even contradictory." Saudi Arabians do gender differently than Argentinians, who in turn do it differently than the Scots or Japanese. The way you perform gender at a formal event like a wedding differs from the way you enact it during a hotly contested soccer match. Wade and Ferree demonstrate that gender roles are flexible — subject to culture, context, and even individual preference. In this engaging selection, they explain how our views of gender are influenced by American culture, how we learn the rules of gender, and how we sometimes break those rules. Lisa Wade (b. 1974) is an Associate Professor of Sociology at Occidental College. She has published numerous journal articles on gender and sexuality as well as critical essays in newspapers and popular magazines; she also founded the award-winning website Sociological Images. Her most recent book is *American Hookup: The New Culture of Sex on Campus* (2017); she coedited *Assigned: Life with Gender* (with Douglas Hartmann, 2017). Myra Marx Ferree (b. 1949) is the Alice H. Cook Professor of Sociology and a member of the Gender and Women's Studies Department at the University of Wisconsin, Madison. She has published many articles on global gender issues and has coedited three books, the most recent of which is *Gender, Violence and Human Security: Feminist Perspectives* (with Aili Tripp and Christina Ewig, 2013). Wade and Ferree wrote the popular sociology text *Gender: Ideas, Interactions, Institutions* (2015), from which this selection is taken.

How to Do Gender

Psychologist Sandra Bem's four-year-old son, Jeremy, decided to wear barrettes to preschool one day. Bem recalls:

> Several times that day, another little boy insisted that Jeremy must be a girl because "only girls wear barrettes." After repeatedly insisting that "wearing barrettes doesn't matter; being a boy means having a penis and testicles," Jeremy finally pulled down his pants to make his point more convincingly. The other boy was not impressed. He simply said, "Everybody has a penis; only girls wear barrettes."[1]

[1]Sandra L. Bem, *The Lenses of Gender: Transforming the Debate on Sexual Inequality* (New Haven: Yale University Press, 1993), 149.

Jeremy's schoolmate stated his objection in the form of a general rule. It wasn't that *he* didn't like it when boys wore barrettes, or that Jeremy *specifically* didn't look fetching in a barrette, it was: *Only girls wear barrettes.* Jeremy's schoolmate articulated a rule for all boys that Jeremy had unwittingly broken.

Sociologists use the phrase **doing gender** to describe the ways in which we actively obey and break gender rules. **Gender rules** are instructions for how to appear and behave as a man or a woman. They are, essentially, the social construction of gender re-stated in the form of an instruction. You could likely brainstorm dozens or hundreds of such rules if you tried. They apply to every area of our lives, specifying how we should decorate our homes, what hobbies and careers we should pursue, with whom we should socialize and how, and much more. Some rules are relatively rigid (e.g., men do not wear makeup), while others are more flexible (e.g., men take showers instead of baths).

Cross- and Intra-Cultural Variation in Gender Rules

Most gender rules are simple cultural agreements. For instance, whereas grown men in the United States are supposed to physically touch each other only in very ritualized ways (e.g., the back slap in the "man hug" or the butt slap in football that means a job well done), in France and Argentina, among other places, heterosexual men exchange friendly kisses of greeting. In some Middle Eastern societies, men even hold hands.

Likewise, whereas skirts are strongly feminized in the United States, men wear kilts in Scotland and, in Arab countries, mean wear a white robe called a *thawb*, often with a pink-and-white head covering. The color pink doesn't have feminine connotations in Arab countries the way it does in the West. And in Belgium, pink isn't gender neutral; it's for boys. Flowers are another icon of femininity in the West, but certain floral patterns on a kimono clearly signal masculinity in Japan.

What women and men *don't* wear is also dictated by gender rules. In the United States, it is against the rules for women to expose their breasts in public. We take this so seriously that whether women should be allowed to breastfeed in public is still a hot debate. This obsession with hiding women's nipples seems unduly conservative from a European standpoint; in some parts of Europe, it is perfectly acceptable for women to sunbathe topless. Americans might be surprised to hear that Europeans describe Americans as irrationally prudish. Many Americans, as well as Europeans, in turn, condemn the "veiling" practices associated with Islam. Of course, many U.S. subcultures—like the Amish and Orthodox Jews—also value modesty for women, requiring that they cover their hair and arms and wear long dresses. Only because the idiosyncrasies of our own culture tend to be invisible to us does it seem obvious that women should cover some parts of their bodies, like their breasts, but not other parts, like their faces or hair.

It often isn't until we travel to or read about a new society or alternative subculture that we encounter rules that are unfamiliar to us, revealing our own rules as culturally contingent. This is the very definition of culture shock.

Historical Variation in Gender Rules

No matter how severe our culture shock, we can often adjust to new gender rules without too much trouble. We are good at such adjustments because we get practice throughout our lives. Gender rules are constantly undergoing both subtle and dramatic shifts.

Consider the earring. An American girl born in the 1930s would likely have worn clip-on earrings.[2] Pierced ears fell out of favor in the 1920s and were, at the time, preferred only by Italian and Spanish women (for whom it was an ethnic practice, similar to the small dot or *bindi* that Hindu women wear on their foreheads) and, oddly, male sailors (who hoped that a gold earring might serve as payment for a proper burial were they to sink, wash ashore, and be found by strangers). Clip-on earrings, however, were passé by the 1960s when pierced ears came back into fashion; Our hypothetical girl, then, might not have gotten her ears pierced until about the age of thirty.

If our hypothetical girl were a boy, he probably wouldn't have worn earrings of any kind. When his sister and all her friends were getting their ears pierced, the only men doing so were hippies and homosexuals. Twenty years later, during the '80s, male musicians and athletes popularized wearing earrings, but only in the left ear. If our now-fifty-year-old man decided to get an ear pierced, he would have gotten it in the left ear if he were straight and the right ear if he were gay. By the time our hypothetical man was seventy, though, the side of the head would be irrelevant: Young men around him would be piercing their left, their right, and even both ears. And these piercings would have signified, essentially, nothing.

Today, both men and women pierce their ears, but *how* we do so is   10 quite different (reflecting a subdivision of the gender binary). Whereas women are more likely to wear either elaborate or dainty earrings to signify femininity, men typically wear simple studs or ear plugs. And now we pierce other things, too—in gendered ways, of course. Belly-button piercings are found almost exclusively on women, whereas men are more likely to stretch their earlobes with plugs. Earrings are a great example of the way that gender rules change, sometimes in ways that seem quite arbitrary. Rules also change from context to context.

Contextual Variation in Gender Rules

Many of us take for granted the rules that guide our own gender display and easily adapt to cultural change. Our flexibility tends to mask the fact that the United States itself is a turbulent mixture of subcultures.

[2]Margo DeMello, *Encyclopedia of Body Adornment* (Westport, CT: Greenwood Press, 2007).

Accordingly, doing gender, even in our daily lives, requires that we simultaneously know the rules of the cultural mainstream as well as those of the subcultures we visit. In other words, we need more than one pair of gender binary glasses.[3]

Many of us adjust our look for different audiences. We all make cultural adjustments throughout our day and week. A guy driving home from a night at the sports bar with his buddies, during which he yelled at the TV, threw back beers, and pounded the table, will likely resort to a polite and professional manner when pulled over by a cop. Both of these self-presentations are versions of masculinity. Likewise, a college student may comfort crying children at her job at a day care center, look to hook up at a party that night, and drag herself to class the next morning prepared to discuss the week's reading. In each context, she does a different version of femininity: the nurturer, the flirt, the smart girl.

The gender rules that apply to varying contexts can be quite nuanced. Knowing exactly what style and behavior rules are appropriate for a wedding (is it a day or night wedding?), a first date (is it coffee or dinner?), and a job interview (do you want to project creativity or reliability?) requires sophisticated calculations. Nevertheless, most of us make these cultural transitions easily, often flawlessly. And thank goodness. People who are incapable of "tuning" their behavior are at risk of coming off as psychologically disturbed or willfully deviant. The same glowing, silver gown that made an actress seem so glamorous on the red carpet at the Oscars would make her look drunk or deranged if she were to wear it at the grocery store the next morning.

We learn a set of gender rules that are specific to our societies. We also learn how that set of gender rules varies—from the funeral home to the classroom, from Savannah to San Francisco, and from age eight to eighty—and how to adjust to those changes. We don't just get a pair of gender binary glasses when we're kids; we get many pairs. And we're constantly getting new prescriptions as needed.

Learning the Rules

Our First Prescription

Since different gender rules apply to different situations and change 15
over time, learning how to do gender appropriately is not easy. Children learn gender from infancy.[4] They can tell the difference between male and female voices by six months old and between men and women in photographs by nine months old. By the time they're one, they know to associate deep voices with men and high voices with women. By two and a half, most children know what sex they are and are "reaching out

[3]**gender binary glasses:** "Gender binary" refers to the false belief that there are only two types of people, male and female; "glasses" refers to the cultural lenses that associate masculine and feminine qualities with things like athletic shoes and high heels. [Eds.]

[4]For a review, see Carol Martin and Diane Ruble, "Children's Search for Gender Cues," *Current Directions in Psychological Science* 13, no. 2 (2004): 69.

to social norms"; they are trying to learn the rules and their brains are built to absorb everything around them.[5] By three years old, they tend to prefer play partners of their own sex and think more positively about their own group compared to the other.

Parents show children that gender matters by teaching them that they are a boy or a girl. Teachers separate school activities and games into boys vs. girls; community and school sports are usually sex segregated, such that girls and boys rarely play alongside or against each other.[6] All these things affirm for children that the distinction is important and meaningful. This is a child's first pair of gender binary glasses. "By the age of 5," psychologists Carol Martin and Diane Ruble write, "children develop an impressive constellation of stereotypes about gender (often amusing and incorrect) that they apply to themselves and others."[7]

Once children have a pair of gender binary glasses, they begin to act in ways that reflect the view, especially if their parents reward gender-stereotype-consistent behavior.[8] They orient themselves to toys they believe are gender appropriate and begin to make assumptions about other people based on their gender. Divisions between boys and girls in play become more strict and defined. Understanding the logic of the gender binary, they try to apply it even to gender-neutral items on the assumption that everything must be gendered. "Men eat pizza and women don't," announced a four-year-old to his parents on the way home from an Italian restaurant.[9]

As children absorb (or invent) new ideas about how girls and boys are supposed to act, they become increasingly rigid about doing things "right." This rigidity peaks around age six, which is exactly when many parents throw their hands up and give their daughters Barbie dolls and sons toy guns. Though this rigidity is often used as evidence that gender is biological, psychologists have shown that it is largely because children aren't yet capable of absorbing and negotiating the rules in their complexity.[10] Childhood rigidity is a learning phase more than proof of biological predispositions toward firepower and fashion.[11] As children learn that gender norms are not quite so strict, they become much more flexible about their own and others' conformity to gender expectations.

[5]Joan Roughgarden, *Evolution's Rainbow: Diversity, Gender and Sexuality in Nature and People* (Berkeley: University of California Press, 2004), 27.

[6]Michael Messner, "Barbie Girls versus Sea Monsters: Children Constructing Gender," *Gender and Society* 14, no. 6 (2000): 765–84; Barrie Thorne, *Gender Play* (New Brunswick, NJ: Rutgers, 1995).

[7]Carol Martin and Diane Ruble, "Children's Search for Gender Cues." *Current Directions in Psychological Science* 13, no. 2 (4002): 67.

[8]Ibid., 67.

[9]David F. Bjorklund, *Children's Thinking: Developmental Function and Individual Differences* (Belmont, CA: Wadsworth, 2000).

[10]Carol Martin and Diane Ruble, "Children's Search for Gender Cues." *Current Directions in Psychological Science* 13, no. 2 (4002): 67–70.

[11]Hanns Trautner et al., "Rigidity and Flexibility of Gender Stereotypes In Childhood: Developmental or Differential?" *Infant and Child Development* 14, no. 4 (2005): 365–81.

Even so, children are not passive recipients of gender socialization. They also actively resist it and, as the story about Jeremy's barrette suggests, they teach each other the rules they (think they) know. Children, then, are participants in their own and others' socialization. We are all negotiating gender rules from the get-go and setting up consequences for one another.

Lifelong Learning

Later, as adults, we navigate gender rules in more sophisticated ways. We become more tolerant of ambiguity and contradictions. But we continue to reach out to gender norms, continually learning and adjusting to new sets of gender rules that we encounter as we interact with new people, in new places, and across a changing social terrain. When we interact with children, we inevitably model and teach gender rules and, as we will explain next, we model and teach gender rules to adults around us as well.

Learning the rules, then, is a lifelong process that we actively negotiate. This means that an **injection model of socialization**, in which genderless children are "dosed" with a gender role in their childhood, never to fully recover, is wrong. Media commentators, when they bemoan the influence of violent video games and skinny actresses on young people, are using this culturalist model of socialization, one that assumes that children are victims of their environment, infected with rigid versions of masculinity or femininity. Children, it is presumed, are exposed to gender roles by "sick" adults and a "diseased" media when their immune system is weak; then they live with the virus for the rest of their lives.

This model of socialization fails on three fronts. First, it suggests that socialization is somehow finished by the time we're adults and doesn't account for our ability to learn new sets of rules and adjust to changing ones. Second, it leaves no room for the possibility that we actively consider and resist gender rules, something that Jeremy was doing even in preschool. Third, because the model fails to give people credit for actively resisting and changing gender rules, the injection model can't explain cultural changes, such as the ones that made pierced ears acceptable at different times for women and men.

Accordingly, sociologists prefer a **learning model of socialization** that suggests that socialization is a lifelong process of learning and re-learning gendered expectations as well as how to negotiate them. Unlike the injection model, the learning model reflects the need to adjust constantly to new contexts as we age, travel, and try new things. We don't *get* socialized once and for all but are constantly *being* socialized to a shifting social terrain.

The learning model gives us credit for being *smart* members of our culture. Because it recognizes that we are socialized to know the rules instead of to act out a role, it acknowledges our ability to think critically about and even reject rules. We aren't cultural dupes; we are cultural *experts* who consciously and strategically adapt our behavior to changes in the social fabric. We do this in negotiation with others who also have some intellectual autonomy from the rules. This is a much more social understanding of socialization than the injection model, which posits a one-way communication from adult to child. We do gender together, learning to manage conflict along the way (usually without resorting to dropping our pants like Jeremy).

Like the contents of the gender binary, then, the rules only *seem* 25 simple and stable over time. Rather, they are complicated, constantly shifting, and even contradictory. Their complexity, however, provides us with little excuse when we do not conform to what others expect.

Why We Follow the Rules

We follow gender rules for a wide range of reasons, including habit, pleasure, and, importantly, the reactions we expect or receive from others.

Habit

Sometimes we follow gender rules simply because they are part of our culture. We become habituated to them. We get used to walking and sitting in a certain way, own a wardrobe of already appropriately gendered clothes, and have experiences in rewarding gendered activities. Practice allows us to do gender without even thinking about it. Psychologists call such behaviors "over-learned"; they are learned not only by our minds but by our bodies—like riding a bike or typing on a keyboard—so we no longer need to think about them. Men's shirts, for example, are typically made so that the buttons are along the right and the button holes along the left; women's shirts are typically made in the opposite way. When is the last time you had to stop and think about the relative location of the buttons and button holes on your clothes while getting dressed? Your hands just automatically go to the right places.

Once we have over-learned a rule, we don't experience it as oppressive but as natural, however arbitrary it may be. Accordingly, it's often *easy* to follow gender rules, especially ones that are fundamental in our culture; we mostly do so unconsciously. American men don't often deliberate, for instance, about whether to pee sitting down or standing up. This is something they have learned (only after being potty trained in the sitting position), but now mostly take for granted. Men in Germany and Japan are much more likely to pee sitting down and whether to do so is more of a conscious choice.

On the flip side, it never occurs to most American women to pee standing up, even though, with enough practice, the majority could probably do so with little mess (or, at least, no more mess than that frequently left behind by men). In some parts of the world, such as Ghana, women do stand up to pee. Many of the gender rules that we follow are simply a matter of habit.

Pleasure

More than simply being habitual, following gender rules can be quite 30 pleasurable. For a man who has over-learned conventional American masculinity, it is rewarding to enact that masculinity at a sports bar with the guys. He knows the script, the beer tastes great, and his team might win. The same is true for enacting those aspects of femininity that are over-learned. Many women, for instance, enjoy dressing up, dancing, and flirting at a club.

For just this reason, we may especially enjoy opportunities to do gender elaborately. You may relish formal events like quinceañeras, bar and bat mitzvahs, your high school prom, and weddings. These events all call for strongly gendered displays: suits or tuxedos for men, dresses or gowns for women. It can be fun to pamper yourself at the salon, bring flowers to your date, and open doors or have them opened for you. It feels great to know that you look especially beautiful in your dress or unusually dashing in your tux. Success is intrinsically rewarding, and that is no less true when the success comes from performing gender.

However, there is a dark side to these success stories. Following rules creates cultural boundaries that are often painful for the people who are on the wrong side of them, by choice or circumstance. Sociologist Michael Kimmel says it beautifully:

> For some of us, becoming adult men and women in our society is a smooth and almost effortless drifting into behaviors and attitudes that feel as familiar to us as our skin. And for others of us, becoming masculine or feminine is an interminable torture, a nightmare in which we must brutally suppress some parts of ourselves to please others — or, simply, to survive. For most of us, though, the experience falls somewhere in between.[12]

The American guy who hates football or has a gluten allergy to beer sometimes feels like an outsider. So, too, does the woman who wants to wear a tux to the prom or can't walk in heels. The American man whose body is limber and powerful and who loves to dance to classical music may in fact train rigorously to be a ballet dancer, but he follows these pleasures at the risk of critical assessments from others that question his gender, his nationality, or his sexuality: He's not a real man, or a real American, and he's probably gay. Likewise, women who are tall and strong and enjoy playing basketball sometimes find that the pleasures of their own bodies can come at a cost to their social life if others judge them to be "unfeminine." We follow the rules voluntarily both out of habit and for pleasure, but also because there are consequences for breaking them.

Policing

Jeremy's schoolmate felt confident that he was entitled to enforce an unwritten rule about barrettes. Despite Jeremy's protestations, his

---

[12]Michael Kimmel, *The Gendered Society* (New York: Oxford University Press, 2004), 94.

schoolmate remained insistent that boys don't wear barrettes. Break-ing the rules can attract negative attention. Sociologists use the term **gender policing** to describe responses to the violation of gender rules aimed at promoting conformity.

When we are policed, we are being taught that we should learn 35 the rules, that these rules warrant conformity, and that we can expect consequences for breaking them. Gender policing happens every day. It comes from our friends, our love interests, our parents, bosses, and mentors. It's part of our daily lives. Some of it can be brutal and pain-ful (especially for people who don't fit in binary boxes), but much of it is friendly and humorous or takes the form of teasing. Consider these stories from our students:

- As James came in from a Saturday night with friends, his father warned, "Get to bed. We're going to the woods tomorrow." "Nah, Dad," the son replied. "I can't." His dad began to tease him, saying: "What? You too good to go huntin' with your dad now?"

- Chandra goes to her economics class wearing sweats, a ponytail, and no makeup. A guy with whom she has been flirting all semes-ter says to her, humorously, "I guess I'm not important enough to dress up for!"

- Sun, waiting in line to use a single-stall bathroom, sees that the men's bathroom is open and starts toward it. As she walks in, her friend says, "You're not going to use the *men's* bathroom, are you!?"

In each of these stories, a person breaks a culturally and historically specific gender rule and is then subjected to policing. In the first example, James's disinterest in going to the woods with his dad broke a rule common in rural working-class communities: *Men should want to hunt.* When Chandra's guy friend used her appearance to remind her that he was interested in her, he affirmed a rule common among young singles: *Women should dress up for men they want to impress.* Sun's friend expressed surprise that she would dare to use a restroom labeled "Men." Whenever there are two bathrooms, even if they each include only one toilet, the rule is clear: *Use the appropriate gender-designated bathroom.*

A raised eyebrow, a derisive laugh, or a comment like "Are you sure you want to wear that?" are small prices to pay for the freedom to be ourselves. But policing isn't always so mild or so fleeting. When women are called "dyke" or "bitch," they are often being policed for being strong or assertive, characteristics that a binary lens sees as mas-culine and unacceptable for women. Conversely, when men are called "pussy" or "girl," they are often being accused of not being strong or assertive, and in the logic of the gender binary, that means not mas-culine. The phrase "nice guys finish last" refers, in part, to women's participation in this same gender policing, by showing a preference for dating men who practice emotional unavailability. Guys who work hard to have a muscular upper body, like women who hide their strength or act deferential when men are around, are using the rules to win friends and protect themselves from censure.

The risks of nonconformity may be much higher than attracting ridicule or being unpopular. We may fear losing friends, lovers, or the support of our parents. We may be fired or passed over for jobs or promotions because our gender display doesn't please clients or co-workers. Gender policing can also be emotionally and physically brutal. The FBI reported 1,572 victims of hate crimes against gays, lesbians, and transgender people in 2011.[13] Gays and lesbians break the rule: *Men should have sex with women and women should have sex with men.* Transgender people break the rule: *People's gender performance should match their apparent biological sex.* It may be odd to think that hate crimes against transgender, gay, and lesbian people are a form of *gender* policing, but they often are. People who cross-dress earnestly, with the intent to pass as the other sex, challenge gender rules and undermine other people's ability to determine their sex in a binary way. People who are committed to a gender binary *trust* these signs as markers of something real and important about others, so they may feel betrayed and act violently to punish people whom they feel are essentially lying to them. Violent gender policing may also aim to produce conformity to the rules by those unwilling to follow them.

Because the rules themselves vary situationally, so does their policing. It is certainly dangerous to be queer in some contexts, but it can be quite fun at Halloween or at friendly gay bars. Middle school boys who study hard may be subjected to constant taunts of "fag," but if they adopt the tough guy performance those taunts are designed to elicit, they may be policed by their teachers and parents. Female athletes may be told to be aggressive on the field but policed toward more traditional gender performances off it. Girls may be pushed to concentrate on their school work and aspire to high-powered careers while at the same time be expected not to be overbearing around their male peers. What happens later when they're asked to deprioritize their own careers in favor of their husbands'?

We, like Jeremy, are policed into multiple and even contradictory gender displays by people with various, often clashing agendas. Some people have more influence than others: Policing is more influential if it comes from someone you care for (like your girlfriend or boyfriend) or who has power over you (such as your boss). We also police ourselves, kindly and cruelly. We watch TV and read fashion blogs to learn how, and how not, to dress. We read the sports section to make sure we can talk about who won the big game last night and why. We stand in front of the mirror and inspect our faces, scrutinize our bodies for too much or not enough hair, and hope for bumps and bulges in gender-appropriate places.

40

---

[13]United States Federal Bureau of Investigation, Hate Crime Statistics 2011, http://www.fbi.gov/about-us/cjis/ucr/hate-crime/2011/narratives/incidents-and-offenses.

We inspect our behavior no less than our bodies: Were we too loud or forward? Too meek or agreeable? Sometimes we call ourselves ugly names or feel shame or disgust. We punish our bodies with overexercise or starvation. We police our words and our tone of voice, watching to ensure that we don't sound too opinionated (if we're women) or too emotional (if we're men). We may force ourselves to major in engineering when we'd really like to take more literature classes because we know we'll later be judged by the size of our paycheck; or we may choose to stay single because our guy friends will never let us hear the end of it if we let them know we're actually in love with that girl or that we're gay; or we may not say anything to the guy we like about the other women he's sleeping with because we fear being called "needy."

We even recruit others to help us police ourselves. We ask each other to evaluate our bodies, our clothes, and our interactions with others: Do I look fat in this dress? Do these shoes look gay? When women get ready for a party together, they frequently ask one another to assess their outfits, looking for a second opinion as to whether they are wearing just the right clothes. Many women try to follow this tricky rule: *Women should dress sexy but not slutty.* "You can wear a short skirt or a low-cut top," we hear, "but not both." There is nothing malevolent in this type of policing; it is simply women trying to help their friends follow the rules that they know apply to them.

We also use media, often unconsciously, to advertise and test gender rules with our friends and family. If you are commented *to*, but not commented *on*, you are still being instructed as to what is and is not acceptable, and these moments help clarify the (ever-changing) rules. When friends get together to watch the Oscars and snark at the outfits on the red carpet or take pleasure in laughing at the women on *Real Housewives*, they are telling one another what makes a person look good or be likeable. Often, our evaluations are gendered. Through these routines, we learn what our friends think is ugly, slutty, sloppy, gay, bitchy, weak, and gross and, accordingly, how we should and should not dress and act around them. Collective reactions to celebrity fashions and personalities, then, can serve to clarify and affirm rules.

And, of course, we participate in policing others directly. We create consequences for those who break the rules. We police others in the name of kindness. We feel we know the rules well and can cue in our friends and family members that they are at risk of being policed by someone less benevolent than we are. Other times we are more deeply disconcerted by rule breaking. We may give in to the temptation to be mean spirited or cruel in our policing when we are personally invested in the rule. We may even feel a sense of injustice or unfairness if the rules we follow—sometimes at a sacrifice—are broken by others who can do so without censure.

Because of policing, our choices about following the rules have 45 real social consequences. Some are mild, some are severe, but they all shape the distribution of rewards and punishments. But—and this is a big "but"—we don't *always* choose to follow the rules; we also break the rules. In fact, we break them all the time.

So the complicated truth is that while we all know the rules, and often follow them, we also break them. How do we do this?

How to Break the Rules

All of us get away with some rule breaking. Breaking rules *is* doing gender. That is, doing gender is about more than just conformity. It's also about negotiating with the rules. In fact, people who *rigidly* conform to a single set of gender rules aren't often considered ideal men or women. Instead, they're often the butt of jokes (a dumb jock or ditzy blonde) or pitied for their one-dimensional lives (the ruthless CEO who never knew his kids or the full-time housewife who never discovered her other talents). Likewise, those who are vicious policers of others' behavior are called rude, intolerant, or worse.

We also break the rules because sometimes it is impossible to follow them, no matter how badly we would like to. The mother undergoing chemotherapy, for example, may not be able to care for her husband and children the way she feels she should; the man with a spinal cord injury, similarly, may not be able to perform sexually the way men are told they must. Likewise, the guy who is five foot two simply can't be taller than most women.

Other times, rules are downright contradictory, like the one that says that men should be able to drink a lot of alcohol but also remain in control. Or maybe we're part of a subculture that requires breaking the rules endorsed by the mainstream, like female farmers. Sometimes we literally can't afford to follow a rule, like the man who doesn't have the extra income to treat women on dates. Sometimes we break a particular rule just because following it is undesirable, like the man who loves romantic comedies. Or perhaps we don't like rules in general and rebel on principle.

So we need a mechanism that allows us to break rules with little or no consequence. How do we do it?   50

We have a creative way to get around the rules. Remember the three stories of policing discussed earlier in this chapter? In each case, it turns out, the rule breaker got away with breaking the rule, despite being policed. Each rule breaker avoided a greater penalty by offering an **account**, or an explanation for why they broke the rule that then excused their behavior. Let's revisit the stories, this time following them through to the end:

- As James came in from a Saturday night with friends, his father warned, "Get to bed. We're going to the woods tomorrow." "Nah, Dad," the son replied. "I can't." His dad began to tease him, saying: "What? You too good to go huntin' with your dad now?" James just said, "No, football tryouts are next week and I was gonna run drills with Mike in the morning." "Go get 'em, son," said his father.

- Chandra goes to her economics class wearing sweats, a ponytail, and no makeup. A guy with whom she has been flirting all semester says to her, humorously, "I guess I'm not important enough to dress up for!" And she smiles and replies, "Hey! I just came from the gym." He reassures her, "I figured. I was just kidding."

- Sun, waiting in line to use a single-stall bathroom, sees that the men's bathroom is open and starts toward it. As she walks in, her friend says, "You're not going to use the *men's* bathroom, are you!?" Sun says, "I wouldn't, but I really have to go!" Her friend nods sympathetically.

As these stories illustrate, we can get away with breaking rules if we have a good excuse.

When the characters above say, "Football tryouts are next week," "I just came from the gym," or "I really have to go," they are offering an account to justify why they are breaking the rule. These accounts may or may not be true, but they offer a sufficient explanation to others that makes gender nonconformity *incidental* rather than *intentional.* If a person has a good account, he or she is likely to get away with it. In all these stories, the "policer" accepts the explanation, responding with "Go get 'em, son," "I was just kidding," or a sympathetic nod.

Accounting does more than excuse one's behavior. In these examples, as often happens, the speakers affirm the rule at the same time that they are explaining why an exception should be made in their specific case. So James is *really* saying: "[Of course I would go hunting], it's just that football tryouts are next week." Chandra is saying: "I [would have dressed up for class, but I] just came from the gym." And Sun is saying, "I wouldn't [use the men's bathroom normally], but I really have to go!"

These speakers didn't respond, "Actually I don't like hunting" 55 or "Who says I can't come to class sloppy!" or "It's stupid that I can't use the men's bathroom!" Such responses reject the rules altogether. Confronting the rules head-on can cause conflict. Instead, if the rule breaker affirms the legitimacy of the rule, the policer is usually satisfied, and conflict can be avoided. Interestingly, affirmation of the rule often works just as well as a change in behavior; infractions are punished only when they aren't excused. That's why transsexuals are more likely to be victims of hate crimes than guys dressed up like women at Halloween. Halloween is an account. It is a way for men to say, "[I would never dress like a woman normally], but it's Halloween!" A transsexual has no such excuse. The Halloween reveler is an exception that proves the rule; the transsexual is an attack on the rule itself.

Accounting is a skill. Jeremy, our intrepid pants dropper, had not yet mastered the art of accounting. He wasn't sophisticated enough to negotiate his gender with his schoolmate and resorted instead to a rather primitive way of proving he was a boy. Explicit conflict over gender rule breaking is typical of younger kids who have just begun to learn the rules and haven't yet mastered the act of explaining violations away. In contrast, because we learn how to do it by watching others and practicing, adults tend to be quite good at offering accounts, though some of us are better at it than others.

Jason Patterson/Conde Nast Publications/The Cartoon Bank

Somewhere between reaching out to learn the rules, learning how to follow them flexibly, accounting for the many instances in which we break them, and seeking subcultures that share our sense of what rules were "made to be broken," we manage to develop a way of doing gender that works for us, given our opportunities and constraints. We grow up into culturally adept, gendered adults and leave some portion of the rigidities of childhood behind.

ENGAGING THE TEXT

1. Why do Wade and Ferree say that doing gender requires us to "know the rules of the cultural mainstream as well as those of the subcultures that we visit"? How does cultural context influence the ways that we enact gender? What cultures or subcultures are you a part of, and what are the expectations of women and men in those contexts?

2. What is "gender policing"? Review Wade and Ferree's discussion of the many ways that policing occurs, and then write about how you may have participated in policing the gender displays of others. Have you policed your own gender expression? If so, how?

3. Working in same-sex groups, brainstorm a list of gender rules for women and men. As a class, compare the results: are the rules consistent or contradictory? Next, debate whether following each rule is a matter of habit (over-learning), pleasure, or policing.

4. Define the "injection model" and the "learning model" of socialization. Why do Wade and Ferree object to the injection model? What do they see as the advantages of the learning model?

5. Think of a time when you either intentionally or accidentally violated the rules of gender conformity. Write a journal entry recounting your experience: What were the unstated rules, and how did you break them? How did others respond to you? Did you offer an account or explanation of why you broke the rules? If so, how effective was it?

6. **Thinking Rhetorically**   Wade and Ferree use stories — like Jeremy wearing barrettes — to illustrate a particular view of gender, and then return to them later in the selection to illustrate a slightly different idea. Why do you think they rely on this technique? Why is this use of stories appropriate in an introductory sociology textbook? How does it work to emphasize the idea of cultural contingency?

EXPLORING CONNECTIONS

7. In Jamaica Kincaid's "Girl" (p. 477), how does the mother police her daughter's gender? To what extent does she emphasize following the rules? Does she ever suggest breaking them? What appears to be the purpose of her instructions?

8. Wade and Ferree argue that "children are not passive recipients of gender socialization" (para. 19); how does Nicole, in Amy Ellis Nutt's narrative (p. 73), resist or reject conventional gender norms? How does she embrace them? How does her family's caution about revealing her trans status acknowledge that gender policing can be "emotionally and physically brutal" (Wade and Ferree, para. 38)?

9. How would Wade and Ferree explain the humor of the cartoon on page 493? What's the effect of the explorer finding traditional female and male symbols on ancient, foreign structures? Does it suggest that the gender binary is universal or that it's completely outmoded?

EXTENDING THE CRITICAL CONTEXT

10. Write an account analyzing your own gender role socialization. How did you first learn the rules? Have you encountered cultural differences that forced you to reevaluate or revise your understanding of the rules? Have you come to resist particular gender rules? What roles have parents, friends, bosses, girl- or boyfriends played in your socialization?

11. If you have lived abroad, traveled in a different country, or become friends with someone from another culture, what surprised you about the gender rules common to that culture? Discuss your experiences in class.

GUYS' CLUB: NO FAGGOTS, BITCHES, OR PUSSIES ALLOWED

CARLOS ANDRÉS GÓMEZ

We acquire our concepts of gender so early in life that they may appear completely natural to us; it's hard to see them as the result of lessons taught and learned. But as this lively, intimate memoir by Carlos Andrés Gómez (b. 1981) demonstrates, the lessons can have an outsized impact on a sensitive child. At six years old, Carlos, fascinated by his sister and aunt painting their fingernails, insists on getting his painted too, only to have an older boy call him "faggot": "Suddenly everyone came running and giggling and pointing at me. . . . I had become the neighborhood freak, all because I had painted fingernails." As he grows older and encounters new people, cultures, and ideas, Carlos comes to resist traditional masculinity and to embrace a more nuanced view of what it means to be a man. A poet, actor, and author, Gómez's work has appeared in literary magazines, journals, and anthologies; he has won a number of awards, including the 2015 Lucille Clifton Poetry Prize and an Andrew W. Mellon Fellowship. He also has appeared on HBO's *Def Poetry Jam***, coauthored and starred in the Emmy Award–winning "Respect Yourself" TV spots, and collaborated with John Legend in the "Senior Orientation Project"—a program for high school students that counteracts bullying and encourages inclusive masculinity. This selection is from his memoir,** *Man Up: Cracking the Code of Modern Manhood* **(2012).**

AT SIX YEARS OLD IT SEEMED SO SIMPLE TO ME. I was visiting my family in Colombia for the summer and bored on a sleepy July afternoon. My sister and aunt were painting their fingernails. The colors were dazzling, mesmerizing, almost *delicious*! And I wanted to get my fingernails painted too.

My aunt tried to laugh off my request. Then she calmly explained to me that this kind of thing was only for girls. And then she started to scold me when the volume of my whining became unbearable. Finally, she gave in.

"Okay," she said. "I guess you'll have to learn the hard way."

And thus, the lesson began. I wanted one hand of each color. Both looked stunning. I wanted to be made pretty as well. So I sat there in my chair, like a king, as my sister thoughtfully painted my left hand with the color she had used and my aunt carefully put two coats of whatever hue she had chosen.

I remember them finishing my nails, and feeling so proud I could ⁵ barely contain myself. I wanted to run all over town and show everyone what they had done to my nails. They were beautiful!

I heard the rising cheers and laughter from the courtyard outside. A soccer game was breaking out, so my sister and I bolted full speed down the stairs to join in the fray. As usual, I was one of the more athletic kids for my age. I sprinted and screamed and dove all over the cobbled square like a madman, trying hard to keep up with the older and bigger kids. There must have been about twenty of us, all huddled around the ball like bees over honey.

Then one of the big kids trapped the ball with his foot and grabbed my hand.

"You can't play," he said quickly, in his gruff Spanish. "Why are your nails painted? What are you, a *faggot?*"

Suddenly everyone came running and giggling and pointing at me. They called to siblings and friends who were still inside their houses to come see. I had become an attraction, an oddity, something to be laughed at and made fun of. I dashed home as fast as I could, hiding my hands in my shirt, hot tears drenching my cheeks in confusion and horror. I had become the neighborhood freak, all because I had painted fingernails.

That's the first lesson in masculinity I can recall. It's pretty hard to ¹⁰ forget being called a hurtful word (one I didn't understand at the time) and then have everyone point and laugh at you in unison. It seemed so strange to me then. My aunt just carefully and tenderly removed the paint from my nails and said, "I tried to tell you, Carlos Andrés, but you wouldn't listen."

I thought to myself, *Tell me what? What did I just do that was so wrong?*

Manhood is something that is enforced. Growing up, my friends and I would always tell each other to stop being a bitch or a pussy anytime someone showed weakness or vulnerability. Staying within the acceptable boundaries of this enforced masculinity (or being "man enough") was a huge issue for me as a kid, especially because I've always been *very* sensitive. I get it from my mom. She's like me: supertough and very vulnerable. As an adult now, I think it is an incredible combination. But when I was little, only the supertough part was an asset.

I don't remember when I learned "faggot" referred to someone who was gay. What I do remember is having friends and classmates who talked about gay people as though they were all pedophiles and molesters. A friend in sixth grade once told me, "Be careful at the pool. That faggot lifeguard might jump on your back while you're not looking."

Even at twelve, I didn't understand the correlation between someone's sexuality and some association with deviance. My friend tried to sell me some story about a guy at the lake one summer who kept trying to climb on his back. Whether or not he believed any of what he was saying, like so much that is about being masculine, I now understand that he was merely signifying to me that he was "safe." He was just proving that he wasn't "one of them." I'd be curious to see who he's dating now.

When I think back to my childhood, there are so many examples and stories of people enforcing my masculinity that I don't know where to start. And in most cases it's a fleeting moment, a passing glance, or an under-breath comment. It's my dad making sure I'm staying in shape and going to the gym. It's friends freezing up and not knowing what to do whenever I get emotional. It's me, caught off guard by my best friend telling me he loves me, and being surprised at the homophobia creeping up in my own chest.

I remember taking a shower after swimming at the gym, having just started puberty and peeking at my friend to see if his body looked like mine. As I glanced over, I realized he was doing the same with me. We both had little hints of pubic hair at the base of our penises, hair starting to emerge from underneath our arms. I'm sure we both giggled and accused each other of being gay, and then kept sneaking peeks when the other wasn't looking. We were curious and young and didn't know yet how high the price could be for breaking this rule among others.

In my first year of high school, one of the kids in my gym class got caught doing much less and almost paid a high price for it. He was checking out one of my teammates on the basketball team as he changed. Just in the longing of the glance, I could tell that this awkward, reticent kid (who I actually had never spoken with) was infatuated with my friend, who turned abruptly and said, "Yo, faggot, don't fuckin' look at me. Unless you want your ass beat." The message was clear and impossible to misunderstand.

I have never felt consciously homophobic about same-sex anything—relationships, affection, marriage. Following the lead of my parents, I've just never really cared who someone dated or was attracted to, nor did I ever feel threatened or put off by it. To me it was just another characteristic that helped tell the story of who a person was. As I headed off to college, I'd read and dialogued and discussed so much regarding homophobia and heterosexism and all the gender-related theory socially conscious kids love to ponder.

Then one day I found out about what was really brewing underneath my open-mindedness. It was the first semester of my freshman year, and four of my girl friends wanted to go to a gay club to go dancing. I did feel turned off by how they were fetishizing gay culture as though it were an accessory (see *Sex and the City* for more), and I was seriously on the prowl for girls most of that year, but I still felt surprised that I didn't want to go with them. It wasn't just that I didn't want to go, I felt very *uncomfortable* with the idea of going to a gay club. And despite my seemingly valid justifications to myself, I had to accept the truth: I was homophobic.

My friends laughed at me when I said I didn't want to go, a couple of them raising their eyebrows in surprise.

"I thought you were different, Carlos. . . . Wow. I didn't think you'd feel like that." I could hear the disappointment in my friend's voice.

"I just don't want to lead anybody on," I blurted out in my defense. "It'd be like colonizing the space," I said proudly, trying to challenge them back.

"Oh, come on," she shot back. "That's bullshit. You're just scared and homophobic like every other guy."

And I was. Those are the moments when you really learn about who you are, when something comes up that cannot be planned for, when you can't prepare or put your best foot forward, and you just stumble into who you are. I had a similar experience when I spent two months in Zambia after my junior year in college.

In the township where I worked, Mtendere, men frequently would   25
walk the streets holding hands. It had no sexual connotation whatsoever (believe me, not in East Africa!), but it was just how people did things. It was so strange for me to see two muscular, maybe even superhomophobic guys with their pinky fingers interlinked walking down the street.

I remember being in college and seeing this girl I had been hooking up with at a party. We would hook up late at night and not really see each other otherwise. At the party, while I was flirting, at one point, I interlinked my fingers with hers.

"Whoa, what are you doing? We're not married, Carlos," she scolded me, pulling her hand quickly away from mine.

I had never held hands with her. And I never did. She had literally sucked my dick probably twenty times, but holding hands was too intimate? Yep. That's America for you.

And it may sound strange, but I actually understand it on a certain level—there is something so beautiful and intimate about holding hands (and sex is just whatever, right?). I wish most guys in the United States could be granted more permission to enter spaces like that with each other, not necessarily in a sexual way, but to develop some kind of emotional literacy among us, especially with each other. As much as I might hope for that, though, that's not to say my handholding experiences in Zambia were any easier.

My good friend Andreas would wrap his pinky around mine while   30
we'd walk. When he would stop and talk to a friend he would keep our fingers interlinked. Sometimes while we talked and joked he would rub his hand against the small of my back. And he wasn't the only guy who did this! In the United States that would be considered flirting by pretty much anyone. But in Zambia it was just the way friendships were signified. I was painfully awkward with Andreas. He probably just thought it was some cultural difference with me being American, or maybe didn't notice it at all, but I was so uncomfortable with all of this handholding and intimate physical interaction among men.

On so many levels, though, I loved it. I thought it was beautiful and powerful and refreshing. I loved how rarely men in Zambia got into conflict or fought when they were out. Unlike when I go out in Brooklyn, I didn't see one fight when I partied with Andreas and Japhet and my other friends in Mtendere. I believe that the language of intimacy and connection that occurs between men there, with handholding and eye contact and listening, prevents violence from erupting so easily. As a man in the United States, I often feel alienated and aloof around my fellow brothers. It's kind of hard not to, with so many rules and boundaries constantly keeping us apart.

Although I consciously may have loved the differences in how men interacted physically in Zambia, my subconscious was screaming. My body was petrified stiff most of the time. As I walked around the township with Andreas I suddenly felt like I no longer knew how to move. My body was no longer my own. When we would stop to talk with someone, I forgot how to stand. My cool, calm aura was completely upended by the simplest detail: two pinkies being intertwined.

My visit to Zambia helped me drop some of my socialized defenses, especially with other men. I now had an easier time embracing my friend Leila's Iranian father when I would visit her family, following the Middle Eastern custom of embracing arms and touching both cheeks. I thought back to my time in Thailand when I was in high school and how easily men embraced and often held hands there as well. On the plane ride home, I thought about how drastically differently people interact and exist outside the United States. As I headed home, I craved that connection I'd discovered in Zambia, arriving back to the "man hugs" and formal handshakes of before.

I don't know how much it was related to the revelations I had in Zambia or not, but something strange and beyond explanation happened that fall. I was visiting Brent during our final year of college. Both of us were struggling through a very tough semester. Brent had just suffered a very painful breakup with his long-term girlfriend, and my mother had just been diagnosed with congestive heart failure and awaited emergency open-heart surgery.

I traveled up to Brent's school, Bates College, for a typical weekend for us: parties, long talks, Mario Kart on his Nintendo 64, and a few drinks. It was our chance to get our feet under ourselves again and do what we always did for each other (and had since we were barely thirteen): pick each other up when we fell.

My first night there we drank like fish. Both got sloppy drunk, hooked up with random girls (whose names and faces remained a blur), and finally stumbled back into his room—where he fell into his bed and I collapsed onto a half-inflated mattress on the floor. I remember being mesmerized by an intense dream. In it, I was talking with my high school sweetheart, Vanessa, and she was stroking my head and kissing me. At this point, she and I hadn't spoken in a year and a half after abruptly breaking off communication when I began briefly dating another girl. For so long she had been a stabilizing support system in my life. Both she and Brent had been my rocks. With my mind swirling with the uncertainty of my mother's health, I needed their support more than ever. I remember how sensuous and soft each kiss was, as we started to kiss some more.

"Carlos." I looked down and saw Brent looking up at me as though he'd seen a ghost. "Carlos. Are you okay?"

I was hovering over Brent, just inches from his face.

"What. . .?" I looked around the room, trying to get my bearings.

"What were you doing?" Brent asked, as if trying to piece it together 40 himself.

"I . . . have no clue. I was just having a dream. And then I was over you." I had no way to either understand *or* explain myself.

"Were you just . . . *kissing* me?" Brent tried to ask, as neutrally as possible, his huge, generous heart doing everything it could not to accuse or shame me.

"I . . . have no idea. What just happened?" I still felt caught in a haze.

God bless Brent for his heart and humanity. He very gingerly brought up the subject the next morning, trying to give me permission to open up about my sexuality. Give me the forum he thought I might need to talk about what I had been hiding from everyone, and him, for so long.

"No," I said, "it's weird. I have no way of understanding or explain- 45 ing what happened. I don't feel any attraction to men at all. At least, not that I'm *conscious* of. That's the best explanation I can give," I told Brent plainly.

He knows when I'm lying. I know when he's hedging on something. He knows when I'm withholding. As he studied my face, I could see his perplexity only grow as he realized that everything I was saying was the truth. Regardless, I started some soul-searching that morning. Was I gay? Did I have something inside of me that was trying to break free? Had I been lying to myself about my sexuality my entire life?

I didn't feel like that was the case, though. Sexuality is just one of those things. It just is. It's an impulse, a moment of kinetic energy in your body. It's not found in a textbook nor can it be explained by a scientist. It just is. That's what's so beautiful about sexuality. And I didn't feel anything romantic or sexual toward my best friend, nor had I toward any other man that I could recall.

Then I considered something even deeper and more powerful—did I just kiss my best friend while I was sleeping as an expression of something else? Was that kiss symbolic of a closeness I craved that I had tasted in Zambia? Was it my desperate attempt to connect to my other best friend, Vanessa, who I had lost? Was it an expression of desperately reaching out, when I felt like I was at risk of losing everyone?

I have no idea what that kiss was about that night. Brent and I ratio- nalized it as me craving intimacy and connection during one of the lowest points of my life. I can't say definitively what it did or did not mean.

There is a writer I very much look up to and respect. He is seventy 50 years old and has been an out gay man since his twenties. One day recently while we were having drinks and talking he told me: "I'm in love with a woman."

"Really?" I asked with genuine surprise. "Who?"

"This twenty-eight-year-old girl who helps me," he began. "Can you believe it? Fifty years all I wanted was dick. And now this woman has climbed into my heart."

I tell that story to say, "Who the fuck knows?" Sexuality is a fluid, changing spectrum of experience and impulse. Who knows? Maybe when I'm seventy I'll be gay. Or bi. Or who knows what. I hope that when I'm his age, I have the same courage to follow my heart. I think we can all learn from his story. Which brings me to another example closer to my own experiences that challenges not just sexuality but also gender.

While living in New York just after college, I developed a friendship with a woman. I always thought she was gorgeous but knew that she was into women. Everything about the way she dressed and moved and acted reinforced my own stereotypes about where she landed on the sexuality spectrum. Over time we got closer and more open with each other. She told me that she had dated one guy in her life, briefly, while she was in high school and still figuring out her sexuality. Besides that lone exception, she had only been with women.

Finally one day she confronted me. "You're not into me, are you?" 55

I was thoroughly confused. My kinda butch, lesbian friend is attracted to me? And I had to admit, what fucked with my head further—I was *very* attracted to her. This woman who said "fuck gender" and spoke and moved like men I knew. Like *I* did! Ultimately, though, it didn't matter to me. I had always been attracted to her but, long before this talk, I had accepted the fact that she wasn't into guys.

"Uh . . . I'm confused. I'm *definitely* into you. But I thought you weren't into guys?" I asked, trying to get some footing.

"Fuck it. It's beyond gender. I like you," she said smiling, as though she were reluctantly conceding something.

In the months we saw each other, I felt challenged by her in how I saw gender and sexuality. Friends and classmates of hers at her university viewed her as "queer," many of them identified similarly, so you should have seen the looks we got when she told them I was staying over for the night. Suddenly she was breaking the rules. She was the Latino with the white mother tucked away somewhere. I could see the nods and betrayal in people's eyes: They didn't like seeing the walls they knew breaking down.

Sexually, things between us were amazing but complex. I could 60
tell that she was the one who was used to being in control. Some of our hook-ups were like wrestling matches, as I struggled to submit and receive, while she became self-aware, and maybe even self-conscious like me, of her own need for dominating. There were so many narratives and energies playing out every time we took off our clothes. I felt both daunted and exhilarated by the explorations that we shared.

Our times together made me rethink what I took for granted in terms of sexuality and gender. I wondered why I was always the one to initiate in my relationships with women. And I mean *initiate* in terms of everything—first contact, sex, the relationship. I wondered why I postured and doted and acted in ways that, after the revelations with my friend, had seemed contrived and programmed.

On the bus ride home after one of my visits, I had the realization that straight men strategically use certain words to police who we are. And three staple words at the center of that enforcement are the ones included in the title of this chapter: faggot, bitch, and pussy. All three of those words share something in common: Men use those words to devalue the feminine.

That day I first recognized how homophobia, although it is usually directed toward other men, is, ultimately, an indictment and an attack on women. Gay men, accurately or not, are often called "effeminate" or "girly" or other names that connote femininity. In a world in which gender is socialized to exist in drastic binaries—with tough guys on one side and dainty ladies on the other—where is there room for any of us to be who we are? Furthermore, and more to the point, where do we see anything associated with women given value?

To have the power of patriarchy and then to surrender it is a threat to all men. When I am not the overbearing, all-powerful man, who am I? When there is a fluid, changing spectrum of sexuality and gender, where actions aren't prescribed and roles aren't all but scripted, how do I know what to do? The truth is, we have no idea what to do. The truth is, only when we move away from what we've subconsciously learned can we ever truly find and know who we are.

That's why I felt lost in Zambia. I felt lost and confused, and then saw a change in myself. It's why I felt liberated and opened up and craved the connections I made while I was there. It may have been why Brent and I woke up mid-kiss, both of us confused, flustered, and embarrassed.

Masculinity is a choke chain. It is a suffocating bar that can never be met. How can every man alive be the toughest? And the most stoic? And the most brave? And the most powerful? And the most "manly"? I realized with my once-lesbian friend that my aspirations toward manhood had been a riddle for my own destruction. I was willingly playing a game I was destined to lose. We all are. By buying into the illusion of power afforded by patriarchy, we as heterosexual men do far more than just oppress women and gay men—ultimately we are oppressing ourselves.

I want more than this narrow slice of humanity I've been given permission to taste. I'm tired of not being able to show affection to my brothers and friends. I'm tired of feeling self-conscious when I kiss or hug my father. I'm tired of feeling like I have to hide my emotion and my sensitivity. I'm tired of being stigmatized for wanting to communicate and express myself. I'm tired of needing to throw hurtful words like "faggot" or "bitch" or "pussy" around to prove that I'm a man.

More than being just tired, though, I wish I could speak to that six-year-old version of myself with beautifully painted nails, that I could be standing in that square in Toledo where my aunt, uncle, and cousin Mauricio used to live in Bogotá and hear those kids yell "¡Maricón!" (which means "faggot" in Spanish) at the top of their lungs. I wish I could circle up the group, like they were one of my classes at Drew

Elementary School in west Philly, where we had a thirty-minute conversation about why the word "faggot" was wrong. I want to ask those kids questions and challenge them, try to break down some of the growing, still-forming hate in their chests, force them to ask the questions their parents and siblings and teachers are allowing them to gloss over, to make sure that they don't live in a world like the one we do now.

I want a different world for my children than the one in which painted nails create a public outcry.

ENGAGING THE TEXT

1. As a child, Gómez feels torn between the things that he likes or wants (like painted fingernails) and the things that are socially acceptable (like playing soccer). What does he learn about being a man, and how does he feel about it?

2. What views do the boys Gómez grows up with have of gay people? Although he claims that he has "never felt consciously homophobic about same-sex anything" (para. 18), what evidence does he offer that he is subconsciously homophobic? Do you agree with his self-assessment? Why or why not?

3. Why does Gómez say, referring to his lesbian friend, "Our times together made me rethink what I took for granted in terms of sexuality and gender" (para. 61)? Why does the role he has always played with women suddenly seem contrived? How does she break the "rules" by sleeping with Gómez? Why does he perceive sexuality and gender as "fluid" (para. 64)?

4. Reflecting on his experience of masculinity, Gómez says, "I want more than this narrow slice of humanity I've been given permission to taste" (para. 67). Do you feel limited by the social expectations of your gender? Write a brief story or journal entry in which you imagine what your life would be like if you weren't constrained by traditional gender roles. Would you feel relieved, confused, or something else? Why?

EXPLORING CONNECTIONS

5. How does gender policing influence Gómez's behavior as a child? How does it continue to affect him as he grows older and begins to reject some of his previous attitudes? How do you think that Lisa Wade and Myra Marx Ferree (p. 480) would analyze the changes that he experiences in his life?

6. Analyze Gómez's experience in Zambia from Wade and Ferree's perspective: How does his reaction to male hand-holding constitute culture shock? How do his ambivalence and physical discomfort reflect "over-learned" gender behavior? Wade and Ferree claim that "Once we have over-learned a rule, we don't experience it as oppressive" (p. 486); how does the cultural change from the United States to Zambia call this into question?

7. How does the image on page 503 reflect both the rewards and the costs of masculinity? How would you interpret the meaning and placement of the "Think Again" message? Do you think that Gómez would sympathize with it? Why or why not?

EXTENDING THE CRITICAL CONTEXT

8. For one full day, keep track of every time you hear the words "gay," "fag," "faggot," "bitch," or "pussy" used in conversation or the media. In each case, is the speaker male or female? Who or what is s/he referring to? Is s/he joking or serious? Bring your notes to class to compare with others' observations. To what extent do your findings bear out Gómez's assertion that "homophobia, although it is usually directed toward other men, is, ultimately, an indictment and an attack on women" (para. 63)?

SISTERHOOD IS COMPLICATED*
RUTH PADAWER

Sisterhood can indeed be complicated. Originally conceived as all-female institutions, women's colleges are currently struggling with what it means to be a woman as they adapt to a new generation of transgender students. In this essay, Ruth Padawer writes about the controversies surrounding transmen, who are demanding recognition and inclusion at Wellesley. Since 1992 Padawer has served as an adjunct professor at Columbia University Graduate School of Journalism, where she teaches reporting and writing. She also serves as a contributing writer for the *New York Times Magazine*, where she has published feature articles on DNA testing, abortion, autism, and gender-fluid children. Her work has been featured in the *Columbia Journalism Review*; on the Public Broadcasting System's "Media Matters"; National Public Radio's "This American Life" and "On the Media"; and internationally in *The Guardian*, *Haaretz Magazine*, and *Internazionale*. This article appeared on October 15, 2014, in the *New York Times Magazine*.

HUNDREDS OF YOUNG WOMEN streamed into Wellesley College on the last Monday of August, many of them trailed by parents lugging suitcases and bins filled with folded towels, decorative pillows and Costco-size jugs of laundry detergent. The banner by the campus entranceway welcoming the Class of 2018 waved in the breeze, as if beckoning the newcomers to discover all that awaited them. All around the campus stood buildings named after women: the Margaret Clapp library, the Betsy Wood Knapp media and technology center, dorms, labs, academic halls, even the parking garage. The message that anything is possible for women was also evident at a fenced-in work site, which bore the sign "Elaine Construction," after a firm named for one woman and run by another.

It was the first day of orientation, and along the picturesque paths there were cheerful upper-class student leaders providing directions and encouragement. They wore pink T-shirts stamped with this year's orientation theme: "Free to Explore" — an enticement that could be interpreted myriad ways, perhaps far more than the college intended. One of those T-shirted helpers was a junior named Timothy Boatwright. Like every other matriculating student at Wellesley, which is just west

© Martin Schoeller/AUGUST

Timothy Boatright (center), a trans man, with his Wellesley classmates.

of Boston, Timothy was raised a girl and checked "female" when he applied. Though he had told his high-school friends that he was transgender, he did not reveal that on his application, in part because his mother helped him with it, and he didn't want her to know. Besides, he told me, "it seemed awkward to write an application essay for a women's college on why you were not a woman." Like many trans students, he chose a women's college because it seemed safer physically and psychologically.

From the start, Timothy introduced himself as "masculine-of-center genderqueer." He asked everyone at Wellesley to use male pronouns and the name Timothy, which he'd chosen for himself.

For the most part, everyone respected his request. After all, he wasn't the only trans student on campus. Some two dozen other matriculating students at Wellesley don't identify as women. Of those, a half-dozen or so were trans men, people born female who identified as men, some of whom had begun taking testosterone to change their bodies. The rest said they were transgender or genderqueer, rejecting the idea of gender entirely or identifying somewhere between female and male; many, like Timothy, called themselves transmasculine. Though his gender identity differed from that of most of his classmates, he generally felt comfortable at his new school.

Last spring, as a sophomore, Timothy decided to run for a seat on the student-government cabinet, the highest position that an openly trans student had ever sought at Wellesley. The post he sought was multicultural affairs coordinator, or "MAC," responsible for promoting

5

"a culture of diversity" among students and staff and faculty members. Along with Timothy, three women of color indicated their intent to run for the seat. But when they dropped out for various unrelated reasons before the race really began, he was alone on the ballot. An anonymous lobbying effort began on Facebook, pushing students to vote "abstain." Enough "abstains" would deny Timothy the minimum number of votes Wellesley required, forcing a new election for the seat and providing an opportunity for other candidates to come forward. The "Campaign to Abstain" argument was simple: Of all the people at a multiethnic women's college who could hold the school's "diversity" seat, the least fitting one was a *white man*.

"It wasn't about Timothy," the student behind the Abstain campaign told me: "I thought he'd do a perfectly fine job, but it just felt inappropriate to have a white man there. It's not just about that position either. Having men in elected leadership positions undermines the idea of this being a place where women are the leaders."

I asked Timothy what he thought about that argument, as we sat on a bench overlooking the tranquil lake on campus during orientation. He pointed out that he has important contributions to make to the MAC position. After all, at Wellesley, masculine-of-center students *are* cultural minorities; by numbers alone, they're about as minor as a minority can be. And yet Timothy said he felt conflicted about taking a leadership spot. "The patriarchy is alive and well," he said. "I don't want to perpetuate it."

In the nineteenth century, only men were admitted to most colleges and universities, so proponents of higher education for women had to build their own. The missions at these new schools both defied and reinforced the gender norms of the day. By offering women access to an education they'd previously been denied, the schools' very existence was radical, but most were nevertheless premised on traditional notions: College-educated women were considered more likely to be engaging wives and better mothers, who would raise informed citizens. Over time, of course, women's colleges became more committed to preparing students for careers, but even in the early 1960s, Wellesley, for example, taught students how to get groceries into the back of a station wagon without exposing their thighs.

By the late 1960s, however, gender norms were under scrutiny. Amid the growing awareness of civil rights and women's liberation, academic separation based on gender, as with race, seemed increasingly outdated. As a vast majority of women opted for coed schools, enrollment at women's colleges tumbled. The number of women's colleges dropped to fewer than 50 today from nearly 300.

In response to shifting ideas about gender, many of the remaining 10 women's colleges redefined themselves as an antidote to the sexism that feminists were increasingly identifying in society. Women's colleges argued that they offered a unique environment where every student leader was a woman, where female role models were abundant, where professors were far more likely to be women and where the message of women's empowerment pervaded academic and campus life. All that seemed to foster students' confidence. Women's colleges say their undergrads are more likely to major in fields traditionally dominated by men. Wellesley alumnae in particular are awarded more science and engineering doctorates than female graduates of any other liberal-arts college in the nation, according to government data. Its alums have become two secretaries of state; a groundbreaking string theorist; a NASA astronaut; and Korea's first female ambassador.

As women's colleges challenged the conventions of womanhood, they drew a disproportionate number of students who identified as lesbian or bisexual. Today a small but increasing number of students at those schools identify as something other than a woman, raising the question of what it means to be a "women's college." Trans students are pushing their schools to play down the women-centric message. At Wellesley, Smith, Mount Holyoke and others, they and their many supporters have successfully lobbied to scrub all female references in student government constitutions, replacing them with gender-neutral language. At Wellesley, they have pressed administrators and fellow students to excise talk of sisterhood, arguing that that rhetoric, rather than being uplifting, excludes other gender minorities. At many schools, they have also taken leadership positions long filled by women: resident advisers on dorm floors, heads of student groups and members of college government. At Wellesley, one transmasculine student was a dorm president. At Mills College, a women's school in California, even the president of student government identifies as male.

What's a women's college to do? Trans students point out that they're doing exactly what these schools encourage: breaking gender barriers, fulfilling their deepest yearnings and forging ahead even when society tries to hold them back. But yielding to their request to dilute the focus on women would undercut the identity of a women's college. While women in coed schools generally outpace men in enrollment and performance, the equation shifts after college: Recent female graduates working full time earn far less than their male counterparts, and more experienced women are often still shut out of corporate and political leadership—all of which prompts women's-college advocates to conclude that a four-year, confidence-building workshop still has its place.

"Sisterhood is why I chose to go to Wellesley," said a physics major who graduated recently and asked not to be identified for fear she'd be denounced for her opinion. "A women's college is a place to celebrate being a woman, surrounded by women. I felt empowered by that every day. You come here thinking that every single leadership position will be held by a woman: every member of the student government, every newspaper editor, every head of the Economics Council, every head of the Society of Physics. That's an incredible thing! This is what they advertise to students. But it's no longer true. And if all that is no longer true, the intrinsic value of a women's college no longer holds."

A few schools have formulated responses to this dilemma, albeit very different ones. Hollins University, a small women's college in Virginia, established a policy several years ago stating it would confer diplomas only to women. It also said that students who have surgery or begin hormone therapy to become men—or who legally take male names—will be "helped to transfer to another institution." Mount Holyoke and Mills College, on the other hand, recently decided they will not only continue to welcome students who become trans men while at school but will also admit those who identify on their applications as trans men, noting that welcoming the former and not the latter seemed unjustifiably arbitrary.

But most women's colleges, including Wellesley, consider only female applicants. Once individuals have enrolled and announced that they are trans, the schools, more or less, leave it to the students to work out how trans classmates fit into a women's college. Two of those students hashed it out last fall after Kaden Mohamed, then a Wellesley senior who had been taking testosterone for seven months, watched a news program on WGBH-TV about the plummeting number of women's colleges. One guest was Laura Bruno, another Wellesley senior. The other guest was the president of Regis College, a women's school that went coed in 2007 to reverse its tanking enrollment. The interviewer asked Laura to describe her experience at an "all-female school" and to explain how that might be diminished "by having men there." Laura answered, "We look around and we see only women, only people like us, leading every organization on campus, contributing to every class discussion."

Kaden, a manager of the campus student cafe who knew Laura casually, was upset by her words. He emailed Laura and said her response was "extremely disrespectful." He continued: "I am not a woman. I am a trans man who is part of your graduating class, and you literally ignored my existence in your interview. . . . You had an opportunity to show people that Wellesley is a place that is complicating the meaning of being an 'all women's school,' and you chose instead to displace a bunch of your current and past Wellesley siblings."

Laura apologized, saying she hadn't meant to marginalize anyone and had actually vowed beforehand not to imply that all Wellesley students were women. But she said that under pressure, she found herself in a difficult spot: How could she maintain that women's colleges would lose something precious by including men, but at the same time argue that women's colleges should accommodate students who identify as men?

Although it may seem paradoxical, Jesse Austin said he chose to attend Wellesley because being female never felt right to him. "I figured if I was any kind of woman, I'd find it there. I knew Wellesley would have strong women. They produce a ton of strong women, strong in all sorts of ways."

When Jesse arrived on campus in the fall of 2009, his name was Sara. Eighteen years old, Sara wore form-fitting shirts and snug women's jeans, because growing up in a small, conservative town in Georgia, she learned that that's what girls were supposed to do—even though she never felt like a girl. As a child, Sara had always chosen to be male characters in pretend plays, and all her friends were boys. In middle

15

school, those boys abandoned her because she was a social liability: not feminine enough to flirt with and not masculine enough to really be one of the guys. In high school, at the urging of well-intentioned female classmates, she started wearing her hair down instead of pulled back and began dressing like they did, even though people kept pointing out that she still acted and carried herself like a boy. "I had no idea that gender was something you could change," Jesse told me recently. "I just thought I needed to make myself fit into these fixed places: There are boys, and there are girls. I knew I didn't fit; I just didn't know what was wrong with me."

Around the middle of Sara's first year at Wellesley, she attended   20
a presentation by trans alums, including one who was in the process of transitioning. As Sara listened, the gender dysphoria she'd always felt suddenly made sense. "It was all so clear to me," Jesse told me. "All I needed were the words." Sara spent the next two weeks scouring the Internet for videos and information on becoming a man. She learned that unlike previous generations, today's trans young adults don't consider physical transformation a prerequisite for identity. Some use hormones; some have their breasts removed in "top" surgery; some reject medical interventions altogether, as unnecessary invasions and expense. She discovered that sexual orientation is independent of gender: Some trans men are attracted to women, some to men, some to both. And she learned that trans men aren't necessarily determined to hide the fact they were raised as girls, or that they once attended a women's college.

Soon after, Sara cut her hair short and bought her first pair of men's jeans. Sara told friends she was a man. By second semester, he was using male pronouns and calling himself Jesse, the other name his mother had considered for her daughter. He also joined a tiny campus group for students who knew or suspected they were trans men. It was called Brothers, a counterweight to the otherwise ubiquitous message of sisterhood.

That summer, Jesse saw a gender therapist, and early in his sophomore year, he began injecting testosterone into his thigh every two weeks, making him one of the first students to medically transform into a man while at Wellesley. He became the administrator of Brothers. Though he felt supported, he also felt alone; all the other trans men on campus had graduated, and the other students in Brothers were not even sure they identified as men. Outside Brothers, everything at Wellesley was still sisterhood and female empowerment. Nevertheless, he said, "I thought of Wellesley as my home, my community. I felt fine there, like I totally belonged."

Jesse decided he wanted to have top surgery over winter break, and his parents agreed to pay for it. He returned for spring semester but only briefly, taking a sudden leave of absence to go home and help care for his ill father. When Jesse re-enrolled at Wellesley a year and a half later, in fall 2012, much had changed in Jesse and at school. Having been on testosterone for two years at that point, Jesse no longer looked like a woman trying to pass as a man. His voice was deep. His facial hair was thick, though he kept it trimmed to a stubble. His shoulders had become broad and muscular, his hips narrow, his arms and chest more defined.

Wellesley was different, too. By then, a whole crowd of people identified as trans—enough for two trans groups. Brothers had officially become Siblings and welcomed anyone anywhere on the gender spectrum except those who identified as women. Meanwhile, Jesse and some transmasculine students continued to meet unofficially as Brothers, though Jesse was the only one on testosterone.

Overall, campus life had a stronger trans presence than ever: At least four of the school's 70 R.A.s did not identify as women. Student organizations increasingly began meetings by asking everyone to state preferred names and pronouns. Around campus, more and more students were replacing "sisterhood" with "siblinghood" in conversation. Even the school's oldest tradition, Flower Sunday—the 138-year-old ceremony that paired each incoming student with an upper-class Big Sister to support her—had become trans-inclusive. Though the school website still describes Flower Sunday as "a day of sisterhood," the department that runs the event yielded to trans students' request and started referring to each participant as a Big or Little "Sister/Sibling"— or simply as Bigs and Littles.

And yet even with the increased visibility of trans students on campus, Jesse stood out. When he swiped his Wellesley ID card to get into friends' dorms, the groundskeepers would stop him and say, "You can't go in there without a woman to escort you." Residential directors who spotted him in the dorm stairwells told him the same thing. In his own dorm, parents who were visiting their daughters would stop him to ask why he was there. Because bathrooms in the dorms are not labeled "women" or "men" but rather "Wellesley only" and "non-Wellesley," students who didn't know Jesse would call him out for using the "Wellesley only" bathroom instead of the one for visitors. When he tried to explain he *was* a Wellesley student, people sometimes thought he was lying.

"Everything felt very different than it had before," he said of that semester. "I felt so distinctly male, and I felt extremely awkward. I felt like an outsider. My voice was jarring—a male voice, which is so distinct in a classroom of women—so I felt weird saying much in class. I felt much more aware of Wellesley as a women's place, even though the college was starting to change."

Once spring semester ended, Jesse withdrew. "I still think of Wellesley as a women's place, and I still think that's a wonderful idea," he said. "It just didn't encompass me anymore. I felt it was a space I shouldn't tread in."

Some female students, meanwhile, said Wellesley wasn't female enough. They complained among themselves and to the administration

© Martin Schoeller/AUGUST

Clockwise from top: Jesse Austin, Alex Poon, and Kaden Mohamad, former Wellesley students.

that sisterhood had been hijacked. "Siblinghood," they argued, lacked the warm, pro-women connotation of "sisterhood," as well as its historic resonance. Others were upset that even at a women's college, women were still expected to accommodate men, ceding attention and leadership opportunities intended for women. Still others feared the changes were a step toward coeducation. Despite all that, many were uneasy: As a marginalized group fighting for respect and clout, how could women justify marginalizing others?

"I felt for the first time that something so stable about our school 30 was about to change, and it made me scared," said Beth, a junior that year, who asked to be identified by only her middle name because she was afraid of offending people she knew. "Changing 'sister' to 'sibling' didn't feel like it was including more people; it felt like it was taking something away from sisterhood, transforming our safe space for the sake of someone else. At the same time, I felt guilty feeling that way." Beth went to Kris Niendorf, the director of residential life, who listened sympathetically and then asked: Why does "sibling" take away from your experience? After thinking about it, Beth concluded that she was connected to her classmates not because of gender but because of their shared experiences at Wellesley. "That year was an epiphany for me. I realized that if we excluded trans students, we'd be fighting on the wrong team. We'd be on the wrong side of history."

Exactly how Wellesley will resolve the trans question is still unclear. Trans students say that aside from making sure every academic building on campus has a unisex bathroom, Wellesley has not addressed what gender fluidity means for Wellesley's identity. Last spring, Alex Poon won Wellesley's 131-year-old hoop-rolling race, an annual spirit-building competition among seniors. Alex's mother was the hoop-rolling champion of the Class of '82 and had long ago taught her daughters the ways of the hoop, on the assumption that they would one day attend her alma mater. (One of Alex's older sisters was Wellesley Class of '11; another went to Bryn Mawr.) Alex was a former Girl Scout who attended an all-girls high school. But unknown to his mother, he was using Google to search for an explanation for his confusing feelings. By the time Alex applied to Wellesley, he secretly knew he was trans but was nonetheless certain Wellesley was a good fit. For one thing, going there was a family tradition; for another, it was a place where gender could be reimagined. In his sophomore year at Wellesley, he went public with his transgender status.

On hoop-rolling day, Alex — wearing a cap backward on his buzz-cut hair — broke through the finish-line streamer. President H. Kim Bottomly took a selfie with him, each with a wide smile. A small local newspaper covered the event, noting that for the first time in the school's history, the winner was a man. And yet the page on Wellesley's website devoted to school traditions continues to describe the race as if it involves only women. "Back in the day, it was proclaimed that whoever won the Hoop Roll would be the first to get married. In the status-seeking 1980s, she was the first to be C.E.O. Now we just say that the winner will be the first to achieve happiness and success, whatever that means to her." But Alex isn't a her, and he told me that his happiness and success includes being recognized for what he is: a man.

That page is not the only place on the site where Wellesley markets itself as a school of only female students. Elsewhere, it crows that "all the most courageous, most provocative, most accomplished people on campus are women." The student body, it says, is "2,300 smart, singular women feeling the power of 2,300 smart, singular women together" on a campus where "our common identity, spirit and pride as Wellesley women" are celebrated. Those sorts of messages, trans students say, make them feel invisible.

"I just wish the administration would at least acknowledge our existence," said Eli Cohen, a Wellesley senior who has been taking testosterone for nearly a year. "I'd be more O.K. with 'We're not going to cater to you, because men are catered to everywhere else in life,' rather than just pretending we don't exist."

Some staff and faculty members, however, are acknowledging the trans presence. Women-and-gender-studies professors, and a handful of others, typically begin each semester asking students to indicate the names and pronouns they prefer for themselves. Kris Niendorf, director of campus and residential life, recruits trans students who want to be R.A.s, as she does with all minorities. Niendorf also initiated informational panels with trans students and alums. And before this school year began, at the urging of trans students, Niendorf required all 200 student leaders to attend a trans-sensitivity workshop focused on how to "create a more inclusive Wellesley College." For the last few years, orientation organizers have also included a trans student as one of the half-dozen upper-class students who stand before the incoming first-years and recount how they overcame a difficult personal challenge.

And yet many trans students feel that more needs to be done. They complain that too many professors assume all their students are women. Students provided numerous examples in courses across subject areas where they've been asked their viewpoint "as a woman." In a course on westerns two years ago, an essay assignment noted that western films and novels were aimed at male audiences and focused on masculinity. The professors asked students for their perspective "as a female reader or watcher" — wording that offended the three trans students in class. When a classmate pointed out the problematic wording to the professors, the instructors asked everyone instead "to explore how your own gender identity changes how you approach westerns."

At times, professors find themselves walking a fine line. Thomas Cushman, who has taught sociology at Wellesley for the last 25 years, first found out about Wellesley's trans population five years ago, after a student in one of his courses showed up at Cushman's office and introduced himself as a trans male. The student pointed out that every example Cushman gave in class referred to women, and every generic pronoun he used was female, as in "Ask your classmate if she. . . ." He told Cushman that Wellesley could no longer call itself a "women's college," given the presence of trans men, and he asked Cushman to use male pronouns and male examples more often, so trans students didn't feel excluded. Cushman said he would abide by whatever pronoun individual students requested for themselves, but he drew the line at changing his emphasis on women.

"All my life here," Cushman told me, "I've been compelled to use the female pronoun more generously to get away from the sexist 'he.' I think it's important to evoke the idea that women are part of humanity. That should be affirmed, especially after being denied for so long. Look, I teach at a women's college, so whenever I can make women's identity central to that experience, I try to do that. Being asked to change that is a bit ironic. I don't agree that this is a 'historically' women's college. It is still a women's college."

On the second day of orientation this fall, Eli Cohen arrived on campus in a muscle T and men's shorts, with a carabiner full of keys hanging from his belt loop. He was elated to be back to the place that felt most like home. It was the first time in four years that Eli had not been part of orientation—first as a newcomer and then two years as an R.A. We hung out in the Lulu Chow Wang Campus Center, known affectionately as Lulu, and watched the excited first-years flutter by, clutching their orientation schedules and their newly purchased Wellesley wear.

Just 12 days earlier, Eli underwent top surgery, which he said gave him a newfound self-assurance in his projection of manhood. It had been nine months since he started testosterone, and the effects had become particularly noticeable over the three-month summer break. His jaw line had begun to square, his limbs to thicken and the hair on his arms and legs to darken. And of course now his chest was a flat wall. As his friends caught sight of him for the first time in months, they hugged him and gushed, "You look sooo good!"

Though Eli secretly suspected in high school that he was a boy, it wasn't until after he arrived at Wellesley that he could imagine he might one day declare himself a man. By his second year, he had buzz-cut his hair and started wearing men's clothes. He asked his friends to call him Beckett, which is similar to his female birth name, which he asked me not to mention. His parents live only 14 miles away and dropped by for short visits. He left his girl nameplate on his dorm door. His friends understood that whenever his parents arrived, everyone was to revert to his female name and its attendant pronouns. He was an R.A. at the time and decided not to reveal his male name to his first-year students, figuring it was too complicated to explain which name to use when.

Given how guarded he had to be, being Beckett was exhausting and anxiety-inducing. Demoralized, he eventually told his pals to just use his birth name. The summer after his sophomore year, he got an internship at a Boston health center serving the L.G.B.T. community, and many of his co-workers were trans. Their confidence gave him confidence. When the Wellesley office that coordinates internships sent out an email to all interns that began, "Good morning, ladies . . . ," he emailed back to say he did not identify as a woman. The coordinator apologized and explained that all the names on her paperwork from Wellesley were female.

By summer's end, he began introducing himself as Eli, a name utterly unlike his birth name. Eli mustered the courage to tell his parents. It took a little while for his mother to accept that her only daughter was actually a son, but she came around.

When I asked Eli if trans men belonged at Wellesley, he said he felt torn. "I don't necessarily think we have a right to women's spaces. But I'm not going to transfer, because this is a place I love, a community I love. I realize that may be a little selfish. It may be a lot selfish." Where, he wondered, should Wellesley draw a line, if a line should even be drawn? At trans men? At transmasculine students? What about students who are simply questioning their gender? Shouldn't students be "free to explore" without fearing their decision will make them unwelcome?

Other trans students have struggled with these questions, too. Last December, a transmasculine Wellesley student wrote an anonymous blog post that shook the school's trans community. The student wrote to apologize for "acting in the interest of preserving a hurtful system of privileging masculinity." He continued: "My feelings have changed: I do not think that trans men belong at Wellesley. . . . This doesn't mean that I think that all trans men should be kicked out of Wellesley or necessarily denied admission." He acknowledged he didn't know how Wellesley could best address the trans question, but urged fellow transmasculine classmates to "start talking, and thinking critically, about the space that we are given and occupying, and the space that we are taking from women."

The reactions were swift and strong. "A lot of trans people on campus felt emotionally unsafe," recalled Timothy, a sophomore that year. "A place that seemed welcoming suddenly wasn't. The difficulty was that because it was a trans person saying it, people who don't have enough of an understanding to appreciate the nuance of this can say, 'Well, even a trans person says there shouldn't be trans people at Wellesley, so it's O.K. for me to think the same thing, too.'"

Students and alums—queer and straight, trans and not—weighed in, sometimes in agreement but other times in anger. Some accused the blogger of speaking on behalf of women as if they were unable to speak for themselves. Others accused him of betraying transmasculine students. (He declined to comment for this article.) But other students, including several transmasculine ones, were glad he had the courage to start a public discussion about Wellesley's deeply conflicted identity. "It's a very important conversation to have," Eli said. "Why can't we have this conversation without feeling hurt or hated?"

In some ways, students are already having that conversation, though perhaps indirectly. Timothy ended up easily winning his seat on the student government last spring, capturing two-thirds of the votes. Given that 85 percent of the student body cast ballots in that race, his victory suggests most students think that transmasculine students—and transmasculine leaders—belong at Wellesley.

Another difficult conversation about trans students touches on the disproportionate attention they receive on campus. "The female-identified students somehow place more value on those students," said Rose Layton, a lesbian who said she views trans students as competitors in the campus dating scene. "They flirt with them, hook up with them. And it's not just the hetero women, but even people in the queer community. The trans men are always getting this extra bit of acknowledgment. Even though we're in a women's college, the fact is men and masculinity get more attention and more value in this social dynamic than women do."

Jesse Austin noticed the paradox when he returned to campus with a man's build and full swath of beard stubble after nearly two years on testosterone. "That was the first time in my life I was popular! People were clamoring to date me."

Trans bodies are seen as an in-between option, Timothy said. "So no matter your sexuality, a trans person becomes safe to flirt with, to explore with. But it's not really the person you're interested in, it's the novelty. For lesbians, there's the safety of 'I may be attracted to this person, but they're "really" a woman, so I'm not actually bi or straight.' And for straight people, it's 'I may be attracted to a woman's body, but he's a male, so I'm not really lesbian or bi.'"

Kaden Mohamed said he felt downright objectified when he returned from summer break last year, after five months of testosterone had lowered his voice, defined his arm muscles and reshaped his torso. It was attention that he had never experienced before he transitioned. But as his body changed, students he didn't even know would run their hands over his biceps. Once at the school pub, an intoxicated Wellesley woman even grabbed his crotch and that of another trans man.

"It's this very bizarre reversal of what happens in the real world," Kaden said. "In the real world, it's women who get fetishized, catcalled, sexually harassed, grabbed. At Wellesley, it's trans men who do. If I were to go up to someone I just met and touch her body, I'd get grief from the entire Wellesley community, because they'd say it's assault—and it is. But for some reason, when it's done to trans men here, it doesn't get read the same way. It's like a free pass, that suddenly it's O.K. to talk about or touch someone's body as long as they're not a woman."

On the last Friday in May, some 5,000 parents, alumnae and soon-to-be graduates streamed onto the rolling field near Severance Hall, named after Elisabeth Severance, a generous 1887 alumna. It was a gorgeous, temperate morning for Wellesley's 136th annual commencement, and once the last baccalaureate degree was conferred, the audience was asked to stand. As is the school's tradition, two graduates led an uplifting rendition of "America, the Beautiful." The lyrics, for those who needed them, were printed in the commencement program, including the chorus: "And crown thy good, with brotherhood, from sea to shining sea!"

Those words were penned by Katharine Lee Bates, an 1880 graduate of Wellesley who defied the expectations of her gender, and not just by becoming a professor, published author and famous poet. A pastor's daughter, she never married, living instead for 25 years with Katharine Coman, founder of Wellesley's economics department, with whom she was deeply in love. When a colleague described "free-flying spinsters" as a "fringe on the garment of life," Bates, then 53, answered: "I always thought the fringe had the best of it."

As parents, professors and graduates joined in the singing of Bates's most famous poem, many felt an intense pride in their connection to the graduates and this remarkable college, which has sent forth so many women who leave impressive marks on the world. As the hundreds of voices rounded the curve on "And crown thy good with . . . ," the unknowing parents continued to "brotherhood," the word that was always supposed to stand in for women too, but never really did. Wellesley women long ago learned that words matter, and for decades, this has been the point in the song when their harmonious choral singing abruptly becomes a bellow as they belt out "sisterhood," drowning out the word that long excluded them and replacing it with a demand for recognition. It's one of the most powerful moments of commencement, followed every year by cheers, applause and tears, evoked by the rush of solidarity with women throughout time, and the thrill of claiming in one of the nation's most famous songs that women matter—even if the world they're about to enter doesn't always agree.

In the last few years, a handful of graduates have changed that word once again, having decided that "sisterhood," no matter how well intended, is exclusionary, and so they instead call out "siblinghood." A few trans men find even that insufficient, and in that instant, they roar the word that represents them best: "brotherhood," not as a sexist stand-in for all humankind, but as an appeal from a tiny minority struggling to be acknowledged.

In truth, it's difficult to distinguish in the cacophony each of the words shouted atop one another. What is clear is that whatever word each person is hollering is immensely significant as a proclamation of existence, even if it's hard to make out what anyone else is saying.

ENGAGING THE TEXT

1. Why were women's colleges first established? How do women's colleges serve as "an antidote to . . . sexism" (para. 10), and how does Wellesley advertise itself to women? Is the idea of all-female institutions out of date or do they continue to fulfill an important purpose? What benefits do women today hope to gain by attending a school like Wellesley?

2. In what ways do trans students threaten to "undercut the identity" (para. 12) of women's colleges? Why do trans students sometimes "feel invisible" (para. 33) at Wellesley?

3. How has Wellesley responded to the presence of trans students on campus? Which of the university's decisions and policies seem wise and which, if any, seem inadequate or misguided? Explain.

4. According to one student, "Men and masculinity get more attention and more value" than women at Wellesley (para. 49). Does the focus on gender-neutral language, the election of trans men to leadership positions, and the "objectification" of transmasculine bodies indicate that "the patriarchy is alive and well" (para. 7) at Wellesley? Why or why not?

5. Why did Timothy Boatwright, Jesse Austin, and Alex Poon decide to attend a women's college? Did they make the right decision? How might their experience have been different had they gone to a mixed-gender school? Write an imaginative alternative history for one of the men.

EXPLORING CONNECTIONS

6. Review the concept of "gender policing" in Lisa Wade and Myra Marx Ferree's "How to Do Gender" (p. 480). How have policing and self-policing affected the lives of Timothy Boatwright, Jesse Austin, and Eli Cohen?

7. Look ahead to Allan G. Johnson's "Patriarchy" (p. 527). How does his description of traditional masculinity differ from the masculinities represented or expressed by the students at Wellesley? In what other ways do Wellesley students challenge patriarchy?

EXTENDING THE CRITICAL CONTEXT

8. What resources for transgender or genderqueer students exist on your campus? For example, is "gender identity or expression" included in your school's antidiscrimination policy? Does your student medical center provide trans-specific services? Are gender-inclusive restrooms, locker rooms, and housing options readily available? Are there trans counselors and support groups? Do some online research to identify other types of support or accommodation that trans students need. Examine your college's website to see how trans-friendly or-unfriendly it is. Write an essay or a journal entry detailing your findings.

VISUAL PORTFOLIO
READING IMAGES OF GENDER

Brittany Werges/Eden Nicole

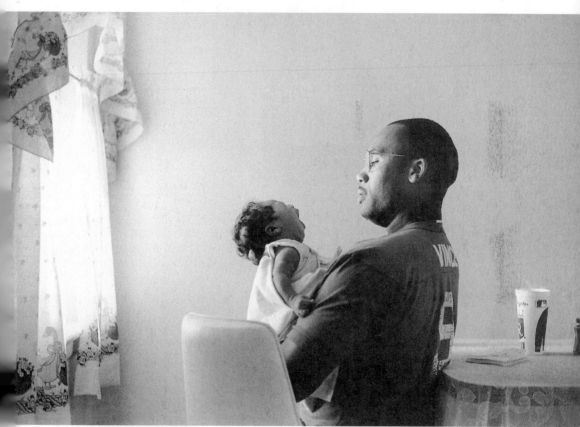

© Eli Reed/Magnum Photos

© Gillian Laub

Kevin Banatte

Damian Dovarganes/AP Images

AP Photo/Evan Vucci

VISUAL PORTFOLIO
READING IMAGES OF GENDER

1. The photo on page 520 was taken at the 2018 Women's March in Denver, Colorado. Eden Nicole, who is Dinè and San Felipe Pueblo, said she attended the march to call attention to "the missing and murdered Indigenous women … [who are] not being talked about."[1] Analyze her stance, her expression, and the messages that she embodies. What is the significance of her raised fist and the red hand print across her mouth? Visit this website to learn more about the issue: https://www.pbs.org/newshour/nation/at-womens-marches-a-spotlight-on-missing-and-murdered-indigenous-women.

   What are the statistics on domestic violence and sexual assault in Native communities? Why do some Native Americans distrust the courts and the police? How are indigenous people fighting back?

2. How would you describe the mood or feeling the photographer has captured in the picture of the father and child (p. 521)? How do the light, the setting, the stance, and the expression of each figure contribute to this impression? Why do you think that "Masculinity" would or would not be an appropriate title for this picture?

3. On page 522, the girl on the left is Cassidy Lynn Campbell with her friend, Victoria Avalos, both male-to-female transgender people. Victoria and Cassidy helped each other come out as transgender and are close friends (you can learn more about their stories at http://time.com/135844/transgender-cassidy-lynn-campbell/). When Cassidy came out during her senior year of high school, her classmates elected her homecoming queen, but her father still refers to her as his son. What does the photographer suggest about transgender identity in this photo? What do each girl's appearance, posture, and expression convey about her? Why are they holding hands?

4. Angela Peoples holds a sign at the Women's March one day after President Trump's inauguration in the image on page 523. The march was organized to protest Trump's election, and many of the protesters wore pink, hand-knit "pussy hats" as symbols of support for women's rights. Although a majority of white women voters (53%) supported Trump, 94% of black female voters did not. What's the significance of the sign: Does it express anger, betrayal, resignation, bitterness, irony, or something else? How would you describe Peoples's attitude toward Trump and the march? How do you interpret her message in relation to the three white women behind her, with their pussy hats and cell phones? What does this photo suggest about feminism, inclusion, and race?

[1]Brittany Werges et al., "30+ People on Why They Participated in the Women's March," 303 Magazine.com.

5. In the photo on page 524, activist Tarana Burke (at center) protests sexual harassment and assault in the Hollywood, CA, #MeToo survivors' march. In 2007, Burke founded the Me Too movement to provide resources for victims of sexual assault and abuse. In 2017, following the Harvey Weinstein scandal, the name was picked up on social media as a hashtag, and people who had experienced sexual harassment were encouraged to respond, "#MeToo." Within twenty-four hours, Facebook was flooded with over 12 million posts.[2] Why was the response so overwhelming? What does the racial diversity of the protesters suggest about the prevalence of sexual harassment? Debate whether this moment marks a permanent change in the public perception of sexual harassment.

6. The image of the Confederate battle flag on page 525 was taken at a Trump rally in Kissimmee, FL. One of the men pictured had purchased the flag from a vendor outside the arena; after a campaign official — and the police — told him to take it down, he complained that Trump would not have asked him to remove it.[3] Read or review Jackson Katz's article, "From Rush Limbaugh to Donald Trump" (p. 583), and explain why you believe that Trump would or would not have allowed him to continue displaying the flag. What messages do the Confederate flag and the cheering men convey about race and masculinity?

[2]Sandra E. Garcia, "The Woman Who Created #MeToo Long Before Hashtags," *New York Times*, Oct. 20, 2017.

[3]Nick Corasaniti, "At a Donald Trump Rally, a Confederate Flag Goes Up, and Quickly Comes Down," *New York Times*, Aug. 11, 2016.

FROM *THE GENDER KNOT:* "PATRIARCHY"

ALLAN G. JOHNSON

In this powerful analysis, Allan Johnson examines patriarchy, the social structure that underlies gender. It is a social order built on male privilege: those qualities associated with men — strength, toughness, and rationality — are more highly valued than those associated with women — cooperation, vulnerability, and empathy. From gender inequality in the workplace to domestic violence, sexual harassment, and rape, the patriarchal system rewards or protects men and disadvantages women. According to Johnson, "We cannot avoid participating in patriarchy. It was handed to us the moment we came into the world. But we can choose *how* to participate in it." An outspoken feminist and social justice advocate, Johnson (1946–2017) taught sociology at Wesleyan University and later taught women's studies and sociology at Hartford College for Women (now the University of Hartford). After volunteering at a rape crisis center, he became particularly interested in male violence against women and served as a consultant to the National Center for the Prevention of Rape. Later in his career, he was well known as a public speaker and diversity trainer focused on issues of gender, race, class, and sexual orientation. In addition to *The Gender Knot* (3rd ed., 2014), his books include *Privilege, Power, and Difference* (3rd ed., 2017) and *The Forest and the Trees: Sociology as Life, Practice, and Promise* (3rd ed., 2014). He wrote fiction as well as nonfiction, including the novel *The First Thing and the Last* (2010), which deals realistically with domestic violence.

WHERE WE ARE IS STUCK. After two decades of sometimes dramatic change in the 1970s and 1980s, progress toward gender equity has slowed to a crawl since 1990. The average man working full time, for example, earns almost 30 percent more than the average woman. In spite of being a majority among college graduates, most employed women are still confined to a narrow range of low-status, low-paid occupations, and those women who have made inroads into previously male-dominated professions, such as medicine, are more likely than men to be in lower-ranked, lower-paid positions. At the same time, men entering occupations such as nursing and elementary school teaching are more highly paid than comparable women and more likely to advance to supervisory positions. In universities, science professors, both male and female, widely regard female students as less competent than comparable males and are less likely to offer women jobs or to pay those they do hire salaries equal to those of men. In politics, women make up just 19 percent of the U.S. Congress and hold less than a quarter of state legislature seats and statewide elective executive offices in spite of being over 50 percent of the population. In families, women still do twice the amount of housework and child care as men, even when they are employed outside the home.[1]

[1]See Cecelia Ridgeway, *Framed by Gender: How Gender Inequality Persists in the Modern World* (New York: Oxford University Press, 2011); Susan J. Douglas, *Enlightened Sexism: The Seductive Message That Feminism's Work Is Done* (New York: Holt, 2010); Barbara J. Berg, *Sexism in America: Alive, Well, and Ruining Our Future* (Chicago: Lawrence Hill, 2009); David Cotter, Joan Hermsen, and Reeve Vanneman, "The End of the Gender Revolution? Gender Role Attitudes from 1977 to 2008," *American Journal of Sociology* 117, no. 1 (2011): 259–289; U.S. Census Bureau, *Current Population Survey, Annual Social and Economic (ASEC) Supplement, Table PINC-05: Work Experience in 2010, People 15 Years Old and Over by Total Money Earnings in 2010, by Race, Age, Hispanic Origin, and Sex* (Washington, DC: U.S. Government Printing Office, 2011); Kenneth Chang, "Bias Persists for Women in Science," *New York Times*, September 24, 2012; Shaila Dewan and Robert Gebeloff, "The New American Job: More Men Enter Fields Dominated by Women," *New York Times*, May 20, 2012, available at http://www.nytimes.com/2012/05/21/business/increasingly-men-seek-success-in-jobs-dominated-by-women.html; Center for American Women and Politics, Eagleton Institute of Politics, Rutgers University, "Women in Elective Office 2013," 2013; Shira Offer and Barbara Schneider, "Revisiting the Gender Gap in Time-Use Patterns: Multitasking and Well-Being among Mothers and Fathers in Dual-Earner Families," *American Sociological Review*, December 2011, pp. 809–833; and Judith Treas and Sonia Drobnic, *Dividing the Domestic: Men, Women, and Household Work in Cross-National Perspective* (Stanford, CA: Stanford University Press, 2010).

We are not only stuck but lost. There is, for example, an ongoing global epidemic of men's violence, including war, terrorism, mass murders, sex trafficking, and rape and battering directed at girls and women. Official responses and public conversations show little understanding of the underlying causes or what to do, including what to make of the fact that the overwhelming majority of violence is perpetrated by men. Worldwide, 30 percent of women report having been sexually or physically assaulted by a current or former partner, and women are more at risk for rape and domestic violence than from cancer, car accidents, war, and malaria *combined*. The U.S. military recently revealed that sexual assault is so pervasive within its ranks that the greatest threat to women's safety comes not from the hazards of military service but from sexual assault by male service members.[2]

Where we are is deep inside an oppressive gender legacy whose consequences in a male-dominated world extend far beyond relations between women and men, from runaway capitalist greed and class inequality to the impending devastation of climate change.

On a scale both large and small, we are faced with the knowledge that what gender is about is tied to a great deal of suffering, injustice, and trouble, but our not knowing what to do with that knowledge binds us in a knot of fear, anger, and pain, of blame, defensiveness, guilt, and denial. We are unsure of just about everything except that something is wrong, and the more we pull at the knot, the tighter it gets.

Patriarchy

We are trapped inside a legacy whose core is patriarchal. To understand what that is and take part in the journey out, we need ways to unravel the knot, and this begins with getting clear about what it means to be inside a patriarchal legacy. To get clear, we first have to get past the defensive reaction of many people—men in particular—to the word "patriarchy" itself, which they routinely interpret as code for "men." Patriarchy is *not* a way of saying "men." Patriarchy is a kind of society, and a society is more than a collection of people. As such, "patriarchy" refers not to me or any other man or collection of men but to a kind of society in which men *and* women participate. By itself this poses enough problems without the added burden of equating an entire society with a group of people.

5

---

[2]See Sanja Bahun-Radunović, *Violence and Gender in the Globalized World* (Burlington, VT: Ashgate, 2008); "Unholy Alliance," *New York Times*, March 11, 2013; Siddharth Kara, *Sex Trafficking: Inside the Business of Modern Slavery* (New York: Columbia University Press, 2010); and Associated Press, "One Third of Women Assaulted by a Partner, Global Report Says," *New York Times*, June 20, 2013. Data on risks to service-women reported on PBS *Newshour*, July 30, 2013.

What is patriarchy? A society is patriarchal to the degree that it promotes male privilege* by being *male dominated, male identified,* and *male centered.* It is also organized around an obsession with control and involves as one of its key aspects the oppression of women.

Male Dominance

Patriarchy is male dominated in that positions of authority — political, economic, legal, religious, educational, military, domestic — are generally reserved for men. Heads of state, corporate CEOs, religious leaders, school principals, members of legislatures at all levels of government, senior law partners, tenured professors, generals and admirals, and even those identified as "head of household" all tend to be male under patriarchy. When a woman finds her way into higher positions, people tend to be struck by the exception to the rule and wonder how she'll measure up against a man. It is a test rarely applied to men ("I wonder if he'll be as good a president as a woman would be") except, perhaps, when men take on the devalued domestic and other caring work typically done by women, such as child care and housework or caring for an elderly parent. Even then, men's failure to measure up can be interpreted as a sign of superiority, a trained incapacity that actually protects their privileged status ("You change the diaper. I'm no good at that.").

In the simplest sense, male dominance creates power differences between men and women. It means, for example, that men can claim larger shares of income and wealth. It means they can shape culture in ways that reflect and serve men's collective interests by, for example, controlling the content of films and television shows, or handling rape and sexual harassment cases in ways that put the victim rather than the defendant on trial.

Male dominance also promotes the idea that men are superior to women. In part this occurs because we don't distinguish between the superiority of *positions* in a hierarchy and the kinds of people who usually occupy them.[3]

---

*I use the term "privilege" according to the definition developed by Peggy McIntosh in her classic paper "White Privilege and Male Privilege: A Personal Account of Coming to See Correspondences through Work in Women's Studies" (Working Paper 189, Wellesley College Center for Research on Women, Wellesley, MA, 1988). Privilege refers to any unearned advantage that is available to members of a social category while being systematically denied to others. In patriarchy, for example, what men say tends to have greater credibility than what women say, even when they're saying the same thing. Access to privilege depends on the prevailing definition of categories such as "male" and "female" and the advantages and disadvantages socially attached to them. It also depends on related characteristics — a man's access to male privilege, for example, varies according to other status characteristics such as race, sexual orientation, disability status, and social class. McIntosh's approach is important to any understanding of privilege because it refers not to individuals but to the organization of social systems in which people live.

[3]See Marilyn French, *Beyond Power: On Men, Women, and Morals* (New York: Ballantine Books, 1985).

This means that if men occupy superior positions, it is a short leap to the idea that men themselves must be superior. If presidents, generals, legislators, priests, popes, and corporate CEOs are all men (with a few token women), then men as a group become identified with superiority. It is true that most men in patriarchies are not powerful individuals and spend their days doing what other men tell them to do whether they want to or not. At the same time, *every* man's standing in relation to women is enhanced by the male monopoly over authority in patriarchal societies.

Male dominance also does not mean that all women are powerless. Former Secretary of State Hillary Rodham Clinton and Supreme Court Justices Sonia Sotomayor, Ruth Bader Ginsberg, and Elena Kagan, for example, are all far more powerful than most men will ever be. But they stand out precisely because they are so unusual in a society in which male dominance is the rule.

Like all subordinate groups, women also manage to have some power by making the most of what is left to them by men. Just as patriarchy turns women into sex objects who are supposed to organize their lives around men's needs, for example, so, too, does this arrangement grant women the power to refuse to have sex with them.[4]

Male Identification

Patriarchal societies are *male identified* in that core cultural ideas about what is considered good, desirable, preferable, or normal are culturally associated with how we think about men, manhood, and masculinity. The simplest example of this is the still-widespread use of male pronouns and nouns to represent people in general. When we routinely refer to human beings as "man" or call women "guys," we construct a symbolic world in which men are in the foreground and women are in the background, marginalized as outsiders[5] (a practice that can back people into some embarrassingly ridiculous corners, as in a biology text that described "man" as "a species that breast-feeds his young").

But male identification amounts to much more than this, for it also takes men and men's lives as the standard for defining what is normal. The idea of a career, for example, with its sixty-hour week, is defined in ways that assume the career holder has something like

---

[4]For more on gender and dominant/subordinate relationships, see Jean Baker Miller, *Toward a New Psychology of Women*, 2nd ed. (Boston: Beacon Press, 1986).

[5]A lot of research shows how such uses of language affect people's perception. See, for example, Mykol C. Hamilton, "Using Masculine Generics: Does Generic 'He' Increase Male Bias in the User's Imagery?" *Sex Roles* 19, nos. 11–12 (1988): 785–799; Wendy Martyna, "Beyond the 'He/Man' Approach: The Case for Nonsexist Language," *Signs* 5, no. 3 (1980): 482–493; Casey Miller and Kate Swift, *Words and Women*, updated ed. (New York: HarperCollins, 1991); and Joseph W. Schneider and Sally L. Hacker, "Sex Role Imagery in the Use of the Generic 'Man' in Introductory Texts: A Case in the Sociology of Sociology," *American Sociologist* 8 (1973): 12–18.

a traditional "wife" at home to perform the vital support work of taking care of children, doing laundry, and making sure there is a safe, clean, comfortable haven for rest and recuperation from the stress of the competitive male-dominated world. Since most women don't have such "wives," they find it harder to identify with and prosper within this male-identified model.

Another aspect of male identification is the cultural description of 15 masculinity and manhood in terms that are virtually synonymous with the core values of society as a whole. These include qualities such as control, strength, competitiveness, toughness, coolness under pressure, logic, forcefulness, decisiveness, rationality, autonomy, self-sufficiency, and control over any emotion that interferes with other core values (such as invulnerability). These male-identified qualities are associated with the work valued most in patriarchal societies—business, politics, war, athletics, law, and medicine—because this work has been organized in ways that require such qualities for success. In contrast, qualities such as cooperation, mutuality, equality, sharing, empathy, compassion, caring, vulnerability, a readiness to negotiate and compromise, emotional expressiveness, and intuitive and other nonlinear ways of thinking are all devalued *and* culturally associated with women and femininity.

Of course, women are not devalued entirely. Women are often prized for their beauty as objects of male sexual desire, for example, but as such they are often possessed and controlled in ways that ultimately devalue them. There is also a powerful cultural romanticizing of women in general and mothers in particular, but it is a tightly focused sentimentality (as on Mother's Day or Secretaries' Day) that has little effect on how women are regarded and treated on a day-to-day basis. And, like all sentimentality, it does not have much weight when it comes to actually doing something to support women's lives by, for example, providing effective and affordable child day care facilities for working mothers or family-leave policies that allow working women to attend to the caring functions for which we supposedly value them so highly, and without compromising their careers.

Because patriarchy is male identified, when most women look out on the world they see themselves reflected as women in a few narrow areas of life such as "caring" occupations and personal relationships. To see herself as a leader, for example, a woman must first get around the fact that leadership itself has been gendered through its identification with manhood and masculinity as part of patriarchal culture. While a man might have to learn to see himself as a manager, a woman has to be able to see herself as a *woman* manager who can succeed in spite of the fact that she is not a man.

As a result, any woman who dares strive for standing in the world beyond the sphere of caring relationships must choose between two very different cultural images of who she is and who she ought to be. For her to assume real public power—as in politics, corporations, or the professions—she must resolve a contradiction between her culturally based identity as a woman, on the one hand, and the male-identified *position* that she occupies on the other. For this reason, the more powerful a woman is under patriarchy, the more "unsexed" she becomes in the eyes of others as her female cultural identity recedes beneath the mantle of male-identified power and the masculine images associated with it. With men the effect is just the opposite: the more powerful they are, the more aware they are of their manhood. In other words, in a patriarchal culture, power looks sexy on men but not on women.

For all the pitfalls and limitations, however, some women do make it to positions of power. What about Margaret Thatcher,[6] for example, or Queen Elizabeth I,[7] Catherine the Great,[8] Indira Gandhi,[9] and Golda Meir?[10] Doesn't their power contradict the idea that patriarchy is male dominated?

The answer is that patriarchy can accommodate a limited number 20 of powerful women as long as the society retains its essential patriarchal character, especially male identification. Although a few individual women have wielded great power in patriarchal societies, each has been surrounded by powerful men — generals, cabinet ministers, bishops, and wealthy aristocrats or businessmen — whose collective interests she must support by embracing core patriarchal values. Indeed, part of what makes these women stand out as so exceptional is their ability to embody values culturally defined as masculine: they have been tougher, more decisive, more aggressive, more calculating, and more emotionally controlled than most men around them.[11]

These women's power, however, has nothing to do with whether women in general are subordinated under patriarchy. It also doesn't mean that putting more women in positions of authority will by itself do much for women unless we also change the patriarchal character of the systems in which they operate. Indeed, without such change, the Hillary Rodham Clintons and Sonia Sotomayors of the world tend to affirm the very systems that subordinate women, by fostering the illusion of gender equality and by embracing the patriarchal values on which male power and privilege rest. This does not mean we shouldn't try to get women into positions of power, only that making some women powerful will not be enough to change the system itself.

Since patriarchal culture identifies power with men, most men who are not themselves powerful can still feel some connection with the *idea*

---

[6]**Margaret Thatcher:** (1925–2013) British stateswoman, leader of the Conservative Party, and prime minister from 1979 to 1990. [Eds.]

[7]**Queen Elizabeth I:** (1533–1603) Queen of England and Ireland, 1558–1603. [Eds.]

[8]**Catherine the Great:** (1729–1796) Catherine II, Empress of Russia, 1762–1796. [Eds.]

[9]**Indira Gandhi:** (1919–1984) Only child of Jawaharlal Nehru, first prime minister of India; served as prime minister herself from 1966 to 1977 and from 1980 until her assassination in 1984. [Eds.]

[10]**Golda Meir:** (1898–1978) Israeli politician and stateswoman, served as prime minister from 1969 until her resignation in 1974. [Eds.]

[11]See, for example, Carole Levin's *The Heart and Stomach of a King: Elizabeth I and the Politics of Sex and Power* (Philadelphia: University of Pennsylvania Press, 1994).

of male dominance and with men who *are* powerful. It is far easier, for example, for an unemployed working-class man to identify with male leaders and their displays of patriarchal masculine toughness than it is for women of any class. When upper-class U.S. president George W. Bush "got tough" with Saddam Hussein, for example, men of all classes could identify with his acting out of basic patriarchal values. The same can be said of President Barack Obama's ordering the mission that resulted in the killing of Osama bin Laden. In this way, male identification gives even the most lowly placed man a cultural basis for feeling a sense of superiority over an otherwise highly placed woman. This is why, for example, a construction worker can feel within his rights as a man when he sexually harasses a well-dressed professional woman who happens to walk by.[12]

When a society identifies a particular group such as men as the standard for human beings in general, it follows that men will be seen as superior, preferable, and of greater value than women. Not only will men be culturally defined as superior, but whatever men do will tend to be seen as having greater value. Occupations performed primarily by men, for example, will tend to be more highly regarded and better paid than occupations done primarily by women even when women's jobs require the same or even higher levels of skill, training, and responsibility. In the nineteenth century, most secretaries, telephone operators, librarians, and nurses were men, and those occupations consequently commanded relatively higher pay and status than they do now, when they are mostly performed by women. At the same time, as men have entered occupations such as nursing and elementary school teaching in search of stable employment following the economic collapse of 2008, they have received better pay than women and are more likely to be elevated to supervisory positions, a phenomenon known as the "glass escalator."[13]

And just as what men do tends to be valued more highly than what women do, those things that are valued in a culture will tend to be associated with men more than with women. The idea of God, for example, is of enormous importance in human life, and so it should come as no surprise that every monotheistic patriarchal religion worships a male-identified God gendered as masculine. As Mary Daly[14] argues in her book *Beyond God the Father,* this, in turn, puts men in the highly favorable position of having God identified with *them*, which further reinforces the position of women as 'other' and the legitimacy of men's claim to privilege and dominance.[15]

---

[12]See Carol Brooks Gardner, *Passing By: Gender and Public Harassment* (Berkeley: University of California Press, 1995).

[13]See Dewan and Gebeloff, "The New American Job"; and Paula England and D. Dunn, "Evaluating Work and Comparable Worth," *Annual Review of Sociology* 14 (1988): 227–248.

[14]**Mary Daly:** (1928–2010) Self-described radical lesbian feminist, philosopher, and theologian, she taught for 33 years at Boston College. [Eds.]

[15]Mary Daly, *Beyond God the Father: Toward a Philosophy of Women's Liberation* (Boston: Beacon Press, 1973).

Male Centeredness

In addition to being male dominated and male identified, patriarchy is 25 *male centered*, which means that the focus of attention is primarily on men and boys and what they do. Pick up any newspaper or go to any movie theater and you will find stories primarily about men and what they've done or haven't done or what they have to say about either. With rare exceptions, women are portrayed as being along for the ride, fussing over their support work of domestic labor and maintaining love relationships, providing something for men to fight over, or being foils that reflect or amplify men's heroic struggle with the human condition. If there is a crisis, what we see is what men did to create it and how men then deal with it.

If you want a story about heroism, moral courage, spiritual trans-formation, endurance, or any of the struggles that give human life its deepest meaning, men and masculinity are usually the terms in which you must see it. Men's experience is what patriarchal culture uses to represent *human* experience, even when it is women who most often live it. Films about single men taking care of children, for example, such as *Sleepless in Seattle*, have far more audience appeal than those focus-ing on women, even though women are much more likely than men to be single parents. And stories that focus on deep bonds of friendship — which men still have a harder time forming than do women — are far more likely to focus on men than women.[16]

In another example, the closing scenes of *Dances with Wolves* show the white male hero and his Native American–raised white wife leaving his recently adopted tribe, which is also the only family *she* has known since early childhood. The focus, however, is clearly on the drama of *his* moment as she looks on supportively. She is leaving her adoptive parents, but we see only the emotionally charged parting (with a touch-ing exchange of gifts) between son-in-law and father-in-law. And the last words we hear are the deeply moving cries of a newfound warrior friend testifying to the depth of feeling between these two men (which, oddly, is the only expression of it we ever see).

By contrast, films that focus on women, such as *Precious, The Queen, Erin Brockovich, Elizabeth, Girlfriends, Leaving Normal, Passion Fish, Strangers in Good Company, Beaches*, and *Thelma and Louise*, are such startling exceptions that they invariably sink quickly into obscurity, are dismissed as clones of male themes ("female buddy movies"), or are subjected to intense scrutiny as aberrations needing to be explained.

[16]For some research on gender differences in friendship, see R. Aukett, J. Ritchie, and K. Mill, "Gender Differences in Friendship Patterns," *Sex Roles* 19, nos. 1–2 (1988): 57–66; R. J. Barth and B. N. Kinder, "A Theoretical Analysis of Sex Differences in Same-Sex Friendship," *Sex Roles* 19, nos. 5–6 (1988): 349–363; Z. Kiraly, "The Relationship between Emotional Self-disclosure of Male and Female Adolescents' Friendship," *Dissertation Abstracts International* 60, no. 7-B (2000): 3619; and D. G. Williams, "Gender, Masculinity-Feminity, and Emotional Intimacy in Same-Sex Friendships," *Sex Roles* 12, nos. 5–6 (1985): 587–600.

TABLE 1   Films Winning the Oscar for Best Picture, 1968–2013

YEAR	FILM	YEAR	FILM
2013	*12 Years a Slave*	1990	*Dances with Wolves*
2012	*Argo*	1989	*Driving Miss Daisy*
2011	*The Artist*	1988	*Rain Man*
2010	*The King's Speech*	1987	*The Last Emperor*
2009	*The Hurt Locker*	1986	*Platoon*
2008	*Slumdog Millionaire*	1985	*Out of Africa*
2007	*No Country for Old Men*	1984	*Amadeus*
2006	*The Departed*	1983	*Terms of Endearment*
2005	*Crash*	1982	*Gandhi*
2004	*Million Dollar Baby*	1981	*Chariots of Fire*
2003	*Lord of the Rings*	1980	*Ordinary People*
2002	*Chicago*	1979	*Kramer vs. Kramer*
2001	*A Beautiful Mind*	1978	*The Deer Hunter*
2000	*Gladiator*	1977	*Annie Hall*
1999	*American Beauty*	1976	*Rocky*
1998	*Shakespeare in Love*	1975	*One Flew Over the Cuckoo's Nest*
1997	*Titanic*	1974	*The Godfather, Part II*
1996	*The English Patient*	1973	*The Sting*
1995	*Braveheart*	1972	*The Godfather, Part I*
1994	*Forrest Gump*	1971	*The French Connection*
1993	*Schindler's List*	1970	*Patton*
1992	*The Unforgiven*	1969	*Midnight Cowboy*
1991	*The Silence of the Lambs*	1968	*Oliver!*

To get a full sense of what I mean, look at the list of films awarded the Oscar for Best Picture since 1968 (Table 1). Of almost fifty films, only four tell a story through the life of someone who is female—*Million Dollar Baby, Chicago, Out of Africa,* and *Terms of Endearment*—and only three of these focus on a serious subject, with the other being a musical.

A male center of focus is everywhere. Research makes clear, for exam- 30 ple, what most women probably already know: that men dominate conversations by talking more, interrupting more, and controlling content.[17]

---

[17]For more on gender and interaction, see Laurie P. Arliss, *Women and Men Communicating: Challenges and Changes,* 2nd ed. (Prospect Heights, IL: Waveland Press, 2000); Robin Lakoff, *Language and Woman's Place,* rev. ed. (New York: Harper and Row, 2004); and Robin Lakoff, *Talking Power: The Politics of Language in Our Lives* (New York: Basic Books, 1992). See also Deborah Tannen, *Conversational Style: Analyzing Talk among Friends* (Norwood, NJ: Ablex, 1984); and *You Just Don't Understand: Women and Men in Conversation* (New York: Morrow, 1990).

When women suggest ideas in business meetings, they often go unnoticed until a man makes the same suggestion and receives credit for it (or, as a cartoon caption put it, "Excellent idea, Ms. Jones. Perhaps one of the men would like to suggest it."). In classrooms at all levels of schooling, boys and men typically command center stage and receive most of the attention.[18] Even when women gather, they must often resist the ongoing assumption that no situation can be complete or even entirely real unless a man is there to take the center position. How else do we understand the experience of groups of women who go out for drinks and conversation and are approached by men who ask, "Are you ladies alone?"

Many men, however, will protest that they do not *feel* at the center, and this is one of the many ironic aspects of male privilege. In *A Room of One's Own*, Virginia Woolf[19] writes that women often serve as "looking-glasses possessing the magic and delicious power of reflecting the figure of man at twice its natural size."[20] Woolf's insight suggests several things about what happens to men in patriarchal societies. As part of men's training, they are affirmed through what they accomplish.[21] This contrasts with women, whose training mirrors them in different ways, affirming them less for what they accomplish than for their ability to empathize and mirror others as they form and maintain personal relationships, If men want to satisfy the human need to be seen and acknowledged by others, it will be through what they do and how well they live up to the standards of patriarchal manhood (which is one reason why male friendships tend to focus so heavily on competition and doing things together). This affects both individual men and patriarchy as a system, for men's focus on themselves ("See me!") and women's focus on others reinforce patriarchy's male-identified, male-centered aspects. These, in turn, support male dominance by making it easier for men to concentrate on enhancing and protecting their own status.

Another consequence of patriarchal mirroring is that heterosexual men in particular are encouraged to relate to women with the expectation of seeing only themselves. When men's reflection is obscured by the reality and demands of women's own lives, men are vulnerable to feeling left out and neglected. Like cold-blooded animals that generate little heat of their own, this dynamic can make it hard for men to feel warm unless the light is shining on them at the moment, something

---

[18]See American Association of University Women, *How Schools Shortchange Girls* (Washington, DC: American Association of University Women, 1995); American Association of University Women, *Gender Gaps: Where Schools Still Fail Our Children* (Washington, DC: AAUW Educational Foundation, 1998); American Association of University Women, *A License for Bias: Sex Discrimination, Schools, and Title IX* (Washington, DC: AAUW Educational Foundation, 2001); and David M. Sadker and Karen Zittleman, *Still Failing at Fairness: How Gender Bias Cheats Girls and Boys in School and What We Can Do about It* (New York: Scribner, 2009).

[19]**Virginia Woolf:** (1882–1941) English feminist, essayist, and fiction writer; committed suicide at the age of 51. [Eds.]

[20]Virginia Woolf, *A Room of One's Own* (New York: Harcourt Brace and World, 1929), 35.

[21]My thanks go to Nora L. Jamieson, who helped me navigate through this psychological territory.

well known to women who spend inordinate amounts of time worrying about whether they're paying enough attention to their male partners, about whether they should be sitting quietly and reading a book or spending time with women friends when they could be paying attention to the men in their lives. It is a worry few men wrestle with unless women complain.

Although men generally do not provide one another with the kind of mirroring they expect from women, they do play a part in fostering the illusion of being larger than life, especially through competition. When men compete, they enter the pumped-up world of winners and losers, in which the number of times a ball goes through a hoop or is carried over a line elevates some men over other men (and, by default, over all women) in ways judged to be important in patriarchal culture. If ever there were an assertion of larger-than-life status, the triumphant shout of "We're number one!" is it. (Not asked is, For how long, compared to whom, and so what?) Even the losers and the male spectators share in the reflected glow of the noble masculine striving after the coveted opportunity to stand before the mirror that makes men look bigger than they are, if only for a little while—until the next season begins or someone faster, stronger, younger, or smarter comes along.

All of this, of course, is impossible for most men to sustain. Women have distracting lives of their own in spite of their training to keep men at the center of attention. And the fleeting moments of actually living up to the expectation of being larger than life are just that. As a result, patriarchal expectations that place men at the center paradoxically perch men just a short drop away from feeling that they are not at the center—and, therefore, on some level, that they don't exist at all.

The Obsession with Control

The fourth characteristic of patriarchy is an obsession with control as a core value around which social and personal life are organized. As with any system of privilege that elevates one group by oppressing another, control is an essential element of patriarchy: men maintain their privilege by controlling both women and other men who might threaten it. Given the primacy of control, it becomes the cultural standard for a truly superior human being, which is then used to justify men's privileged position. Men are assumed (and expected) to be in control at all times, to be unemotional (except for anger and rage), to present themselves as invulnerable, autonomous, independent, strong, rational, logical, dispassionate, knowledgeable, always right, and in command of every situation, especially those involving women. These qualities, it is assumed, mark them as superior and justify male privilege. Women, in contrast, are assumed (and expected) to be just the opposite, especially in relation to men.

It would be misleading to suggest that control is inherently bad or that it inevitably leads to oppression. Control is, after all, one of the hallmarks of our species. It is our only hope to bring some order out of chaos or to protect ourselves from what threatens our survival. We imagine, focus, and act—from baking bread to planting a garden to designing a national health plan—and all of this involves control. Even small children delight in a sense of human agency, in being able to make things happen. Under patriarchy, however, control is more than an expression of human essence or a way to get things done. It is valued and pursued to a degree that gives social life an oppressive form by taking a natural human capacity to obsessive extremes.

Under patriarchy, control shapes not only the broad outlines of social life but also men's inner lives. The more that men see control as central to their sense of self worth, well being, and safety, the more driven they feel to go after it and to organize their lives around it. This takes men away from connection to others and themselves and toward disconnection. This is because control involves a relationship between controller and controlled, and disconnection is an integral part of that relationship. To control something, we have to see it as a separate "other." Even if we are controlling ourselves, we have to mentally split ourselves into a "me" who is being controlled and an "I" who is in control.

Patriarchy is not organized around simply an obsession with control, but a male-identified obsession with control. As a result, the more that men participate in the system, the more likely they are to see them-selves as separate, autonomous, and disconnected from others. They may become versions of the western hero who rides into town from nowhere, with no past, and leaves going nowhere, with no apparent future. Women's lives, of course, also involve control, especially in rela-tion to children. But the idea and practice of control as a core principle of social life is part of what defines patriarchal *man*hood, not woman-hood, and so women are discouraged from pursuing it and criticized if they do. A woman perceived as controlling a man is typically labeled a castrating bitch or a ball buster, and the man she supposedly controls is looked down on as henpecked, pussy whipped, and barely a man at all. But there are no insulting terms for a man who controls a woman—by having the last word, not letting her work outside the home, deciding when she'll have sex, or limiting her time with other women—or for the woman he controls. There is no need for such words because men controlling women is culturally defined as a core aspect of patriarchal manhood.

Women and Patriarchy

An inevitable consequence of patriarchy is the oppression of women, which takes several forms. Historically, for example, women have been excluded from major institutions such as church, state, universities, and the professions. Even when they have been allowed to participate, it has generally been at subordinate, second-class levels. Marilyn French goes so far as to argue that historically women's oppression has amounted to a form of slavery:

> What other term can one use to describe a state in which people do not have rights over their own bodies, their own sexuality, marriage, reproduction or divorce, in which they may not receive education or practice a trade or profession, or move about freely in the world? Many women (both past and present) work laboriously all their lives without receiving any payment for their work.[22]

Because patriarchy is male identified and male centered, women 40 and the work they do tend to be devalued, if not made invisible, and women are routinely repressed in their development as human beings through neglect and discrimination in schools[23] and in occupational hiring, development, promotion, and rewards. Anyone who doubts that patriarchy is an oppressive system need only consult the growing literature documenting not only economic, political, and other institutionalized sexism but pervasive violence, from pornography to the everyday realities of battering, sexual harassment, and sexual assault.[24] And there are also the daily headlines—such as recent revelations of a long history of pervasive sexual harassment and assault in the U.S. military that went on for years before a public scandal prompted demands for corrective action, which, as of this writing, has yet to materialize.

This is not to deny that much has changed in women's position over the last hundred years—from the appointment of women to the U.S. Supreme Court to assigning women to combat zones in Iraq and Afghanistan. There is less tolerance for overtly sexist behavior toward women in many settings. An elite of women has managed to enter the professions and, to a degree, upper levels of corporate management. And most laws that blatantly discriminate against women have been repealed.

[22]French, *Beyond Power*, 132.

[23]See American Association of University Women, *How Schools Shortchange Girls*; American Association of University Women, *Gender Gaps*; American Association of University Women, *A License for Bias*; and Sadker and Zittleman, *Still Failing at Fairness*.

[24]See Heather McLaughlin, Christopher Uggen, and Amy Blackstone, "Sexual Harassment, Workplace Authority, and the Paradox of Power," *American Sociological Review*, August 2012, pp. 1–23; Susan Brownmiller, *Against Our Will: Men, Women, and Rape* (New York: Simon and Schuster, 1975); Andrea Dworkin, *Woman Hating* (New York: Dutton, 1974); Susan Faludi, *Backlash: The Undeclared War against American Women* (New York: Crown, 1991); Marilyn French, *The War against Women* (New York: Summit Books, 1992); Carol Brooks Gardner, *Passing By: Gender and Public Harassment* (Berkeley and Los Angeles: University of California Press, 1995); Laura Lederer, ed., *Take Back the Night: Women on* Pornography (New York: Morrow, 1980); Catharine A. MacKinnon, *Only Words* (Cambridge, MA: Harvard University Press, 1993); Catharine MacKinnon, *Sex Equality: Rape Law* (New York: Foundation Press, 2001); "Medical News and Perspectives," *Journal of the American Medical Association* 264, no. 8 (1990): 939; Diana E. H. Russell, *Rape in Marriage* (New York; Macmillan, 1982); Diana E H. Russell, *Sexual Exploitation: Rape, Child Sexual Abuse, and Workplace Harassment* (Beverly Hills, CA: Sage, 1984); Diana E. H. Russell, ed., *Making Violence Sexy: Feminist Views on Pornography* (New York: Teachers College Press, 1993); and Diana E. H. Russell and Roberta A. Harmes, *Femicide in Global Perspective* (New York: Teachers College Press, 2001).

To a great degree, however, such highly publicized progress supports an illusion of fundamental change. In spite of new laws, for example, violence and sexual harassment against women are still pervasive. Inequality of income and wealth has not changed much from the 1980s, and women are still heavily concentrated in a small number of low-level service and pink-collar occupations. In spite of the huge influx of married women, many of them mothers, into the paid labor force, and in spite of a great deal of talk about the joys of fatherhood, there has been no substantial increase in men's sense of responsibility for domestic labor or their willingness to actually participate.[25] And, as we saw earlier, women's share of authority in major institutions—from the state to organized religion to corporations to science, higher education, and the mass media—remains low. In short, the basic features that define patriarchy as a type of society have barely budged, and the women's movement has been stalled in much the same way that the civil rights movement was stalled after the hard-won gains of the 1960s.

Thus far, mainstream women's movements have concentrated on the liberal agenda, whose primary goal has been to allow women to do what men do in the ways that men do it, whether in science, the professions, business, government, or the military. More serious challenges to patriarchy have been silenced, maligned, and misunderstood for reasons that are not hard to fathom. As difficult as it is to change overtly sexist* sensibilities and behavior, it is much harder to raise critical questions about how sexism is embedded in major institutions such as the economy, politics, religion, health care, and the family. It is easier to allow women to assimilate into patriarchal society than to question society itself. It is easier to allow a few women to occupy positions of

---

[25]See Joan Acker, *Class Questions: Feminist Answers* (Lanham, MD: Rowman and Littlefield, 2006); Ridgeway, *Framed by Gender*; and Maria Charles and David Grusky, *Occupational Ghettos: The Worldwide Segregation of Women and Men* (Stanford, CA: Stanford University Press). This is true even in socialist societies such as Sweden. For research on men and domestic work, see R. L. Blumberg, ed., *Gender, Family, and Economy: The Triple Overlap* (Newbury Park, CA: Sage, 1991); C. Goldin, *Understanding the Gender Gap: An Economic History of American Women* (New York: Oxford University Press, 1990); L. Haas, *Equal Parenthood and Social Policy: A Study of Parental Leave in Sweden* (Albany: State University of New York Press, 1992); Arlie Hochschild, *The Second Shift: Working Parents and the Revolution at Home*, rev. ed. (New York: Viking/Penguin, 2012); M. J. Intons-Peterson, *Gender Concepts of Swedish and American Youth* (Hillsdale, NJ: Erlbaum, 1988); and J. R. Wilkie, "Changes in U.S. Men's Attitudes towards the Family Provider Role, 1972–1989," *Gender and Society* 7, no. 2 (1993): 261–279. For statistics on men's and women's housework and child care contributions, see U.S. Department of Commerce Economics and Statistics Division, *Women in America: Indicators of Social and Economic Well-Being* (Washington, DC: U.S. Department of Commerce, 2011).

*The words "sexism" and "sexist" are commonly used to describe a personal prejudice or the person who holds it. As sociologist David Wellman argues in *Portraits of White Racism* (New York: Cambridge University Press, 2012), however, that approach is far too narrow to be of use because male privilege requires far more than this to continue. Following his lead, I use the term to indicate anything that has the effect of promoting male privilege, regardless of the intentions of the people involved. By judging actions, policies, and institutional arrangements solely in terms of their consequences, Wellman's conceptualization allows us to focus on the full range of forces that perpetuate male privilege, and saves us from the trap of personalizing what is essentially a social and systemic phenomenon.

authority and dominance than to question whether social life should be organized around principles of hierarchy, control, and dominance at all, to allow a few women to reach the heights of the corporate hierarchy rather than question whether people's needs should depend on an economic system based on dominance, control, and competition. It is easier to allow women to practice law than to question adversarial conflict as a model for resolving disputes and achieving justice. It has even been easier to admit women to military combat roles than to question the acceptability of warfare and its attendant images of patriarchal masculine power and heroism as instruments of national policy. And it has been easier to elevate and applaud a few women than to confront the cultural misogyny that is never far off, available to anyone who wants to use it to bring women down and put them in their place.

Easier, yes, but not easy or anything close to it. Like all movements that work for basic change, women's movements have come up against the depth to which the status quo is embedded in virtually every aspect of social life. The power of patriarchy is especially evident in the ongoing resistance even to the liberal agenda of women's movements—including the Supreme Court's retreat on women's reproductive rights, the routine trashing of feminism resulting in women's reluctance to embrace or identify with it, misogynist attacks on women running for public office, and a vocal movement of men who portray themselves as victims not only of the sex/gender system but of women's struggle to free themselves from their own oppression under it.

The power of patriarchy is also reflected in its ability to absorb the   45
pressures of superficial change as a defense against deeper challenges. Every social system has a certain amount of give that allows some change to occur and in the process leaves deep structures untouched and even invisible. Indeed, the 'give' plays a critical part in maintaining the status quo by fostering illusions of fundamental change and acting as a systemic shock absorber. It keeps the focus on symptoms while root causes go unnoticed and unremarked, and it deflects the power we need to take the risky deeper journey that leads to the heart of patriarchy and our involvement in it.

Obviously, we are in something much larger than ourselves, and it is not us. But equally obvious is our profound connection to it through the social conditions that shape our sense of who we are and what kinds of alternatives we can choose from. As a system, patriarchy encourages men to accept male privilege and perpetuate women's oppression, if only through silence. And it encourages women to accept and adapt to their oppressed position even to the extent of undermining movements to bring about change. We cannot avoid participating in patriarchy. It was handed to us the moment we came into the world. But we can choose *how* to participate in it.

Garry Trudeau/Doonesbury/Andrews McMeel Syndication

ENGAGING THE TEXT

1. What does Johnson mean when he says that "Patriarchy is *not* a way of saying 'men'" (para. 5)? In his view, why aren't most men powerful in a patriarchal society? In what ways do ordinary men benefit from patriarchy?

2. According to Johnson, what kinds of value and power do women have in a patriarchal society? How do politically powerful women like Indira Gandhi

and Golda Meir succeed? Why does he claim that their power "has nothing to do with whether women in general are subordinated under patriarchy" (para. 21)? Do you agree with him? Why or why not?

3. What roles do women and men play in "patriarchal mirroring" (para. 32)? In Johnson's view, how does it reinforce male dominance? How is male competition another kind of mirroring?

4. Why is a woman who appears to control a man or men "typically labeled a castrating bitch or a ball buster" (para. 38) when there are no derogatory labels for a man who is controlling? Have you heard comments like these about powerful women, such as female bosses or politicians? If so, what was the gender of the person or people who made the remarks, what did they say, and how did you react?

5. Johnson acknowledges that women have gained significant power over the last century; why does he imply that women's movements have made only superficial changes in patriarchy as a whole? What do you think he means when he says, "We cannot avoid participating in patriarchy. . . . But we can choose *how* to participate in it" (para. 46)? Working in small groups, brainstorm all the ways that you might work to challenge patriarchal attitudes, and then share your strategies with the class as a whole. What benefits and drawbacks do you see in each approach? Is there any consensus about the best ways to effect change?

EXPLORING CONNECTIONS

6. **Thinking Rhetorically**   In their essays, Lisa Wade and Myra Marx Ferree (p. 480) and Johnson rely on central metaphors ("gender binary glasses" and "the gender knot") to develop their arguments. What is the effect of each metaphor? What's the significance of "constantly getting new prescriptions as needed" (p. 483)? What's the effect of being bound "in a knot of fear, anger, and pain, of blame, defensiveness, guilt, and denial" (Johnson, para. 4)? What do the metaphors say about the flexibility or the strength of gender roles and socialization? Are these metaphors compatible, contradictory, or both? Explain.

7. Review Johnson's discussion of male dominance and male identification. How would he explain Carlos Andrés Gómez's observation that "To have the power of patriarchy and then to surrender it is a threat to all men" (p. 502)?

8. Analyze the Doonesbury cartoon on page 543. Why does Sam claim that she's not a feminist? Do you think she would agree with Johnson about the persistence and strength of patriarchy? Why or why not?

9. Look at the photos in the Visual Portfolio (p. 520) and discuss with a classmate whether they illustrate or challenge Johnson's view of patriarchy. Are you in agreement about all of them, some, or none? Why?

EXTENDING THE CRITICAL CONTEXT

10. Following the #MeToo and #TimesUp movements, there has been extensive discussion of sexism in the movie industry and of Hollywood's "old boys' club." Update Johnson's list of Best Picture Oscars: Have recent winners included more women in leading roles? Have the stories been less male centered? Do you feel that movies and the movie business are becoming more open to women? Why or why not?

11. Working in single-sex groups, identify at least half a dozen men living today who are widely admired in American culture. To what extent do these men reflect the qualities traditionally associated with masculinity, such as toughness, competitiveness, and decisiveness? Do they embody any characteristics that are typically associated with women, such as compassion, vulnerability, or willingness to compromise? Compare your results: if there are differences among the groups, how do you explain them?

"TWO WAYS A WOMAN CAN GET HURT": ADVERTISING AND VIOLENCE
JEAN KILBOURNE

Most of us like to think of ourselves as immune to the power of ads — we know that advertisers use sex to get our attention and that they make exaggerated claims about a product's ability to make us attractive, popular, and successful. Because we can see through these subtle or not-so-subtle messages, we assume that we're too smart to be swayed by them. But Jean Kilbourne argues that ads affect us in far more profound and potentially damaging ways. The way that ads portray bodies — especially women's bodies — as objects conditions us to see each other in dehumanizing ways, thus "normalizing" attitudes that can lead to sexual aggression. Kilbourne (b. 1946) has spent most of her professional life teaching and lecturing about the world of advertising. She has produced award-winning documentaries on images of women in ads (*Killing Us Softly, Slim Hopes*) and tobacco advertising (*Pack of Lies*). She has also been a member of the National Advisory Council on Alcohol Abuse and Alcoholism and has twice served as an adviser to the surgeon general of the United States. Currently she serves as an ambassador for the National Eating Disorders Association and is a senior scholar at the Wellesley Centers for Women (WCW) at Wellesley

5

College. Her most recent book, coauthored by Diane E. Levin, is *So Sexy So Soon: The New Sexualized Childhood and What Parents Can Do to Protect Their Kids* (2008). The following selection is taken from her 1999 book *Can't Buy My Love: How Advertising Changes the Way We Think and Feel* (formerly titled *Deadly Persuasion*).

SEX IN ADVERTISING IS MORE ABOUT DISCONNECTION and distance than connection and closeness. It is also more often about power than passion, about violence than violins. The main goal, as in pornography, is usually power over another, either by the physical dominance or preferred status of men or what is seen as the exploitative power of female beauty and female sexuality. Men conquer and women ensnare, always with the essential aid of a product. The woman is rewarded for her sexuality by the man's wealth, as in an ad for Cigarette boats in which the woman says, while lying in a man's embrace clearly after sex, "Does this mean I get a ride in your Cigarette?"

Sex in advertising is pornographic because it dehumanizes and objectifies people, especially women, and because it fetishizes products, imbues them with an erotic charge — which dooms us to disappointment since products never can fulfill our sexual desires or meet our emotional needs. The poses and postures of advertising are often borrowed from pornography, as are many of the themes, such as bondage, sadomasochism, and the sexual exploitation of children. When a beer ad uses the image of a man licking the high-heeled boot of a woman clad in leather, when bondage is used to sell neckties in the *New York Times*, perfume in *The New Yorker*, and watches on city buses, and when a college magazine promotes an S&M Ball, pornography can be considered mainstream.

Most of us know all this by now and I suppose some consider it kinky good fun. Pornography is more dangerously mainstream when its glorification of rape and violence shows up in mass media, in films and television shows, in comedy and music videos, and in advertising. Male violence is subtly encouraged by ads that encourage men to be forceful and dominant, and to value sexual intimacy more than emotional intimacy. "Do you want to be the one she tells her deep, dark secrets to?" asks a three-page ad for men's cologne. "Or do you want to be her deep, dark secret?" The last page advises men, "Don't be such a good boy." There are two identical women looking adoringly at the man in the ad, but he isn't looking at either one of them. Just what is the deep, dark secret? That he's sleeping with both of them? Clearly the way to get beautiful women is to ignore them, perhaps mistreat them.

"Two ways a woman can get hurt," says an ad for shaving gel, featuring a razor and a photo of a handsome man. My first thought

Two Ways A Woman Can Get Hurt.

(Heartbreaker)

(Soap and water shave)

Skintimate® Shave Gel Ultra Protection formula contains 75% moisturizers, including vitamin E, to protect your legs from nicks, cuts and razor burn. So while guys may continue to be a pain, shaving most definitely won't.

SKINTIMATE® SHAVE GEL.
LOVE YOUR LEGS

is that the man is a batterer or date rapist, but the ad informs us that he is merely a "heartbreaker." The gel will protect the woman so that "while guys may continue to be a pain, shaving most definitely won't." Desirable men are painful—heartbreakers at best.

Wouldn't it be wonderful if, realizing the importance of relation- 5 ships in all of our lives, we could seek to learn relational skills from women and to help men develop these strengths in themselves? In fact, we so often do the opposite. The popular culture usually trivializes these abilities in women, mocks men who have real intimacy with women (it is almost always married men in ads and cartoons who are jerks), and idealizes a template for relationships between men and women that is a recipe for disaster: a template that views sex as more important than anything else, that ridicules men who are not in control of their women

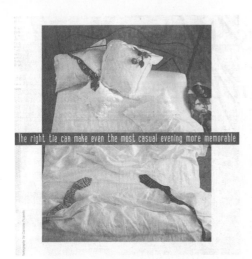

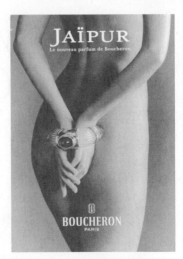

(who are "pussy-whipped"), and that disparages fidelity and commitment (except, of course, to brand names).

Indeed the very worst kind of man for a woman to be in an intimate relationship with, often a truly dangerous man, is the one considered most sexy and desirable in the popular culture. And the men capable of real intimacy (the ones we tell our deep, dark secrets to) constantly have their very masculinity impugned. Advertising often encourages women to be attracted to hostile and indifferent men while encouraging boys to become these men. This is especially dangerous for those of us who have suffered from "condemned isolation" in childhood: like heat-seeking missiles, we rush inevitably to mutual destruction.

Men are also encouraged to never take no for an answer. Ad after ad implies that girls and women don't really mean "no" when they say it, that women are only teasing when they resist men's advances.

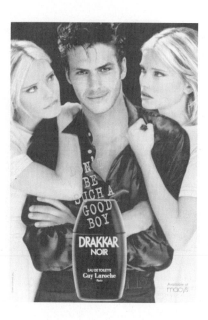

"NO" says an ad showing a man leaning over a woman against a wall. Is she screaming or laughing? Oh, it's an ad for deodorant and the second word, in very small print, is "sweat." Sometimes it's "all in good fun," as in the ad for Possession shirts and shorts featuring a man ripping the clothes off a woman who seems to be having a good time.

And sometimes it is more sinister. A perfume ad running in several teen magazines features a very young woman, with eyes blackened by makeup or perhaps something else, and the copy, "Apply generously to your neck so he can smell the scent as you shake your head 'no.'" In other words, he'll understand that you don't really mean it and he can respond to the scent like any other animal.

Sometimes there seems to be no question but that a man should force a woman to have sex. A chilling newspaper ad for a bar in Georgetown features a closeup of a cocktail and the headline, "If your date won't listen to reason, try a Velvet Hammer." A vodka ad pictures a wolf hiding in a flock of sheep, a hideous grin on its face. We all know what wolves do to sheep. A campaign for Bacardi Black rum features shadowy figures almost obliterated by darkness and captions such as "Some people embrace the night because the rules of the day do not apply." What it doesn't say is that people who are above the rules do enormous harm to other people, as well as to themselves.

These ads are particularly troublesome, given that between 10
one-third and three-quarters of all cases of sexual assault involve alcohol
consumption by the perpetrator, the victim, or both.[1] "Make strangers
your friends, and your friends a lot stranger," says one of the ads in
a Cuervo campaign that uses colorful cartoon beasts and emphasizes
heavy drinking. This ad is especially disturbing when we consider the
role of alcohol in date rape, as is another ad in the series that says, "The
night began with a bottle of Cuervo and ended with a vow of silence."
Over half of all reported rapes on college campuses occur when either
the victim or the assailant has been drinking.[2] Alcohol's role has different meaning for men and women, however. If a man is drunk when he
commits a rape, he is considered less responsible. If a woman is drunk
(or has had a drink or two or simply met the man in a bar), she is considered more responsible.

In general, females are still held responsible and hold each other
responsible when sex goes wrong—when they become pregnant or are
the victims of rape and sexual assault or cause a scandal. Constantly
exhorted to be sexy and attractive, they discover when assaulted that that
very sexiness is evidence of their guilt, their lack of "innocence." Sometimes the ads play on this by "warning" women of what might happen if
they use the product. "Wear it but beware it," says a perfume ad. Beware
what exactly? Victoria's Secret tempts young women with blatantly sexual ads promising that their lingerie will make them irresistible. Yet when
a young woman accused William Kennedy Smith of raping her, the fact
that she wore Victoria's Secret panties was used against her as an indication of her immorality. A jury acquitted Smith, whose alleged history of
violence against women was not permitted to be introduced at trial.

It is sadly not surprising that the jury was composed mostly of
women. Women are especially cruel judges of other women's sexual

---

[1]Wilsnack, Plaud, Wilsnack, and Klassen, 1997, 262. [All notes are Kilbourne's unless
otherwise indicated.]
[2]Abbey, Ross, and McDuffie, 1991. Also Martin, 1992, 230–37.

behavior, mostly because we are so desperate to believe we are in control of what happens to us. It is too frightening to face the fact that male violence against women is irrational and commonplace. It is reassuring to believe that we can avoid it by being good girls, avoiding dark places, staying out of bars, dressing "innocently." An ad featuring two young women talking intimately at a coffee shop says, "Carla and Rachel considered themselves open-minded and non-judgmental people. Although they did agree Brenda was a tramp." These terrible judgments from other women are an important part of what keeps all women in line.

If indifference in a man is sexy, then violence is sometimes downright erotic. Not surprisingly, this attitude too shows up in advertising. "Push my buttons," says a young woman, "I'm looking for a man who can totally floor me." Her vulnerability is underscored by the fact that she is in an elevator, often a dangerous place for women. She is young, she is submissive (her eyes are downcast), she is in a dangerous place, and she is dressed provocatively. And she is literally asking for it.

"Wear it out and make it scream," says a jeans ad portraying a man sliding his hands under a woman's transparent blouse. This could be a seduction, but it could as easily be an attack. Although the ad that ran in the Czech version of *Elle* portraying three men attacking a woman seems unambiguous, the terrifying image is being used to sell jeans *to women*. So someone must think that women would find this image compelling or attractive. Why would we? Perhaps it is simply designed to get our attention, by shocking us and by arousing unconscious anxiety. Or perhaps the intent is more subtle and it is designed to play into the fantasies of domination and even rape that some women use in order to maintain an illusion of being in control (we are the ones having the fantasies, after all, we are the directors).

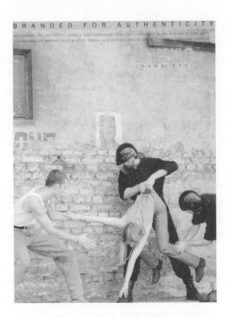

A camera ad features a woman's torso wrapped in plastic, her hands 15 tied behind her back. A smiling woman in a lipstick ad has a padlocked chain around her neck. An ad for MTV shows a vulnerable young woman, her breasts exposed, and the simple copy "Bitch." A perfume ad features a man shadowboxing with what seems to be a woman.

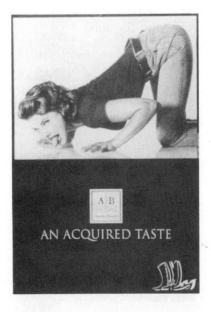

Sometimes women are shown dead or in the process of being killed. "Great hair never dies," says an ad featuring a female corpse lying on a bed, her breasts exposed. An ad in the Italian version of *Vogue* shows a man aiming a gun at a nude woman wrapped in plastic, a leather briefcase covering her face. And an ad for Bitch skateboards, for God's sake, shows a cartoon version of a similar scene, this time clearly targeting young people. We believe we are not affected by these images, but most of us experience visceral shock when we pay conscious attention to them. Could they be any less shocking to us on an unconscious level?

Most of us become numb to these images, just as we become numb to the daily litany in the news of women being raped, battered, and

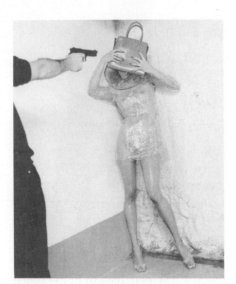

La Borsa è la Vita

killed. According to former surgeon general Antonia Novello, battery is the single greatest cause of injury to women in America, more common than automobile accidents, muggings, and stranger rapes combined, and more than one-third of women slain in this country die at the hands of husbands or boyfriends.[3] Throughout the world, the biggest problem for most women is simply surviving at home. The Global Report on Women's Human Rights concluded that "Domestic violence is a leading cause of female injury in almost every country in the world and is typically ignored by the state or only erratically punished."[4] Although usually numb to these facts on a conscious level, most women live in a state of subliminal terror, a state that, according to Mary Daly,[5] keeps us divided both from each other and from our most passionate, powerful, and creative selves.[6]

Ads don't directly cause violence, of course. But the violent images contribute to the state of terror. And objectification and disconnection create a climate in which there is widespread and increasing violence. Turning a human being into a thing, an object, is almost always the first step toward justifying violence against that person. It is very difficult, perhaps impossible, to be violent to someone we think of as an equal, someone we have empathy with, but it is very easy to abuse a thing. We see this with racism, with homophobia. The person becomes an object and violence is inevitable. This step is already taken with women. The violence, the abuse, is partly the chilling but logical result of the objectification.

[3]Novello, 1991. Also Blumenthal, 1995.
[4]Wright, 1995, A2.
[5]**Mary Daly:** Radical feminist scholar and author (1928–2010). [Eds.]
[6]Weil, 1999, 21.

bitch skateboards

An editorial in *Advertising Age* suggests that even some advertisers are concerned about this: "Clearly it's time to wipe out sexism in beer ads; for the brewers and their agencies to wake up and join the rest of America in realizing that sexism, sexual harassment, and the cultural portrayal of women in advertising are inextricably linked."[7] Alas, this editorial was written in 1991 and nothing has changed.

It is this link with violence that makes the objectification of women 20 a more serious issue than the objectification of men. Our economic system constantly requires the development of new markets. Not surprisingly, men's bodies are the latest territory to be exploited. Although we are growing more used to it, in the beginning the male sex object came as a surprise. In 1994 a "gender bender" television commercial in which a bevy of women office workers gather to watch a construction worker doff his shirt to quaff a Diet Coke led to so much hoopla that you'd have thought women were mugging men on Madison Avenue.[8]

There is no question that men are used as sex objects in ads now as never before. We often see nude women with fully clothed men in ads (as in art), but the reverse was unheard of, until recently. These days some ads do feature clothed and often aggressive women with nude men. And women sometimes blatantly objectify men, as in the Metroliner ad that says," 'She's reading Nietzsche,' Harris noted to himself as he walked towards the café car for a glass of cabernet. And as he passed her seat, Maureen looked up from her book and thought, 'Nice buns.'"

Although these ads are often funny, it is never a good thing for human beings to be objectified. However, there is a world of difference between the objectification of men and that of women. The most important difference is that there is no danger for most men, whereas objectified women are always at risk. In the Diet Coke ad, for instance, the women are physically separated from the shirtless man. He is the one in control. His body is powerful, not passive. Imagine a true role

[7]Brewers can help fight sexism, 1991, 28.
[8]Kilbourne, 1994, F13.

reversal of this ad: a group of businessmen gather to leer at a beautiful woman worker on her break, who removes her shirt before drinking her Diet Coke. This scene would be frightening, not funny, as the Diet Coke ad is. And why is the Diet Coke ad funny? Because we know it doesn't describe any truth. However, the ads featuring images of male violence against women do describe a truth, a truth we are all aware of, on one level or another.

When power is unequal, when one group is oppressed and discriminated against *as a group*, when there is a context of systemic and historical oppression, stereotypes and prejudice have different weight and meaning. As Anna Quindlen[9] said, writing about "reverse racism": "Hatred by the powerful, the majority, has a different weight—and often very different effects—than hatred by the powerless, the minority."[10] When men objectify women, they do so in a cultural context in which women are constantly objectified and in which there are consequences—from economic discrimination to violence—to that objectification.

For men, though, there are no such consequences. Men's bodies are not routinely judged and invaded. Men are not likely to be raped, harassed, or beaten (that is to say, men presumed to be heterosexual are not, and very few men are abused in these ways by women). How many men are frightened to be alone with a woman in an elevator? How many men cross the street when a group of women approaches? Jackson Katz, who writes and lectures on male violence, often begins his workshops by asking men to describe the things they do every day to protect themselves from sexual assault. The men are surprised, puzzled, sometimes amused by the question. The women understand

[9]**Anna Quindlen:** Novelist and Pulitzer Prize–winning journalist who often writes about women's issues (b. 1953). [Eds.]
[10]Quindlen, 1992, E17.

where women are women
and men are
roadkill.

harley-davidson motorclothes

the question easily and have no trouble at all coming up with a list of responses. We don't list our full names in the phone directory or on our mailboxes, we try not to be alone after dark, we carry our keys in our hands when we approach our cars, we always look in the back seat before we get in, we are wary of elevators and doorways and bushes, we carry pepper sprays, whistles, Mace.

Nonetheless, the rate of sexual assault in the United States is the highest of any industrialized nation in the world.[11] According to a 1998 study by the federal government, one in five of us has been the victim of rape or attempted rape, most often before our seventeenth birthday. And more than half of us have been physically assaulted, most often by the men we live with. In fact, three of four women in the study who responded that they had been raped or assaulted as adults said the perpetrator was a current or former husband, a cohabiting partner or a date.[12] The article reporting the results of this study was buried on page twenty-three of my local newspaper, while the front page dealt with a long story about the New England Patriots football team.

A few summers ago, a Diet Pepsi commercial featured Cindy Crawford being ogled by two boys (they seemed to be about twelve years old) as she got out of her car and bought a Pepsi from a machine. The boys made very suggestive comments, which in the end turned out to be about the Pepsi's can rather than Ms. Crawford's. There was no outcry: the boys' behavior was acceptable and ordinary enough for a soft-drink commercial.

Again, let us imagine the reverse: a sexy man gets out of a car in the countryside and two preteen girls make suggestive comments,

25

[11]Blumenthal, 1995, 2.
[12]Tjaden and Thoennes, 1998.

seemingly about his body, especially his buns. We would fear for them and rightly so. But the boys already have the right to ogle, to view women's bodies as property to be looked at, commented on, touched, perhaps eventually hit and raped. The boys have also learned that men ogle primarily to impress other men (and to affirm their hetero-sexuality). If anyone is in potential danger in this ad, it is the woman (regardless of the age of the boys). Men are not seen as *property* in this way by women. Indeed if a woman does whistle at a man or touches his body or even makes direct eye contact, it is still *she* who is at risk and the man who has the power.

"I always lower my eyes to see if a man is worth following," says the woman in an ad for men's pants. Although the ad is offensive to everyone, the woman is endangering only herself.

"Where women are women and men are roadkill," says an ad for motorcycle clothing featuring an angry-looking African American woman. Women are sometimes hostile and angry in ads these days, especially women of color who are often seen as angrier and more threatening than white women. But, regardless of color, we all know that women are far more likely than men to end up as roadkill—and, when it happens, they are blamed for being on the road in the first place.

Even little girls are sometimes held responsible for the violence 30 against them. In 1990 a male Canadian judge accused a three-year-old girl of being "sexually aggressive" and suspended the sentence of her molester, who was then free to return to his job of baby-sitter.[13] The deeply held belief that all women, regardless of age, are really temptresses in disguise, nymphets, sexually insatiable and seductive, conveniently transfers all blame and responsibility onto women.

[13]Two men and a baby, 1990, 10.

All women are vulnerable in a culture in which there is such widespread objectification of women's bodies, such glorification of disconnection, so much violence against women, and such blaming of the victim. When everything and everyone is sexualized, it is the powerless who are most at risk. Young girls, of course, are especially vulnerable. In the past twenty years or so, there have been several trends in fashion and advertising that could be seen as cultural reactions to the women's movement, as perhaps unconscious fear of female power. One has been the obsession with thinness. Another has been an increase in images of violence against women. Most disturbing has been the increasing sexualization of children, especially girls. Sometimes the little girl is made up and seductively posed. Sometimes the language is suggestive. "Very cherry," says the ad featuring a sexy little African American girl who is wearing a dress with cherries all over it. A shocking ad in a gun magazine features a smiling little girl, a toddler, in a bathing suit that is tugged up suggestively in the rear. The copy beneath the photo says, "short BUTTS from FLEMING FIREARMS."[14] Other times girls are juxtaposed with grown women, as in the ad for underpants that says "You already know the feeling."

This is not only an American phenomenon. A growing national obsession in Japan with schoolgirls dressed in uniforms is called "Loli-con," after Lolita.[15] In Tokyo hundreds of "image clubs" allow Japanese men to act out their fantasies with make-believe schoolgirls. A magazine called *V-Club* featuring pictures of naked elementary-school

[14]Herbert, 1999, WK 17.
[15]**Lolita:** The title character of Vladimir Nabokov's 1955 novel, Lolita is a young girl who is sexually pursued by her stepfather. [Eds.]

girls competes with another called *Anatomical Illustrations of Junior High School Girls*.[16] Masao Miyamoto, a male psychiatrist, suggests that Japanese men are turning to girls because they feel threatened by the growing sophistication of older women.[17]

In recent years, this sexualization of little girls has become even more disturbing as hints of violence enter the picture. A three-page ad for Prada clothing features a girl or very young woman with a barely pubescent body, clothed in what seem to be cotton panties and perhaps a training bra, viewed through a partially opened door. She seems surprised, startled, worried, as if she's heard a strange sound or glimpsed someone watching her. I suppose this could be a woman awaiting her lover, but it could as easily be a girl being preyed upon.

The 1996 murder of six-year-old JonBenet Ramsey[18] was a gold mine for the media, combining as it did child pornography and violence. In November of 1997 *Advertising Age* reported in an article entitled "JonBenet Keeps Hold on Magazines" that the child had been on five magazine covers in October, "Enough to capture the Cover Story lead for the month. The pre-adolescent beauty queen, found slain in her home last Christmas, garnered 6.5 points. The case earned a *triple play* [italics mine] in the *National Enquirer*, and one-time appearances on *People* and *Star*."[19] Imagine describing a six-year-old child as "pre-adolescent."

---

[16]Schoolgirls as sex toys, 1997, 2E.
[17]Ibid.
[18]**JonBenet Ramsey:** Six-year-old beauty-pageant winner who was sexually molested and murdered in her Boulder, Colorado, home in 1996. [Eds.]
[19]Johnson, 1997, 42.

Sometimes the models in ads are children, other times they just   35
look like children. Kate Moss was twenty when she said of herself, "I
look twelve."[20] She epitomized the vacant, hollow-cheeked look known
as "heroin chic" that was popular in the mid-nineties. She also often
looked vulnerable, abused, and exploited. In one ad she is nude in the
corner of a huge sofa, cringing as if braced for an impending sexual
assault. In another she is lying nude on her stomach, pliant, available,
androgynous enough to appeal to all kinds of pedophiles. In a music
video she is dead and bound to a chair while Johnny Cash sings "Delia's
Gone."

It is not surprising that Kate Moss models for Calvin Klein, the fashion
designer who specializes in breaking taboos and thereby getting himself public outrage, media coverage, and more bang for his buck. In
1995 he brought the federal government down on himself by running a
campaign that may have crossed the line into child pornography.[21] Very
young models (and others who just seemed young) were featured in las-
civious print ads and in television commercials designed to mimic child
porn. The models were awkward, self-conscious. In one commercial, a
boy stands in what seems to be a finished basement. A male voiceover
tells him he has a great body and asks him to take off his shirt. The
boy seems embarrassed but he complies. There was a great deal of protest, which brought the issue into national consciousness but which also
gave Klein the publicity and free media coverage he was looking for.
He pulled the ads but, at the same time, projected that his jeans sales
would almost double from $115 million to $220 million that year, partly
because of the free publicity but also because the controversy made his
critics seem like prudes and thus positioned Klein as the daring rebel, a
very appealing image to the majority of his customers.

[20]Leo, 1994, 27.
[21]Sloan, 1996, 27.

Having learned from this, in 1999 Klein launched a very brief advertising campaign featuring very little children frolicking in their underpants, which included a controversial billboard in Times Square.[22] Although in some ways this campaign was less offensive than the earlier one and might have gone unnoticed had the ads come from a department store catalog rather than from Calvin Klein, there was the expected protest and Klein quickly withdrew the ads, again getting a windfall of media coverage. In my opinion, the real obscenity of this campaign is the whole idea of people buying designer underwear for their little ones, especially in a country in which at least one in five children doesn't have enough to eat.

Although boys are sometimes sexualized in an overt way, they are more often portrayed as sexually precocious, as in the Pepsi commercial featuring the young boys ogling Cindy Crawford or the jeans ad portraying a very little boy looking up a woman's skirt. It may seem that I am reading too much into this ad, but imagine if the genders were reversed. We would fear for a little girl who was unzipping a man's fly in an ad (and we would be shocked, I would hope). Boys are vulnerable to sexual abuse too, but cultural attitudes make it difficult to take this seriously. As a result, boys are less likely to report abuse and to get treatment.

Many boys grow up feeling that they are unmanly if they are not always "ready for action," capable of and interested in sex with any woman who is available. Advertising doesn't cause this attitude, of course, but it contributes to it. A Levi Strauss commercial that ran in Asia features the shock of a schoolboy who discovers that the seductive young woman who has slipped a note into the jeans of an older student is his teacher. And an ad for BIC pens pictures a young boy wearing X-ray glasses while ogling the derriere of an older woman. Again, these

---

[22]Associated Press, 1999, February 18, A7.

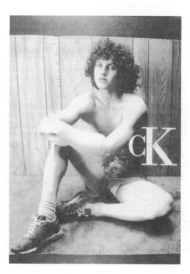

ads would be unthinkable if the genders were reversed. It is increasingly difficult in such a toxic environment to see children, boys or girls, as *children*.

In the past few years there has been a proliferation of sexually 40 grotesque toys for boys, such as a Spider Man female action figure whose exaggerated breasts have antennae coming out of them and a female Spawn figure with carved skulls for breasts. Meantime even children have easy access to pornography in video games and on the World Wide Web, which includes explicit photographs of women having intercourse with groups of men, with dogs, donkeys, horses, and snakes; photographs of women being raped and tortured; some of these women made up to look like little girls.

It is hard for girls not to learn self-hatred in an environment in which there is such widespread and open contempt for women and girls. In 1997 a company called Senate distributed clothing with inside labels that included, in addition to the usual cleaning instructions, the line "Destroy all girls." A Senate staffer explained that he thought it was "kind of cool."[23] Given all this, it's not surprising that when boys and girls were asked in a recent study to write an essay on what it would be like to be the other gender, many boys wrote they would rather be dead. Girls had no trouble writing essays about activities, power, freedom, but boys were often stuck, could think of nothing.

It is also not surprising that, in such an environment, sexual harassment is considered normal and ordinary. According to an article in the journal *Eating Disorders*:

> In our work with young women, we have heard countless accounts of this contempt being expressed by their male peers: the girls

[23]Wire and *Times* staff reports, 1997, D1.

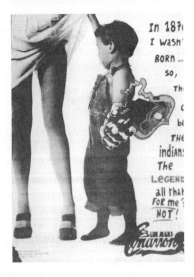

who do not want to walk down a certain hallway in their high school because they are afraid of being publicly rated on a scale of one to ten; the girls who are subjected to barking, grunting and mooing calls and labels of "dogs, cows, or pigs" when they pass by groups of male students; those who are teased about not measuring up to buxom, bikini-clad [models]; and the girls who are grabbed, pinched, groped, and fondled as they try to make their way through the school corridors.

Harassing words do not slide harmlessly away as the taunting sounds dissipate. . . . They are slowly absorbed into the child's identity and developing sense of self, becoming an essential part of who she sees herself to be. Harassment involves the use of words as weapons to inflict pain and assert power. Harassing words are

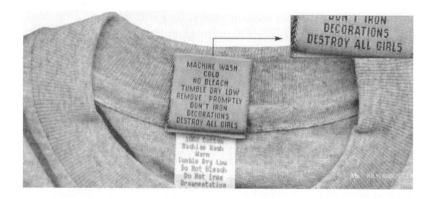

meant to instill fear, heighten bodily discomfort, and diminish the sense of self.[24]

It is probably difficult for those of us who are older to understand how devastating and cruel and pervasive this harassment is, how different from the "teasing" some of us might remember from our own childhoods (not that that didn't hurt and do damage as well). A 1993 report by the American Association of University Women found that 76 percent of female students in grades eight to eleven and 56 percent of male students said they had been sexually harassed in school.[25] One high-school junior described a year of torment at her vocational school: "The boys call me slut, bitch. They call me a ten-timer, because they say I go with ten guys at the same time. I put up with it because I have no choice. The teachers say it's because the boys think I'm pretty."[26]

High school and junior high school have always been hell for those who were different in any way (gay teens have no doubt suffered the most, although "overweight" girls are a close second), but the harassment is more extreme and more physical these days. Many young men feel they have the right to judge and touch young women and the women often feel they have no choice but to submit. One young woman recalled that "the guys at school routinely swiped their hands across girls' legs to patrol their shaving prowess and then taunt them if they were slacking off. If I were running late, I'd protect myself by faux shaving—just doing the strip between the bottom of my jeans and the top of my cotton socks."[27]

Sexual battery, as well as inappropriate sexual gesturing, touching, and fondling, is increasing not only in high schools but in elementary and middle schools as well.[28] There are reports of sexual assaults by students on other students as young as eight. A fifth-grade boy in Georgia repeatedly touched the breasts and genitals of one of his fellow

45

[24]Larkin, Rice, and Russell, 1996, 5–26.
[25]Daley and Vigue, 1999, A12.
[26]Hart, 1998, A12.
[27]Mackler, 1998, 56.
[28]Daley and Vigue, 1999, A1, A12.

students while saying, "I want to get in bed with you" and "I want to feel your boobs." Authorities did nothing, although the girl complained and her grades fell. When her parents found a suicide note she had written, they took the board of education to court.[29]

A high-school senior in an affluent suburban school in the Boston area said she has been dragged by her arms so boys could look up her skirt and that boys have rested their heads on her chest while making lewd comments. Another student in the same school was pinned down on a lunch table while a boy simulated sex on top of her. Neither student reported any of the incidents, for fear of being ostracized by their peers.[30] In another school in the Boston area, a sixteen-year-old girl, who had been digitally raped by a classmate, committed suicide.[31]

According to Nan Stein, a researcher at Wellesley College:

> Schools may in fact be training grounds for the insidious cycle of domestic violence. . . . The school's hidden curriculum teaches young women to suffer abuse privately, that resistance is futile. When they witness harassment of others and fail to respond, they absorb a different kind of powerlessness—that they are incapable of standing up to injustice or acting in solidarity with their peers. Similarly, in schools boys receive permission, even training, to become batterers through the practice of sexual harassment.[32]

This pervasive harassment of and contempt for girls and women constitute a kind of abuse. We know that addictions for women are rooted in trauma, that girls who are sexually abused are far more likely to become addicted to one substance or another. I contend that all girls growing up in this culture are sexually abused—abused by the pornographic images of female sexuality that surround them from birth, abused by all the violence against women and girls, and abused by the constant harassment and threat of violence. Abuse is a continuum, of course, and I am by no means implying that cultural abuse is as terrible as literally being raped and assaulted. However, it hurts, it does damage, and it sets girls up for addictions and self-destructive behavior. Many girls turn to food, alcohol, cigarettes, and other drugs in a misguided attempt to cope.

As Marian Sandmaier said in *The Invisible Alcoholics: Women and Alcohol Abuse in America*, "In a culture that cuts off women from many of their own possibilities before they barely have had a chance to sense them, that pain belongs to all women. Outlets for coping may vary widely, and may be more or less addictive, more or less self-destructive. But at some level, all women know what it is to lack access to their own power, to live with a piece of themselves unclaimed."[33]

[29]Shin, 1999, 32.
[30]Daley and Vigue, 1999, A12.
[31]Daley and Abraham, 1999, B6.
[32]Stein, 1993, 316–17.
[33]Sandmaier, 1980, xviii.

Today, every girl is endangered, not just those who have been physically and sexually abused. If girls from supportive homes with positive role models are at risk, imagine then how vulnerable are the girls who have been violated. No wonder they so often go under for good—ending up in abusive marriages, in prison, on the streets. And those who do are almost always in the grip of one addiction or another. More than half of women in prison are addicts and most are there for crimes directly related to their addiction. Many who are there for murder killed men who had been battering them for years. Almost all of the women who are homeless or in prisons and mental institutions are the victims of male violence.[34]

Male violence exists within the same cultural and sociopolitical context that contributes to addiction. Both can be fully understood only within this context, way beyond individual psychology and family dynamics. It is a context of systemic violence and oppression, including racism, classism, heterosexism, weightism, and ageism, as well as sexism, all of which are traumatizing in and of themselves. Advertising is only one part of this cultural context, but it is an important part and thus is a part of what traumatizes.

Sources

Abbey, A., Ross, L., and McDuffie, D. (1991). Alcohol's role in sexual assault. In Watson, R., ed. *Addictive behaviors in women.* Totowa, NJ: Humana Press.

Associated Press (1999, February 18). Calvin Klein retreats on ad. *Boston Globe,* A7.

Blumenthal, S. J. (1995, July). *Violence against women.* Washington, DC: Department of Health and Human Services.

Brewers can help fight sexism (1991, October 28). *Advertising Age,* 28.

Daley, B., and Vigue, D. I. (1999, February 4). Sex harassment increasing amid students, officials say. *Boston Globe,* A1, A12.

Hart, J. (1998, June 8). Northampton confronts a crime, cruelty. *Boston Globe,* A1, A12.

Herbert, B. (1999, May 2). America's littlest shooters. *New York Times,* WK 17.

Johnson, J. A. (1997, November 10). JonBenet keeps hold on magazines. *Advertising Age,* 42.

Kilbourne, J. (1994, May 15). "Gender bender" ads: Same old sexism. *New York Times,* F13.

Larkin, J., Rice, C., and Russell, V. (1996, Spring). Slipping through the cracks: Sexual harassment. *Eating Disorders: The Journal of Treatment and Prevention,* vol. 4, no. 1, 5–26.

Leo, J. (1994, June 13). Selling the woman-child. *U.S. News and World Report,* 27.

Mackler, C. (1998). Memoirs of a (sorta) ex-shaver. In Edut, O., ed. (1998). *Adios, Barbie.* Seattle, WA: Seal Press, 55–61.

Martin, S. (1992). The epidemiology of alcohol-related interpersonal violence. *Alcohol, Health and Research World,* vol.16, no. 3, 230–37.

Novello, A. (1991, October 18). Quoted by Associated Press, AMA to fight wife-beating. *St. Louis Post Dispatch,* 1, 15.

Quindlen, A. (1992, June 28). All of these you are. *New York Times,* E17.

Sandmaier, M. (1980). *The invisible alcoholics: Women and alcohol abuse in America.* New York: McGraw-Hill.

Schoolgirls as sex toys. *New York Times* (1997, April 16), 2E.

Shin, A. (1999, April/May). Testing Title IX. *Ms.,* 32.

[34]Snell, 1991.

Sloan, P. (1996, July 8). Underwear ads caught in bind over sex appeal. *Advertising Age*, 27.

Snell, T. L. (1991). *Women in prison*. Washington, DC: U.S. Department of Justice.

Stein, N. (1993). No laughing matter: Sexual harassment in K-12 schools. In Buchwald, E., Fletcher, P. R., and Roth, M. (1993). *Transforming a rape culture*. Minneapolis, MN: Milkweed Editions, 311–31.

Tjaden, R., and Thoennes, N. (1998, November). *Prevalence, incidence, and consequences of violence against women: Findings from the National Violence Against Women Survey*. Washington, DC: U.S. Department of Justice.

Two men and a baby (1990, July/August). *Ms.*, 10.

Vigue, D. J., and Abraham, Y. (1999, February 7). Harassment a daily course for students. *Boston Globe*, B1, B6.

Weil, L. (1999, March). Leaps of faith. *Women's Review of Books*, 21.

Wilsnack, S. C., Plaud, J. J., Wilsnack, R. W., and Klassen, A. D. (1997). Sexuality, gender, and alcohol use. In Wilsnack, R. W., and Wilsnack, S. C., eds. *Gender and alcohol: Individual and social perspectives*. New Brunswick, N.J.: Rutgers Center of Alcohol Studies, 262.

Wire and *Times* Staff Reports (1997, May 20). Orange County skate firm's "destroy all girls" tags won't wash. *Los Angeles Times*, D1.

Wright, R. (1995, September 10). Brutality defines the lives of women around the world. *Boston Globe*, A2.

ENGAGING THE TEXT

1. What parallels does Kilbourne see between advertising and pornography? How persuasive do you find the evidence she offers? Do the photos of the ads she describes strengthen her argument? Why or why not?

2. Why is it dangerous to depict women and men as sex objects, according to Kilbourne? Why is the objectification of women *more* troubling, in her view? Do you agree?

3. How does Kilbourne explain the appeal of ads that allude to bondage, sexual aggression, and rape — particularly for female consumers? How do you respond to the ads reproduced in her essay?

4. **Thinking Rhetorically** What does Kilbourne mean when she claims that the depiction of women in advertising constitutes "cultural abuse"? How does she go about drawing connections between advertising images and social problems like sexual violence, harassment, and addiction? Which portions of her analysis do you find most and least persuasive, and why?

EXPLORING CONNECTIONS

5. How might Allan G. Johnson (p. 527) respond to Kilbourne's analysis of advertising images? How do the ads she discusses reflect the values of patriarchy? How do they represent male dominance, male identification, male centeredness, and an obsession with control?

6. Drawing on the selections by Kilbourne, Jackson Katz (p. 583), Jessie Daniels (p. 298), and Noreen Malone (p. 285), write an essay exploring the power of media, including social media, to promote or curb violence.

EXTENDING THE CRITICAL CONTEXT

7. Kilbourne claims that popular culture idealizes dangerous, exploitative, or dysfunctional relationships between women and men. Working in small groups, discuss the romantic relationships depicted in movies you've seen recently. Does her critique seem applicable to those films? List the evidence you find for and against her argument, and compare your results with those of other groups.

8. In her analysis of two ads (the Diet Pepsi commercial featuring Cindy Crawford and the Diet Coke ad with the shirtless construction worker), Kilbourne applies a gender reversal test in order to demonstrate the existence of a double standard. Try this test yourself on a commercial or ad that relies on sexual innuendo. Write a journal entry describing the ad and explaining the results of your test.

9. Working in pairs or small groups, survey the ads in two magazines — one designed to appeal to a predominantly female audience and one aimed at a largely male audience. What differences, if any, do you see in the kinds of images and appeals advertisers use in the two magazines? How often do you see the kinds of "pornographic" ads Kilbourne discusses? Do you find any ads depicting the "relational skills" that she suggests are rarely emphasized in popular culture?

THE LONGEST WAR

REBECCA SOLNIT

When we read about women being stoned in Afghan villages or gang-raped by men on buses in rural India, we often assume that we've made progress on issues of violence against women here in the United States. But, as Rebecca Solnit argues in this selection, nothing could be further from the truth. She once wrote that she "was a battered little kid" who "grew up in a really violent house where everything feminine and female . . . was hated."[1] It may be no surprise, then, that she feels that even in America there's a continuing "pandemic of violence by men against women." Since the 1980s, Solnit (b. 1961) has worked for human rights and environmental causes; an independent writer, historian, and activist, she has received two NEA fellowships in literature, a Guggenheim Fellowship, and a Lannan literary award for nonfiction. She is the author of seventeen books, among them *River of Shadows:*

---

[1]Caitlin Donohue. "Why Can't I Be You: Rebecca Solnit." Rookiemag.com. 4 September 2014. [All notes are the editors', except 5.]

Eadweard Muybridge and the Technological Wild West (2004), which links the biography of Muybridge (who first photographed high-speed motion in the late nineteenth century) to the rise of Hollywood and Silicon Valley. The book won multiple awards, including the National Book Critics Circle Award for criticism. In 2008 she was invited to Iceland to be the first international writer in residence at the Library of Water. Solnit's *The Faraway Nearby* (2013) was nominated for a National Book Award and deals with — among other things — storytelling and the loss of her mother to Alzheimer's disease. "The Longest War" appeared in her 2014 collection of feminist essays, *Men Explain Things to Me*.

HERE IN THE UNITED STATES, where there is a reported rape every 6.2 minutes, and one in five women will be raped in her lifetime, the rape and gruesome murder of a young woman on a bus in New Delhi on December 16, 2012, was treated as an exceptional incident. The story of the sexual assault of an unconscious teenager by members of the Steubenville High School football team in Ohio was still unfolding, and gang rapes aren't that unusual here either. Take your pick: some of the twenty men who gang-raped an eleven-year-old in Cleveland, Texas, were sentenced shortly beforehand, while the instigator of the gang rape of a sixteen-year-old in Richmond, California, was sentenced in that fall of 2012 too, and four men who gang-raped a fifteen-year-old near New Orleans were sentenced that April, though the six men who gang-raped a fourteen-year-old in Chicago that year were still at large. Not that I went out looking for incidents: they're everywhere in the news, though no one adds them up and indicates that there might actually be a pattern.

There is, however, a pattern of violence against women that's broad and deep and horrific and incessantly overlooked. Occasionally, a case involving a celebrity or lurid details in a particular case get a lot of attention in the media, but such cases are treated as anomalies, while the abundance of incidental news items about violence against women in this country, in other countries, on every continent including Antarctica, constitute a kind of background wallpaper for the news.

If you'd rather talk about bus rapes than gang rapes, there was the rape of a developmentally disabled woman on a Los Angeles bus that November and the kidnapping of an autistic sixteen-year-old on the regional transit train system in Oakland, California—she was raped repeatedly by her abductor over two days this winter—and a gang rape of multiple women on a bus in Mexico City recently, too. While I was writing this, I read that another female bus rider was kidnapped in India and gang-raped all night by the bus driver and five of his friends who must have thought what happened in New Delhi was awesome.

We have an abundance of rape and violence against women in this country and on this Earth, though it's almost never treated as a civil rights or human rights issue, or a crisis, or even a pattern. Violence doesn't have a race, a class, a religion, or a nationality, but it does have a gender.

Here I want to say one thing: though virtually all the perpetrators of such crimes are men, that doesn't mean all men are violent. Most are not. In addition, men obviously also suffer violence, largely at the hands of other men, and every violent death, every assault is terrible. Women can and do engage in intimate partner violence, but recent studies state that these acts don't often result in significant injury, let alone death; on the other hand, men murdered by their partners are often killed in self-defense, and intimate violence sends a lot of women to the hospital and the grave. But the subject here is the pandemic of violence by men against women, both intimate violence and stranger violence.

What We Don't Talk About When We Don't Talk About Gender

There's so much of it. We could talk about the assault and rape of a seventy-three-year-old in Manhattan's Central Park in September 2012, or the recent rape of a four-year-old and an eighty-three-year-old in Louisiana, or the New York City policeman who was arrested in October of 2012 for what appeared to be serious plans to kidnap, rape, cook, and eat a woman, any woman, because the hate wasn't personal (although maybe it was for the San Diego man who actually killed and cooked his wife in November and the man from New Orleans who killed, dismembered, and cooked his girlfriend in 2005).

Those are all exceptional crimes, but we could also talk about quotidian assaults, because though a rape is reported only every 6.2 minutes in this country, the estimated total is perhaps five times as high. Which means that there may be very nearly a rape a minute in the United States. It all adds up to tens of millions of rape victims. A significant portion of the women you know are survivors.

We could talk about high-school- and college-athlete rapes, or campus rapes, to which university authorities have been appallingly uninterested in responding in many cases, including that high school in Steubenville, Notre Dame University, Amherst College, and many others. We could talk about the escalating pandemic of rape, sexual assault, and sexual harassment in the U.S. military, where Secretary of Defense Leon Panetta estimated that there were nineteen thousand sexual assaults on fellow soldiers in 2010 alone and that the great majority of assailants got away with it, though four-star general Jeffrey Sinclair was indicted in September for "a slew of sex crimes against women."

Never mind workplace violence, let's go home. So many men murder their partners and former partners that we have well over a thousand homicides of that kind a year—meaning that every three years the death toll tops 9/11's casualties, though no one declares a war on this particular kind of terror. (Another way to put it: the more than 11,766 corpses from domestic-violence homicides between 9/11 and 2012 exceed the number of deaths of victims on that day *and* all American soldiers killed in the "war on terror.") If we talked about crimes like these and why they are so common, we'd have to talk about what kinds of profound change this society, or this nation, or nearly every nation needs. If we talked about it, we'd be talking about masculinity, or male roles, or maybe patriarchy, and we don't talk much about that.

Instead, we hear that American men commit murder-suicides — at the rate of about twelve a week — because the economy is bad, though they also do it when the economy is good; or that those men in India murdered the bus rider because the poor resent the rich, while other rapes in India are explained by how the rich exploit the poor; and then there are those ever-popular explanations: mental problems and intoxicants — and for jocks, head injuries. The latest spin is that lead exposure was responsible for a lot of our violence, except that both genders are exposed and one commits most of the violence. The pandemic of violence always gets explained as anything but gender, anything but what would seem to be the broadest explanatory pattern of all.

Someone wrote a piece about how white men seem to be the ones who commit mass murders in the United States and the (mostly hostile) commenters only seemed to notice the white part. It's rare that anyone says what this medical study does, even if in the driest way possible: "Being male has been identified as a risk factor for violent criminal behavior in several studies, as have exposure to tobacco smoke before birth, having antisocial parents, and belonging to a poor family."

It's not that I want to pick on men. I just think that if we noticed that women are, on the whole, radically less violent, we might be able to theorize where violence comes from and what we can do about it a lot more productively. Clearly the ready availability of guns is a huge problem for the United States, but despite this availability to everyone, murder is still a crime committed by men 90 percent of the time.

The pattern is plain as day. We could talk about this as a global problem, looking at the epidemic of assault, harassment, and rape of women in Cairo's Tahrir Square that has taken away the freedom they celebrated during the Arab Spring — and led some men there to form defense teams to help counter it — or the persecution of women in public and private in India from "Eve-teasing" to bride-burning, or "honor killings"[2] in South Asia and the Middle East, or the way that South Africa has become a global rape capital, with an estimated six hundred thousand rapes last year, or how rape has been used as a tactic and "weapon" of war in Mali, Sudan, and the Congo, as it was in the former

10

---

[2]**Eve-teasing:** street harassment of women; **bride-burning:** burning a woman alive when her family refuses to pay more for her dowry; **honor killing:** the murder of a woman by a family member for bringing "dishonor" to the family by refusing an arranged marriage, being raped, being in a relationship that the family disapproves of, or dressing "inappropriately." [Eds.]

Yugoslavia, or the pervasiveness of rape and harassment in Mexico and the femicide in Juarez,[3] or the denial of basic rights for women in Saudi Arabia and the myriad sexual assaults on immigrant domestic workers there, or the way that the Dominique Strauss-Kahn case in the United States revealed what impunity he and others had in France, and it's only for lack of space I'm leaving out Britain and Canada and Italy (with its ex-prime minister known for his orgies with the underaged),[4] Argentina and Australia and so many other countries.

Who Has the Right to Kill You?

But maybe you're tired of statistics, so let's just talk about a single incident that happened in my city while I was researching this essay in January 2013, one of many local incidents that made the local papers that month in which men assaulted women:

> A woman was stabbed after she rebuffed a man's sexual advances while she walked in San Francisco's Tenderloin neighborhood late Monday night, a police spokesman said today. The 33-year-old victim was walking down the street when a stranger approached her and propositioned her, police spokesman Officer Albie Esparza said. When she rejected him, the man became very upset and slashed the victim in the face and stabbed her in the arm, Esparza said.[5]

The man, in other words, framed the situation as one in which his [15] chosen victim had no rights and liberties, while he had the right to control and punish her. This should remind us that violence is first of all authoritarian. It begins with this premise: I have the right to control you.

Murder is the extreme version of that authoritarianism, where the murderer asserts he has the right to decide whether you live or die, the ultimate means of controlling someone. This may be true even if you are obedient, because the desire to control comes out of a rage that obedience can't assuage. Whatever fears, whatever sense of vulnerability may underlie such behavior, it also comes out of entitlement, the entitlement to inflict suffering and even death on other people. It breeds misery in the perpetrator and the victims.

As for that incident in my city, similar things happen all the time. Many versions of it happened to me when I was younger, sometimes involving death threats and often involving torrents of obscenities: a man approaches a woman with both desire and the furious expectation that the desire will likely be rebuffed. The fury and desire come in a package, all twisted together into something that always threatens to turn *eros* into *thanatos*, love into death, sometimes literally.

---

[3]**femicide in Juarez:** In Juarez, Mexico, the disappearance and murders of women became an international sensation in the 1990s. [Eds.]

[4]**ex–prime minister . . . underaged:** Refers to Silvio Berlusconi, the seventy-six-year-old politician who was accused of paying for sex with underaged girls. [Eds.]

[5]"Woman Stabbed Walking Down Tenderloin Street," KTVU, January 2013.

It's a system of control. It's why so many intimate-partner murders are of women who dared to break up with those partners. As a result, it imprisons a lot of women, and though you could say that the Tenderloin attacker on January 7, or a brutal would-be rapist near my own neighborhood on January 5, or another rapist here on January 12, or the San Franciscan who on January 6 set his girlfriend on fire for refusing to do his laundry, or the guy who was just sentenced to 370 years for some particularly violent rapes in San Francisco in late 2011, were marginal characters, rich, famous, and privileged guys do it, too.

The Japanese vice-consul in San Francisco was charged with twelve felony counts of spousal abuse and assault with a deadly weapon in September 2012, the same month that, in the same town, the ex-girlfriend of Mason Mayer (brother of Yahoo CEO Marissa Mayer) testified in court: "He ripped out my earrings, tore my eyelashes off, while spitting in my face and telling me how unlovable I am . . . I was on the ground in the fetal position, and when I tried to move, he squeezed both knees tighter into my sides to restrain me and slapped me." According to *San Francisco Chronicle* reporter Vivian Ho, she also testified that "Mayer slammed her head onto the floor repeatedly and pulled out clumps of her hair, telling her that the only way she was leaving the apartment alive was if he drove her to the Golden Gate Bridge 'where you can jump off or I will push you off.'" Mason Mayer got probation.

The summer before, an estranged husband violated his wife's restraining order against him, shooting her—and killing or wounding six other women—at her workplace in suburban Milwaukee, but since there were only four corpses the crime was largely overlooked in the media in a year with so many more spectacular mass murders in this country (and we still haven't really talked about the fact that, of sixty-two mass shootings in the United States in three decades, only one was by a woman, because when you say *lone gunman*, everyone talks about loners and guns but not about men—and by the way, nearly two-thirds of all women killed by guns are killed by their partner or ex-partner). [20]

What's love got to do with it, asked Tina Turner, whose ex-husband Ike once said, "Yeah I hit her, but I didn't hit her more than the average guy beats his wife." A woman is beaten every nine seconds in this country. Just to be clear: not nine minutes, but nine seconds. It's the number-one cause of injury to American women; of the two million injured annually, more than half a million of those injuries require medical attention while about 145,000 require overnight hospitalizations, according to the Centers for Disease Control, and you don't want to know about the dentistry needed afterwards. Spouses are also the leading cause of death for pregnant women in the United States.

"Women worldwide ages 15 through 44 are more likely to die or be maimed because of male violence than because of cancer, malaria, war and traffic accidents combined," writes Nicholas D. Kristof, one of the few prominent figures to address the issue regularly.

The Chasm Between Our Worlds

Rape and other acts of violence, up to and including murder, as well as threats of violence, constitute the barrage some men lay down as they attempt to control some women, and fear of that violence limits most women in ways they've gotten so used to they hardly notice—and we hardly address. There are exceptions: last summer someone wrote to me to describe a college class in which the students were asked what they do to stay safe from rape. The young women described the intricate ways they stayed alert, limited their access to the world, took precautions, and essentially thought about rape all the time (while the young men in the class, he added, gaped in astonishment). The chasm between their worlds had briefly and suddenly become visible.

Mostly, however, we don't talk about it—though a graphic has been circulating on the Internet called *Ten Top Tips to End Rape*, the kind of thing young women get often enough, but this one had a subversive twist. It offered advice like this: "Carry a whistle! If you are worried you might assault someone 'by accident' you can hand it to the person you are with, so they can call for help." While funny, the piece points out something terrible: the usual guidelines in such situations put the full burden of prevention on potential victims, treating the violence as a given. There's no good reason (and many bad reasons) colleges spend more time telling women how to survive predators than telling the other half of their students not to be predators.

Threats of sexual assault now seem to take place online regularly. 25 In late 2011, British columnist Laurie Penny wrote,

> An opinion, it seems, is the short skirt of the Internet. Having one and flaunting it is somehow asking an amorphous mass of almost-entirely male keyboard-bashers to tell you how they'd like to rape, kill, and urinate on you. This week, after a particularly ugly slew of threats, I decided to make just a few of those messages public on Twitter, and the response I received was overwhelming. Many could not believe the hate I received, and many more began to share their own stories of harassment, intimidation, and abuse.

Women in the online gaming community have been harassed, threatened, and driven out. Anita Sarkeesian, a feminist media critic who documented such incidents, received support for her work, but also, in the words of a journalist, "another wave of really aggressive, you know, violent personal threats, her accounts attempted to be hacked. And one man in Ontario took the step of making an online video game where you could punch Anita's image on the screen. And if you punched it multiple times, bruises and cuts would appear on her image." The difference between these online gamers and the Taliban men who, last October, tried to murder fourteen-year-old Malala Yousafzai for speaking out about the right of Pakistani women to education is one of degree. Both are trying to silence and punish women for claiming voice, power, and the right to participate. Welcome to Manistan.

The Party for the Protection of the Rights of Rapists

It's not just public, or private, or online either. It's also embedded in our political system, and our legal system, which before feminists fought for us didn't recognize most domestic violence, or sexual harassment and stalking, or date rape, or acquaintance rape, or marital rape, and in cases of rape still often tries the victim rather than the rapist, as though only perfect maidens could be assaulted—or believed.

As we learned in the 2012 election campaign, it's also embedded in the minds and mouths of our politicians. Remember that spate of crazy pro-rape things Republican men said last summer and fall, starting with Todd Akin's notorious claim that a woman has ways of preventing pregnancy in cases of rape, a statement he made in order to deny women control over their own bodies (in the form of access to abortion after rape). After that, of course, Senate candidate Richard Mourdock claimed that rape pregnancies were "a gift from God," and soon after another Republican politician piped up to defend Akin's comment.

Happily the five publicly pro-rape Republicans in the 2012 campaign all lost their election bids. (Stephen Colbert tried to warn them that women had gotten the vote in 1920.) But it's not just a matter of the garbage they say (and the price they now pay). Congressional Republicans refused to reauthorize the Violence Against Women Act because they objected to the protection it gave immigrants, transgender women, and Native American women. (Speaking of epidemics, one of three Native American women will be raped, and on the reservations 88 percent of those rapes are by non-Native men who know tribal governments can't prosecute them. So much for rape as a crime of passion—these are crimes of calculation and opportunism.)

And they're out to gut reproductive rights—birth control as well as abortion, as they've pretty effectively done in many states over the last dozen years. What's meant by "reproductive rights," of course, is the right of women to control their own bodies. Didn't I mention earlier that violence against women is a control issue?

And though rapes are often investigated lackadaisically—there is a backlog of about four hundred thousand untested rape kits in this country—rapists who impregnate their victims have parental rights in thirty-one states. Oh, and former vice-presidential candidate and current congressman Paul Ryan (R-Manistan) is reintroducing a bill that would give states the right to ban abortions and might even conceivably allow a rapist to sue his victim for having one.

All the Things That Aren't to Blame

Of course, women are capable of all sorts of major unpleasantness, and there are violent crimes by women, but the so-called war of the sexes is extraordinarily lopsided when it comes to actual violence. Unlike the last (male) head of the International Monetary Fund, the current (female) head is not going to assault an employee at a luxury hotel; top-ranking female officers in the U.S. military, unlike their male counterparts, are not accused of any sexual assaults; and young female athletes, unlike those male football players in Steubenville, aren't likely to urinate on unconscious boys, let alone violate them and boast about it in YouTube videos and Twitter feeds.

No female bus riders in India have ganged up to sexually assault a man so badly he dies of his injuries, nor are marauding packs of women terrorizing men in Cairo's Tahrir Square, and there's just no maternal equivalent to the 11 percent of rapes that are by fathers or stepfathers. Of the people in prison in the United States, 93.5 percent are not women, and though quite a lot of the prisoners should not be there in the first place, maybe some of them should because of violence, until we think of a better way to deal with it, and them.

No major female pop star has blown the head off a young man she took home with her, as did Phil Spector. (He is now part of that 93.5 percent for the shotgun slaying of Lana Clarkson, apparently for refusing his advances.) No female action-movie star has been charged with domestic violence, because Angelina Jolie just isn't doing what Mel Gibson and Steve McQueen did, and there aren't any celebrated female movie directors who gave a thirteen-year-old drugs before sexually assaulting that child, while she kept saying "no," as did Roman Polanski.

In Memory of Jyoti Singh

What's the matter with manhood? There's something about how masculinity is imagined, about what's praised and encouraged, about the way violence is passed on to boys that needs to be addressed. There are lovely and wonderful men out there, and one of the things that's encouraging in this round of the war against women is how many men I've seen who get it, who think it's their issue too, who stand up for us and with us in everyday life, online and in the marches from New Delhi to San Francisco this winter.

Increasingly men are becoming good allies — and there always have been some. Kindness and gentleness never had a gender, and neither did empathy. Domestic violence statistics are down significantly from earlier decades (even though they're still shockingly high), and a lot of men are at work crafting new ideas and ideals about masculinity and power.

Gay men have redefined and occasionally undermined conventional masculinity—publicly, for many decades—and often been great allies for women. Women's liberation has often been portrayed as a movement intent on encroaching upon or taking power and privilege away from men, as though in some dismal zero-sum game, only one gender at a time could be free and powerful. But we are free together or slaves together. Surely the mindset of those who think they need to win, to dominate, to punish, to reign supreme must be terrible and far from free, and giving up this unachievable pursuit would be liberatory.

There are other things I'd rather write about, but this affects everything else. The lives of half of humanity are still dogged by, drained by, and sometimes ended by this pervasive variety of violence. Think of how much more time and energy we would have to focus on other things that matter if we weren't so busy surviving. Look at it this way: one of the best journalists I know is afraid to walk home at night in our neighborhood. Should she stop working late? How many women have had to stop doing their work, or been stopped from doing it, for similar reasons? It's clear now that monumental harassment online keeps many women from speaking up and writing altogether.

One of the most exciting new political movements on Earth is the Native Canadian indigenous rights movement, with feminist and environmental overtones, called Idle No More. On December 27, shortly after the movement took off, a Native woman was kidnapped, raped, beaten, and left for dead in Thunder Bay, Ontario, by men whose remarks framed the crime as retaliation against Idle No More. Afterward, she walked four hours through the bitter cold and survived to tell her tale. Her assailants, who have threatened to do it again, are still at large.

The New Delhi rape and murder of Jyoti Singh, the twenty-three-year-old who was studying physiotherapy so that she could better herself while helping others, and the assault on her male companion (who survived) seem to have triggered the reaction that we have needed for one hundred, or one thousand, or five thousand years. May she be to women—and men—worldwide what Emmett Till,[6] murdered by white supremacists in 1955, was to African Americans and the then-nascent U.S. civil rights movement.

We have far more than eighty-seven thousand rapes in this country every year, but each of them is invariably portrayed as an isolated incident. We have dots so close they're splatters melting into a stain, but hardly anyone connects them, or names that stain. In India they did. They said that this is a civil rights issue, it's a human rights issue, it's everyone's problem, it's not isolated, and it's never going to be acceptable again. It has to change. It's your job to change it, and mine, and ours.

40

Sources

"Is Delhi So Different from Steubenville?," *New York Times*, op ed, January 13, 2013, p. SR1.

"Online Harassment Gets Real for Online Gamers." Boston: WBUR.

Wright, J. P., Dietrich, K. N., Ris, M. D., Hornung, R. W., Wessel, S. D., Lanphear, B. P. et al. (2008). "Association of Prenatal and Childhood Blood Lead Concentrations with Criminal Arrests in Early Adulthood," *PLoS Med* 5(5): e101. doi:10.1371/journal.pmed.0050101.

[6]**Emmett Till:** The 1955 murder of 14-year-old Emmett Till by two white men in Mississippi galvanized the civil rights movement. [Eds.]

Ted Rall, Dist. by Andrews McMeel Syndication

ENGAGING THE TEXT

1. What is the significance of Solnit's title, "The Longest War"? In what ways does she view violence against women as a war?

2. Solnit writes that gendered violence is "almost never treated as a civil rights or human rights issue, or a crisis, or even a pattern" (para. 4). How would violence against women be treated differently if it were considered a matter of civil or human rights? How would news or political coverage differ if it were considered a crisis? Do you agree with Solnit's assessment that violence against women follows a pattern? Why or why not?

3. Solnit contends that violence against women is "a system of control" (para. 18). How does she support this claim? Which aspects of her argument do you find most and least compelling, and why?

4. Solnit ends the essay with these words: "It has to change. It's your job to change it, and mine, and ours" (para. 41). Explain why you think her conclusion is or is not justified. What might you do to "change it"?

5. **Thinking Rhetorically** Solnit deploys shocking statistics and horrifying stories of crimes against women to bolster her argument. Do you think she overstates her case? Do Solnit's periodic concessions to men—acknowledging that most men aren't violent (para. 5) and that many men "get it" (para. 35)—make her claims less alienating for men? Who is her intended audience in this essay?

EXPLORING CONNECTIONS

6. Read or review Peggy Orenstein's essay, "Blurred Lines, Take Two" (p. 193), which discusses campus rape and sexual assault. To what extent would Orenstein agree with Solnit about the causes of and possible solutions to gendered violence?

7. According to Solnit, "There's something about how masculinity is imagined, about what's praised and encouraged, about the way violence is passed on to boys that needs to be addressed" (para. 35). Write or role-play a panel discussion among Solnit, Jean Kilbourne (p. 545), Carlos Andrés Gómez (p. 495), and Jessie Daniels (p. 298) in which they discuss how masculinity is imagined and how it's conveyed to boys. How should we imagine, model, or teach it differently?

8. Examine the images of Anita Sarkeesian on page 311. How do these pictures support or undercut Solnit's contention that the difference between the online gamers and the Taliban is merely "one of degree" (para. 26)?

EXTENDING THE CRITICAL CONTEXT

9. Solnit describes a "college class in which the students were asked what they do to stay safe from rape" (para. 23). Working in single-sex groups, take a few minutes to list the strategies you use to avoid sexual assault. Then compare your lists to those of other groups. If there are noticeable differences between the men's and the women's lists, how do you explain them?

10. Solnit charges that sexual violence against women is "incessantly overlooked" (para. 2). Has the #MeToo movement brought more attention to this problem? Research online "sexual harassment and women of color" or "sexual harassment and transgender women." To what extent does #MeToo address violence against all women?

11. Recently, a fraternity at Cornell University was put on two-year probation because some members had sponsored a "pig roast"—a competition in which pledges earned points for having sex with overweight women. What attitudes toward women does this contest reflect? Do you think that probation is an appropriate punishment? Why or why not?

12. Watch *The Hunting Ground*, a 2015 documentary that deals with campus rape and colleges' reluctance to address the issue. Then write an essay in which you evaluate the case that the film makes.

FROM RUSH LIMBAUGH TO DONALD TRUMP: CONSERVATIVE TALK RADIO AND THE DEFIANT REASSERTION OF WHITE MALE AUTHORITY

JACKSON KATZ

Many Americans were stunned by the election of Donald Trump, who was caught on a 2005 video bragging that "You can do anything" to women, "Grab 'em by the pussy." During the presidential campaign, he mocked a disabled man, called undocumented Mexicans drug-dealers and rapists, and proposed a total ban on Muslims entering the country. But as Jackson Katz argues in this essay, Trump's outrageous rhetoric had already been normalized by conservative talk radio and cable TV hosts, who were "selling a brand of authoritarian, bellicose, and at times verbally abusive White masculinity." Their brand of misogyny and "hatred as entertainment" had, over three decades, developed a popular following and made extreme views more acceptable to conservative audiences. Katz (b. 1960) has a PhD in cultural studies and education, and lectures in the United States and internationally on gender, sexual orientation, race, violence, and media. He cofounded the Mentors in Violence Prevention (MVP) program at Northeastern University, which is designed to prevent sexual assault and relationship abuse. He has worked extensively with the military on gender violence prevention, and has produced the award-winning *Tough Guise* educational videos. He is the author of many articles as well as two books, *Man Enough? Donald Trump, Hillary Clinton, and the Politics of Presidential Masculinity* (2016) and *The Macho Paradox: Why Some Men Hurt Women and How All Men Can Help* (2006). The following essay appears in *Gender, Race, and Class in Media: A Critical Reader* (2017), edited by Gail Dines and Jean M. Humez.

DONALD TRUMP'S 2016 campaign slogan "Make America Great Again" (MAGA) is one of those catchy phrases that carries much greater weight than the sum of its words. While an object of derision and caricature on the cultural and political left—mostly for the putatively racist implications of its timing after two terms of the first African American president, Barack Obama—for millions of (mostly White) Americans, MAGA captured an essential truth. The America they remembered and romanticized was fading from view amidst the dizzying pace of social change over the past half-century, especially the changes associated with the country's intensifying racial, ethnic, gender, and sexual diversity.

A popular progressive restatement of the right-wing catchphrase alleged that Trump wanted to "Make America White Again." But a careful examination of the Trump campaign's rhetoric and stage-managed rallies, bolstered by exit poll results, reveals that race *and* gender anxieties and resentments animated the bombastic real estate developer's political rise. A more finely tuned rewrite of the famous phrase might read: "Put White Men Back on Center Stage Again," which aptly captures Trumpism as an aspirational political movement.

But White men were already on center stage in a critically important theater in U.S. media culture: conservative talk radio. In fact, the same reactionary sociocultural forces that fueled the phenomenal success of Rush Limbaugh and other conservative talkers over the past generation arguably paved the way for Trump's election as president of the United States. This article outlines some of those forces, with particular attention to the ways in which conservative talk radio, like Trumpism, champions the reassertion of an idealized, throwback White masculinity as the solution to America's myriad problems at home and abroad.

The Rise of Conservative Talk Radio

The recent historical context for the rise of Trumpism was set at least as far back as the 1990s, long before the real estate developer and reality TV star who energized the movement emerged as a serious candidate for the 2016 Republican presidential nomination. In particular, that decade saw the rise of a militantly antigovernment conservatism, which was catalyzed in part by White men's continuing loss of economic power and an accompanying loss of familial and cultural authority, especially in the working and middle classes. Not coincidentally, the 1990s was also the decade in which the influence of conservative talk radio increased dramatically. Over the past three decades, Rush Limbaugh, Sean Hannity,[1] and a number of charismatic White male talk radio and cable TV hosts have risen to cultural prominence and have done so—like Donald Trump—by selling a brand of authoritarian, bellicose, and at times verbally abusive White masculinity, which for reasons of identity politics and history has touched a nerve with millions of listeners—especially (but not exclusively) White men.

In the real world of the 21st century, White men's unquestioned   5
dominance in the family and workplace are in the process of a long-term decline. But not when you turn on right-wing AM talk radio or *Fox News Channel*, which together reach an audience of as many as 50 million people (Draper, 2016). People don't generally travel to those precincts to seek out new ideas about the possibilities of democratic governance and citizenship in an increasingly diverse and interconnected world—and they don't get it there. Instead, right-wing hosts

---

[1]**Sean Hannity:** (b. 1961) Conservative radio talk show host, Fox News commentator, and enthusiastic Trump supporter. [All notes are the editors'.]

typically speak with an old-school masculine authority that recalls an idealized past, when (White) men were in control in the public and private spheres, and no one was in a position to actively challenge their power. They provide their listeners with an alternate media universe where the old order of male dominance and White supremacy is still intact, even if they've (sometimes) cleaned up the cruder rhetorical expressions of sexism and racism. It is both fitting and revealing that one of the signature on-air promotions for Rush Limbaugh's top-rated radio program features an announcer boldly proclaiming that Rush is "America's anchorman," slyly invoking association with the memory (if not the liberal politics) of the late Walter Cronkite, a paternal and authoritative television presence as the chief anchor of the CBS Evening News in the 1960s and 1970s who was known as the "most trusted man in America."

Of course not all conservative talk hosts are White men. There are women, such as Laura Ingraham, a former law clerk for Supreme Court Justice Clarence Thomas, and a handful of men of color, such as the African American conservative libertarian Larry Elder. The Los Angeles–based Elder's signature characteristic, and perhaps the key feature of his popularity with a largely White male audience, is his performance of an angry Black man persona. But unlike the angry Black man who elicits fear and resentment in the White racist imagination, Elder's anger typically is directed at the usual objects of conservative scorn: antiracist White liberals, feminists, and progressives of all stripes. Elder is the Black man who literally gives voice to sentiments— especially about race—that White conservatives are reluctant to say out loud, for fear of being labeled as racists.

But women and Black men are the exceptions on conservative talk radio, which remains a bastion of White men's power and center stage for the airing of a myriad of cultural and political grievances on the part of conservative White men. On the air and in their public personae, the (White) men who personify the genre—such as Limbaugh, Hannity, Mark Levin[2] and Michael Savage[3]—typically shun nuance, rarely concede points in arguments, or even acknowledge the validity of opposing viewpoints. This is, arguably, less a result of their personal stubbornness than it is an occupational imperative: the simplicity of their ideology and arguments and their exaggerated self-confidence are the very source of their popularity. In the midst of a society in transition, in which the old *Father Knows Best*[4] certainties are a figment of the idealized

---

[2]**Mark Levin:** (b. 1957) Conservative lawyer, author, radio host, and Fox News personality; proponent of many extreme views.

[3]**Michael Savage:** (b. 1942) Real name Michael Weiner, conservative radio host and author, who since 2009 has been banned from the U.K, for "engaging in unacceptable behavior by seeking to provoke others to serious criminal acts and fostering hatred which might lead to intercommunity violence." ["Who is on UK 'Least Wanted' List?" BBC News, May 5, 2009.]

[4]***Father Knows Best:*** 1950s television sitcom about a middle-class family; the title is self-explanatory.

past, these men provide a comforting patriarchal presence, just as the reactionary ideology they champion seeks to roll back the democratizing social changes that have disrupted White men's cultural centrality.

In recent years, bloggers, journalists, and scholars have begun to move beyond dismissive caricatures of talk radio as merely entertainment or simplistic populist chatter and pay closer attention to its cultural and political influence. This is long overdue. There is ample data that demonstrate the powerful role talk radio plays in elections; one study showed that in the 2010 midterm elections 78% of talk radio listeners voted, compared to 41% of eligible voters (Harrison, 2011). There has been some discussion of the racial politics of talk radio. In a book-length study of "outrage media," the authors suggest that many conservatives fear being perceived as racist, and thus find comfort in the "safe political environs" provided by "outrage" programs in which conservative racial resentment is normalized and defended (Berry & Sobieraj, 2014). But with the exception of ongoing feminist criticism of the crude sexism that persists among too many male political commentators in media, there has been very little gendered analysis of talk radio's role in establishing and enforcing a certain kind of old school White manhood.

Talk Radio and the Promotion of Traditional Gender Ideology

Conservative talk radio programs are typically hosted by strong, charismatic White men whose personal style ranges from verbal bomb throwers like Michael Savage to more cerebral and less-caffeinated types like Michael Medved.[5] But almost all of them share a belief not only in conservative orthodoxies like "smaller government" and the virtues of a "free market," but also in traditional gender and sexual ideologies. One way this traditionalist belief plays out conversationally is in the near-constant refrain from right-wing talkers that the problems of the country are linked to the supposed "softness" of liberal men. For example, it is common to hear qualities like compassion and empathy—especially in men—equated with weakness and femininity; a major theme of Rush Limbaugh's social commentary is that the "chickification" of American society is linked to our cultural decline (Limbaugh, 2011). In fact, one of the most popular rhetorical techniques conservative talk hosts use is a variation of the rational-public sphere/emotional-private sphere binary. Men in patriarchal cultures have employed this binary for centuries to justify the perpetuation of their familial, religious, economic, and political control over women. The idea is that men are more rational, and hence better equipped to handle public matters of the economy and foreign policy than women, who

---

[5]**Michael Medved:** (b. 1948) Film critic, author, political commentator, and conservative radio show host, who has referred to Trump as "insecure, unprepared, and angrily unhinged." [Hadas Gold, "Michael Medved Suffers for His Anti-Trump Stance." *Politico*, 6, Nov. 2016.]

are said to be more "emotional," and thus more suited to the private sphere of caregiving and maintaining relationships. Feminist theorists and popular writers have critiqued—and discredited—this falsely gendered dichotomy for decades, but it continues to animate conservative talk radio—one of the chief sources of news and political commentary for millions of White men.

On his nationally syndicated radio program, the Los Angeles–based conservative talk host Dennis Prager regularly declares that liberal thought is based on the heart, not on the mind. In his book *Still the Best Hope: Why the World Needs American Values to Triumph*, Prager (2012) outlines what he calls the "feelings-based nature" of liberalism. Of course the "feelings" of empathy or compassion that Prager and other conservatives deride as incapable of competing with conservative "logic" has long been devalued in public discourse as feminine. In fact, conservative propagandists have so thoroughly feminized the word "liberal" that in recent years few Democratic candidates of either sex wanted to claim the label. Male candidates feared being unmanned, while female politicians didn't want to be seen in narrow, stereotypical terms as merely a "women's candidate."

Critiquing these linguistic practices is not merely a rhetorical exercise, because all of this talk has significant material consequences. For example, talk radio plays an important role in national debates about military spending and foreign policy, because daily discussion and on-air dialogue and disputation about these matters helps to define what course of action "manly" men should support. This, in turn, helps to define the political space in which politicians, especially presidents, have to operate. As many observers have noted, for decades Democrats have often supported or acquiesced in the advancement of militaristic policies in part out of fear of being accused of being "soft" on defense. Even before he was elected president, Barack Obama had been the target of relentless mockery and ridicule on conservative talk radio. The line of attack varied from issue to issue, but its essence was usually the same: Obama was Jimmy Carter II: a weak and vacillating leader who (in Obama's case) gave good speeches but was in way over his head. The growing troubles in the world were the result not of complex historical and economic forces, but instead were caused by weak leadership in the White House. This right-wing narrative—replayed endlessly on talk radio for nearly a decade—played a crucial role in setting the stage for the emergence of a leader—Donald Trump—who would "get tough" and (finally) get things done.

Rush Knows Best

Any serious discussion about the cultural and political significance of talk radio has to begin with Rush Limbaugh. Since the early 1990s Limbaugh's astounding political influence on the right—and in the Republican Party—has been an open secret. He has been the top-rated radio talk show host in America since *Talkers* magazine started the rankings in 1991. His weekly audience is estimated at approximately 15 million listeners. Over the past two decades Limbaugh's influence has grown to the point that David Frum[6] described him as the "unofficial spokesman for the Republican Party." Limbaugh's audience is made up not only of casual listeners and die-hard "dittoheads," but includes a significant percentage of the political class in and outside of the Washington Beltway, especially conservatives. In 1994, dubbed "The Year of the Angry White Male," when Republicans gained control of Congress for the first time in 40 years, Limbaugh was asked to address the new GOP legislators and was named an honorary member of the freshman class (Chafets, 2010). As Karl Rove[7] said of Limbaugh, "He's a leader. If Rush engages on an issue, it gives others courage to engage" (Wilson, 2011, p. 252).

It is notable—although hardly surprising—that Rush Limbaugh's listeners are 72% male, over 90% White, and skew 50+ years old. Presumably, a key part of the appeal of conservative talk radio to its predominantly older White male audience resides in its reinforcement of traditional masculinity in the face of a culture where epochal economic transformations and progressive social movements have shaken old certainties about what constitutes a "real man." In this context it is important to note that Limbaugh not only articulates a set of conservative moral precepts and reactionary politics. He also performs a kind of cartoonish masculinity from an era gone by. For example, he loves to talk about football, and he is frequently photographed smoking expensive cigars. He regularly celebrates the military and in the mid-2000s was a prominent defender of the conduct of U.S. service members in the disgraceful episode of the Abu Ghraib[8] prison in Iraq, which he dismissed as a "fraternity prank."

Limbaugh's retrograde attitudes toward women are well-known. According to his biographer, the thrice-divorced Limbaugh has "a fair amount" of Hugh Hefner[9] in him (Chafets, 2010, p. 204). Limbaugh has a long history of making explicitly sexist and dismissive statements about women—especially feminists. Early in his career, he published his "Undeniable Truths of Life," which included this: "Feminism was established so as to allow unattractive women easier access to the mainstream of society" (Limbaugh, 2008). He is also the media personality most responsible for popularizing the term *feminazi,* which links feminists, who are among those at the forefront of democratic advocacy and nonviolence, with Nazis, the embodiment of masculine cruelty and violence. In Limbaugh-land, Democratic women who demand to be treated as men's equals are castrating "feminazis," and Democratic men are either neutered wimps or gay. This antiwoman and antifeminist anger

---

[6]**David Frum:** (b. 1960) Canadian-American writer, conservative political commentator, and speechwriter for George W. Bush; currently a senior editor at *the Atlantic.*

[7]**Karl Rove:** (b. 1950) Republican political consultant who served as Senior Advisor and Deputy Chief of Staff to George W. Bush; he now writes a weekly column for the *Wall Street Journal.*

[8]**Abu Ghraib:** Prison in Iraq used from 2003 to 2006 as a U.S. Army detention center for captured Iraqis; in 2004, photos surfaced of Iraqis being tortured and humiliated, and an investigation led to eleven U.S. soldiers being convicted of crimes.

[9]**Hugh Hefner:** (1926–2017) Founder and editor of *Playboy* magazine.

finds expression in the commercial world of talk radio in a way that is inconceivable in other forms of mainstream political discourse.

In fact, the source of Limbaugh's immense popularity on AM radio has some interesting parallels to Howard Stern's popularity on FM, and later on satellite radio. Under the guise of self-consciously constructed personae—Limbaugh as the fun-loving conservative truth-teller, Stern as naughty rock-and-roll bad boy—both men function as the id of their respective audiences. They say things that men in more responsible or respectable contexts may believe but would never say out loud. For example, few men in public life—particularly Republican candidates and officeholders—would dare criticize sexual harassment laws when women comprise 53% of the electorate. But Rush Limbaugh, who repeatedly refers to accomplished women, including women in politics, as "babes," female journalists as "infobabes" and "anchorettes," and lesbians as "lesbos," boasts that a sign on his door reads "Sexual harassment at this work station will not be reported. However . . . it will be graded" (Edsall, 2006). Outside of a handful of short-lived boycotts by feminist activists that resulted in some of his advertisers pulling their support for his program, Limbaugh has largely sidestepped significant financial repercussions for his repeated expressions of open misogyny. Nonetheless it is notable that in 2016–17, two of the most powerful figures in conservative media, Fox News Channel founding president and CEO Roger Ailes, and that network's biggest star, Bill O'Reilly, lost their jobs at Fox due to multiple allegations of sexual harassment against them.

To be sure, Limbaugh is not without his many critics and detractors. For many years he has been the subject of mainstream media interest—and concern. One *Time* magazine cover story that appeared as far back as 1995 was headlined "Is Rush Limbaugh Good for America? Talk Radio is only the beginning. Electronic populism threatens to short-circuit representative democracy" (*Time*, 1995). A 2008 cover story in the *New York Times Magazine* profiled Limbaugh's political influence, as well as offered readers a glimpse at the lavish lifestyle afforded him due to his financial success (Chafets, 2008). But not everyone recognizes the extent of his political clout. When the controversy over Limbaugh's misogynous tirade against Georgetown law student Sandra Fluke[10] erupted in 2012, Al Neuharth, founder of *USA Today*, wrote that "the real problem with Rush Limbaugh is that people take him seriously. He's a clown. If you listen to his radio program regularly, it should be to get your daily laugh" (Neuharth, 2012).

Critics of Limbaugh and other right-wing talk radio hosts often point to the coarsening of political discourse to which the talkers have contributed. Former vice-president Al Gore describes what he terms the "Limbaugh-Hannity-Drudge[11] axis" as a kind of "fifth column in

---

[10]**Sandra Fluke:** (b. 1981) When the feminist activist spoke in support of requiring religiously-affiliated hospitals and universities to cover the costs of medical contraceptives, Rush Limbaugh attacked her as a "slut" and a "prostitute." Fluke is now an attorney who focuses on social justice issues.

[11]**Drudge:** Matt Drudge (b. 1966), creator and editor of the *Drudge Report,* a conservative news website.

the fourth estate" that is made up of "propagandists pretending to be journalists" (Gore, 2007, p. 66). Gore claims that what most troubles him about these right-wing polemicists is their promotion of hatred as entertainment—particularly their mean-spirited hostility toward liberals and progressives. But what most of right-wing radio's progressive critics overlook or downplay is the gendered nature of Limbaugh and company's contempt for liberals. Embedded firmly within the talk radio hosts' scathing critique of liberalism is a barely suppressed well of anger at the progressive changes in the gender and sexual order over the past 40 years and the concomitant displacement of traditional patriarchal power. Limbaugh is perhaps the most overt in his open hostility not only toward feminist women, but also the men who support them. He calls these men the "new castrati," and ridicules them for having "lost all manhood, gonads, guts and courage throughout our culture and our political system" (Media Matters, 2011).

In the media character he self-created, Limbaugh's unrestrained narcissism drives him to broadcast to his audience an inflated sense of himself as a "man's man," while his political agenda seeks to reinforce the link between manly strength and political conservatism. He accomplishes this rhetorically, in part, by relentlessly attacking the femininity of feminist women, and the masculinity of men who support gender equality. Limbaugh's brash and boorish persona, and his belief that White men's cultural centrality is, in the title of his first book, "The Way Things Ought to Be," helped set the stage for the political rise of another bombastic media performer: Donald J. Trump.

Limbaugh and Other Conservative Talkers Provide the Template for Trump

During the 2016 presidential campaign, Sean Hannity—who is the second most highly-rated talk radio host (after Limbaugh) and a Fox News Channel mainstay—became a vociferous supporter of Donald Trump, providing the eventual Republican nominee and president with many millions of dollars of free (and largely fawning) media coverage. But while Hannity eagerly insinuated himself into the Trump story, Rush Limbaugh's entire career can be seen as an extended prelude to Trump's climb to the pinnacle of power. In fact, when Rush Limbaugh praised a Donald Trump speech on June 22, 2016 that the *New York Times* said contained a "torrent of criticism" aimed at Hillary Clinton, he was really congratulating himself. Trump "basically said things about Hillary Clinton that you just do not hear Republicans saying," the right-wing talk radio icon said. "You just do not hear Mitt Romney[12] say this, for example. You would not hear the Bush family talk this way about Hillary. You . . . would not hear it" (Schwartz, 2016, para. 2). Limbaugh's point—variations of which he has made for years—is that

[12]**Mitt Romney:** (b. 1947) Businessman and politician, governor of Massachusetts from 2003 to 2007, and unsuccessful Republican nominee for president in 2012.

"establishment types" can't or won't be this blunt in their criticism. "But Trump can say this as an outsider, he can say this stuff as a nonmember of the elite or the establishment" (Schwartz, 2016, para. 3).

Limbaugh might outwardly have been lauding the brashness of the billionaire real estate developer, but any critical Limbaugh-listener could hear the gushing self-congratulation just beneath the surface of those remarks. For perhaps the best way to describe the Big Talker is the "outsider who can say stuff that is normally out of bounds in polite company"—a cleverly constructed persona that the college drop-out from Cape Girardeau, Missouri, has parlayed into a long and amazingly lucrative career in conservative talk radio. Limbaugh's unparalleled popularity owes a great deal to his willingness to say things—especially sexist, racist, and homophobic things—that more respectable Republicans would never utter in public: especially those who have to face the voters. And for close to 30 years his legions of fans have loved him for it. In this sense, Limbaugh's affection for Donald Trump is about more than his recognition of a kindred spirit; it is actually yet another manifestation of his narcissism.

Consider the many similarities between the two men. They're both aging heterosexual White men of German American ethnicity who were born 5 years apart and grew up as the sons of authoritarian, deeply patriarchal, and professionally highly successful fathers. They both have reaped rich rewards in life despite—or is it because of?—displaying levels of narcissistic toxicity that are notable even in the puffed-up precincts of New York City real estate and conservative media. They are both frequent supporters of aggressive military action, including torture, but each deftly avoided military service during the Vietnam War era. Trump avoided serving through a series of deferments common to members of his social class, Limbaugh by claiming an anal boil rendered him unfit for service. They are both members of the 1% who inhabit worlds of almost unimaginable wealth and privilege, living in luxury dwellings in New York City and mansions in south Florida, flying around the world on private jets. They both love to golf. They both repeatedly make misogynous comments and refuse to apologize for them. They both have had at least three wives. And they are both fake populists who have used aggressive language and verbal bullying tactics against their adversaries to wrangle their way to the heights of cultural and political influence in the United States of America.

Consider how Rush Limbaugh's career in talk radio might have paved the way for Donald Trump's political ascension. For almost three decades, Limbaugh fashioned himself a tribune of the people, a man with the guts to defend average (White) folks from an ongoing assault waged by liberal politicians and cultural elites against traditional American values. Many liberals and progressives see Limbaugh as a pompous and bigoted blowhard, and they are perplexed and dismayed by his continuing popularity. At the same time, Limbaugh is revered on the right as a champion of the little White guy (and gal) who have been trampled for a generation by multiculturalism, feminism, the gay rights movement, and the myriad of unsettling cultural transformations they have catalyzed. While progressives look at Limbaugh and see a bloated bully who routinely targets individuals and groups with less power, his fans see him as a man armed only with a very large microphone and the confidence and courage to shovel sand against the rising tides of social change.

Perhaps the most concise way to explain these radically different perceptions is that while the left sees many of Limbaugh's pronouncements as offensive, the right sees them as defensive. And because he's defending them, they're willing to overlook or excuse his more than occasional intemperate outbursts. It's quite similar to how millions of Trump supporters see the reality TV star who was elected to be the 45th president of the United States. Like Limbaugh, Trump is a man of privilege whose class sympathies lie with the rich, but who nonetheless has been able to market himself as someone who is on the side of average (White) Americans. A crucial part of Trump's appeal to downwardly mobile White men is his image as the "blue-collar billionaire" who will do what it takes to bring back good jobs for working-class people. He has managed to maintain this illusion despite the reality that, as Matt Taibbi[13] wrote, "Trump had spent his entire career lending his name to luxury properties that promised exclusivity and separation from exactly the sort of struggling Joes who turned out for his speeches" (Taibbi, 2015) and despite his enthusiasm for the failed idea of trickle-down economics—that is, cutting taxes on the wealthy as a way to create jobs for the working class (Taibbi, 2015).

But in Trumpworld, you're a "populist" not because you advocate economic policies that actually benefit working people, but because you're dismissive of "politically correct" elites who refuse to talk honestly and say what every red-blooded White American man supposedly knows to be true—especially about matters of race, gender, and sexuality. Trump learned during his campaign for the presidency what Rush Limbaugh has known for decades. On the right, the way to build an audience—or a voter base—is to convince people you're on their side and are willing to fight back—and hit hard—against the forces that are holding them down. For Limbaugh, those forces are, generally speaking, the enemy within: snobby "libs," the "drive-by media," "feminazis," "environmentalist wackos," Black Lives Matter activists. The objects of Trump's rhetorical aggression are more likely to be "outsiders," either far-away actors like China and ISIS, or closer to home, Mexican and Muslim immigrants (and Muslim Americans).

What these men's rhetorical appeals have in common is they identify and target specific enemies for people to get angry with—especially those who reside on the lower rungs of economic and social power. It's much easier to direct people's anger downward (or sideways) than it is to level with them that their very real problems—including the loss of millions of well-paying jobs and a chance for social mobility for the next generation—are rooted in the impersonal forces of global

25

[13]**Matt Taibi:** (b. 1970) Liberal journalist and author, currently a contributing editor at *Rolling Stone.*

capitalism. It's much easier to bash Democrats or dark-skinned others than it is to critique decades of conservative economic and social policy — promulgated by class-peers and ideological fellow-travelers of the real estate mogul and radio star — that have gutted the middle class and dramatically exacerbated income inequality.

Conclusion

This chapter outlined some of the ways that conservative talk radio is not simply "entertainment." Rather, it has a profound influence not only on elections, but on the very nature of public discourse, and thus ultimately on public policy, on issues ranging from women's health to climate change. Until now, little attention has been paid in cultural studies scholarship to the important cultural and political role of conservative talk radio, and even less to how this cultural phenomenon functions in the gender order. Considering the important "public pedagogical" role that charismatic hosts play in their embodiment and modeling of an influential version of conservative White masculinity, and the influence this has on contemporary American political dialogue and debate, much more empirical research and analysis of conservative talk radio's social and political impact is necessary. This need has taken on even greater urgency since the stunning political success of Donald Trump, a former reality TV star who performs a kind of crude, loud-mouthed, throwback White masculinity that has been a regular presence on the airwaves for the past generation, but which is now ensconced at the pinnacle of cultural and political power.

References

Berry, J., & Sobieraj, S. (2014). *The outrage industry: Political opinion media and the new incivility*. New York: Oxford University Press.

Chafets, Z. (2008, July 6). Late period Limbaugh. *The New York Times Magazine*, 3. Retrieved from http://www.nytimes.com/2008/07/06/magazine/06Limbaugh.html?pagewanted=all&_r=0.

Chafets, Z. (2010). *Rush Limbaugh: An army of one*. New York: Sentinel.

Draper, R. (2016, October 2). How Donald Trump's candidacy set off a civil war within the right-wing media. *The New York Times Magazine*, 38.

Edsall, T. (2006). *Building red America: The New Conservative Coalition and the drive for permanent power*. New York: Basic Books.

Gore, A. (2007). *The assault on reason*. New York: Penguin.

Harrison, M. (2011, October). Qualitative aspects of the talk radio audience. *Talkers Magazine*, 8.

Limbaugh, R. (2011). Chickification of America: NFL cancels game because of snow. RushLimbaugh.com. Retrieved from http://www.rushlimbaugh.com/daily/2011/01/04/chickification_of_america_nfl_cancels_game_because_of_snow.

MacNicol, G. (2011, May 2). Rush Limbaugh MOCKS the idea that Obama is responsible for capture of Bin Laden: "Thank God for President Obama!" *Business Insider*. Retrieved from http:///www.businessinsider.com/rush-limbaugh-thank-god-for-president-obama-2011–5.

Media Matters. (2011, March 8). Limbaugh describes the new castrati.

Neuharth, A. (2012, March 19). Limbaugh is a clown so let's laugh at him. *USA Today*.

Politico. (2011, May 2). Limbaugh mocks Obama for Bin Laden hit. Retrieved from http://www.politico.com/blogs/onmedia/0511/Limbaugh_mocks_Obama_for_bin_Laden_hit.html.

Prager, D. (2012). *Still the best hope: Why the world needs American values to triumph.* New York: Broadside Books.

Schwartz, I. (2016, June 23). Limbaugh on Trump: Finally, a Republican (other than me) tells the truth about Hillary Clinton. *Real Clear Politics.* Retrieved from http://www.realclearpolitics.com/video/2016/06/23/limbaugh_on_trump_finally_a_republican_other_than_me_tells_the_truth_ about_hillary_clinton.html.

Taibbi, M. (2015, December 29). "In the year of Trump, the joke was on us." *Rolling Stone.*

Time magazine. (1995, January 23). Cover.

Wilson, J. (2011). *The most dangerous man in America: Rush Limbaugh's assault on reason.* New York: St. Martin's.

ENGAGING THE TEXT

1. In what ways is "White men's unquestioned dominance in the family and work-place" declining in twenty-first-century America, according to Katz (para. 5)?

2. What recent cultural changes threaten white male authority, according to Katz? How do conservative talk shows provide "an alternate media universe (para. 5)" that reassures those who feel displaced?

3. Katz asserts that "conservative propagandists have so thoroughly feminized the word 'liberal'" (para. 10) that few politicians are now willing to embrace it. How has the word itself become gendered?

4. How does Rush Limbaugh appeal to his older, white male listeners? How, according to Katz, is Limbaugh's demonizing of women and feminists "inconceivable in . . . mainstream political discourse" (para. 14)? Do you think this is still the case? Why or why not?

5. How have Rush Limbaugh and other "outrage media" personalities helped to prepare the way for Donald Trump's political career? In what ways do Trump's attitudes toward women, minorities, and gay rights advocates mirror Limbaugh's? Why do Trump's supporters see his "rhetorical aggression" (para. 24) as justifiable?

6. How does Katz explain the basis of Trump's appeal? What "specific enemies" does Trump encourage his followers to blame for their economic hardships? Why does Katz say, "It's much easier to direct people's anger downward (or sideways) than it is to level with them that their very real problems . . . are rooted in the impersonal forces of global capitalism" (para. 25)? Explain why you agree or disagree with his analysis.

EXPLORING CONNECTIONS

7. Review the vitriolic online responses to the student whose "rape accusations resulted in the suspension of a fraternity" (para. 17) in Peggy Orenstein's "Blurred Lines, Take Two" (p. 193) and the raging antifeminism of Gamergate in Noreen Malone's "Zoë and the Trolls" (p. 285). How does Limbaugh's overt sexism parallel the younger men's online threats against women? How does it differ? Write an imaginary conversation among Orenstein, Malone, and Katz in which they analyze the motives that underlie this behavior.

8. Compare the values, rhetoric, and behavior of the white supremacists that Jessie Daniels describes (p. 298) with those of the "outrage media" hosts that Katz analyzes. What are their views on immigration, multiculturalism, race, and gender? What do they admire, whom do they despise, and what do they fear? How do they hope to change American culture? Why do they use outrageous language, and how do they enforce their messages? Do you believe that right-wing media hosts'"promotion of hatred as entertainment (para. 17)" is dangerous? Why or why not?

EXTENDING THE CRITICAL CONTEXT

9. Listen to and evaluate one of Rush Limbaugh's shows: What kind of persona does he present to listeners? Is Katz's assessment — that he's "selling a brand of authoritarian, bellicose, and at times verbally abusive White masculinity" (para. 4) — fair or unfair? Why?

10. Watch one or two episodes of *Full Frontal with Samantha Bee*, who, as an outspoken feminist and satirist, could be called the anti-Limbaugh. Who is Sam Bee's audience and how does it differ from Limbaugh's? What kinds of targets does she skewer, and why? Do you prefer her humor to Limbaugh's or vice versa? Explain.

FURTHER CONNECTIONS

1. Compare the rhetorical strategies and effectiveness of any two of the selections in this chapter. What is each writer's purpose and what audience is he or she addressing? To what extent and how does each author appeal to readers' reason and emotions? What kind of persona does each writer project? What kinds of evidence does each author rely on? How persuasive or compelling do you find each selection, and why?

2. Research the issue of domestic violence. How is it defined? How prevalent is domestic violence nationwide, in your state, and in your community? What are the risk factors for abusers and their victims? Investigate the resources in your community that offer assistance to victims of domestic abuse: hotlines, shelters, organizations, and government agencies that provide counseling or legal aid. Do these services focus on punishing abusers or "curing" them? Write a paper evaluating the effectiveness of different approaches to protecting victims from abusive partners.

3. Research the status of women in the field or profession you plan to pursue. Are women's salaries and compensation comparable to those of men with similar credentials and experience? What is the ratio of women to men in the field as a whole, in entry-level positions, and in executive or high-status positions? Interview at least one woman in this line of work: In what ways, if any, does she feel that her work experience has differed from a man's? Report your findings to the class.

4. Title IX, the law mandating equal funding for women's sports at publicly funded schools, has been praised for opening new opportunities for women athletes and criticized for siphoning money away from some popular men's sports. Research the impact of Title IX on athletics programs at your college or university: How has the picture of women's and men's sports changed since 1972, the year Title IX was enacted? Have women's and men's athletics attained equality at your school?

5. Some religious groups argue that laws and policies that prohibit harassment of or discrimination against homosexuals infringe on their religious freedom. Investigate a specific case in which a religious organization has made this claim. What arguments have been advanced on both sides of the case? What values and assumptions underlie these arguments? What rights and freedoms are at stake for each party in the dispute?

CREATED EQUAL
Myths of Race

Alex Garland

FAST FACTS

1. In 2017, black people were three times more likely to be killed by police than white people. 152 victims of police killings were unarmed, and over half of them were people of color.

2. 92% of blacks think that whites enjoy some to many advantages over them, whereas over half of whites (54%) believe that their race offers few to no advantages. Blacks are nearly twice as likely as whites to see discrimination as a major reason that they have a harder time getting ahead.

3. 71% of blacks state that they have personally experienced racial or ethnic discrimination. A large majority of whites (70%) and Latinos (67%) say that antiblack discrimination arises from individual prejudice; fewer than half of blacks agree, and 40% think that discrimination is built into U.S. laws and institutions.

4. In 2016, the median household income for Native Americans was 69% of the national average. The Native American poverty rate is about three times that of whites, and over a third of indigenous children live in poverty.

5. Three-quarters of Muslims report that there is "a lot" of prejudice against them in the United States, and almost half (48%) say that they've experienced discrimination in the past year; however, 89% feel proud to be both Muslim and American.

6. 65% of Americans believe that immigrants' talent and hard work benefit the United States, rather than drain the country of resources, and an equal number favor allowing undocumented immigrants to remain in the United States and eventually apply for citizenship.

7. From 2000 to 2015, the Asian population of the United States increased by 72%; by 2055, Asians are expected to become the largest immigrant group in the country. Overall, Asians do well economically, with some subgroups (Japanese, Sri Lankans, Filipinos, and Indians) earning household incomes higher than average American families, but with others (Bangladeshis, Hmong, Nepalese, and Burmese) earning significantly less.

Data from (1) Mapping Police Violence: "2017 Police Violence Report"; (2) Pew Research Center: "Views about Whether Whites Benefit from Societal Advantages Split Sharply along Racial and Partisan Lines," 9/28/2017; Pew Research Center: "How Blacks and Whites View the State of Race in America," 6/27/2016; (3) Pew Research Center: "On Views of Race and Inequality, Blacks and Whites Are Worlds Apart," 2/29/2018–5/8/2018; (4) Economic Policy Institute: "2016 ACS Shows

Stubbornly High Native American Poverty . . ."; U.S. Department of Commerce: "Income and Poverty in the United States 2016"; (5) Pew Research Center: "U.S. Muslims Concerned about Their Place in Society, but Continue to Believe in the American Dream," 1/23/2017–5/2/2017; (6) Pew Research Center: "The Partisan Divide on Political Values Grows Even Wider," 10/5/2017; Chicago Council on Global Affairs: "What Americans Think about America First," 2017; (7) American Community Survey 1-Year Estimates, 2015; Pew Research Center analysis of 2013–2015 American Community Survey.

MYTHS OF RACE long predate the American Revolution. White Europeans, when they arrived in North America, considered Native Americans to be primitive and inferior; one colonist described them as "ignorant of Civilitie, of Arts, of Religion; more brutish than the beasts they hunt; more wild and unmanly than the unmanned wild Countrey, which they range rather than inhabite; captivated also to Satans tyranny in foolish pieties, mad impieties, wicked idlenesse, busie and bloudy wickednesse." When the first Africans were brought to Jamestown in 1619, there was no legal distinction between black and white indentured servants; however, by the mid-seventeenth century, as the economy began to rely more heavily on forced labor, the laws began to change, and in 1705, Virginia lawmakers passed the first slave codes, clearly denoting the relative superiority of white servants over black slaves. According to these codes, intermarriage between blacks and whites was punishable by imprisonment; a slave who was found with a weapon of any kind was subject to twenty lashes; and a runaway slave could be killed by his master, who could then request reimbursement from the court for his loss.

With the Revolution, a more optimistic myth of race emerged. In 1782, a year before the Peace of Paris formally ended the Revolutionary War, J. Hector St. John de Crèvecoeur envisioned the young American republic as a crucible that would forge its disparate immigrant population into a vigorous new society with a grand future:

> What, then, is the American, this new man? He is neither an European, or the descendant of an European. . . . He is an American, who leaving behind him all his ancient prejudices and manners, receives new ones from the new mode of life he has embraced, the new government he obeys, and the new rank he holds. . . . Here individuals of all nations are melted into a new race of men, whose labours and posterity will one day cause great changes in the world.

Crèvecoeur's metaphor has remained a powerful ideal for many generations of American scholars, politicians, artists, and ordinary citizens. Ralph Waldo Emerson, writing in his journal in 1845, celebrated the national vitality produced by the mingling of immigrant cultures: "In this continent — asylum of all nations, — the energy of . . . all the European tribes, — of the Africans, and of the Polynesians — will construct a new race, a new religion, a new state, a new literature." An English Jewish writer named Israel Zangwill, himself an immigrant, popularized the myth in his 1908 drama, *The Melting Pot*. In the play, the hero rhapsodizes, "Yes East and West, and North and South, the palm and the pine, the pole and the equator, the crescent and the cross — how the great Alchemist melts and fuses them with his purging flame! Here shall they all unite to build the Republic of Man and the Kingdom of God." The myth was perhaps most vividly dramatized, though, in a pageant staged by Henry Ford in the early 1920s. Decked out in the costumes of their native lands, Ford's immigrant workers sang traditional songs from their homelands as they danced their way into an enormous replica of a cast-iron pot. They then emerged from the other side wearing identical "American" business suits, waving miniature American flags, and singing "The Star-Spangled Banner."

The drama of becoming an American has deep roots: immigrants take on new identities — and a new set of cultural myths — because they want to become members of the community, equal members with all the rights, responsibilities, and opportunities of their fellow citizens. The force of the melting pot myth lies in this implied promise that all Americans are indeed "created equal." However, the myth's promises of openness, harmony, unity, and equality were deceptive from the beginning. Crèvecoeur's exclusive concern with the mingling of *European* peoples (he lists the "English, Scotch, Irish, French, Dutch, Germans, and Swedes") utterly ignored the presence of some three-quarters of a million Africans and African Americans who then lived in the United States, as well as the indigenous people who had lived on the land for thousands of years before European contact. Crèvecoeur's vision of a country embracing "all nations" clearly applied only to northern European nations. Benjamin Franklin, in a 1751 essay, was more blunt: since Africa, Asia, and most of America were inhabited by dark-skinned people, he argued, the American colonies should consciously try to increase the white population and keep out the rest: "Why increase the Sons of Africa, by Planting them in America, where we have so fair an opportunity, by excluding Blacks and Tawneys, of increasing the lovely White?" If later writers like Emerson and Zangwill saw a more inclusive cultural mix as a source of hope and renewal for the United States, others throughout this country's history have, even more than Franklin, feared that mix as a threat.

Thomas Jefferson, in his *Notes on the State of Virginia* (1785), openly expressed his anxiety about freeing the slaves. Proposing that the new state of Virginia gradually phase out slavery, he recommended that the newly emancipated slaves be sent out of the state to form separate colonies, because allowing them to remain could lead to disastrous racial conflict:

> It will probably be asked, Why not retain and incorporate the blacks into the State, and thus save the expense of supplying by importation of white settlers, the vacancies they will leave? Deep-rooted prejudices entertained by the whites; ten thousand recollections, by the blacks, of the injuries they have sustained; new provocations; the real distinctions which nature has made; and many other circumstances, will divide us into parties, and produce convulsions, which will probably never end but in the extermination of the one or the other race.

Jefferson unambiguously asserted white racial superiority as he compared the "physical and moral" characteristics of whites and blacks: "Are not the fine mixtures of red and white, the expressions of every passion by greater or less suffusions of color in the one, preferable to that eternal monotony, which reigns in the countenances, that immovable veil of black which covers the emotions of the other race?" And, in one of the more shocking passages, Jefferson claimed that blacks themselves preferred white features "as uniformly as is the preference of the Oranootan[1] for the black woman over those of his own species. The circumstance of superior beauty, is thought worthy of attention in the propagation of our horses, dogs, and other domestic animals; why not in that of man?"

Considering African Americans' intellect and capacity for the arts, Jefferson found that aside from their musical talent, "in imagination they are dull, tasteless, and anomalous." The Indians, he says,

> will often carve figures on their pipes not destitute of design and merit. They will crayon out an animal, a plant, or a country, so as to prove the existence of a germ in their minds which only wants cultivation. They astonish you with strokes of the most sublime oratory; such as prove their reason and sentiment strong, their imagination glowing and elevated. But never yet could I find that a black had uttered a thought above the level of plain narration; never saw even an elementary trait of painting or sculpture. . . . Misery is often the parent of the most affecting touches in poetry. Among the blacks is misery enough, God knows, but no poetry.

Jefferson concluded that "this unfortunate difference of color, and perhaps of faculty, is a powerful obstacle to the emancipation of these people." Comparing the black slave to the white Roman slave, he disclosed that a primary reason he favored the removal of African Americans was to prevent black and white intermarriage: "Among the Romans emancipation required but one effort. The slave, when made free, might mix with, without staining the blood of his master. But with us a second is necessary, unknown to history. When freed, he is to be removed beyond the reach of mixture."

The myth of white supremacy is a powerful American fantasy — it is the negative counterpart of the melting pot ideal: instead of the equal and harmonious blending of cultures, it proposes a racial and ethnic hierarchy based on the "natural superiority" of Anglo-Americans. Under the sway of this myth, differences become signs of inferiority, and "inferiors" are treated as childlike or even subhuman. Jefferson was far from the last politician to advocate solving the nation's racial problems by removing African Americans from its boundaries. In 1862, the Great Emancipator himself, Abraham Lincoln, called a delegation of black leaders to the White House to enlist their support in establishing a colony for African Americans in Central America. Congress had appropriated money for this project, but it was abandoned after the governments of Honduras, Nicaragua, and Costa Rica protested the plan.

The myth of white superiority has given rise to some of the most shameful passages in our national life: slavery, segregation, and lynching; the near extermination of tribal peoples and cultures; the denial of citizenship and constitutional rights to African Americans, American Indians, Chinese, and Japanese immigrants; the brutal exploitation of Mexican and Asian laborers. The catalog

---

[1]**Oranootan:** Orangutan. [Eds.]

of injustices is long and painful. The melting pot ideal itself has often masked the myth of racial and ethnic superiority. "Inferiors" are expected to "melt" into conformity with Anglo-American behavior and values. Henry Ford's pageant conveys the message that ethnic identity is best left behind — exchanged for something "better," more uniform, less threatening.

This chapter explores how racial categories are defined and how they sometimes operate to divide us. These issues become crucial as the population of the United States grows increasingly diverse. The first half of the chapter focuses on the origins and lingering consequences of racism. It opens with an award-winning essay, Ta-Nehisi Coates's "The Case for Reparations," that raises profound questions about the treatment of African Americans throughout the nation's history. Coates charges that white supremacy has dominated the black experience and continues to inflict damage on the bodies and psyches of black people. He calls this shameful history a "crime [that] indicts the American people themselves, at every level, and in nearly every configuration" and suggests that reparations are in order. The selection "Theories and Constructs of Race," by Linda Holtzman and Leon Sharpe, provides an academic overview of racism and offers a number of useful terms and concepts for discussing racial issues. Next comes Sherman Alexie's amusing, provocative short story, "Gentrification," in which an unnamed narrator tackles the job of removing an unsightly, smelly, perhaps rat-infested mattress from his neighbor's property. "Nobody," Marc Lamont Hill's impassioned essay about the killing of Michael Brown in Ferguson, Missouri, examines the racial and class inequality that "expose life on the underside of American democracy."

The second half of the chapter offers a Visual Portfolio that gives individual faces to abstractions like race and racism. Here, you'll find images that challenge you to ponder the centrality of race in American culture and to consider what it means today in our divided country. The readings that follow the portfolio represent distinctive voices that address contemporary inequalities. In "Muslim Girl," Amani Al-Khatahtbeh discusses the development of her website, the rise of Islamophobia in the United States after 9/11, her encounters with anti-Muslim attitudes on Snapchat, and the "commercial exploitation" of modest fashion. Her eclectic subject matter and lively style reflect Al-Khatahtbeh's identity as a media-savvy millennial who is also a veiled Muslim woman. The final two selections deal with the complexities of immigration. "Passport to the New West," a chapter from José Orduña's memoir, provides a moving firsthand look at the overwhelming difficulties faced by migrants who cross the border illegally; it also presents a searing account of politics on the border. Finally, in "How Immigrants Become 'Other,'" Marcelo M. Suárez-Orozco and Carola Suárez-Orozco argue that our immigration system is broken, and explore the human costs to unauthorized immigrants — the poverty, fear, insecurity, families torn apart — that result from that brokenness.

Sources

"An act concerning Servants and Slaves." *Encyclopedia Virginia*. 1705 (transcription from the original). https://www.encyclopediavirginia.org/_An_act_concerning_Servants _and_Slaves_1705.

Franklin, John Hope. *Race and History: Selected Essays, 1938–1988*. Baton Rouge: Louisiana State University Press, 1989. 321–31. Print.

Gordon, Milton M. *Assimilation in American Life: The Role of Race, Religion, and National Origins*. New York: Oxford University Press, 1964. Print.

Harvey, Sean P. "Ideas of Race in Early America." *Oxford Research Encyclopedias: American History*, April 2016. http://americanhistory.oxfordre.com/view/10.1093/acrefore/9780199329175.001.0001/acrefore-9780199329175-e-262#acrefore-9780199329175-e-262-note-6.

Jefferson, Thomas. *Notes on the State of Virginia*. 1785. Print.

Njeri, Itabari. "Beyond the Melting Pot." *Los Angeles Times* 13 Jan. 1991: E1+. Print.

Pitt, Leonard. *We Americans*. 3rd ed. Vol. 2. Dubuque: Kendall/Hunt, 1987. Print.

Stevenson, Bryan. "A Presumption of Guilt: The Legacy of America's History of Racial Injustice." In *Policing the Black Man*, ed. Angela J. Davis. New York: Pantheon, 2017. 3–30.

Takaki, Ronald. "Reflections on Racial Patterns in America." In *From Different Shores: Perspectives on Race and Ethnicity in America*. Ed. Ronald Takaki. New York: Oxford University Press, 1987. 26–37. Print.

BEFORE READING

- Survey images in the popular media (newspapers, magazines, online sources, TV shows, movies, and pop music) for evidence of racial harmony or conflict. How well or poorly do these images reflect your experience of interactions with other ethnic and racial groups? Explore these questions in a journal entry, and then discuss in class.

- Investigate the language used to describe racial and ethnic group relations or interactions between members of different groups on your campus and in your community. Consult local news sources and campus publications, and keep your ears open for conversations that touch on these issues. What metaphors, euphemisms, and clichés are used to discuss group interactions? Do some freewriting about what you discover and compare notes with classmates.

- The photo on page 597 was taken at the Water Protectors' encampment at the Standing Rock Sioux Reservation on the Missouri River in North Dakota. Hundreds of tribes from all over the country joined the Sioux to stop the Dakota Access Pipeline (DAPL) from crossing land they consider sacred and to prevent it from traveling under the river that provides the tribe's water. The protest began in early spring 2016 and at its height involved thousands; it lasted until February 2017, when law enforcement moved in to destroy the camp. To learn more about the protest, watch this eight-minute YouTube video:

    https://www.youtube.com/watch?v=4FDuqYld8C8

    What's the overall effect of this photo? How does it combine traditional tribal and contemporary American elements, and what do these details suggest about the protesters? What's the significance of the upside-down flag, and what do you think it means in this context? How do you interpret the central figures of the young man and his horse, and what visual details support your reading of the image? Share responses with your classmates.

6

THE CASE FOR REPARATIONS

TA-NEHISI COATES

Between 1951 and 1998, the government of West Germany paid the state of Israel and survivors of the Nazi Holocaust more than 102 billion marks — or about 62 billion in 1998 U.S. dollars — in reparation for crimes committed against the Jewish people during World War II. In 2013, the Federal Republic of Germany provided the equivalent of an additional $1 billion to care for the 56,000 remaining Holocaust survivors. Similarly, in 1988, the U.S. Congress issued a formal apology to Japanese Americans who had been detained in internment camps between 1943 and 1945 and passed legislation providing a payment of $20,000 for each internee. Eventually, nearly $2 billion was allocated to acknowledge the suffering of Japanese Americans. Why, then, hasn't a single dollar ever been given to compensate the black victims of white supremacy in the United States? Initially, Ta-Nehisi Coates (b. 1975) opposed reparations for black Americans, saying that "Blame is useless to me. Blame is for the dead."[1]

Then, as he did more research and engaged with scholars of black history, he gradually began to change his mind: "[W]e should never forget that this world was 'made.' Whiteness and blackness are not a fact of providence, but of policy — of slave codes, black codes, Jim Crow, redlining, GI Bills, housing covenants, New Deals, and mass incarcerations. I did not understand it at the time, but this way of thinking pushed me toward reparations."[2] Several years of reading and study led Coates to believe that a monstrous crime — 250 years in the making — has been committed against black people in America and that a logical response is to seek reparations. When *The Atlantic* published "The Case for Reparations" as its cover story in June 2014, the article generated more web traffic in a single day than any story in the history of the magazine; it won the 2014 George Polk Award for Commentary as well as the Harriet Beecher Stowe Center Prize for Writing to Advance Social Justice. As a senior editor and blogger for *The Atlantic*, Coates has written extensively about race, including his 2012 cover story, "Fear of a Black President." His first book, *The Beautiful Struggle: A Memoir* (2008), is about growing up in a tough West Baltimore neighborhood; his

---

[1] "Inverse Nationalism." *The Atlantic*, April 26, 2010.
[2] "How Racism Invented Race in America." *The Atlantic*, June 23, 2014.

second, *Between the World and Me* (2015), is a meditation on racism and American history addressed to his fifteen-year-old son. *We Were Eight Years in Power* (2017) collects a number of his essays from *The Atlantic,* including "The Case for Reparations."

> And if thy brother, a Hebrew man, or a Hebrew woman, be sold unto thee, and serve thee six years; then in the seventh year thou shalt let him go free from thee. And when thou sendest him out free from thee, thou shalt not let him go away empty: thou shalt furnish him liberally out of thy flock, and out of thy floor, and out of thy winepress: of that wherewith the LORD thy God hath blessed thee thou shalt give unto him. And thou shalt remember that thou wast a bondman in the land of Egypt, and the LORD thy God redeemed thee: therefore I command thee this thing today.
>
> —DEUTERONOMY 15: 12–15

> Besides the crime which consists in violating the law, and varying from the right rule of reason, whereby a man so far becomes degenerate, and declares himself to quit the principles of human nature, and to be a noxious creature, there is commonly injury done to some person or other, and some other man receives damage by his transgression: in which case he who hath received any damage, has, besides the right of punishment common to him with other men, a particular right to seek reparation.
>
> —JOHN LOCKE, "SECOND TREATISE"

> By our unpaid labor and suffering, we have earned the right to the soil, many times over and over, and now we are determined to have it.
>
> —ANONYMOUS, 1861

I. "So That's Just One of My Losses"

Clyde Ross was born in 1923, the seventh of 13 children, near Clarksdale, Mississippi, the home of the blues. Ross's parents owned and farmed a 40-acre tract of land, flush with cows, hogs, and mules. Ross's mother would drive to Clarksdale to do her shopping in a horse and buggy, in which she invested all the pride one might place in a Cadillac. The family owned another horse, with a red coat, which they gave to Clyde. The Ross family wanted for little, save that which all black families in the Deep South then desperately desired—the protection of the law.

In the 1920s, Jim Crow[3] Mississippi was, in all facets of society, a kleptocracy.[4] The majority of the people in the state were perpetually robbed of the vote — a hijacking engineered through the trickery of the poll tax[5] and the muscle of the lynch mob. Between 1882 and 1968, more black people were lynched in Mississippi than in any other state. "You and I know what's the best way to keep the nigger from voting," blustered Theodore Bilbo, a Mississippi senator and a proud Klansman. "You do it the night before the election."

The state's regime partnered robbery of the franchise with robbery of the purse. Many of Mississippi's black farmers lived in debt peonage, under the sway of cotton kings who were at once their landlords, their employers, and their primary merchants. Tools and necessities were advanced against the return on the crop, which was determined by the employer. When farmers were deemed to be in debt — and they often were — the negative balance was then carried over to the next season. A man or woman who protested this arrangement did so at the risk of grave injury or death. Refusing to work meant arrest under vagrancy laws and forced labor under the state's penal system.

Well into the twentieth century, black people spoke of their flight from Mississippi in much the same manner as their runagate ancestors had. In her 2010 book, *The Warmth of Other Suns*, Isabel Wilkerson tells the story of Eddie Earvin, a spinach picker who fled Mississippi in 1963, after being made to work at gunpoint. "You didn't talk about it or tell nobody," Earvin said. "You had to sneak away."

When Clyde Ross was still a child, Mississippi authorities claimed his father owed $3,000 in back taxes. The elder Ross could not read. He did not have a lawyer. He did not know anyone at the local courthouse. He could not expect the police to be impartial. Effectively, the Ross family had no way to contest the claim and no protection under the law. The authorities seized the land. They seized the buggy. They took the cows, hogs, and mules. And so for the upkeep of separate but equal, the entire Ross family was reduced to sharecropping.

This was hardly unusual. In 2001, the Associated Press published a three-part investigation into the theft of black-owned land stretching back to the antebellum period. The series documented some 406 victims and 24,000 acres of land valued at tens of millions of dollars. The land was taken through means ranging from legal chicanery to terrorism. "Some of the land taken from black families has become a country club in Virginia," the AP reported, as well as "oil fields in Mississippi" and "a baseball spring training facility in Florida."

Clyde Ross was a smart child. His teacher thought he should attend a more challenging school. There was very little support for educating

---

[3]**Jim Crow:** Collective term for southern segregation laws. [All notes are the editors'.]
[4]**kleptocracy:** A government ruled by thieves.
[5]**poll tax:** A tax paid to register to vote. Following passage of the Fifteenth Amendment, which gave blacks voting rights, poll taxes were imposed in many states, effectively denying the vote to blacks, Native Americans, and poor people.

black people in Mississippi. But Julius Rosenwald, a part owner of Sears, Roebuck, had begun an ambitious effort to build schools for black children throughout the South. Ross's teacher believed he should attend the local Rosenwald school. It was too far for Ross to walk and get back in time to work in the fields. Local white children had a school bus. Clyde Ross did not, and thus lost the chance to better his education.

Then, when Ross was 10 years old, a group of white men demanded his only childhood possession—the horse with the red coat. "You can't have this horse. We want it," one of the white men said. They gave Ross's father $17.

"I did everything for that horse," Ross told me. "Everything. And they took him. Put him on the racetrack. I never did know what happened to him after that, but I know they didn't bring him back. So that's just one of my losses."

The losses mounted. As sharecroppers, the Ross family saw their wages treated as the landlord's slush fund.[6] Landowners were supposed to split the profits from the cotton fields with sharecroppers. But bales would often disappear during the count, or the split might be altered on a whim. If cotton was selling for 50 cents a pound, the Ross family might get 15 cents, or only five. One year Ross's mother promised to buy him a $7 suit for a summer program at their church. She ordered the suit by mail. But that year Ross's family was paid only five cents a pound for cotton. The mailman arrived with the suit. The Rosses could not pay. The suit was sent back. Clyde Ross did not go to the church program.

It was in these early years that Ross began to understand himself as an American—he did not live under the blind decree of justice, but under the heel of a regime that elevated armed robbery to a governing principle. He thought about fighting. "Just be quiet," his father told him. "Because they'll come and kill us all."

Clyde Ross grew. He was drafted into the Army. The draft officials offered him an exemption if he stayed home and worked. He preferred to take his chances with war. He was stationed in California. He found that he could go into stores without being bothered. He could walk the streets without being harassed. He could go into a restaurant and receive service.

Ross was shipped off to Guam. He fought in World War II to save the world from tyranny. But when he returned to Clarksdale, he found that tyranny had followed him home. This was 1947, eight years before Mississippi lynched Emmett Till and tossed his broken body into the Tallahatchie River. The Great Migration, a mass exodus of 6 million African Americans that spanned most of the 20th century, was now in its second wave. The black pilgrims did not journey north simply seeking better wages and work, or bright lights and big adventures. They were fleeing the acquisitive warlords of the South. They were seeking the protection of the law.

[6]**slush fund:** A secret stash of money used for illegal or dishonest purposes.

Clyde Ross was among them. He came to Chicago in 1947 and took a job as a taster at Campbell's Soup. He made a stable wage. He married. He had children. His paycheck was his own. No Klansmen stripped him of the vote. When he walked down the street, he did not have to move because a white man was walking past. He did not have to take off his hat or avert his gaze. His journey from peonage to full citizenship seemed near-complete. Only one item was missing—a home, that final badge of entry into the sacred order of the American middle class of the Eisenhower years.

In 1961, Ross and his wife bought a house in North Lawndale, a 15 bustling community on Chicago's West Side. North Lawndale had long been a predominantly Jewish neighborhood, but a handful of middle-class African Americans had lived there starting in the '40s. The community was anchored by the sprawling Sears, Roebuck headquarters. North Lawndale's Jewish People's Institute actively encouraged blacks to move into the neighborhood, seeking to make it a "pilot community for interracial living." In the battle for integration then being fought around the country, North Lawndale seemed to offer promising terrain. But out in the tall grass, highwaymen, nefarious as any Clarksdale kleptocrat, were lying in wait.

Three months after Clyde Ross moved into his house, the boiler blew out. This would normally be a homeowner's responsibility, but in fact, Ross was not really a homeowner. His payments were made to the seller, not the bank. And Ross had not signed a normal mortgage. He'd bought "on contract": a predatory agreement that combined all the responsibilities of homeownership with all the disadvantages of renting—while offering the benefits of neither. Ross had bought his house for $27,500. The seller, not the previous homeowner but a new kind of middleman, had bought it for only $12,000 six months before selling it to Ross. In a contract sale, the seller kept the deed until the contract was paid in full—and, unlike with a normal mortgage, Ross would acquire no equity in the meantime. If he missed a single payment, he would immediately forfeit his $1,000 down payment, all his monthly payments, and the property itself.

The men who peddled contracts in North Lawndale would sell homes at inflated prices and then evict families who could not pay— taking their down payment and their monthly installments as profit. Then they'd bring in another black family, rinse, and repeat. "He loads them up with payments they can't meet," an office secretary told *The Chicago Daily News* of her boss, the speculator Lou Fushanis, in 1963. "Then he takes the property away from them. He's sold some of the buildings three or four times."

Ross had tried to get a legitimate mortgage in another neighborhood, but was told by a loan officer that there was no financing available. The truth was that there was no financing for people like Clyde Ross. From the 1930s through the 1960s, black people across the country were largely cut out of the legitimate home-mortgage market through means both legal and extralegal. Chicago whites employed every measure, from "restrictive covenants"[7] to bombings, to keep their neighborhoods segregated. . . .

Their efforts were buttressed by the federal government. In 1934, Congress created the Federal Housing Administration. The FHA insured private mortgages, causing a drop in interest rates and a decline in the size of the down payment required to buy a house. But an insured mortgage was not a possibility for Clyde Ross. The FHA had adopted a system of maps that rated neighborhoods according to their perceived stability. On the maps, green areas, rated "A," indicated "in demand" neighborhoods that, as one appraiser put it, lacked "a single foreigner or Negro." These neighborhoods were considered excellent prospects for insurance. Neighborhoods where black people lived were rated "D" and were usually considered ineligible for FHA backing. They were colored in red. Neither the percentage of black people living there nor their social class mattered. Black people were viewed as a contagion. Redlining went beyond FHA-backed loans and spread to the entire mortgage industry, which was already rife with racism, excluding black people from most legitimate means of obtaining a mortgage.

"A government offering such bounty to builders and lenders could 20 have required compliance with a nondiscrimination policy," Charles Abrams, the urban-studies expert who helped create the New York City Housing Authority, wrote in 1955. "Instead, the FHA adopted a racial policy that could well have been culled from the Nuremberg laws."[8]

The devastating effects are cogently outlined by Melvin L. Oliver and Thomas M. Shapiro in their 1995 book, *Black Wealth/White Wealth*:

> Locked out of the greatest mass-based opportunity for wealth accumulation in American history, African Americans who desired and were able to afford home ownership found themselves consigned to central-city communities where their investments were affected by the "self-fulfilling prophecies" of the FHA appraisers: cut off from sources of new investment[,] their homes and communities deteriorated and lost value in comparison to those homes and communities that FHA appraisers deemed desirable.

In Chicago and across the country, whites looking to achieve the American dream could rely on a legitimate credit system backed by the government. Blacks were herded into the sights of unscrupulous lenders who took them for money and for sport. "It was like people who like to go out and shoot lions in Africa. It was the same thrill," a housing attorney told the historian Beryl Satter in her 2009 book, *Family Properties*. "The thrill of the chase and the kill."

---

[7]**restrictive covenants:** Legally enforceable real estate contracts that prevented a particular group of people (like African Americans or Jews) from buying or occupying the property.

[8]**Nuremberg laws:** In 1935, the Nazi Party passed a series of laws that deprived German Jews of their rights as citizens. These laws represented the first step toward the wholesale murder of Jews and other "undesirables."

The kill was profitable. At the time of his death, Lou Fushanis owned more than 600 properties, many of them in North Lawndale, and his estate was estimated to be worth $3 million. He'd made much of this money by exploiting the frustrated hopes of black migrants like Clyde Ross. During this period, according to one estimate, 85 percent of all black home buyers who bought in Chicago bought on contract. "If anybody who is well established in this business in Chicago doesn't earn $100,000 a year," a contract seller told *The Saturday Evening Post* in 1962, "he is loafing."

Contract sellers became rich. North Lawndale became a ghetto.

Clyde Ross still lives there. He still owns his home. He is 91, and the   25
emblems of survival are all around him—awards for service in his community, pictures of his children in cap and gown. But when I asked him about his home in North Lawndale, I heard only anarchy.

"We were ashamed. We did not want anyone to know that we were that ignorant," Ross told me. He was sitting at his dining-room table. His glasses were as thick as his Clarksdale drawl. "I'd come out of Mississippi where there was one mess, and come up here and got in another mess. So how dumb am I? I didn't want anyone to know how dumb I was.

"When I found myself caught up in it, I said, 'How? I just left this mess. I just left no laws. And no regard. And then I come here and get cheated wide open.' I would probably want to do some harm to some people, you know, if I had been violent like some of us. I thought, 'Man, I got caught up in this stuff. I can't even take care of my kids.' I didn't have enough for my kids. You could fall through the cracks easy fighting these white people. And no law."

But fight Clyde Ross did. In 1968 he joined the newly formed Contract Buyers League—a collection of black homeowners on Chicago's South and West Sides, all of whom had been locked into the same system of predation. There was Howell Collins, whose contract called for him to pay $25,500 for a house that a speculator had bought for $14,500. There was Ruth Wells, who'd managed to pay out half her contract, expecting a mortgage, only to suddenly see an insurance bill materialize out of thin air—a requirement the seller had added without Wells's knowledge. Contract sellers used every tool at their disposal to pilfer from their clients. They scared white residents into selling low. They lied about properties' compliance with building codes, then left the buyer responsible when city inspectors arrived. They presented themselves as real-estate brokers, when in fact they were the owners. They guided their clients to lawyers who were in on the scheme.

The Contract Buyers League fought back. Members—who would eventually number more than 500—went out to the posh suburbs where the speculators lived and embarrassed them by knocking on their neighbors' doors and informing them of the details of the contract-lending trade. They refused to pay their installments, instead holding monthly payments in an escrow account. Then they brought a suit against the contract sellers, accusing them of buying properties and reselling in such a manner "to reap from members of the Negro race large and unjust profits."

In return for the "deprivations of their rights and privileges under the Thirteenth and Fourteenth Amendments," the league demanded "prayers for relief"—payback of all moneys paid on contracts and all moneys paid for structural improvement of properties, at 6 percent interest minus a "fair, non-discriminatory" rental price for time of occupation. Moreover, the league asked the court to adjudge that the defendants had "acted willfully and maliciously and that malice is the gist of this action."

Ross and the Contract Buyers League were no longer appealing to the government simply for equality. They were no longer fleeing in hopes of a better deal elsewhere. They were charging society with a crime against their community. They wanted the crime publicly ruled as such. They wanted the crime's executors declared to be offensive to society. And they wanted restitution for the great injury brought upon them by said offenders. In 1968 Clyde Ross and the Contract Buyers League were no longer simply seeking the protection of the law. They were seeking reparations.

II. "A Difference of Kind, Not Degree"

According to the most-recent statistics, North Lawndale is now on the wrong end of virtually every socioeconomic indicator. In 1930 its population was 112,000. Today it is 36,000. The halcyon talk of "interracial living" is dead. The neighborhood is 92 percent black. Its homicide rate is 45 per 100,000—triple the rate of the city as a whole. The infant-mortality rate is 14 per 1,000—more than twice the national average. Forty-three percent of the people in North Lawndale live below the poverty line—double Chicago's overall rate. Forty-five percent of all households are on food stamps—nearly three times the rate of the city at large. Sears, Roebuck left the neighborhood in 1987, taking 1,800 jobs with it. Kids in North Lawndale need not be confused about their prospects: Cook County's Juvenile Temporary Detention Center sits directly adjacent to the neighborhood.

North Lawndale is an extreme portrait of the trends that ail black Chicago. Such is the magnitude of these ailments that it can be said that blacks and whites do not inhabit the same city. The average per capita income of Chicago's white neighborhoods is almost three times that of its black neighborhoods. When the Harvard sociologist Robert J. Sampson examined incarceration rates in Chicago in his 2012 book, *Great American City*, he found that a black neighborhood with one of the highest incarceration rates (West Garfield Park) had a rate more than 40 times as high as the white neighborhood with the highest rate (Clearing). "This is a staggering differential, even for community-level comparisons," Sampson writes. "A difference of kind, not degree."

In other words, Chicago's impoverished black neighborhoods—characterized by high unemployment and households headed by single parents—are not simply poor; they are "ecologically distinct." This "is not simply the same thing as low economic status," writes Sampson. "In this pattern Chicago is not alone."

The lives of black Americans are better than they were half a century ago. The humiliation of WHITES ONLY signs [is] gone. Rates of black poverty have decreased. Black teen-pregnancy rates are at record lows—and the gap between black and white teen-pregnancy rates has shrunk significantly. But such progress rests on a shaky foundation, and fault lines are everywhere. The income gap between black and white households is roughly the same today as it was in 1970. Patrick Sharkey, a sociologist at New York University, studied children born from 1955 through 1970 and found that 4 percent of whites and 62 percent of blacks across America had been raised in poor neighborhoods. A generation later, the same study showed, virtually nothing had changed. And whereas whites born into affluent neighborhoods tended to remain in affluent neighborhoods, blacks tended to fall out of them.

This is not surprising. Black families, regardless of income, are significantly less wealthy than white families. The Pew Research Center estimates that white households are worth roughly 20 times as much as black households, and that whereas only 15 percent of whites have zero or negative wealth, more than a third of blacks do. Effectively, the black family in America is working without a safety net. When financial calamity strikes—a medical emergency, divorce, job loss—the fall is precipitous.

And just as black families of all incomes remain handicapped by a lack of wealth, so too do they remain handicapped by their restricted choice of neighborhood. Black people with upper-middle-class incomes do not generally live in upper-middle-class neighborhoods. Sharkey's research shows that black families making $100,000 typically live in the kinds of neighborhoods inhabited by white families making $30,000. "Blacks and whites inhabit such different neighborhoods," Sharkey writes, "that it is not possible to compare the economic outcomes of black and white children."

The implications are chilling. As a rule, poor black people do not work their way out of the ghetto—and those who do often face the horror of watching their children and grandchildren tumble back.

Even seeming evidence of progress withers under harsh light. In 2012 the Manhattan Institute cheerily noted that segregation had declined since the 1960s. And yet African Americans still remained—by far—the most segregated ethnic group in the country.

With segregation, with the isolation of the injured and the robbed, comes the concentration of disadvantage. An unsegregated America might see poverty, and all its effects, spread across the country with no particular bias toward skin color. Instead, the concentration of poverty has been paired with a concentration of melanin. The resulting conflagration has been devastating.

One thread of thinking in the African American community holds that these depressing numbers partially stem from cultural pathologies that can be altered through individual grit and exceptionally good behavior. (In 2011, Philadelphia Mayor Michael Nutter, responding to violence among young black males, put the blame on the family: "Too many men making too many babies they don't want to take care of, and then we end up dealing with your children." Nutter turned to those presumably fatherless babies: "Pull your pants up and buy a belt, because no one wants to see your underwear or the crack of your butt.") The thread is as old as black politics itself. It is also wrong. The kind of trenchant racism to which black people have persistently been subjected can never be defeated by making its victims more respectable. The essence of American racism is disrespect. And in the wake of the grim numbers, we see the grim inheritance.

The Contract Buyers League's suit brought by Clyde Ross and his allies took direct aim at this inheritance. The suit was rooted in Chicago's long history of segregation, which had created two housing markets — one legitimate and backed by the government, the other lawless and patrolled by predators. The suit dragged on until 1976, when the league lost a jury trial.

Securing the equal protection of the law proved hard; securing reparations proved impossible. If there were any doubts about the mood of the jury, the foreman removed them by saying, when asked about the verdict, that he hoped it would help end "the mess Earl Warren made with *Brown v. Board of Education* and all that nonsense."

III. "We Inherit Our Ample Patrimony"

In 1783, the freedwoman Belinda Royall petitioned the commonwealth of Massachusetts for reparations. Belinda had been born in modern-day Ghana. She was kidnapped as a child and sold into slavery. She endured the Middle Passage[9] and 50 years of enslavement at the hands of Isaac Royall[10] and his son. But the junior Royall, a British loyalist, fled the country during the Revolution. Belinda, now free after half a century of labor, beseeched the nascent Massachusetts legislature:

> The face of your Petitioner, is now marked with the furrows of time,
> and her frame bending under the oppression of years, while she,
> by the Laws of the Land, is denied the employment of one morsel
> of that immense wealth, apart whereof hath been accumulated by
> her own industry, and the whole augmented by her servitude.

---

[9]**Middle Passage:** The middle leg of a triangular trade route beginning and ending in Europe. Ships would leave European ports with items — such as iron, guns, and liquor — that could be traded in Africa for slaves, who would then be taken to the Americas and exchanged for sugar or cotton, which was then shipped back to Europe. Conditions on these ships were horrific: between 10 and 25 percent of the human "cargo" died en route.

[10]**Isaac Royall:** Slaves were often given the last names of their masters.

WHEREFORE, casting herself at your feet if your honours, as to a body of men, formed for the extirpation of vassalage, for the reward of Virtue, and the just return of honest industry — she prays, that such allowance may be made her out of the Estate of Colonel Royall, as will prevent her, and her more infirm daughter, from misery in the greatest extreme, and scatter comfort over the short and downward path of their lives.

Belinda Royall was granted a pension of 15 pounds and 12 shillings, 45 to be paid out of the estate of Isaac Royall — one of the earliest successful attempts to petition for reparations. At the time, black people in America had endured more than 150 years of enslavement, and the idea that they might be owed something in return was, if not the national consensus, at least not outrageous.

"A heavy account lies against us as a civil society for oppressions committed against people who did not injure us," wrote the Quaker John Woolman in 1769, "and that if the particular case of many individuals were fairly stated, it would appear that there was considerable due to them."

As the historian Roy E. Finkenbine has documented, at the dawn of this country, black reparations were actively considered and often effected. Quakers in New York, New England, and Baltimore went so far as to make "membership contingent upon compensating one's former slaves." In 1782, the Quaker Robert Pleasants emancipated his 78 slaves, granted them 350 acres, and later built a school on their property and provided for their education. "The doing of this justice to the injured Africans," wrote Pleasants, "would be an acceptable offering to him who 'Rules in the kingdom of men.'"

Edward Coles, a protégé of Thomas Jefferson who became a slaveholder through inheritance, took many of his slaves north and granted them a plot of land in Illinois. John Randolph, a cousin of Jefferson's, willed that all his slaves be emancipated upon his death, and that all those older than 40 be given 10 acres of land. "I give and bequeath to all my slaves their freedom," Randolph wrote, "heartily regretting that I have been the owner of one."

In his book *Forever Free*, Eric Foner recounts the story of a disgruntled planter reprimanding a freedman loafing on the job:

Planter: "You lazy nigger, I am losing a whole day's labor by you."
Freedman: "Massa, how many days' labor have I lost by you?"

In the 20th century, the cause of reparations was taken up by a 50 diverse cast that included the Confederate veteran Walter R. Vaughan, who believed that reparations would be a stimulus for the South; the black activist Callie House; black-nationalist leaders like "Queen Mother" Audley Moore; and the civil-rights activist James Forman. The movement coalesced in 1987 under an umbrella organization called the National Coalition of Blacks for Reparations in America (N'COBRA). The NAACP endorsed reparations in 1993. Charles J. Ogletree Jr., a professor at Harvard Law School, has pursued reparations claims in court.

But while the people advocating reparations have changed over time, the response from the country has remained virtually the same. "They have been taught to labor," the *Chicago Tribune* editorialized in 1891. "They have been taught Christian civilization, and to speak the noble English language instead of some African gibberish. The account is square with the ex-slaves."

Not exactly. Having been enslaved for 250 years, black people were not left to their own devices. They were terrorized. In the Deep South, a second slavery ruled. In the North, legislatures, mayors, civic associations, banks, and citizens all colluded to pin black people into ghettos, where they were overcrowded, overcharged, and undereducated. Businesses discriminated against them, awarding them the worst jobs and the worst wages. Police brutalized them in the streets. And the notion that black lives, black bodies, and black wealth were rightful targets remained deeply rooted in the broader society. Now we have half-stepped away from our long centuries of despoilment, promising, "Never again." But still we are haunted. It is as though we have run up a credit-card bill and, having pledged to charge no more, remain befuddled that the balance does not disappear. The effects of that balance, interest accruing daily, are all around us.

Broach the topic of reparations today and a barrage of questions inevitably follows: Who will be paid? How much will they be paid? Who will pay? But if the practicalities, not the justice, of reparations are the true sticking point, there has for some time been the beginnings of a solution. For the past 25 years, Congressman John Conyers Jr., who represents the Detroit area, has marked every session of Congress by introducing a bill calling for a congressional study of slavery and its lingering effects as well as recommendations for "appropriate remedies."

A country curious about how reparations might actually work has an easy solution in Conyers's bill, now called HR 40, the Commission to Study Reparation Proposals for African Americans Act. We would support this bill, submit the question to study, and then assess the possible solutions. But we are not interested.

"It's because it's black folks making the claim," Nkechi Taifa, who helped found N'COBRA, says. "People who talk about reparations are considered left lunatics. But all we are talking about is studying [reparations]. As John Conyers has said, we study everything. We study the water, the air. We can't even study the issue? This bill does not authorize one red cent to anyone." 55

That HR 40 has never—under either Democrats or Republicans— made it to the House floor suggests our concerns are rooted not in the impracticality of reparations but in something more existential. If we conclude that the conditions in North Lawndale and black America are not inexplicable but are instead precisely what you'd expect of a community that for centuries has lived in America's crosshairs, then what are we to make of the world's oldest democracy?

One cannot escape the question by hand-waving at the past, disavowing the acts of one's ancestors, nor by citing a recent date of ancestral immigration. The last slaveholder has been dead for a very long time. The last soldier to endure Valley Forge has been dead much longer. To proudly claim the veteran and disown the slaveholder is patriotism à la carte. A nation outlives its generations. We were not there when Washington crossed the Delaware, but Emanuel Gottlieb Leutze's[11] rendering has meaning to us. We were not there when Woodrow Wilson took us into World War I, but we are still paying out the pensions. If Thomas Jefferson's genius matters, then so does his taking of Sally Hemings's[12] body. If George Washington crossing the Delaware matters, so must his ruthless pursuit of the runagate Oney Judge.[13]

In 1909, President William Howard Taft told the country that "intelligent" white southerners were ready to see blacks as "useful members of the community." A week later Joseph Gordon, a black man, was lynched outside Greenwood, Mississippi. The high point of the lynching era has passed. But the memories of those robbed of their lives still live on in the lingering effects. Indeed, in America there is a strange and powerful belief that if you stab a black person 10 times, the bleeding stops and the healing begins the moment the assailant drops the knife. We believe white dominance to be a fact of the inert past, a delinquent debt that can be made to disappear if only we don't look.

There has always been another way. "It is in vain to alledge, that *our ancestors* brought them hither, and not we," Yale President Timothy Dwight said in 1810.

> We inherit our ample patrimony with all its incumbrances; and are bound to pay the debts of our ancestors. *This* debt, particularly, we are bound to discharge: and, when the righteous Judge of the Universe comes to reckon with his servants, he will rigidly exact the payment at our hands. To give them liberty, and stop here, is to entail upon them a curse.

IV. "The Ills That Slavery Frees Us From"

America begins in black plunder and white democracy, two features 60 that are not contradictory but complementary. "The men who came together to found the independent United States, dedicated to freedom and equality, either held slaves or were willing to join hands with those who did," the historian Edmund S. Morgan wrote. "None of them felt entirely comfortable about the fact, but neither did they feel responsible

---

[11]**Emanuel Gottlieb Leutze:** German-born historical and landscape painter (1816–1868), best known for his monumental *Washington Crossing the Delaware*, 1851.

[12]**Sally Hemings:** A Jefferson family slave (1773–1835), who is rumored to have borne six children to Thomas Jefferson; DNA and other evidence suggests that Jefferson was the likely father.

[13]**Oney Judge:** A slave of Martha Custis Washington, Judge (1773–1848) escaped in 1796 and fled to New Hampshire, where she met and married a free black man. George Washington made several failed attempts to return Judge to his wife. She remained a fugitive for the rest of her life, and her children, though born in New Hampshire to a free father, were legally considered "property" of the Custis estate.

for it. Most of them had inherited both their slaves and their attachment to freedom from an earlier generation, and they knew the two were not unconnected."

When enslaved Africans, plundered of their bodies, plundered of their families, and plundered of their labor, were brought to the colony of Virginia in 1619, they did not initially endure the naked racism that would engulf their progeny. Some of them were freed. Some of them intermarried. Still others escaped with the white indentured servants who had suffered as they had. Some even rebelled together, allying under Nathaniel Bacon[14] to torch Jamestown in 1676.

One hundred years later, the idea of slaves and poor whites joining forces would shock the senses, but in the early days of the English colonies, the two groups had much in common. English visitors to Virginia found that its masters "abuse their servantes with intollerable oppression and hard usage." White servants were flogged, tricked into serving beyond their contracts, and traded in much the same manner as slaves.

This "hard usage" originated in a simple fact of the New World — land was boundless but cheap labor was limited. As life spans increased in the colony, the Virginia planters found in the enslaved Africans an even more efficient source of cheap labor. Whereas indentured servants were still legal subjects of the English crown and thus entitled to certain protections, African slaves entered the colonies as aliens. Exempted from the protections of the crown, they became early America's indispensable working class — fit for maximum exploitation, capable of only minimal resistance.

For the next 250 years, American law worked to reduce black people to a class of untouchables and raise all white men to the level of citizens. In 1650, Virginia mandated that "all persons except Negroes" were to carry arms. In 1664, Maryland mandated that any English-woman who married a slave must live as a slave of her husband's master. In 1705, the Virginia assembly passed a law allowing for the dismemberment of unruly slaves — but forbidding masters from whipping "a Christian white servant naked, without an order from a justice of the peace." In that same law, the colony mandated that "all horses, cattle, and hogs, now belonging, or that hereafter shall belong to any slave" be seized and sold off by the local church, the profits used to support "the poor of the said parish." At that time, there would have still been people alive who could remember blacks and whites joining to burn down Jamestown only 29 years before. But at the beginning of the 18th century, two primary classes were enshrined in America.

---

[14]**Nathaniel Bacon:** Bacon (1647–1676), a Virginia planter, led an armed rebellion against Governor William Berkeley; he was particularly angry at Berkeley's perceived failure to protect white settlements against Indian raids. Bacon, promising freedom to slaves and indentured servants who would join his cause, attracted a large following. In 1676, Bacon and his men captured Jamestown and burned it to the ground. Shortly thereafter, Bacon died of dysentery and the rebellion collapsed.

"The two great divisions of society are not the rich and poor, but white and black," John C. Calhoun, South Carolina's senior senator, declared on the Senate floor in 1848. "And all the former, the poor as well as the rich, belong to the upper class, and are respected and treated as equals." ⁶⁵

In 1860, the majority of people living in South Carolina and Mississippi, almost half of those living in Georgia, and about one-third of all Southerners were on the wrong side of Calhoun's line. The state with the largest number of enslaved Americans was Virginia, where in certain counties some 70 percent of all people labored in chains. Nearly one-fourth of all white Southerners owned slaves, and upon their backs the economic basis of America — and much of the Atlantic world — was erected. In the seven cotton states, one-third of all white income was derived from slavery. By 1840, cotton produced by slave labor constituted 59 percent of the country's exports. The web of this slave society extended north to the looms of New England, and across the Atlantic to Great Britain, where it powered a great economic transformation and altered the trajectory of world history, "Whoever says Industrial Revolution," wrote the historian Eric J. Hobsbawm, "says cotton."

The wealth accorded America by slavery was not just in what the slaves pulled from the land but in the slaves themselves. "In 1860, slaves as an asset were worth more than all of America's manufacturing, all of the railroads, all of the productive capacity of the United States put together," the Yale historian David W. Blight has noted. "Slaves were the single largest, by far, financial asset of property in the entire American economy." The sale of these slaves — "in whose bodies that money congealed," writes Walter Johnson, a Harvard historian — generated even more ancillary wealth. Loans were taken out for purchase, to be repaid with interest. Insurance policies were drafted against the untimely death of a slave and the loss of potential profits. Slave sales were taxed and notarized. The vending of the black body and the sundering of the black family became an economy unto themselves, estimated to have brought in tens of millions of dollars to antebellum America. In 1860 there were more millionaires per capita in the Mississippi Valley than anywhere else in the country.

Forced partings were common in the antebellum South. A slave in some parts of the region stood a 30 percent chance of being sold in his or her lifetime. Twenty-five percent of interstate trades destroyed a first marriage and half of them destroyed a nuclear family.

When the wife and children of Henry Brown, a slave in Richmond, Virginia, were to be sold away, Brown searched for a white master who might buy his wife and children to keep the family together. He failed:

> The next day, I stationed myself by the side of the road, along which the slaves, amounting to three hundred and fifty, were to pass. The purchaser of my wife was a Methodist minister, who was about starting for North Carolina. Pretty soon five waggon-loads of little children passed, and looking at the foremost one, what should I see but a little child, pointing its tiny hand towards me,

exclaiming, "There's my father; I knew he would come and bid me good-bye." It was my eldest child! Soon the gang approached in which my wife was chained. I looked, and beheld her familiar face; but O, reader, that glance of agony! may God spare me ever again enduring the excruciating horror of that moment! She passed, and came near to where I stood. I seized hold of her hand, intending to bid her farewell; but words failed me; the gift of utterance had fled, and I remained speechless. I followed her for some distance, with her hand grasped in mine, as if to save her from her fate, but I could not speak, and I was obliged to turn away in silence.

In a time when telecommunications were primitive and blacks 70 lacked freedom of movement, the parting of black families was a kind of murder. Here we find the roots of American wealth and democracy—in the for-profit destruction of the most important asset available to any people, the family. The destruction was not incidental to America's rise; it facilitated that rise. By erecting a slave society, America created the economic foundation for its great experiment in democracy. The labor strife that seeded Bacon's rebellion was suppressed. America's indispensable working class existed as property beyond the realm of politics, leaving white Americans free to trumpet their love of freedom and democratic values. Assessing antebellum democracy in Virginia, a visitor from England observed that the state's natives "can profess an unbounded love of liberty and of democracy in consequence of the mass of the people, who in other countries might become mobs, being there nearly altogether composed of their own Negro slaves."

V. The Quiet Plunder

The consequences of 250 years of enslavement, of war upon black families and black people, were profound. Like homeownership today, slave ownership was aspirational, attracting not just those who owned slaves but those who wished to. Much as homeowners today might discuss the addition of a patio or the painting of a living room, slaveholders traded tips on the best methods for breeding workers, exacting labor, and doling out punishment. Just as a homeowner today might subscribe to a magazine like *This Old House*, slaveholders had journals such as *De Bow's Review*, which recommended the best practices for wringing profits from slaves. By the dawn of the Civil War, the enslavement of black America was thought to be so foundational to the country that those who sought to end it were branded heretics worthy of death. Imagine what would happen if a president today came out in favor of taking all American homes from their owners: the reaction might well be violent.

"This country was formed for the *white*, not for the black man," John Wilkes Booth wrote, before killing Abraham Lincoln. "And looking upon *African slavery* from the same standpoint held by those noble framers of our Constitution, I for one have ever considered *it* one of the greatest blessings (both for themselves and us) that God ever bestowed upon a favored nation."

In the aftermath of the Civil War, Radical Republicans attempted to reconstruct the country upon something resembling universal equality—but they were beaten back by a campaign of "Redemption," led by White Liners, Red Shirts, and Klansmen bent on upholding a society "formed for the *white*, not for the black man." A wave of terrorism roiled the South. In his massive history *Reconstruction*, Eric Foner recounts incidents of black people being attacked for not removing their hats; for refusing to hand over a whiskey flask; for disobeying church procedures; for "using insolent language"; for disputing labor contracts; for refusing to be "tied like a slave." Sometimes the attacks were intended simply to "thin out the niggers a little."

Terrorism carried the day. Federal troops withdrew from the South in 1877. The dream of Reconstruction died. For the next century, political violence was visited upon blacks wantonly, with special treatment meted out toward black people of ambition. Black schools and churches were burned to the ground. Black voters and the political candidates who attempted to rally them were intimidated, and some were murdered. At the end of World War I, black veterans returning to their homes were assaulted for daring to wear the American uniform. The demobilization of soldiers after the war, which put white and black veterans into competition for scarce jobs, produced the Red Summer of 1919: a succession of racist pogroms against dozens of cities ranging from Longview, Texas, to Chicago to Washington, D.C. Organized white violence against blacks continued into the 1920s—in 1921 a white mob leveled Tulsa's "Black Wall Street," and in 1923 another one razed the black town of Rosewood, Florida—and virtually no one was punished.

The work of mobs was a rabid and violent rendition of prejudices that extended even into the upper reaches of American government. The New Deal is today remembered as a model for what progressive government should do—cast a broad social safety net that protects the poor and the afflicted while building the middle class. When progressives wish to express their disappointment with Barack Obama, they point to the accomplishments of Franklin Roosevelt. But these progressives rarely note that Roosevelt's New Deal, much like the democracy that produced it, rested on the foundation of Jim Crow.

"The Jim Crow South," writes Ira Katznelson, a history and political-science professor at Columbia, "was the one collaborator America's democracy could not do without." The marks of that collaboration are all over the New Deal. The omnibus programs passed under the Social Security Act in 1935 were crafted in such a way as to protect the southern way of life. Old-age insurance (Social Security proper) and unemployment insurance excluded farmworkers and domestics—jobs heavily occupied by blacks. When President Roosevelt signed Social Security into law in 1935, 65 percent of African Americans nationally and between 70 and 80 percent in the South were ineligible. The NAACP protested, calling the new American safety net "a sieve with holes just big enough for the majority of Negroes to fall through."

The oft-celebrated GI Bill similarly failed black Americans, by mirroring the broader country's insistence on a racist housing policy. Though ostensibly color-blind, Title III of the bill, which aimed to give veterans access to low-interest home loans, left black veterans to tangle with white officials at their local Veterans Administration as well as with the same banks that had, for years, refused to grant mortgages to blacks. The historian Kathleen J. Frydl observes in her 2009 book, *The GI Bill*, that so many blacks were disqualified from receiving Title III benefits "that it is more accurate simply to say that blacks could not use this particular title."

In Cold War America, homeownership was seen as a means of instilling patriotism, and as a civilizing and anti-radical force. "No man who owns his own house and lot can be a Communist," claimed William Levitt, who pioneered the modern suburb with the development of the various Levittowns, his famous planned communities. "He has too much to do."

But the Levittowns were, with Levitt's willing acquiescence, segregated throughout their early years. Daisy and Bill Myers, the first black family to move into Levittown, Pennsylvania, were greeted with protests and a burning cross. A neighbor who opposed the family said that Bill Myers was "probably a nice guy, but every time I look at him I see $2,000 drop off the value of my house."

The neighbor had good reason to be afraid. Bill and Daisy Myers 80 were from the other side of John C. Calhoun's dual society. If they moved next door, housing policy almost guaranteed that their neighbors' property values would decline.

Whereas shortly before the New Deal, a typical mortgage required a large down payment and full repayment within about 10 years, the creation of the Home Owners' Loan Corporation in 1933 and then the Federal Housing Administration the following year allowed banks to offer loans requiring no more than 10 percent down, amortized over 20 to 30 years. "Without federal intervention in the housing market, massive suburbanization would have been impossible," writes Thomas J. Sugrue, a historian at the University of Pennsylvania. "In 1930, only 30 percent of Americans owned their own homes; by 1960, more than 60 percent were home owners. Home ownership became an emblem of American citizenship."

That emblem was not to be awarded to blacks. The American real-estate industry believed segregation to be a moral principle. As late as 1950, the National Association of Real Estate Boards' code of ethics warned that "a Realtor should never be instrumental in introducing into a neighborhood . . . any race or nationality, or any individuals whose presence will clearly be detrimental to property values." A 1943 brochure specified that such potential undesirables might include madams, bootleggers, gangsters—and "a colored man of means who was giving his children a college education and thought they were entitled to live among whites."

The federal government concurred. It was the Home Owners' Loan Corporation, not a private trade association, that pioneered the practice of redlining, selectively granting loans and insisting that any property it insured be covered by a restrictive covenant—a clause in the deed forbidding the sale of the property to anyone other than whites. Millions of dollars flowed from tax coffers into segregated white neighborhoods.

"For perhaps the first time, the federal government embraced the discriminatory attitudes of the marketplace," the historian Kenneth T. Jackson wrote in his 1985 book, *Crabgrass Frontier*, a history of suburbanization. "Previously, prejudices were personalized and individualized; FHA exhorted segregation and enshrined it as public policy. Whole areas of cities were declared ineligible for loan guarantees." Redlining was not officially outlawed until 1968, by the Fair Housing Act. By then the damage was done—and reports of redlining by banks have continued.

The federal government is premised on equal fealty from all its citizens, who in return are to receive equal treatment. But as late as the mid-20th century, this bargain was not granted to black people, who repeatedly paid a higher price for citizenship and received less in return. Plunder had been the essential feature of slavery, of the society described by Calhoun. But practically a full century after the end of the Civil War and the abolition of slavery, the plunder—quiet, systemic, submerged—continued even amidst the aims and achievements of New Deal liberals.

VI. Making the Second Ghetto

Today Chicago is one of the most segregated cities in the country, a fact that reflects assiduous planning. In the effort to uphold white supremacy at every level down to the neighborhood, Chicago—a city founded by the black fur trader Jean Baptiste Point du Sable—has long been a pioneer. The efforts began in earnest in 1917, when the Chicago Real Estate Board, horrified by the influx of southern blacks, lobbied to zone the entire city by race. But after the Supreme Court ruled against explicit racial zoning that year, the city was forced to pursue its agenda by more-discreet means.

Like the Home Owners' Loan Corporation, the Federal Housing Administration initially insisted on restrictive covenants, which helped bar blacks and other ethnic undesirables from receiving federally backed home loans. By the 1940s, Chicago led the nation in the use of these restrictive covenants, and about half of all residential neighborhoods in the city were effectively off-limits to blacks.

It is common today to become misty-eyed about the old black ghetto, where doctors and lawyers lived next door to meatpackers and steelworkers, who themselves lived next door to prostitutes and the unemployed. This segregationist nostalgia ignores the actual conditions endured by the people living there—vermin and arson, for instance—and ignores the fact that the old ghetto was premised on denying black people privileges enjoyed by white Americans.

In 1948, when the Supreme Court ruled that restrictive covenants, while permissible, were not enforceable by judicial action, Chicago had other weapons at the ready. The Illinois state legislature had already given Chicago's city council the right to approve—and thus to veto—any public housing in the city's wards. This came in handy in 1949, when a new federal housing act sent millions of tax dollars into Chicago and other cities around the country. Beginning in 1950, site selection for public housing proceeded entirely on the grounds of segregation. By the 1960s, the city had created with its vast housing projects what the historian Arnold R. Hirsch calls a "second ghetto," one larger than the old Black Belt but just as impermeable. More than 98 percent of all the family public-housing units built in Chicago between 1950 and the mid-1960s were built in all-black neighborhoods.

Governmental embrace of segregation was driven by the virulent racism of Chicago's white citizens. White neighborhoods vulnerable to black encroachment formed block associations for the sole purpose of enforcing segregation. They lobbied fellow whites not to sell. They lobbied those blacks who did manage to buy to sell back. In 1949, a group of Englewood Catholics formed block associations intended to "keep up the neighborhood." Translation: keep black people out. And when civic engagement was not enough, when government failed, when private banks could no longer hold the line, Chicago turned to an old tool in the American repertoire—racial violence. "The pattern of terrorism is easily discernible," concluded a Chicago civic group in the 1940s. "It is at the seams of the black ghetto in all directions." On July 1 and 2 of 1946, a mob of thousands assembled in Chicago's Park Manor neighborhood, hoping to eject a black doctor who'd recently moved in. The mob pelted the house with rocks and set the garage on fire. The doctor moved away.

In 1947, after a few black veterans moved into the Fernwood section of Chicago, three nights of rioting broke out; gangs of whites yanked blacks off streetcars and beat them. Two years later, when a union meeting attended by blacks in Englewood triggered rumors that a home was being "sold to niggers," blacks (and whites thought to be sympathetic to them) were beaten in the streets. In 1951, thousands of whites in Cicero, 20 minutes or so west of downtown Chicago, attacked an apartment building that housed a single black family, throwing bricks and firebombs through the windows and setting the apartment on fire. A Cook County grand jury declined to charge the rioters—and instead indicted the family's NAACP attorney, the apartment's white owner, and the owner's attorney and rental agent, charging them with conspiring to lower property values. Two years after that, whites picketed and planted explosives in South Deering, about 30 minutes from downtown Chicago, to force blacks out.

When terrorism ultimately failed, white homeowners simply fled the neighborhood. The traditional terminology, *white flight*, implies a kind of natural expression of preference. In fact, white flight was a triumph of social engineering, orchestrated by the shared racist presumptions of America's public and private sectors. For should any nonracist white families decide that integration might not be so bad as a matter of principle or practicality, they still had to contend with the hard facts of American housing policy: When the mid-20th-century white home-owner claimed that the presence of a Bill and Daisy Myers decreased his property value, he was not merely engaging in racist dogma—he was accurately observing the impact of federal policy on market prices. Redlining destroyed the possibility of investment wherever black people lived.

Speculators in North Lawndale, and at the edge of the black ghettos, knew there was money to be made off white panic. They resorted to "block-busting"—spooking whites into selling cheap before the neigh-borhood became black. They would hire a black woman to walk up and down the street with a stroller. Or they'd hire someone to call a num-ber in the neighborhood looking for "Johnny Mae." Then they'd cajole whites into selling at low prices, informing them that the more blacks who moved in, the more the value of their homes would decline, so bet-ter to sell now. With these white-fled homes in hand, speculators then turned to the masses of black people who had streamed northward as part of the Great Migration, or who were desperate to escape the ghet-tos; the speculators would take the houses they'd just bought cheap through block-busting and sell them to blacks on contract.

To keep up with his payments and keep his heat on, Clyde Ross took a second job at the post office and then a third job delivering pizza. His wife took a job working at Marshall Field. He had to take some of his children out of private school. He was not able to be at home to supervise his children or help them with their homework. Money and time that Ross wanted to give his children went instead to enrich white speculators.

"The problem was the money," Ross told me. "Without the money, 95 you can't move. You can't educate your kids. You can't give them the right kind of food. Can't make the house look good. They think this neighborhood is where they supposed to be. It changes their outlook. My kids were going to the best schools in this neighborhood, and I couldn't keep them in there."

Chicago, like the country at large, embraced policies that placed black America's most energetic, ambitious, and thrifty countrymen beyond the pale of society and marked them as rightful targets for legal theft. The effects reverberate beyond the families who were robbed to the community that beholds the spectacle. Don't just picture Clyde Ross working three jobs so he could hold on to his home. Think of his North Lawndale neighbors—their children, their nephews and nieces—and consider how watching this affects them. Imagine yourself as a young black child watching your elders play by all the rules only to have their possessions tossed out in the street and to have their most sacred possession—their home—taken from them. . . .

VII. Toward a New Country

Scholars have long discussed methods by which America might make reparations to those on whose labor and exclusion the country was built. In the 1970s, the Yale Law professor Boris Bittker argued in *The Case for Black Reparations* that a rough price tag for reparations could be determined by multiplying the number of African Americans in the population by the difference in white and black per capita income. That number—$34 billion in 1973, when Bittker wrote his book—could be added to a reparations program each year for a decade or two. Today Charles Ogletree, the Harvard Law School professor, argues for something broader: a program of job training and public works that takes racial justice as its mission but includes the poor of all races.

To celebrate freedom and democracy while forgetting America's origins in a slavery economy is patriotism à la carte.

Perhaps no statistic better illustrates the enduring legacy of our country's shameful history of treating black people as sub-citizens, sub-Americans, and sub-humans than the wealth gap. Reparations would seek to close this chasm. But as surely as the creation of the wealth gap required the cooperation of every aspect of the society, bridging it will require the same.

Perhaps after a serious discussion and debate—the kind that HR 40 100 proposes—we may find that the country can never fully repay African Americans. But we stand to discover much about ourselves in such a discussion—and that is perhaps what scares us. The idea of reparations is frightening not simply because we might lack the ability to pay. The idea of reparations threatens something much deeper—America's heritage, history, and standing in the world.

The early American economy was built on slave labor. The Capitol and the White House were built by slaves. President James K. Polk traded slaves from the Oval Office. The laments about "black pathology," the criticism of black family structures by pundits and intellectuals, ring hollow in a country whose existence was predicated on the torture of black fathers, on the rape of black mothers, on the sale of black children. An honest assessment of America's relationship to the black family reveals the country to be not its nurturer but its destroyer.

And this destruction did not end with slavery. Discriminatory laws joined the equal burden of citizenship to unequal distribution of its bounty. These laws reached their apex in the mid-20th century, when the federal government—through housing policies—engineered the wealth gap, which remains with us to this day. When we think of white supremacy, we picture COLORED ONLY signs, but we should picture pirate flags.

On some level, we have always grasped this.

"Negro poverty is not white poverty," President Johnson said in his historic civil-rights speech.

> Many of its causes and many of its cures are the same. But there are differences—deep, corrosive, obstinate differences—radiating painful roots into the community and into the family, and the nature of the individual. These differences are not racial differences. They are solely and simply the consequence of ancient brutality, past injustice, and present prejudice.

We invoke the words of Jefferson and Lincoln because they say [105] something about our legacy and our traditions. We do this because we recognize our links to the past—at least when they flatter us. But black history does not flatter American democracy; it chastens it. The popular mocking of reparations as a harebrained scheme authored by wild-eyed lefties and intellectually unserious black nationalists is fear masquerading as laughter. Black nationalists have always perceived something unmentionable about America that integrationists dare not acknowledge—that white supremacy is not merely the work of hotheaded demagogues, or a matter of false consciousness, but a force so fundamental to America that it is difficult to imagine the country without it.

And so we must imagine a new country. Reparations — by which I mean the full acceptance of our collective biography and its consequences—is the price we must pay to see ourselves squarely. The recovering alcoholic may well have to live with his illness for the rest of his life. But at least he is not living a drunken lie. Reparations beckons us to reject the intoxication of hubris and see America as it is—the work of fallible humans.

Won't reparations divide us? Not any more than we are already divided. The wealth gap merely puts a number on something we feel but cannot say—that American prosperity was ill-gotten and selective in its distribution. What is needed is an airing of family secrets, a settling with old ghosts. What is needed is a healing of the American psyche and the banishment of white guilt.

What I'm talking about is more than recompense for past injustices— more than a handout, a payoff, hush money, or a reluctant bribe. What I'm talking about is a national reckoning that would lead to spiritual renewal. Reparations would mean the end of scarfing hot dogs on the Fourth of July while denying the facts of our heritage. Reparations would mean the end of yelling "patriotism" while waving a Confederate flag. Reparations would mean a revolution of the American consciousness, a reconciling of our self-image as the great democratizer with the facts of our history.

Something more than moral pressure calls America to reparations. We cannot escape our history. All of our solutions to the great problems of health care, education, housing, and economic inequality are troubled by what must go unspoken. "The reason black people are so far behind now is not because of now," Clyde Ross told me. "It's because of then." In the early 2000s, Charles Ogletree went to Tulsa, Oklahoma, to meet with the survivors of the 1921 race riot that had devastated "Black Wall Street." The past was not the past to them. "It was amazing seeing these black women and men who were crippled, blind, in wheelchairs," Ogletree told me. "I had no idea who they were and why they wanted to see me. They said, 'We want you to represent us in this lawsuit.'"

A commission authorized by the Oklahoma legislature produced a report affirming that the riot, the knowledge of which had been suppressed for years, had happened. But the lawsuit ultimately failed, in 2004. Similar suits pushed against corporations such as Aetna (which insured slaves) and Lehman Brothers (whose co-founding partner owned them) also have thus far failed. These results are dispiriting, but the crime with which reparations activists charge the country implicates more than just a few towns or corporations. The crime indicts the American people themselves, at every level, and in nearly every configuration. A crime that implicates the entire American people deserves its hearing in the legislative body that represents them.

John Conyers's HR 40 is the vehicle for that hearing. No one can know what would come out of such a debate. Perhaps no number can fully capture the multi-century plunder of black people in America. Perhaps the number is so large that it can't be imagined, let alone calculated and dispensed. But I believe that wrestling publicly with these questions matters as much as—if not more than—the specific answers that might be produced. An America that asks what it owes its most vulnerable citizens is improved and humane. An America that looks away is ignoring not just the sins of the past but the sins of the present and the certain sins of the future. More important than any single check cut to any African American, the payment of reparations would represent America's maturation out of the childhood myth of its innocence into a wisdom worthy of its founders.

In 2010, Jacob S. Rugh, then a doctoral candidate at Princeton, and the sociologist Douglas S. Massey published a study of the recent foreclosure crisis. Among its drivers, they found an old foe: segregation. Black home buyers—even after controlling for factors like creditworthiness—were still more likely than white home buyers to be steered toward subprime loans. Decades of racist housing policies by the American government, along with decades of racist housing practices by American businesses, had conspired to concentrate African Americans in the same neighborhoods. As in North Lawndale half a century earlier, these neighborhoods were filled with people who had been cut off from mainstream financial institutions. When subprime lenders went looking for prey, they found black people waiting like ducks in a pen.

"High levels of segregation create a natural market for subprime lending," Rugh and Massey write, "and cause riskier mortgages, and thus foreclosures, to accumulate disproportionately in racially segregated cities' minority neighborhoods."

Plunder in the past made plunder in the present efficient. The banks of America understood this. In 2005, Wells Fargo promoted a series of Wealth Building Strategies seminars. Dubbing itself "the nation's leading originator of home loans to ethnic minority customers," the bank enrolled black public figures in an ostensible effort to educate blacks on building "generational wealth." But the "wealth building" seminars were a front for wealth theft. In 2010, the Justice Department filed a discrimination suit against Wells Fargo alleging that the bank had shunted blacks into predatory loans regardless of their creditworthiness. This was not magic or coincidence or misfortune. It was racism reifying itself. According to the *New York Times*, affidavits found loan officers referring to their black customers as "mud people" and to their subprime products as "ghetto loans."

"We just went right after them," Beth Jacobson, a former Wells 115 Fargo loan officer, told the *Times*. "Wells Fargo mortgage had an emerging-markets unit that specifically targeted black churches because it figured church leaders had a lot of influence and could convince congregants to take out subprime loans."

In 2011, Bank of America agreed to pay $355 million to settle charges of discrimination against its Countrywide unit. The following year, Wells Fargo settled its discrimination suit for more than $175 million. But the damage had been done. In 2009, half the properties in Baltimore whose owners had been granted loans by Wells Fargo between 2005 and 2008 were vacant; 71 percent of these properties were in predominantly black neighborhoods.

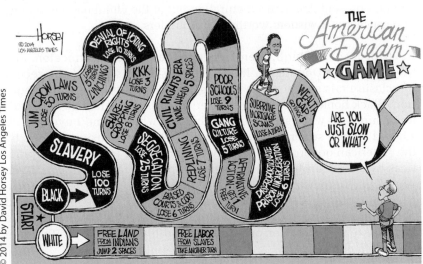

ENGAGING THE TEXT

1. Why does Coates devote so much time to the story of Clyde Ross? In what ways do Ross's experiences reflect the experience of black Americans more generally?

2. In part 2 of this essay ("A Difference of Kind, Not Degree") Coates paints a grim picture of black Chicago, citing statistics on homicide, infant mortality, incarceration rate, income, and household wealth. How does he use these statistics to construct his argument, and how persuasive is it? Why does Coates reject "cultural pathology" as an explanation for black poverty?

3. Coates argues that "America begins in black plunder and white democracy, two features that are not contradictory but complementary" (para. 60). How was democracy intertwined with and dependent upon slavery, according to Coates?

4. Coates asserts that "one cannot escape the question" of reparations "by hand-waving at the past, disavowing the acts of one's ancestors, nor by citing a recent date of ancestral immigration" (para. 57). How, according to Coates, do contemporary white Americans, who had little or nothing to do with slavery, still reap benefits from the historic oppression of African Americans? Why does he believe that there remains a debt to be paid?

5. In "The Case for Reparations," Coates makes only passing reference to reparations in the first two sections. He discusses the concept in detail in part 3 ("We Inherit Our Ample Patrimony"), but devotes the next four parts to the history of black exploitation and white supremacy, returning to the topic of reparations in the final section. Why does he wait so long to introduce the main subject of his essay? How does he develop the case for reparations in the four parts that never mention the idea? What would be the effect of focusing more exclusively on reparations throughout the essay?

6. **Thinking Rhetorically** Coates's language can appear extreme: He describes the "tyranny" of "the acquisitive warlords of the South" (para. 13), condemns America's 250-year "war upon black families and black people" (para. 71), and refers to the "plunder" of black bodies and labor over a dozen times. He also draws extensively on scholarship, quoting historians, sociologists, and law professors throughout the essay. Write a paper analyzing Coates's style: Do you find his language engaging or off-putting? How does he deploy supporting evidence? Is it convincing? How might opponents of reparations object to his arguments, and how might he respond?

EXPLORING CONNECTIONS

7. Linda Holtzman and Leon Sharpe (p. 631) claim that the tendency to see "contemporary racial oppression as interpersonal and episodic gets in the way of our ability to come to grips with its fundamental nature, which is structural and systemic" (para. 5). Using specific examples from Coates, explain the distinction between individual and structural racism.

8. Linda Holtzman and Leon Sharpe discuss how racial oppression can lead to "intergenerational trauma" and "post-traumatic slave syndrome" affecting many generations of individuals (Holtzman and Sharpe, para. 12). Review Coates's essay and write a journal entry in which you imagine the impact of slavery, Jim Crow, red-lining, and continued economic disadvantage on black Americans. How might the destruction of families during slavery, the experience of two-and-a-half centuries of violent racism and segregation, and the daily insults of everyday discrimination affect black family stories and individual attitudes today?

9. Write an imaginary conversation among Coates, Marc Lamont Hill (p. 651), and Sheryll Cashin (p. 88) about the relative merits of reparations, activism, and cultural dexterity as possible solutions to inequality. What are the practical benefits and drawbacks of each? Do you think they're equally effective or not? Why?

10. While Coates is deliberately vague about the form that reparations should take, Alan Aja and his coauthors (p. 382) propose two concrete policies — Child Trust Accounts and a Federal Job Guarantee — to bridge the "persistent racial gaps in employment and wealth" (para. 5). How far would these policies go toward satisfying Coates's call for reparations? What would they accomplish and what would they fail to address?

11. Examine David Horsey's "American Dream Game" on page 628. How does the white character interpret the black character's slower progress toward the American Dream? What is the cartoonist suggesting about white privilege and racial blindness?

EXTENDING THE CRITICAL CONTEXT

12. Work in small groups to brainstorm a plan for reparations. Should it target blacks alone, or include "the poor of all races"? Should it pay people directly or aim for "job training and public works" (para. 97)? What kinds of public works would be most beneficial? Do some background research on the Rosewood massacre reparations, Japanese internment reparations, and German Holocaust reparations to find out who was paid, how much, and how it was distributed. Present and debate each group's ideas: Are the plans fair? Do they adequately address economic disadvantage? Would they stimulate the national soul-searching that Coates calls for?

13. In 2013, a divided Supreme Court voted 5 to 4 to strike down a key section of the Voting Rights Act of 1965. Do some online research about the case, *Shelby County v. Holder*. Why was the Voting Rights Act passed in the first place? Why did the Court's majority rule that this section of the law was unconstitutional? Why did the dissenters disagree? How have some states changed the voting laws since this decision, and how have these changes affected minority, poor, elderly, and student voters?

14. According to the website of the Legacy Museum and the National Memorial for Peace and Justice, which recently opened in Montgomery, Alabama,

"confronting the truth about our history is the first step towards recovery and reconciliation." Visit the website and examine the links — including videos, audio files, news stories, and graphics — to learn more about the purpose and design of the memorial and museum:

https://museumandmemorial.eji.org

How do the museum and memorial challenge the history of the South? What truth do they emphasize, and how do they convey it? Do you think their message is effectively presented? Why or why not?

THEORIES AND CONSTRUCTS OF RACE
LINDA HOLTZMAN AND LEON SHARPE

At a time when 55 percent of white people believe that antiwhite discrimination has become as big a problem as discrimination against minority groups,[1] Linda Holtzman and Leon Sharpe provide a necessary corrective. In the following excerpt from their book *Media Messages: What Film, Television, and Popular Music Teach Us About Race, Class, Gender, and Sexual Orientation* (2nd edition, 2014), Holtzman and Sharpe offer a critical look at race, racism, and the belief that we now live in a "postracial" society. Linda Holtzman is an emeritus professor of journalism and communications at Webster University, where she taught media theory and research for twenty-five years. She has won many awards for her work as an antiracism facilitator for national social justice organizations and school districts in Illinois and Missouri. In addition, she has received grants for her work on human rights activism in the United States, Israel, and Palestine. Leon Sharpe teaches at Webster University, where he is an adjunct professor of communications. He is also founder of The Praxis Group, which has conducted workshops and training sessions for institutions and organizations nationwide, including the Coalition of Essential Schools, Focus St. Louis, and the Anti-Defamation League.

Theories and Constructs of Race

The shifting meaning of race throughout U.S. history provides important clues to its definition. It is not biological, nor is it based primarily on skin

[1]PRRI/MTV, "Diversity, Division, and Discrimination," 2017.

color. It is not necessarily based on ethnicity nor is it based on country of origin. Rather, race is constructed socially, culturally, politically, and economically. "Various racial categories have been created or changed to meet the emerging economic and social needs of white United States culture. Racial categories artificially emphasize the relatively small external physical differences among people and leave room for the creation of false notions of mental, emotional, and intellectual differences as well" (Adams, Bell, and Griffin 1997, 83).

While race itself is fiction, the consequences of racism are a historical and contemporary fact of American life. "Racism is based on the concept of whiteness—an identity concept invented and enforced by power and violence. Whiteness is a constantly shifting boundary separating those who are entitled to have certain privileges from those whose exploitation and vulnerability to violence is justified by their not being white" (Kivel 1996, 17). The historical mutability of race is significant because of how it has been used as a marker of group identity and a means of access to privilege in this country and elsewhere. The possession of whiteness represents a valued status that confers upon its owners a set of exclusive citizenship rights (Lipsitz 1998).

The centrality of race in our society is one of the core tenets of **critical race theory (CRT)**. CRT emerged originally in the 1980s as an outgrowth of critical legal studies (Crenshaw et al. 1995; Delgado and Stefancic 2001; Taylor, Gillborn, and Ladson-Billings 2009). Over the years, CRT has expanded to other disciplines such as education. Its ideas and methodologies have also been applied in other areas of focus such as LatCrit, AsianCrit, TribalCrit, FemCrit, and QueerCrit. One of the key concepts of critical race theory is that racism is a core component of the systems and structures of power in our nation. Racial inequity is so deeply embedded in our institutional practices, so integral to our interpersonal relationships and individual attitudes, so inextricably woven into the warp and woof of everyday life, that it has become a permanent feature of the American experience. Therefore, racism, in all its manifestations, must be continuously critiqued and challenged.

Not surprisingly, foundational elements of racial inequity often go unexamined, underanalyzed, or misrepresented by the mainstream media: "Specific media frames select out limited aspects of an issue in order to make it salient for mass communication, a selectivity usually promoting a narrow reading of that issue. . . . A particular frame structures the thinking process and shapes what people see or do not see, in important societal settings" (Feagin 2009, 27). A 2007 study of print media coverage of racial disparities in health care, education, early child development, and employment determined that because racism is framed, for the most part, as being rooted in interpersonal relationships between individuals or among groups of individuals, the systemic nature of race-based power dynamics is rarely reported. In examining the explanatory frames of 140 news articles published by major outlets in eight metropolitan areas nationwide, the study found that articles provided clear and unambiguous accounts of how racism can exist in a number of institutions and were easy for a wide audience to identify as racist. However, the dominance of such stories reinforces the notion that racism is primarily about individual actions rather than embedded in social structures. Furthermore, overt and blatant acts of racism were framed as aberrant occurrences that were unfortunate, but did not effectively challenge the perception that the United States has largely transcended its racial past. (O'Neil 2009)

The mischaracterization of contemporary racial oppression as interpersonal and episodic gets in the way of our ability to come to grips with its fundamental nature, which is structural and systemic. Young people today have grown up and come of age during an era when *legally sanctioned* racial segregation of public facilities appears to be a thing of the past. Overt acts of racial violence, although they still occur, are less common than they were prior to the civil rights era. Youth of color and their white counterparts form friendships and interact socially across racial lines more freely today than at any other time in America's past. Yet despite the popular notion that we now live in a "postracial" society, racial injustice continues to thrive in the United States. Glaring racial disparities continue to exist in education, employment, healthcare, housing, bank lending policies, the criminal justice and penal system, household income, household net worth, and a host of other areas. Thus, what has been referred to as America's "pathology of denial" about race (Leary 2006) impedes our ability to develop systemic solutions that will lead to the dismantling of the **racialized** institutional foundations of our country. It prevents us from devising strategies that are structurally transformative.

The Social and Psychological Impact of Race

The continuous racial targeting of people of color and the privileging of whites, along with misinformation about race passed along from one generation to the next and reinforced through the media, has imbued people of all races with a distorted sense of personal and group identity. Not surprisingly, given the centuries of racial stereotyping and negative messaging directed at people of color, research indicates that a majority of white Americans continue to have strong feelings of racial bias (Banaji and Greenwald 2013, 169–188; Greenwald and Krieger 2006). Many white people in the United States are socialized to regard their race as representing not only the majority group but also the societal norm—the cultural standard and benchmark for what it means to be American. According to one writer, "For many white people, the idea that we have racial identities is difficult to come to terms with. We usually see ourselves simply as people. Whiteness, by virtue of its status as the dominant social position, is unmarked. It is relatively easy for white persons to go through life never thinking about their own racial identity. Whiteness functions as the normative ideal against which other people are categorized and judged" (Kaufman 2001).

This illusory standard of a white societal norm reinforces the notion that people of color are not merely different but also deficient. Studies indicate that, despite a decline in overt expressions of racial bigotry, a large percentage of white Americans continue to consciously or unconsciously regard white identity as positive and black identity as negative (Schmidt and Nosek 2010). The unconscious belief among whites in the superiority of their own racial group relative to blacks and other people of color is a form of *implicit bias*—learned social stereotypes that are sometimes triggered automatically in individuals without their awareness (Greenwald and Banaji 1995). There is evidence to indicate that implicit racial bias exists in children as young as six years old and endures through adulthood (Baron and Banaji 2006). Implicit bias has the capacity to influence people's judgments in regard to how they think about and treat individuals who are racially different from them even when they openly express non-prejudicial views; "to characterize the nature of an individual's prejudice correctly, one must consider both explicit racial attitudes as well as implicit, automatic biases" (Son Hing et al. 2008).

The espousing of racial openness and egalitarianism while simultaneously harboring negative racial attitudes is prevalent in contemporary society. The acting out of biased beliefs through jokes, slurs, and other racial actions and commentary is less likely to occur openly in what sociologist Joe R. Feagin refers to as the *frontstage* of public, professional, and mixed-race gatherings where a diverse range of people is present. Yet such behaviors occur quite frequently in *backstage* settings among friends and close acquaintances where whites with negative feelings toward people of color can comfortably express their beliefs without fear of being judged or marginalized socially (Feagin 2009, 184). A study analyzing more than 600 personal journals from college students throughout the nation revealed thousands of instances of racially bigoted behavior such as name-calling, inappropriate racial humor, and references to stereotypes. Although often characterized as innocent fun, such actions reinforce racial polarization and antagonism (Feagin 2009, 185–190).

In addition, the toleration of duplicitous frontstage/backstage behavior contributes to the perpetuation of an American societal norm that enables schools, employers, public service providers, real estate brokers, law enforcement agencies, and a host of other institutions to publicly embrace equal opportunity policies while privately engaging in practices that deny equal access and fair treatment to members of racially targeted groups. While many white individuals are overtly racist, millions of others benefit from institutionally sanctioned racial privilege in ways that are often invisible to them. When Linda [Holtzman] wrote earlier of her personal story, she discussed the anti-Semitism her grandparents faced in Russia and as new immigrants to the United States. But because they and their descendants would ultimately be considered white, they were allowed to find work and housing and education from which African Americans and Japanese Americans were prohibited. Without ever initiating or participating in one overtly hateful act, they benefited from racism.

Misinformation about race and identity also contributes adversely 10 to the socialization of people of color in the United States. The myth of racial inferiority and superiority has been upheld not only by physical violence and discriminatory policies but also by the psychological violence conveyed through the stereotyping and racist messaging to which people of color, beginning early in childhood, are continuously exposed. In the interest of dominant-group hegemony, false notions of a race-based hierarchy are promulgated relentlessly through virtually every mainstream institution in our society. "Oppressed people come to embody in their very being the negations imposed on them and thus, in the reproduction of their lives, harbor a tendency to contribute to the perpetuation of their own oppression" (Outlaw 2005, 14).

People of color in America have always had to wage a battle against **internalized racism**, a condition that can cause an individual to assume self-deprecating attitudes and engage in self-destructive behaviors that reflect the traumatizing effects of racial targeting. When people are regularly subjected to the physical and psychological abuse of overt and covert racial oppression, they sometimes respond by re-enacting that abuse on themselves and other members of their racial group. When Leon [Sharpe] wrote earlier about the stories he heard his adult family members telling with such vividness and ironic humor, he was speaking of the unremitting conversations of self-empowerment and cultural affirmation that many African Americans draw upon as a source of healing strength and collective power to counteract the insidious impact of internalized racism. Such stories have been as much a part of the black resistance movement in American history as any civil rights march, economic boycott, or slave uprising.

Internalized racism, which is always involuntary, is a direct byproduct of historical and ongoing racial targeting. It works in many ways. For instance, social psychologist Claude M. Steele has advanced the theory of *stereotype threat* to explain the extent to which a person's performance can be detrimentally affected by the psychological triggering of negative stereotypes assigned to one's social group identity (Steele and Aronson 1995; Steele 1997; Steele 2010). Laura Padilla has written about the manner in which many Latinos accept the negative stereotypes directed at their own group and thus question the qualifications of other Latinos who are successful. She refers to this phenomenon as *envidia* or intragroup jealousy and regards it as a clear example of how behaviors resulting from internalized racism can sabotage communities of color (Padilla 2001). Social researcher Dr. Joy DeGruy (formerly Leary) posits the concept of intergenerational trauma resulting from what she has termed *post-traumatic slave syndrome*, a consequence of multigenerational oppression of Africans and their descendants resulting from centuries of chattel slavery followed by decades of institutionalized racism that continues to inflict emotional injury (Leary 2006). In a similar vein, social worker Maria Yellow Horse Brave Heart, through her research and clinical work examining manifestations of intergenerational trauma among Native Americans, has focused on diagnosing and treating what she identifies as *historical unresolved grief* (Brave Heart 2000). Internalized racism among people of color and implicit racial bias among whites are unhealthy psychosocial reactions to the toxic power of racial targeting. Because of their detrimental effects, they must be actively addressed and rigorously interrupted whenever possible. Nevertheless, the injury they cause can only be fully healed as racism in our society is eliminated.

The Science and Pseudoscience of Race

Is race a scientifically verifiable concept? Does racial difference actually exist among human beings? According to biologists, a race is a distinct evolutionary lineage within a species that is sharply defined by measurable genetic differences. Genetic differences between populations are necessary but not sufficient to define race (Templeton 2002). Obviously, differences exist between populations within the human species. Members of what we regard as different racial groups have visibly diverse physical characteristics (skin color, hair texture, facial features). Thus, the question becomes, do diverse human populations exhibit sufficient differences at the genetic level to constitute a scientific basis for establishing the existence of separate races within our species?

A segment of the 2003 documentary *Race: The Power of Illusion* depicts a multiethnic group of students meeting with a DNA expert. They compare their skin colors, submit blood and DNA samples, and then discuss their thoughts as to which of their classmates share the closest genetic similarity with them. Most, if not all, of them assume that the students within their own "racial" group will be the closest to them genetically. When their DNA is analyzed, the students are surprised to learn that their assumptions are wrong. The white students do not share the same genetic traits with one another, nor do the African American, Latino, or Asian students. In fact, what they all discover is that, according to the scientific evidence upon which the film is based, there is just as much genetic variation among people of the same so-called "race" as there is among people across racial populations (Gould 1981, 323; Lewontin 1970; Templeton 2002). Differences indeed exist among humans, but they are not racial.

Skin color, the most common visual cue that most of us use as a [15] determinant of race, does not reflect extreme genetic difference, nor does it reflect a distinct evolutionary history. Diversity of skin color merely indicates the geographical adaptation of various populations as they migrated out of equatorial Africa and moved further north to regions where ultraviolet rays from the sun were less concentrated.

Overexposure to certain UV rays can destroy folic acid in the body, thus having a detrimental effect on reproduction. In tropical regions, humans evolved with darker skin and large stores of melanin, which protects the body from the harmful effects of solar radiation. On the other hand, insufficient exposure to UV rays can impede the body's ability to produce vitamin D, thus preventing the absorption of calcium by the intestines. As some human populations migrated north and south into the temperate regions, their bodies gradually adapted by developing lighter skin complexions and the ability to tan so as to make optimum use of the available ultraviolet light. Difference in skin color among humans is nothing more than an indicator of the areas of the world to which one's ancestors migrated (Jablonski and Chaplin 2000; 2003). In short, there are no available data to support racial classifications or any form of social hierarchy based on racial or ethnic group membership (Cartmill 1998, 653).

So does that completely answer our question? Is race merely an optical illusion—a trick of the sun? No, it is much more complex than that. Lani Guinier writes, "If we think in categories and think about race only in one category, we conflate many different spheres of racial meaning. We fail to specify if we mean biological race, political race, historical race, or cultural race. We simplify race as a fixed category from which many people want to escape" (Guinier and Torres 2002, 4). Despite the scientific refutation of racial taxonomy as a legitimate means for biologically differentiating and categorizing diverse populations within the human species, it continues to endure as a reality in the social realm. "That race is a social construct rather than a biological fact does not minimize its impact on our lives . . . racial distinctions have powerful social meaning with profound real-world consequences" (Croteau and Hoynes 1997, 138). Most people in our society have a sense of themselves as possessing a racial identity and belonging to a racial group. Various official forms and surveys continue to have checkboxes for designating one's race. Most people harbor conscious and unconscious stereotypes and biases about other racial groups in comparison with their own. People still laugh at racial humor, people still spout racial slurs, and those racial slurs still have the capacity to sting and enrage. People still live in racially segregated communities. People are still denied jobs and promotions because of race. People are still discriminated against economically, incarcerated disproportionately, and educated less effectively because of race. People still attack and kill people because of race.

Stories and Counterstories: Decoding the Master Script

The identity and relationship dynamics of race are so pervasive in our lives today that it feels as though current notions of race have existed since the beginning of historical time. Yet that is far from true. Prior to the fifteenth century, the idea of racial divisions among humans was of minimal significance and had little impact on people's interactions with one another (Vaughan 1995). The early European aggression and hostility toward the indigenous people of Africa, Asia, and the Americas was driven by economic interests and justified primarily by a belief in the right of Christian nations such as Spain, Portugal, Great Britain, and the Netherlands to conquer any civilization and claim any land that was not under the sovereign domain of Christians.

Erecting a social construct with the epic staying power, counterrational robustness, and destructive force that has been exhibited by "race" over the centuries was not a brief or simple process. Our present-day concept of race is based on false ideas, myths, and fabrications that accumulated over the centuries to form a grand, sweeping story or **meta-narrative** to justify the exploitation of entire populations of human beings and the appropriation of their labor, land, natural resources, cultural artifacts, and intellectual property. The social construction of the American meta-narrative—the master script on race and racial hierarchy—has been formulated and upheld through an elaborate system of dehumanizing **schemas**. These racial schemas are mental models created through the telling and retelling of stories that reinforce the idea of a racial hierarchy with the white race at the top, other races beneath, and the black race at the very bottom. Such stories have been utilized to frame our history from a perspective that upholds the language, logic, and worldview of the dominant group and suppresses the language, logic, and worldviews of those who have been targeted for racial oppression.

Throughout our history, there have been an untold number of assaults on the humanness of people of color in the interest of white hegemony. These assaults prime, activate, and reinforce racial schemas and uphold the meta-narrative. They range from the creation of stereotypes and the passage of oppressive laws to the wholesale enslavement, colonization, and genocide of entire populations. In addition to attacks on life, land, and liberty, Africans, Asians, Latinos, Native Americans, and Pacific Islanders have been subject to relentless assaults on their linguistic and cultural traditions, their communal and kinship bonds, their ancestral ties, and their spiritual beliefs.

We have learned that many of the stories we have been told about race are demonstrably false. Yet if those stories go uncontested, we will accept them as truth because of the way we have been socialized. One of the strategies for challenging these stories is through the development of counterstories that refute the assumptions upon which the original stories are based. A counterstory (also referred to as a counternarrative) is a tool utilized by critical race theorists as a means of contesting the race meta-narrative. Counterstories reframe the dehumanizing schemas by revealing additional facts, examining the same facts from different perspectives, personalizing the experiences of the targeted, humanizing the voices of the oppressed, and critically analyzing the misinformation that the dominant group has heretofore represented as unimpeachable.

Let us turn our attention now to an example of how a critical counternarrative can be used to challenge a dehumanizing schema. One of the prevailing beliefs about America's past is that the indigenous people of the Western Hemisphere were primitive, uncivilized, and underdeveloped, with little or no understanding of science and technology prior to the arrival of Europeans from more sophisticated and advanced civilizations. This is a schema—a pattern of thinking that influences the way we organize and simplify our knowledge of the world around us. Let us call it the "primitive people" schema. This schema about American Indians has been repeated in various versions so often over the years that many people accept it as historical fact even though it is just a story—a story told by one group about another. The false beliefs based on this schema can be activated in our minds by a variety of stereotypical words or images, such as "redskins" or "tomahawks," which have become embedded in our popular culture. The schema is dehumanizing because it perpetuates the myth that American Indians were simple people of inferior culture and intelligence. Moreover, this "primitive people" schema contributes to the global meta-narrative of racial hierarchy by implying that, despite the brutality suffered at the hands of whites, the Indians were better off because they had the opportunity to be exposed to more "civilized" people with superior science and technology.

In reality, the notion of Native American technology as limited is grounded in Eurocentric cultural assumptions and misconceptions. If we can acknowledge that simple fact, then we can begin to craft a counternarrative that gets us closer to the truth. Native American science and technology appear to have been highly developed within the context of the Native American social, cultural, and ecological worldview. Conversely, given what we know of the adverse environmental impact that some European technology has had on the North American continent and the rest of the planet, it seems neither appropriate nor accurate to regard European technology as particularly advanced or superior. From the vantage point of twenty-first-century hindsight, the early encounters between the people of the Americas and the people of Europe could more accurately be described as the interrupted development of the technologies of one civilization in service to the overdevelopment of the technologies of another. In other words, it was a missed opportunity for mutually constructive technological synergy. Had the prevailing paradigm of the time been one of cultural reciprocity rather than cultural conquest, it is conceivable that, today, earth-dwellers of all cultures—and all species, for that matter—might be the grateful beneficiaries of the best of both technological frameworks.

Summary

Students in elementary school and high school in the United States receive limited and often distorted information about our country's racial history. Most of us learned primarily about the immigrant experiences of Europeans in the New World and only bits and pieces about the enslavement of Africans and the conquest of American Indians and Mexicans. We have rarely learned about the immigration experiences of Puerto Ricans, Cubans, Vietnamese, Chinese, or Japanese. Often the information that we get is limited or glossed over to eliminate elements of racial cruelty, violence, or suppression. Sometimes the information that we get is taught to us as African American history or Asian American history — as if it is something completely separate from American history. At best, perhaps we have been taught that while there are unfortunate aspects of racism (slavery) and conquest (American Indians) in our history, there have been many efforts to right these wrongs so that racially the United States now has a level playing field in which people of all races have equal life chances. Rarely is there any analysis of the connection between individual acts of racial hatred and the institutional or structural racism in laws or private businesses that discriminate in housing, health care, education, and employment. And seldom is there any mention of the individuals, groups, and movements that have worked to undo the policies and effects of racism.

There are hard facts in U.S. history. There have been times when dehumanizing a whole group of people has merged with individual acts of hatred and with laws and policies that promote violence and oppression, causing many, many people to die because of racism. While the omission or revision of this part of our history may be intended to keep children from learning such painful parts of our past, the consequences of the distortion of U.S. racial history are far-reaching. "Education as socialization influences students simply to accept the rightness of our society. American history textbooks overtly tell us to be proud of America. The more schooling, the more socialization, and the more likely the individual will conclude that America is good" (Loewen 1995, 307). Education that does not lie is not equivalent to socializing students to believe that America is "bad" rather than "good." Rather it calls for teaching students about the complexities of our stories and how to make inquiries and draw conclusions that allow for critical thinking and autonomous decision making.

The combination of our personal experiences, our formal education, and our exposure to entertainment media constitutes our socialization about race. If this socialization tells us that all is well racially and that everyone has equal life chances regardless of race or ethnicity, we are likely to see any racial problem or failure as strictly the fault of an individual. If we believe that there are no racial barriers to employment, then we will see unemployment among people of color as lazy or slovenly. If we believe that education is equitable for everyone, we will not be open to discuss or vote for remedies to address defects in the educational system that have an adverse impact on students of color. The lump sum of these distortions can be dehumanizing for everyone.

Acclaimed writer and activist Audre Lorde wrote, "In our work and in our living, we must recognize that difference is a reason for celebration and growth, rather than a reason for destruction." While our history regarding race may be painful, we must learn it in much the same way that Germans must learn about the Holocaust: to understand our part in it, to understand its impact on the present, to learn how to act on its contemporary implications, and to ensure that it will never happen again. Past history cannot be changed. It can only be rediscovered, reexamined, and revealed. Presenting counternarratives is an essential stage of that revelatory process. But it is only the beginning. We not only have to tell the counterstories, we have to live them. It is only through the liberatory cycle of continuous collective action, personal reflection, honest dialogue, and more action that we can transform our society, purge the toxic racist strains from the American meta-narrative, and put a process in motion that will enable future generations to write it anew.

Key Terms

critical race theory (CRT): An academic discipline that analyzes race in the United States through the lens of power and law. CRT is based on several core tenets, including the permanence of racism, critique of liberalism, whiteness as property, interest convergence, intersection of racism with other forms of oppression, centrality of personal experience, and use of the counternarrative as an explanatory and analytical tool.

internalized racism: The process by which people of color take in negative messages of overt and covert racism, superiority, and inferiority, and apply those messages to themselves and others in ways that are self-destructive rather than self-affirming. Internalized racism, which is always involuntary, is the direct by-product of historical and ongoing racial targeting.

meta-narrative: A comprehensive "story" of history and knowledge that unifies and simplifies the culture and value of a group or nation. When meta-narratives are applied to nations, they frequently are used to explain and justify the existing power structure.

racialize: To see or describe something from a racial perspective; to emphasize race or to make something seem racial. For example, in the early twentieth century; Jews were racialized in Europe, Russia, and most of the United States. Today, in much of the United States, Judaism is regarded as a religion rather than a race. Another example occurred in the aftermath of the 9/11 terrorist attacks with the widespread racialization of Muslims and people of Middle Eastern descent.

schema: A mental model or pattern of thinking that influences the way we organize and simplify our knowledge of the world around us.

white privilege: A set of unearned advantages and opportunities created by racism that are often far more visible to people of color than they are to whites. Despite the pervasiveness of racism in the history and current structures of the United States, many white people believe that racism was eradicated by the late twentieth century and that individual achievement and success are based solely on individual intelligence, motivation, and hard work. As a result of this type of misinformation and socialization, many whites believe that all of their successes are built exclusively on their own talent, skills, merit, and hard work. In fact, in many small and large ways, whites have access to different opportunities and are treated differently than people of color, giving them an often invisible boost to this success to which people of color do not have the same access. For example, white parents rarely need to think about the danger present for their sons at a mall or on the street if they are stopped by a police officer. Ample research and statistics indicate that young African American or Latino men are far more likely to be harassed, abused, and/or arrested by police than young white men. The privilege here is that white parents generally only need to think about this danger if their son will be in an area in which there is high crime. But the danger there is potential criminals, not the police. Whites are rarely asked to speak on behalf of their whole race or justify the criminal activity or failure of other whites, while people of color are frequently asked to do all of these things. White privilege allows whites the luxury and advantage of living in a world where their personal worth, rightness, and personhood are continually validated in ways that do not apply for people of color (Olson, n.d).

Bibliography

Adams, Maurianne, Lee Anne Bell, and Pat Griffin, eds. 1997. *Teaching for Diversity and Social Justice: A Sourcebook.* New York: Routledge.

Banaji, Mahzarin R., and Anthony G. Greenwald. 2013. *Blindspot: Hidden Biases of Good People.* New York: Delacorte Press.

Baron, Andrew S., and Mahzarin Banaji. 2006. "The Development of Implicit Attitudes: Evidence of Race Evaluations from Ages 6 and 10 and Adulthood." *Psychological Science* 17, no. 1: 53–58.

Brave Heart, MariaYellow Horse. 2000. "Wakiksuyapi: Carrying the Historical Trauma of the Lakota." *Tulane Studies in Social Welfare* 21–22: 245–266.

Cartmill, Matt. 1998. "The Status of Race Concept in Physical Anthropology." *American Anthropologist* (New Series) 100, no. 3: 651–660.

Crenshaw, Kimberle, Neil T. Gotanda, Gary Peller, and Kendall Thomas, eds. 1995. *Critical Race Theory: The Key Writings That Formed the Movement.* New York: The New Press.

Croteau, David, and William Hoynes. 1997. *Media/Society: Industries, Images, and Audiences.* Thousand Oaks, CA: Pine Forge Press.

Delgado, Richard, and Jean Stefancic. 2001. *Critical Race Theory: An Introduction.* New York: New York University Press.

Feagin, Joe R. 2009. *The White Racial Frame: Centuries of Racial Framing and Counter-Framing.* New York: Routledge.

Gould, Stephen Jay. 1981. *The Mismeasure of Man.* New York: W. W. Norton.

Greenwald, Anthony G., and Linda H. Krieger. 2006. "Implicit Bias: Scientific Foundations." *California Law Review* 94, no. 4.

Greenwald, Anthony G., and Mahzarin Banaji. 1995. "Implicit Social Cognition: Attitudes, Self-Esteem, and Stereotypes." *Psychological Review* 1: 4–27.

Guinier, Lani, and Gerald Torres. 2002. *The Miner's Canary: Enlisting Race, Resisting Power, Transforming Democracy.* Cambridge, MA: Harvard University Press.

Jablonski, Nina G., and George Chaplin. 2000. "The Evolution of Human Skin Colorization." *Journal of Human Evolution* 39(1): 57–106.

———. 2003. "Skin Deep." *Scientific American,* 13, no. 2 (August): 72–79.

Kaufman, Cynthia. 2001. "A User's Guide to White Privilege." *Radical Philosophy Review* 4, no. 1/2: 30–38.

Kivel, Paul. 1996. *Uprooting Racism: How White People Can Work for Racial Justice.* Gabriola Island. BC: New Society.

Leary, Joy DeGruy. 2006. *Post-Traumatic Slave Syndrome: America's Legacy of Enduring Injury and Healing.* Milwaukie, OR: Uptone Press.

Lewontin, Richard C. 1970. "Further Remarks on Race and the Genetics of Intelligence." *Bulletin of the Atomic Scientists* 26(5): 23–25.

Lipsitz, George, ed. 1998. *The Possessive Investment in Whiteness: How White People Profit from Identity Politics.* Philadelphia: Temple University Press.

Loewen, James W. 1995. *Lies My Teachers Told Me: Everything Your American History Textbook Got Wrong.* New York: Touchstone.

Olson, Joan. (n.d.) "The Four Faces of Racism." Unpublished handout adapted from Cultural Bridges Training. Posted in the compilation *We're All In It Together* by North American Students of Co-operation (NASCO). http://kalamazoo.coop/sites/default/filesWe're%20all%20in%20it%20together.pdf.

O'Neil, Moira. 2009. *Invisible Structures of Opportunity: How Media Depictions of Race Trivialize Issues of Diversity and Disparity.* Washington, DC: FrameWorks Institute.

Outlaw, Lucius T. 2005. *Critical Social Theory in the Interests of Black Folks.* Lanham, MD: Rowman & Littlefield.

Padilla, Laura M. 2001. "But You're Not a Dirty Mexican": Internalized Oppression, Latinos & Law. *Texas Hispanic Journal of Law & Policy* 7: 1.

Schmidt, Kathleen, and Brian A. Nosek. 2010. "Implicit (and Explicit) Racial Attitudes Barely Changed During the Campaign and Early Presidency of Barack Obama." *Journal of Experimental Social Psychology* 46: 308–314.

Son Hing, Leanne S., Greg A. Chun-Yang, Leah K. Hamilton, and Mark P. Zanna. 2008. "A Two-Dimensional Model That Employs Explicit and Implicit Attitudes to Characterize Prejudice." *Journal of Personality and Social Psychology* 94(6): 971–987.

Steele, Claude M. 1997. "A Threat in the Air: How Stereotypes Shape Intellectual Identity and Performance." *American Psychologist* 52: 613–629.

———. 2010. *Whistling Vivaldi: And Other Clues to How Stereotypes Affect Us.* New York: W. W. Norton.

Steele, Claude M., and Joshua Aronson. 1995. "Stereotype Threat and the Intellectual Test Performance of African Americans." *Journal of Personality and Social Psychology* 69(5): 797–811.

Taylor, Edward, David Gilborn, and Gloria Ladson-Billings, eds. 2009. *Foundations of Critical Race Theory in Education.* New York: Routledge.

Templeton, Alan R. 2002. "Out of Africa Again and Again." *Nature* 416: 45–51.

Vaughan, Alden T. 1995. *Roots of American Racism: Essays on the Colonial Experience.* New York: Oxford University Press.

Wells, Kathleen. 2013. "Prof. Robert Jensen Discusses Racism, White Supremacy and White Privilege (Part 2)." *The Blog/HuffPost Black Voices.* www.huffingtonpost. com/kathleen-wells/prof-robert-jensen-discus_b_2500184.html.

ENGAGING THE TEXT

1. What evidence do Holtzman and Sharpe offer that "race itself is a fiction" (para. 2)? What evidence do they provide that race nevertheless "continues to endure as a reality in the social realm" (para. 16)?

2. How do Holtzman and Sharpe distinguish "frontstage" from "backstage" behavior? Have you witnessed or experienced backstage behavior (racial jokes, offensive stereotypes, or racist name-calling)? Write a journal entry describing one of these incidents and detailing your response to it. Do you view such behavior as "innocent fun" or feel that it "reinforce[s] racial polarization and antagonism" (para. 8)? Why?

3. According to Holtzman and Sharpe, "Racial inequity . . . has become a permanent feature of the American experience. Therefore, racism, in all its manifestations, must be continuously critiqued and challenged" (para. 3). How would you go about challenging racism? Is the idea that racism must be "critiqued and challenged" enough, or should more be done? If so, what?

4. Holtzman and Sharpe assert that "students in elementary school and highschool in the United States receive limited and often distorted information about our country's racial history" (para. 23). In what ways do they claim that students are misinformed or that U.S. racial history is "glossed over"? Write a journal entry or an essay evaluating the extent to which this has been true in your experience.

5. **Thinking Rhetorically** This selection is an excerpt from an introductory college textbook. How do its organization, vocabulary, style, and typography identify it as such? Choose a short passage and rewrite it for a nonacademic audience. For example, how would your language and style have to change if you were writing it for your younger sister or if you were composing a blog?

EXPLORING CONNECTIONS

6. As Holtzman and Sharpe note, "Throughout our history, there have been an untold number of assaults on the humanness of people of color in the interest of white hegemony" (para. 19). Analyze how Coates's essay (p. 604) links segregation and violence against black people to the maintenance of white supremacy; focus particularly on section 5 ("The Quiet Plunder"). How persuasive is his argument?

7. Holtzman and Sharpe discuss counterstories as a way of refuting false but widely accepted stories about race (p. 637). How does Ta-Nehisi Coates use counterstories or counternarratives to reframe dominant views of American history? Does he succeed in reframing the Federal Housing Administration, the New Deal, and the GI Bill? Do you think that he manages to reframe reparations? Explain your response.

8. What is the source of humor in Barry Deutsch's cartoon below? What does the white woman assume about the black woman's role, and why is the black character so irritated with her?

EXTENDING THE CRITICAL CONTEXT

9. The *Journal of Blacks in Higher Education* has posted a comprehensive list of reported campus racial incidents dating from September 2011 to the present. Visit the journal's website (www.jbhe.com/incidents) and read a half dozen of the nearly 200 summaries of the incidents; coordinate with other class members to cover different portions of the list. Jointly report your findings to the class: Do you see any patterns in the issues that are raised? How many are overtly hostile acts? How many involve students, professors, or administrators? How does the college respond? What steps might be taken to prevent similar incidents in the future?

10. Write a journal entry describing an experience that made you question a preconception you had about another race, ethnicity, religion, or nationality. What did you believe about the group before this experience, and what happened to make you question your view? Did you change as a result? If so, how and why?

11. Watch Jordan Peele's horror/comedy *Get Out* and write an analysis of the white characters' frontstage and backstage behavior. What's the source of comedy when Chris, the black protagonist, meets the slightly too-friendly white parents of his fiancée? In what ways are the neighbors' interactions with Chris both creepy and funny? When and how do the backstage attitudes of the white characters become clear?

GENTRIFICATION

SHERMAN ALEXIE

This short story packs a punch: in a scant three pages, Sherman Alexie manages to explore the racial dynamics of city life with his trademark humor. Alexie (b. 1966) grew up on the Spokane Indian Reservation in Washington State but attended a high school where, in his words, he was "the only Indian . . . except the school mascot." He has written four novels, including *Reservation Blues* (1995), which won an American Book Award; *Indian Killer* (1996); *Flight* (2007); and the semi-autobiographical young adult novel *The Absolutely True Diary of a Part-Time Indian* that won the 2007 National Book Award for Young People's Literature. In addition, he's produced seventeen volumes of poems and short stories, among them *War Dances* (2009), winner of the 2010 PEN/Faulkner Award for Fiction. He coauthored the script for the prize-winning film *Smoke Signals* (1998), wrote and directed *The Business of Fancydancing* (2002), and in 2014 produced a film adaptation of James Welch's classic novel *Winter in the Blood*. In 2017, he was accused of sexual harassment; Alexie admitted "there are women telling the truth about my behavior" and apologized to the people he had hurt. Previously, the American Library Association (ALA) had announced that Alexie's memoir, *You Don't Have to Say You Love Me* (2017) was the winner of its Carnegie Medal for nonfiction, but because of the harassment scandal, Alexie declined the award. The ALA also rescinded its 2008 award for Best Young Adult novel. This selection comes from *Blasphemy: New and Selected Stories* (2012).

A MONTH AGO, MY NEXT-DOOR NEIGHBORS tossed a horribly stained mattress onto the curb in front of their house. I suppose they believed the mattress would be collected on our next regular garbage day. But the city charges thirty dollars to dispose of bulky items and you have to go online and schedule the pickup. Obviously, my neighbors had not bothered to schedule such an appointment. I'd thought the city, once they'd learned of the abandoned mattress, would have collected it anyway and automatically added the charge, plus a fine, to my neighbors' utility bill.

But four garbage collection days passed and nothing happened. The mattress, dank and dirty to begin with, had begun to mold. There were new holes in the fabric that I assumed were made by rats. We live in a large waterfront city so there are millions of rodents. It's an expected, if rather unwelcome, part of urban life. In every city in the world, there are more rats than people. But one doesn't throw a potential home for them onto the curb in front of one's house. That mattress was an apartment building for rats. Or at least a vacation home.

I'd thought to call the city and tell them about the mattress, but I doubted that I would have remained anonymous.

I am the only white man living on a block where all of my neighbors are black. Don't get me wrong. My neighbors are like any other group of neighbors I've ever had. They are the same self-appointed guardians, social directors, friendly alcoholics, paranoid assholes, overburdened parents, sullen teenagers, flirty housewives, elderly misers, amateur comedians, and hermits that exist in every neighborhood of every city in the country. They are people, not black people; and I am a person, not a white person. And that is how we relate to one another, as people. I'm not treated as the white guy on the block, at least not overtly or rudely, and I do not treat my neighbors as if they are some kind of aliens. We live as people live, aware of racial dynamics but uninterested in their applications as it applies to our neighborhood.

My next-door neighbors, an older couple with two adult sons living at home, are kind. All four of them often sit on their front porch, sharing snacks and drinks, and greeting everybody who walks past. But they'd been sitting only a few feet away from the mattress they'd so haphazardly tossed onto the curb. How could they have continued to live as if creating such a mess were normal? I wanted to ask them what they planned to do about the mattress, though I wasn't even sure of the older son's name. It's something ornately African-sounding that I hadn't quite understood when I'd first met him, and it was too late, a year later, to ask for the proper pronunciation. And that made me feel racist. If his name were something more typical, like Ron or Eddie or Vlad or Pete or Carlos or Juan, then I would have remembered it later. The simple names are easier to remember. So, in this regard, perhaps I am racist.

And, frankly, it felt racist for me to look out my front window at that abandoned mattress and wonder about the cultural norms that allowed my neighbors, so considerate otherwise, to create a health hazard.

And why hadn't my other neighbors complained? Or maybe they had complained and the city had ignored the mattress because it was a black neighborhood? Who was the most racist in that situation? Was it the white man who was too terrified to confront his black neighbors on their rudeness? Was it the black folks who abandoned the mattress on their curb? Was it the black people who didn't feel the need to judge the behavior of their black neighbors? Was it the city, which let a mattress molder on the street in full view of hundreds, if not thousands, of people? Or was it all of us, black and white, passively revealing that, despite our surface friendliness, we didn't really care about one another?

In any case, after another garbage day had passed, I rented a U-Haul truck, a flatbed with enough room to carry the mattress, and parked it—hid it, really—two blocks away. I didn't want to embarrass or anger my neighbors so I set my alarm for three A.M. I didn't turn on the lights as I donned gloves, coveralls, and soft-soled shoes. Perhaps I was being overcautious. But it was fun, too, to be on a secret mission.

I slowly opened my front door, worried the hinges might creak, and took step after careful step on the porch, avoiding the loose boards. Then I walked across my lawn rather than on the sidewalk. A dog barked. It was slightly foggy. A bat swooped near a streetlight. For a moment, I felt like I'd walked into a werewolf movie. Then I wondered what the police would do if they discovered a clean-cut white man creeping through a black neighborhood.

"Buddy," the cops would say. "You don't fit the profile of the neighborhood."

I almost laughed out loud at my joke. That would have been a stu- 10
pid way to get caught.

Then I stood next to the mattress and realized that I hadn't figured out how I was supposed to carry that heavy, awkward, water-logged thing two blocks to the truck.

Given more time, I probably could have rigged up a pulley system or a Rube Goldberg contraption that would have worked. But all I had that night was brute strength, without the brute.

I kicked the mattress a few times to flush out any rats. Then I grabbed the mattress's plastic handles—thank God they were still intact—and tried to lift the thing. It was heavier than I expected, and smelled and felt like a dead dolphin.

At first I tried to drag the mattress, but that made too much noise. Then I tried to carry it on my back, but it kept sliding from my grip. My only option was to carry the mattress on my head, like an African woman gracefully walking with a vase of water balanced on her head, except without her grace.

Of course, the mattress was too heavy and unbalanced to be car- 15
ried that way for long. It kept slipping off my head onto the sidewalk. It didn't make much noise when it fell; I was more worried that my lung-burning panting would wake everybody.

It took me twenty minutes to carry that mattress to the truck and another ten to slide it into the flatbed. Then I got behind the wheel and drove to the city's waste disposal facility in the Fremont neighborhood. But it wouldn't open for another two hours so I parked on the street, lay across the seat, and fell asleep in the truck.

I was awakened by the raw noise of recycling and garbage trucks. I wiped my mouth, ran my fingers through my hair, and hoped that I wouldn't offend anybody with my breath. I also hoped that the facility workers wouldn't think that filthy mattress was mine. But I shouldn't have worried. The workers were too busy to notice one bad-breathed man with one rat-stained mattress.

They charged me forty bucks to dispose of the mattress, and it was worth it. Then I returned the truck to the U-Haul rental site and took a taxi back to my house.

I felt clean. I felt rich and modest, like an anonymous benefactor.

When I stepped out of the taxi I saw my neighbors—mother, father, 20 and two adult sons—sitting in the usual places on their porch. They were drinking Folgers instant coffee, awful stuff they'd shared with me on many occasions.

I waved to them but they didn't wave back. I pretended they hadn't noticed me and waved again. They stared at me. They knew what I had done.

"You didn't have to do that," said the son with the African name. "We can take care of ourselves."

"I'm sorry," I said.

"You think you're better than us, don't you?"

I wanted to say that, when it came to abandoned mattresses, I was 25 better.

"Right now, I feel worse," I said.

I knew I had done a good thing, so why did I hurt so bad? Why did I feel judged?

"You go home, white boy," the son said. "And don't you bother us anymore."

I knew the entire block would now shun me. I felt pale and lost, like an American explorer in the wilderness.

ENGAGING THE TEXT

1. What's the significance of the title, "Gentrification"? Is it serious, ironic, or both? Why?

2. How would you describe the unnamed narrator of this story? When he considers calling the city about the abandoned mattress, why is he concerned about remaining anonymous? Why does he hide the flatbed truck two blocks away from his neighbors' house? Why does he collect the mattress at 3:00 A.M. and take multiple precautions not to make any noise? Is he afraid of something? If so, what?

3. Mentioning that he is the only white man in an all-black neighborhood, the narrator explains, "We live as people live, aware of racial dynamics but uninterested in their applications as it applies to our neighborhood" (para. 4). Do you see any evidence in the story that suggests he's mistaken, self-deluded, or lying?

4. How would you respond to the series of questions that the narrator raises in paragraph 6: "Who was the most racist in that situation? Was it the white man . . . Was it the black folks . . . Was it the city . . . Or was it all of us, black and white . . . ?" Keeping in mind that the narrator may be unreliable, discuss these questions in small groups and try to come to a consensus. Report your group's conclusions to the class: If there are differences of interpretation, how do you account for them?

5. How does the narrator feel after disposing of the mattress? Why do his neighbors resent what he did, and why does he feel judged? Do you ever sympathize with the narrator? How do you interpret the final sentence of the story: "I felt pale and lost, like an American explorer in the wilderness" (para. 29)? Can you read it in more than one way? If so, how?

EXPLORING CONNECTIONS

6. To what extent does Linda Holtzman and Leon Sharpe's definition of "implicit bias" in "Theories and Constructs of Race" (p. 631) apply to the narrator? Look closely at his rationale for not remembering the older son's name: "It's something ornately African-sounding. . . . If his name were something more typical, like Ron or Eddie or Vlad or Pete or Carlos or Juan, then I would have remembered it later" (para. 5). Does his admission that "perhaps" he's a racist get him off the hook? Do you see any other indications in the story that the narrator may be operating out of internalized stereotypes or a sense of innate superiority?

EXTENDING THE CRITICAL CONTEXT

7. Watch the short documentary "White People" (at www.lookdifferent.org) in which the director, Jose Antonio Vargas, talks to millennials about what it means to be young and white. What's your reaction to the film? Do you identify with any of the individuals depicted in it? If so, who and why? Write a journal entry exploring these issues.

8. According to a story by National Public Radio, Alexie "traded on his literary celebrity to lure [women] into uncomfortable sexual situations." To find out how his behavior has affected young women and Native American writers, read the following report:

> https://www.npr.org/2018/03/05/589909379/it-just-felt-very-wrong-sherman-alexies-accusers-go-on-the-record

In light of Alexie's misconduct, do you think that his work should or should not be included in textbooks like *Rereading America*? Why?

NOBODY

MARC LAMONT HILL

Writing of Michael Brown's killing and the months of protest that followed, social activist Marc Lamont Hill claims, "There is no formal poll tax to march against any more, no segregation of the lunch counter. But the kind of injustice that the story of Ferguson illuminates is just as insidious as the earlier battles of the freedom struggle." In "Nobody," Hill contends that Brown and other victims of police violence illustrate our failure to care for the poor, the young, the neglected, the vulnerable — the Nobodies. Hill is the Steve Charles Professor of Media, Cities, and Solutions at Temple University. He has published *Gentrifier* (2017, with John Joe Schlichtman and Jason Patch), *The Classroom and the Cell: Conversations on Black Life in America* (2012, with Mumia Abu-Jamal), and *Beats, Rhymes, and Classroom Life: Hip-Hop Pedagogy and the Politics of Identity* (2009). He has also coedited two collections of essays on media and hip-hop education. Hill is the host of BET News and HuffPost Live and a frequent political contributor to CNN. In 2011, *Ebony* named him one of their Power 100, a list of inspiring African Americans. This essay comes from Hill's best-seller *Nobody: Casualties of America's War on the Vulnerable from Ferguson to Flint and Beyond* (2016).

TO BE NOBODY IS TO BE VULNERABLE. In the most basic sense, all of us are vulnerable; to be human is to be susceptible to misfortune, violence, illness, and death. The role of government, however, is to offer forms of protection that enhance our lives and shield our bodies from foreseeable and preventable dangers. Unfortunately, for many citizens — particularly those marked as poor, Black, Brown, immigrant, queer, or trans — State power has only increased their vulnerability, making their lives more rather than less unsafe.

To be Nobody is to be subject to State violence. In recent years, thousands of Americans have died at the hands of law enforcement, a reality made even more shameful when we consider how many of these victims were young, poor, mentally ill, Black, or unarmed. The cases of Michael Brown in Ferguson, Missouri; Eric Garner[1] in New York City; Kathryn Johnston[2]

---

[1]**Eric Garner:** (1970–2014) Arrested for selling individual cigarettes illegally, Garner was put in a chokehold and held face down on the sidewalk; he repeated, "I can't breathe" eleven times, lost consciousness, and died. [All notes are the author's except 1–10, 25, 50, 51, and 56.]

[2]**Kathryn Johnston:** (1914–2006) 92-year old Johnston was shot and killed by undercover police during an illegal raid on her home.

in Atlanta; Trayvon Martin[3] in Sanford, Florida; Freddie Gray[4] in Baltimore; and Sandra Bland[5] in Hempstead, Texas, have forced a stubborn nation to come to terms with the realities of police corruption, brutality, and deeply entrenched racism. While media coverage and global activism have turned these individuals into household names, they are not, sadly, exceptional. Instead, they represent the countless Americans who die daily, and unnecessarily, at the hands of those who are paid to protect and serve them.

To be Nobody is to also confront systemic forms of State violence. Long before he was standing in front of the barrel of Darren Wilson's gun, Michael Brown was the victim of broken schools and evaporated labor markets. Prior to being choked to death by Daniel Pantaleo, Eric Garner lived in a community terrorized by policing practices that transform neighborhoods into occupied territories and citizens into enemy combatants. Sandra Bland's tragic death sequence did not begin with a negligent jailer or an unreasonable cop but with a criminal justice system that has consistently neglected the emotional, physical, and psychological well-being of Black women and girls. For the vulnerable, it is the violence of the ordinary, the terrorism of the quotidian, the injustice of the everyday, that produces the most profound and intractable social misery.

To be Nobody is to be abandoned by the State. For decades now, we have witnessed a radical transformation in the role and function of government in America. An obsession with free-market logic and culture has led the political class to craft policies that promote private interests over the public good. As a result, our schools, our criminal justice system, our military, our police departments, our public policy, and virtually every other entity engineered to protect life and enhance prosperity have been at least partially relocated to the private sector. At the same time, the private sector has kept its natural commitment to maximizing profits rather than investing in people. This arrangement has left the nation's vulnerable wedged between the Scylla of negligent government and the Charybdis of corporate greed, trapped in a historically unprecedented state of precarity.

*   *   *

Forty years from now, we will still be talking about what happened   5
in Ferguson. It will be mentioned in high school history textbooks.

---

[3]**Trayvon Martin:** (1995–2012) A high school junior, Martin had gone to a convenience store for a snack and was walking back to the town home he was visiting; George Zimmerman, a neighborhood watch coordinator, followed him and called 911 to report a suspicious person. Martin's girlfriend, who was on the phone with him, heard him say, "Why are you following me?" In an ensuing altercation, Zimmerman shot and killed Martin.

[4]**Freddie Gray:** (1989–2015) Police arrested Gray for having a knife in his pocket (it was legal). They loaded him into a van, handcuffed, without a seatbelt; forty-five minutes later, he was found unconscious in the van with a nearly severed spinal cord. He died in the hospital a week later.

[5]**Sandra Bland:** (1987–2015) Stopped for failing to signal a turn, Bland was ordered to put out her cigarette, and she asked why; the conflict with the police officer grew heated and he arrested her for assault. Bland had experienced depression and attempted suicide in the past, and three days after her arrest, she hanged herself in her cell.

Hollywood studios will make movies about it, as they now make movies about Selma. Politicians will talk about "how far we have come since Ferguson" in the same way they talk today about how far we have come since Little Rock, Greensboro, or Birmingham.[6]

Ferguson is that important.

But why?

After all, to some, Ferguson isn't as worthy as other markers on the historical timeline of social-justice struggle. And Ferguson's native son Michael Brown, whose tragic death in 2014 put the small Missouri town on the map, was certainly no traditional hero. He did not lead a march or give a stirring speech. He did not challenge racial apartheid by refusing to sit in the back of a bus, attempting to eat at a "Whites only" lunch counter, or breaking the color barrier in a major professional sport. He wrote no books, starred in no movies, occupied no endowed chair at a major university, and held no political office. He was no Jackie Robinson,[7] no Rosa Parks,[8] no Bayard Rustin,[9] no Fannie Lou Hamer,[10] no Barack Obama. If he could see what has happened in reaction to his death, he would likely be stunned.

Brown was just eighteen years old on the morning of Saturday, August 9, 2014, when he decided to meet up with his friend Dorian Johnson—who would later become Witness 101 in the Department of Justice (DOJ) federal investigation report—and together they settled on a mission to get high. Johnson, who was twenty-two, had not known Brown very long but, being older, considered himself as somewhat of a role model to the teen. Although he was unemployed, Johnson worked whenever he could find available jobs, paid his rent on time, and consistently supported his girlfriend and their baby daughter.

Brown had just graduated, albeit with some difficulty, from Normandy High School, part of a 98 percent African-American school district where test scores are so low that it lost state accreditation in 2012.[11] In addition to low test scores, incidents of violence have become so common at Normandy that it is now considered one of the most dangerous schools

10

---

[6]**Little Rock, Greensboro, and Birmingham:** All touchstones of the civil rights movement. In 1957, nine African American students enrolled in Little Rock, Arkansas's segregated Central High School and persisted in the face of violent demonstrations by whites; in 1960, four black college students staged the first sit-in at a lunch counter in Greensboro, North Carolina, to protest segregation; in 1963, white supremacists bombed the 16th Street Baptist Church in Birmingham, Alabama, killing four little girls.

[7]**Jackie Robinson:** (1919–1972) In 1947 became the first black player in the modern era to integrate Major League Baseball.

[8]**Rosa Parks:** (1913–2005) Civil rights activist whose arrest for refusing to give up her seat on the bus to a white man sparked the Montgomery Bus Boycott of 1955–56.

[9]**Bayard Rustin:** (1912–1987) Civil rights organizer, openly gay man, and adviser to Martin Luther King Jr.

[10]**Fannie Lou Hamer:** (1917–1977) Civil rights leader who helped register black voters in Mississippi and, with an integrated group of activists, challenged the all-white Mississippi delegation at the Democratic National Convention in 1964.

[11]Jessica Bock, "State Votes to Strip Normandy Schools of Accreditation," *St. Louis Post-Dispatch*, September 18, 2012, http://www.stltoday.com/news/local/education/state-votes-to-strip-normandy-schools-of-accreditation/article_d5a11724-01a4-11e2-87a5-0019bb30f31a.html.

in Missouri.[12] Conditions in the Normandy School District are so dire that it has become a talking point in the school-choice debate, with conservatives pointing to the schools' failures as evidence that privatized educational options are necessary.[13] Despite this troublesome academic environment, Brown, like many teenagers of color, had a positive and eclectic set of aspirations. He wanted to learn sound engineering, play college football, become a rap artist, and be a heating and cooling technician; he also wanted to "be famous."[14,15] All of this was part of the conversation between Brown and Johnson that morning.

In need of cigarillos to empty out for rolling paper for their marijuana blunts, Brown and Johnson entered Ferguson Market and Liquor, a popular convenience store at 9101 West Florissant Avenue. As video footage shows, Brown swiped the cigarillos from the counter without paying. The store's owner, an immigrant from India[16] who did not speak English, came around to challenge him. Brown, whose nickname "Big Mike"[17] derived from his six-foot-four-inch and nearly three-hundred-pound frame, gave a final shove[18] to the shopkeeper before departing. While the surveillance camera captured the entire interaction, it did not show how badly the incident shocked Johnson. He had never seen Brown commit a crime, nor had Brown given him any reason to think he would. "Hey, I don't do stuff like that," he said to Brown as they walked home, knowing that the shopkeeper had promised to call the police. Quickly, Johnson's feelings shifted from shock and anxiety about being caught on camera to genuine concern for Brown. He turned to him and asked, "What's going on?"[19]

While interesting, all of this was mere overture to the main event that tragically awaited Brown and Johnson, one that would make both

---

[12] Elisa Crouch, "Normandy High: The Most Dangerous School in the Area," *St. Louis Post-Dispatch*, May 5, 2013, http://www.stltoday.com/news/local/education/normandy-high-the-most-dangerous-school-in-the-area/article_49a1b882-cd74-5cc4-8096-fcb1405d8380.html.

[13] While the widespread media exposure of the Brown shooting has made the Normandy School District part of the national education debate, it has been part of the statewide conversation for years. For an example of the conservative argument, see James V. Shuls's op-ed, "School Choice Must Be an Option," in the *St. Louis American*, May 27, 2015, http://www.stlamerican.com/news/editorials/article_c1e39f38-04e2-11e5-bde2-3b8a2d8949e9.html.

[14] Jessica Lussenhop, "Family of Michael Brown, Teenager Shot to Death by Ferguson Police, Talks About His Life," *Riverfront Times*, August 10, 2014, http://www.riverfronttimes.com/newsblog/2014/08/10/family-of-michael-brown-teenager-shot-to-death-by-ferguson-police-talks-about-his-life.

[15] Catherine E. Shoichet, "Missouri Teen Shot by Police Was Two Days Away from Starting College," CNN.com, August 13, 2014, http://www.cnn.com/2014/08/11/justice/michael-brown-missouri-teen-shot/index.html.

[16] Paul Hampel, "Ferguson Market and Liquor," *St. Louis Post-Dispatch*, August 3, 2015, http://www.stltoday.com/news/special-reports/multimedia/ferguson-market-liquor/article_ead8b0f8-e91c-507c-a45f-7a53c574b75f.html.

[17] Gore Perry Reporting, Video transcript of grand jury hearing in *State of Missouri v. Darren Wilson*, vol. 4, September 10, 2014, 19, http://www.documentcloud.org/documents/1370541-grand-jury-volume-4.html.

[18] Ibid., 36.

[19] Ibid., 38.

of them unlikely entries in the history books. Brown and Johnson were in the middle of residential Canfield Drive a few minutes later when twenty-eight-year-old police officer Darren Wilson saw the two jaywalking "along the double yellow line."[20] According to Johnson, Wilson told them to "get the fuck on the sidewalk," though Wilson denies using profanity.[21,22] Regardless of the tone of their initial exchange, the interaction created room for Wilson to link Johnson and Brown to the robbery report and suspect description that had been given over the police radio. The next forty-five seconds—disputed, dissected, and debated ad nauseam throughout the ensuing months—would soon became the focus of international attention.

But how could such a random encounter, in the largely unknown St. Louis suburb of Ferguson, possibly mean so much?

* * *

There was, and is, no disagreement as to the result of Darren Wilson's confrontation with Michael Brown. After a brief struggle at Wilson's car,[23] Brown fled the scene and was pursued by the officer in a chase that ended with the unarmed Brown struck dead by bullets fired from Wilson's Sig Sauer S&W 40-caliber semiautomatic pistol. What remains, however, is the dispute about whether the shooting was criminal. Both the St. Louis County grand jury, which met for twenty-five days over a three-month period and heard a total of sixty witnesses,[24] as well as a separate investigation done by the USDOJ[25] that investigated potential civil-rights violations, determined that there was no cause to indict Wilson for his actions. The seven men and five women who made up that

[20]Ibid, vol. 5, September 16, 2014, https://www.documentcloud.org/documents/1370494-grand-jury-volume-5.html.

[21]Gore Perry, transcript of grand jury, vol. 4, 45.

[22]According to a March 2015 Department of Justice memorandum: "When pressed by federal prosecutors, Wilson denied using profane language, explaining that he was on his way to meet his fiancée for lunch, and did not want to antagonize the two subjects. Witness 101 responded to Wilson that he was almost to his destination, and Wilson replied, 'What's wrong with the sidewalk?'" United States Department of Justice, "Department of Justice Report Regarding the Criminal Investigation into the Shooting Death of Michael Brown by Ferguson, Missouri Police Officer Darren Wilson," March 4, 2015, 12, http://www.justice.gov/sites/default/files/opa/press-releases/attachments/2015/03/04/doj_report_on_shooting_of_michael_brown_l.pdf.

[23]From the DOJ memorandum summarizing its findings: "Wilson and other witnesses stated that Brown then reached into the SUV through the open driver's window and punched and grabbed Wilson. This is corroborated by bruising on Wilson's jaw and scratches on his neck, the presence of Brown's DNA on Wilson's collar, shirt, and pants, and Wilson's DNA on Brown's palm. While there are other individuals who stated that Wilson reached out of the SUV and grabbed Brown by the neck, prosecutors could not credit their accounts because they were inconsistent with physical and forensic evidence, as detailed throughout this report." United States Department of Justice, "Department of Justice Report Regarding the Criminal Investigation into the Shooting Death of Michael Brown," 6.

[24]Erik Eckholm, "Witnesses Told Grand Jury That Michael Brown Charged at Darren Wilson, Prosecutor Says," New York Times, November 24, 2014, http://www.nytimes.com/2014/11/25/us/witnesses-told-grand-jury-that-michael-brown-charged-at-darren-wilson-prosecutor-says.html.

[25]**USDOJ:** United States Department of Justice.

grand jury—three Black and nine White, chosen to reflect the racial makeup of St. Louis county, though not the overwhelmingly Black population of Ferguson itself—and the FBI investigators working on the federal study concluded that Brown had not been shot in the back, as some had initially said. Assertions that Brown had put his hands in the air and said "Don't shoot" in the moments before he was killed—an image so disturbing, it became a rallying cry for protesters determined to see that Wilson was indicted—were also not supported by witnesses who watched the encounter. Those conclusions, when matched with Wilson's testimony that he feared for his life in the confrontation with Brown and with Missouri's broad latitude for police use of deadly force,[26] left little legal room to justify an indictment. But the law does not tell the full story.

The law is but a mere social construction, an artifact of our social, economic, political, and cultural conditions. The law represents only one kind of truth, often an unsatisfying truth, and ultimately not the truest of truths. The rush of public emotion that spilled into the streets after the killing of Michael Brown alerted the world to the existence of a multitude of other, competing truths. Whatever the facts may have shown in this instance—including the forensic evidence and the parade of witnesses who recanted earlier statements—Michael Brown's life was taken with disturbingly casual ease. This indifference unmoored racial and class antagonisms long held in awkward restraint. 15

There was not only Brown's shooting to consider; there was also the aftermath. There was Brown's body, left for hours on the hot pavement, his crimson blood puddling next to his young head, staining the street, flowing in a crisscross pattern, a tributary running slowly to the gutter. Eventually, an officer produced a bedsheet and placed it over Brown's frame, a figure so large that the cover could not shield it all, the oversized teenager's legs left peeking out from the bottom. Though it was early August, a wintry stillness set in over the next four hours, as police officers stood stone-faced and crowds of passers-by gazed in astonishment. While this was happening, Michael Brown remained on the street, discarded like animal entrails behind a butcher shop. As Keisha, a local resident who I interviewed a week after the shooting, said to me, "They just left him there . . . Like he ain't belong to nobody."

Nobody.

No parents who loved him. No community that cared for him. No medical establishment morally compelled to save him. No State duty-bound to invest in him, before or after his death. Michael Brown was treated as if he was not entitled to the most basic elements of democratic citizenship, not to mention human decency. He was treated as if he was not a person, much less an American. He was disposable.

Despite the heated claims by many observers, Michael Brown was not "innocent," as either a moral or legal designation. To the contrary,

---

[26]Missouri Rev. Statues, Ann. § 563.046.1 (Missouri General Assembly 2015), http://www.moga.mo.gov/mostatutes/stathtml/56300000461.html.

it is virtually indisputable that Brown made bad choices, both in the convenience store and in his subsequent interactions with Darren Wilson. But the deeper issue is that one should not need to be innocent to avoid execution (particularly through extrajudicial means) by the State. After all, theft, even strong-arm theft, is not a capital offense in the United States.

It is also not clear that Wilson was acting with racist intentions—but, like debates about Mike Brown's "innocence," this is beyond the point. Even if Wilson operated with the best of conscious intentions, he was nonetheless following the logic of the current moment, one marked by what Princeton race scholar Imani Perry calls "post-intentional racism."[27] Perry argues that contemporary understandings of racism cannot be reduced to intentional acts of bigotry, beliefs in biological determinism, or even subconscious prejudices. Instead, we must rely on a thicker analysis, one that accounts for the structural, psychological, and cultural dimensions of racism. With regard to Darren Wilson, even if he held no personal racial animus, he nonetheless approached Michael Brown carrying a particular set of assumptions about the world. Like everyone else's, Wilson's assumptions included socially constructed narratives about Black men, Ferguson residents, and even what constituted a lethal threat.[28] Beyond the level of the personal, Wilson also obediently and uncritically followed the protocol of a system already engineered to target, exploit, and criminalize the poor, the Black, the Brown, the queer, the trans, the immigrant, and the young.

For many of the thousands who erupted in protest after Michael Brown's death, and again after the grand jury's subsequent decision not to indict Darren Wilson, the motivating factor for their anger was not shock.[29] To the contrary, the incident between Brown and Wilson was animated by a set of beliefs and conditions that were all too familiar: the assumptions that all people of color are violent criminals from birth; that petty crimes are the neon arrow pointing to someone already involved in, or destined to commit, more serious crimes; that there is money to be made in overpolicing minor offenses; and that poverty, race, and gender nonconformity are identifiers of moral failings so rich that there is no longer any reason to recognize the rights, the citizenship, or the humanity of those so identified.

[27]See Imani Perry, *More Beautiful and More Terrible: The Embrace and Transcendence of Racial Inequality in the United States* (New York: New York University Press, 2011).

[28]Wilson's beliefs on these topics were made clear in Jake Halpern's article in the August 10 & 17, 2015, issue of the *New Yorker*, "The Man Who Shot Michael Brown." In it, Wilson argues that Black people lack initiative to find jobs. While he acknowledges the scarcity of employment, he adds, "There's also lack of initiative to get a job. You can lead a horse to water, but you can't make it drink." He also discusses parenting, attitudes toward police, and other issues in the Black community. The article is viewable at http://www.newyorker.com/magazine/2015/08/10/the-cop.

[29]This lack of shock stands in contrast to the narratives of surprise and sentiments suggesting that "This shouldn't happen here" that accompany tragedies in majority-White areas. For an examination of such narratives, see Marc Lamont Hill, "This Shouldn't Happen Here: Sandy Hook, Race, and the Pedagogy of Normalcy," *Journal of Curriculum and Pedagogy* 10, no. 2 (2013): 109–12.

This attitude—most visible in the conduct of law enforcement, but pervasive throughout the halls of power—is not a phenomenon limited to Ferguson or even St. Louis. In response to the grand jury's decision not to indict Darren Wilson, crowds of protesters appeared in Oakland, Los Angeles, Dallas, Denver, Washington, Minneapolis, Chicago, Atlanta, and New York to stand in solidarity. They wanted not only to see justice prevail in this particular instance but also to assert the deeper symbolic importance of the story. They wanted to express its clear resonance, to speak to their own sense of familiarity with the circumstances that in an instant left an unarmed eighteen-year-old Black boy holding a pack of stolen cigarillos dead in the street. "Enough," read placards raised by marchers in Atlanta. "We are all one bullet away from being a hashtag."[30]

The teenager and the police officer had become like characters in a national morality play with so many rich ironies and plot twists, so many double meanings in the language of its participants, that it was hard not to feel that we were witnessing the playing out of a civic parable. "As he is coming towards me, I . . . keep telling him to get on the ground," the sandy-haired Wilson told the grand jury, using phrases that made him sound like he was a game hunter confronting a wildebeest:

"He doesn't. I shoot a series of shots. I don't know how many I shot, I just know I shot it."

"It." Not "him," not "Brown," not "the teenager," not even "the perp." Wilson told the grand jury that he had shot "It."[31]

"I know I missed a couple, I don't know how many, but I know I hit him at least once because I saw his body kind of jerk."[32]

The aim was not mere incapacitation; it was execution.

"At this point I start backpedaling and again, I tell him get on the ground, get on the ground, he doesn't. I shoot another round of shots . . ."

An invader who had burst through the neighborhood barriers.

"It looked like he was almost bulking up to run through the shots, like it was making him mad that I'm shooting at him."

A Magical Negro with superhuman powers.

"And the face that he had was looking straight through me, like I wasn't even there, I wasn't even anything in his way."

---

[30]Steve Almasy and Holly Yan, "Protestors Fill Streets Across Country as Ferguson Protests Spread Coast to Coast," CNN.com, November 26, 2014, http://www.cnn.com/2014/11/25/us/national-ferguson-protests/index.html.

[31]It is disputable whether Wilson was referring to Brown when using the term "it." Some argue that he was referring to his gun, while others suggest "it" referred to Brown's head, which is also referenced in the transcript. After careful reading of the text, however, I strongly believe that Wilson was referring to Brown. This is also supported by other statements made by Wilson, in which he describes Brown as subhuman in his response to being shot.

[32]Rachel Clarke and Mariano Castillo, "Michael Brown Shooting: What Darren Wilson Told the Ferguson Grand Jury," CNN.com, November 26, 2014, http://www.cnn.com/2014/11/25/justice/ferguson-grand-jury-documents/index.html; Juliet Lapidos, "How Darren Wilson Saw Michael Brown," nytimes.com, November 25, 2014, http://takingnote.blogs.nytimes.com/2014/11/25/how-darren-wilson-saw-michael-brown-in-ferguson/.

In Wilson's account, it is the Magical Negro who dehumanizes the courageous officer. Ironically, this process humanizes the officer and dehumanizes the Magical Negro to the jury and the broader public.

"And then when [the bullet] went into him, the demeanor on his face went blank, the aggression was gone . . . the threat was stopped."

Nobody.

*   *   *

In a mockery of the city's longstanding efforts to maintain segregation, St. Louis's inner ring of suburbs, once nearly exclusively White, became home to thousands of poor and middle-class Blacks. One reason for the shift was economic: there were simply too few opportunities for employment in St. Louis. Another was the opportunity for better housing; as Whites moved out to shinier, newer developments, housing in the older suburbs opened up. But while the Black population in Ferguson had grown from just 1 percent in 1970 to roughly 25 percent in 1990, the 2010 census revealed an even more dramatic shift to 67 percent Black. Over the course of forty years, Ferguson had become a majority-Black city, indicative of a trend that extended beyond St. Louis. Amazing as it may seem, there are now more poor people and more African-American people living in American suburbs than in American cities.[33]

The problem in Ferguson, of course, was that the administration of the city did not change with these demographic shifts. While the city itself was becoming largely African-American, most positions of authority — including the mayoralty, most of the city council, and all but three police officers in a fifty-three-officer department — were held by Whites.[34] But much more important than that, as the second part of the DOJ investigation of the killing of Michael Brown revealed, the social distance between those in positions of authority — particularly the police, but others as well — and those who actually lived in Ferguson was now vast. As the city became African-American, the Ferguson Police Department (FPD) shifted from being the protector of the people of Ferguson to their user and abuser.

How else to explain the DOJ's finding that Ferguson officers "routinely conduct[ed] stops that [had] little relation to public safety and a questionable basis in law," often issuing multiple citations for

[33]*The Avenue* (blog of the Brookings Institution); "On Ferguson, Fragmentation, and Fiscal Disparities," blog entry by Bruce Katz and Elizabeth Kneebone, April 2, 2015, http://www.brookings.edu/blogs/the-avenue/posts/2015/04/02-ferguson-fragmentation-fiscal-disparities-katz-kneebone; see also Alana Semuels, "Suburbs and the New American Poverty," *Atlantic*, January 7, 2015, http://www.theatlantic.com/business/archive/2015/01/suburbs-and-the-new-american-poverty/384259/. For a more detailed analysis of the experiences of African-Americans in the suburbs, as well as the material consequences of such population shifts, see R. L'Heureux Lewis-McCoy's *Inequality in the Promised Land: Race, Resources, and Suburban Schooling* (Palo Alto, CA: Stanford University Press, 2014).

[34]Paulina Firozi, "5 Things to Know About Ferguson Police Department," USA Today Network, August 19, 2014, http://www.usatoday.com/story/news/nation-now/2014/08/14/ferguson-police-department-details/14064451/.

the same violation, and all in the interest of increasing revenue to the department?[35] How else to understand that in the FPD budgets, "fines and fees" accounted for nearly one quarter of the department's operating revenue ($3.09 million in 2015), and that it urged officers in performance reviews to help achieve this number, as if they were a sales team needing to make their fourth-quarter projection? What else are we to make of the fact that at the time of the DOJ investigation, more than sixteen thousand people—this out of a population of twenty thousand—had some form of outstanding arrest warrant, nearly all of them relating to a missed payment or court appearance on a traffic fine or a (usually minor) municipal code violation?[36] As a report in the *Washington Post* revealed, it was not unusual for towns in St. Louis County to cite residents for loud music, unkempt property, disruptive behavior, and even "saggy pants."[37] These penalties reflect a long history of public-nuisance laws being used in ways that further marginalize the vulnerable, and reinforce the idea that poverty, mental illness, and even Blackness are threats to the public good.[38]

In the course of their study, the DOJ investigators also discovered repeated instances of Ferguson police issuing arrest warrants without probable cause, in direct violation of the Fourth Amendment, and of police being unaware, in general, of the constitutional restrictions on their conduct. Confronted, for instance, about one situation in which Ferguson officials arrested a man without a warrant (and, as it turned out, on false conclusions), the officers explained away objections by asserting that the detainee was held in an "air-conditioned" environment. They also told investigators that the disproportionate arrest of African-Americans in Ferguson was indicative of the lack of "personal responsibility" among members of the Black race.

Finally, the DOJ investigation report, released only days before the commemoration of the fiftieth anniversary of the Selma voting rights march known as "Bloody Sunday," found despicable racial stereotypes in e-mails routinely sent within the department, including e-mails comparing President Obama to a chimpanzee and mocking Black citizens' use of language. Others repeated age-old stereotypes of Black people as lazy, ignorant, and "on the take." These Ferguson officials were merely reenacting the quintessentially American ritual of humiliating

40

---

[35]All quoted materials are taken directly from the DOJ report: United States Department of Justice, Civil Rights Division, "Investigation of the Ferguson Police Department," March 4, 2015. You can read the entire DOJ report at http://www.justice.gov/sites/default/files/opa/press-releases/attachments/2015/03/04/ferguson_police_department_report.pdf.

[36]Ibid.

[37]Radley Balko, "How Municipalities in St. Louis County, Mo., Profit from Poverty," *Washington Post*, September 3, 2014, https://www.washingtonpost.com/news/the-watch/wp/2014/09/03/how-st-louis-county-missouri-profits-from-poverty/.

[38]For an excellent conceptual and empirical analysis, see Matthew Desmond and Nicol Valdez, "Unpolicing the Urban Poor: Consequences of Third-Party Policing for Inner-City Women," *American Sociological Review* 78, no. 1 (2003): 117–41. See also Cari Fais, "Denying Access to Justice: The Cost of Applying Chronic Nuisance Laws to Domestic Violence," *Columbia Law Review* 108, no. 5 (2008): 1181–225.

and dehumanizing Black bodies while at the same time exploiting them for economic gain.

A few months after the DOJ report was issued, another study of Ferguson[39] conducted by a Missouri state commission appointed by Governor Jay Nixon, issued a call for reforms, including an expansion of Medicare eligibility, an increase in the minimum wage, a reform of zoning laws, and a new scrutiny of police incidents requiring the use of force. "We know that talking about race makes a lot of people uncomfortable," asserted the authors of the report. "But make no mistake: This is about race."[40]

Yes, except that the story of Ferguson, Missouri—the epic tale that prompts us to keep talking about it—is not only about race. It is not only about the death of a Black teenager at the hands of a White policeman in a department that routinely abused and exploited the city's majority African-American population, not only about the virtual exoneration of Darren Wilson for acting in a manner that, if not criminal, was certainly reckless and avoidably deadly.

Despite the widespread outrage about the grand jury's failure to indict Darren Wilson, the deeper meanings of Ferguson have become more apparent in the aftermath of the non-indictment. If an indictment had been made, a trial convened, and perhaps even a conviction secured, the story of Ferguson would have been reduced to the story of a single act of injustice in a single place at a single time. Such an analysis would only have given comfort to those who would like see the error here as Wilson's (or even Brown's) alone, rather than a signpost of a much deeper and more intractable set of problems.

Michael Brown died at the hands of police in Ferguson, but his killing was preceded by the death of seventeen-year-old Trayvon Martin—armed only with a hoodie, an Arizona Iced Tea, and a bag of Skittles—who was shot dead not as a victim of the police, but of the vigilante George Zimmerman, who was then exonerated in a trial that played out in minute detail on CNN; and by the death of Jordan Davis, who was killed neither by the police nor a vigilante but by Michael Dunn, a White software developer who became irritated by the sound of "thug music" coming from Davis's car.

Michael Brown's death was succeeded by Cleveland, Ohio, police officer Timothy Loehmann's killing of twelve-year-old Tamir Rice in a playground when Rice's toy gun was mistaken for the real thing;[41] by

---

[39]Forward Through Ferguson, "This Report," http://forwardthroughferguson.org/report/executive-summary/clarifying-our-terms/.

[40]Wesley Lowery, "Missouri Commission Formed After Ferguson Concludes: 'Make No Mistake. This Is About Race,'" *Washington Post*, September 14, 2015, https://www.washingtonpost.com/news/post-nation/wp/2015/09/14/missouri-commission-formed-after-ferguson-concludes-make-no-mistake-this-is-about-race/.

[41]Mitch Smith, "Two Reviews of Tamir Rice Shooting in Cleveland Are Seen as Shielding Police," *New York Times*, October 11, 2015, http://www.nytimes.com/2015/10/12/us/tamir-rice-outside-reviews-cleveland-police-charges.html?_r=0.

the killing of Samuel DuBose after University of Cincinnati police officer Ray Tensing stopped DuBose for driving a car without a front license plate and then, when DuBose appeared to be getting ready to drive away, shot him in the head;[42,43] by the killing of Walter Scott after North Charleston, South Carolina, police officer Michael Slager stopped him for a broken taillight. Scott was unarmed and sprinting from the scene when Slager shot him eight times in the back.[44,45]

Michael Brown's death came after the death of Eric Garner, suffocated by New York City policeman Daniel Pantaleo as he arrested Garner for selling loose cigarettes; and before that of Sandra Bland, who allegedly hung herself in a jail cell after she had been arrested for refusing to cooperate with an aggressive Waller County, Texas, officer who had stopped her for changing lanes without signaling.[46] Finally, it came before the death of Freddie Gray from injuries suffered in a Baltimore police van while Gray was in custody for possession of a legal knife. It was this last death—suspicious as it was tragic—that led to weeks of rebellion in Baltimore. These incidents were not extraordinary circumstances, but representations of a chilling pattern of deadly encounters between Black bodies and State power.

Back in 2009, in the heady days of enthusiasm that accompanied the election of a Black man, Barack Obama, to the presidency, the nation was riveted by the "teachable moment" offered when a Cambridge, Massachusetts, police sergeant arrested Henry Louis Gates Jr., the eminent Harvard African-American studies professor, in front of his home. Gates had been dealing with a faulty door key when a passerby, mistaking the scene as a break-in, called the police. Gates verbally challenged Sergeant James Crowley for investigating the scene—the citation refers to "loud and tumultuous behavior"—and in turn, Crowley arrested Gates for disorderly conduct. Amid the ensuing public outcry, President Obama intervened, resulting in what became known as the "Beer Summit," with Crowley, Obama, and Gates engaging in "guy talk and trouser hitching"—Darryl Pinckney's wonderful

---

[42]Richard Pérez-Peña, "University of Cincinnati Officer Indicted in Shooting Death of Samuel Dubose," *New York Times*, July 29, 2015, http://www.nytimes.com/2015/07/30/us/university-of-cincinnati-officer-indicted-in-shooting-death-of-motorist.html.

[43]Charles M. Blow, "The DuBose Family: Grieving, But Determined," *New York Times*, July 30, 2015, http://www.nytimes.com/2015/07/31/opinion/charles-blow-the-dubose-family-grieving-but-determined.html.

[44]Michael S. Schmidt and Matt Apuzzo, "South Carolina Officer Is Charged with Murder of Walter Scott," *New York Times*, April 7, 2015, http://www.nytimes.com/2015/04/08/us/south-carolina-officer-is-charged-with-murder-in-black-mans-death.html.

[45]Alan Blinder and Manny Fernandez, "North Charleston Prepares for Mourning and Protest in Walter Scott Shooting," *New York Times*, April 10, 2015, http://www.nytimes.com/2015/04/11/us/north-charleston-prepares-for-weekend-of-mourning-and-protest-in-walter-scott-shooting.html?_r=2.

[46]Katie Rogers, "The Death of Sandra Bland: Questions and Answers," *New York Times*, July 23, 2015, http://www.nytimes.com/interactive/2015/07/23/us/23blandlisty.html.

image in the *New York Review of Books*[47] — over a few cold-and-frosties at the White House.

The unfortunate and dishonest conclusion of that incident — the first landmark episode of the Obama presidency — was a kind of twenty-first-century retort to Rodney King's 1994 plea for peace: "Yes, we can all get along." Maybe now, with a Black man in the White House, the American Empire was finally prepared to enter its much-desired post-racial era, in which race would no longer be a central organizing feature of our social world. As wrongheaded as the idea was then, it seems downright absurd today. In light of Ferguson, the Beer Summit is quite easily exposed for what it was: a gross trivialization of the racial, cultural, and economic divides that continue to starkly define American life well into the twenty-first century.

Given that it occurred in an upper-middle-class town known for its conspicuously liberal allegiances, and with a protagonist in the form of the very distinguished and respected Gates, one could see how so many were deluded into thinking that the confrontation was all one big, unfortunate misunderstanding. Such an analysis, however, would be nothing short of delusional. The "presumption of guilt," as Harvard law professor Charles Ogletree described it,[48] that characterized Crowley's initial attitude toward Gates was no mere accident. Rather, it has always been the governing logic for White officers engaging Black men and women in America. As the ensuing years have demonstrated so vividly, the Gates-Crowley incident was only the most polite demonstration of this logic.

Indeed, thanks to the Beer Summit, the implicit understanding reached about this event was not that Black America should not be made to suffer such unfortunate and degrading indignities, but that Henry Louis Gates Jr. — prosperous, educated, friend of the president, a commingler with White society — should not be made to suffer such unfortunate and degrading indignities. And precisely why should he not? Because Gates was, in fact, "one of us" who had tragically been mistaken for "one of them."

It is this same dynamic that informed then-senator Joe Biden's 2007 comments about fellow presidential candidate Barack Obama when

50

---

[47] "A week later, at a news conference about health care, President Obama was asked about the incident and he said that Skip Gates was a friend and that the Cambridge police had 'acted stupidly' in arresting somebody who had proven that he was in his own home. The uproar that followed led Obama to invite both Gates and Crowley to the White House for guy talk and trouser hitching as they drank beer. Obama seemed to be scrambling to defend his image as the national reconciler, while having to absorb the warning implicit in the protests of policemen's unions that white America was made uneasy by the nation's first black president speaking as a black man or identifying with the black man's point of view." See Darryl Pinckney, "Invisible Black America," *New York Review of Books*, March 11, 2010, http://www.nybooks.com/articles/archives/2011/mar/10/invisible-black-america/.

[48] See Charles Ogletree, *The Presumption of Guilt: The Arrest of Henry Louis Gates, Jr. and Race, Class and Crime in America* (New York: St. Martin's Press, 2012). Kindle edition.

he said that Obama was the "first mainstream African-American who is articulate and bright and clean and a nice-looking guy."[49] In each case, the inference is that Black men who fit in deserve respect—but what about those who do not? What about Black Americans who do not look like Henry Louis Gates Jr., who do not have his pedigree, his eloquence, his stature, his paycheck, who do not fit the White mainstream's conception of "bright," "clean," or "nice-looking"? What about those who look like Michael Brown or Freddie Gray, Renisha McBride[50] or CeCe McDonald,[51] Sandra Bland or Jordan Davis? What about the single mothers, the welfare recipients like those who a generation ago lived at Pruitt-Igoe? Do they deserve fairness too, or is fairness the privilege of the well-turned-out, the conformist, the employed, the happy, the "accepted"?

It is worth contemplating how "Gates and Crowley" and "Brown and Wilson" form the same basic narrative: a Black person doing something ordinary is subjected to heightened scrutiny for a suspected criminal act. Police confront the Black suspect, who responds with verbal hostility, whereupon that hostility becomes, for the arresting officer, the very confirmation of criminal behavior. This confirmation of criminality then becomes the justification for the use of force. Gates was doing something ordinary as he fiddled with his key; Brown and his friend, the dreadlocked Dorian Johnson, were doing something ordinary as they jaywalked in their own neighborhood. Brown, like Gates, reacted to the police officer's questioning with "lip." In Gates's case, the result was an embarrassing arrest that turned into a national incident. The Brown episode, as with many other incidents involving America's vulnerable, ended with his death.

That Brown's story also contained a petty crime—the stealing of the cigarillos—and a physical tussle may cloud the picture for some. This was likely the reason that the Ferguson Police Department released video footage of Brown's store theft during the same press conference in which they were forced to release Darren Wilson's name to the public. Their hope was that the public, including the Black community, would not invest its support in Brown if he was marked as a criminal. But, in fact, Brown's story highlights how respectability politics around who deserves public support and protection within the Black community, as well as the expansion of the market-driven punishment state, creates

---

[49]Xuan Thai and Ted Barrett, "Biden's Description of Obama Draws Scrutiny," CNN .com, February 9, 2007, http://www.cnn.com/2007/POLITICS/01/31/biden.obama/.

[50]**Renisha McBride:** (1994–2013) After wrecking her car late at night, McBride walked to a house and knocked to ask for help; the white homeowner shot her through the screen door with a shotgun.

[51]**CeCe McDonald:** (b. 1989) A transgender woman, McDonald and three friends were walking to the grocery store when four people stepped out of a bar and started hurling racist and antitrans insults at them; a fight ensued, and McDonald stabbed one of the men to death with scissors. McDonald was convicted of second-degree murder and served nineteen months in a men's prison.

an environment where constitutional affordances like due process and protection from cruel and unusual punishment are reflexively denied to those considered part of the "criminal class."[52] Brown's story is a testament to how race and class, as well as other factors like gender, sexuality, citizenship, and ability status, conspire to create a dual set of realities in twenty-first-century America. For the powerful, justice is a right; for the powerless, justice is an illusion.

This is why the discourse of race is at once indispensable and insufficient when telling the story of Ferguson and other sites of State-sanctioned violence against Black bodies. Michael Brown, Tamir Rice, Jordan Davis, and Trayvon Martin were not killed simply because they were Black, although it is entirely reasonable to presume that they would still be alive if they were White. They were killed because they belong to a disposable class for which one of the strongest correlates is being Black. While it is hard to imagine that Brown would be dead if he were White, his death was only made more certain because he was young, male, urban, poor, and subject to the kinds of legal and social definitions that devalue life and compromise justice. His physical presence on Canfield Drive was due not only to his own personal experiences and choices but also a deeply rooted set of policy decisions, institutional arrangements, and power dynamics that made Ferguson, and Canfield, spaces of civic vulnerability. There is no formal poll tax to march against anymore, no segregation of the lunch counter.[53] But the kind of injustice that the story of Ferguson illuminates is just as insidious as the targets of earlier battles of the freedom struggle.

This is why the death of Michael Brown is not merely a throw-back to a wounded racial past but also a thoroughly modern event. It is not only the repeat of an age-old racial divide but also a statement of a relatively new public chasm that has been growing for years. This

55

[52]I borrow the term "respectability politics" from Evelyn Brooks Higginbotham, whose conceptualization of "politics of respectability" is often cited and frequently mis-represented. In this instance, Brown's behavior in the store compromised his moral author-ity in the eyes of many observers. This moral authority is necessary in order to present Brown, and the broader Black community, as being worthy of respect in the eyes of the general public. As Higginbotham has recently argued, the term "politics of respectability" has been wrongly associated with passivity, class arrogance, and an antiresistance pos-ture. For a full explication of Higginbotham's idea, see *Righteous Discontent: The Women's Movement in the Black Baptist Church, 1880–1920* (Cambridge, MA: Harvard Univer-sity Press, 1993). For a more recent analysis of the idea in light of the Black Lives Matter movement, see Higginbotham's interview with the feminist website *For Harriet*: Kimberly Foster, "Wrestling with Respectability in the Age of #BlackLivesMatter: A Dialogue," *For Harriet*, October 2015, http://www.forharriet.com/2015/10/wrestling-with-respect-ability-in-age-of.html#axzz3ve5FZd4s.

[53]I use the term "formal" to stress the ways in which de facto poll taxes, in the form of voter ID laws, continue to obstruct access to full voting rights for people of color and poor people. For a thorough examination of this issue, read Judge Richard Posner's dissenting opinion on the issue in *Ruthelle Frank et al. v. Scott Walker, Governor of Wisconsin et al.*, and *League of United Latin American Citizens (LULAC) of Wisconsin et al., v. David G. Deininger, Member, Government Accountability Board et al.*, Nos. 14-2058 & 14-2059, 2014 US App (4th Cir. October 10, 2014): https://s3.amazonaws.com/s3.documentcloud.org/documents/1312285/posner.pdf.

divide is characterized by the demonization and privatization of public services, including schools, the military, prisons, and even policing; by the growing use of prison as our primary resolution for social contradictions; by the degradation and even debasement of the public sphere and all those who would seek to democratically occupy it; by an almost complete abandonment of the welfare state; by a nearly religious reverence for marketized solutions to public problems; by the growth of a consumer culture that repeatedly emphasizes the satisfaction of the self over the needs of the community; by the corruption of democracy by money and by monied interests, what Henry Giroux refers to as "totalitarianism with elections";[54] by the mockery of a judicial process already tipped in favor of the powerful; by the militarization of the police; by the acceptance of massive global inequality; by the erasure of those unconnected to the Internet-driven modern economy; by the loss of faith in the very notion of community; and by the shrinking presence of the radical voices, values, and vision necessary to resist this dark neoliberal moment.[55]

The stories of Ferguson, Baltimore, Flint,[56] and countless other sites of gross injustice remind us of what it means to be largely erased from the social contract. They expose life on the underside of American democracy, where countless citizens are rendered disposable through economic arrangements, public policy, and social practice. They spotlight the nagging presence of the exploited, the erased, the vulnerable, the dehumanized—those who are imagined, treated, and made to feel like Nobody.

[54]See Henry A. Giroux, "Barbarians at the Gates: Authoritarianism and the Assault on Public Education," *Truthout*, December 30, 2014, http://www.truth-out.org/news/item/28272-barbarians-at-the-gates-authoritarianism-and-the-assault-on-public-education. Giroux argues: "What unites all of these disparate issues is a growing threat of authoritarianism—or what might be otherwise called totalitarianism with elections. Neoliberal societies embrace elections because they 'exclude and alienate most people from political power' and thus provide a kind of magical defense for the authoritarian project of depoliticizing the public while removing all obstacles to their goal of defending massive inequities in power, wealth and the accumulation of capital. It is impossible to understand the current assault on public education without coming to grips with the project of neoliberalism and its devaluation of the social, critical agency and informed thinking as part of its attempt to consolidate class power in the hands of a largely white financial and corporate elite."

[55]Throughout the book, I use the term "neoliberal" to describe not only the liberalization of the market but the accompanying processes of privatization, austerity, deregulation, and "free" trade. In addition to its economic dimensions, neoliberal ideology promotes the fragmentation of community, hyperindividualism, a conflation of citizenship with consumership, and an obsession with market values at the expense of deeper and more democratic moral, ethical, and social commitments. For a deeper analysis of neoliberalism, see David Harvey's *A Brief History of Neoliberalism* (New York: Oxford University Press, 2005) and Wendy Brown's *Undoing the Demos: Neoliberalism's Stealth Revolution* (Brooklyn, NY: Zone Books, 2015).

[56]**Flint:** In 2014, Flint, Michigan, a majority black city, began to experience a severe water-contamination crisis, which at first appeared to be caused by bacterial contamination, but the following year, tests revealed high levels of lead leeched from old pipes. By 2016, President Obama declared a federal state of emergency, and people were urged not to drink or cook with the water. A number of criminal cases were filed against local and state officials.

ENGAGING THE TEXT

1. Why does Hill say that Michael Brown is "Nobody"? How, according to his analysis, are Eric Garner, Kathryn Johnston, Trayvon Martin, Freddie Gray, and Sandra Bland "not exceptional" (para. 2)? Why have their deaths nevertheless been significant?

2. In what ways is Brown not a typical civil rights hero, and why does Hill emphasize this point? How does he justify his claim that what happened in Ferguson is as important as earlier civil rights struggles?

3. Why does Hill conclude that the grand jury had "little legal room to justify an indictment" of Darren Wilson for the death of Michael Brown? What does he mean when he adds, "But the law does not tell the full story"? What "other, competing truths" emerged from the protests that erupted in Ferguson (paras. 14–15)?

4. According to Hill, why is it beside the point whether or not Darren Wilson had "racist intentions" (para. 20)? What common assumptions about race, poverty, and criminality does he contend influenced Wilson's response to Brown? In what ways does he argue that Wilson perceived Brown as a "Magical Negro" (para. 31)? Do you agree with Hill's analysis? Why or why not?

5. Following months of angry protests over Michael Brown's death and the failure to indict Darren Wilson, a Department of Justice investigation found a number of flagrant abuses in the city of Ferguson: a largely African American city patrolled by an almost exclusively white police department, the extensive and unjustified use of "fines and fees" to bolster the city's finances, and gross racial stereotypes circulated by both police and city officials. In Hill's view, how do these details reveal "the deeper meanings of Ferguson" (para. 43)?

6. Discuss the significance of the Beer Summit: What similarities and differences does Hill see in the incidents involving Michael Brown and Henry Louis Gates Jr.? Why does he call the Beer Summit "a gross trivialization of the racial, cultural, and economic divides" (para. 48) that run through American life? Do you agree with Hill's assessment? Explain.

7. In what ways is the "discourse of race" both essential and insufficient to explain what happened in Ferguson (para. 54) as well as in other deadly incidents involving race? What other factors does Hill contend contributed to the deaths of Michael Brown, Eric Garner, and Sandra Bland?

8. **Thinking Rhetorically**   Hill cites many people who, like Brown, died unjustly; some — like Eric Garner, Trayvon Martin, Jordan Davis, Tamir Rice, and Sandra Bland — he mentions several times in different contexts. In each case, why does he mention them (in paras. 2–3, 44–46, 51, and 54)? What are the rhetorical effects of naming them and of repeating some names? Do you find the strategy effective or ineffective and why?

EXPLORING CONNECTIONS

9. In Sara Goldrick Rab's "City of Broken Dreams" (p. 210), to what extent does the higher education system available to poor and minority students illustrate what it means to be "abandoned by the State" (Hill, para. 4)? What do the struggles of Alicia, José, and Anne to get a higher education in Milwaukee suggest about Michael Brown's ambitions for college (para. 10)? Which of his goals, if any, do you think he could have fulfilled, and why?

10. Read or review Gregory Mantsios's "Class in America" (p. 347) and write an imaginary conversation between Hill and Mantsios in which they discuss the ways that class status and "respectability politics" (Hill, para. 53) affect the lives of people like Michael Brown.

11. In Darren Bell's cartoon (p. 667), Clyde describes a dream he had: "I dreamt didn't nobody ever shoot no one." Why does he imply that this was a "weird, fantastical" dream? Do you think that Hill would agree with him? Why or why not?

EXTENDING THE CRITICAL CONTEXT

12. Oscar Grant, Kendrec McDade, Yvette Smith, Eric Garner, Samuel DuBose, John Crawford, Ezell Ford, Tanisha Anderson, Tamir Rice, Jerame Reid, Walter Scott, Freddie Gray, Alton Sterling, Philando Castile, Korryn Gaines, Stephon Clark — all were unarmed blacks killed by police under questionable circumstances. Research one or more of them: What led to the confrontation? What different accounts were given about the killing? What role, if any, did video play in the public's perception of the incident? What role did the courts and the U.S. Department of Justice play? What role did social media, organized protest, and public outrage play? How do you explain the outcome of the case (if an outcome has been reached), and was any measure of justice attained?

13. Hill observes that when the grand jury declined to indict Darren Wilson, "crowds of protesters appeared" in cities throughout the country (para. 22). In the conclusion of "Nobody," he offers the hope that grassroots activism will prevail over State violence and injustice. Investigate some of the following activist movements: Moral Mondays, Black Lives Matter, Dream Defenders, Black Youth Project 100, Hands Up United, Millennial Activists United, Lost Voices, and Internet campaigns like #SayHerName, #IfIDieInPoliceCustody, #NeverAgain. What led to their establishment, and what are their aims? What types of resistance do they sponsor or engage in? How effective have they been in promoting their goals? Explain your response.

VISUAL PORTFOLIO

READING IMAGES OF RACE

STEPHEN LAM/REUTERS/Newscom

Chip Somodevilla/Getty Images

ANDREW CABALLERO-REYNOLDS/AFP/Getty Images

Michael S. Williamson/The Washington Post/Getty Images

National Socialist Movement

Justin Sullivan/Getty Images

VISUAL PORTFOLIO
READING IMAGES OF RACE

1. Demonstrations erupted in many cities following the grand jury's decision not to indict the police officer who killed Michael Brown in Ferguson, Missouri. The photo on page 669 shows a protester in Oakland, California: notice the sign the protester is holding, the fire burning behind him, the graffiti on the dumpster, the bottles and debris in the street. What does the picture say to you? How would you describe the protester's state of mind, and how would you support your interpretation?

2. After white supremacist Dylann Roof murdered nine African Americans in South Carolina in order to "start a race war," the tragedy inspired a national debate over racism and Confederate symbols. Public officials in many communities pledged to tear down Confederate monuments or move them to private property. On August 12, 2017, a rally involving white nationalists, the Ku Klux Klan, neo-Nazis, and alt-right groups was organized to protest the removal of the Robert E. Lee statue in Charlottesville, Virginia's Emancipation Park. A large crowd of civil rights activists and counterprotesters gathered, and the two sides clashed violently. Many were injured in the melée, and one activist died when a white supremacist deliberately plowed his car into the crowd. For dramatic photos of the clash, see this website:

   http://time.com/charlottesville-white-nationalist-rally-clashes/

   The photo on page 670 shows a face-off between a white nationalist and a counterprotester. The black X on a white shield symbolizes a far-right nationalist group "devoted to preserving the traditional culture of the South."[1] How are the shield and the Confederate flag behind it at odds with the man's stars-and-stripes shirt? What's the significance of the black protester's chains in the context of the Confederate monuments debate? What does each man's stance and expression say about his intentions? What does the photographer's helmet tell you about the nature of the conflict?

3. What messages are the men in this photo (p. 671) sending, and what do you make of their banners and t-shirts (on the extreme right, the man's shirt reads "Allah is Satan," and the man next to him is wearing a shirt that says, "Ask me why you deserve Hell"). What do you think of the combined antigay, anti-Muslim, and hellfire-and-damnation messages, and to whom are these men appealing? Do people like this demonstrate why Amani Al-Khatahtbeh needed to publish "a crisis safety manual for Muslim women just to live" (p. 679), or are they harmless cranks? Explain your response.

4. The photo on page 672 shows Nour Obeidallah at the 2017 Women's March in Washington, DC. Why do you think she chose to carry a frame rather than a poster

---

[1] Pearse, Matt. "A Guide to Some of the Far-Right Symbols Seen in Charlottesville." *Los Angeles Times,* Aug. 14, 2017. http://www.latimes.com/nation/la-na-far-right-symbols-20170814-story.html.

or sign, and how do you interpret the statement at the bottom of the frame? Why do you think she evokes the Constitution with the words "We the people"? How does her American flag hijab and her message contrast to the shirt, shield, and Confederate flag of the white nationalist at the Charlottesville rally (p. 670)? Do her words and image represent a refutation of the anti-Muslim slogans on the previous page? Why or why not?

5. These members of a neo-Nazi militia group unofficially patrol the American–Mexican border (p. 673). As José Orduña points out, "many groups operate with the tacit consent of some local authorities. They're regularly allowed to . . . hold people under false pretenses until they can be handed over to Border Patrol" (p. 687). Why are the men posing with this sign, and what do their camouflage, guns, and facial expressions signify for anyone traveling through the desert? Why do you think that armed vigilantes are allowed to patrol here and not in urban areas? What does the Border Patrol's tolerance of militias on the border suggest about the authorities' view of immigrants?

6. Mauricio Hernandez is pictured with his daughter Emily at the Deported Veterans Support House in Tijuana, Mexico, which was established by another deported vet (p. 674). Hernandez is a veteran of the U.S. Marine Corps who served in both Afghanistan and Iraq following 9/11. He was discharged "under honorable conditions,"[2] but had developed a severe case of post-traumatic stress disorder (PTSD). Hernandez held a green card, but once back in the States, he was convicted on drug charges and deported. Read his personal story here:

http://www.vvaw.org/veteran/article/?id=3382

Was his deportation just? Do you think that any veteran who has served honorably should be subject to deportation? Why or why not?

FROM *MUSLIM GIRL*

AMANI AL-KHATAHTBEH

Amani Al-Khatahtbeh was a fourth-grader in East Brunswick, New Jersey, when the disaster of 9/11 occurred. Following the attacks on the World Trade Center and the Pentagon, the media equated Islam with terrorism: news reports proliferated about the firebombing of mosques and about Muslims who were arrested, attacked, even killed. Al-Khatahtbeh was bullied at school, her father faced harassment at work, her mother's tires were slashed, and people threw rotten eggs at her house. By the time she was eleven, she was too embarrassed to wear a headscarf, and two years later her family moved back to Jordan, fleeing

[2]Clark, James. "Desperate to Return Home, Deported Veterans Face Exile." *Task and Purpose*, Dec. 17, 2015. https://taskandpurpose.com/desperate-to-return-home-deported-veterans-face-exile/.

the hatred and violence. She found that living in a Muslim country, the profound contrast between the image of Islam in the U.S. media and the reality of a peaceful Islamic society was transformative. When she and her family returned to the United States a year later, she began wearing a hijab both to defy Islamophobia and to reclaim her identity. She realized that she was living a "unique and trying experience as a millennial Muslim, the daughter of an immigrant and a refugee, born and raised in the United States — ostracized through bullying, heightened Islamophobia, and the difficult task of growing up as a young girl in a misogynistic and hypersexualized society."[1] She founded MuslimGirl.com at age seventeen to give a voice to girls like herself, publishing blogs that she wrote with friends from her mosque. Since then, the site has grown into an influential media presence with fifty editors and writers and over a million unique visitors; about half of the audience is non-Muslim. At twenty-three, Al-Khatahtbeh was named one of *Forbes* magazine's 30 under 30 in media — and her site became the first Muslim company to make the list. In 2018 CNN named her one of 25 Influential American Muslims. This excerpt is from *Muslim Girl: Coming of Age* (2016), which was selected as an Editor's Pick on the *New York Times* Bestseller List.

HERE ARE THE ROUGH, GENERAL, immediate guidelines as to how Muslims react whenever a public act of violence takes place: 1) Pray to God that the perp is not Muslim. Dear God, spare us this one. Please. 2) Compulsively follow any convenient corporate news outlet or subsequent trending hashtag on developments, oscillating between mourning the victims and fearing for the sanctity of your life. 3) If the perp is identified to be white and/or non-Muslim, emotionally prepare yourself for the trauma of having the double standard dangled in your face again that they are just "mentally disturbed," because, remember, the word *terrorism* only applies to people that are shades of brown. 4) If they're identified as Muslim and then inevitably as a terrorist, or having ties to some terrorist organization, or, even more conveniently, as having outwardly proclaimed loyalty to a terrorist group somehow, mentally prepare for the — possibly violent — backlash. 5) In the case of our highly digital Muslim community, prepare a corresponding Facebook status: whether offering thoughts and prayers for the respective Western city, exasperation at the hypocritical label of a "lone white shooter," or an urgent and woeful reminder that all Muslim and "Muslim-passing" friends stay safe in the ensuing media frenzy of another terrorist attack.

The mistreatment of the definition of terrorism — did you know the United Nations doesn't even have an established definition of what it

---

[1]Al-Khatahtbeh, Amani. *Muslim Girl: A Coming of Age.* New York: Simon & Schuster, 2016, 78.

is? But the U.S. sure does, and it's quite an exclusive and broad one all at the same time—really skews people's perceptions of Muslims and the atrocities taking place around the world.

In the summer of 2016, MTV aired a new web show with me on the issues that impact Muslim Americans on their Snapchat Discover channel to millions of viewers, an episode of which listed several of my recent and ridiculous encounters with the Transportation Security Agency. They were pretty tragic cases of racial profiling, but spun to be hilarious and understandable to the network's preteen audience. I'm all for packaging an otherwise marginalized message in a way that will be digestible to its recipients—hey, that's what Prophet Muhammad did, wasn't it? One Snapchat user responded to the TSA episode by saying, "Instead of complaining about things we need to do to be safe, how about you talk about how terrorists should stop killing people." While I usually ignored such inquiries without even batting an eyelash, I took the bait and engaged, maybe because of how deep the stupidity of his comments hit a nerve.

I replied to this dude with a data plan and social media access and thus opinions worth sharing with, "Racial profiling people at airport security is actually a detriment to our safety. Think about it—there could be a white person passing through a gate with a bomb on him because we didn't search him properly, because TSA was too busy being fixated on people that look like me." As I was leaving the Nice airport after the Cannes Lions festival, I passed through the security machine, and it didn't even beep, but the French National Police still stopped me for an additional search. They gave me a very invasive and public pat down, cupping my boobs and butt, hands too close for comfort in my groin area, straight down to the bottom soles of my shoes to check for a bomb. It was humiliating. The white girl behind me passed through and actually set off the detector beeping, and she was let through without any additional inconvenience.

He responded, "No one else is killing innocent people like Muslims!"   5

"It's easy to think that way," I Snapchatted him back. "What happens is that whenever Muslims do something wrong, they are always in the news and identified as their religion. When people of other faiths commit horrible acts, we are never told what religion they are because it's deemed irrelevant, and they get to enjoy the privilege of being held accountable as individuals for their actions rather than having their background be collectively held accountable or blamed on their behalf.

"The term 'terrorism' is only ever applied to Muslims, but never when it's people of other faiths. Like the KKK, Christian conservatives that bomb abortion clinics, etc.," I continued. In this way, it's easy to see how the public garners a skewed perception of Muslims and Islam. Zoom in on the fringe minority of any group—rather than, in this case, the 1.6 billion[2] majority of all the other Muslims in the world that come from all walks of life and live peacefully in their societies (if Islam was

[2]Bill Chapeli, "World's Muslim Population Will Surpass Christians This Century, Pew Says," NPR, April 2, 2015, http://www.npr.org/sections/thetwo-way/2015/04/02/397042004/muslim-population-will-surpass-christians-this-century-pew-says.

really founded on terrorism, imagine the havoc of 1.6 billion terrorists in the world? Or even just half that many? *Allahu akbar,* for real.)—and *obviously* that would create a super limited and distorted image of a people. Like, imagine if we only focused on racists like Dylann Roof[3] and said that's what all white people are like? Imagine if I demanded an apology from my local Starbucks barista for the racial slur her white peer hurled at me from his car window as I walked into the store? Would that make any sense at all? Of course not.

This, my friends, is how you manufacture hate.

The winter of 2015 was a tumultuous and difficult one to navigate. The second Paris attack[4] of the year had just taken place in November, and the Muslim American community was still dealing with imminent backlash as a result of the sensational media coverage when the San Bernardino shooting[5] happened only a few weeks later. The oncoming confusion with all the mixed information surrounding the shooters came to a head when the *New York Post* published a cover photo of San Bernardino victims with the large overset headline MUSLIM KILLERS. The irresponsible journalism and hysterical, propagandized coverage wildly legitimized anti-Muslim sentiment and made leaving our homes all the more difficult.

The aftermath brought with it a series of attacks on the Muslim American community in rapid, head-spinning succession. In Seattle, a Somali teenager was beaten and thrown off the roof of a six-story building. Bigots shot at a Muslim woman as she was leaving a mosque in Tampa. A little sixth-grade girl was taunted with the name "ISIS" as her boy classmates in the Bronx ripped the scarf off of her head and physically beat her on the playground. Two days after Trump's call for a Muslim ban, our team at Muslim Girl felt compelled to publish a "Crisis Safety Manual for Muslim Women" for basic survival in the aftermath of the San Bernardino shooting. I started distancing myself from social media at this time, lessening the log-ins and the amount of posts—only staying plugged in long enough to stay informed for our Muslim Girl coverage. Unfortunately, there were no trigger warnings for "vilifying you for your religion," "subjugation & dehumanization," or "delegitimizing your existence."

As a veiled Muslim woman, I was yet again overcome with a fear of leaving my house in the morning. The type of rhetoric Trump was using—banning all Muslims from the country, like we were different, incompatible with American life, like we didn't belong—made even a born and raised Jersey girl like me feel like an outsider all over again. I was frustrated, because I had already been through this before. I already

10

---

[3]**Dylann Roof:** (b. 1994) White supremacist convicted of murdering nine African Americans during a prayer service at Emanuel African Methodist Episcopal Church on June 17, 2015, in Charleston, South Carolina. [Eds.]

[4]**The second Paris attack:** On November 13, 2015, a series of terrorist attacks in Paris, France, left 137 people dead; several groups of suicide bombers and gunmen, sponsored by ISIS, attacked a theater, a soccer stadium, and several open-air restaurants. [Eds.]

[5]**The San Bernardino shooting:** On December 2, 2015, fourteen people died and twenty-two were injured in a mass shooting at the Inland Regional Center in San Bernardino, California; a U.S.-born citizen and his wife, a permanent resident of the U.S., fled the scene but were killed in a shootout with police four hours later. [Eds.]

lived through and survived this assault on my identity. And as a society, we're supposed to be progressing forward, not backward. The Muslim community worked tirelessly against this type of hatred since 2001,[6] and suddenly, like a slippery slope, Trump had us falling right back down to where we started. The thought that another generation of little girls would have to endure an experience that almost broke me, that was the most difficult thing in my life to navigate, was truly heartbreaking. And so Muslim Girl decided that this time, instead of wasting space on our platform to talk back to Donald Trump—engaging in the same broken-record disputes and responding to the same unfair attacks on our humanity that we have collectively been facing since 9/11—we would stop giving Trump any space on our platform at all. He didn't deserve it, and we deserved better.

It was during this time that I started actively pitching Muslim Girl so that we could sustain our increasingly critical work. *The Harvard Law Review* published Nancy Leong's analysis on racial capitalism in June 2013, which analyzes "the process of deriving social and economic value from the racial identity of another person." While we were dishing out Muslim Girl's neatly streamlined numbers in pretty PowerPoint slides at shiny conference tables, trying to quantify and convince in dollar signs why Muslim women's voices are valuable, all I could really think about was how our site had to resort to publishing a crisis safety manual for Muslim women just to live. All the hateful rhetoric in the media—Paris, San Bernardino, now Trump—wasn't made in a void. The social complacency that Muslim Girl was created to combat has real life or death consequences for Muslim women in Western societies. While the world scapegoats Islam, Muslim women quickly become the most vulnerable targets, and yet, the fashion industry and corporations are simultaneously eager to profit off of them.

At the same time, 2015 saw the trending topic of modest fashion and a huge surge of interest in Muslim women as consumers. Leong argues that "nonwhiteness has acquired a unique value because, in many contexts, it signals the presence of the prized characteristic of diversity," yet warns that "the 'thin' version of the diversity objective—emphasizes numbers and appearances. That is, it is exclusively concerned with improving the superficial appearance of diversity."[7] This can be said of many of the media outlets cashing in on hijab headlines while maintaining often racially or religiously uniform newsrooms, but also of the fashion industry's treatment of modest fashion. Many brands, from DKNY to Dolce & Gabbana, started launching their own modest fashion lines catered to Muslim women. Global media outlets heralded H&M for

---

[6]**2001:** On September 11, 2001, nineteen Al-Qaeda terrorists boarded four airliners in the northeast United States and, during the flights, highjacked the planes. Two of the planes flew into the Twin Towers in Manhattan; one crashed into the Pentagon; the fourth plane, in which passengers attacked the highjackers, crashed in a field near Shanksville, Pennsylvania. Nearly 3,000 people died in the attacks, most from the collapse of the Twin Towers. [Eds.]

[7]Nancy Leong, "Racial Capitalism," *Harvard Law Review*, June 2013, 2152, 2169, http://harvardlawreview.org/wp-content/uploads/pdfs/vol16_leong.pdf.

including a headscarf-clad model in their marketing campaign. Yet few brands have successfully integrated Muslim women fashion designers, consultants, or models into their lines, nor have they championed causes that would benefit the women from whom they'd gain the profit. In this way, what would otherwise appear to be a positive step in social inclusivity could have adverse effects on Muslim women, by putting out of business the designers that have been creating headscarves and abayas long before they became an Instagram sensation.

And then there's this question: In the midst of the severe backlash and threat against Muslim women's bodies, how many companies claiming to represent Muslim women actually made statements in support of them? How many blogs celebrating modest fashion also covered our stories of discrimination?

Muslim women are hot right now. The thing is, we can't be cool with society vilifying our identities while at the same time trying to profit off them. One thing became clear: Muslim Girl became a start-up because it had to. For us, entrepreneurialism is a means to an end. It's survival.

On top of all this, law enforcement and the media are usually slow to consider obviously biased incidents as hate crimes. This results in frequent media misrepresentation of the severity of anti-Muslim bigotry, which has a profound negative effect on our community, especially on those Muslim women by whom they are so fascinated. Yusor Abu-Salha was shot execution-style in her Chapel Hill, North Carolina, apartment in February 2015, along with her husband and little sister. The murders, committed by their angry and admittedly anti-religion neighbor, were dismissed in the media far and wide as simply being "a parking dispute." It pains me to think that people would have been more interested in how Yusor styled her scarf than in what caused the senseless violence that took her life.

Trump discovered that milking anti-Muslim sentiment, with complete disregard to the dangers it poses to our very lives, keeps him in the spotlight and gets him more airtime. Since his ascension to the national stage, I have been receiving press requests around the clock during his media circuses to explain, again and again, "the current climate for Muslim women." By the time the Muslim-ban comments came, I had run out of different palatable ways to say, "Our lives are under threat right now"—ironically, not from ISIS extremism or the brown men that our society is raising pitch forks against, but from our own Western society itself.

Amid all the chaos, I witnessed one interesting development for the first time in my entire life since 9/11. When Trump's words rang around the country, many Americans were roused to rise to the defense of their Muslim neighbors. Social and broadcast media highlighted heartwarming stories of extended hands between Muslims and non-Muslims, images popped up on my feed of non-Muslim Americans going the extra distance to make Muslims feel safe here in their own hometowns, and my Muslim friends from across the country recorded moments of increased acts of warmth and kindness towards them—seemingly as though our fellow countrymen were making an effort to remind us that this was our country, too. It was as if, through Trump's outrageously hateful rhetoric, America had awoken to the reality that now was time to defend and protect a minority community that needed it. Even though Trump represented the racist underbelly of a nation, light rose to the surface, even through the most negligible of cracks, to resist it.

On September 11, 2015, I received a text message from my friend Hebah, Muslim Girl's creative director at the time, that was just as much unexpected as it was totally natural.

"Yo should I be nervous to go to *jummah*? I can't tell," it said.   20

Jummah is the Arabic word for Friday, the Muslim holy day of the week. In this case, she was referring to Friday prayer, our weekly religious service. We regularly attended *jummah* prayer at the Islamic Center of New York University (ICNYU). I had come to love the ICNYU for the space it provided, and I saw it as a home away from home—and my fellow worshipers as a second family, even though I had never personally met most of the people there. That's why, for a brief moment, I was confused, and I texted Hebah back, "Why?" I watched as the iMessage bubbles popped up. "9/11," she responded.

I almost forgot that it was the anniversary of a tragedy that became one of the worst days of our lives—a tragedy not only for the horrible terrorist act on our soil that became a symbol of our empirical resolve and the lives lost on Ground Zero, but also for the countless people still paying the collective price for an action that had nothing to do with them.

"Oh yeah, I'm wearing a turban. #incognito," I sent Hebah. For hijabis, we enjoy the privilege of being able to style our head-scarves like turbans, which evoke a kind of religious ambiguity for us—they're seen as more trendy on women than religious, as they are usually expected to be worn by brown men. That's a privilege Sikh men will never enjoy. They've been just as much victimized by Islamophobia for their publicly identifiable religious garment—whether or not people can tell the religious difference. Shame. I didn't realize it until that moment that I had based my scarf style that day on the level of negative attention I would likely be subjected to in public. And it wasn't until that moment, through Hebah's texts, that I realized she had done the same—and verbalized a lived experience familiar to many Muslim women for the past decade. Our text conversation was the materialization of what goes on just beneath the surface of our everyday lives. This constant negotiation. These adaptations. The breathing, quivering epitome of the millennial generation of Muslim women. They are microdefenses, the conditioned changes we make for our safety on a day to day basis.

Another behavorial phenomenon that I've witnessed become prevalent among Muslim women is how we protect ourselves on the subway. It's almost become inscribed among Muslim women to stand further away from the edge of the platform, for fear of getting pushed onto the tracks by some rabid Islamophobe. Any New Yorker is in danger of this happening, but we, especially those of us who are veiled, are increasingly vulnerable targets of this kind of crime and so have trained ourselves to take extra precautions. In 2013, a woman killed a Hindu man by shoving him onto the tracks of an oncoming train because, as she later stated, she hated Muslims ever since 9/11 happened. Think about that. It's like the perfect perverted intersection of the typical American's ignorance of those she mindlessly hates—in this case, conflating a Hindu, or often-times a Sikh, with a Muslim, because, you know, brown skin—and the collective blame and incitement of violence against a people as a whole.

Another form of a microdefense that has become innate among Muslim millennials is avoiding use of the slang word *bomb*, no matter the context. It's been a really long time since I've exclaimed the common school phrase, "Man, I totally bombed that exam." This applies in public so that we don't cause any discomfort or alarm to the people around us hearing this word uttered from a Muslim mouth, as do the series of Ara-bic-speakers kicked off their flights after fellow passengers become sus-picious of the use of their native language in such a hostile context. This also applies in private, given the invasive surveillance policies placed on Muslim communities that effectively kill our due process rights and have caused the type of language we use to come under bewildering scrutiny. In my case, I even get uneasy when my friends message me words that are on the NSA hotlist. One year, an article was published online claiming that the NSA has a list of words[8] that, when sent in electronic form, automatically prompt surveillance; one of my Muslim friends humorously Facebook chatted me a series of messages using those terms in all their glory. "Ha! Now I got the NSA on you!" he joked.

The youngins that we are, we have often turned to humor to help us cope with our mind-bogglingly ridiculous reality, though that doesn't negate the treacherous threat that language really poses to our lives. At the very beginning of the Summer of Hustle, I had just finished grab-bing coffee with two acquaintances that worked at Al Jazeera America.[9] We were standing outside of a Starbucks in Manhattan, discussing the internal condition of the network, which was then only creeping toward its eventual demise less than a year later. My colleagues were both Arabs—one a fair-skinned woman with straight jet-black hair, the other, a dark burly man with a thick black beard.

As the conversation moved forward, the other woman and I noticed a blond, blue-eyed white guy hovering near us, almost eavesdropping, and acting kind of weird. Eventually, the producer said something to the effect of, "We have to hit the reset button on the entire thing," regard-ing Al Jazeera America's operations, and that was it. Weird White Guy abruptly interrupted us and jumped into the middle of our conversation.

"Excuse me," he said. "I'm going to be super quick and I'm just going to get right to it: When you say 'reset,' does that mean, like,

25

---

[8]Dylan Love, "These Are Supposedly the Words That Make the NSA Think You're a Terrorist," *Business Insider,* June 13, 2013, http://www.businessinsider.com/nsa-prism-keywords-for-domestic-spying-2013-6.

[9]**Al Jazeera America:** American satellite news channel launched in 2013 and closed in 2016; owned by Al Jazeera Media Network, a Middle Eastern multinational conglomerate.

starting over?" We all gave him a New York stare, super confused and highly offended at his imposition.

"Huh? What are you talking about?" we all asked.

"You said you want to hit the reset button," he continued. "Are you talking about a bomb? Are you planning to blow this place up? Are you going to kill me? I just want to know if I should call a police officer over . . ."

That was that. My colleagues both began to address him in their own assertive ways, the woman saying she'd worked for the govern-ment and was going to call a cop on *him* if he didn't walk away and stop making her feel so uncomfortable, the man giving him an intimidat-ing death glare and demanding that he get the hell away from us. But me? I was suddenly confronted by my own suffocating vulnerability: the intense self-realization that, among the three of us, I was the only one wearing a headscarf—the only one "visibly" Muslim, that was dressed like those people on the news, and thus would be a lightning rod of attention for someone inclined to make such an outrageously racist and horrifying assumption. In seconds, I saw an imaginary series of reactive events flash before my eyes: handcuffs, NYPD ransacking my apart-ment, my entire life dissected and twisted, the carpet of the judicial system ripped right out from under my feet at the conceivable threat of terror. I thought of the Patriot Act, of one of my friends saying that someone he knew in college disappeared, the illegal police surveillance compound that was secretly erected on our Rutgers University campus so law enforcement could surveil our Muslim Student Association. In the age of the War on Terror, due process is no right for Muslims.

I hadn't realized the deeply subconscious reaction it would trig-ger in me. It was truly instinctual—the type of innate response that is ignited upon threat against one's survival—and, while my friends could afford the time to respond and challenge, my immediate need was to get as far away from him as possible. "Please, can we please leave," I begged them in a low voice between clenched teeth, so as not to panic. "Stop responding, please, let's just go." Finally, I took off, trying to put as much space between me and that individual as possible. It was so distressing that I kept looking over my shoulder, even across streets, expecting to see him following me. I was so shaken that when I finally felt that I was a safe enough distance away from him, I walked into the first café I could find and collapsed onto a wooden chair, where I would sit motionless for almost an hour.

I really don't know why that prompted such an emotional reaction out of me. Actually, I wouldn't even call it emotional—it was definitely instinctual. And I know what people would say: Well, if you're innocent, you have nothing to worry about. That's the usual response given to people who dare criticize the Patriot Act, legalizing an intrusion on our private lives across the board. But the thing is, this isn't about innocence or guilt. This is about a government with absolutely no accountability, with the legal power to do what it wants with your body simply because of your religion, which it could hold against you as an inherent threat. Bodies of color are criminalized. Black Americans can be shot dead in

the seat of their cars, with a seatbelt on, for reaching for their wallets. Undocumented people can be extorted with deportation for not complying with the smallest arbitrary assertion of authority. Muslims can face the threat of torture cells and prison compounds for, I guess, making the mistake of saying the word "reset" in public. Sometimes these identities meet at one treacherous intersection. It's moments like these that compel our microdefensiveness at the most basic level.

ENGAGING THE TEXT

1. Review the five guidelines that Al-Khatahtbeh says Muslims follow "whenever a public act of violence takes place" (para. 1). Among other reactions, she mentions praying that the perpetrator isn't Muslim, fearing for her life, preparing for trauma, preparing for potentially violent backlash, and worrying about the safety of friends. Write a journal entry detailing how you react to public acts of violence. Do you have concerns about the religious identity of the perpetrator or about your own safety? Share your entries in class and discuss how and why the responses vary.

2. Al-Khatahtbeh makes a number of generalizations about terrorism, for example, that "the word only applies to people that are shades of brown" (para. 1)

and that the term "is only ever applied to Muslims" (para. 3). To what extent does she justify these assertions?

3. After the second Paris attack and the San Bernardino shootings, why do the sensational media reports and the attacks on Muslims make Al-Khatahtbeh fearful of leaving her home? Why does she feel particularly vulnerable as a veiled Muslim woman? In referring to Trump's anti-Muslim rhetoric, what does she mean when she says, "I already lived through and survived this assault on my identity" (para. 10)?

4. What is "racial capitalism" (para. 11), and how does the current popularity of modest fashion reflect a "thin" or superficial version of it? In what ways does Al-Khatahtbeh suggest that media outlets, fashion houses, and blogs could represent Muslim women more substantially?

5. What are microdefenses? How do styling a hijab as a turban, standing further from the edge of the subway platform, avoiding the word *bomb*, and not speaking Arabic on an airplane constitute microdefenses? Why are such precautions necessary?

6. Why does Al-Khatahtbeh respond so viscerally to the white man who interrupts the conversation with her colleagues? Is she exaggerating when she calls her reaction an instinctual response to "a threat against one's survival" (para. 29)? Is her comparison of racism against Muslims to racism against black Americans and undocumented immigrants fair? Why or why not?

7. **Thinking Rhetorically** How do you respond to Al-Khatahtbeh's style? At times her tone sounds breezy — as in the passage about "the dude with a data plan" (para. 4) — yet she also talks about serious issues like racism and fearing for her life. Who is her audience and what is her purpose? Is her tone appropriate? Try rewriting one of her passages in a consistently serious, academic style; what's the effect?

EXPLORING CONNECTIONS

8. In their discussion of racialization, Linda Holtzman and Leon Sharpe (p. 631) note that following 9/11 there was "widespread racialization of Muslims and people of Middle Eastern descent" (p. 641). To what extent can the bigoted and violent responses that Al-Khatahtbeh details in her essay be attributed to racialization?

9. As Holtzman and Sharpe note in "Theories and Constructions of Race," media frames shape people's thought processes by influencing what they see or what they overlook in a story (para. 4). How does media framing help to explain the misrepresentation of the triple murder in North Carolina? How do media frames partially explain the many reports, following Trump's Muslim ban, of non-Muslims defending Muslims, "as though our fellow countrymen were making an effort to remind us that this was our country, too" (Al-Khatahtbeh, para. 17)?

EXTENDING THE CRITICAL CONTEXT

10. In this selection, Al-Khatahtbeh is clearly doing her best to refute the Muslim-as-terrorist stereotype. If you have ever consciously attempted to disprove a stereotype about a group that you are part of, write a short essay or journal entry describing your experience. Why did you feel the need to refute the stereotype, how did you go about combating it, and what was the result of your efforts, if any?

11. Explore muslimgirl.com, Amani Al-Khatahtbeh's website: click on the articles that interest you and check out the Twitter, Facebook, Instagram, and YouTube links. What impressions do you get? If you're not Muslim, did you learn anything new, and if so, what? If you are Muslim, did you find the site helpful or not, and why?

12. Research why Islamophobia has become more common. The following website argues that there is a well-financed network supporting Islamophobia in the United States and spreading false anti-Muslim information:

> https://www.americanprogress.org/issues/religion/reports/2015/02/11/ 106394/fear-inc-2-0

How persuasive is the site? What other influences may have caused an increase in anti-Muslim feeling?

PASSPORT TO THE NEW WEST
JOSÉ ORDUÑA

This provocative essay comes from José Orduña's *The Weight of Shadows: A Memoir of Immigration and Displacement* (2016). While unauthorized immigrants are sometimes demonized as murderers and rapists, Orduña reminds us of their humanity and the deadly risks they take in search of a better life. As a volunteer with No More Deaths, a humanitarian aid group that works in the U.S.–Mexico borderlands, Orduña experiences the unforgiving desert that migrants must survive and witnesses the casual cruelty of Border Patrol agents who deny them water when they're exhausted and dehydrated. "There is some rage in this book,"[1] Orduña says — rage against American apathy in the face of suffering, rage against an immigration system that holds no one accountable for migrants' deaths. A Mexican immigrant himself, Orduña applied for naturalization while studying for his MFA at the University of Iowa's Nonfiction Writing Program; he became a citizen in 2011. He is currently Assistant Professor of Creative Writing at the University of Nevada, Las Vegas. His essays

[1]Kuperman, Benjamin. "Writer José Orduña on the U.S.' Inconsistent Immigration Policies, Trump Rhetoric, and the Scapegoating of Immigrants." *Little Village Magazine*, April 21, 2016.

have appeared in *TriQuarterly, Buzzfeed, After Montaigne: Contemporary Writers Cover the Essays* (2015), and other publications.

I ARRIVE BY BUS IN TUCSON LATE ONE afternoon and walk to a gas station where a volunteer will be picking me up. I signed up with a humanitarian aid group that leaves water in the desert for people attempting to cross the border, provides emergency medical treatment for those who may need it, and documents abuse suffered by people at various points in their journeys. By the time I make it there I'm dripping sweat because it's late July, I have a fifty pound bag strapped to my back, and the sun feels like it's a few feet away from my face. A rusted-out SUV pulls up and a young white guy with a scruffy beard rolls down his window.

"You José?"

"Yeah."

"Hop in."

Orientation for new volunteers starts a few hours later at a space the group has arranged in a small local church and school building in Tucson. A handful of young people, mostly white, sit around smoking in the courtyard for a while. We gather in a small classroom where an attorney comes in to give us some information so that we can make informed decisions in the desert. A couple of summers back, a jury of twelve convicted a volunteer of "knowingly littering"—for leaving gallons of water for people in the 110-degree desert. We're told that people drink cow tank water—stagnant pools that cows wade, urinate, and defecate in—out of necessity. A former volunteer tells us that Border Patrol and Wackenhut GS_4, a contractor paid by the government to transport migrants, don't often give people water or medical attention even though they know they've been journeying through the desert for days. We're told that two volunteers, a young woman and man, were arrested, and that a grand jury charged them with two felonies: conspiracy to transport an "illegal immigrant" and transporting an "illegal immigrant." The volunteers had come upon a group of migrants who'd been traveling through the desert for four days, two days without food or water during the week that turned out to be, until then, the deadliest in Arizona history.[2] It was over one hundred degrees Fahrenheit for forty straight days, and seventy-eight people were known to have died. The volunteers were arrested while evacuating three men to a medical facility in Tucson. They rejected a plea that would have seen all charges dropped for an admission of guilt, instead risking a sentence of up to fifteen years in prison and fines of up to five hundred thousand dollars. The proceedings dragged on for about a year and a half. Eventually the charges were dropped.

A tall older man who looks like a cowboy joins us in the classroom. He takes off his beige felt hat and wipes the white hair on his sweaty forehead. He introduces himself as John Fife, a retired Presbyterian minister and cofounder of No More Deaths (NMD). In the eighties Fife also cofounded

[2]John Fife, "My Tucson: Once Jailed, Pair Become Heroes," *Tucson Citizen*, May 2, 2007. John Fife's criminal history: "Sanctuary Activists Lose Conspiracy Trial," *Chicago Tribune*, May 2, 1986.

the sanctuary movement in the United States, a network that helped Central American refugees flee US-backed death squads in El Salvador and Guatemala. He was arrested with others, and in 1986 Fife was found guilty of "conspiracy and two counts of aiding and abetting the illegal entry of Central American refugees into the US," for which he served five years of probation. He tries to talk to all the volunteer groups. He tells us what he thinks this work means and that he's glad we're here. Leaning on the wall behind him is a large map glued to a poster board. Depicting the border region south of Tucson, it's covered with hundreds of red dots, which he tells us represent the loss of human life. Almost six thousand deaths are marked on the map, and those are just the ones that have been counted.

After Fife leaves, a wilderness EMT shows us how to irrigate a wound and treat severe blisters. We learn that a moderately to severely dehydrated person needs to be given small amounts of water in intervals and that pinching someone's skin and seeing how long it takes to return to its shape is a way to gauge how dehydrated a person may be. We're told to ask everyone we encounter if they're urinating or defecating blood, because that can be a sign of a severe infection from drinking contaminated water. Each gallon of water, we're told, weighs eight and a half pounds, so it's impossible for people to carry enough. The border is eleven miles from where we'll be staying, a region of jagged mountains and arroyos that rise and fall in brutal configurations. It usually looks like a barren lunar landscape, but after monsoon season, which it is now, it's lush, and the arroyos can flood in seconds and sweep away anyone who may be walking in them to avoid detection.

Volunteers sleep in small classrooms at the church. Just before turning out the lights I see a translucent scorpion the size of a domino in the corner and crush it with one of my boots. I arrange foldout chairs in a row and manage to sleep on them. The next morning we drive sixty miles south to Arivaca with the windows down. It rained at dawn, and things are a lot more lush than I'd expected. I draw in thick air with a deep clean smell. A young woman in the car says that people think the smell is rain, but it's really rain mixing with the waxy resin of the creosote bush that gives the desert its fresh, wide-open smell after a downpour. She points out the window at brittle-looking scrub along the road. It looks unimpressive, but it may have been the bush through which God spoke to Moses in fire, and it can live for two, sometimes three years without a drop of rain. She says one of the oldest living organisms on earth is a ring of creosote that's been cloning itself for almost twelve thousand years in the Mojave.

Someone else says there's a checkpoint up ahead and that we might be asked to identify ourselves. I finger my new US passport[3] in a Ziploc bag in my pocket. According to a 2005 report[4] by the US Government

---

[3]**new U.S. Passport:** Orduña had recently been naturalized as a citizen of the United States. [Eds.]

[4]Border checkpoint figures and their history: *Border Patrol: Available Data on Interior Checkpoints Suggest Differences in Sector Performance* (Washington: Government Accountability Office, 2005), http://www.gao.gov/assets/250/247179.pdf; "The Constitution in the 100-Mile Border Zone," American Civil Liberties Union, https://www.aclu.org/constitution-100-mile-border-zone.

Accountability Office, there are thirty-three "permanent" checkpoints in the Southwest border states. The number of checkpoints actually in operation is not publicly known because there are an undisclosed number of "tactical" and "temporary" ones deployed. Some news outlets report that the number is around 170. The one up ahead has "temporarily" been there for about five years, and the residents of Arivaca have to go through it whenever they need to go to a store bigger than the mercantile exchange, a small convenience store in town, or go to work, school, or anywhere other than Arivaca, really. When the Border Patrol started in 1924, it was "a handful of mounted agents patrolling desolate areas along U.S. borders." They operated within "a reasonable distance" of the boundary line, but in 1953 the federal government defined this distance as "100 air miles" from all external borders, including coasts. That means that today the more than twenty-one thousand agents of Customs and Border Protection (CBP) stomp around violating the Fourth Amendment[5] on a land area on which about two-thirds of the US population lives. The ACLU reports that "Connecticut, Delaware, Florida, Hawaii, Maine, Massachusetts, New Hampshire, New Jersey, New York, Rhode Island and Vermont lie entirely or almost entirely within this area," and that the area contains "New York City, Los Angeles, Chicago, Houston, Philadelphia, Phoenix, San Antonio, San Diego and San Jose." I remember that a few years ago an old friend of mine was snatched off a Greyhound bus on his way home to Chicago from Cornell University.

When we pull up to the checkpoint, an agent looks inside the truck at everyone's faces. He's uninterested because we're headed toward Arivaca instead of coming from there. He asks the group if everyone's a citizen. We all say yes, and he waves us through.

Within twenty-five miles of the border, CBP agents have been given the authority to enter private property (except dwellings) without a warrant.[6]

We drive through Arivaca to Ruby Road. After a bit, the asphalt gives way to severe dirt terrain, so the car slows as the morning burns off and the early afternoon makes the inside of the truck feel like a dry sauna. All morning I've been thinking about that map—the red dots that looked like spilled blood covering thousands of miles, and the number of lives that have been ended on this political line. The figure comes from the Border Patrol's own tabulations, which are almost certainly low because of the unstructured, sporadic, and prohibitive ways the dead are counted. Even this low estimate means that since 1998, nearly as many people have died trying to cross the southern border

[5]**Fourth Amendment:** This amendment to the Constitution guarantees the right of people to be "secure in their persons, houses, papers, and effects against unreasonable searches and seizures." [Eds.]

[6]CBP agents able to enter private property within twenty-five miles of the border without a warrant: "Know Your Rights With Border Patrol," American Civil Liberties Union of Arizona, http://www.acluaz.org/sites/default/files/documents/ACLU%20Border%20 Rights%20ENGLISH.pdf.

into the United States as there were US soldiers killed in Iraq.[7] Whenever I'm confronted with that figure I try to imagine them embodied, in a group, taking up space and still breathing. A room wouldn't be enough to contain the dead, nor would a warehouse—it would have to be an arena, something like a minor league baseball park packed with men, women, and children, some of whom look like they could be my aunts, uncles, cousins, nephews, parents. But most likely it would be two, three, maybe four arenas, because many bodies are never recovered and so never counted. I think about how, even if all the dead were recovered, the figure wouldn't come close to reflecting the embodied traumas of these ongoing killings. Lives aren't units to be weighed like commodities. Each one of these people was a needed member of a family. Officially there are six thousand dead—six thousand forever-open wounds. In reality the devastation is much greater than this.

The beauty of the desert doesn't hit me until dusk. Before that all I can feel is the sun, a searing orb too bright to look toward, burning me through my clothes, and all I can think is how horrific it must be to not have any way to escape it. When we'd done a little bit of walking earlier in the day, each step was arduous, with loose rock under every footfall shifting my ankles violently. Nothing was flat or smooth, and massive boulders required significant climbing at points. Within minutes it became obvious how easy it would be to succumb, even for a young person in good health. On our drive into camp I'd seen long stretches of jagged terrain with no more to make shade than waist-high mesquite trees, sprawling clusters of nopales, and ocotillo, a succulent that resembles a cat-o'-nine-tails or a group of spindly coral fingers. It wasn't like anything I'd imagined. The residents of Arivaca and the Tohono O'odham people live in this desert and interact with it knowingly and casually on a daily basis. The climate and terrain are harsh, but they need not be deadly. It isn't exposure or the natural danger of this terrain that ends people's lives. In the Border Patrol's own articulation of their plan to militarize the border, a document titled "Border Patrol Strategic Plan 1994 and Beyond" the agency accepted "that absolute sealing of the border is unrealistic." The plan instead was "to prioritize ... efforts by geographic area." The document includes a brief assessment of the environment of border areas where "illegal entrants crossing through remote, uninhabited expanses of land and sea ... can find themselves in mortal danger." The plan specifies that cities split by the boundary line "are the areas of greatest risk for illegal entry," because these "urban areas offer accessibility to roads, rail lines, airports and bus routes to the interior of the country." The document identifies and names specific sectors that are "the locations of heaviest illegal immigration activity."

---

[7]Border Patrol number for migrant remains recovered on the US side of the boundary in the southwestern sectors: 6,330 between 1998 and 2014. The number of US soldiers killed in Iraq through August 8, 2015 (6,840): "Faces of the Fallen," *Washington Post*, http://apps.washingtonpost.com/national/fallen.

At dusk a meeting is called, and as I'm waiting on a folding chair around an extinguished campfire for the rest of the group to gather, I feel utterly overwhelmed by the desert. I'd expected to see something barren, reflective of death and dying, but everything is fecund, verdant—teeming. Just beside me, shooting up through the hard earth, are a few long stalks punctuated at their ends by bursts of purple and yellow flowers smaller than an infant's pinky nail. Beyond the edge of the clearing the brush is so thick it seems impossible to walk through without a machete to clear a path. In the middle distance, perhaps a thousand yards from the edge of camp, rise two hills in black silhouette against an indigo, cerulean, and fuchsia sky. This is the first time I see the group together—a motley collection, mostly white women, two women of Mexican lineage, me, and three or four white men. One of the young white women facilitates the meeting. Mostly it's about how the water drops are done and protocols for situations we may encounter. She finishes by saying it'll be important for us to stay in larger groups this week because a PBS program that used NMD footage aired last night.[8]

Just over two months ago, on the morning of May 14, a camera placed   15
by volunteers captured three agents in bulky green gear walking along a trail at the edge of a cliff. There are six plastic gallons of water visible. The middle agent, who appears to be a blonde white woman, kicks the gallons off the ledge one by one. Some explode when her boot meets them, their tops bursting off, and some survive the initial kick only to tear open on the jagged rocks below. The agent in front, also white, stops to watch and smile. The third agent's face is obscured by his movements.

The kind of cruelty captured on the video isn't an anomaly. NMD conducted a study in which they found that denial of food and water is common, even when migrants are in custody for multiple days and even though most people taken into custody are already experiencing some form of dehydration. Ten percent of interviewees, including teens and children, reported physical abuse, and "of the 433 incidents in which emergency medical treatment or medications were needed, Border Patrol provided access to care in only 59 cases." One interviewee, a woman who said she had lived in the United States for seventeen years with three children, said agents had made her strip naked. "Then they took her clothes and touched her breasts." A man from Chiapas reported being kicked to the ground while being apprehended and having a cactus needle lodged in his eye. He was held in custody for forty-eight hours and did not receive medical attention before being repatriated. One female interviewee reported seeing a pregnant woman with a fever requesting to go to the hospital. The guards didn't believe she was pregnant, and she suffered a miscarriage. A sixteen-year-old boy from Guatemala reported being struck in the back of the head with a flashlight and being held in custody for three days, during which time he only received a packet of cookies and one juice box each day.

---

[8]NMD footage in "Crossing the Line, Part 2," PBS, July 20, 2012, http://www.pbs.org/wnet/need-to-know/video/video-crossing-the-line/14291.

Several men recounted being hit with the butt of a gun during apprehension. One man reported that migra corridos, macabre songs about death and killing in the desert, were played twenty-four hours a day at extreme volumes, and that every two hours shouting guards would rush their cells and make them line up for inspection.[9] The report concluded:

> It is clear that instances of mistreatment and abuse in Border Patrol custody are not aberrational. Rather, they reflect common practice for an agency that is part of the largest federal law enforcement body in the country. Many of them plainly meet the definition of torture under international law.

In this border region, the horizon between natural violence and state violence has been collapsed. The arid climate, the flash floods, the diamondbacks, the mountain impasses, the distance, and the heat of the sun have all been weaponized. People's apathy, disregard, and xenophobia have been weaponized. The situation in which death occurs has been manufactured as such. This is murder without a murderer, administered through bureaucracy and policy planning, murder with the most refined form of impunity, where not only is no one held responsible for the killing of an individual, but no one *can* be held responsible for the individuals who succumb to the journey. The responsibility of having set off into the desert is put solely on the migrants themselves.

A few days later the reality of being in a militarized zone becomes impossible to ignore. Another humanitarian aid group calls to let us know that after a water drop they found a sign on one of their vehicles saying they were being watched. It was signed "Arizona Border Recon," the name of a vigilante group that patrols the border and is listed as a "nativist extremist group" by the Southern Poverty Law Center.[10] I knew before coming out here that encountering militia or armed vigilante groups was a possibility, especially considering many groups operate in the area with the tacit consent of some local authorities. They're regularly allowed to make citizen's arrests, go on armed patrols wearing colors, gear, and identifying patches with logos and names that resemble law enforcement uniforms, and hold people under false pretenses until they can be handed over to Border Patrol. When we take to the trails I try to focus on how it's statistically unlikely for someone in Arizona to be killed or maimed by a member of one of these groups, but I can't help feeling that my odds are different as a brown person on the border. A little over two months before I arrived in the desert, I'd read about how Jason Todd Ready, a neo-Nazi, former candidate for state legislature, and founder of two armed border vigilante groups (Minutemen Civil Defense Corps and the US Border

---

[9] All information about abuse in short-term border patrol custody comes from *A Culture of Cruelty: Abuse and Impunity in Short-Term U.S. Border Patrol Custody* (Tucson: No More Deaths, 2011), http://forms.nomoredeaths.org/wp-content/uploads/2014/10/CultureOfCruelty-full.compressed.pdf.

[10] "'Nativist Extremist' Groups Decline Again," Southern Poverty Law Center, February 25, 2014, https://www.splcenter.org/fighting-hate/intelligence-report/2014/%E2%80%98nativist-extremist%E2%80%99-groups-decline-again-0.

Guard), entered the home he shared with his girlfriend, Lisa Mederos, and fatally shot her, her twenty-three-year-old daughter Amber, Amber's fiancée Jim, and Lisa's fifteen-month-old daughter Lilly, before killing himself.[11] Authorities retrieved a small arsenal, including six grenades from the home. At the time of his death, Ready was being investigated by the FBI for domestic terrorism charges in connection with migrants who had been found shot dead near the border in southern Arizona.

A year and a half before that, one of Ready's associates, Jeffrey Harbin, was arrested on a public highway in Arizona while in possession of an explosive device that contained ball bearings that upon detonation would tear into more human flesh, break more bones, and destroy more body parts than an explosion alone could.[12] In May 2009, Shawna Forde, the founder of a group called Minutemen American Defense, planned and executed a home invasion in Arivaca with two accomplices.[13] The target was Raul Flores, a man Forde and her associates believed was a drug smuggler with large amounts of drugs and money in his home. Their plan was to impersonate Border Patrol agents and rob smugglers in order to fund their operations on the border. When they entered the Flores home, they found no money or drugs but shot and killed Raul and his nine-year-old daughter anyway.

It would be easy to dismiss these events as outliers and the individuals who carried them out as extremist lunatics, but many enjoyed camaraderie and privileged positions at speaking events attended by state officials and members of local governments. Ready even ran for a Mesa City Council seat in 2006 and was called a "true patriot" by former Arizona state senator Russell Pearce.[14] Mainstream elected officials like Pearce, Jan Brewer (governor of Arizona from 2009 to 2015), and Joe Arpaio[15] (sheriff of Arizona's Maricopa County) made careers out of appealing to white supremacists, nativists, hate groups, and their sympathizers, counting them among their voters and donors. They accrued political capital from remaining ambiguous about people like Ready, their racist rhetoric, and the climate of violent xenophobia these individuals have fomented. Their policy initiatives have often been supported by those who identify as white supremacists and, more broadly, by a sizable population of Arizonans who don't.

[margin] 20

---

[11]Information about the murders committed by J.T. Ready can be found in Michael Muskal, "Border Guard Founder J.T. Ready Blamed in Arizona Murder-Suicide," *Los Angeles Times*, May 3, 2012. FBI investigation of Ready before he committed the murders: Tim Gaylord, "FBI Investigating Arizona Neo-Nazi Before Shooting," Reuters, May 5, 2012, http://www.reuters.com/article/2012/05/06/us-usa-arizona-shooting-idUSBRE84500020120506.

[12]"Valley Man Sentenced to 24 Months for Possessing and Transporting Improvised Explosive Devices," press release, Federal Bureau of Investigation, February 7, 2012, https://www.fbi.gov/phoenix/press-releases/2012/valley-man-sentenced-to-24-months-for-possessing-and-transporting-improvised-explosive-devices.

[13]Arizona Vigilante Found Guilty of Murdering Latino Man, Daughter," CNN, February 15, 2011, http://www.cnn.com/2011/CRIME/02/14/arizona.double.killing.verdict.

[14]"J.T. Ready," Extremist Files, Southern Poverty Law Center, https://www.splcenter.org/fighting-hate/extremist-files/individual/jt-ready.

[15]**Joe Arpaio:** (b. 1942) was sheriff until he was defeated in 2017; convicted of criminal contempt of court but pardoned by President Trump. [Eds.]

This kind of crossover between hate groups and the general voters of Arizona is disturbing, but even more disturbing is that liberal policy makers' calls for a national security paradigm are not so different from a white supremacist wish list. The grim reality is that the manipulation of migrant flows into the deadliest parts of the Sonoran Desert has been a bipartisan affair. This national policy, and how we choose to think of and delineate our political community, has killed and continues to kill more people than Ready, Forde, or any other armed terrorist ever could.

Five of us are in a pickup truck when suddenly there's a violent gust of wind and a rushing staccato *thuk thuk thuk thuk* sound rushing toward us. An all-black helicopter with blacked-out windows and no markings rips across the landscape fifty feet in front of the truck. It's flying so low it's framed in the windshield. The driver slams on the brakes, and the helicopter tips forward, kicking up a huge cloud of dust. When it dissipates, the helicopter is gone. After the *thuk thuk thuk thuk* is in the distance and then gone completely, the driver says that BP helicopters are green and white, and that we may have activated one of the seismic sensors buried in undisclosed locations throughout the desert. "Then why the fuck was this one black?" asks someone in the backseat. The truck has started rolling again, and before anyone has time to posit a theory about the color of the chopper, a BP SUV pops over a hill and cuts down fast in front of our truck, blocking our path and almost causing a head-on collision. Several other SUVs and three men on ATVs wearing dark helmets, clad in body armor, and carrying assault rifles surround us. All of them scream commands at the same time so we can't understand any of their words. After a few tense moments, when they've calmed down a bit and verified all of our identities and immigration statuses, they still remain openly hostile, and a few of the agents duck and peer into the backseat of the car, locking onto my brown face. It all happens too fast for me to become scared in the moment, but later, after we're back at camp, I wonder how much danger we were actually in. A study conducted by the Police Executive Research Forum examined cases when BP officers discharged their firearms. One scenario they examined was agents shooting into vehicles, and they found that "most reviewed cases involved non-violent suspects who posed no threat other than a moving vehicle." The study found that, in many cases, agents "intentionally put themselves into the exit path of the vehicle, thereby exposing themselves to additional risk and creating justification for the use of deadly force." According to the report, "The cases suggest that some of the shots at suspect vehicles are taken out of frustration." It concludes, "As with vehicle shootings, some cases suggest that frustration is a factor motivating agents to shoot."

On one of my last days in the desert a group of us drives toward a drop location deep in the Buenos Aires National Wildlife Refuge. Almost two weeks at camp has been a dose of concentrated something, but I'm not sure what. Later, when I get back to my life, the effects of being out here really start to become apparent. When a news helicopter flies overhead in Tucson I wince, and for a long time I can't look white people in the eye without feeling a pinprick of rage I have to work hard to contain. I can't concentrate on anything because the August sun on my skin and the record-breaking heat in which I move keep me constantly thinking about how, *now, right now*, there are people walking in the desert. I spend the rest of the summer drinking heavily, compulsively, with the intended purpose of blacking out. And when this feeling of catastrophic urgency starts to fade, I feel a paralyzing guilt. In the backseat of the pickup between two volunteers I'm trying to formulate in language why I've come out here, not an explanation for them, just for me, inside my head, but there isn't a singular reason I can pin down. It's more like an accumulation of intensity that has reached a point of saturation and needed to be spent, a sense of obligation, and a rage.

On a dirt road not far from camp, we see six men struggling to remain upright and moving forward. When they hear the truck, four of them let themselves fall to the ground, and the other two throw their arms up to flag us down. As we approach, our driver, a tall white woman volunteer, tells us she has medical training and thinks a Spanish speaker should stay with her. She says the truck should be driven to camp and not come back for at least an hour. She explains that since they're on a main road approaching town, BP has probably already been alerted of their presence. We'll want to treat the men as quickly and as best we can before agents arrive. So many people go through the entire process of apprehension and repatriation without receiving medical attention, being given any or enough water, or being fed much (if at all), and almost no one is informed of rights. She also explains that we want to stay and observe the apprehension because our presence might deter a beating or other forms of abuse, at least during these moments.

The two of us get out of the truck with a backpack full of emergency medical supplies, four gallons of water each, and a few packs of food. The truck takes off down the road. Two of the men, the two still standing, are unmistakably brothers, in their late twenties or early thirties.

"Hola, muchachos, somos amigos. Por qué no nos sentamos aquí en la sombra?"[16] I say.

"Gracias, gracias."[17]

They all nod, and we help the ones who are already sitting to stand back up, which looks painful for all of them but especially agonizing to one who pulls hard on my hand as he stands without bending his left leg.

"Me jodí la pierna, carnal."[18]

Their eyes look the kind of tired no amount of sleep can fix. They're all wearing tattered blue jeans and their shoes are curled upward from walking countless miles on uneven terrain. We help them all sit in a small clearing near a tree that provides a few slivers of shade. I tell them we're friends, friends with a humanitarian aid group, as we crack

[16]**Hola, muchachos, somos amigos. ¿Por qué no nos sentamos aquí en la sombra?:** Hey, guys, we're friends. Why don't we sit here in the shade? [Notes 16–26 are the editors'.]
[17]**Gracias, gracias:** Thank you, thank you.
[18]**Me jodí la pierna, carnal:** I screwed up my leg, dude.

open a gallon of water for each of them and advise them to drink it slowly or they won't be able to keep it down. One of the brothers says they want to turn themselves in to Border Patrol—*no more, no more, we want to go home.*

One of the brothers has been smiling at me as I speak, and when I pause he asks me if I'm from Puebla. I smile and tell him I'm from Veracruz, recognizing that he asked because we both have the flat accent of central Mexico, specifically the accent that Poblanos have. Jarochos, people from Veracruz, usually speak a bit more emphatically, while Poblanos have a slower, rounder cadence. I tell him my mother is from Puebla, but since I wasn't raised in Veracruz, and since my mother was the one whose Spanish I modeled because my old man was always working, I spoke Spanish like a Poblano without ever having lived in Puebla. The group cracks up.

"Cabrón,"[19] says one of them, slapping the ground laughing.

A few of them have ripped open Clif Bars and crackers and are struggling to swallow what they've chewed. One man says they've been walking for four days and that the night before last they went to sleep, and when they woke up, the rest of the group, including their guide, was gone. They had run out of water the following morning. Another man asks me how long I've lived "on this side" and how my family got here. I tell him as briefly as I can, and when I finish, the younger brother from Puebla asks what my mother's maiden name is. I tell him, and I also tell him *her* mother's maiden name and my grandfather's name. He says he knows some people with the last name Flores, who live near his family. I brush it off, until he says the grandfather is tall, abnormally so, and very dark with light-colored eyes and white hair, so they sometimes call him El Puro because he looks like a lit cigar. I remember Yoli[20] showing me a photo of her father as a young man standing with five of his brothers, a couple of them towering over the others, and her telling me some of my great uncles were over six feet tall. The photo was sepia, and all of them were a deep brown with shiny foreheads, slicked back hair, and strangely light eyes.

For a moment it feels like I'm among family.

We all hear a car in the distance. Some of the men who'd been lying down sit up. The other volunteer is finishing wrapping one of their feet. I tell them to put the card we gave them in their pockets and to remember they're entitled to a phone call. Their faces change, tighten, and the man with the knot on his knee extends his hand to the other volunteer.

"Gracias, muchacha,"[21] he says.

"De nada," she answers, shaking his hand.

Both brothers look at me, their faces communicating more than they ever could with words: the arbitrariness of why I'm helping them rather than the other way around; the meaninglessness of it; how this absence of meaning may not make the brutality worse but somehow casts it in an even harsher light; and some relief because they think it's over, and

35

---

[19]**Cabrón:** Bastard.
[20]**Yoli:** Orduña's mother.
[21]**Muchacha:** Young woman.

the worst of it might be, but it might not. We shake hands. One of them pats me on the chest with his open palm after he lets go of my hand.

"Gracias, hermano."[22]

The green-and-white SUV skids to a halt on the dirt road. We hear 40 a car door open and close. We walk toward the road and I round a bush into visibility. When I do, the agent, a tall blond white man with a flattop, takes a step back, extending one hand while the other hand reaches back toward his belt.

"What the hell!" he yells.

"Hi, hi, hi," I say, putting my hands out with my palms open and turned upward. "We're volunteers, we're with the church."

"Get down! Sit down! On the ground!" He's yelling and signaling violently with his outstretched hand, the other one still back, hovering above his gun. We sit down.

"You—come over here," he says, pointing at the other volunteer.

She stands up slowly and walks toward him. They go to the back of 45 the vehicle, and from where I'm sitting I can see the agent looking and signaling in my direction, obviously asking questions about me. After a minute or so they walk back, he stares at me with his eyebrows furrowed, looking perhaps a little confused. My beard was already three weeks long before I arrived in the desert, so now it's a little over an inch and unruly. It curls upward on one side along my jaw line with a few ringlets by my ears and none of it stays matted down. I'm wearing expensive cargo pants my dad insisted on buying at an outdoor store before I came out, and screen-printed on my T-shirt is a photo of an old-timey man panning for gold, with a caption that reads: "I'm not a gold digger, I'm a panhandler."

"You—come here." He signals for me to stand and follow.

The three of us walk to the group of men. When we get there, the agent radios for another vehicle. He tells us to sit, and he approaches the men who are all still in a half moon under the shade of a scraggly tree. He gets uncomfortably close, towering over them as he yells, "Yo,[23] Steven. Okay? Bway-no?[24] Okay. Ha ha ha." A few of the men strain to smile and nod as he says this, and a few of the others just look toward the ground.

"See, I'm nice. I'm a nice guy. Okay? Bway-no?"

He stands over me so that I have to crane my neck back at an extreme angle, looking almost directly up. He lowers his volume and changes his tone dramatically, like he's trying to make small talk.

"So, you from around here?" he asks me, ignoring the other volunteer. 50

"No, I live in the Midwest."

"Oh, yeah? Where? I have some family out there."

"Iowa."

I don't want to flat out refuse to answer his questions because I don't want to anger him so that he might take his frustration out on the men, or someone else he encounters after we've split.

[22]**Hermano:** Brother.
[23]**Yo:** I; the Border Patrol agent is speaking fractured Spanish ("I, Steven.").
[24]**Bway-no:** More fractured Spanish; he means *bueno*—good.

"Oh, wow. Ha! So are you *from* Iowa?" 55

"I lived in Illinois before that."

"So, is English your, uh, fir—uh, first language?"

"I speak mostly English now, yes."

A voice comes over his radio, and he steps back to the vehicle for a moment. We tell the men to keep drinking water and eating. When he comes back he points at me and tells me to translate what he's going to say. He asks the men a few questions through me and then says, "Well, if you'd only done things the right way, I wouldn't have to slap these cuffs on you. I don't know why so many people can't just follow the law. It's the law. Lah-*lay*.[25] Lah-*lay*." Instead of translating what he's just said, I remind the men they don't have to sign voluntary departure papers if they think they may qualify for some kind of immigration relief, and that someone at the number on the card can help determine if they might qualify.

"Okay, well, you two better take off now," he says, signaling to me 60 and the other volunteer. "I'm nice, as you can see, but my partner who's on his way now is crazy. *I* don't care if you're here, but he's crazy. You better get outta here."

The other volunteer tells him we're waiting for our ride and they should be arriving any minute. He shakes his head at us.

"Don't say I didn't warn you."

He approaches the men and begins taking their backpacks and bags of food, tossing them into a pile. He tells them to put down the gallons of water and starts riffling through the bags.

"Back up, then. Go over there, on the other side," he points across the road where he wants us to move. The other volunteer starts to pick up our supplies, putting them in the medical pack one by one. She looks me in the eye as she's doing it, communicating that I should also start picking up garbage and supplies as slowly as possible, one by one, so we can remain within eyesight longer.

Another BP vehicle arrives, this one a pickup with a cage on the 65 bed. The first agent approaches it. A man who looks like a caricature of police—a close-cropped haircut, aviators, and a push-broom mustache—gets out of the car. He too juts back when he sees me.

"What the fuck! Who the fuck is *that*?" he says to the first agent, pointing at me.

The first agent grabs him by the shoulder, turning him away from us. They whisper to each other for a minute, and then the newly arrived agent goes to the men. The first agent stands above us.

"Go to the other side. Now. *Now!*"

We stand in the middle of the road where we can still see the men. The agents tell them to stand. They struggle to get up. The agents grab the gallons of water and start dumping them out.

"Come on, man," I say. 70

Both of them look at us, and then at each other.

---

[25]**Lah-lay:** He means, *la ley*—the law.

"Please let them take some water," says the other volunteer calmly.

"No, no, no. We can't. We don't know what's in these.'

"We have sealed ones. Please. They're dehydrated," says the other volunteer.

They look at each other again.   75

"Okay, give me the sealed ones. We'll take them in the truck with us."

"Can't they take them in the back with them? Please."

"No."

The agents make the men turn toward the tree, interlock their fingers on the backs of their heads, and spread their legs. They begin manhandling and patting them down one by one. It becomes apparent that what I'm witnessing is an act of empire-building. Here, in this zone, and on these bodies, America defines itself by what it's not. Each rejection, each death in the desert, is a re-articulation of our foundational violence. This is America. Each passage and inscription of a human being as "illegal" is a reiteration. We are in the zone where justice reaches its vanishing point, sheds its veneer, and reveals itself fully as punishment.

The agents have the men at the back of the pickup. The one with   80
the mustache unlocks the cage and opens the door. The agent shoves the younger brother forward, and the young man braces himself on the frame and looks over to us.

"Adiós,[26] carnales."

Each man says good-bye before they're shoved in. One of them pokes his fingers through small slots in a metal grate at the very back of the cage and waves them as the truck pulls away and disappears over the horizon.

26**Adios:** Goodbye.

ENGAGING THE TEXT

1. What is the purpose of the stories about people charged with littering, charged with transporting illegal immigrants, and convicted of "aiding and abetting the illegal entry of Central American refugees" (para. 6)? What were they actually doing, and how does Orduña feel about their actions?

2. The Border Patrol is authorized to operate within 100 miles of any external border, enabling them to "stomp around violating the Fourth Amendment . . . [where] about two-thirds of the US population lives" (para. 9). Orduña's language indicates that he sees this as excessive power. Explain why you agree or disagree with him.

3. In paragraph 12, Orduña tries to grasp the number of people who have died in the desert; the red dots on the map that mark individual deaths "looked like spilled blood covering thousands of miles." What other comparisons does he make to convey the enormity of such numbers, and why does he say the tally of deaths is much higher than the official body count? What point is he making when he says, "each one of these people was a needed member of a family"? What is the cumulative effect of this paragraph?

4. Orduña describes a video that shows Border Patrol agents destroying six gallons of water that volunteers had left for people traversing the desert (para. 15). He also provides a number of shocking details about the Border Patrol's treatment of migrants, including denial of water, food, and medical attention; sexual harassment; and physical or psychological abuse. How do these details affect you as a reader?

5. What does Orduña mean when he observes that the desert itself has become "weaponized"? Who is he referring to when he says, "people's apathy, disregard, and xenophobia have been weaponized"? Do you agree with his claim that "this is murder without a murderer" (para. 17)? Why or why not?

6. What links does Orduña see between violent extremists and mainstream conservative politicians? What connects all of them to liberal politicians and to national policy (paras. 18–20)? He says that the U.S. government "has killed and continues to kill more people than . . . [an] armed terrorist ever could" (para. 20). What point is he making here? Explain why you find his presentation persuasive or not.

7. What effects does Orduña experience once he's returned to Iowa, and how do you account for them? Why does he drink "heavily, compulsively, with the intended purpose of blacking out"? Why does he feel "a sense of obligation, and a rage" (para. 22)?

8. **Thinking Rhetorically** Orduña clearly identifies with undocumented immigrants and deplores their inhumane treatment by the Border Patrol. How does his own position as a Mexican immigrant influence the narrative? Do you sympathize with him, distrust his bias, or both? What image of himself does he present in this selection, and how does his character affect your reading of "Passport to the New West"?

EXPLORING CONNECTIONS

9. Why does Orduña say, "Each rejection, each death in the desert, is a re-articulation of our foundational violence. This is America" (para. 78)? Do you think that Ta-Nehisi Coates (p. 604) would agree with this conclusion? Explain your reasoning.

10. Linda Holtzman and Leon Sharpe discuss counterstories — stories that reframe or disrupt common misunderstandings of race (p. 637). What dominant stories are Marc Lamont Hill (p. 651), Amani Al-Khatahtbeh (p. 676), and Orduña trying to overturn? What counterstories do their essays present, and how effectively do they challenge the dominant narratives?

11. Read Ted Rall's cartoon on page 700. What does the cartoonist suggest about the difficulties facing kids who were brought to the United States illegally? How humane is the practice of deporting young migrants who have spent most of their lives in the United States? What's Rall saying about millennials?

EXTENDING THE CRITICAL CONTEXT

12. All of Orduña's examples of detainee abuse are taken from a report issued by No More Deaths in 2011. Do some online research to find more current sources of information about the treatment of migrants by the Border Patrol. To what extent do your findings support Orduña's claims about the inhumane treatment of undocumented immigrants?

HOW IMMIGRANTS BECOME "OTHER"

MARCELO M. SUÁREZ-OROZCO AND CAROLA SUÁREZ-OROZCO

Illegal immigration is a contentious issue. Extremists liken those who enter the United States illegally to criminals and advocate construction of a wall on the Mexican border monitored by predator drones. Marcelo M. Suárez-Orozco and Carola Suárez-Orozco suggest that immigration is more complex and emphasize instead the conditions that often drive unauthorized immigrants to flee their countries — including poverty, violence, and war. Marcelo M. Suárez-Orozco is Distinguished Professor of Education and the Wasserman Dean of the Graduate School of Education and Information Studies at

UCLA, where his wife, Carola, is also a Professor of Education. Both are leading experts in immigration studies, having jointly won Harvard's Virginia and Warren Stone Prize for Outstanding Book on Education and Society (2007) for their *Learning a New Land: Immigrant Students in American Society*. Together and separately, they have edited a number of books on Latinos and immigration, and cowrote *Children of Immigration: The Developing Child* (2002). In 2009–2010, Marcelo M. Suárez-Orozco served as Special Advisor to the Chief Prosecutor at the International Criminal Court in The Hague, Netherlands. This essay originally appeared in *Arizona Firestorm: Global Immigration Realities, National Media, and Provincial Politics*, edited by Otto Santa Ana and Celeste González de Bustamante (2012).

Unauthorized Immigration

No human being can be "illegal." While there are illegal actions — running a red light or crossing an international border without the required authorization, one action should not come to define a person's existence. The terms *illegal, criminal*, and *alien*, often uttered in the same breath, conjure up unsavory associations.[1] Unsettling and distancing ways to label people, they have contributed to the creation of our very own caste of untouchables.

In many cases, "illegal status," or what we prefer to term unauthorized status, may not be voluntary. We prefer this term to *undocumented immigrant* as many have documents or could have documents but often find themselves in a limbo state pending a formal legal outcome.

In the mid-1990s, Sonia Martinez, mother of four children, all under the age of ten, became a young widow when her husband was stricken with cancer. With a limited education and no means to support her family on a rancho in rural southern Mexico, she reluctantly left her children behind in the care of her mother and crossed the border without papers. The week after arriving Sonia took up a job as a live-in housekeeper and nanny in the Southwest. Every month she faithfully sent money home to her family. She called them every week. Each time she called, they had less and less to say to her. Lovingly, she selected presents for each of her children over the course of the year. By Christmas she would make the pilgrimage back to her rancho to see her children and, Santa-like, shower them with American gifts.

---

[1]Santa Ana, O. (2002). *Brown tide rising: Metaphoric representations of Latinos in contemporary public discourse*. Austin: University of Texas Press. [All notes are the Suárez-Orozcos', except 13.]

But the sweet visits home were always too short and she would soon have to face the dangerous and expensive crossing back to California, relying on the help of treacherous *coyotes* (smugglers) she hired each time. After September 11, as border controls tightened, she no longer dared to make the trek back and forth. She has stayed behind the trapdoor on this side of the border and has not seen her children since then.[2]

Sonia found herself a young widow and in a post–NAFTA [North Atlantic Free Trade Agreement] Mexican economy with promised jobs that simply never materialized and in an unforgiving economy for poorly educated, unskilled, rural workers. Plentiful jobs in the Southwest economy in the mid-1990s, relatively comfortable working conditions as a live-in housekeeper and nanny in a middle-class neighborhood, and an extremely advantageous wage differential proved irresistible. Although not raising her children came at a high emotional cost, the ability to support them was its own reward.

In 1998, Hurricane Mitch devastated Honduras, leaving little in the way of work opportunities. Like many others, Gustavo Jimenez made his way north, dangerously riding atop trains through Central America and Mexico and then crossed with a hired *coyote* into Texas. He worked a series of odd jobs but found it difficult to find steady work. Then, yet another hurricane changed his fate. When Katrina devastated New Orleans in 2005, ample work opportunities opened—dirty work in horrific conditions were hard to fill over the long haul of the cleanup and reconstruction. Mr. Jimenez quickly found work: "Who but us migrants would do these hard jobs without ever taking a break? We worked day and night in jobs Americans would never do, so that the Gulf could be rebuilt." But he found that he would be treated with disdain. It left him mystified. On one hand, "I know that by coming here illegally I am breaking the law," but he added, "I did not come to steal from anyone. I put my all in the jobs I take. And I don't see any of the Americans wanting to do this work."[3] Gustavo's story is both old and new. Unauthorized immigrants have always been called upon to do the jobs on the dark side of the American economy. The post-Katrina cleanup is a fitting example. Adding insult to injury, these workers are the target of disdain and disparagement. The stigma of the work gets attached to them—as if those doing dirty, demanding, and dangerous jobs themselves by mimesis become dirty, despised, and dispensable.

Hervé Fonkou Takoulo is a college-educated professional with a knack for stock trading in his spare time. Mr. Takoulo arrived in the

5

---

[2]Note that we have used a pseudonym; this case is from IS @ NYU data—see http://steinhardt.nyu.edu/scmsAdmin/media/users/ef58/metrocenter/Online_Supplemental_Notes.pdf.

[3]Gustavo's quotes are to be found in Orner, P. (Ed.). (2008). *Underground America: Narratives of undocumented lives.* San Francisco, CA: McSweeney's.

United States in 1998 on a valid visa from the troubled African nation of Cameroon. He took to New York like a duck to water. He graduated with an engineering degree from the State University of New York and married a U.S. citizen hailing from California. She was the vice president of a Manhattan media advertising company. The biracial professional couple was ecstatic when President Obama spoke of his dual African and American roots. Takoulo's wife, Caroline Jamieson, "recalled that she cried when Mr. Obama said during a 2008 campaign speech, 'With a mother from Kansas and a father from Kenya' — I said, 'Oh, Hervé, even the alliteration is right — with a mother from California and a father from Cameroon, our child could do the same!'" She cried again but for a very different reason when the letter she wrote to President Obama resulted in her husband's arrest. The letter to the president "explained that Ms. Jamieson, 42, had filed a petition seeking a green card for her husband on the basis of their 2005 marriage. But before they met, Mr. Takoulo, who first arrived in the country on a temporary business visa, had applied for political asylum and had been denied it by an immigration judge in Baltimore, who ordered him deported." Surely, this president with his extensive personal experience in Africa would understand that Cameroon had a horrendous record of human rights abuses. Instead of the hoped-for presidential reprieve, the asylum seeking Obamista was met by two immigration agents, "in front of the couple's East Village apartment building. He says one agent asked him, 'Did you write a letter to President Obama?' When he acknowledged that his wife had, he was handcuffed and sent to an immigration jail in New Jersey for deportation."[4]

When she was four, Marieli's father was assassinated in front of his wife and children. Left as a widow responsible for her family, Marieli's mother reluctantly left Guatemala for the United States, as she put it, "in order to be able to feed my family." Once in California, she applied for asylum status and waited patiently for her papers to be processed. The unforgiving bureaucratic labyrinth took six years and a small fortune to complete. Only then could she begin the process of applying to reunite with her children. In the meantime, the grandmother, who had been raising the children in her absence, died. With no one to care for them and after having patiently waited for years, Marieli's mother made the drastic choice of having her children make the crossing without papers. Finally, at age eleven, after having spent more than half her childhood away from her mother, Marieli arrived in northern California after being smuggled into the country by *coyotes*. Recognizing she "owed everything" to her mother but at the same time angry she had been left behind for so long, the reunification with the mother she barely knew was a rocky and bittersweet one. Marieli is now an unauthorized immigrant waiting in limbo.

[4]Bernstein, N. (2010, June 18). Plea to Obama led to an immigrant's arrest. *New York Times*.

The Reagan-inspired U.S. wars of proxy in El Salvador, Guatemala, and Nicaragua of the 1980s resulted in systematic killings—largely of noncombatant civilians, massive displacements of people, and the beginning of an international exodus of biblical proportions not only to the United States but also to neighboring Latin American countries. The U.S. invasion of Iraq has made Iraqis top the list of formally admitted refugees in the United States in 2009. While those escaping our foreign policy debacles often make it through the legal maze, thousands of others fall through every year.

The cases reveal how war and conflict drive human migration. But the heart also plays an unanticipated but powerful role. Work, war, and love are behind almost every migrant journey—authorized or unauthorized.

Many come here fully aware that they will be breaking a law by 10 crossing without the proper documents, but in other cases accidents, misunderstandings, and an unforgiving bureaucracy can turn good faith errors into labyrinths without exit.

During his tour of duty in Iraq, Lt. Kenneth Tenebro "harbored a fear he did not share with anyone in the military. Lieutenant Tenebro worried that his wife, Wilma, back home in New York with their infant daughter, would be deported. Wilma, who like her husband was born in the Philippines, is an illegal immigrant. . . . That was our fear all the time." When he called home, "She often cried about it. . . . Like, hey, what's going to happen? Where will I leave our daughter?" The Tenebros' story, like many others, began as a love story and an overstayed visa. They met several years ago while Wilma was on vacation in New York at the end of a job as a housekeeper on a cruise ship. Love kept her from returning to the Philippines, and ultimately she overstayed her visa. Today, the lieutenant and the wife face an unhappy choice: "Wilma is snagged on a statute, notorious among immigration lawyers, that makes it virtually impossible for her to become a legal resident without first leaving the United States and staying away for 10 years." Lt. Tenebro is not alone—thousands of U.S. soldiers facing dangerous tours of duty have the additional burden of worrying that loved ones close to them will be deported.[5]

Combined, these testimonies embody the varieties of unauthorized journeys into the United States. Synergetic "push" and "pull" factors coalesce, luring immigrants away from familiar but relatively scarce surroundings to an alluring unknown. Immigrant optimism springs eternal. While some fly in with documents and visas and simply overstay, more immigrants come undetected through the southern border. Often they hire dangerous *coyotes* (typically from Mexico or Central America) or *snakeheads* (working from as far away as China, India, or Russia). Immigrants pay a very high price for these unauthorized

---

[5]Preston, J. (2010, May 8). Worried about deploying with family in limbo. *New York Times*.

journeys. While the crossing from Mexico to the United States can run approximately $3,000, the costs of longer passages are substantially higher, running up to an exorbitant $30,000 per journey. Those who arrive under the long shadow of transnational smuggling syndicates often face a period of protracted indentured servitude, as they must pay back exorbitant crossing fees. Whether the journey begins in Fujian, China, or Puebla, Mexico, tough border controls have made the crossing more dangerous than ever before—on average more than a person a day dies at the southern border attempting to cross.

The Children of Unauthorized Immigrants

Unauthorized immigrants are neither from Mars nor Venus. The majority have roots in American society. While some are married to U.S. citizens, others partner with migrants already here. Nearly half of unauthorized immigrants live in households with a partner and children. The vast majority of these children—79 percent—are U.S. citizens by birth.[6] The number of U.S.-born children in mixed-status families has expanded rapidly from 2.7 million in 2003 to 4 million in 2008.[7] Adding the 1.1 million unauthorized children living in the United States (like Marieli) means that there are 5.1 million children currently living in "mixed-status" homes.[8]

Nowhere is the story of the unauthorized immigration more dystopic than for the children who grow up in the shadows of the law. On an unbearable steamy afternoon in July 2010, Carola Suárez-Orozco found herself in a somber congressional chamber testifying on behalf of the American Psychological Association in front of an ad hoc committee of the United States House of Representatives headed by Arizona's Congressman Raúl Grijalva (D-Tucson). At her side were two children—precocious, overly serious. A congressional photographer afterward whispered to Carola that in over twenty years on the job he had never seen such young children testify before the U.S. Congress.

> Eleven-year-old Mathew Parea was poised and collected as he spoke in the august chamber. At a tender age, he had already been active in social justice causes for several years including a four-day fast honoring the patron saint of migrant workers, César Chávez. Mathew spoke on behalf of thousands of children of migrant families. His steady voice was riveting: "I am here to tell you about my fears growing up in Arizona. Children want to be with their parents because we know that our parents love us. The laws in Arizona are just unjust and make me fear for my family. I am always worried when my family leaves the house that

[6]Passel, J. S., & Taylor, P. (2010). Unauthorized immigrants and their U.S.-born children. Washington, DC: Pew Research Center. Retrieved from pewhispanic.org/reports/report.php?ReportID=125.
[7]Ibid.
[8]Ibid.

something might happen to them. I think about it when my dad goes to work that he might not come back or when I go to school that there might not be someone to pick me up when I get out."[9]

Heidi Portugal physically appeared younger than twelve, yet she carried herself in an unsettling serious manner. Her story embodies the immigrant dream turned nightmare: "At only 10 years of age I had a sad awakening the day of February 11th. When I woke up, I found out that my mother had been arrested. . . . My biggest preoccupation was my two little brothers and sister. What was going to happen to them? And what about my little brother that my mother was breast feeding?" She went on to explain how as the eldest sister, she took on the responsibility of caring for her younger siblings, how her mother was deported, and how she has never seen her mother again. She went on, "Before, I would admire all uniformed people that protect our country . . . [but they] took away the most precious thing that children can have, our mother. With one hit, they took away my smile and my happiness."[10]

Mathew and Heidi are part of an estimated one hundred thousand citi-   15
zen[11] children whose parents have been deported. They face an impossible choice no child should have to make—staying in the United States with relatives or going with their parents to a country they do not know. These youngsters are a caste of orphans of the state, citizen children who day in and day out lose "the right to have rights"[12]—for them the protections of the Fourteenth Amendment[13] are an elusive mirage. Children whose parents are detained and/or deported by Immigration and Customs Enforcement exhibit multiple behavioral changes in the aftermath of parental detention, including anxiety, frequent crying, changes in eating and sleeping patterns, withdrawal, and anger. Such behavioral changes were documented for both short-term after the arrest as well as in the long-term at a nine-month follow-up.[14]

They also experience dramatic increases in housing instability and food insecurity—both important dimensions of basic developmental well-being. Such insecurities, while heightened for children whose parents are detained, is ongoing for children growing up in mixed-status households. These insecurities exist even though unauthorized immigrants have very high levels of employment; among men, fully 94 percent are active in the labor force (a rate substantially higher than for U.S.-born citizens—83 percent and legal immigrants—85 percent). At the same time, more than 30 percent of children growing up

[9]See Testimony of Carola Suárez-Orozco before the United States House of Representatives, www.apa.org/about/gr/issues/cyf/immigration-enforcement.aspx.
[10]Ibid.
[11]Ibid.
[12]Arendt, H. (1966). *The origins of totalitarianism.* New York: Harcourt.
[13]**Fourteenth Amendment:** Provides equal protection and due process under the law. [Eds.]
[14]Chaudry, A., Pedroza, J., Castañeda, R. M., Santos, R., & Scott, M. M. (2010). *Facing our future: Children in the aftermath of immigration enforcement.* Washington, DC: Urban Institute.

in unauthorized households live below the poverty line. Harvard psychologist Hiro Yoshikawa, in his detailed study of infants and their families, documents the range of penalties American-born preschool children of unauthorized parents face. First, the children's housing and economic situation was often quite fragile. Second, unauthorized parents were less likely to take advantage of a range of benefits to which their citizen children are entitled (like Temporary Assistance to Needy Families, Head Start, the Women, Infants and Children Nutritional Program, Medicaid, and others). Lastly, they had less access to extended social networks that can provide information, babysit, or lend money in a crisis.[15]

While the majority of children of unauthorized immigrants are citizen children (4 million), there are some 1.1 million children who just like Marieli have no papers. Many arrive when they are very young, others in their teen years. These children grow up in America, attending American schools, making American friends, learning English, and developing an emerging American identity. Every year approximately 65,000 young people graduate from high schools without the requisite papers either to go on to college or to legally enter the work force.

Unauthorized immigrants live in a parallel universe. Their lives are shaped by forces and habits that are unimaginable to many American citizens. Work and fear are the two constants. They lead to routines, where the fear of apprehension and deportation is an ever-present shadow in their lives. Dropping off a child to school, a casual trip to the supermarket, a train or bus ride, expose them to the threat of apprehension, deportation, and the pain of being separated from their loved ones.

Mass unauthorized immigration has become a social phenomenon with deep structural roots in American institutions. The responsibility must be shared beyond the immigrants themselves to the businesses that thrive on their labor, the middle-class families who rely on them for housekeeping, babysitting, landscaping, and other amenities, consumers who have come to expect their affordable produce and rapid delivery services, and all citizens who have consciously or unconsciously enabled a dysfunctional system to flourish. Above all the political class shares the bulk of the responsibility by oscillating between denial, grandstanding, and hysterical scapegoating. They have brought us demagogic, unworkable, and self-defeating policy proposals.

Broken Lines

Outcry over our broken immigration system is focused on the borderline. Frustrated and fearful, Americans ask, "Why won't these illegals get in line like everybody else?" On the surface that is a perfectly reasonable question.

---

[15]Yoshikawa, H. (2011). *Immigrants raising citizens: Undocumented parents and their young children.* New York: Russell Sage Foundation.

The reality, however, is that there is no orderly line to join. The ter- 20 rorist attacks of September 11 threw sand in an already rusty machinery of legal immigration. In countless U.S. consulates and embassies the world over and in U.S. Citizenship and Immigration Services offices all over the country, millions wait in interminable queues. New security considerations brought an already inefficient system to a near standstill.

There are nearly 3.5 million immediate family members of U.S. citizens and permanent lawful immigrants waiting overseas for their visas.[16] In U.S. consulates in Mexico alone, approximately a quarter of a million spouses and minor children of U.S. citizens and permanent lawful residents wait to legally join their immediate relatives north of the border. In the Philippines, approximately 70,000 spouses and minor children are in the same situation. The average wait in line for these countries is from four to six years for spouses and under-age children. If you are a U.S. citizen and your sister is in the Philippines, you will have to wait twenty years before she can join you. If you are a U.S. citizen and would like to sponsor your unmarried adult child in Mexico, you will wait sixteen years and spend considerable resources.

The visa allocation system for work permits is no more functional.[17] The annual quota for work visas is 140,000 per year; as this includes spouses and children, the actual number of workers is much lower. There is no systematic queue for low-skilled workers. There are a million people waiting in Mexico alone in any given year.[18] As Roxanna Bacon, the chief counsel for the United States Citizenship and Immigration Services in Washington, D.C., succinctly stated, "Our housing industry, our service industry, our gardening, landscape industry, you name it—it's been dependent for decades on Mexican labor. None of these people qualify for an employment-based visa. So when the hate mongers say, 'Why can't they wait in line? Can't they get a visa?'—there aren't any visas to get! There is no line to wait in! And that's why everyone who knows this area of law says without comprehensive immigration reform you really aren't going to solve any of these pop-up issues."[19]

Reasonable voices have been driven off stage, while demagogic venting, grandstanding, and obfuscation saturate the airwaves, the print media, the Internet, and town halls throughout the nation. Rather than offering new solutions, an amalgamation of cultural xenophobes and economic nativists has joined together to fuel the fire. Xenophobes see mass immigration, especially from Latin America, as a growing menace to the pristine tapestry of American culture that would be

[16]Anderson, S. (2010). Family immigration: The long wait to immigrate. Arlington, VA: National Foundation for American Policy. Retrieved from www.nfap.com/.

[17]Anderson, S. (2009). *Employment-based green card projections point to decade-long waits.* Arlington, VA: National Foundation for American Policy. Retrieved from www.nfap.com/.

[18]U.S. State Department (2009). Annual report on immigrant visa applicants in the family sponsored and employment based preferences registered at the National Visa Center as of November 1. Annual Report on Immigrant Visas. Washington, DC: U.S. State Department.

[19]Bacon, R. (2010, May 22). One border, many sides. *New York Times.* Retrieved on 22 February 2012 from www.nytimes.com/2010/05/23/opinion/23deavere-smith.html?sc=8&sq-Deveare-Smith&st=cse&pagewanted=1.

stained by new arrivals from the "Brown" continent. Economic nativists wring their hands: immigration presents unfair competition for ever-scarcer jobs as well as putting downward pressure on wages. For them, immigration has come to embody the globalization in all its pathologies. Immigrants are tangible representations of enormous and amorphous problems—the globalization of terror, the outsourcing of jobs, and the discomfort of being surrounded by strangers (dis)figuring the social sphere with exotic languages, cultural habits, and uncanny ways.

References

Anderson, S. (2009). *Employment-based green card projections point to decade-long waits.* Arlington, VA: National Foundation for American Policy. Retrieved from www.nfap.com/.

Anderson, S. (2010). *Family immigration: The long wait to immigrate.* Arlington, VA: National Foundation for American Policy. Retrieved from www.nfap.com/.

Arendt, H. (1966), *The origins of totalitarianism.* New York: Harcourt.

Bernstein, N. (2006, May 22). 100 years in the back door, out the front. *New York Times.* Retrieved on July 31, 2011 from www.nytimes.com/learning/teachers/featured_articles/20060522monday.html?scp=10&sq=Ari%20Zolberg&st=cse.

Bernstein, N. (2010, June 18). Plea to Obama led to an immigrant's arrest. *New York Times.*

Chaudry, A., Pedroza, J., Castañeda, R. M., Santos, R., & Scott, M. M. (2010). *Facing our future: Children in the aftermath of immigration enforcement.* Washington, DC: Urban Institute.

Orner, P. (Ed.). (2008). *Underground America: Narratives of undocumented lives.* San Francisco, CA: McSweeney's.

Passel, J. S., & Taylor, P. (2010). Unauthorized immigrants and their U.S.-born children. Washington, DC: Pew Research Center. Retrieved from pewhispanic.org/reports/report.php?ReportID=125.

Preston, J. (2010, May 8). Worried about deploying with family in limbo. *New York Times.*

Santa Ana, O. (2002). *Brown tide rising: Metaphoric representations of Latinos in contemporary public discourse.* Austin: University of Texas Press.

Yoshikawa, H. (2011), *Immigrants raising citizens: Undocumented parents and their young children.* New York: Russell Sage Foundation.

Zolberg, A. (2008). *A nation by design: Immigration policy in the fashioning of America.* Cambridge, MA: Harvard University Press.

ENGAGING THE TEXT

1. According to the Suárez-Orozcos, how do the stories of immigrants like Sonia Martinez suggest that unauthorized immigration "may not be voluntary" (para. 2)? What "push and pull factors" do these stories reflect?

2. In what ways do the children of unauthorized immigrants routinely face insecurity and deprivation? What physical, psychological, and emotional problems do U.S.-born children experience when their parents are detained or deported? How is it that "for them the protections of the Fourteenth Amendment are an elusive mirage" (para. 14)?

3. How do the Suárez-Orozcos respond to the suggestion that unauthorized immigrants "get in line like everybody else" (para. 19)? How did the terrorist attacks of 9/11 complicate legal immigration? How long do U.S. citizens'

immediate family members have to wait for a visa? What further problems do people seeking work visas face?

4. If the decision were up to you, which of the immigrants named by the Suárez-Orozcos would you allow to stay in the United States legally? Would you grant green cards to all of them, some of them, or none of them? What is the rationale for your decision? Compare your response to those of your class-mates and debate.

5. **Thinking Rhetorically**   What emotional or logical impact do the individual immigration stories have on the essay? What effect does the first-person tes-timony of the children have? The Suárez-Orozcos supplement the stories with statistics and expert testimony: How does this influence their argument? How would relying exclusively on storytelling affect the essay's credibility? Do the authors succeed in convincing you that "unauthorized immigrants live in a parallel universe" (para. 17)? Why or why not?

EXPLORING CONNECTIONS

6. According to Marc Lamont Hill (p. 651), Nobodies are defined as vulnera-ble "to misfortune, violence, illness, and death"; they confront both indi-vidual and systemic forms of State violence; and they are "abandoned by the State." Are the immigrants described by the Suárez-Orozcos and José

Orduña (p. 702) Nobodies? To what extent do they conform to each of these definitions?

7. In Darrin Bell's cartoon on page 712, what does he imply about the long history of anti-immigrant attitudes in the United States? What does he suggest about the immigrants themselves, and why does he construct the cartoon in reverse chronological order? To what extent would he agree with the Suárez-Orozcos that in the immigration debate, "reasonable voices" have been drowned out by "cultural xenophobes and economic nativists" (para. 23)?

EXTENDING THE CRITICAL CONTEXT

8. Examine the language used by news reporters, politicians, or pro- and anti-immigrant groups in discussing immigration issues. What terms are used to describe unauthorized immigrants, what metaphors are used for the number of immigrants entering the United States, and what are their implications? What racial frames underlie this language?

9. The Trump administration is dramatically reshaping U.S. immigration policy. Research any one of these issues to find out how laws, policies, and implementation have recently changed:

> DACA (Deferred Action for Childhood Arrivals)
>
> Deportation of noncriminals
>
> Separation of immigrant children from their parents
>
> Reduction of legal immigration
>
> Temporary Protected Status (TPS) for refugees
>
> Denial of asylum for victims of domestic abuse and gang violence
>
> Denaturalization Task Force
>
> Military discharge of immigrant recruits who were promised citizenship

What is the rationale for this change, if it's been articulated? What impact, if any, will it have on the economy? Who supports and who objects to the change? How will it affect legal or unauthorized immigrants, and how is it affecting them now? Look for stories of individuals who have been or are likely to be affected by this change, and write a position paper supported by evidence from reliable sources.

10. In 2018, on her satirical TV news show *Full Frontal*, Samantha Bee proposed the elimination of Immigration and Customs Enforcement (ICE), and since then, a number of politicians and activist groups have taken up the call to abolish ICE. As you review this segment of the show, take notes on the key arguments and evidence Bee presents to support her position:

> https://www.youtube.com/watch?v=AiBtPy0EOno

Discuss the strengths and weaknesses of her analysis with classmates: What do you think of Bee's proposal? Does her satiric approach to ICE make her argument more effective or less? Why?

FURTHER CONNECTIONS

1. Research the history of the native peoples of your state. What tribal groups inhabited the area before Europeans arrived? What is known about the cultures and languages of these tribes? How much and why did the native population decrease following European contact? What alliances and treaties were made between the tribes and the newcomers as non-natives began to occupy native lands? To what extent were treaties upheld or abandoned, and why? How were local native populations affected by relocation, the establishment of reservations, the creation of Indian boarding schools, the Dawes Act, or other legislation? What role has the Bureau of Indian Affairs played in protecting or failing to protect tribal interests? What issues are of greatest concern to the tribes in your area today? Write up the results of your research and present them to the class.

2. Some states and communities have responded to the rise in illegal immigration by enacting laws or ordinances that ban any language other than English, deny government services to undocumented immigrants, and penalize citizens (such as employers, landlords, and merchants) who "assist" them. Has your state or community adopted any such regulations? Research the arguments for and against such legislation, and discuss your findings in class. Which arguments are the most compelling, and why?

3. Investigate a recent conflict between ethnic, racial, or cultural groups on your campus or in your community. Research the issue, and interview people on each side. What event triggered the conflict? How do the groups involved perceive the issue differently? What tension, prior conflict, or injustice has contributed to the conflict and to the perceptions of those affected by it? Has the conflict been resolved? If so, write a paper discussing why you feel that the resolution was appropriate or not. If the conflict is continuing, write a paper proposing how a fair resolution might be reached.

4. Contentious debates over issues like affirmative action often hinge on whether or not the debaters accept the idea of structural racism (also called systemic racism). Proponents argue that structural racism is largely responsible for persistent racial disparities in wealth, income, home ownership, education, health care, and life expectancy. What evidence and examples of systemic racism do proponents cite? How do opponents of the concept explain racial inequalities, and what supporting evidence do they offer? Argue a position: Is it necessary to address structural discrimination in order to achieve racial equality in the United States?

ACKNOWLEDGMENTS

Alan Aja, Daniel Bustillo, William Darity Jr., and Darrick Hamilton, "From a Tangle of Pathology to a Race-Fair America," from *Dissent*, Summer 2014, pp. 39–43. Copyright © 2014 by *Dissent* Magazine. All rights reserved. Reprinted with permission of the University of Pennsylvania Press.

Sherman Alexie, excerpts from *Blasphemy* by Sherman Alexie, copyright © 2012 by Falls Apart Productions, Inc. Used by permission of Grove/Atlantic, Inc. and Nancy Stauffer Associates. Any third party use of this material, outside of this publication, is prohibited.

Amani Al-Khatahtbeh, from *Muslim Girl: A Coming of Age* by Amani Al-Khatahtbeh. Copyright © 2016 by Amani Al-Khatahtbeh. Reprinted with the permission of Simon & Schuster, Inc. All rights reserved.

Jean Anyon, excerpt from "Social Class and Curriculum of Work." Reprinted by permission of the Estate of Jean Anyon.

Mehrsa Baradaran, from *How the Other Half Banks: Exclusion, Exploitation, and the Threat to Democracy* by Mehrsa Baradaran, Cambridge, Mass: Harvard University Press. Copyright © 2015 by the President and Fellows of Harvard College. Reprinted with permission.

Rutger Bregman, from *Utopia for Realists: How We Can Build the Ideal World* by Rutger Bregman, translated from the Dutch by Elizabeth Manton. Copyright © 2016 by The Correspondent. English translation copyright © 2017 by Elizabeth Manton. Reprinted by permission of Little Brown and Company. All rights reserved.

Sheryll Cashin, from *Loving: Interracial Intimacy in America and the Threat to White Supremacy* by Sheryll Cashin. Copyright © 1990 by Sheryll Cashin. Reprinted by permission of Beacon Press, Boston.

Ta-Nehisi Coates, "The Case for Reparations," *The Atlantic*, June 2014. © 2014 The Atlantic Media Co., as first published in *The Atlantic* Magazine. All rights reserved. Distributed by Tribune Content Agency, LLC.

Stephanie Coontz, "What We Really Miss About the 1950's," from *The Way We Really Are* by Stephanie Coontz, copyright © 1998. Reprinted by permission of Basic Books, an imprint of Hachette Book Group, Inc.

Jessie Daniels, "Twitter and White Supremacy, A Love Story," DAME Magazine, October 19, 2017. Reprinted by permission of Dame Media, LLC.

Barbara Ehrenreich, "Serving in Florida," from *Nickel and Dimed: On (Not) Getting By in America* by Barbara Erhenreich. Copyright © 2001 by Barbara Ehrenreich. Used by permission of Henry Holt & Company. All rights reserved.

John Taylor Gatto, "Against School." Copyright © 2003 by *Harper's* magazine. All rights reserved. Reproduced from the September issue by special permission.

Naomi Gerstel and Natalia Sarkisian, "The Color of Family Ties: Race, Class, Gender, and Extended Family Involvement," in *American Families: A Multicultural Reader*, 2nd ed, edited by Stephanie Coontz. Copyright © 2008 Naomi Gerstel. Reprinted by permission.

Sara Goldrick-Rab, *Paying the Price: College Costs, Financial Aid, and the Betrayal of the American Dream*. Copyright © 2016 by The University of Chicago. Reprinted by permission of University of Chicago Press.

Kenneth Goldsmith, "Introduction: Let's Get Lost" (pp. 1–22, 24–27, + Endnotes, pp. 239–40), from *Wasting Time on the Internet* by Kenneth Goldsmith. Copyright © 2016 by Kenneth Goldsmith. Reprinted by permission of HarperCollins Publishers.

Carlos Andrés Gómez, excerpts from *Man Up: Cracking the Code of Modern Manhood* by Carlos Andrés Gómez, copyright © 2012 by Carlos Andrés Gómez. Used by permission of Gotham Books, an imprint of Penguin Publishing Group, a division of Penguin Random House LLC. All rights reserved.

Marc Lamont Hill, from *Nobody: Casualties of America's War on the Vulnerable, from Flint to Ferguson and Beyond* by Marc Lamont Hill. Copyright © 2016 by Marc Lamont Hill. Reprinted with the permission of Atria Books, a division of Simon & Schuster, Inc. All rights reserved.

Linda Holtzman and Leon Sharpe, with the assistance of Joseph Farand Gardner, from "Racing in America: Fact or Fiction," from *Media Messages: What Film, Television, and Popular Music Teach Us About Race, Class, Gender, and Sexual Orientation*. Copyright © 2014 by Taylor & Francis. Permission granted via Copyright Clearance Center.

Allan G. Johnson, excerpt from "Where Are We?," from *The Gender Knot: Unraveling Our Patriarchal Legacy*, 3rd edition, by Allan G. Johnson. Used by permission of Temple University Press. © 2014 by Allan G. Johnson. All Rights Reserved.

Jackson Katz, "From Rush Limbaugh to Donald Trump: The Defiant Reassertion of White Male Authority," from Gail Dines, Jean M. Humez, Bill Yousman, Lori Bindig Yousman, eds., *Gender,*

Race, and Class in Media: A Critical Reader, Fifth Edition, pp. 146–152. Copyright © 2018 by SAGE Publications, Inc. Reprinted by permission of SAGE Publications, Inc.

Diana Kendall, "Framing Class," from *Framing Class.* Copyright © 2011 by Rowman & Littlefield Publishers, Inc. Reprinted by permission of The Rowman & Littlefield Publishing Group.

Jean Kilbourne, from *Can't Buy My Love: How Advertising Changes the Way We Think and Feel* by Jean Kilborne. Copyright © 1999 by Jean Kilbourne. Previously published in hardcover under the title *Deadly Persuasion.* Reprinted by permission of Free Press, a Division of Simon & Schuster, Inc. All rights reserved.

Jamaica Kincaid, "Girl," from *At the Bottom of the River* by Jamaica Kincaid. Copyright © 1983 by Jamaica Kincaid. Reprinted by permission of Farrar, Straus and Giroux.

Larissa MacFarquhar, "When Should a Child Be Taken from His Parents?," originally published in *The New Yorker.* Copyright © 2017 Larissa MacFarquhar, used by permission of The Wylie Agency LLC.

Noreen Malone, from "Zoe and the Trolls," *New York Magazine,* July 24, 2017. Reprinted by permission of New York Media, LLC.

Gregory Mantsios, "Class in America: Myths and Realities." © by Gregory Mantsios. Reprinted by permission of the author.

Amy Ellis Nutt, excerpts from *Becoming Nicole: The Transformation of an American Family* by Amy Ellis Nutt, copyright © 2015 by Amy Ellis Nutt. Used by permission of Random House, an imprint and division of Penguin Random House LLC. All rights reserved.

José Orduña, from *The Weight of Shadows: A Memoir of Immigration & Displacement* by José Orduña. Copyright © 2016 by José Orduña. Reprinted by permission of Beacon Press, Boston.

Peggy Orenstein, "Blurred Lines: Take Two" (pp. 176–83, 185–89, 192–201, + Notes, pp. 261–66), from *Girls & Sex* by Peggy Orenstein. Copyright © 2016 by Peggy Orenstein. Reprinted by permission of HarperCollins Publishers.

Ellen K. Pao, excerpts from *Reset: My Fight for Inclusion and Lasting Change* by Ellen K. Pao, copyright © 2017 by Ellen K. Pao. Used by permission of Spiegel & Grau, an imprint of Random House, a division of Penguin Random House LLC. All rights reserved.

Mike Rose, from *Lives on the Boundary: The Struggles and Achievements of America's Underprepared* by Mike Rose. Copyright © 1989 by Mike Rose. Reprinted with the permission of The Free Press, a division of Simon & Schuster, Inc. All rights reserved.

Mimi Schippers, from *Beyond Monogamy: Polyamory and the Future of Polyqueer Sexualities* by Mimi Schippers. Copyright © 2016 by New York University Press. Reprinted by permission of New York University Press.

Eric Schmidt and Jared Cohen, excerpts from *The New Digital Age: Reshaping the Future of People, Nations and Business* by Eric Schmidt and Jared Cohen, copyright © 2013 by Google Inc. and Jared Cohen. Used by permission of Alfred A. Knopf, an imprint of Knopf Doubleday Publishing Group, a division of Random House LLC. All rights reserved.

Bruce Schneier, "How We Sold Our Souls—and More—to the Internet Giants," *The Guardian,* May 17, 2015, https://www.schneier.com/essays/archives/2015/05/how_we_sold_our_soul.html. Reprinted by permission of the author.

Rebecca Solnit, "The Longest War," from *Men Explain Things to Me* (Haymarket Press).Used by permission of the author. Copyright © 2014 by Rebecca Solnit.

Gary Soto, "Looking for Work," from *Living Up the Street,* copyright © 1985 by Gary Soto. Reprinted by permission of the author.

Marcelo M. Suárez-Orozco and Carola Suárez-Orozco, "Immigration in the Age of Global Vertigo," from *Arizona Firestorm,* edited by Otto Santa Ana. Copyright © 2012 by Rowman & Littlefield Publishers, Inc. Reprinted by permission of The Rowman & Littlefield Publishing Group.

Sherry Turkle, excerpts from *Reclaiming Conversation: The Power of Talk in a Digital Age* by Sherry Turkle, copyright © 2015 by Sherry Turkle. Used by permission of Penguin Press, an imprint of Penguin Publishing Group, a division of Penguin Random House LLC. All rights reserved.

Jean M. Twenge, "Has the Smartphone Destroyed a Generation?," *The Atlantic,* September 2017. © 2017 The Atlantic Media Co., as first published in *The Atlantic* Magazine. All rights reserved. Distributed by Tribune Content Agency, LLC.

Lisa Wade and Myra Marx Ferree, from *Gender: Ideas, Interactions, Institutions* by Lisa Wade and Myra Marx Ferree. Copyright © 2015 by W.W. Norton & Company, Inc. Used by permission of W.W. Norton & Company, Inc.

INDEX OF AUTHORS AND TITLES